SMITH'S GUIDE™ TO STATE HABEAS CORPUS RELIEF
FOR STATE PRISONERS

Also by Zachary A. Smith

SMITH'S GUIDE to Habeas Corpus Relief
for State Prisoners Under 28 U.S.C. §2254

SMITH'S GUIDE to Executive Clemency
for State and Federal Prisoners

SMITH'S GUIDE to Chapter 7 Bankruptcy
for Prisoners

SMITH'S GUIDE to Second or Successive
Federal Habeas Corpus Relief
for State and Federal Prisoners

*Available through Amazon.com
and distributed by Ingram*

SMITH'S GUIDE™
to
State Habeas Corpus Relief

for
State Prisoners

By
Zachary A. Smith

redbat books
2017

First Edition, August 15, 2017

Copyright © 2017 by Zachary A. Smith
All rights reserved

No part of this book may reproduced in any form whatsoever, whether by graphic, visual, electronic, film, microfilm, tape recording, or any other means, without prior written permission of the author, except in the case of brief passages embodied in critical reviews or articles.

ISBN-10: 0989592464
ISBN-13: 978-0-9895924-6-8
    Library of Congress Control Number: 2017950424

Published by
redbat books
2901 Gekeler Lane
La Grande, OR 97850
www.redbatbooks.com

Text set in Chaparral Pro.

Book design by Kristin Summers, redbat design | www.redbatdesign.com

DISCLAIMER

This book is not an alternative to professional assistance by an attorney. This book does not provide licensed, professional legal advice. It's author is a paralegal, not a lawyer; it's text is for informational purposes only. The material contained herein is not intended to substitute for professional assistance by an attorney. Never disregard professional legal advice, and never delay in seeking it or hiring an attorney to represent you, because of anything you read in this book. It is the responsibility of you, the reader, to seek out and secure legal advice on how to proceed with state habeas corpus proceedings.

The information in this book has been carefully researched, and all efforts have been made to ensure accuracy. The author and publisher assume no responsibility for any damages or losses incurred during, or as a result of, the application of the information presented here. All information should be carefully studied and clearly understood before taking any action based on the contents of this book. The reader assumes full responsibility for the consequences of his or her own actions, filings, and strategic decisions.

INTRODUCTION

I have studied and practiced law for over nineteen years. Throughout those years, I've talked with dozens of prisoners about their frustration with nonprofit organizations like the Midwest Innocence Project (MIP), the Center for Wrongful Convictions, etc. Prisoners fill out information packets for these organizations but almost never receive any serious consideration of their cases.

It's as if most of these organizations only offer assistance to prisoners with high profile cases, cases that attract media attention.

Like most prisoners, I do not have a high profile case. But in the early stages of preparing my own state habeas corpus petition, I decided to investigate and write some of these nonprofit organizations claiming they help prisoners prove their innocence or overturn their wrongful convictions. I started with the MIP. They mailed me the following response:

April 9, 2014

Dear Mr. Smith,

Thank you for your April 2, 2014 letter. It is clear you have done research and understand the process.

In reviewing your letter and clemency petition, it appears you have wrongful conviction issues. Unfortunately, MIP does not work on wrongful conviction cases unless it is a claim of actual innocence. Nothing in your application or clemency letter asserts such a claim. For those reasons, we will be unable to assist you.

There are organizations that do work on wrongful conviction cases, regardless of innocence claims. While many are out of state, you can contact them for assistance.

    KU Project for Innocence & Post-Conviction Remedies
    Green Hall
    1535 West 15th Street
    Lawrence, KS 66045

    Innocence and Justice Clinic
    Wake Forest University
    1834 Wake Forest Road
    Winston Salem, NC 27109

    Center on Wrongful Convictions
    Northwestern University School of Law

INTRODUCTION

<blockquote>

375 East Chicago Ave.
Chicago, IL 60611

We are sorry you have been the subject of such misconduct and wish you the best of luck in your case. Unfortunately, your case is outside of our mission, and for that reason, we are unable to assist.

Sincerely,

Penelope Kress
Intake Analyst

</blockquote>

After receiving this letter from the MIP, I wrote to every organization listed, and later got back the following letters:

<blockquote>

April 22, 2014

Dear Mr. Smith,

We received your letter asking for assistance with your case. Unfortunately, we are only able to offer assistance on cases originating from North Carolina courts. Because your case is from Missouri, we recommend that you contact:

> Midwest Innocence Project
> 605 W. 47th, Ste 222
> Kansas City, MO 64112
> Phone: 816.221.2166

We wish you the best of luck in your continued pursuit of justice. By sending you this letter, we are not agreeing to represent you in any legal matter.

Sincerely,

Wake Forest University
Innocence and Justice Clinic

</blockquote>

* * *

<blockquote>

April 22, 2014

Dear Mr. Smith:

We have received your letter requesting help from the Project for Innocence. Unfortunately the Project cannot assist inmates who are not confined in Kansas institutions. We simply do not have the resources or time.

</blockquote>

INTRODUCTION

We are sorry we cannot do more to help you, and wish you the best.

Sincerely,

Elizabeth Cateforis
Supervising Attorney

* * *

May 2, 2014

Dear Mr. Smith:

We have received your letter dated April 14, 2014, and thank you for writing.

The Center on Wrongful Convictions' primary mission is to identify and rectify wrongful convictions through representation, research, and public education. We are rarely if ever able to accept cases outside of that mission. We have carefully reviewed your letter, but are unable to offer you any assistance.

We may review additional correspondence that we receive from you but those requests may not result in additional responses from us.

Thank you again for writing. Your documents are enclosed. We wish you well in your pursuit of justice.

Sincerely,

Sara Sornmervold
Case Coordinator
Center on Wrongful Convictions

To say writing these organizations was a complete waste of time is an understatement; I was given the runaround from day one. I wrote to let the MIP's legal director know what I thought about my treatment:

May 5, 2015

Dear Ms. Bushnell:

The MIP has been gathering information about me and about my criminal case for a number of years. The MIP's last letter to me, dated April 9, 2014, has clearly stated that it cannot assist me in overturning my criminal conviction. As such, I hereby make a written request for the entire file the MIP gathered while investigating my case over the years.

And for full disclosure, I've enclosed copies of letters I received back from two organizations that the MIP referred to me to ask assistance from. Not surprisingly, I was given the runaround (see the Wake Forest letter). I have yet to hear of any actual case that the

INTRODUCTION

MIP was able to get overturned. It has tried to take credit for cases they didn't have any direct involvement in. The Ryan Ferguson case being one of them, filing an amicus curiae brief for a case one wasn't needed on. The man was represented by KATHLEEN ZELLNER! And the MIP didn't get involved in Robert E. Nelson's case until O'Sullivan was appointed to represent him by the court, assuring that the legal fees would be paid by the State of Missouri. And it wasn't the MIP who provided Nelson with the DNA motion to file, it was given to his sister by Court Administrator Sharon Snyder who was later fired, days after Nelson's release.

Remember, I was only asking for a little help and was shunned.

* * *

May 16, 2014

Dear Mr. Smith,

Thank you for your letters dated April 11, 2014, and May 5, 2014.

In order to properly review your case, we need copies of your transcripts, appellate documents, and police reports as requested in our February 8, 2013 letter to you. We understand from your subsequent letters that you either do not have access to them, do not want to send what you have, and/or cannot afford to send them to us. To date, we have no documents of yours other than your clemency petition and a couple of police reports that you provided to us. Pursuant to your May 5, 2014 request, copies of those documents are enclosed herewith.

Because the demands upon our program are so great, the Midwest Innocence Project is not able to represent all the claims of innocence that we receive. Without the above-requested documents, we cannot properly review your case, and therefore are unable to assist you. If you find that you are able to send us copies of your documents, we will be happy to review them, but make no guarantees that we will ultimately be able to assist you. Otherwise, please know that our decision to close your file in no way reflects the merit of your case.

We do wish you the best of luck.

Sincerely,

Penelope Kress
Intake Analyst

INTRODUCTION

After I provided the requested information, the MIP sent me a letter stating law students had been assigned to investigate my case. That was over two years ago. I've filed six state habeas corpus petitions since then.

The point is this: many prisoners waste time writing these organizations, desperate for help with their cases that can't be found elsewhere, only to be put through pointlessly long delays or put off altogether in an endless cycle of recommendations. Note that I also asked the MIP for several public-information documents easily obtainable from the internet, which I did not have access to, just to see if they would send them to me. They said no. How helpful is an organization, well funded and amply staffed, if they will not even mail an occasional printout to a prisoner so clearly in need?

This book was written for every prisoner who has been given the runaround—or who wants to sidestep these organizations—and wants to fight for his or her own freedom.

In the following pages, I have laid out the process for attacking a conviction by way of a state habeas corpus petition. You can find the statutes that govern your state in the appendix.

And as a trademark feature of all *Smith's Guide* titles, you will find examples throughout, from actual cases, to assist you in preparing your own state habeas corpus petition.

I did not provide case citations for the relief available in all fifty states (although it would be helpful and may be included in a potential second edition). Too many prisoners get stuck searching for that one case that will guarantee him or her relief, then waste years without ever finding it.

Prisoners should focus on procedure and actively get involved in the practice of law. Rarely have I won a case based solely on perfect case law. More often than not, I won because I made a compelling argument, applying the correct legal standard to the irrefutable facts of the case. I'm not saying it doesn't happen, I'm only saying a prisoner should never use the excuse of doing legal research as the reason not to file a petition challenging his or her conviction.

Once you become familiar with the civil and criminal procedural rules, there isn't any legal issue you can't litigate. And through practice, you will gain confidence in your own abilities, winning every case that should be won.

—Zachary A. Smith

TABLE OF CONTENTS

Disclaimer 5

Introduction 7

<1> Overview of State Habeas Corpus Relief 19
   History of Habeas Corpus 19
   State Habeas Corpus Relief 19
   Habeas Corpus Process by State 19
   Timeliness of Petition for State Habeas Corpus Relief 20
   Procedural Default 20
   Grounds for State Habeas Corpus Relief 20
      Jurisdictional Issues—Personal and Subject Matter 20
      Sentencing Defect 21
      Actual Innocence Claims—Manifest Injustice and Freestanding 22
      Brady Claims 22
   Legal Standard of Review—Preponderance of the Evidence 23

<2> Investigating Case and Collecting Evidence 25
   Investigating Case—Objective Observation 25
   Collecting Evidence 27
      Case File 27
      Public Records 28
      Records Open to Public 28
      State, County, and Federal Records 28
      Records Reviewable Only Upon Proof of a Legal Need 29
      Records Available Only Upon Written Request 29
      Freedom of Information Act 29
      Finding Potential Witnesses 30
      Finding Expert Witnesses 30

<3> Petition for Writ of Habeas Corpus in State Court 33
   Preparation of Petition 33
   State Forms and Cover Page 33
   Petition for Writ of Habeas Corpus with Suggestions in Support 34
   Jurisdictional Statement 34
   Statement of the Case 34
   C. Newly Discovered Evidence 34

D. Cause to Overcome Procedural Default 34
Reasons for Granting the Writ 34
Conclusion 35
Verification of Petition 35
Certificate of Service 35
Example Verification of Petition 36
Example Petition for Writ of Habeas Corpus (*Smith v. Pash*) 37
Example Petition for Writ of Habeas Corpus #2 (*Engel v. Dormire*) 47
Example Petition for Writ of Habeas Corpus #3 (*Woodworth v. Denney*) 104

<4> Preparation of Appendix for Accompanying Exhibits in Support of Petition 127
Preparation of Appendix for Accompanying Exhibits 127
Affidavits 127
Appendix for Accompanying Exhibits 130
Page Numbering (Optional) 130
Binding 130
Example Accompanying Exhibits in Support of Petition for Writ of Habeas Corpus 131
Example Affidavit of Zachary A. Smith 133

<5> Filing Petition and Accompanying Exhibits with the Court 137
Filing with the Court 137
Filing Fee 137
Proceeding in Forma Pauperis 137
Application for Change of Judge 138
Motion for Bail 138
Mailing Petition and Exhibits 138
Example Motion for Leave to Proceed in Forma Pauperis 139
Example Application for Change of Judge 141
Example Motion to be Admitted to Bail 143

<6> Court's Order to Show Cause Why Writ Should Not be Granted 145
Show Cause Order 145
Respondent's Motion for Extension of Time to File Response 146
Respondent's Response 146
Petitioner's Request for Extension of Time to File Reply 146
Petitioner's Reply 146
Court's Judgment 147
Example Order to Show Cause 148
Example Respondent's Motion for Extension of Time 150
Example Respondent's Response to Show Cause Order 152
Example Petitioner's Motion for Extension of Time 160
Example Petitioner's Statement, Brief and Argument 163
Example Petitioner's Reply Brief 197
Example Reply in Opposition to Respondent's Motion for Rehearing or Transfer ... 214

<7> Discovery 221
- Scope of Discovery 221
- Written Interrogatories 221
- Depositions—Oral and Written... 222
- Production of Things and Places 223
- Inspection of Things and Places 224
- Requests for Admissions 224
- Objections and Motions to Compel Discovery 225

<8> Evidentiary Hearing 227
- Evidentiary Hearing.. 227
- Writ of Habeas Corpus ad Testificandum 227
- Courtroom Appearance 227
- Presenting Yourself and Reading Others... 228
  - *Posture* 228
  - *Tells* 228
  - *Vocalization* 229
- Conducting Hearing and Introducing Evidence 231
  - *Securing Attendance of Witnesses* 231
  - *Frames, Frame Control, and Reframing*... 231
  - *Direct Examination of Witnesses* 231
  - *Introducing Exhibits* 233
  - *Cross-Examination of Witnesses* 233
  - *Expert Witnesses* 235
  - *Frye and Daubert Tests* 236
  - *Objections* 237
- Example Writ of Habeas Corpus ad Testificandum..................................... 238

<9> Case Disposition and Appellate Remedies 239
- Case Disposition 239
- Appellate Remedies... 239
- Remedies in Federal Court 239
- Writ of Certiorari 240
- Conclusion 241
- Example Order (*Smith v. Pash*) 242
- Example Order #2 (*Smith v. Pash*) 243
- Example Letter from Missouri Supreme Court (*Smith v. Pash*) 245
- Example Opinion (*Thornton v. Denny*)... 246
- Example Order Denying Application to Transfer (*Thornton v. Denney*) 259
- Example Opinion (*Engel v. Dormire*) 260
- Example Opinion #2 (*Woodworth v. Denney*) 264

Acknowledgments 297

Appendix 299

To every prisoner that refuses to give up the fight for freedom

<1> OVERVIEW OF STATE HABEAS CORPUS RELIEF

History of Habeas Corpus

The writ of habeas corpus* originated in England. Its first recorded use was in 1305, but the use of similar writs occurred as early as the 12th century. In 1679, the English Parliament passed the Habeas Corpus Amendment Act which served to prevent the King of England from locking people up in secret dungeons and forgetting about them, a common practice of kings in medieval times. The amended act codified the procedure for issuing a writ of habeas corpus, removing the king's power to detain a prisoner against the wishes of Parliament and the courts.

The procedure permitted a prisoner, or a third party on his or her behalf, to petition for a writ of habeas corpus. The court would then issue a summons, commanding the custodian or jailer to produce the prisoner so the court could determine whether the prisoner's confinement was legal. If it wasn't, the court would issue the writ and set the prisoner free.

The concept of habeas corpus was adopted by the Founding Fathers of the United States, to preserve liberty, justice, and democracy for the people. It was made the first article of the United States Constitution. Article One, Section 9, states, "The privilege of the writ of habeas corpus shall not be suspended, unless when in cases of rebellion or invasion the public safety may require it."

State Habeas Corpus Relief

The writ of habeas corpus is a civil proceeding and is governed by each particular state's rules of civil procedure. A court's inquiry is limited to whether a prisoner is being confined legally. The relief available depends upon each particular case, but a court may order bail, credit for time served, resentencing, or discharge from custody.

Habeas Corpus Process by State

The habeas corpus process varies from state to state. You can find the statutory procedure for your state listed in the appendix of this book.

---

* The Latin term *habeas corpus* means "You (i.e., the accuser) are to produce the body."

Timeliness of Petition for State Habeas Corpus Relief

The time limitations for filing a petition for a writ of habeas corpus will vary, depending upon each states' habeas corpus process. You can find the time limitations, if any, for your state listed in the appendix of this book.

Procedural Default

A petitioner who fails to raise a challenge to his or her conviction on direct appeal or in a timely post-conviction proceeding is said to have procedurally defaulted on those claims, forfeiting the right to raise them. Most states have adopted the federal standard, which states that a petitioner can overcome a procedural bar defense if he or she can show cause for not presenting his or her claims in earlier state court proceedings, as well as prejudice resulting from constitutional error, or a fundamental miscarriage of justice. See *Coleman v. Thompson, 501 U.S. 722 (1991)*. Cause, as defined in *Murray v. Carrier, 477 U.S. 478 (1986)*, is a factor external to the defense or for which the defense is not responsible.

A petitioner can establish the presence of an objective factor external to the defense, which impeded the petitioner's ability to comply with the procedural rules for review of his or her claims, by making a showing that the factual or legal basis for a claim was not reasonably available to him or her. See *Coleman v. Thompson, 501 U.S. 722 (1991)*. The procedural default must have been caused by something that cannot fairly be attributed to the petitioner (e.g., the evidence is newly discovered, the state withheld evidence, the law was changed and made retroactive, etc.).

Grounds for State Habeas Corpus Relief

State habeas corpus review is extremely limited to grounds such as: jurisdictional issues, sentencing defects, actual innocence claims, and Brady claims. Although this is not an exhaustive list of every possible ground for habeas corpus relief, below is a brief legal summary of the grounds just mentioned.

Jurisdictional Issues—Personal and Subject Matter

The term *personal jurisdiction* refers to the power of a court to require a person to answer to a legal proceeding, criminal or civil, that may affect his or her rights or interests. Since *Pennoyer v. Neff, 95 U.S. 714, 24 L.Ed. 565 (1877)*, the power of a state's courts over people within and without the territory of the state has been a matter of due process of law under the Fourteenth Amendment to the United States Constitution. Before *Pennoyer*, the power of the state courts to exercise jurisdiction over people within the state and the interests of people in property within the state was unquestioned. The Due Process Clause limits the power of the state over people outside the state; the needs of interstate and international commerce have expanded the notions of what extraterritorial power a state court may exercise. See *International Shoe v. Washington, 326 U.S. 310, 66 S.Ct. 154, 90 L.Ed. 95 (1945)* and its progeny.

To facilitate the economic advantages of having those with business in a state be answerable in the state's courts, most states have enacted statutes and rules that explicitly, or by judicial interpretation, expand the state courts' jurisdictional reach to the maximum extent permitted by the federal constitution.

In modern times, when a court says that it lacks personal jurisdiction, it means simply that the constitutional principle of due process bars it from affecting the rights and interests of a particular person, whether the "person" be an individual or an entity such as a corporation.

Subject matter jurisdiction, in contrast to personal jurisdiction, is not a matter of a state court's power over a person, but the court's authority to render a judgment in a particular category of cases. In the federal courts, unlike most states, subject matter jurisdiction is set forth in statutes passed within the authority granted to Congress by Article III of the United States Constitution. Pursuant to this constitutional authority, Congress has the power to increase or decrease the kinds and categories of cases heard in the federal courts.

Federal courts are referred to as courts of limited jurisdiction because they are courts of a sovereign whose authority is limited to those subjects the United States Constitution assigns to the national government. States, on the other hand, are sovereigns of general powers—powers that are limited only by the authority granted exclusively to the federal government or served by the state or federal constitution to the people themselves. All of this is set forth by the Tenth Amendment to the United States Constitution.

The subject matter jurisdiction of most states is governed directly by that state's constitution or statutes. For example, in Missouri, Article V, Section 14, sets forth the subject matter jurisdiction of the circuit courts in plenary terms, providing that "[t]he circuit court shall have original jurisdiction over all cases and matters, civil and criminal. Such courts may issue and determine original remedial writs and shall sit at times and place within the circuit as determined by the circuit court."

By contrast, there are subject-matter limits that can be placed by statute. When a statute speaks in jurisdictional terms or can be read in such terms, it is proper to read it as merely setting statutory limits on remedies or elements of claims for relief that courts may grant. Statutory restrictions on judicial powers also may be subject to the constitutional principle of separation of powers.

Sentencing Defect

A claim that the sentencing court has imposed a sentence in excess of that authorized by statute may be raised in a petition for a writ of habeas corpus and is considered a jurisdictional defect. Even if a petitioner has failed to timely raise a claim in a post-conviction motion, it is settled in most states that the imposition of a sentence beyond that permitted by the applicable statute or rule may be raised by way of a writ of habeas corpus.

Actual Innocence Claims—Manifest Injustice and Freestanding

A petitioner may be granted relief on a claim not raised in a direct appeal or in a post-conviction proceeding if he or she can show manifest injustice. This standard is met when a petitioner shows newly discovered evidence of actual innocence coupled with a claim of constitutional violation at trial. *Actual innocence* means that the petitioner must show that it is more likely than not that no reasonable juror would have found him or her guilty beyond a reasonable doubt. See *Schlup v. Delo*, 115 S.Ct. 851 (1995).

If a petitioner presents evidence of innocence so strong that a court cannot have confidence in the outcome of the trial, he or she should be permitted to argue the merits of underlying constitutional claims. In this instance, the claim of innocence itself is not a constitutional claim but instead a "gateway" through which a petitioner must pass before his or her procedurally defaulted constitutional claims can be considered on the merits. Again, see *Schlup v. Delo*, 115 S.Ct. 851 (1995).

In *Herrera v. Collins*, 113 S.Ct. 853 (1993), the United States Supreme Court considered the question of whether or not, in the absence of a constitutional violation at trial, a petitioner's claim of actual innocence could serve as the basis for federal habeas relief.

The Court concluded, in *Herrara, 506 U.S. at 418-19*, that Herrera failed to make a "truly persuasive demonstration of actual innocence" because his new evidence fell "far short of that which would have to be made in order to trigger the sort of constitutional claim which we have assumed, arguendo, to exist." Without defining a standard for a freestanding claim, the Court only said that, in the interest of finality, a threshold showing would have to be "extraordinarily high."

Since the Herrera decision, a number of states have considered the same question and have concluded that a freestanding claim of actual innocence, while not currently available under federal habeas review, is available for state habeas relief—states such as California, Connecticut, Illinois, and Missouri. (There are thirty-eight states that permit some form of relief based on newly discovered evidence of innocence.)

At least two states, Ohio and Virginia, have rejected freestanding claims of actual innocence as a basis for habeas relief. Instead, these states have opted to follow the federal standard in *Schlup*, recognizing an actual innocence claim only as a gateway to consider a procedurally defaulted constitutional violation at trial. (Missouri only recognizes freestanding claims in death penalty cases. See *In re Lincoln v. Cassaday*, 2016 Mo.App. LEXIS 1006 (Mo.App.WD 2016)).

Brady Claims

In *Brady v. Maryland*, 373 U.S. 83 (1963), the Supreme Court held that "the suppression by the prosecution of evidence favorable to an accused upon request violates due process where the evidence is material either to guilt or to punishment, irrespective of the good faith of the prosecution." Later, in *Strickler v. Greene*, 527 U.S. 263 (1999), the court more precisely articulated the three essential elements for establishing a Brady claim: "the evidence at issue must be favorable to the accused, either because it is exculpatory, or because it is impeaching; that evidence must have been suppressed by the state, either willfully or inadvertently; and prejudice must have ensued." It is also well settled that the Brady rule encompasses evidence "known only to police investigators and not the prosecutor [...] in order to comply with Brady, therefore, the individual prosecutor has a duty to learn of any favorable evidence known to others acting on the government's behalf in the case, including [the] police." See Strickler quoting *Kyles v. Whitley, 514 U.S. 419, 437 (1995)*.

To establish Brady materiality, a petitioner must convince the court that "there is a reasonable probability" that the result of his or her trial would have been different if the suppressed evidence had been disclosed to the defense. As the court stressed, in *Kyles*, "[T]he adjective is important. The question is not whether the defendant would more likely than not have received a different verdict with the evidence, but whether in its absence he received a fair trial, understood as a trial resulting in a verdict worthy of confidence."

As the *Kyles* court made clear, the materiality inquiry is not just a matter of determining whether, after discounting the inculpatory evidence in light of the undisclosed evidence, the remaining evidence is sufficient to support the jury's conclusions. Rather, the question is whether "the favorable evidence could reasonably be taken to put the whole case in such a different light as to undermine confidence in the verdict."

Legal Standard of Review

Because a habeas corpus proceeding is a civil action, the legal standard of review is governed by the preponderance of evidence standard. "The burden of showing something by a preponderance of evidence requires the trier of fact to believe that the existence of a fact is more probable than its nonexistence before [he] may find in favor of the party who has the burden to persuade the [judge] of the fact's existence." See *Concrete Pipe & Products of Cal., Inc. v. Construction Laborers Pension Trust for Southern Cal., 508 U.S. 602, 622 (1993)*.

In other words, the preponderance standard goes to how convincing the evidence in favor of a fact must be in comparison with the evidence against it before that fact may be found, but does not determine what facts must be proven as a substantive part of a claim or defense. See *Greenwich Collieries v. Director, OWCP, 990 F.2d 730, 736 (CA 1993)*, which defines a preponderance of evidence as "evidence which is [...] more convincing than the evidence [...] offered in opposition to it."

<2> INVESTIGATING A CASE AND COLLECTING EVIDENCE

Investigating a Case—Objective Observation

In 1903, George Edalji, a resident of Great Wyrley, England, was convicted for the mutilation death of a pony and sentenced to seven years hard labor, despite having an alibi. George was also the prime suspect in fifteen other animal mutilations but was not tried for those crimes. The method of killing was the same: each animal had a shallow cut across its underbelly, causing the animal to suffer a slow, agonizing death.

The evidence used to convict George was circumstantial: bloody razors found at his home; his muddy clothes; some anonymous letters he supposedly wrote, implicating himself in the animal mutilations; and the physical location of where the pony was found, in a pit near his home.

The case attracted a lot of attention. George's supporters collected signatures and sent two petitions to the Home Office, protesting his innocence. Finally, in 1906, he was released. However, because he hadn't been exonerated of the crime, he was prohibited from returning to his law practice as a solicitor (a kind of attorney qualified to draw up wills and other legal documents).

That same year, Arthur Conan Doyle, the famous author of the Sherlock Holmes detective stories, also developed an interest in George's bizarre case. Doyle was convinced of the man's innocence after objectively observing him on just one occasion. Doyle wrote:

> [George] had come to my hotel by appointment, but I had been delayed, and he was passing the time by reading the paper. I recognized my man by his dark face, so I stood and observed him. He held the paper close to his eyes and rather sideways, proving not only a high degree of myopia, but marked astigmatism. The idea of such a man scouring fields at night and assaulting cattle while avoiding the watching police was ludicrous....There, in a single physical defect, lay the moral certainty of his innocence.

After meeting with George, Doyle made a trip to Great Wyrley, England. He questioned the locals, went to the crime scenes, and looked at all the evidence used to obtain the conviction. Doyle also went to George's old school to look over records of anonymous letters and pranks made against young George and his family. Doyle even investigated the handwriting expert who testified against the man at trial. When his investigation was completed, Doyle assembled his findings and sent them to the Committee of Inquiry at the Home Office.

In his findings, Doyle debunked the evidence, piece by piece: the razors were not covered in animal blood but rust and could not have possibly been used to cut the animals' bellies; the dirt on George's clothes did not come from the crime scene where the pony had been found; the handwriting expert had made erroneous conclusions in other cases, leading to wrongful convictions; and George's defective eyesight, which made it highly improbable that a man with strong myopia and marked astigmatism could navigate through farmers' fields in the dark and mutilate animals with precise, meticulous cuts—all without falling under the watchful eyes of police.

George was fully exonerated in 1907 by the Committee of Inquiry, which found, "The police commenced and carried on their investigation for the purpose of finding evidence against Edalji, who they were already sure was the guilty man."

The concept of objective observation is a mindset, an acquired skill, a way of looking at things, the practice of thinking as a scientist by applying the scientific method: 1) identify the problem; 2) make observations and collect information; 3) make a hypothesis, or an educated guess; 4) test the hypothesis and deduce; and 5) repeat.

In *A Study in Scarlet*, Doyle, through his character Sherlock Holmes, describes objective observation like this:

> From a drop of water, a logician could infer the possibility of an Atlantic or a Niagara without having seen or heard of one or the other. So all life is a great chain, the nature of which is known whenever we are shown a single link of it. Like all other arts, the Science of Deduction and Analysis is one which can only be acquired by long and patient study, nor is life long enough to allow any moral and mental aspects of the matter which present the greatest difficulties, let the inquirer begin by mastering more elementary problems. Let him on meeting a fellow-mortal, learn at a glance to distinguish the history of the man, and the trade or profession to which he belongs. Puerile as such an exercise may seem, it sharpens the faculties of observation, and teaches one where to look and what to look for. By a man's fingernails, by his forefinger and thumb, by his expression, by his shirt-cuffs—by each of these things a man's calling is plainly revealed. That all united should fail to enlighten the competent inquirer in any case is almost inconceivable.

And to elaborate further, Holmes provides a specific example of objective observation, as applied to human interaction, in action:

> Observation with me is second nature. You [Dr. John Watson] appeared to be surprised when I told you, on our first meeting, that you had come from Afghanistan. From long habit the train of thoughts ran so swiftly through my mind that I arrived at the conclusion without being conscious of intermediate steps. There were such steps, however. The train of reasoning ran, "Here is a gentleman of a medical type, but with the air of a military man. Clearly an army doctor, then. He has just come from the tropics, for his face is dark, and that is not the natural tint of his skin, for his wrists are fair. He has undergone hardship and sickness, as his haggard face says clearly. His left arm has been injured. He holds it in a stiff and unnatural manner. Where in the tropics could an English army doctor have seen

much hardship and got his arm wounded? Clearly in Afghanistan." The whole train of thought did not occupy a second. I then remarked that you came from Afghanistan, and you were astonished.

The same way Doyle depicts Sherlock Holmes's deductive reasoning, you will have to apply the scientific method when investigating your case: objectively observe and glean important facts from the information available to you; collect all the possible information, look at all the evidence, ask yourself and others questions, consult experts, investigate people, search for public records, research applicable law; develop a theory of why something is or is not the way it should be, based on known and observed facts; then test your theory, compare it to the evidence, eliminating each deduction until the one that remains, however improbable, must be correct. Having done this, do it again. By repeating the exact same process, your deductions, if correct, should produce the same conclusions.

Collecting Evidence

Collecting evidence to overturn a conviction will be an arduous task, but it is one that can be accomplished through patience and unrelenting tenacity. This section will provide information to help you find whatever you need—case files, public records, documents, potential witnesses, expert witnesses, etc.

Case File

When an attorney is retained or assigned to a case, the attorney will prepare a case file (typically called trial counsel's file or trial file). This file will consist of a copy of the discovery, which should include items such as police reports, witness statements, crime scene photos and diagrams, forensic reports, investigator notes, and lawyers' trial notes.

After the case is disposed of, either through trial or a guilty plea, the attorney will keep the file unless it is requested by one of the attorneys perfecting an appeal or a motion for post-conviction relief (PCR).

At the conclusion of a direct appeal, the appellate attorney usually keeps the trial file and combines it with the appellate file.

In cases where a PCR motion is initiated, the PCR attorney will prepare a PCR file. He or she will also make requests for case files from the trial and appellate attorneys.

Upon the completion of the PCR proceedings, the PCR attorney usually keeps possession of the trial, direct appeal, and PCR case files—that is, unless the trial and direct appellate attorneys ask for return of their case files.

You are entitled to everything contained in the case files; they belong to you, not the attorneys. To obtain these files yourself, make a written request for them from each attorney who represented you. Most attorneys will first send an acknowledgment for you to sign, stating that once they are sent to you, the attorney or public defender's office is no longer responsible for storing the case files.

Some attorneys prefer to send clients copies of the case file while retaining custody of the original file. This is done to preserve the integrity of the files' contents.

At times this is beneficial, especially if a Brady claim is made. The attorney's testimony, along with the original case file, can then be used to prove that the Brady material was never disclosed during discovery.

Oftentimes, when an attorney is called to testify at a hearing, he or she will not remember whether the police report, witness's statement, etc., was in the case file. The issue then quickly becomes a question of credibility: the prosecutor versus the petitioner. In such instances, the court will, more often than not, make a factual finding that the prosecutor provided the discovery and deny the petitioner's Brady claim on that basis. It is nearly impossible to overcome the court's factual finding.

Public Records

There are basically four kinds of public records: records you can look up online; records you can view at state or federal offices or agencies; records that are only attainable upon proof of a legal need, such as birth certificates, death certificates, and marriage licenses; and records that are not made public but must be disclosed upon request.

Everyone leaves behind a trail of records throughout his or her lifetime: birth certificate, school records, addresses and phone numbers in the White Pages, driver's licenses, utility records, voter registry information, college degrees, military records, marriage certificates, property records, liens, transcripts of court proceedings, tickets for traffic offenses and city ordinance violations, criminal conviction records, inmate locator records, sex offender registry listings, bankruptcy filings and discharges, divorce decrees, and death certificate.

Records Open to Public

There are documents and databases open to the public online. This is problematic for prisoners, due to the lack of Internet access. The incarcerated must either have someone look up the desired information online or make a request for the information in writing. Oftentimes, the requested information will be sent to you free of charge; sometimes you will have to pay for the copies.

State, County, and Federal Records

You may be doing an investigation to see if a witness was given a lesser sentence in exchange for providing testimony against you. If this is your aim, write a letter to the court clerk where the witness was sentenced, requesting copies of the presentencing report and sentencing transcripts. (Courts usually charge for copies of these documents.)

If the witness testified at your trial that he or she wasn't expecting any favorable consideration in exchange for testifying against you, but at his or her sentencing, stated that this *was* the understanding, then that may be grounds for a new trial based upon the witness's perjury. This is especially true if the witness was explicitly asked at your trial whether he or she was expecting some kind of consideration for testifying against you and answered no.

This situation arises frequently. Most prosecutors will postpone such witnesses' cases to delay sentencing until after said witnesses have testified in other cases. Later on, a prosecutor will provide a letter on a witness's behalf, stating that a conviction wouldn't have been possible without the witness's testimony and asking the sentencing court to take his or her cooperation into consideration when imposing sentence.

Records Reviewable Only upon Proof of a Legal Need

Records that are only reviewable upon proof of a legal need consist of birth certificates, death certificates, and marriage licenses. Despite the restrictions, most information contained in these records can be found in other documents. For example, if a person filed for bankruptcy or divorce, or probated a will upon the death of a family member, that is public information and, as such, documentation of those actions is available from the state or federal courts, containing all the information you may be looking for.

Records Available Only Upon Written Request

State and federal agencies retain documents and other records that are only made available upon written request. If a Freedom of Information Act (FOIA) letter is received, these agencies must produce whatever requested information is not privileged or protected by law. This is usually done by sending you documents with any privileged or protected information redacted or blotted out.

Freedom of Information Act

The Freedom of Information Act establishes your right to obtain information from federal government agencies.

If your request is denied, it is the government's burden to explain why the record should not be provided to you. There are nine types of records the FOIA protects:

- Classified matters of national defense or foreign policy
- Internal personnel rules and practices
- Trade secrets and commercial or financial information
- Investigatory records compiled for law enforcement purposes
- Records of financial institutions

- Information specifically exempted by other statutes
- Privileged inter-agency or intra-agency memoranda or letters
- Geographical and geophysical information concerning wells
- Personal information affecting an individual's privacy

The Department of Justice provides a guide for FOIA, explaining what the FOIA can and cannot provide to you. A copy may be requested by writing to

United States Department of Justice, Civil Division
Freedom of Information/Privacy Act Officer, Room 808
901 E Street, NW
Washington, DC 20530-0001

Each state has its own version of the FOIA. Before making a request, you should thoroughly review your state's statutes.

Finding Potential Witnesses

Not having access to the Internet is a huge disadvantage. Finding potential witnesses from prison can be difficult, but it is not impossible. You may have friends and family members who can access the Internet for you.

The quickest and easiest way to find someone is through social media—Facebook, LinkedIn, Twitter, etc. If you know the person's correct name and city, he or she likely can be found online.

Of course, if the person doesn't want to get involved with your case, it would be better to find out his or her address so that you can serve them with a subpoena and depose them. However, learning someone's address is a little trickier than finding them on a social media site. Your computer-savvy friend or family member may be able to find the person's address by searching an online directory, such as: AnyWho.com, WhoWhere.com, or 411.com.

Finding Expert Witnesses

Whether you are looking for information that discredits the state's expert witness or trying to find an expert of your own, you can do a Google search for the expert's name and area of expertise. Professionals (e.g., doctors, forensic pathologists, ballistics experts, etc.) advertise their services.

If you are a lone wolf and have to do everything yourself, you can write to any public library's reference librarian, explaining your situation, and ask for help finding an expert in a certain scientific field or specific information from such an expert. Be sure to send a self-addressed, stamped envelope for their reply.

Also, writing to more than one public library betters your chances of receiving what you're searching for.

You might be able to find an expert through a search on your law library's computer. Doing so will also show you whether or not the scientific method has been used in other cases.

When doing research and investigating anything or anyone, you have to think "outside the box" and get creative. Sometimes the person or piece of information you need will be found by someone not known to you, from a place least expected. The effort you put into investigating your case, collecting information, could make the difference between overturning your conviction or losing more years of your life to prison.

<3> PETITION FOR WRIT OF HABEAS CORPUS IN STATE COURT

Preparation of Petition

As in all *Smith's Guide* titles, you can find, at the end of this chapter, examples to look to while preparing your petition. Two of this chapter's examples have writ summaries and two do not. In Missouri, any original writ (habeas corpus, mandamus, or prohibition) filed in the appellate or supreme court is required to have a writ summary, but this is not the rule of the circuit courts.

Although the format recommended by *Smith's Guide* is similar to that used in the examples, your state's statutes may require additional information that the examples do not include. Check your state's statutes, provided in the appendix of this book.

Note that, although *application* and *petition* refer to the same thing, you should use whichever term your state uses to describe its instrument for state habeas corpus relief.

When preparing your petition, each material fact should be numbered and set forth in separate paragraphs. This practice will make it easier for the court to determine which facts are undisputed and which present genuine material facts in dispute, requiring resolution by the court via evidentiary hearing.

Should you need to use several exhibits to prove your claim(s), it may be more practical to prepare your appendix for accompanying exhibits before preparing your petition. If this applies to you, see the next chapter.

State Forms and Cover Page

The State of Virginia requires prisoners to use specific forms. In such instances, fill in all information for which space on the form is provided, writing "see attached petition" where there is not enough space to fully answer any question. Place the completed state form(s) on the top of your petition.

As shown in the example petitions, the cover page should have a caption at the top; a title in the middle; and your name, DOC number, and address at the bottom right.

Petition for Writ of Habeas Corpus with Suggestions in Support

Your petition should start with a caption, a title such as "PETITION FOR WRIT OF HABEAS CORPUS WITH SUGGESTIONS IN SUPPORT," and an introduction. The introduction should be brief, stating your name, the relief you are asking for, and the rule or statutory authority that invokes the court's jurisdiction.

Jurisdictional Statement

Depending upon your state's statutory requirements, the jurisdictional statement should state the name and address of the place where you're confined, the name and address of the person confining you (e.g., the warden or jailer), whether a petition for a writ of habeas corpus has been filed in any other court, and a brief description of your illegal confinement.

Statement of the Case

The statement of the case should have two sections, "A. Procedural History" and "B. Statement of Facts." The first should succinctly state the procedural history of your case, including conviction(s), sentence(s), appellate direct appeals, and any post-conviction proceedings in state or federal court.

The statement of facts should supply all the necessary information to your claim(s) for relief. Each material fact should be followed by a citation—a reference to the trial transcript, appendix of accompanying exhibits, affidavit(s), or other document(s) where the fact comes from.

C. Newly Discovered Evidence

This section, if applicable to your case, should state the newly discovered evidence that establishes your basis for relief—what evidence you discovered, as well as how and when you discovered it.

D. Cause to Overcome Procedural Default

In this section, you should state the factual and legal basis that you intend to use to overcome any state procedural default. This might include the state's failure to disclose Brady material, newly discovered evidence, jurisdictional defect, actual innocence, or other basis.

Reasons for Granting the Writ

Here you will state your claim(s), showing exactly why you are entitled to relief. Your claim(s) should each include the facts of the claim(s), the controlling law, and an application of that law to the facts. (You may, alternatively, state the law first, *then* apply it to the facts of your claim(s).)

By following a simple format, you will present concise and convincing legal arguments for the court's consideration.

Conclusion

Your conclusion should be brief, stating that you are entitled to relief, what form that relief should take, and a short prayer for that relief.

Verification of Petition

Some states require the petitioner to verify his or her petition by stating that he or she is aware of its contents, and that the contents are true and correct to the best of the petitioner's knowledge and belief. Such verifications must be signed and notarized.

An example verification is provided at the end of this chapter.

Certificate of Service

The certificate of service should state that your petition was mailed, postage prepaid, on a certain date, and that a copy was sent to the court and the respondent or his or her attorney (e.g., the jailer, warden, or attorney general).

Example—Verification of Petition

STATE OF [insert name of state]   )
) ss.
COUNTY OF [insert name of county]   )

VERIFICATION OF PETITION

I,_____, the Petitioner, hereby verify that I know the contents of this Petition for a Writ of Habeas Corpus; that the facts stated in this petition are true and correct to the best of my knowledge and belief.

_____
Petitioner

Subscribed and sworn to before me, a Notary Public, this___day of _____, 20__.

_____
Notary Public

My commission expires:

Example Petition for Writ of Habeas Corpus—Smith v. Pash

Case No. _____

**IN THE CIRCUIT COURT OF DEKALF COUNTY, MISSOURI
AT MAYSVILLE**

ZACHARY A. SMITH,

Petitioner,

v.

**RHONDA PASH, WARDEN
CROSSROADS CORRECTIONAL CENTER,**

Respondent.

PETITION FOR WRIT OF HABEAS CORPUS

ZACHARY A. SMITH,
Reg. No. 521163
Crossroads Corr. Center
1115 E. Pence Road
Cameron, Missouri 64429

Petitioner

Example Petition for Writ of Habeas Corpus—Smith v. Pash (cont.)

IN THE CIRCUIT COURT OF DEKALB COUNTY, MISSOURI
AT MAYSVILLE

ZACHARY A. SMITH,)
)
        Petitioner,)
)
v.) Case No. _____
)
RHONDA PASH, WARDEN,)
)
        Respondent.)

PETITION FOR WRIT OF HABEAS CORPUS

WITH SUGGESTIONS IN SUPPORT

COMES NOW Petitioner, Zachary A. Smith, and petitions this Court for a writ of habeas corpus vacating his Jackson County convictions for first degree murder and armed criminal action, pursuant to Missouri Supreme Court Rule 91.01. In support of petition, Zachary states:

JURISDICTIONAL STATEMENT

1. Zachary is incarcerated at Crossroads Correctional Center, 1115 E. Pence Road, Cameron, Missouri 64429. Rhonda Pash is the Warden of Crossroads Correctional Center and is the proper named Respondent in this matter.

2. No petition for writ of habeas corpus has been filed in any other court in connection with this newly discovered evidence, the subject of this petition.

3. Zachary was denied his right to effective assistance of counsel, as guaranteed by the Sixth and Fourteenth Amendments to the United States Constitution, and Article I, Sections 10 and 18(a) of the Missouri Constitution, in that Zachary's defense attorney failed to advise him of a seventeen year plea offer.

1

STATEMENT OF THE CASE

A. PROCEDURAL HISTORY

4. Zachary was convicted of the murder of Derek Hoskins and sentenced to life without the possibility of probation or parole and ninety-nine years, after three jury trials. The first jury was unable to reach a verdict. At the second trial, Zachary was convicted and sentenced to life without parole and one hundred years; however, the conviction was reversed for a failure to instruct on second degree murder. **State v. Smith**, 966 S.W.2d 1 (Mo.App. 1997).

5. At the third trial, Zachary was again convicted of first degree murder. The conviction was affirmed on direct appeal. **State v. Smith**, 90 S.W.3d 132 (Mo.App. 2002). State postconviction proceedings were filed; relief was denied in the motion court and on appeal in an unpublished opinion.

6. Zachary then filed a habeas corpus actin in federal court. His petition was denied but was granted a certificate of appealability on an issue of ineffective assistance of counsel. However, the Eighth Circuit denied relief, concluding that Zachary failed to establish prejudice. Zachary filed a petition for a Writ of Certiorari; it was denied on November 19, 2009.

B. STATEMENT OF FACTS

7. On February 6, 1996, attorney Fredrick A. Duchardt Jr. advised Zachary of a plea offer for two life sentences. Zachary declined the States's offer and proceeded to trial; the trial resulted in a hung jury (Petitioner's Exhibit A).

2

Example Petition for Writ of Habeas Corpus—Smith v. Pash (cont.)

8. Prior to second trial, Fred advised Zachary of a twenty-five year plea offer. He declined the State's offer and proceeded to trial; Zachary was convicted and sentenced to life without the possibility of probation or parole and one hundred years. The conviction, however, was reversed on direct appeal, and the case was remanded for a new trial (Petitioner's Exhibits A and D).

9. When Zachary returned to the Jackson County Detention Center to await the third trial, Fred visited him, sometime in June of 1998. During the visit, Fred said, "Let's cut the shit, what plea would you take?" Zachary answered, "I'll take ten years." Fred grinned and said, "I bet you would. I can't take the State an offer like that. It is 'highly unlikely' they would agree to it" (Petitioner's Exhibit A).

10. Nevertheless, Fred told Ms. Werner, the assistant prosecuting attorney, about Zachary's offer to plead to ten years. And when Zachary talked to Fred over the phone, he said Ms. Werner laughed for a solid ten minutes. When she regained her composure, she said, "Tell him I'll meet him half way from the ten years he offered to take and the twenty-five I offered him last time." Fred said it would be an eighteen year sentence (Petitioner's Exhibit A).

11. Remembering a comment Ms. Werner made when the judge declared a hung jury, saying Zachary's case wasn't one she wanted to retry, Zachary countered with an offer to take ten and three, consecutive. He was hoping Ms. Werner would come down to fifteen. With the two years he already served, Zachary would of been eligible to serve his sentence at a level three institution, possibly at Algoa Correctional Center, the institution his father was at serving a thirteen years sentence, instead of at the violent and highly restricted level five he had just

Example Petition for Writ of Habeas Corpus—Smith v. Pash (cont.)

come from (Petitioner's Exhibits A and B).

12. When Fred told Ms. Werner of Zachary's counter offer, she became angry and took back her eighteen year plea offer, telling Fred, "He has until December 31, 1998, to take twenty-five years or I'll give him life without parole again" (Petitioner's Exhibits A and C).

13. At that point, Zachary asked Fred to move for a bond. And at the hearing, Ms. Werner objected, stating she was unable to locate her witnesses (Petitioner's Exhibits A and D).

14. A few months later, Zachary met an attorney named Daniel L. Franco. Zachary discussed a 1983 civil rights case with him. But Franco was more interested in Zachary's criminal case, asking him who the prosecutor was. When Zachary told him Bronwyn Werner, he smiled. He said he wanted to read Zachary's trial transcripts, so he retrieved them for him. Franco then said he'd see Zachary in a few weeks (Petitioner's Exhibit A).

15. A few weeks later, Franco visited Zachary and told him he wanted to take his case, saying he was Ms. Werner's study partner in law school. Franco further said Werner was a good person until she went to the "dark side." Franco said he could beat her and wanted to take Zachary's case to teach her a lesson. Zachary told him he didn't have any money. Franco said he would take the case if Zachary would agree to pay him ten thousand dollars upon being acquitted. Figuring he didn't have anything to lose, Zachary agreed to the terms of his representation. He didn't want to go to trial again but with no plea offer forthcoming, Zachary felt he had no other choice. He also figured that Ms. Werner might relent on her promise and offer him the eighteen

4

again before trial, especially since she knew Franco personally and was having trouble locating her witnesses. At the time, Zachary believed that's how the legal system worked, hire the right attorney, get a better plea (Petitioner's Exhibits A and D).

16. But Franco never spoke to Zachary about _any_ plea offers, ever. And the next time Zachary talked with Franco, months later, he told Zachary he saw Ms. Werner at a Big Twelve Basketball Conference. She told Franco that she was having problems at the prosecutor's office--something to do with her sexual orientation and how she was being treated--and put in her resignation. Franco joked about Ms. Werner wearing shorts and having hairy legs when he saw her. Zachary wasn't amused, his hope of getting the eighteen year plea back were dashed. Zachary knew Daniel Miller would take first chair and his reputation wasn't earned by making plea offers (Petitioner's Exhibit A).

17. Zachary's case proceeded to trial on April 24, 2000, and he was convicted and sentenced to life without the possibility of probation or parole and ninety-nine years (Petitioner's Exhibits A and D).

18. On February 20, 2002, Daniel L. Franco was charged in an Information filed by the Region IV Disciplinary Committee with ten counts of professional misconduct. (Petitioner's Exhibt H). On October 7, 2002, Franco filed an application to surrender his license to practice law in Missouri (Petitioner's Exhibit I). On April 18, 2003, Franco was found guilty of dishonest behavior in connection with him practicing law in Kansas without a license (Petitioner's Exhibit J).

C. NEWLY DISCOVERED EVIDENCE

19. Sometime after Zachary's federal habeas corpus remedy was

5

exhausted, his habeas attorney, Elizabeth Unger Carlyle, had lost the case files. Almost five years later, Elizabeth sent Zachary a letter stating she found the files and asked if he wanted them. Zachary called her and told her he did. He received three boxes on or about March 23, 2015, including the appellate and postconviction files (Petitioner's Exhibits A and E).

20. Shortly after, Zachary went to the property room and looked through the files. Inside the appellate file--a file Zachary never had possession of--he found a memo of a conversation Nancy Wiebe had with Daniel Franco, dated November 1, 2000. The last sentence of the memo read: "He [Franco] also added that he [Franco] had a 17yr. plea offer that Zach refused to accept" (Petitioner's Exhibits A, F, and G).

21. Zachary felt sick when he read the memo because Franco never discussed a 17yr. plea offer with him or any other plea offers. Had Zachary known that there was a 17yr. plea offer available after Ms. Werner took the eighteen off the table, he would have accepted it instead of proceeding to trial. Until he read the November 1, 2000, memo, Zachary believed he had no choice but to proceed to trial because there was no plea offer available to him (Petitioner's Exhibit A).

D. CAUSE TO OVERCOME PROCEDURAL DEFAULT

22. In Missouri, a habeas petitioner may show cause for a procedural default by demonstrating that his claim was not "known to him" in time to include it in a direct appeal or a post-conviction motion. **State ex rel. Engel v. Dormire**, 304 S.W.3d 120, 125-26 (Mo.banc. 2010)(quoting **State ex rel. Simmons v. White**, 866 S.W.2d 443, 446

Example Petition for Writ of Habeas Corpus—Smith v. Pash (cont.)

(Mo.banc. 1993). See also **Gehrke v. State**, 280 S.W.3d 54, 58-59 (Mo.banc. 2009); **Brown v. State**, 66 S.W.3d 721, 726 (Mo.banc. 2002).

23. Cause to overcome any procedural default in this case is established because Zachary was not made aware that his attorney Daniel L. Franco failed to advise him of the State's 17yr. plea offer until he read the November 1, 2000, memo. Zachary never had possession of the appellate or postconviction files until Elizabeth Carlyle found them, after being lost for five years, and sent them to him the end of March, 2015 (Petitioner's Exhibits A, E, and G). And because Franco lied about Zachary rejecting the plea, the claim would not of been recognizable to his appellate or postconviction attorneys. But Zachary immediately recognized the claim once he seen the memo because Franco never advised him of <u>any</u> seventeen year plea offer or any other plea offer (Petitioner's Exhibit A).

REASONS FOR GRANTING THE WRIT
CLAIM ONE

ZACHARY IS ENTITLED TO THE ISSUANCE OF A WRIT OF HABEAS CORPUS, DISCHARGING HIM FROM HIS UNCONSTITUTIONAL CONVICTIONS FOR FIRST DEGREE MURDER AND ARMED CRIMINAL ACTION, BECAUSE HIS ATTORNEY FAILED TO ADVISE HIM OF A SEVENTEEN YEAR PLEA OFFER BY THE STATE, IN VIOLATION OF ZACHARY'S RIGHT TO EFFECTIVE ASSISTANCE OF COUNSEL, AS GUARANTEED BY THE SIXTH AND FOURTEENTH AMENDMENTS TO THE UNITED STATES CONSITUTION, AND ARTICLE I, SECTIONS 10 AND 18(A) OF THE MISSOURI CONSTITUTION.

24. Defense counsel has a duty to communicate formal offers from the prosecutor to accept a plea on terms and conditions that may be favorbale to the accused. When defense counsel allows an offer to expire

without advising the defendant or allowing him to consider it, defense counsel does not render the effective assistance the Constitution requires. **Missouri v. Frye,** 132 S.Ct. 1399 (2012).

25. In the present case, Daniel Franco failed to advise him of a seventeen year plea offer (Petitioner's Exhibit A). Instead, Franco let the plea offer expire when Ms. Werner put in her resignation at the Jackson County Prosecutor's Office (Petitioner's Exhibit A). Had Zachary been advised that there was a seventeen year plea offer available after the December 31, 1998, twenty-five year plea offer had expired, he would have accepted it. Zachary was prejudiced by Franco's failure to advise him of the plea offer because he was forced to proceed to trial and was convicted of first degree murder and armed criminal action and sentenced to life without the possibility of probation or parole and ninety-nine years in prison (Petitioner's Exhibits A and D).

CONCLUSION

In light of Franco's failure to advise Zachary of a seventeen year plea offer, Zachary prays this Court, after holding a hearing, and examining the evidence and applicable law, issue a writ of habeas corpus vacating his convictions for first degree murder and armed criminal action and discharge him from custody. He further prays for any other and further relief as the Court deems just and equitable.

Example Petition for Writ of Habeas Corpus—Smith v. Pash (cont.)

Respectfully Submitted,

/s/ Z.A. Smith
Zachary A. Smith,
Reg. No. 521163
Crossroads Corr. Center
1115 E. Pence Road
Cameron, Missouri 64429

Petitioner

CERTIFICATE OF SERVICE

I hereby certify that on this 27th day of May, 2015, a true and correct copy of the foregoing was mailed, postage prepaid, to: Chris Koster, Attorney General, P.O. Box 899, Jefferson City, Missouri 65102, attorney for Respondent.

/s/ Z.A. Smith
Zachary A. Smith

Example Petition for Writ of Habeas Corpus #2—Engel v. Dormire

IN THE SUPREME COURT OF MISSOURI

GARY W. ENGEL,)
)
  Petitioner,)
)
) Case No. 090014
v.)
)
DAVE DORMIRE,)
  Superintendent,)
)
  Respondent.)

WRIT SUMMARY

Identity of the parties and their attorneys in the underlying action, if any: N/A

Nature of underlying action, if any: N/A

Action of respondent being challenged, including date thereof: Judgment and sentence of Clay County, Missouri, Case No. CR 190-1698FX, dated October 4, 1991.

Relief sought by relator or petitioner: Vacate petitioner's illegal and unconstitutional convictions for the crimes of kidnapping (2 cts) and armed criminal action (2 cts).

Date case set for trial, if set, and date of any other event bearing upon relief sought (e.g., date of deposition or motion hearing): N/A

Date, Court and disposition of previous writ proceedings: Rule 91 petitions: Circuit Court of Cole County No. 06AC-CC01100; denied July 11, 2007; Missouri Court of Appeals, Western District, No. WD69561; denied October 31, 2008.

Example Petition for Writ of Habeas Corpus #2—Engel v. Dormire (cont.)

IN THE SUPREME COURT OF MISSOURI

In re:

GARY W. ENGEL,)
)
       Petitioner,)
)
vs.) Case No. 090314
)
DAVE DORMIRE,)
       Superintendent,)
)
       Respondent.)

<u>**PETITION FOR A WRIT OF HABEAS CORPUS**</u>

FILED

AUG 0 6 2009

Thomas F. Simon
CLERK, SUPREME COURT

KENT E. GIPSON #34524
Law Office of Kent Gipson, LLC
301 E. 63rd Street
Kansas City, Missouri 64113
816-363-4400 / fax: 816-363-4300
kent.gipson@kentgipsonlaw.com

Counsel for Petitioner

Example Petition for Writ of Habeas Corpus #2—Engel v. Dormire (cont.)

IN THE
SUPREME COURT OF MISSOURI

GARY W. ENGEL,)
)
    Petitioner,)
)
)
) Case No._____
)
DAVE DORMIRE,)
    Superintendent,)
)
    Respondent.)

PETITION FOR A WRIT OF HABEAS CORPUS

COMES NOW petitioner, Gary W. Engel, pursuant to Missouri Supreme Court Rule 91, and petitions this Court for a writ of habeas corpus vacating his Clay County convictions for two counts of kidnapping and two counts of armed criminal action. In the support of his petition, petitioner states:

SUGGESTIONS IN SUPPORT

I.

INTRODUCTION AND SUMMARY OF ARGUMENT

This habeas corpus case presents the court with an extraordinary set of facts, involving petitioner Gary Engel and his co-defendant Steven Manning, two ex-Chicago police officers who were convicted nearly twenty years ago in Clay County for kidnapping and holding for ransom two drug dealers. Steven Manning was freed more than five years ago after the Eighth Circuit reversed his convictions in *Manning v. Bowersox*, 310 F.3d 571 (8th Cir. 2002) and Clay County prosecutors elected to dismiss the charges rather than seek a retrial.

Mr. Manning then pursued a federal lawsuit under *Bivens v. Six Unknown Agents*, 403 U.S. 388 (1971) against the FBI agents who brought this case to Clay County for prosecution, alleging that these agents committed numerous *Brady v. Maryland*, 373 U.S. 83 (1963) violations and suborned perjury at his trial. In 2005, a federal jury in Chicago found in favor of Mr. Manning and awarded him over six million dollars in damages. (*See* Exh. F).

Gary Engel, in stark contrast, has languished in prison for over nineteen years because he had the misfortune to be appointed incompetent counsel during his federal habeas corpus action. Petitioner's appointed counsel missed a mandatory deadline that resulted in the denial of his petition. *Engel v. Dormire*, #03-0798-CV-W-GAF (Judgment of February 24, 2005).

Mr. Manning's attorneys, during his federal habeas corpus action and subsequent lawsuit against the investigating officers, uncovered compelling evidence that FBI Agent Robert Buchan and the Buffalo Grove, Illinois Police Department withheld *Brady* material and suborned perjury from three of the state's key witnesses against Manning and petitioner: Anthony Mammolito, Sharon Dugan, and Carolyn Heldebrand. Among other things, it was revealed during the *Manning* litigation that

2

Example Petition for Writ of Habeas Corpus #2—Engel v. Dormire (cont.)

both Mammolito and Dugan were paid by the government for their testimony, a fact that was not revealed to Mr. Engel prior to his trial. (*See* Exh.'s B, C, D, F).

Apart from establishing a clear-cut due process violation, the evidence uncovered by Manning and his attorneys also provides cause and prejudice to overcome any procedural default arising from the fact that Mr. Engel did not present these *Brady*/perjured testimony claims in his state court appeals, which were exhausted in 1993, *because* the factual basis supporting these claims was not available due to the fact that this evidence was concealed by the government. *See State ex. rel Nixon v. Jaynes*, 63 S.W.3d 210, 214 (Mo. banc 2001), *Amadeo v. Zant*, 486 U.S. 214, 222 (1988). Thus, this case presents a rare situation in which this Court should exercise its discretionary power to intervene under Rule 91 to correct a clear injustice.

Having established that no procedural impediment to this Court's discretionary review exists, the present petition presents three grounds for relief: (1) a *Brady* claim; (2) an interrelated due process claim involving the use of perjured testimony; and (3) a claim that petitioner's Armed Criminal Action convictions are unlawful because they were filed after the statute of limitation had expired. After a full and fair review of the following facts and applicable law, petitioner Gary Engel respectfully requests that, like his co-defendant, his constitutionally tainted convictions be set aside.

3

II.

STATEMENT OF JURISDICTION

Jurisdiction lies with this Court pursuant to Missouri Supreme Court Rule 91, and 508.010 R.S. Mo. (2000), in that the petitioner is a prisoner in the State of Missouri, and is being held in the custody of respondent within Cole County, Missouri, and service upon respondent can be made within Cole County, Missouri. Pursuant to Rule 91.04, petitioner states that no petition for relief has been made to a higher court.

III.

STATEMENT OF PARTIES

Petitioner, Gary W. Engel, # 182067, is a prisoner of the State of Missouri, due to a criminal conviction. Petitioner is being held at the Jefferson City Correctional Center, 8200 Fenceline Road, Jefferson City, Missouri, 65101. Service can be made upon petitioner at this address.

Petitioner is represented by Kent E. Gipson, 301 E. 63rd Street, Kansas City, Missouri, 64113. Service can be made upon petitioner's counsel at this address.

Respondent, Dave Dormire, is employed by the State of Missouri, as the Superintendent of Jefferson City Correctional Center, 8200 No More Victims Road,

Jefferson City, Missouri, 65101. Service can be made upon respondent at this address.

Respondent will be represented by Attorney General's Office for the State of Missouri, Jeremiah (Jay) Nixon, P.O. Box 899, Jefferson City, Missouri, 65102. Service can be made upon respondent's counsel at this address.

IV.

STATEMENT OF THE CASE

A. PROCEDURAL HISTORY

Petitioner was charged by way of complaint in the Circuit Court of Clay County, Missouri, on July 20, 1990, with two counts of kidnapping and two counts of armed criminal action. The complaint alleged that petitioner kidnapped Charles Ford and Mark Harris at gunpoint on an unspecified day in February, 1984. Petitioner was arrested on July 26, 1990, on a Clay County warrant and was placed in the Cook County Jail in Chicago, Illinois, to await extradition.

Petitioner retained Kansas City attorney F.A. White to represent him. Petitioner proceeded to trial on subsequent information (case # CR190-1698FX) on June 24, 1991, before the Honorable John R. Hutcherson, which resulted in a jury verdict of conviction on all counts. (Tr. 630-31; L.F. 46-49).[1] On October 4, 1991,

---

[1] Citations to the State Court record will be designated as follows: trial

Example Petition for Writ of Habeas Corpus #2—Engel v. Dormire (cont.)

Judge Hutcherson sentenced petitioner to consecutive thirty-year terms for each count of kidnapping and consecutive fifteen year sentences on the counts of armed criminal action, for a total of ninety years imprisonment. (L.F. 58-59).

Thereafter, petitioner filed a notice of appeal and a motion for state post-conviction relief, pursuant to Rule 29.15. (L.F. 61). On May 26, 1992, after holding a hearing, Judge Hutcherson denied petitioner's 29.15 motion in all respects. On consolidated appeal, the Court of Appeals affirmed petitioner's convictions and the denial of post-conviction relief. *State v. Engel*, 859 S.W. 2d 822 (Mo. App. W.D. 1993).

On February 24, 2003, petitioner filed a *pro se* Petition for Writ of Habeas Corpus, in the Nineteenth Judicial Circuit Court, Cole County, Missouri (case # 03-CV-323479). This case was assigned to the Honorable Richard G. Callahan. On April 28, 2003, Judge Callahan rendered a decision, denying the Petition for Writ of Habeas Corpus in all respects. On May 9, 2003, petitioner filed a timely Motion for Reconsideration with the Circuit Court. On May 16, 2003, the Circuit Court Judge denied Petitioner's Motion for Reconsideration.

---

transcripts will be "Tr.; legal file, "L.F.". A partial trial transcript, containing the testimony of the key prosecution witnesses, is attached as Exhibit Q.

6

Example Petition for Writ of Habeas Corpus #2—Engel v. Dormire (cont.)

On May 29, 2003, petitioner filed an appeal with the Missouri Court of Appeals, Western District (case # WD62850). On June 30, 2003, the Court of Appeals dismissed this appeal.

On July 7, 2003, petitioner timely filed a petition for discretionary review with this Court (case # SC85404). On August 26, 2003, this petition was denied.

On September 2, 2003, petitioner filed, *pro se*, a petition for a writ of habeas corpus pursuant to 28 U.S.C. § 2254 (case # 03-0798-CV-W-GAF-P) in the United States District Court, Western District of Missouri. On May 4, 2004, the District Court (the Honorable Gary Fenner) appointed Kansas City attorney Philip Klawuhn to represent petitioner in all further proceedings.

On November 19, 2004, after receiving numerous extensions of time, Klawuhn filed an amended petition for writ of habeas corpus on behalf of petitioner. On January 28, 2005, the State of Missouri filed its response to the petition.

On February 24, 2005, nearly one month later, after receiving no reply (traverse) from petitioner's court-appointed attorney to the State's response, in violation of Local Rule 9.2(I),[2] and because no timely request for an extension to

---

[2] This local rule requires a traverse or reply to be filed within seven days. The failure to file a timely traverse results in an admission that all facts pleaded in the state's response are true.

7

reply was filed, the District Court entered an order denying petitioner's petition for writ of habeas corpus.

On March 10, 2005, Klawuhn filed a motion for reconsideration (F.R.C.P. Rule 59e) and a motion to expand the record to include newly discovered evidence, (§2254 Rule 7). These motions were denied by the District Court on April 6, 2005.

Petitioner appealed this judgment to the Eighth Circuit Court of Appeals, (Case # 05-2439). On February 7, 2006, an Eighth Circuit panel denied petitioner's application for Certificate of Appealability and dismissed the appeal. On February 21, 2006, Klawuhn filed a petition for rehearing, which was denied on March 16, 2006.

Petitioner thereafter filed another Rule 91 petition in the Circuit Court of Cole County, Missouri with the assistance of undersigned counsel, raising the same claims he raised in his federal habeas action based upon newly discovered *evidence* that did not become available until it was unearthed by civil litigation involving co-defendant Steve Manning. *Engel v. Dormire*, No. 06-AC-CC01100. The case was assigned to Circuit Judge Richard Callahan, who ordered the State of Missouri to answer the petition. After full briefing and oral argument, Judge Callahan issued an order and judgment on July 11, 2007 denying the petition, primarily on procedural grounds. (*See* Exh. L). Judge Callahan's order copied verbatim much of the state's response to the petition and incorporated nearly identical language in his order denying habeas relief. (*See* Exh. M).

8

On April 18, 2008, petitioner filed a Rule 91 petition in the Missouri Court of Appeals Western District. *Engel v. Dormire*, WD 69561. The Court ordered the State of Missouri to answer the petition. The State filed a response to the petition on May 1, 2008. Petitioner filed a reply on May 6, 2008. Judge Holliger issued a one-line order denying the motion on October 31, 2008, with Judge Lowenstein concurring. (Exh. P).

B. PROCEDURAL BACKGROUND OF CO-DEFENDANT STEVEN MANNING

After petitioner and his co-defendant Steve Manning were convicted in Missouri, Manning was returned to Chicago, Illinois to stand trial on murder charges involving the murder of James Pellegrino. In October of 1993, Manning was convicted of First Degree Murder and sentenced to death. The murder investigation was conducted for the most part by Chicago FBI agent Robert Buchan, who was also the lead investigator in the Missouri kidnapping case. Manning then appealed his murder conviction to the Illinois Supreme Court. In April 1998, Manning's murder conviction was reversed and the case was remanded for a new trial. *People v. Manning*, 695 N.E.2d 423 (Ill. 1998). Because of the improprieties in that case, Cook County, Illinois prosecutors determined not to pursue Manning further, and dropped the case. Manning was then released from Illinois' death row and returned to Missouri to serve out his kidnapping sentences. In January 2002, Manning filed a federal civil suit against FBI Agent Buchan and others, alleging he was framed by Buchan for the Pellegrino murder. Mills, *Ex-Death Row Inmate Sues: "FBI Prosecutors 'Fixed' Murder Case, Lawyer Says"*, Chicago Tribune, January 17, 2002.

In November 2002, Manning's convictions in Missouri were reversed by the Eighth Circuit Court of Appeals. *Manning v. Bowersox*, 310 F3d 571 (8th Cir. 2002). The Eighth Circuit sidestepped the *Brady*/perjured testimony issues presented here because a new trial was granted on other grounds and those issues could be more thoroughly examined at retrial. *Id.* at 574 n. 3. In September 2003, Manning was released from the Missouri Department of Corrections and returned to Clay County, Missouri, for retrial there. On February 26, 2004, Clay County prosecutors elected to dismiss the charges, and Manning was released.[3]

Manning was then allowed to amend his original federal civil suit to include his Missouri convictions, where he again alleged that FBI Agent Buchan had manufactured false evidence, suborned the perjury of witnesses, and secretly paid a

---

[3] The undersigned counsel was appointed by the district court and Eighth Circuit to represent Mr. Manning in his federal habeas action. After Mr. Manning was released, counsel agreed to represent Mr. Engel, *pro bono*, in the present Rule 91 proceedings.

Example Petition for Writ of Habeas Corpus #2—Engel v. Dormire (cont.)

witness to testify. In December 2004, a civil trial was held before District Court Judge Mathew Kennelly and a jury in United States District Court in Chicago. *See Manning v. Buchan and Miller et al.*, case # 02C372 (N.D. IL.), hereinafter referred to as "Civil Trial."

After nearly three weeks of testimony and a week more of deliberations, on January 24, 2005, the jury issued a *unanimous* verdict in favor of Manning, awarding him over 6.5 million dollars in damages. (*See* Pet. Exh. F). This verdict was entered into the record March 25, 2005.

Attorneys for the FBI agents and the Federal Government then filed motions to overturn the jury verdict before the District Court. On November 14, 2005, District Court Judge Kennelly issued his Memorandum, Opinion and Order (hereinafter referred to as "Memorandum") denying this request. (*See* Pet. Exh. G).

On February 14, 2006, co-defendant Manning then filed a federal civil suit against the Village of Buffalo Grove, Illinois, and its then police officers, Sgt. Robert Quid (RET) and former Cmdr. Gary Del Re, for their roles in falsely convicting Manning concerning the Missouri kidnapping case. (*See Manning v. Quid and Del Re, et al.*, Case # 06C820 (N.D. IL.)

On September 28, 2006 Judge Kennelly issued an order ruling against Mr. Manning on his claim against the FBI under the Federal Tort Claims Act (FTCA).

11

However, as Judge Kennelly pointed out, to prevail on a claim under the FTCA the government is entitled to prevail if there was probable cause to prosecute Manning, and the issue of fabricated or hidden evidence is irrelevant. As Judge Kennelly pointed out at the outset: "The court's conclusion that there was probable cause to prosecute Manning is in no way inconsistent with the jury's finding on the constitutional law claims against the two FBI agents. On those claims, the jury reasonably concluded that the evidence that the agents fabricated and/or withheld was 'material' and made the difference in his state court convictions." (9/28, 2006 Order at p. 2). Later in this same opinion, Judge Kennelly stated: "There is no question that a deal was made at some point before Mammolito testified at Manning's Kansas City trials to pay him some amount of money... The deal to pay Mammolito was not disclosed to Manning's attorney's in the Missouri case." (*Id.* at p. 23).

Judge Kennelly's subsequent order of December 26, 2006 setting aside the jury verdict on Manning's *Bivens* claims also does not impact the jury's findings regarding the *Brady*/perjured testimony claims against the law enforcement officers who investigated the case. As Judge Kennelly pointed out, his decision to vacate the jury verdict had nothing to do with the merits of the claims involved, but instead hinged upon a statutory provision under the FTCA precluding dual recovery. In this regard, the decision to vacate the jury verdict on the *Brady* claims was based upon the plain

12

language of 28 U.S.C § 2676, which states: "The judgment in any action under §1346(b) of this title shall constitute a complete bar to any action by the claimant by reason of the same subject matter, against the employee of the government whose act or omission gave rise to the claim."[4] Because the legal questions are entirely distinct under the FTCA, it is clear that the jury's findings in *Manning* remain the most powerful evidence in this case, demonstrating that the investigating officers violated Manning's and Engel's rights, resulting in their wrongful convictions.

C. STATEMENT OF FACTS

Petitioner was convicted of multiple charges arising from the armed kidnapping of Charles Ford and Mark Harris that allegedly occurred in Clay County, Missouri, in February 1984. Mr. Ford, who was a major drug dealer, did not report this kidnapping until months later, while negotiating a plea bargain in connection with pending federal drug charges against him. (Exh. Q p. 30). Authorities did not actively investigate this kidnapping until 1989, when they interviewed Anthony Mammolito at a federal prison facility on an unrelated matter.

---

[4] Judge Kennelly's order was affirmed by the Seventh Circuit in *Manning v. United States*, 546 F.3d 430 (7th. Cir. 2008). A petition for a writ of certiorari was filed by Manning in the United States Supreme Court on June 24, 2009. *Manning v. United States*, No. 08-1595, 78 USLW 3015.

13

Example Petition for Writ of Habeas Corpus #2—Engel v. Dormire (cont.)

Neither of the victims could identify their assailants (*Id.* 2-117). No evidence connected petitioner Engel to this crime until federal prisoner Anthony Mammolito told Sgt. Robert Quid of the Buffalo Grove, Illinois Police Department, and agent Robert Buchan, FBI, Chicago Office, about the kidnapping, in 1989. At that time, Mammolito gave a statement to the authorities that he recruited Engel, Steven Manning, and Thomas McKillip, all from Chicago, to kidnap Mr. Ford and to hold him for ransom, because Mammolito knew that Ford had substantial amounts of cash he had acquired through his illegal drug dealing activities. Throughout the proceedings, including pre-trial examinations, Anthony Mammolito repeatedly denied that he received *any* deals or favorable treatment from the government for his testimony against petitioner Engel and his co-defendant Steven Manning, other than an understanding that he would not be prosecuted for the kidnapping. (*Id.* 177).

The only other direct evidence against petitioner Engel came from Sharon Dugan, the ex-wife of petitioner, who testified that in 1984, she picked Engel up from Midway Airport in Chicago, and that Engel told her (Dugan) he had been to Kansas City, Mo, and had scored down there. Dugan also testified that she took, without his knowledge, a diamond ring from Engel upon his return from Kansas City that Engel told her was a part of the score. (*Id.* 207-220).

14

Example Petition for Writ of Habeas Corpus #2—Engel v. Dormire (cont.)

The jury returned a verdict of guilty on all counts. Petitioner was sentenced to a total of 90 years imprisonment and was remanded to the Missouri Department of Corrections, where he continues to serve these sentences in the custody of respondent.

D. **NEWLY DISCOVERED EVIDENCE**

The newly discovered evidence that forms the basis for this habeas corpus petition establishes that:

1. Agent Buchan (FBI) and Sgt. Quid (Buffalo Grove, IL Police Department) conspired together to frame petitioner and his co-defendant for crimes they did not commit.

2. Agent Buchan and Sgt. Quid failed to disclose to petitioner and the Clay County prosecutors a deal they had made with State's star witness Anthony Mammolito, whereby Mammolito would receive monetary compensation and other inducements, as well as intervention by the investigators in securing his (Mammmolito's) release from federal prison, in exchange for his testimony against Engel and Manning.

3. Buchan and Quid hid from Clay County prosecutors their investigative technique of disseminating information to witnesses before their testimony to make them appear credible.

15

4. Buchan and Quid produced false documentation of witness statements in an effort to persuade Clay County prosecutors to accept and file this case.

5. Newly discovered exculpatory and impeachment evidence, which was never disclosed to Manning or petitioner, was discovered for the first time during Manning's civil trial fifteen years later.

U.S. District Court Judge Kennelly's Memorandum of November 2005 provides a clear and concise summary of the evidence that supported Manning's civil jury verdict. (*See* Exh. G). Remarkably, the Clay County prosecutors simply failed to investigate their own case, and instead relied on the word of these out-of-state rogue law enforcement agents to make their case. In sum, Clay County prosecutors were hoodwinked into providing a courtroom setting for a malicious prosecution.

After Manning's civil trial ended, these FBI agents, in a post-trial motion for a new trial, attempted to lay blame for Manning's wrongful conviction at the feet of the Clay County prosecutors. They argued that "even if they did taint witness testimony," there was no *Brady* violation because Clay County prosecutors knew about it from the beginning. This argument was emphatically rejected by Judge Kennelly in his Memorandum at p. 18. (*See* Exh. G).

As evidenced by Manning's civil trial, this was not the only case where Agent Buchan committed misconduct. After securing false convictions against petitioner

16

and his co-defendant in Missouri, Agent Buchan returned to Illinois and conspired with fellow agent Gary Miller to falsely convict (co-defendant) Manning for a murder in Illinois that landed Manning on death row. Manning became the thirteenth man released from Illinois death row after being wrongly convicted, which influenced former Governor George Ryan to place a moratorium on state executions in Illinois.

The civil jury verdict, as well as Judge Kennelly's Memorandum, shows that once again, as with Mammolito in Missouri, Buchan paid a state witness (Tommy Dye) $2,000.00 to make false statements and/or to fabricate claims about the Pellegrino murder, and concealed that fact from Illinois prosecutors. In short, Manning offered compelling proof at his civil trial that Buchan and Quid secured his conviction by fabricating evidence and withholding exculpatory and impeachment evidence which would have exonerated him.[5]

---

[5] Because the sequence of events, beginning with the initial investigation of the case in 1989 through the Manning civil litigation, is critical to the resolution of petitioner's claims, a chronological summary of these events is attached to this petition as Exhibit N.

REASONS FOR GRANTING THE WRIT

CLAIM ONE

PETITIONER'S CONVICTIONS VIOLATE DUE PROCESS OF LAW, IN VIOLATION OF THE FOURTEENTH AMENDMENT TO THE UNITED STATES CONSTITUTION, AND ART. I, § 18(a) OF THE CONSTITUTION OF THE STATE OF MISSOURI FOR THE REASON THAT EXCULPATORY AND IMPEACHMENT EVIDENCE THAT UNDERMINED CONFIDENCE IN THE OUTCOME OF PETITIONER'S CRIMINAL TRIAL WAS WITHHELD FROM PETITIONER PRIOR TO AND DURING HIS TRIAL.

In 1998, petitioner's co-defendant, Steven Manning, was in the midst of appealing his Missouri convictions before the federal courts pursuant to 28 U.S.C. § 2254. During those proceedings, District Judge Ortrie Smith ordered discovery, directing the Clay County Prosecutor's Office and Buffalo Grove, IL Police Department to produce all documents from its files regarding the Manning and Engel investigation and prosecution.

It was during this discovery process that the "smoking gun" letters from Mammolito to Sgt. Quid and Clay County prosecutor...now Judge Rex Gabbert...came to light. (*See* Pet. Exh's B; D). The Gabbert letter was written by Mammolito and received by the Clay County Prosecutor's Office prior to petitioner's

18

trial. Although prosecutor Bryan Klopfenstein and Judge Gabbert gave sworn testimony at the Manning civil trial that they had never seen this letter, or were even aware of its existence, both of the letters were considered by the jury in Manning's civil trial. Both letters clearly indicate that Mammolito reached an agreement to be paid for his testimony against Manning and Engel.

A different letter surfaced at Manning's civil trial that was never turned over by the Buffalo Grove Police Department in response to Judge Smith's order for discovery. In addition to the other letters Mammolito had written averring to a secret deal for monetary compensation, this newly discovered letter corroborated Mammolito's assertions that a deal for payment in exchange for testimony existed. This letter, written by Buffalo Grove P.D. Cmdr. Del Re to Mammolito's mother, with an enclosed check for $500.00, states that he wished they could have sent Mammolito more money "for the help Tony provided in this very important case." (*See* Pet. Exh. C).

It was also revealed at Manning's civil trial for the first time that Mammolito had made statements, prior to petitioner's trial, to a Clay County prosecutor that were contrary to his trial testimony. Prosecutor Klofenstein gave sworn testimony that Mammolito told him that there had been a different person involved in the Missouri kidnapping scenario who Mammolito refused to name because that person had since

Example Petition for Writ of Habeas Corpus #2—Engel v. Dormire (cont.)

died. (C.T. V15: 192-94).[6] The statement was never documented in any report, nor was it relayed to petitioner in any manner prior to or during trial.

Additional undisclosed evidence surfaced at the Manning civil trial that Sgt. Quid had made an additional visit to Mammolito in Louisiana in July, 1990 that was withheld from petitioner. (C.T. V14: 172). Quid was adamant that he made a report of this visit (when Mammolito changed his story to comport with law enforcement's new version of events), but this report was never disclosed to petitioner prior to or at his criminal trial, nor to Manning pursuant to Judge Smith's discovery order, or at Manning's civil trial. Coincidentally, this document is the only "critical" report missing from Buffalo Grove's entire file. (C.T. V14: 174-77).

During the civil trial, Cmdr. Del Re and Sgt. Quid insisted there was no deal made with Mammolito, but when pressed by Manning's attorney, neither could explain why they did not respond with any sort of denial when they received Mammolito's letter demanding they honor their deal. (C.T. V15: 15-16; V16: 204-06). The fact is, they sent Mammolito's mother $500 in a letter expressing regret that

---

[6] Petitioner will designate citations from Manning's civil trial as "C.T." followed by the volume number then page number. Transcript excerpts from Manning's civil trial are attached to the petition as Exhibit O.

20

died. (C.T. V15: 192-94).[6] The statement was never documented in any report, nor was it relayed to petitioner in any manner prior to or during trial.

Additional undisclosed evidence surfaced at the Manning civil trial that Sgt. Quid had made an additional visit to Mammolito in Louisiana in July, 1990 that was withheld from petitioner. (C.T. V14: 172). Quid was adamant that he made a report of this visit (when Mammolito changed his story to comport with law enforcement's new version of events), but this report was never disclosed to petitioner prior to or at his criminal trial, nor to Manning pursuant to Judge Smith's discovery order, or at Manning's civil trial. Coincidentally, this document is the only "critical" report missing from Buffalo Grove's entire file. (C.T. V14: 174-77).

During the civil trial, Cmdr. Del Re and Sgt. Quid insisted there was no deal made with Mammolito, but when pressed by Manning's attorney, neither could explain why they did not respond with any sort of denial when they received Mammolito's letter demanding they honor their deal. (C.T. V15: 15-16; V16: 204-06). The fact is, they sent Mammolito's mother $500 in a letter expressing regret that

---

[6] Petitioner will designate citations from Manning's civil trial as "C.T." followed by the volume number then page number. Transcript excerpts from Manning's civil trial are attached to the petition as Exhibit O.

20

they could not send him more for his efforts in securing petitioner's and Manning's convictions. (*See* Exh. C).

After considering the evidence, Manning's civil jury found that Buchan, Quid, and Mammolito had a "deal" in place prior to his testimony at petitioner's trial. (Exh. F). Judge Kennelly's assessment of the evidence concerning this finding buttresses the civil jury verdict. There is no longer any question whether this undisclosed deal with Mammolito existed; Manning has proven that it did, and the civil jury's verdict confirms it. (*See* Exh. F).

In addition, evidence was presented at Manning's civil trial that an agreement was made between Buchan, Quid, and Mammolito prior to petitioner's trial for the investigators to assist Mammolito in securing his release from federal prison. (*See* Pet. Exh. E). In fact, prosecutor Klopfenstein was duped by Quid (and possibly Buchan) into sending a letter to U.S. Attorney Paul Becker on behalf of Mammolito, touting Mammolito's unquestioned cooperation in this case. (*See* Pet. Exh. I).

The civil jury also found that Carolyn Heldenbrand's false identification of Manning constituted undisclosed exculpatory evidence which could have been used to impeach her. (*See* Exh. G at 17). Petitioner was also not apprized of this exculpatory evidence at his trial.

21

Example Petition for Writ of Habeas Corpus #2—Engel v. Dormire (cont.)

In preparing for the civil trial, Manning's Chicago attorneys began noticing up depositions. On July 29, 2004, the deposition of Anthony Mammolito was taken in Kansas City, Missouri. During that proceeding, Mammolito gave sworn testimony, for the first time, that he had written a letter to the Buffalo Grove police prior to being brought back to Missouri for his testimony. (*See* Pet. Exh. J; Mammolito deposition at 40). Mammolito stated that this letter was written approximately ten days after Quid's undisclosed July 1990 meeting with Mammolito in Louisiana. (*See* Pet. Exh. J; Mammolito deposition at 9). This newly discovered evidence of a third undisclosed letter demanding payment was also intentionally withheld from petitioner. (*See* Pet. Exh. H; p. 2). This alleged exculpatory and impeachment evidence was withheld throughout Manning's two trials, the federal discovery orders issued by Judge Smith in 1998, and is either still being withheld by Quid, or is also an additional document "missing" from Buffalo Grove's files. In any event, this undisclosed letter was *Brady* material that should have been disclosed prior to petitioner's trial.

In addition, during the pre-civil trial deposition of Sharon Dugan taken on October 7, 2004, Dugan gave sworn testimony revealing for the first time that she received a monetary reward for her testimony. (*See* Pet. Exh. K; Dugan deposition at 55). Not only were her transportation and lodging costs in Kansas City paid for by

22

Example Petition for Writ of Habeas Corpus #2—Engel v. Dormire (cont.)

the FBI, but she brought along her new husband (who was not involved in this case whatsoever) and they were given an additional spending allowance during their stay in Kansas City. This *Brady* material was never disclosed by law enforcement to the prosecutor or to petitioner prior to, or at trial.

One of the victims in this case, Charles Ford, gave sworn testimony at the civil trial that he told Buchan at the first interview that he believed one of the actual kidnappers was Carl Spero, (C.T. V11: 183-86), an individual that Ford knew personally. Documentation of this exculpatory statement was withheld by both Buchan and Quid from prosecutors and petitioner at his trial, but finally surfaced during Manning's second trial.

Despite the fact that Clay County prosecutors were found (by the civil jury) to have been totally in the dark about all the withheld exculpatory and impeachment evidence, they are still *de facto* responsible for the actions of Buchan and Quid. It is well-settled that the *Brady* rule encompasses evidence "known only to police investigators and not the prosecutor...In order to comply with *Brady*, therefore, 'the individual prosecutor has a duty to learn of any favorable evidence known to the others acting on the government's behalf in this case, including the police.'" *Strickler v. Greene*, 527 U.S. 263, 280-281 (1999); quoting *Kyles v. Whitley*, 514 U.S. at 437 (1995).

23

Further illuminating this point is *United States v. Ramos-Cartagena*, 9 F.Supp.2d 88, 90 (D. Puerto Rico 1998). That court stated:

A question usually addressed by courts is who is to be considered as part of the prosecution for *Brady* purposes. It is clear, for example, that any information possessed by any member of the United Stated Attorney's Office may be attributed to the prosecution (citation omitted). The 'prosecution' also includes police officers, federal agents, other investigatory personnel who participated in the investigation and prosecution of the instant case. *U.S. v. Brooks*, 966 F. 2d 1500, 1503 (D.C. Cir. 1984). *Carey v. Duckworth*, 738 F. 2d 875, 878-79 (7th Cir. 1984). Id. at 90-91. Accord, *U.S. v. Guerrerio*, 670 F. Supp. 1215 (D. NY 1987).

A prisoner asserting a *Brady* claim must show that the evidence at issue was both exculpatory or impeaching and "material." *See Smith v. Holtz*, 210 F.3d. 186, 198 (3rd Cir. 2000). Undisclosed evidence is "material only if there is a reasonable probability that, had the evidence been disclosed to the defense, the result would have been different." *Strickler v. Greene*, 527 U.S. 263, 289-90 (1999). In other words, the withheld evidence must "undermine confidence in the conviction." *Kyles v.*

Whitley, 514 U.S. 419, 434-37 (1995); *United States v. Bagley*, 473 U.S. 667, 682 (1985).

In the courts below, respondent has asserted various procedural bar defenses arising from the undisputed fact that this *Brady* claim was not presented in petitioner's 29.15 or direct appeal. A petitioner can overcome a procedural bar defense if he can show "cause" for not presenting his claims in state court and "prejudice" resulting from constitutional error, or a fundamental miscarriage of justice. *Coleman v. Thompson*, 501 U.S. 722, 750 (1991). "Cause" as defined in *Murray v. Carrier*, 477 U.S. 478, 488 (1986), is a factor external to the defense or a cause for which the defense is not responsible.

Cause is established in this case to excuse any procedural bar because the factual basis for these claims was not reasonably available to the defense during prior state court appellate and post-conviction proceedings. Cause is also established because interference by law enforcement officials made it impossible for petitioner to advance his claims in state court in a procedurally correct manner. *See Amadeo v. Zant*, 486 U.S. 214 (1987); *Strickler v. Greene*, 527 U.S. 263 (1999); and *Williams v. Taylor*, 529 U.S. 420 (2000).

In *Strickler*, the court found that the prisoner established cause to overcome a procedural default for not raising a *Brady* claim during state court proceedings because state post-conviction counsel did not have knowledge of the suppressed exculpatory evidence at the time this *Brady* claim could have been timely advanced in state post-conviction proceedings. 527 U.S. at 281-84. The Supreme Court in *Strickler* held that this cause existed because the factual basis for this claim was not reasonably available to state post-conviction counsel. *Id.* at 284.

In assessing prejudice arising from claims of this nature, reviewing courts must consider all available evidence uncovered following trial in determining whether a petitioner is entitled to habeas relief. *State ex rel. Amrine v. Roper*, 102 S.W.3d 541, 545 (Mo. banc 2003) (reviewing court under Rule 91 must assess the totality of all of the evidence uncovered over the years between various judicial reviews to determine whether a claim of innocence can be established); *Kyles v. Whitley*, 514 U.S. 419, 436-437 (1995) (reviewing court must consider the collective effect of all excluded evidence in assessing whether a *Brady* violation occurred).

After petitioner filed his prior Rule 91 petition in 2003, as the present petition reveals, additional evidence supporting a *Brady* claim was uncovered during the course of Steven Manning's civil trial. Under prevailing law, this Court is required to consider the cumulative effect of all of this excluded evidence in assessing whether a *Brady* violation occurred.

In the Rule 91 proceeding in the Circuit County of Cole County below, Judge Callahan, quoting verbatim from the state's response, found that this *Brady* claim was not cognizable because it was successive in light of the fact the petitioner filed a prior Rule 91 action in 2003. (*See* Exh.'s L, M). In reaching this conclusion, the circuit court, citing *State ex rel Simmons v. White*, 866 S.W.2d 443, 446 (Mo. banc 1993), held that Rule 91 does not allow for successive claims. (See Exh. L). This finding is clearly erroneous.

There is nothing in the text of Rule 91, nor the *Simmons* decision to support the position that Rule 91 does not allow successive claims. In any event, under either a cause/prejudice or ends of justice test, reconsideration of this *Brady* claim is warranted based upon the fact that new evidence has surfaced in the Manning civil lawsuit, as demonstrated by the jury verdict and Judge Kennelly's memorandum, that was unavailable to petitioner during the 2003 Rule 91 litigation. Where the factual predicate for a claim was not available in earlier proceedings, there is no procedural bar in a subsequent Rule 91 action. *See White v. State*, 779 S.W.2d 571, 573 (Mo. banc 1989); *Merriweather v. Grandison*, 904 S.W.2d 485, 489 (Mo. App. W.D. 1995). In any event, there can be no successive writ bar in the instant case because this is the first time petitioner has filed a Rule 91 petition before this Court.

It is well-settled that when the factual basis for a constitutional claim is concealed by the government, as was done in this case, so that there is no reasonable factual basis to raise this claim during state post-conviction (Rule 29.15) proceedings, this government interference constitutes adequate cause to overcome a procedural default. *Amadeo v. Zant, supra.* It is patently unfair for the state to hide exculpatory evidence and then later, after the evidence is discovered, assert that a constitutional claim based upon hidden evidence is procedurally barred because the evidence was not presented earlier. As the court stated in *Strickler*, "a defendant cannot conduct the 'reasonable and diligent investigation' mandated by *McCleskey* to preclude a finding of procedural default when the evidence is in the hands of the state." 527 U.S. at 287-88.

Similarly, in *Williams v. Taylor*, supra, the Supreme Court rejected the government's argument that trial counsel could have discovered the factual basis for the claim by checking public records. 529 U.S. at 443. The Manning civil trial supplemental verdict, as well as District Judge Kennelly's Memorandum, viewed in conjunction with applicable caselaw, removes any doubt that petitioner can establish cause to overcome any procedural default to his claims.

Actual prejudice can be established to overcome a default if the defaulted claim is sufficiently meritorious to entitle the prisoner to relief. *Ivy v. Caspari*, 173 F 3d

Example Petition for Writ of Habeas Corpus #2—Engel v. Dormire (cont.)

1136, 1141-44 (8th Cir. 1998). In the context of the due process claims presented here involving Mammolito and Dugan, prejudice can be established if petitioner can meet the materiality test to prevail on the merits of the underlying claim for relief. *Strickler* 527 U.S. at 289-90. To do so, petitioner must establish that there is a reasonable probability that the result of the trial would have been different, but for the governmental misconduct and the perjured testimony of Mammolito, Dugan, and Carolyn Hildebrand. *Id; see also Kyles v. Whitley,* 514 U.S. 419, 434 (1995).

The U.S. Supreme Court set forth the framework for evaluating the materiality of *Brady* evidence as follows: "evidence is material only if there is a reasonable probability that, had the evidence been disclosed to the defense, the result of the proceedings would have been different ." *United States v. Bagley*, 473 U.S. at 682 The court further defined a "reasonable probability" as "a probability sufficient to undermine confidence in the outcome ." *Id.*

On remand, the Ninth Circuit in *Bagley*, 798 F.2d 1297, 1298 (9th Cir.1986), held that a non-disclosed payment "undermines confidence in the outcome of a trial," and reversed the conviction. The court stated that the government's payments to the two important witnesses for expense money for their part in the investigation of defendant constituted inducements from the government for their actions. *Id.* at 1299. As here, the court found that "When the 'reliability of a given witness may well be

29

determinative of guilt or innocence,' nondisclosure of evidence affecting credibility falls within the general rule of *Brady*." *Id.* at 1300, quoting *Giglio v. United States*, 405 U.S. 150, 154 (1972).

The court in *Bagley* stressed the fact that the record revealed that undisclosed payments were made and that the witnesses lied under oath about them. 798 F.2d at 1301. The court stated: "When the evidence shows that government's only witness lied under oath, it is contrary to reason that confidence in the outcome of the case would not objectively be undermined." *Id.* "When the witnesses' testimony is central to the government's case, their credibility is an important issue of the case." *Id.* Additionally, a showing of bias on the part of the witness would have a tendency to make the facts to which he testified less probable in the eyes of the jury. *Id.* at 1302. The "reasonable probability of a different outcome" test is also met here where the government failed to disclose the existence of contract to pay "expenses" of two prosecution witnesses, resulting in undisclosed payments of $300.00 and $500.00. *Id.* at 1299. More recently, the Ninth Circuit found a *Brady* violation where it was not disclosed that a key prosecution witness was paid $150.00 for his testimony. *Benn v. Lambert*, 283 F.3d 1040, 1056-1057 (9th Cir. 2002).

The Eighth Circuit has also extensively discussed the relevant standard of review for *Brady* violations where the undisclosed material would have shown

30

perjury on the part of the witness. *United States v. Duke*, 50 F.3d 571, 577-78 (8th Cir. 1995). In such a case, the standard used to determine whether the undisclosed evidence is "material" is whether there is a "reasonable probability" that, had the evidence been disclosed to the defense, the result of the proceedings would have been different. A "reasonable probability" is a probability sufficient to undermine confidence in the outcome, citing *United States v. Bagley*, 473 U.S. at 682.

The Eighth Circuit in *Duke* also stated:

> Yet another standard applies to a motion for a new trial based on newly discovered evidence that a conviction was obtained by the prosecutor's knowing use of perjured testimony. (citation omitted). The Supreme Court has held that a conviction so obtained 'must set aside if there is any reasonable likelihood that the false testimony could have affected the judgment of the jury.' The Supreme Court subsequently described this test as a materiality standard under which 'the fact that the testimony is perjured is considered material unless failure to disclose it would be harmless beyond a reasonable doubt.' *Bagley*, 473 U.S. at 580. In *Napue v. Illinois*, the court explained that the principle that the prosecution may not knowingly use false evidence did not cease to apply 'merely because the false testimony goes only to the credibility of the

31

Example Petition for Writ of Habeas Corpus #2—Engel v. Dormire (cont.)

witness' because the jury's estimate of a given witness 'may well be determinative of guilt or innocence.' 360 U.S. at 269." 50 F.3d at 577.

In *Killian v. Poole*, 282 F.3d 1204 (9th Cir. 2002), the Ninth Circuit granted habeas relief to a prisoner due to the presentation of perjured testimony of the prosecution's star witness. *Id.* at 1209-10. As in this case, the star witness against Killian falsely denied that he received any deals for his testimony. Id. at 1208-09. Remarkably, part of the evidence establishing perjury in *Killian* consisted of letters that the witness had written after the trial. *Id.* at 1208-09. Finally, the decision in *Killian* is significant because the Ninth Circuit held that Killian could prevail on her perjured testimony claim regardless of whether or not the prosecutor actually knew that the witness committed perjury during his trial testimony. *Id.* at 1208 and n.4. *See also United States ex rel Smith v. Fairman*, 769 F 2d 386, 391-98 (7th Cir. 1985) (due process violated where police failed to disclose exculpatory evidence before trial); *Newsom v. McCabe*, 260 F.3d 824 (7th Cir. 2001) (recognizing that a police officer's duty to disclose *Brady* material was clearly established not later than 1988).

Petitioner contends that it has clearly been proven through Manning's civil jury trial that the undisclosed *Brady* material was solely in the hands of law enforcement prior to trial and was intentionally hidden by law enforcement from the prosecutors

32

Example Petition for Writ of Habeas Corpus #2—Engel v. Dormire (cont.)

as well as petitioner. Some of the still "missing" *Brady* material may remain in the hands of law enforcement since they have not been forthcoming when ordered by the federal courts to do so. This misconduct amply satisfies the "cause" prong under *Murray*. Petitioner was, therefore, unable to develop the true facts supporting this claim in any prior proceedings.

Regarding the materiality aspect of these claims, petitioner submits that there can be no stronger argument for "materiality" or "prejudice" than the findings of Manning's civil jury. The court here is in the highly unique position of having the benefit of a jury verdict finding that exculpatory and impeachment evidence was withheld from petitioner's and Manning's trial counsel. This civil jury verdict clearly rebuffs any procedural bar defense and shows an entitlement to habeas relief on the merits of the underlying claims.

The following evidence was presented and findings made by the jury and judge in Manning's *Bivens* action:

1. Mammolito was promised and paid money by government agents and was induced to give false testimony against Manning and Engel. (Pet. Exh. F, Supp. Form at 2).

2. Carolyn Hildebrand was induced to falsely identify Manning, and Sharon Dugan was induced to make false statements. (*Id.*, Exh. G at 17).

33

Example Petition for Writ of Habeas Corpus #2—Engel v. Dormire (cont.)

3. Mammolito's undisclosed letter to Buffalo Grove Police in July 1990. (Pet. Exh. J at 40).

4. Sgt. Quid's undisclosed visit to Mammolito on July 12, 1990. (C.T. V14:172).

5. Quid's now "missing" report depicting Mammolito's new revelations at the above undisclosed visit. (C.T. V14: 174-77).

6. Dugan's undisclosed "spending allowance" for her testimony. (Pet. Exh. K at 55).

7. Quid's undisclosed additional meetings with Dugan. (Tr. 442, 494).

8. Quid's "missing" (or intentionally withheld) reports regarding undisclosed meetings with Dugan. (C.T. V14: 174-75).

9. Buchan or Quid's intentional withholding of documentation of (victim) Ford's exculpatory information relating to Carl Spero. (C.T. V11:183-86).

10. Mammolito's undisclosed and undocumented statements to prosecutor Klopfestein regarding a different perpetrator of this kidnapping. (C.T. V15: 192-94).

11. Mammolito's undisclosed letter to Clay County prosecutors prior to the criminal trial. (Pet. Exh. B).

All of the above stated evidence was exculpatory and impeachment evidence and is therefore *Brady* material, which should have been turned over to the defense as requested prior to trial.

Even when this case was tried in 1991, the evidence of petitioner's guilt was tenuous at best. Both Mammolito and Dugan had inherent credibility problems even then. Mammolito was a multiple convicted felon and "snitch." (*See* Exh. Q pp. 118-119). Dugan's credibility was called into question because she was the bitter ex-wife of petitioner. (*Id.* pp. 208, 226-229). In light of the evidence that has emerged during litigation involving co-defendant Steven Manning that further undermines their credibility, it is not a close question that this additional impeaching information, had it been disclosed to the jury, is sufficiently compelling to entitle petitioner to a new trial because there is a reasonable probability the result at trial would have been different. *Strickler v. Greene*, 527 U.S. 263, 289-290 (1999).

Mammolito's letter to the Buffalo Grove Police Department referencing a deal (Pet. Exh. D) and Del Re's letter to Mammolito's mother enclosed with a five hundred dollar check (Pet. Exh. C), along with Buffalo Grove's letter (Pet. Exh. E) and Klopfenstein's letter (Pet. Exh. I) to the U.S. Parole Board on behalf of Mammolito for leniency, all indicate that Mammolito's trial testimony was false. These facts present a textbook case of a *Brady* violation as demonstrated by the

Example Petition for Writ of Habeas Corpus #2—Engel v. Dormire (cont.)

verdict in Manning's civil trial and the fact that Clay County prosecutor, when confronted with this newly discovered evidence, dismissed all charges against Steven Manning.

Article IV, Section 1 of the United States Constitution dictates that full faith and credit shall be given by each state to foreign judicial proceedings. Had Mr. Engel been the plaintiff against the United States, Buchan, and Miller, this Court would be collaterally estopped from re-adjudicating the *Brady* violations with respect to Engel because these very same violations were previously adjudicated with respect to the same defendants in *Manning v. United States*. "The doctrine of collateral estoppel, or issue preclusion, precludes the same parties or those in privity from relitigating issues that were necessarily and unambiguously decided in a previous judgment." *Deatherage v. Cleghorn*, 115 S.W.3d 447 (Mo.App. S. D. 2003), quoting *Jeffrey v. Cathers*, 104 S.W.3d 424, 430 (Mo.App. E.D. 2003).

The elements of collateral estoppel are: (1) the issue decided in the prior adjudications mirrors that in the present action; (2) the prior adjudication resulted in a final decision on the merits; (3) the party against whom collateral estoppel may apply participated as a party or in privity with a party to the prior adjudication; and (4) the party against whom the doctrine may apply has had a full and fair opportunity to litigate the issue. *In re Marriage of Evans*, 155

36

S.W.3d 90, at 96 (Mo.App. S.D. 2004).

All four elements would clearly be met, and Missouri is obligated to recognize a foreign judgment "unless that judgment is void for lack of jurisdiction over the person or over the subject matter, or is obtained by fraud." *Phillips v. Fallen*, 6 S.W.3d at 864 (Mo. 1999). The same holds true concerning federal judgments. *Creative Walking, Inc. v. American States Ins. Co.*, 25 S.W.3d 682, 687 (Mo.App. E.D. 2000).

Petitioner has spent nineteen years in prison for a crime he did not commit. Like Steven Manning, petitioner deserves a new trial and his freedom because of egregious governmental misconduct. Because the record establishes that the government withheld material exculpatory evidence from petitioner prior to trial, habeas relief is warranted.

CLAIM TWO

PETITIONER'S CONVICTIONS WERE SECURED IN VIOLATION OF PETITIONER'S RIGHT TO DUE PROCESS OF LAW BY THE GOVERNMENT'S USE OF PERJURED TESTIMONY, THE FABRICATION OF FALSE POLICE REPORTS, PROVIDING MONETARY PAYMENT AND OTHER INDUCEMENTS TO SECURE FALSE TESTIMONY, AND BY PROVIDING THE KEY WITNESS WITH COPIES OF ALL POLICE

37

REPORTS AND PRE-TRIAL DEPOSITIONS OF ALL THE STATE'S WITNESSES TO ENHANCE THE CREDIBILITY OF THEIR FALSE TESTIMONY.

In addition to the *Brady* claim set forth above, the same evidence reveals a distinct, yet related due process violation arising from the fact that petitioner's conviction was secured through the use of perjured testimony. Manning's jury found that Agent Buchan suborned the perjury of Mammolito, Dugan, and Carolyn Heldenbrand, as will be discussed below. (*See* Pet. Exh. F; Supplemental Verdict Form at 1). The civil jury also found that the FBI failed to inform Clay County prosecutors that they had manipulated and fabricated the testimony of those witnesses. (*Id.*) The FBI documented the fabricated statements of each witness in official police reports, and misrepresented to Clay County prosecutors that the statements made by each witness were the witness' own recollection of events to the alleged kidnapping.

Quid (and Buchan) were very fortunate to have found Mammolito to be such a malleable witness. Their misfortune was that Mammolito, whom the investigators were desperately trying to get to corroborate their false scenario of events, just could not keep this manufactured script straight in his own mind. To get around this dilemma, the agents arranged for Mammolito to receive copies of all the witness

38

statements and pre-trial depositions at the Platte County Jail where he was being held prior to his criminal trial testimony. The fact that he received them is evidenced by Mammolito's handwritten February 1992 letter to Sgt. Quid (*See* Pet. Exh. D) and is corroborated by the affidavit of Harold Bascom, who saw and read these documents for himself. (*See* Pet. Exh. A).

In sworn testimony presented to the civil jury, Judge Gabbert and prosecutor Klopfenstein adamantly denied giving Mammolito any of these documents. The responsibility for this misconduct has to fall on the only two people, other than the prosecutors, to have possession of these documents, Buchan and Quid, since these documents could not have come from any other source. This misconduct constitutes a due process violation as set forth in *United States v. Agurs*, 427 U.S. 97 (1976) and *Napue v. Illinois*, 360 U.S. 264 (1959).

A. **Witness Anthony Mammolito**

As noted earlier under Claim Two, the civil jury in *Manning* unanimously found that Buchan (and Quid) had manipulated the criminal trial testimony of Anthony Mammolito, the State's star witness, and hid this fact from Missouri (Clay County) prosecutors. (*See* Pet. Exh. F., Supplemental Verdict Form at 1). The civil jury also unanimously found that Mammolito had a "deal" in place with Buchan and Quid prior to his criminal trial testimony, where he (Mammolito) would be secretly

39

Example Petition for Writ of Habeas Corpus #2—Engel v. Dormire (cont.)

paid for his testimony against petitioner and his co-defendant, and that information of this deal was withheld from Missouri prosecutors by Buchan (and Quid). (*See* Pet. Exh. F., Supplemental Verdict Form at 2). Both of these unanimous jury findings are bolstered by District Judge Kennelly's assessment of the evidence in his Memorandum (pp. 17-18). (*See* Exh. G).

Prior to his criminal trial, the petitioner, through his attorney, had made <u>two</u> motions for discovery, specifically requesting information of any deals, understandings or agreements, or offer of such, with Mammolito or any other witness. (*See* Pet. Exh. H). While the prosecutors were found to be unaware of any such deal, it has now been proven that Buchan, Quid, and Mammolito *knew* such a deal was in place prior to Mammolito's trial testimony.

When Mammolito testified at the trials of Manning and petitioner, he was specifically asked by then prosecutor Gabbert if there had been any agreements for his testimony to which Mammolito responded, "No nothing whatsoever, no agreements." (Exh. Q, Tr. 177). Buchan and Quid *knew* that Mammolito was perjuring himself and failed to inform either prosecutor of the situation. This evidence nevertheless constitutes prosecutorial misconduct, in that the prosecutors while in the dark, are still responsible for the actions (or inactions) of law enforcement personnel who investigated the case.

40

In addition, Buchan and Quid withheld from the prosecutors the method they employed, and how and under what circumstances they successfully manipulated Mammolito's testimony, by providing Mammolito with witness statements of the other witnesses. (*See* Pet. Exh. A; Exh. D; Exh. G at 20, n. 6). Mammolito's undisclosed February 1992 letter to Sgt. Quid (Pet. Exh. D) is significant for other reasons apart from the money issue. Just before demanding his promised payoff, Mammolito mentions that, "as (they) know" he has "read all investigative reports." The obvious inference is that Mammolito is exerting his leverage over the investigators by flaunting the fact that the agents provided him these documents to help convict petitioner and his co-defendant, and the agents had better stand by the entire deal.

B. Witness Sharon Dugan

In previous appeals, the respondent has always relied upon the testimony of Sharon Dugan to bolster Mammolito's credibility. This argument is no longer viable. The civil jury in *Manning* found that Dugan's testimony had been manipulated and fabricated as well, by Agent Buchan (and Quid). (*See* Exh. F). The civil jury was entitled to find (and did find) that Dugan's trial testimony was not credible. Everything about this witness revealed at the civil trial suggested that her testimony at the criminal trial was tainted. (*See* C.T. V13:172-202). Manning's civil jury

41

Example Petition for Writ of Habeas Corpus #2—Engel v. Dormire (cont.)

concluded that Buchan and Quid withheld from the Clay County prosecutors the manner in which they had disseminated critical information to Dugan. (*See* Exh. G at 20). As was done with Mammolito, Buchan and Quid failed to inform the Clay County prosecutors that they had armed Dugan with facts of the case she otherwise would not have known facts which gave her the necessary credibility to convict petitioner and his co-defendant at their respective trials.

As an example, civil trial testimony revealed that Quid started out this "fishing trip" (his own words) by asking Dugan in 1989 if she remembered her former husband (petitioner) ever going to Kansas City, and whether 1984 would be the right year, to which she replied "probably." (C.T. V14: 161-162). By the time of the criminal trial...after several undocumented meetings with Buchan and Quid...Dugan provided a vivid account of details and events she claimed occurred in February 1984, (C.T. V13: 191-95). How she went from point A ("probably") to point B (vivid dates and details) is a mystery and cannot be explained in any police report or witness statement.

Another example occurred during Dugan's first meeting with Quid, where Quid described for Dugan a ring they were seeking, even showing Dugan a drawing of the ring that Quid had made. It took Dugan about a week to come up with such a ring (from among several diamond rings that she insisted petitioner had given her,

42

although she bizarrely stated she had thrown the rest of them in the garbage). (C.T. V13: 182-84). However, the ring she produced did not match the number of diamonds the ring contained as described by Ford, or even the drawing Quid had made and memorialized in his report, nor the official report submitted by Agent Buchan. (C.T. V13: 185-86).

The most telling example of the government's manipulation of Dugan involved Buchan showing Dugan a paperback book titled: "How to Rip off Drug Dealers," that Buchan allegedly recovered from a briefcase belonging to petitioner. Thereafter, Dugan suddenly "remembered" having seen petitioner reading this book approximately *seven months* prior to the alleged kidnapping. Buchan quickly documented this sudden revelation in an official report. Months later, Dugan repeated this reference to the book in a sworn deposition. After that deposition, and to Buchan's dismay, he learned the paperback book was not published until *one month* prior to the alleged kidnapping. By the time of the trial, and after numerous undocumented meetings with Buchan (Exh. Q pp. 236), Dugan changed her prior sworn testimony and stated that she saw this book at a time that comported with its date of publication (*See* Exh. O, Tr. 478-81). During the civil trial, when it became time for Dugan to confirm that she had actually told law enforcement what they had documented in their official reports, she could not do so. (C.T. V13: 172-202).

43

Finally, like Mammolito, Dugan also admitted receiving payment for her testimony. (*See* Pet. Exh. K; Dugan deposition at 55).

C. <u>Witness Carolyn Heldenbrand</u>

Although this witness never identified petitioner as being a perpetrator of the alleged kidnapping, her discredited identification of co-defendant Manning had a detrimental "spillover effect" on petitioner's criminal jury. Throughout petitioner's trial, the name Manning became synonymous with Engel in the jury's mind. Heldenbrand's manufactured identification of Manning had no relevance to petitioner's guilt, and was used solely to bolster Mammolito's fabricated story. Manning's civil jury found that Heldenbrand's criminal trial testimony regarding events of the alleged kidnapping was tainted and had been manipulated by Buchan and Quid, and that these actions by these agents had been withheld from Missouri prosecutors. (*See* Pet. Exh. F., Supplemental Verdict Form at 1). The civil jury also concluded that Heldenbrand was coerced into falsely identifying Manning as the person who picked up the ransom money. (*See* Exh. G at 14-17). Moreover, these agents created false official documents of this "alleged" identification (Buchan's report has Heldenbrand's I.D. of Manning being 100% positive) and presented those reports to Clay County prosecutors in an effort to get them to file charges in this case.

Furthermore, evidence was presented at the civil trial of other questionable actions by Buchan involving Heldenbrand. Almost one year after visiting Heldenbrand and securing her identification of Manning, Agent Buchan happened to be re-inventorying the results of a 1986 search of Manning's storage locker (that was originally not relevant to this case) when he discovered that Manning owned a hat "with side flaps." (C.T. V11: 170). As Buchan had previously done with Dugan, he (Buchan) alleged that Heldenbrand called him out of the blue one year later and reported that she had "just remembered" that the "bagman" wore a hat with side flaps. (*Id*. at 170-73). It is apparent that the civil jury did not believe Buchan's explanation for Heldenbrand's revelation in reaching its verdict.

D. Victim Charles Ford

It should now be abundantly apparent that Buchan and Quid left no stone unturned in their crusade to secure the convictions of petitioner and his co-defendant. In a final insult to the justice system, even one of the victims (Charles Ford) was manipulated by Buchan and Quid into giving false testimony.

Ford gave sworn testimony that the agents had "pressured" him into changing his recollection of the events and dates in his story to comport with Buchan's and Quid's version or script. (C.T. V11: 183-86). Ford further testified about how he (Ford) kept telling Buchan that it was his firm belief that one of the kidnappers was

45

Carl Spero (a person known to the victim), who was blown up and killed by someone thirty days after the alleged kidnapping. Buchan's insistence on ignoring this legitimate lead, and Mammolito's undisclosed statement to prosecutor Klopfenstein that there was a different person involved in this kidnapping whom he (Mammolito) refused to name because that person had since died (C.T. V15: 192-94), lends additional credence to the civil jury verdict and the premise that petitioner and his co-defendant were framed by Buchan and Quid.

Respondent, in previous filings in past appeals, has always alluded to Ford's "positive identification" of the ring that Dugan was alleged to have turned over to the investigators as unassailable proof of petitioner's involvement. Ford's original statement to Buchan and Quid was that a ring had been taken from him by the kidnappers, and the ring contained *five* diamonds, according to Buchan's reports. The ring that Dugan was alleged to have turned over to authorities, almost six years later, contained *seven* diamonds. Ford's oddly-equivocal identification of the ring at the petitioner's trial was "It *looks* like my ring." (Exh. Q 24, 25, 71). The ring allegedly turned over by Dugan may very well have resembled or was even shaped like Ford's stolen ring, but diamonds have never been known to reproduce. One would expect that Ford, who testified the stolen ring was "made special for (him)," and who had to pay for each diamond in that ring, would know exactly how many diamonds that this ring contained.

Petitioner submits that, in the initial interview with Buchan, Ford correctly described his stolen ring as having *five* diamonds on it. It was only through Buchan's "pressure" (Ford's words) that Ford made the half-hearted attempt to identify the *seven* diamond ring as, "it looks like it."

E. <u>**Agent Buchan and Sgt. Quid**</u>

Both Agent Buchan and Sgt. Quid testified at petitioner's and his co-defendant's trials that the statements of the witnesses they set forth in their official reports were the recollections of the witnesses themselves. Manning's civil jury verdict now refutes that aspect of the sworn testimony of Buchan and Quid. This verdict leads to the conclusion that both Buchan and Quid knowingly perjured themselves at petitioner's criminal trial, and willfully created documents containing false witness statements. Buchan and Quid *knew* that their sworn trial testimony was false, and they *knew* that the direct sworn testimony of all the witnesses had been manipulated through their actions, and failed to inform the prosecutors of what they had done. Instead, they simply remained mute and knowingly and intentionally perpetuated fraud upon the trial court. These repugnant actions on the part of these agents undoubtedly violated the Constitution. Additionally, as noted by Judge

47

Kennelly (Exh. G at 16), Agent Buchan did everything possible at the civil trial to obstruct Manning's presentation of much of this compelling government misconduct evidence.

In addition, the circumstances surrounding co-defendant Manning's reversal and remand, and the Clay County prosecutor's decision to dismiss Manning's remaining charges, raises the inference that they lacked reasonable grounds to pursue the prosecution. A lack of probable cause is indicative of innocence. *See Velez v. Avis Rent-A-Car Systems, Inc.*, 721 N.E. 2d 652 (Ill. App. 1999) (Failure to prosecute case despite "ample opportunity" to do so indicated that "the disposition was premised upon a lack of probable cause and was indicative of the innocence of the petitioner"). Even before the newly discovered evidence of the civil trial and jury verdict was known, the Clay County prosecutors, one year earlier, felt that they could not secure Manning's conviction in light of the evidence of misconduct that had been exposed at that time. If Manning is innocent of these charges in the eyes of the law, logic compels the conclusion that petitioner's innocence is also established. Habeas relief is warranted.

48

CLAIM THREE

PETITIONER'S CONVICTIONS AND SENTENCES FOR THE CHARGES OF ARMED CRIMINAL ACTION WERE SECURED IN VIOLATION OF THE LAWS OF THE STATE OF MISSOURI BECAUSE THESE CHARGES WERE NOT FILED WITHIN THE THREE YEAR STATUTE OF LIMITATION PERIOD.

The Clay County Prosecutor's Office lacked the jurisdiction to charge, and the trial court lacked the jurisdiction to proceed to trial on the two armed criminal action charges. Petitioner's charges arose from an alleged crime that occurred on or about February 9, *1984*, in Clay County, Missouri. Petitioner was charged by way of complaint in the Seventh Judicial Circuit Court of Clay County on July 20, *1990*, with two counts of kidnapping (Class A felony) and two counts of armed criminal action, over six years after the alleged crime. Armed criminal action charges must be filed within a three year statute of limitation period. *State v. Hyman*, 37 S.W. 3d. 384 (Mo. App. W.D. 2001). In *Hyman*, the Missouri Court of Appeals held that because the felony of armed criminal action has no classification, and includes its own penalty, it is an unclassified code offense that is subject to the three year statute of limitation period. *Id.* at 389-390; *see also*, § 556.036 R.S. Mo. (2000).

49

Example Petition for Writ of Habeas Corpus #2—Engel v. Dormire (cont.)

The circuit court below declined to address this claim finding it to be procedurally barred because it was not raised on direct appeal or at the time of trial. (See Exh. L at p. 15-16). The circuit court also expressed the view that petitioner could not show cause and prejudice because he and his attorney "were fully able to raise this claim at the time of trial and chose not to do so." (*Id.* 16).

The circuit court's procedural bar analysis fails to take into account the fact that the intervening *Hyman* case created the legal basis for raising a statute of limitations challenge to the armed criminal action statute. Since the *Hyman* case was decided ten years after petitioner's trial and long after his direct appeal had been concluded, there is cause and prejudice to overcome any default because the legal basis for such a challenge to the armed criminal action charges was unavailable to him. *See Reed v. Ross*, 468 U.S. 1, 12-15 (1984).

This Court, in striking down the juvenile death penalty, rejected an identical procedural bar argument from the Missouri Attorney General. *State ex. rel. Simmons v. Roper*, 112 S.W.3d 397, 400-401 (Mo. banc. 2003) *affd., sub. nom., Roper v. Simmons*, 543 U.S. 551 (2005). Like the *Atkins* decision in *Simmons*, the *Hyman* decision establishes cause under the novelty exception to the procedural bar rule. *Id.* If respondent's procedural bar argument he advanced in the circuit court had merit, Christopher Simmons would have been executed in 2003.

50

Example Petition for Writ of Habeas Corpus #2—Engel v. Dormire (cont.)

At the time *Hyman* was decided, the armed criminal action statute had been on the books for approximately 25 years. Prior to the *Hyman* litigation, no criminal defense lawyer in this state had ever believed they had a legal ground to argue that ACA charges must be brought within a three year statute of limitation. Because the *Hyman* decision was a "bolt from the blue," this novel legal development establishes cause under *Reed* because there was no reasonable basis in existing law for Engel's trial or appellate counsel to raise a time bar challenge to these charges in the early 1990s. 468 U.S. at 14-16. Because there was no lack of diligence or deliberate bypass, the lack of knowledge of the legal basis for this claim overcomes any procedural bar. *See Brown v. Gammon*, 947 S.W.2d 437, 440 (Mo. App. W.D. 1997).

In light of *Hyman*, the prosecutor's office lacked the jurisdiction to charge this crime in 1990, since the statute of limitation had expired more than three years prior to the time of the original complaint. Furthermore, when co-defendant Manning was returned to Clay County, Missouri for possible retrial there, the charges of armed criminal action were immediately dismissed when the *Hyman* ruling was brought to the attention of the prosecutors, before their decision to dismiss the remaining charges. Petitioner's armed criminal action convictions and sentences should be set aside.[7]

---

[7] Phillip Thompson, a third year law student from Indiana University,

51

CONCLUSION

In light of all of the evidence of governmental misconduct and deception that has been presented here, petitioner submits that this court can come to only one determination. As was found by the Manning civil jury, Buchan's and Quid's purposeful and intentional manipulation of all the State's witnesses and fabrication of evidence violated the Constitution. Even the Clay County prosecutors were manipulated and exploited (albeit unwittingly) into assisting these two rogue out-of-state law enforcement agents in their zeal to obtain unlawful convictions of the petitioner and his co-defendant. Buchan and Quid were able to pull this off by keeping the prosecution in the dark in a successful effort to get Clay County to accept and file this case from the outset.

Manning's civil jury has found that Buchan violated Manning's rights. Under normal circumstances in a case such as this one, a prisoner faces a difficult hurdle in establishing misconduct by law enforcement. However, in light of Manning's civil jury verdict and Judge Kennelly's conclusions, any presumption that law enforcement acted properly no longer exists. It should now be incumbent on the respondent, who justifiably faces a considerable hurdle, to refute the logical conclusion that Mr. Engel should receive the same result as Manning.

---

provided substantial assistance to counsel in drafting this petition.

The Assistant U. S. Attorney in Chicago, Jonathan Haile, in defending the FBI and its agents, basically retried the entire kidnapping case before a jury of fair and impartial citizens, (Exh. G at 7-8, f.n. 2). That jury, after hearing all the exculpatory and impeachment evidence that was withheld from petitioner's criminal jury, in effect, found Manning not guilty and condemned and severely punished the misconduct of the investigating officers. Co-defendant Steven Manning is today a free man, and he and his attorneys have fought a long hard battle to gain him that freedom. Gary Engel is entitled to the same result.

WHEREFORE, petitioner requests that, for all the forgoing reasons advanced in his petition, that this Court issue a writ of habeas corpus discharging petitioner from his unconstitutional convictions and sentences *with prejudice*, or grant such other relief that this Court deems just and proper under the circumstances.

Respectfully submitted,

KENT E. GIPSON #34524
301 E. 63rd Street
Kansas City, Missouri 64113
816-363-4400 / fax: 816-363-4300
kent.gipson@kentgipsonlaw.com

Counsel for Petitioner

CERTIFICATE OF SERVICE

I, Kent E. Gipson, attorney for petitioner, hereby certify that on the 5th day of August, 2009, a true and correct copy of the foregoing Petition for Writ of Habeas Corpus, with supporting Exhibits was mailed, postage prepaid, to:

Jeremiah (Jay) W. Nixon
Attorney General
State of Missouri
P.O. Box 899
Jefferson City, MO 65102

Kent E. Gipson

Case no. 091021

IN THE MISSOURI SUPREME COURT

MARK WOODWORTH,

Petitioner,

v.

LARRY DENNEY, WARDEN
CROSSROADS CORRECTIONAL
CENTER,

Respondent.

WRIT SUMMARY

Identity of parties and their attorneys in the underlying action, if any:

Mark Woodworth
Represented by Robert B Ramsey
Law Offices of Michael R. Bilbrey, P.C.
104 Magnolia Drive, Suite B
Glen Carbon, IL 62034
Phone: (618) 288-6784
Fax: (618) 288-6726

Larry Denney, Warden, Crossroads Correctional Center
Represented by Chris Koster
Missouri Attorney General
207 W. High Street
Jefferson City, MO 65102
Phone: (573) 751-3321
Fax: (573) 751-0774

PETITION FOR WRIT OF HABEAS CORPUS IN STATE COURT

Example Petition for Writ of Habeas Corpus #3—Woodworth v. Denney (cont.)

Nature of the underlying action, if any: On January 19, 2000, Petitioner was sentenced by the Circuit Court of Clinton County, Missouri, (on change of venue from Livingston County Missouri) Hon. Stephen K. Griffin (retired) presiding, to four consecutive life sentences for Murder 2nd degree, Assault 1st degree, and two counts of Armed Criminal Action, and an additional consecutive sentence of 15 years for Burglary 1st Degree, Cause # CR793-59F

Action of Respondent being challenged, including date thereof: Unlawful custody of Petitioner by the Respondent.

Relief sought by Relator or Petitioner: Writ of Habeas Corpus

Date case set for trial, if set, and date of any other event bearing upon relief sought (e.g., date of deposition or motion hearing): N/A

Date, court and disposition of any previous or pending writ proceeding concerning the action or related matter: Originally Petition for Writ of Habeas Corpus was filed in the Circuit of DeKalb County State of Missouri on September 22, 2009, Cause # 09DK-CC00155. The Petition was denied on February 3, 2010. Subsequently Petitioner filed a Petition of Writ of Habeas Corpus in the Missouri Court of Appeals Western District on April 9, 2010, Cause # WD 72334. The Petition was denied on May 25, 2010.

Example Petition for Writ of Habeas Corpus #3—Woodworth v. Denney (cont.)

Case no. 091021

IN THE MISSOURI SUPREME COURT

MARK WOODWORTH,

Petitioner,

v.

LARRY DENNEY, WARDEN
CROSSROADS CORRECTIONAL
CENTER,

Respondent.

FILED
JUL X 6 2010
Thomas F. Simon
CLERK, SUPREME COURT

PETITION FOR WRIT OF HABEAS CORPUS

COMES NOW Petitioner Mark A. Woodworth, by and through his attorney, Robert B. Ramsey, and for his Petition for Writ of Habeas Corpus pursuant to Missouri Supreme Court Rule 91 states as follows:

1. Petitioner is currently being held as a prisoner at the Crossroads Correctional Center in Cameron, DeKalb County, Missouri.

2. The warden at the Crossroads Correctional Center is Larry Denney, Respondent herein.

3. No petition for writ of habeas corpus has been made to any higher court, and no court has denied any such petition.

Page 1 of 18

Example Petition for Writ of Habeas Corpus #3—Woodworth v. Denney (cont.)

4. A petition for writ of habeas corpus was denied without a hearing by the Circuit Court, 43rd Judicial Circuit of Missouri on or about February 3, 2010, and a similar action was denied by the Missouri Court of Appeals, Western District on May 25, 2010.

5. Petitioner's incarceration is illegal, improper and unconstitutional in that his rights under the 5th and 6th Amendments to the U.S. Constitution, as well as the corresponding sections of the Missouri Constitution in the following particulars:

Issues Presented by This Petition

A. Whether the deliberate or inadvertent concealment by the State of Missouri of exculpatory evidence that the shooting victim had identified and demanded the prosecution of a person not Petitioner 3 years prior to Petitioner being charged with the shootings, and had committed perjury regarding this fact at pre-trial deposition and trial, violated Petitioner's right to Due Process under *Brady v. Maryland*; and

B. Whether Petitioner's rights to Due Process and a Fair and Impartial Judge were violated when, despite having had ex parte communications with the shooting victim and despite having personal knowledge of controversial facts about the shooting victim's identification of a person other than Petitioner, a Livingston County circuit judge assumed the role of chief prosecutor by disqualifying a county prosecutor, who had "boycotted" the grand jury empanelled by the said judge and who had refused to seek indictments against Petitioner, and by appointing a special prosecutor who would present only one side of the evidentiary controversy of whether the victim had, years before, identified and actively sought the prosecution of another.

Factual and Legal Background

6. On January 19, 2000, Petitioner was sentenced by the Circuit Court of Clinton County, Missouri, Hon. Stephen K. Griffin (retired) presiding, to four consecutive life sentences for Murder 2nd degree, Assault 1st degree, and two counts of Armed Criminal Action, and an additional consecutive sentence of 15 years for Burglary 1st degree, arising out of the shootings of Lyndel and Catherine Robertson at their farm near Chillicothe, Missouri on November 13, 1990.

7. This was Petitioner's second trial on the same charges, the Court having reversed and remanded the first convictions, and sentences case for a new trial in *State v. Woodworth*, 941 S.W.2d 679 (Mo.App.W.D.1997).

8. In March 1995, the first jury had recommended the drastically lower (and) minimum sentences of 10 years each on the Class A felonies of Murder 2nd degree and Assault 1st degree and five, three and three years on Armed Criminal action and burglary. However, the trial court ordered the sentences to be served consecutively for a total sentence of 31 years.[1]

---

[1] The Due Process issue of retaliation in the drastic increase in sentences is presently pending, along with several other overlapping issues, before the Missouri Court of Appeals, Western District, Case No. WD 72334 in a direct appeal from the denial by the trial court of Petitioner's 29.15 motion. (Petitioner incorporates by reference herein the

Example Petition for Writ of Habeas Corpus #3—Woodworth v. Denney (cont.)

9. This second conviction and sentence was affirmed without an opinion on August 14, 2001. *State v. Woodworth* 55 S.W.3d 865 (Mo.App.W.D.2001).

10. Petitioner filed a motion under Rule 29.15 to vacate the second convictions and sentences, alleging unlawful sentencing, ineffective assistance of counsel, prosecutorial misconduct, the denial of the right to a fair and impartial judge, grand jury and trial jury improprieties, which was denied by the Court on January 13, 2009.

11. Petitioner incorporates by reference herein the allegations and matters contained in said 29.15 motion.

12. Petitioner filed an appeal from that ruling and that appeal is pending in the Missouri Court of Appeals, Western District, Case Number WD 70685.

13. In 1993, approximately three years after the shootings, victim Lyndel Robertson hired a private investigator to "assist" the Livingston County Missouri Sheriff's Department in its investigation of the shootings, and charges were brought against Mark Woodworth by a Livingston County grand jury, empanelled by Livingston County Circuit Judge Kenneth Lewis and directed by the special assistant attorney general, appointed by Judge Lewis, Kenny Hulshof.

14. Mark Woodworth, the son of Lyndel Robertson's former farming partner and neighbor, Claude Woodworth, was 16 years old at the time of the shootings.

---

allegations contained in his motion under Missouri Supreme Court Rule 29.15 and attaches a copy as Exhibit O.)

Newly Discovered Evidence

15. Unbeknownst to Petitioner, until August 2009, a series of correspondence between Livingston County Prosecuting Attorney Doug Roberts, Judge Kenneth Lewis, shooting victim Lyndel Robertson and Special Prosecutor Kenny Hulshof were concealed within the case file maintained by the Missouri Attorney General, containing the following highly exculpatory and/or impeaching evidence:

   a. **EXHIBIT A.**- An October 5, 1993 letter from Livingston County prosecuting Attorney Doug Roberts to Judge Kenneth Lewis regarding the grand jury proceedings against Petitioner, states in part:

   "It has come to my attention that the complaining witness in this matter (Lyndel Robertson) has requested you to disqualify me for "lack of enthusiasm". Mr. Robertson confuses my desire to make a thorough review of all the reports in this case with a lack of enthusiasm. I can understand his frustration, **but recall that soon after this crime, Mr. Robertson was adamant that we charge another man.** Had his decision been rubber-stamped by this office, an innocent person might have been prosecuted."

   b. **EXHIBIT B.** - A September 24, 1993 letter in which shooting victim Lyndel Robertson complained to Judge Lewis that Doug Roberts showed a "lack of enthusiasm" in not pursuing charges against Petitioner. The letter clearly proves that there had been ex parte communications between

Judge Lewis and the victim, all prior to Judge Lewis's empanelling of the grand jury which ultimately indicted Petitioner.

c. **EXHIBIT C.-** An October 7, 1993 letter from Judge Lewis to Assistant Attorney General Kenny Hulshof wherein Judge Lewis acknowledged his appointment of Hulshof as special prosecutor, after he had forced his county prosecuting attorney Roberts out of the case (and providing him with Exhibits A and B), in which Judge Lewis states:

> "...(T)o state that Doug Roberts has been uncooperative would be a monumental understatement. He boycotted the grand jury proceeding this morning, which is simply unheard-of in my experience..."

Materiality of the Evidence

16. One of the reasons Petitioner's first conviction was reversed was that Petitioner had been unfairly deprived of the ability to present evidence that another person, Brandon Hagen (a/k/a Thomure) had the motive and opportunity to commit the crimes. Further, the state was unlawfully allowed to present irrelevant evidence ostensibly on the issue of Mark's motive. See *State v. Woodworth*, 941 S.W.2d 679 (Mo.App.W.D.1997).

17. The court specifically found that Lyndel Robertson denied during his trial testimony that he had ever identified Brandon Thomure as the shooter. (His testimony at the second trial was consistent).

18. The Court further emphasized that "...Certainly the state's case was thin, and had we been on the jury we might have voted to acquit..." (p.689)

19. During a pre-trial deposition on January 24, 1995, attended by Mr. Hulshof, Lyndel Robertson testified on questioning by Petitioner's counsel that, prior to Mark's indictment;

    "...Well, the question always was who possibly could have done it, and I never did point my finger at anybody" (Exhibit D, Lyndel Robertson deposition, 1/24/95, p. 43) (emphasis added).

20. Although directly contrary to statements attributed to Robertson immediately after the shootings in medical and police reports that he was "almost 100% sure" it was Brandon Thomure (Exhibit G), and contrary to the newly discovered evidence in 2009, Robertson maintained throughout all the proceedings against Petitioner that he had not identified Brandon Thomure at any time, but had merely offered suggestions as to who "might" have committed the crime. (Thomure had been the boyfriend of Lyndel's daughter, Rochelle, and had been forbidden by the Robertson's from seeing her.)

21. The newly discovered evidence directly contradicts this and proves that Robertson not only had identified Thomure but also had expended considerable time and energy in adamantly seeking Thomure's prosecution.

22. The complicity of the State and the Circuit Court in allowing Robertson to falsely conceal these facts from the defense, the Court, two juries, and probably the grand jury is proved by the state's continuous possession of the 1993 correspondence

Example Petition for Writ of Habeas Corpus #3—Woodworth v. Denney (cont.)

and the physical presence of the state's attorney at the deposition two years later, wherein Robertson totally concealed his adamantly seeking the prosecution of a person other than Petitioner.

23. The evidence of the identification of a person, other than Petitioner, by the only living survivor of the shootings is material in that it goes to the very heart of the defense and was clearly relevant to the impeachment of Robertson, as well as those law enforcement officers involved with him during the period of time when he was "adamant" to the court and the prosecutor that Thomure, not Petitioner, be prosecuted. It was relevant to the motives of the state as well. It is entirely likely that, had the exculpatory, impeaching evidence not been concealed, Petitioner neither would have been prosecuted nor convicted.

24. Defense evidence against Thomure included the following:

    a. Thomure was the only suspect who tested positive for gunpowder residue within twenty-four hours after the shooting.

    b. Contrary to Thomure's alibi, witnesses identified Thomure as being in Chillicothe on the evening of the shootings.

    c. Victim Catherine Robertson had recently obtained an order of protection against Thomure because of his threatening behavior.

25. The suppressed *Brady* evidence would have significantly strengthened Petitioner's theory of defense and weakened the State's case against Petitioner.

26. The commission of perjury by Robertson as the only living eye witness in this matter about an issue directly related to the theory of defense, and the conduct and

contrived theory of the prosecution was necessarily material and highly prejudicial to the defense.

27. The evidence was also material to the issue of whether Petitioner was denied the right to a fair and impartial judge.

28. Throughout all legal proceedings, Petitioner has consistently and specifically requested in discovery, inter alia, all statements of witnesses and all exculpatory evidence known to or within the possession or control of the State.

29. Petitioner has requested unsuccessfully all the Courts in this state to order the state to produce all records pertaining to the empanelling and conduct of the grand jury which indicted him.

30. Petitioner has exhibited that his attempts to obtain grand jury information was no mere fishing expedition in the following particulars, to wit:

31. Affidavit of the foreperson of the Grand Jury, John Cook, (Exhibit I) directly contradicts the State's assertion throughout, that the only grand jury testimony transcribed by a court reporter was that of Claude and Jacqueline Woodworth, in that, according to him, a court reporter was present and transcribing witness testimony at all times during the grand jury proceedings involving Petitioner.

32. No Court has yet seen fit to allow Petitioner to present the testimony of Mr. Cook at a hearing nor has Petitioner been allowed to obtain any information from the Court or the Circuit Clerk about such grand jury proceedings.

33. The nature and sequence of events strongly suggest that the State, through Mr. Hulshof, deliberately concealed the transcripts and Exhibits A, B and C, thus

effectively preventing Petitioner from obtaining proof that the Grand Jury was misled or that the prosecution was guilty of concealment and other misconduct.

34. The state has never at any time produced Exhibits A, B and C to the defense.

35. This exculpatory, impeaching evidence has been concealed by the state since at least some time in 1993 and was found by a reporter in 2009, either by accident or by deliberate leak. (See affidavit of Robert Ramsey, Exhibit J).

Denial of a Fair and Impartial Judge

36. Additionally, Petitioner was clearly denied his Due Process right to a fair and impartial judge presiding over the grand jury considering whether or not to indict him for Murder.

37. The written words of Judge Lewis, Doug Roberts and Lyndel Robertson, evidence violations of the following provisions of The Missouri Code of Judicial Conduct, Missouri Supreme Court Rule 2:

    a. Rule 203B. (5), Canon 1. "A judge shall perform judicial duties without bias or prejudice...A judge must perform judicial duties impartially and fairly. A judge who manifests bias or prejudice on any basis in a proceeding impairs the fairness of the proceeding and brings the judiciary into disrepute."

    b. Rule 203B. (7), Canon 1. "...A judge shall not initiate, permit or consider ex parte communications, or consider other communications made to the judge outside the presence of the parties concerning a pending or impending proceeding..."

c. Rule 203E. (1), Canon 1. "A judge shall recuse in a proceeding in which the judge's impartiality might reasonably be questioned…"

d. Rule 203E. (1)(a), Canon 1. "A judge shall recuse where …the judge has a personal bias or prejudice concerning a party or a party's lawyer, or **personal knowledge of disputed evidentiary facts concerning the proceeding…**"

e. Rule 203, Canon 2, A. "A judge shall respect and comply with the law and shall act at all times in a manner that promotes public confidence in the integrity and impartiality of the judiciary."

f. Rule 203, Canon 2, B. "A judge shall not allow family, social, political or other relationships to influence the judge's judicial conduct or judgment. A judge shall not lend the prestige of judicial office to advance the private interests of the judge or others…"

40. Judge Lewis, by his conduct, specifically assumed the role of chief prosecutor, not for the purpose of conducting a fair grand jury investigation, but to bring about prosecution of Petitioner before the statute of limitations ran on the non-homicide offenses, as he specifically states in Exhibit C.

41. Once he received ex parte communications from the victim about the prosecution, he should have recused himself from any further proceedings, especially where, as here, the judge was knowledgeable of disputed facts regarding the victim's identification of another. Instead, it is clear that Judge Lewis forced the county

prosecutor to remove himself from the case rather than allowing him to exercise his prosecutorial discretion not to seek formal charges against Petitioner.

42. Further, Judge Lewis unlawfully exceeded his authority and interfered with the absolute discretion of the Livingston County prosecuting attorney whether or not to charge a particular suspect and thus assumed the role of de facto Chief Prosecutor against Petitioner.

43. In Missouri, the law is clear that county prosecuting attorneys have absolute discretion to prosecute or not. §§ 56.06 and 56.087 (RSMo)

44. A circuit judge has no discretion or jurisdiction to interfere with a prosecutor's decision in a particular case. *State ex rel Griffin v. Smith*, 258 SW.2d 590 (Mo Banc 1953).

45. It is imperative that a trial judge maintains absolute impartiality during criminal proceedings to ensure a defendant receives a fair trial. *State v. Houston*, 139 SW 3d 223 (Mo.App.W.D. 2004)

46. In this case, it is clear that Judge Lewis was not impartial and that his conduct deprived Petitioner of Due Process.

Cause and Prejudice and Manifest Injustice

47. The theory and conduct of the State's eventual prosecution of Petitioner at both trials depended upon the concealment from the Court, the jury and Petitioner, the exculpatory, impeaching evidence that Lyndel Robertson had not only identified someone other than Petitioner as the shooter but had been "adamant" about seeing that other person be prosecuted.

48. Not only did Mr. Hulshof permit Lyndel Robertson's misleading deposition testimony to be given, but also he never saw to it that it was corrected, thus leaving the defense without the available means to impeach Robertson at trial or to present crucial evidence clearly supportive of the defense theory that another person committed the crimes. Circumstances suggest direct complicity by Hulshof in misleading the defense.

48. The opening statement of Kenny Hulshof on March 14, 1995 at Petitioner's first trial contains no reference to Robertson's previous identification of Brandon Thomure as the shooter and his demands that Thomure be prosecuted. (Attached hereto as Exhibit E, 1st trial transcript, PP.225-249)

49. In fact, Mr. Hulshof stated, (and Robertson ultimately testified in both trials), that not only did Robertson **not remember** making ANY statements implicating another person, **but did not, in fact, see who shot him.** Hulshof went a step further in the deception by stating "...he (Robertson) has blocked it out or the trauma has caused him not to be able to remember anything and perhaps that's best..." (Exhibit E, p. 236). Ironically, Robertson must not have had this trauma – induced memory problem when he demanded after the shooting that Brandon Thomure be prosecuted.

Page 13 of 18

50. The defense, being unaware of this exculpatory evidence, was unable to either adequately impeach the victim or to effectively cross-examine Robertson and law enforcement witnesses on this critical issue[2].

51. The same conduct and theory was repeated by the state in Petitioner's second trial.

52. During an April 26, 2006, deposition pursuant to Petitioner's 29.15 motion, Lyndel Robertson falsely denied that he had ever been told that Doug Roberts, Livingston County Prosecutor, was not going to pursue charges against Mark Woodworth, thereby demonstrably perpetuating the scheme to conceal from the defense the exculpatory, impeaching evidence referred to in Exhibits A, B, and C. (Exhibit H). This testimony is directly contradicted by the suppressed evidence.

53. The defense was also deprived of the opportunity to investigate or conduct discovery regarding the circumstances under which Robertson demanded that Thomure be prosecuted, i.e. whether law enforcement and other crucial witnesses were aware of Robertson's identification of a different person when they participated in the investigation and prosecution of Petitioner and the extent to which all participated in concealing exculpatory, impeaching evidence supportive of Petitioner's defense. It is clear that Robertson's demand for Thomure's prosecution was known by Judge Lewis, Hulshof and Doug Roberts.

---

[2] One of the issues to be decided in Petitioner's 29.15 appeal is whether his trial counsel was ineffective in failing to adequately impeach the credibility, and testimony of State's witness Brandon Thomure

54. Because Petitioner's claims were cognizable in his direct appeal and post-conviction 29.15 motion, he is entitled to review in this action, only if he can show "manifest injustice, cause and prejudice, or a jurisdictional defect." *Engel v. Dormire*, (Supra, at p. 125).

55. Petitioner has established the cause necessary to overcome procedural bar by showing that the exculpatory, impeaching evidence and information was not revealed until August 2009, when it was uncovered for the first time by Associated Press reporter Alan Zagier.

56. The suppressed evidence was favorable to Petitioner in that it supported the defense theory that another person (Brandon Thomure) had the motive and opportunity to commit the crime and was material and impeaching evidence with which Petitioner would likely have undermined the credibility of two of the crucial state's witnesses against him, Lyndel Robertson and sheriff's deputy Gary Calvert.

57. The totality of the circumstances prove unequivocally, that this favorable evidence was suppressed by the State, and that Petitioner was prejudiced thereby.

58. The State had been in possession of the evidence since before Petitioner's indictment in 1993, yet never disclosed it to the defense.

61. This evidence could not have been discovered through due diligence by Petitioner because:

   a. The evidence was concealed by the State.

   b. At a deposition on April 26, 2006, Lyndel Robertson falsely denied that he had ever been told that Doug Roberts was not going to pursue charges against Mark Woodworth, thereby concealing his attempts to have Appellant prosecuted and Doug Roberts removed from the case. (Attached hereto as Exhibit H, Page 1 and page 15 of Lyndel Robertson's deposition dated April 26, 2006.)

c. Petitioner, from the onset of the proceedings against him, has repeatedly requested the production of exculpatory evidence, in the possession of the State.

d. The courts deciding Petitioner's case have consistently denied Petitioner's attempts and requests to obtain grand jury records and for authority to take the deposition of Judge Lewis, which would likely have unmasked this concealment.

e. The Sixth Amendment requires that the State has a continuing duty to disclose exculpatory facts and information, yet they did not do so.

f. Livingston County prosecuting attorney Doug Roberts was interviewed by Petitioner's counsel, and he did not disclose this information. (See Exhibit J, attached affidavit of Petitioner's counsel.)

g. This Petitioner's right to Due Process as set for in *Brady v. Maryland*, 373 U.S. 83 (1983) has been violated.

Petitioner is Actually Innocent

62. As this Court noted when it reversed Petitioner's first conviction, the evidence against Petitioner was "thin". It did not get better with age, nor did it change appreciably from the first trial to the second.

63. The following additional facts support Petitioner's contentions that he is innocent and that he was denied Due Process:

   a. Affidavit of Ron Motley (attached hereto as Exhibit K), in which the witness testifies to hearing Kenny Hulshof remark, during jury deliberations in Petitioner's first trial, that he did not believe Petitioner was guilty, but that he believed the real killer would come forward as a result of the Petitioner being tried for murder.

   b. Affidavit of Wes Ferguson (attached hereto as Exhibit L), who heard the same remarks from Hulshof in the first trial and heard the court bailiffs, during the jury deliberations in the second trial, remark that the judge had ordered no food or drink would be given to jury until they reached a verdict.

   c. Affidavit of Bonnie Penn (attached hereto as Exhibit M), who also heard the court bailiffs, during the jury deliberations of the second trial, remark that the judge had ordered no food or drink would be given to jury until they reached a verdict.

WHEREFORE, Petitioner prays this Court for the following orders:

64. That the Petition for Writ of Habeas Corpus be sustained and that Petitioner be ordered released from custody forthwith, or, in the alternative, the following:

    a. That Respondent be ordered to bring Petitioner to Court;

    b. That respondent show cause why the Writ of Habeas Corpus should not be granted; and/or

    c. That a full evidentiary hearing be granted to determine the facts.

Respectfully Submitted,

By: _____
Robert B. Ramsey, #28312
Law Offices of Michael R. Bilbrey, P.C.
104 Magnolia Drive, Suite B
Glen Carbon, IL 62034
Ph: (618) 288-6784
Fx: (618) 288-6726

ATTORNEY FOR PETITIONER

Case no. _____

IN THE MISSOURI SUPREME COURT

MARK WOODWORTH,

Petitioner,

v.

LARRY DENNEY, WARDEN
CROSSROADS CORRECTIONAL
CENTER,

Respondent.

CERTIFICATE OF SERVICE

Petitioner certifies that a copy of Petitioner's Habeas Corpus Petition has been served on this 2 day of **July, 2010** via U.S. Mail, postage pre-paid, and addressed to the following:

Mr. Chris Koster

207 W. High Street

Jefferson City, MO 65102

Missouri Attorney General

Attorney for Respondent

Phone: (573) 751-3321 Fax: (573) 751-0774

Example Petition for Writ of Habeas Corpus #3—Woodworth v. Denney (cont.)

Larry Denney

1115 E. Pence Road

Cameron, MO 64429

Warden, Crossroads Correctional Center

Respondent

Phone: (816) 632-2727 Fax: (816) 632-2754

Respectfully Submitted,
The Law Offices of Michael R. Bilbrey

_____
Robert B. Ramsey, #28312
104 Magnolia Drive, Suite B
Glen Carbon, IL 62034
Ph: (618) 288-6784
Fx: (618) 288-6726

<4> PREPARATION OF APPENDIX FOR ACCOMPANYING EXHIBITS IN SUPPORT OF PETITION

Preparation of Appendix

As stated in the previous chapter, it may be more practical to prepare your appendix before preparing your petition. Doing so allows the appendix to be used as an aid while preparing your petition, enabling you to easily cite each specific exhibit that establishes a material fact and where the exhibit can be found in the appendix—all in the logical sequence shown in the example petitions.

If your testimony is necessary to prove your claim(s)—and it most likely will be—then your affidavit should be the first exhibit listed in the appendix. That is, of course, unless your state's statute requires you to provide specific legal pleadings with your petition (e.g., the complaint, the arrest warrant, etc.), in which instance, these pleadings should be listed first, then your affidavit, followed by any other exhibits.

At the end of this chapter, you can find an example affidavit to assist you with preparing your own. It may also be useful when preparing affidavits for other witnesses whose testimony is necessary to prove your claim(s).

You will notice, after reading the example affidavit, that the only difference between some of the sentences constructed in the first example petition is that they were written in third person, whereas the affidavit itself was written in first person. You can do the same when writing your petition, saving valuable time and effort by simply changing any affidavits' perspective from first to third person, then incorporating that text into your petition.

Affidavits

German psychologists developed a system they called *"Statement Validity Assessment"* (SVA) which is now used to determine the credibility of children in sexual abuse cases. The system can also be used in assessing the credibility of adults. The SVA is a list of nineteen indicators to look for when determining whether a story someone is telling is true or false.

Aldert Vrij, the author of *Detecting Lies and Deceit*, discusses how the SVA systeill can be used in everyday situations to help spot liars and deceivers. SVA is widely known and used by law enforcement, including police officers, detectives, prosecutors, defense attorneys, judges, etc.

PREPARATION OF APPENDIX FOR ACCOMPANYING EXHIBITS IN SUPPORT OF PETITION

Below are thirteen of the most notable and applicable indicators, which can be embedded in your own affidavit, and the affidavits of other witnesses, lending them more credibility.

1. Unstructured Production
True stories tend to jump around in time, moving forward and backward, when being told. For example, the person telling the story may start with the reason for the story and what he or she wants to convey first before giving the narrative, providing more details as the story progresses. The less likely a story was rehearsed, the more likely it is true, especially when it is of a serious incident.

2. Quantity of Details
When a person lies, he or she may not give a lot of details. Instead, that person will likely just continue to repeat what was already said, when asked for more specific details. The more detailed a story is, the more likely it is true. Usually when a person makes up a story, he or she is only concerned with telling a basic outline, something easy to remember and deliver, especially when under pressure. Of course, if the person has a sufficient amount of time to make the story up and then rehearse it, he or she can tell a very convincing lie.

3. Contextual Embedding
"I was talking to Mike about coming over to take me to the store. And it being a nice day, I though I'd wait outside for him. As I walked to the door, I heard three gunshots and saw a green Chevy speed off." This is contextual embedding, injecting information about the speaker's daily life before describing some other event. Contextual embedding doesn't usually happen when the story is made up.

4. Descriptions of Interactions
When a story is true, the person telling it will usually provide details about what other people said and did. For example, "When I went back to the Jackson County Detention Center to await my third trial, Fred asked me, 'Let's cut the shit, what plea would you take?' I answered, 'I'll take ten years.' Fred grinned and said, 'I bet you would. I can't take the State an offer like that. It's highly unlikely they would agree to it.'"

5. Reproduction of Speech
Liars do not usually reproduce parts of dialogue between them or other people in their story. For example, he or she would say something like, "I told him to stop and put his hands up, but he didn't do it. I was afraid. I fired seventeen warning shots. I didn't mean to kill him." This example sounds extreme, but the point is that when someone is telling the truth he or she wants to give the listener a play-by-play of everything that was said and done by everyone in the story.

6. Unusual Details
"Between the dates of July 17 and July 19, 2004, I personally visited the above listed address on three (3) occasions. At my first attempt, on July 17, 2004, no one answered the door. At my second attempt, on July 18, 2004, a woman

answered the door. She indicated that Mr. Franco did not reside at that location, nor did she know a Daniel Franco or where I might locate him. At my third attempt, on July 19, 2004, a second woman answered the door. She indicated she is Daniel Franco's sister and that my earlier contact was with Mr. Franco's mother. The woman indicated that Mr. Franco previously resided at this location; however, he no longer resides there. She was not able to provide an address at which Mr. Franco could be contracted." The more unusual the details, the more credible the story is. In this example, it is the context of the statements made by the two women that make the situation unusual, pointing out the untruthful statements by the first woman.

7. Accurately Reported Details Misunderstood
This happens in contexts where a person is describing a situation about which he or she doesn't have all the facts to fully understand, but the person listening does. This indicator is mostly applicable to the telling of a story by a child, in naive terms, of a sexual situation he or she was put in by a pedophile. But it can be powerful evidence in a case where a witness provides testimony that fills in the gaps of other evidence.

8. Accounts of Subjective Mental State
Truthful accounts generally include the thoughts and feelings of the person telling them. For example, "the gunshots were so close that I grabbed my chest and fell to the ground. I was scared I was hit."

9. Attribution of the Perpetrator's Mental State
This is when a person describes what he or she believes another person was feeling. For example, "He was jittery, pacing back and forth, looking around the room as if he knew something was about to happen."

10. Spontaneous Corrections
If a person is excited when telling a true story, he or she may make corrections and add facts during their account, as if reliving it and recalling events clearer as the story being told progresses.

11. Admitting Lack of Memory
Sometimes things happen so fast or appear to be so inconsequential that certain details don't get stored in the person's long-term memory. A person telling the truth will usually admit a lack of memory if the story is true. But when a person says, "I can't remember," or, "I don't recall," to a direct question, the person is likely being evasive and doesn't want to incriminate themselves or someone else.

12. Raising Doubts About One's Own Testimony
When someone is being truthful, he or she may admit to being wrong about something he or she heard or witnessed. This doesn't mean the person is lying, it just shows that the person isn't sure and doesn't want to provide misinformation.

13. Self-deprecation
When someone is telling the truth, he or she will give information that may be incriminating or make him or her look foolish. For example, "When those guys started arguing at the party, I left because I didn't want to get beat up in front of the girls from my neighborhood."

The above list is not all-inclusive of signs that an account is true or false, but it is a useful guide. Look for these indicators in the example affidavit and implement them when writing your own and those of your witnesses.

Appendix for Accompanying Exhibits

The appendix for accompanying exhibits should have a caption and a title, followed by a list of all exhibits in support of your petition for writ of habeas corpus. These exhibits should be listed alphabetically, unless there are more than twenty-six exhibits, in which instance you should use numbers instead of letters.

Page Numbering (Optional)

If your appendix has a lot of pages, you may want to number them starting at the first exhibit. Just use a pen and write the page number at the bottom-right corner of each page. You may then refer to actual page numbers in the appendix when citing sources for certain material facts. (Note: do not mark your original exhibits, only the copies.)

Binding

Most courts today use electronic filing, so it is unnecessary to staple your pleadings. However, it may be a good idea to put at least one staple in the top-left corner of your appendix, ensuring that your pleadings stay neatly bound together. The court clerk can remove the staple, if he or she wishes, when filing your pleadings with the court.

PREPARATION OF APPENDIX FOR ACCOMPANYING EXHIBITS IN SUPPORT OF PETITION

Example—Accompanying Exhibits in Support of Petition

IN THE CIRCUIT COURT OF DEKALB COUNTY, MISSOURI
AT MAYSVILLE

FILED
JUN 0 1 2015
JULIE WHITSELL
Circuit Clerk
DeKalb County, MO

ZACHARY A. SMITH,

    Petitioner,

v.   Case No. 15DK-CC00031

RHONDA PASH, WARDEN,

    Respondent.

ACCOMPANYING EXHIBITS IN SUPPORT OF
PETITION FOR WRIT OF HABEAS CORPUS

1. Affidavit of Zachary A. Smith, Petitioner's Exhibit A.
2. Transcript page from first trial, Petitioner's Exhibit B.
3. Fax by Bronwyn E. Werner, Petitioner's Exhibit C.
4. Docket Sheet Entries in State v. Zachary Smith, Petitioner's Exhibit D.
5. Letter by Elizabeth Unger Carlyle, Petitioner's Exhibit E.
6. Memo to Case File, Petitioner's Exhibit F.
7. Affidavit of Nancy Wiebe, Petitioner's Exhibit G.
8. Chief Disciplinary Counsel's Report and Recommendation, Petitioner's Exhibit H.
9. Daniel L. Franco's Application to Surrender License, Petitioner's Exhibit I.
10. In RE: Daniel L. Franco, Supreme Court of Kansas, Petitioner's Exhibit J.

PREPARATION OF APPENDIX FOR ACCOMPANYING EXHIBITS IN SUPPORT OF PETITION

Example—Accompanying Exhibits in Support of Petition (cont.)

Respectfully Submitted,

Z.A. Smith
Zachary A. Smith,
Reg. No. 521163
Crossroads Corr. Center
1115 E. Pence Road
Cameron, Missouri 64429

Petitioner

CERTIFICATE OF SERVICE

I hereby certify that on this 27th day of May, 2015, a true and correct copy of the foregoing was mailed, postage prepaid, to: Chris Koster, Attorney General, P.O. Box 899, Jefferson City, Missouri 65102, attorney for Respondent.

Z.A. Smith
Zachary A. Smith

Example—Affidavit of Zachary A. Smith

State of Missouri)
) ss
County of Dekalb)

AFFIDAVIT OF ZACHARY A. SMITH

My name is Zachary A. Smith. I am over eighteen years of age, of sound mind, and capable of executing this affidavit. Being duly sworn, I depose and state, to the best of my knowledge and belief, the following.

1. On February 6, 1996, my attorney Frederick A. Duchardt Jr. advised me of a plea offer for two life sentences. I declined the State's offer and proceeded to trial; the trial resulted in a hung jury.

2. Prior to second trial, Fred advised me of a twenty-five year plea offer. I declined the State's offer and proceeded to trial; I was convicted and sentenced to life without the possibility of probation or parole and one hundred years. The conviction, however, was reversed on direct appeal, and my case was remanded for a new trial.

3. When I returned to the Jackson County Detention Center to await the third trial, Fred visited me, sometime in June of 1998. During our visit, Fred said, "Let's cut the shit, what plea would you take?" I answered, "I'll take ten years." Fred grinned and said, "I bet you would. I can't take the State an offer like that. It is 'highly unlikely' they would agree to it."

4. Nevertheless, Fred told Ms. Werner, the assistant prosecuting attorney, about my offer to plead to ten years. And when I talked with him over the phone, Fred said Ms. Werner laughed for a solid ten minutes. When she regained her composure, she said, "Tell him I'll

1

Example—Affidavit of Zachary A. Smith (cont.)

meet him half way from the ten years he offered to take and the twenty-five I offered him last time." Fred said it would be an eighteen year sentence.

5. Remembering a comment Ms. Werner made when the judge declared a hung jury, saying my case wasn't one she wanted to retry, I foolishly pushed my luck by countering with an offer to take ten and three, consecutive. I was hoping Ms. Werner would come down to fifteen. With the two years I already served, I would of been eligible to serve my sentence at a level three insititution, possibly at Algoa Correctional Center, the institution my father was at serving a thirteen year sentence, instead of at the violent and highly restricted level five I had just come from.

6. When Fred told Ms. Werner of my counter offer, she became angry and took back her eighteen year plea offer, telling Fred, "He has until December 31, 1998, to take twenty-five years or I'll give him life without parole again.

7. At that point, I asked Fred to move for a bond. And at the hearing, Ms. Werner objected, stating she was unable to locate her witnesses.

8. A few months later, I met an attorney named Daniel L. Franco. I discussed a 1983 civil rights case with him. But Franco was more interested in my criminal case, asking me who the prosecutor was. When I told him Bronwyn Werner, he smiled. He said he wanted to read my trial transcripts, so I retrieved them for him. Franco then said he'd see me in a few weeks.

9. A few weeks later, Franco visited me and told me he wanted to take my case, saying he was Ms. Werner's study partner in law school.

2

PREPARATION OF APPENDIX FOR ACCOMPANYING EXHIBITS IN SUPPORT OF PETITION

Example—Affidavit of Zachary A. Smith (cont.)

Franco further said Werner was a good person until she went to the "dark side." Franco said he could beat her and wanted to take my case to teach her a lesson. I told him I didn't have any money. Franco said he would take my case if I agreed to pay him ten thousand dollars upon being acquitted. Figuring I didn't have anything to lose, I agreed to the terms of his representation. I didn't want to go to trial again but with no plea offer forthcoming, I felt I had no other choice. I also figured that Ms. Werner might relent on her promise and offer me the eighteen again before trial, especially since she knew Franco personally and was having trouble locating her witnesses. At the time, I believed that's how the legal system worked, hire the right attorney, get a better plea.

10. But Franco never spoke to me about any plea offers, ever. And the next time I talked with Franco, months later, he told me he saw Ms. Werner at a Big Twelve Basketball Conference. She told Franco that she was having problems at the prosecutor's office--something to do with her sexual orientation and how she was being treated--and put in her resignation. Franco joked about Ms. Werner wearing shorts and having hairy legs when he saw her. I wasn't amused, my hope of getting the eighteen year plea back were dashed. I knew Daniel Miller would take first chair and his reputation wasn't earned by making plea offers.

11. My case proceeded to trial on April 24, 2000, and I was convicted and sentenced to life without the possibility of probation or parole and ninety-nine years.

12. Sometime after my federal habeas corpus remedy was exhausted, my habeas attorney, Elizabeth Unger Carlyle, had lost the case files.

3

PREPARATION OF APPENDIX FOR ACCOMPANYING EXHIBITS IN SUPPORT OF PETITION

Example—Affidavit of Zachary A. Smith (cont.)

Almost five years later, Elizabeth sent me a letter stating she found the files and asked if I wanted them. I called her and told her I did. I received three boxes on or about March 23, 2015, including the appellate and postconviction files.

13. Shortly after, I went to the property room and looked through the files. Inside the appellate file--a file I never had possession of--I found a memo of a conversation Nancy Wiebe had with Daniel L. Franco, dated November 1, 2000. The last sentence of the memo read: "He [Franco] also added that he [Franco] had a 17yr. plea offer that Zach refused to accept."

14. I felt sick when I read the memo because Franco never discussed a 17yr. plea offer with me or any other plea offers. Had I known that there was a 17yr. plea offer available after Ms. Werner took the eighteen off the table, I would have accepted it instead of proceeding to trial. Until I read the November 1, 2000, memo, I believed I had no choice but to proceed to trial because there was no plea offer available to me.

Zachary A. Smith
Zachary A. Smith

Subscribed and sworn to before me, a Notary Public, this 28 day of June, 2015.

Notary Public

My commission expires:

VINCENT NEGUS
Notary Public - Notary Seal
STATE OF MISSOURI
DeKalb County
Commission # 13898623
My Commission Expires: 11-18-2017

4

<5> FILING PETITION AND ACCOMPANYING EXHIBITS WITH THE COURT

Filing with the Court

When a petition or other civil pleading is filed, most circuit courts require the original and two copies, plus a filing fee. To determine how much the filing fee is, and to learn the correct number of copies to send, write a letter to the court clerk of the county where your petition will be filed or look up the circuit court's rules in your prison's law library.

After the court clerk receives your petition, he or she will send you a notice stating the filing date, the case number issued, and an order of any action taken. If you are required to provide further information, to comply with a local rule or practice, an order will be issued. In such an instance, the court will grant you additional time to comply with the order (usually thirty days). If you need longer, you may ask the court for an extension of time to comply with order.

Filing Fee

The filing fee will vary from state to state. Some states do not require a filing fee in habeas corpus proceedings. If a filing fee is required in your state and you are unable to pay it, you may proceed in forma pauperis.

Proceeding in Forma Pauperis

Most states have enacted statutes that provide remedies for when a prisoner files a civil action or appeals a judgment in a civil action and cannot prepay the required filing fees and costs. It is a standard practice, from state to state, for an indigent prisoner to include the following with his or her petition: 1) a request for leave to proceed without prepayment of the costs and filing fees; and 2) a certified copy of their prison account for the six-month period immediately proceeding the filing. (See example Motion for Leave to Proceed in Forma Pauperis.)

Upon receipt of a prisoner's request to proceed in forma pauperis, the court will determine whether or not the prisoner is able to pay the full amount of the filing fee or costs. If the court

---

* The Latin term *in forma pauperis* means "as a poor person."

finds that the prisoner cannot pay, it will assess a partial payment based upon the average monthly deposits or average monthly balance of that prisoner's institutional account.

The court will calculate the amount of this partial payment, then notify the prisoner and the corrections agency of the amount, along with an order for its payment by installments. Twenty percent of any funds deposited into the prisoner's account will be withdrawn and sent to the court until the full filing fees or costs are paid in full. The corrections agency will automatically forward these payments whenever funds exist.

Application for Change of Judge

In most states, the rules of civil practice and procedure provide petitioners the opportunity for one change of judge without showing cause. If you believe that a certain judge will rubber-stamp your petition, dismissing your case, you should file an application for a change of judge. (See example Application for Change of Judge.)

Motion for Bail

Depending on the circumstances of your case, you may want to file a motion to be admitted to bail. If so, check the statutory rules for your state in the appendix of this book, then refer to the example Motion to Be Admitted to Bail, located at the end of this chapter.

Mailing Petition and Exhibits

When everything is in proper order, sign, date, and mail your petition, its accompanying exhibits, and any other pleadings to the court clerk and respondent. Be sure to keep a copy of each pleading for your records.

Example—Motion for Leave to Proceed in Forma Pauperis

IN THE CIRCUIT COURT OF DEKALB COUNTY, MISSOURI
AT MAYSVILLE

ZACHARY A. SMITH,   )
)
            Petitioner,   )
)
     v.   )   Case No.
)
RHONDA PASH, WARDEN,   )
)
            Respondent.   )

MOTION FOR LEAVE TO PROCEED IN FORMA PAUPERIS

COMES NOW Petitioner, Zachary A. Smith, and asks this Court for leave to proceed in forma pauperis. In support of motion, Zachary states as follows.

1. Zachary is incarcerated, is unemployed, and is therefore unable to pay the filing fee in this case. (See attached certified printout of prison account for the last six months).

2. Zachary believes that he is entitled to relief and should prevail if granted leave to proceed in forma pauperis.

3. Zachary therefore asks this Court to grant him leave to proceed in forma pauperis.

For the foregoing reasons, Zachary prays this Court grant the requested relief. He further prays for any further relief which this Court may deem just and proper under the circumstances.

Respectfully Submitted,

_____
Zachary A. Smith,
Reg. No. 521163
Crossroads Corr. Center
1115 E. Pence Road
Cameron, Missouri 64429

Petitioner

Example—Motion for Leave to Proceed in Forma Pauperis (cont.)

CERTIFICATE OF SERVICE

I hereby certify that on this___day of _____, 2015, a true and correct copy of the foregoing was mailed, postage prepaid, to: Chris Koster, Attorney General, P.O. Box 899, Jefferson City, Missouri 65102, attorney for Respondent.

_____
Zachary A. Smith

FILING PETITION AND ACCOMPANYING EXHIBITS WITH THE COURT

Example—Application for Change of Judge

IN THE CIRCUIT COURT OF DEKALB COUNTY, MISSOURI
AT MAYSVILLE

ZACHARY A. SMITH,)
)
       Petitioner,)
)
v.) Case No. _____
)
RHONDA PASH, WARDEN,)
)
       Respondent.)

APPLICATION FOR CHANGE OF JUDGE

COMES NOW Petitioner, Zachary A. Smith, and moves this Court for an Order for a Change of Judge, pursuant to Supreme Court Rule 51.05. In support, Zachary states the following.

1. "A change of judge shall be ordered in any civil action upon the timely filing of a written application therefor by a party." **Rule 51.05(A)**. See also **State ex rel. Manion v. Elliott**, 305 S.W.3d 462 (Mo.2010).

2. Zachary moves this Court to issue an Order to disqualify Judge Bartley Spear and transfer this action to another judge, pursuant to Rule 51.05(A).

Respectfully Submitted,

Z.A. Smith
Zachary A. Smith,
Reg. No. 521163
Crossroads Corr. Center
1115 E. Pence Road
Cameron, Missouri 64429

Petitioner

CERTIFICATE OF SERVICE

I hereby certify that on this 29th day of May_____, 2015, a true

1

Example—Application for Change of Judge (cont.)

and correct copy of the foregoing was mailed, postage prepaid, to: Chris Koster, Attorney General, P.O. Box 899, Jefferson City, Missouri 65102, attorney for Respondent.

　　　　　　　　　　　　　　　Z. A. Smith
　　　　　　　　　　　　　　　Zachary A. Smith

Example—Motion to be Admitted to Bail

IN THE CIRCUIT COURT OF DEKALB COUNTY, MISSOURI
AT MAYSVILLE

ZACHARY A. SMITH,)
)
      Petitioner,)
)
v.) Case No. 15DK-CC00051
)
RHONDA PASH, WARDEN,)
)
      Respondent.)

MOTION TO BE ADMITTED TO BAIL
AND RELEASED ON OWN RECOGNIZANCE

COMES NOW Petitioner, Zachary A. Smith, and moves this Court for an order admitting him to bail and releasing him from custody on his own recognizance, pursuant to Supreme Court Rule 91.14. In support, Zachary states the following.

1. Zachary has already served twenty years of the seventeen year plea offer. Had it not been for his attorney's failure to advise Zachary of the plea offer, Zachary would have accepted it and been released from the department of corrections three years ago.

2. Zachary's further incarceration is a irreparable injury. He moves this Court to enter an order releasing him on his own recognizance until a hearing can be held and case disposed of.

For the foregoing reason, Zachary prays this Court grant the requested relief. He further prays for any other and further relief the Court may deem just and proper under the circumstances.

Respectfully Submitted,

Z.A. Smith
Zachary A. Smith,
Reg. No. 521163
Crossroads Corr. Center
1115 E. Pence Road

1

FILING PETITION AND ACCOMPANYING EXHIBITS WITH THE COURT

Example—Motion to be Admitted to Bail (cont.)

Cameron, Missouri 64429

Petitioner

CERTIFICATE OF SERVICE

I hereby certify that on this 11th day of June, 2015, a true and correct copy of the foregoing was mailed, postage prepaid, to: Chris Koster, Attorney General, P.O. Box 899, Jefferson City, Missouri 65102, attorney for Respondent.

Z.A. Smith
Zachary A. Smith

<6> COURT'S ORDER TO SHOW CAUSE WHY WRIT SHOULD NOT BE GRANTED

Show Cause Order

Only when it is clear, from the petition and supporting exhibits, that the petitioner is entitled to relief must a court order the respondent to show cause why a writ of habeas corpus should not be granted. Unless such a finding is made, a court will usually summarily dismiss the case without ordering the respondent to show cause why the petitioner's confinement is legal. A court could also write findings of fact and conclusions of law, detailing its decision for denying relief without issuing a show cause order.

A court's order of dismissal, with or without written findings of fact and conclusions of law, doesn't necessarily mean that the petitioner wasn't entitled to relief. The courts deny relief on a daily basis to those who are actually entitled to relief. The judicial system is imperfect, but the appellate courts are designed to correct erroneous legal conclusions by the lower courts, acting as a set of scales to balance out injustices and provide relief to those who have been grievously wronged.

The examples provided at the end of this chapter are from such a case. After being denied relief in the lower circuit court, the petitioner prevailed in the Missouri Court of Appeals. In a case where the issue is a question of law, the appellate court is the most likely venue to grant a petitioner relief. Appellate courts, however, do not make findings of fact. That is done by the lower courts, after an evidentiary hearing.

A material fact is a fact that, if proven, could determine the outcome of the proceedings, either for or against the petitioner. In a case where a material fact is in dispute, a hearing will need to be held. This phase of the habeas corpus process is, in essence, similar to a motion for summary judgment in a civil action, a process that permits a court to grant relief or dismiss the case without holding an evidentiary hearing.

A court will only issue a show cause order if the petition, along with supporting exhibits, establishes that the petitioner is entitled to relief. The burden is upon the petitioner to prove his or her claim(s) by a preponderance of evidence.

The petition, along with supporting exhibits, must present sufficient evidence to meet each and every element of the claim(s), both legally and factually, before a court will order the respondent to show cause why a writ of habeas corpus should not be granted. (See example Order to Show Cause.)

For instance, if a show cause order is issued and the respondent files a response alleging that the petitioner failed to show that the state withheld favorable evidence from the defense, the petitioner's reply must then present evidence disputing the respondent's contention, showing that there is, indeed, a genuine issue as to whether the state withheld material evidence.

Respondent's Motion for Extension of Time to File Response

Typically, when a court orders the respondent to show cause, the respondent will file a Motion for an Extension of Time to file a response, usually requesting thirty to sixty additional days. Although the example provided requests an extension of time to file a brief, the format is the same when requesting additional time to file a response to a show cause order.

Respondent's Response

A respondent's response is similar to a motion for summary judgment: it makes a legal argument and attaches exhibits to establish certain facts to support it. (See example Respondent's Suggestions in Opposition to Petition.)

Whether a case only involves a question of law or has a genuine issue of fact to be decided, the respondent's response will attempt to persuade a court that the petitioner is entitled to no relief under the law. The most common defense made by a respondent is a procedural default argument. Any respondent's goal is to get the case disposed of without a hearing.

Petitioner's Request for Extension of Time to File Reply

A petitioner's Motion for Extension of Time is of similar format to that of the respondent. It will need to be modified to request time to file a reply rather than a brief. (See example Petitioner's Motion for Extension of Time.)

You may ask a court to grant you a thirty- or sixty-day extension of time to file a reply to the respondent's response, stating that you need time to research respondent's contentions, gather additional documents, or obtain additional affidavits. Without an extension, a court normally expects a reply within seven working days.

Petitioner's Reply

In the example Order to Show Cause, the Missouri Court of Appeals denied the petitioner's request for time to respond to Respondent's Suggestions in Opposition to Petition. Instead, it ordered the parties to file briefs. For example purposes, those briefs are presented in this chapter rather than a typical reply. A Reply in Opposition to Respondent's Motion for Rehearing or Transfer is also provided as an example.

Although the brief format is not necessary for preparing a reply to the respondent's response (unless an appellate court orders you to file briefs), these examples will assist you with preparing your reply. The only difference is, you will not need to prepare a cover page, a table of contents, etc. Your reply should only contain a caption, title, and argument disputing the respondent's contentions.

Court's Judgment

A court will render a judgment after the petitioner's reply is filed and the case is taken up for consideration. A court may set a hearing and order discovery; issue a summary dismissal; or issue a written opinion of findings of fact and conclusions of law, granting or denying petitioner relief.

In most states, when a court issues a judgment, the petitioner may simply refile a new petition in a higher court. Some states permit the filing of a notice of appeal to challenge a lower court's judgment. To learn if yours is such a state, check your state's appellate practice in deciding habeas corpus proceedings. (This issue is further discussed in Chapter 9.)

Example—Order to Show Cause

**In the
Missouri Court of Appeals
Western District**

IN RE FREDERICK THORNTON,)
       Petitioner,)
v.)
)
LARRY DENNEY, WARDEN,) WD77276
Crossroads Correctional Center,)
)
       Respondent.)

ORDER TO SHOW CAUSE PURSUANT TO RULE 91.05

This Court acknowledges Petitioner Frederick Thornton's Petition for Writ of Habeas Corpus filed February 20, 2014, (Petition) requesting the issuance of a Writ of Habeas Corpus pursuant to Rule 91.

Respondent's Suggestions in Opposition to the petition were filed on March 24, 2014. Petitioner's Motion to Request Permission and Time to Respond to State's Suggestions in Opposition to Petition for Writ of Habeas Corpus filed on March 27, 2014, is hereby **denied** as moot.

The Court hereby issues an Order to Show Cause Why the Writ of Habeas Corpus should not be issued pursuant to Rule 91.05.

Pursuant to Rule 91.09(b)(1) and (2) the Respondent would normally be required to answer the petition. However, the Respondent has filed Suggestions in Opposition to the petition which may have incorporated the requirements in Rule 91. If not, the appropriate responses should be made in the briefs in complying with Rule 91.

Example—Order to Show Cause (cont.)

The parties will comply with the following briefing schedule pursuant to Rule 84.24(i):

The brief of the petitioner or relator shall be filed within 30 days from the date of this order, respondent's brief shall be filed within 20 days thereafter; and if petitioner or relator desires to file a reply brief, it shall be filed within 10 days thereafter.

Without limiting the scope of the parties' briefs, the Court requests that the parties address the following questions:

1) Whether under *State ex rel. Koster v. Jackson*, 301 S.W.3d 586, 590 (Mo. App. W.D. 2010), Thornton's argument presents a "jurisdictional defect" which may be raised in a petition for writ of habeas corpus, whether or not the issue could have been raised earlier, and without the necessity for movant to establish "cause and prejudice";

2) Whether the appropriate standard for determining the retroactive application of the *Turner* decision is the three-part test announced in *Summers v. Summers*, 701 S.W. 2d 720, 724 (Mo. Banc 1985), and applied in, e.g., *Trout v. State*, 231 S.W.3d 140 (Mo. Banc 2007), and *Trans UCU, Inc. v. Dir. Of Revenue*, 808 S.W.2d 374 (Mo. Banc 1991); and

3) In determining the retroactivity of *Turner v. State*, 245 S.W.3d 826 (Mo. Banc 2008), the relevance of the Missouri Supreme Court's statements in *State v. Severe*, 307 S.W.3d 640, 644 (Mo. Vanc 2010), that "*Turner* created no new law, " and that "[t]he state was on notice by the plain language of section 577.023.16 that a guilty plea followed by a suspended imposition of sentence in 'municipal court' was not to be treated as a prior conviction."

Consistent with the authority described in Rule 91.01(a), further details of procedure as may be necessary to the orderly course of this action shall be subject to further order of this Court.

Dated this 1st day of April, 2014.

/s/ THOMAS H. NEWTON
Thomas H. Newton
Presiding Judge, Writ Division

Joseph M. Ellis, Judge, concurs
Alok Ahuja, Judge, concurs.

cc: Mr. Frederick Thornton
 Mr. Stephen D. Hawke, Esq.
 Mr. Andrew Bailey, Esq.

COURT'S ORDER TO SHOW CAUSE WHY WRIT SHOULD NOT BE GRANTED

Example—Respondent's Motion for Extension of Time

IN THE
MISSOURI COURT OF APPEALS
WESTERN DISTRICT

IN RE FREDERICK THORNTON,	)	
Petitioner,	)))	
v.	))	WD77276
LARRY DENNEY, Warden, Crossroads Correctional Center,	)))	
Respondent.	)	

AMENDED MOTION FOR EXTENSION OF TIME IN WHICH TO FILE RESPONDENT'S BRIEF

COMES NOW Respondent, by and through counsel, and hereby moves that this Court grant the Respondent additional time to file Respondent's brief, and in support states:

1. On June 16, 2014, Petitioner filed his brief with this Court.

2. Respondent's brief is due to the Court on or about July 6, 2014.

3. Undersigned counsel has been travelling extensively in the month of June 2014, covering court appearances in various counties throughout the State. Due to these court appearances and case preparation related to those appearances, respondent's brief in this matter is not yet complete.

4. The requested extension is not designed to vex or harass Appellant. Appellant's substantive right should not be adversely affected.

Example—Respondent's Motion for Extension of Time (cont.)

WHEREFORE, for the reasons herein stated, Respondent prays that the Court grant his motion for extension of time for an additional 30 days to file Respondent's brief in this matter.

Respectfully submitted,

CHRIS KOSTER
Attorney General

/s/ Andrew Bailey
ANDREW BAILEY
Assistant Attorney General
Missouri Bar No. 65758
P. O. Box 899
Jefferson City, MO 65102
(573) 751-1508
(573) 751-1336 fax
Andrew.Bailey@ago.mo.gov
Attorneys for Respondent

CERTIFICATE OF SERVICE

I hereby certify that a true and correct copy of the foregoing was electronically filed by using the CM/ECF system. Service to counsel for plaintiff is performed by the filing and service through that system, this 7 day of July, 2014, to:

/s/ Andrew Bailey
ANDREW BAILEY
Assistant Attorney General

Example—Respondent's Response to Show Cause Order

IN THE MISSOURI COURT OF APPEALS FOR THE
WESTERN DISTRICT

In re: FREDERICK THORNTON,)
)
      Petitioner,)
)
      v.)   Case No.   WW77276
)
LARRY DENNEY,)
)
      Respondent.)

SUGGESTIONS IN OPPOSITION TO PETITION

Statement of Custody and Parties

Petitioner Frederick Thornton is incarcerated at the Crossroads Correctional Center located in Cameron, due to the sentence and judgment of the Circuit Court of DeKalb County. Thornton pleaded guilty to the class D felony of driving while intoxicated-persistent offender, and the trial court sentenced Thornton to four years in the Department of Corrections. Thornton has completed the prison portion of this sentence with the conditional release portion to be served after Thornton is released from other sentences.[1]

---

[1] Originally, the trial court retained jurisdiction under Section 559.015. After his release on probation, Thornton committed the new offenses of second-degree murder and the class C felony of driving while intoxicated – aggravated offender. The trial court revoked Thornton's probation on this case and imposed consecutive sentences in the new case. Thornton is

Example—Respondent's Response to Show Cause Order (cont.)

Warden Larry Denney is petitioner's custodian and is the proper respondent. Missouri Supreme Court Rule 91.01, .07.

List of Exhibits

1. Respondent's Exhibit A is a copy of the Information.

2. Respondent's Exhibit B is a copy of the plea petition.

3. Respondent's Exhibit C is a copy of the November 2011 sentence and judgment.

4. Respondent's Exhibit D is a copy of Thornton's redacted current face sheet in the Department of Corrections.

Summary of Case

On August 24, 2007, the State filed an information charging Thornton with the class D felony of driving while intoxicated. Respondent's Exhibit A. For the prior alcohol-related traffic offenses, the State alleged a 2002 plea in the Cameron Municipal Division of the Circuit Court of Clinton County and a 2006 plea in the Dekalb County Circuit Court. Respondent's Exhibit A.

On October 24, 2007, Thornton entered his plea of guilty to the class D felony of driving while intoxicated, and the Dekalb County Circuit Court sentenced Thornton to four years in the Department of Corrections under the

currently serving the prison portion of the twenty-five year sentence with a consecutive five-year sentence for aggravated DWI.

2

Example—Respondent's Response to Show Cause Order (cont.)

provisions of Section 559.115. Respondent's Exhibit B; Respondent's Exhibit C; Respondent's Exhibit D. On November 5, 2007, the Department of Corrections received Thornton on this sentence. On February 29, 2008, the sentencing court granted Thornton probation. Respondent's Exhibit C; Respondent's Exhibit D.

On March 4, 2008, the Missouri Supreme Court issued its opinion in *Turner v. State*, 245 S.W.3d 826 (Mo. banc 2008), holding that a municipal driving while intoxicated offense on which the court suspended imposition of sentence did not qualify as an intoxication-related offense for the purposes of Section 577.023, RSMo. Supp. 2005.

On or about May 5, 2008, the time for Thornton to file for post-conviction relief challenging his plea and sentence expired without Thornton filing a pro se motion.

Statement Regarding Availability of Habeas Relief

Article I, Section 12 of the Missouri Constitution recognizes the right of individuals to seek a writ of habeas corpus. As the Missouri Supreme Court has explained, however, the writ of habeas corpus in Missouri is the common law writ of habeas corpus. *State ex rel. Zinna v. Steele*, 301 S.W.3d 510, 513 (Mo. banc 2010). With some exceptions, the general rule is that the review provided on a petition for writ of habeas corpus is limited to determining the facial validity of a petitioner's confinement based on the records of the

3

Example—Respondent's Response to Show Cause Order (cont.)

proceedings underlying that confinement. *Id.; see also State ex rel. Nixon v. Jaynes,* 63 S.W.3d 210, 214 (Mo. banc 2001).

Habeas review is not meant to be a substitute for post-conviction review under Rule 24.035 or Rule 29.15 or for direct appeal. *State ex rel. Green v. Moore,* 131 S.W.3d 803, 805 (Mo. banc 2004). As such, to receive habeas review on a challenge to the validity of the conviction, a petitioner must: 1) demonstrate the existence of a jurisdictional defect; 2) make a claim of actual innocence; 3) or demonstrate cause and prejudice for the failure to make the claim on direct appeal or post-conviction review. *Green,* 131 S.W.3d at 805 n. 5.

Thornton asserts that he should be allowed to file this petition because he could not have been aware of the decision in *Turner* at the time of his plea and that, if he had timely filed a post-conviction motion, his claim would have been rejected under the governing case law. Suggestions, pages 8. While it may be true that Thornton would not have known about *Turner* at the time of his plea or the time of his release from custody, neither date is the controlling fact for determining cause.

In *State ex rel. Koster v. Jackson,* 301 S.W.3d 586 (Mo. App. W.D. 2010), the Missouri Court of Appeals, Western District held that an inmate could raise a *Turner* claim in a habeas proceeding when the time for filing a post-conviction motion expired before the decision in *Turner. Id.* at 591. While

4

Example—Respondent's Response to Show Cause Order (cont.)

file a post-conviction claim. *See State ex rel. Taylor v. Moore*, 136 S.W.3d 799, 801-02 (Mo. banc 2004). Any allegation that Thornton did not personally learn that *Turner* might apply to his conviction would not justify allowing this untimely claim.

This Court should deny this petition.

Claims Raised

A.   Thornton's claim

Thornton alleges that his conviction is invalid as the State used a municipal offense on which he received a suspended imposition of sentence to enhance his sentence.

B.   Evidence

The State alleged in the information that Thornton had two prior offenses: 1) a 2002 plea to driving while intoxicated in the Cameron Municipal Division; and 2) a 2006 plea in Dekalb County Circuit Court. Respondent's Exhibit A. Thornton entered a plea of guilty to those charges. Respondent's Exhibit B; Respondent's Exhibit C.

In his pleadings, Thornton attaches court records from two driving while intoxicated cases from the Cameron Municipal Division – one for a 1998 conviction which contains no indication that Thornton was represented

Example—Respondent's Response to Show Cause Order (cont.)

by counsel and one for a 2000 suspended imposition of sentence[3] in which Thornton was represented by counsel.

C. Analysis

Under the 2005 version of Section 577.023 (which controls this case) as interpreted by *Turner,* an alcohol-related offense was a municipal conviction for driving while intoxicated at which the defendant had counsel or waived counsel in writing or a state plea/finding for driving while intoxicated, excessive blood alcohol or the "intoxicated driving" provisions of assault in the second degree and involuntary manslaughter. The proper classification and range of punishment depended on the number (and timing) of the prior offenses.

The *Turner* decision does not apply retrospectively to Thornton to upset the conviction and sentence. As noted, Thornton resolved any factual controversy by pleading guilty on October 24, 2007 (Respondent's Exhibit B). Thornton did not appeal his conviction so it became final ten days later on

---

[3]As best as respondent can determine, based on Thornton's criminal history and driving record and the charges in Thornton's new case, the information in this case contained a typographical error and the reference to the 2002 driving while intoxicated case is actually the 2000 municipal case included in Thornton's exhibits.

7

November 3, 2007. Missouri Supreme Court Rule 30.03. The Missouri Supreme Court did not decide *Turner* until months later on March 4, 2004. So the legal question is whether *Turner* applies retrospectively to vacate this conviction. The answer is no.

Guidance on this question comes from *State v. Ferguson*, 887 S.W.2d 585 (Mo. banc 1994). Giving Thornton the benefit of saying *Turner* is a substantive rule, then *Turner* applies prospectively and retrospectively to cases subject to direct appeal or to pending cases "not finally adjudicated." *Id.* When *Turner* was decided, Thornton's conviction was not on direct appeal and his criminal case was final. Accordingly, the Court should not extend the benefit of *Turner* to upset Thornton's conviction.

Thornton does not contest that the 2006 offense from DeKalb County counts as a valid prior offense. As such, even if Thornton's other claims are correct, his remedy would be resentencing on a class A misdemeanor as a prior alcohol-related offender under Section 577.023.2.

Assuming that Thornton is correct that neither of his prior pleas qualified in 2007 as prior alcohol-related offenses, this flaw would, if it had been timely raised, only have invalidated the enhancement to the Class D felony, not the entire plea. *Cf. Turner*, 245 S.W.3d at 827 (describing challenge as to the maximum authorized sentence, not the validity of the plea).

Example—Respondent's Response to Show Cause Order (cont.)

Conclusion

This Court should dismiss this petition with prejudice.

Respectfully submitted,

CHRIS KOSTER
Attorney General

/S/ Stephen D. Hawke
STEPHEN D. HAWKE
Assistant Attorney General
Missouri Bar No. 35242

P. O. Box 899
Jefferson City, MO 65102
(573) 751-3321
(573)751-3825 fax
stephen.hawke@ago.mo.gov
Attorneys for Respondent

CERTIFICATE OF SERVICE
I hereby certify that a true and correct copy of the foregoing was mailed, postage prepaid, this 24 day of March, 2014, to:

Frederick W. Thornton
Inmate Number 1168395
Crossroads Correctional Center
1115 East Pence Road
Cameron, Missouri 64429

/S/ Stephen D. Hawke
_____
Stephen D. Hawke
Assistant Attorney General

COURT'S ORDER TO SHOW CAUSE WHY WRIT SHOULD NOT BE GRANTED

Example—Petitioner's Motion for Extension of Time

IN THE
MISSOURI COURT OF APEALS
WESTERN DISTRICT

IN RE: FREDERICK W. THORNTON, III,)
)
    Petitioner,)
)
vs.)   Case No. WD77276
)
LARRY DENNEY, Superintendent)
  Crossroads Correctional Center,)
)
    Respondent.)

**MOTION FOR EXTENSION OF TIME
IN WHICH TO FILE PETITIONER'S BRIEF**

COMES NOW Sean D. O'Brien, counsel for Petitioner Frederick Thornton, III, and moves this Court for an extension of time in which to file Petitioner's brief. In support of this motion, counsel states:

1. This Court on April 1, 2014, issued a briefing schedule pursuant to Rule 84.24(i) directing Petitioner to file his brief within thirty days, making his brief presently due on or about May 1, 2014.

2. Thereafter on April 10, 2014, this Court sustained Mr. Thornton's Motion to Appoint Counsel, and appointed the undersigned counsel to represent Mr. Thornton. Counsel entered his appearance on April 11, 2014.

3. Undersigned counsel has obtained Mr. Thornton's file and is researching the issues presented. However, he requires additional time because of pre-existing professional obligations. Counsel teaches full time at UMKC School of Law. In addition to those duties,

1

COURT'S ORDER TO SHOW CAUSE WHY WRIT SHOULD NOT BE GRANTED

Example—Petitioner's Motion for Extension of Time (cont.)

he is counsel of record in two cases involving the death penalty, United States v. Jeffery Paul, WD Ark. 05-2107, and Dale W. Eaton v. Eddie Wilson, D. Wyo. 09-CV-261. These and other professional duties prevent counsel from completing the brief as currently scheduled.

4. Counsel anticipates that he can file Petitioner's brief within an additional month. Since the thirtieth day after the current due date falls on a Saturday, counsel respectfully requests an extension of time until Monday, June 2, 2014, within which to complete Mr. Thornton's brief.

WHEREFORE, for the foregoing reasons, counsel for Petitioner' respectfully requests an extension of time until June 2, 2014, within which to file Petitioner's brief in this matter.

Respectfully submitted,

/s/ Sean D. O'Brien
Sean D. O'Brien, MoBar # 30116
4920 N. Askew
Kansas City, MO 64119
Telephone (816) 235-6152
Facsimile (816) 235-5276
E-mail: obriensd@umkc.edu

2

CERTIFICATE OF SERVICE

I hereby certify that the foregoing document was served upon the parties by e-mail through this Court's eFiling system this 25th day of April, 2014, at the following addresses:

Andrew Bailey
Assistant Attorney General
andrew.bailey@ago.mo.gov

Stephen D. Hawke
Assistant Attorney General
stephen.hawke@ago.mo.gov

P.O. Box 899
Jefferson City, MO 65102

/s/ Sean D. O'Brien
Sean D. O'Brien

COURT'S ORDER TO SHOW CAUSE WHY WRIT SHOULD NOT BE GRANTED

Example—Petitioner's Statement, Brief and Argument

IN THE MISSOURI COURT OF APPEALS

WESTERN DISTRICT

Case No. WD77276

IN RE: FREDERICK W. THORNTON, III,

Petitioner,

v.

LARRY DENNNEY, Superintendent,
Crossroads Correctional Center

Respondent.

PETITIONER'S STATEMENT, BRIEF AND ARGUMENT

Respectfully submitted,

SEAN D. O'BRIEN #30116
4920 N. Askew
Kansas City, MO 64119
816/235-6152 • Fax 816/235-5276

Counsel for Petitioner

Example—Petitioner's Statement, Brief and Argument (cont.)

i
TABLE OF CONTENTS

Page

TABLE OF AUTHORITIES iii

JURISDICTIONAL STATEMENT vi

STATEMENT OF THE CASE 1

POINTS AND AUTHORITIES 19

STANDARD OF REVIEW 23

ARGUMENT I

ARGUMENT II.

ARGUMENT III. 69

ARGUMENT IV. 74

CONCLUSION 83

STATEMENT OF THE CASE

Petitioner Frederick Thornton, III, seeks habeas corpus relief from custody pursuant to the judgment and orders of the Honorable Thomas Campbell in DeKalb County Case No. 07K4-00429, revoking his probation and imposing a five year sentence of imprisonment based on a conviction for the Class D felony of Driving While Intoxicated-Third Offense, consecutive to sentences imposed in DeKalb County Case No. 11DK-CR00036-01.[1] The crux of Mr. Thornton's petition is that his October 27, 2007 felony conviction and sentence must be vacated because under *Turner v. State,* 245 S.W.3d 826 (Mo. Banc 2008), the

---

[1] Mr. Thornton's appeal of the denial of his motion under Rule 24.035 challenging his conviction and sentence in DeKalb County Case No. 11DK-CR00036-01 is pending before this Court. On the same day that Mr. Thornton's probation was revoked in Case No. 07K4-CR00429, he was sentenced in Case No. 11DK-CR00036-01 to twenty-five years for Class A felony of Murder in the Second Degree as an Aggravated Driving While Intoxicated offender pursuant to RSMo. § 577.023 and to five years' imprisonment for Driving While Intoxicated as an Aggravated DWI offender. All sentences were ordered to run consecutively to one another, for a total of thirty five years imprisonment. See *Thornton v. State,* WD76734, Legal File on Appeal, pp. 18-19.

COURT'S ORDER TO SHOW CAUSE WHY WRIT SHOULD NOT BE GRANTED

Example—Petitioner's Statement, Brief and Argument (cont.)

circuit court lacked jurisdiction to impose and execute a Class D felony sentence of five years' imprisonment. A simple chronology provides all the relevant facts.

Mr. Thornton was charged in the Circuit Court of DeKalb County in No. 07K4-00429 on October 24, 2007, pursuant to RSMo. § 577.010 with Driving While Intoxicated on or about August 19, 2007. Petition for Writ of Habeas Corpus, Exhibit A. The Information alleged that Mr. Thornton's offense was a Class D felony, pursuant to RSMo. § 577.023, because he had two prior driving-while-intoxicated convictions, which were described as follows:

> on or about August 22, 2002, defendant had pleaded guilty to driving while intoxicated in the Circuit Court of Clinton County, Missouri, Cameron Municipal Division and the defendant was represented by an attorney, and

> on or about September 27, 2006, defendant had pleaded guilty to driving while intoxicated in the Circuit Court of DeKalb County, Missouri.

Petition for Writ of Habeas Corpus, Exhibit A. The State did not provide relevant case numbers, and no August 22, 2002 Cameron Municipal Court judgment or

Example—Petitioner's Statement, Brief and Argument (cont.)

guilty plea record pertaining to Mr. Thornton can be found.[2] The Information may attempt to refer to Mr. Thornton's August 22, 2000, plea of guilty to driving while intoxicated in *City of Cameron v. Frederick Thornton, III*, No. 00648, pursuant to which imposition of sentence was suspended. Exhibits in Support of Petition for Writ of Habeas Corpus, p. 30-31. Mr. Thornton was placed on probation for two years, which he successfully completed. *Id.*, at 40. Potential notice defects aside, under *Turner v. State*, 245 S.W.3d 826 (Mo. Banc 2008), this plea should not have been admissible to trigger the enhancement provisions of RSMO § 577.023.

The second prior offense alleged in the indictment was probably intended to be *State of Missouri v. Frederick Thornton, III*, DeKalb County No. 06K4-CR00284-01, in which Mr. Thornton pled guilty to the Class B misdemeanor of

---

[2] Mr. Thornton provided two court records in support of his petition. In *City of Cameron v. Frederick Thornton*, Case No. 98-56, Mr. Thornton on April 10, 1998, entered a pro se plea of guilty to the charge of driving under the influence, imposition of sentence was suspended, and he completed a period of probation. Petitioner's Exhibit B, p. 22. This is clearly not the plea of guilt that was alleged in the information, nor does it affect the underlying issue in this case since it, too, is a municipal court suspended imposition of sentence, and Mr. Thornton was not represented by counsel.

Example—Petitioner's Statement, Brief and Argument (cont.)

driving while intoxicated, and on October 10, 2006, was sentenced to six months, the execution of which was suspended. Mr. Thornton does not challenge the validity of that conviction. Therefore, at the time of Mr. Thornton's plea of guilty in DeKalb County Case No. 07K4-00429 to driving while intoxicated, he had only one prior alcohol related driving offense that would have qualified to enhance his crime, making him a prior offender under RSMo. § 577.023.1(6), as interpreted in *Turner v. State, supra.* A person found guilty of such an offense as a prior offender "shall be guilty of a class A misdemeanor." RSMo. § 522.013.2.

Mr. Thornton on December 4, 2007, was found guilty of the Class D Felony of driving while intoxicated as a persistent alcohol offender, and sentenced to five years in prison. L.F. ___. Thereafter on February 8, 2008, the trial court entered a 120-Day Order of Probation, suspending the execution of the balance of Mr. Thornton's five-year sentence and placing him on probation for a period of five years.[3] On March 4, 2008, the Missouri Supreme Court filed its opinion in *Turner*

---

[3] This was the maximum term of probation authorized for a felony. RSMo. § 559.016.1(1). Under *Turner,* Mr. Thornton's probation would have been "subject to revocation" for "[a] term not less than six months and not to exceed two years for a misdemeanor." RSMo. § 559.016.1(2).

v. State, supra, holding that "the use of prior municipal offenses resulting in an SIS cannot be used to enhance punishment under section 577.023." 245 S.W.3d at 829.

Mr. Thornton was still serving the term of probation imposed by the DeKalb County Circuit Court in Case No. 07K4-00429 nearly four years later when, on January 28, 2011, while he was driving in an intoxicated condition and ran a red light, tragically causing the death of Laura Fisher. Based on this event and Mr. Thornton's driving record, he was charged with Second Degree Murder, § 565.021, and related charges. See *Thornton v. State,* WD76374, Legal File p. 7.[4] Pursuant to his plea of guilty to Second Degree Murder and the Class C Felony of Driving While Intoxicated, Mr. Thornton on November 21, 2011, was sentenced to 25 years and five years, respectively, in the Missouri Department of Corrections, to run consecutive to one another. *Thornton v. State*, WD76374, Legal File p. 18. The trial court further ordered "both charges to be served consecutively with case 07K4-CR00429-01." *Id.* Based on the January 28, 2011 offense, Mr. Thornton's

---

[4] In WD76374, Mr. Thornton appeals the denial of his motion pursuant to Missouri Rule 24.035 seeking to vacate his plea of guilty because he was sentenced in excess of his and his attorney's expectations based on his plea negotiations with the prosecuting attorney.

COURT'S ORDER TO SHOW CAUSE WHY WRIT SHOULD NOT BE GRANTED

Example—Petitioner's Statement, Brief and Argument (cont.)

probation in DeKalb County Case No. 07K4-CR00429-01 was revoked and the sentence executed, for a total of thirty-five years.

Mr. Thornton on June 19, 2012, petitioned for habeas corpus relief from his conviction and sentence in DeKalb County Case No. 07K4-CR00429-01, alleging that he was entitled to the benefit of *Turner v. State, supra.* L.F. ____. Respondent alleged that Mr. Thornton should be denied the benefit of *Turner* because he did not file a motion under Rule 24.035 challenging his 2007 conviction, conceding that "If he had filed a timely motion, he would have had a claim under the case law in effect in May, 2008." L.F. ___ (Ex. ___, p. 51). The DeKalb County Circuit Court on October 2, 2013 summarily denied Mr. Thornton's petition. L.F. ___ (Ex. ___, p. 55.

Mr. Thornton now seeks habeas corpus relief from this Court based on the Supreme Court's ruling in *Turner v. State, supra.* On April 1, 2014, this Court issued a briefing schedule, and further ordered:

Without limiting the scope of the parties' briefs, the Court requests that the parties address the following questions:

1) Whether under *State ex rel. Koster v. Jackson*, 301 S.W.3d 586, 590 (Mo. App. W.D. 2010), Thornton's argument presents a "jurisdictional defect" which may be raised in a petition for writ of habeas corpus, whether or

Example—Petitioner's Statement, Brief and Argument (cont.)

not the issue could have been raised earlier, and without the necessity for movant to establish "cause and prejudice";

2) Whether the appropriate standard for determining the retroactive application of the Turner decision is the three-part test announced in *Summers v. Summers*, 701 S.W. 2d 720, 724 (Mo. Banc 1985), and applied in, e.g., *Trout v. State*, 231 S.W.3d 140 (Mo. Banc 2007), and *Trans UCU, Inc. v. Dir. Of Revenue*, 808 S.W.2d 374 (Mo. Banc 1991); and

3) In determining the retroactivity of *Turner v. State*, 245 S.W.3d 826 (Mo. Banc 2008), the relevance of the Missouri Supreme Court's statements in *State v. Severe*, 307 S.W.3d 640, 644 (Mo. banc 2010), that "Turner created no new law, " and that "[t]he state was on notice by the plain language of section 577.023.16 that a guilty plea followed by a suspended imposition of sentence in 'municipal court' was not to be treated as a prior conviction."

Example—Petitioner's Statement, Brief and Argument (cont.)

In re Thornton v. Denney, No. WD77276, Order to Show Cause Pursuant to Rule 91.05, filed April 1, 2014.

not the issue could have been raised earlier, and without the necessity for movant to establish "cause and prejudice";

2) Whether the appropriate standard for determining the retroactive application of the Turner decision is the three-part test announced in *Summers v. Summers*, 701 S.W. 2d 720, 724 (Mo. Banc 1985), and applied in, e.g., *Trout v. State*, 231 S.W.3d 140 (Mo. Banc 2007), and *Trans UCU, Inc. v. Dir. Of Revenue*, 808 S.W.2d 374 (Mo. Banc 1991); and

3) In determining the retroactivity of *Turner v. State*, 245 S.W.3d 826 (Mo. Banc 2008), the relevance of the Missouri Supreme Court's statements in *State v. Severe*, 307 S.W.3d 640, 644 (Mo. banc 2010), that "Turner created no new law, " and that "[t]he state was on notice by the plain language of section 577.023.16 that a guilty plea followed by a suspended imposition of sentence in 'municipal court' was not to be treated as a prior conviction."

Example—Petitioner's Statement, Brief and Argument (cont.)

In re Thornton v. Denney, No. WD77276, Order to Show Cause Pursuant to Rule 91.05, filed April 1, 2014.

Example—Petitioner's Statement, Brief and Argument (cont.)

ARGUMENT I

THIS COURT SHOULD ISSUE THE WRIT OF HABEAS CORPUS BECAUSE, UNDER *TURNER V. STATE*, 245 S.W.3D 826 (MO. BANC 2008), WHICH APPLIES RETROACTIVELY TO MR. THORNTON'S CASE, THE TRIAL COURT LACKED JURISDICTION TO SENTENCE HIM TO A TERM OF YEARS IN THE PENITENTIARY FOR THE OFFENSE OF DRIVING WHILE INTOXICATED, AND LACKED JURISDICTION TO REVOKE HIS PROBATION BEYOND THE TWO-YEAR MAXIMUM TERM OF SUPERVISION AUTHORIZED FOR A MISDEMEANOR UNDER RSMO. § 559.016.

Frederick Thornton, III, petitions for habeas corpus relief from his conviction and sentence of five years imprisonment imposed and ordered executed in *State v. Thornton*, DeKalb County Case No. 07K4-00429, for driving under the influence of alcohol in violation of RSMo. § 577.010. The state alleged that Mr. Thornton's conviction should be enhanced to a class D felony pursuant to RSMo. § 577.023 based on two previous pleas of guilty to driving while intoxicated:

> on or about August 22, 2002, defendant had pleaded guilty to driving while intoxicated in the Circuit Court of Clinton County, Missouri, Cameron Municipal Division and the defendant was represented by an attorney, and

> on or about September 27, 2006, defendant had pleaded guilty to driving while intoxicated in the Circuit Court of DeKalb County, Missouri.

Exhibits in Support of Petition, pp __-__. As explained in Mr. Thornton's Statement of the Case, August 22, 2002, does not correspond with any plea or

COURT'S ORDER TO SHOW CAUSE WHY WRIT SHOULD NOT BE GRANTED

Example—Petitioner's Statement, Brief and Argument (cont.)

finding of guilt; it is the day on which his probation expired in *City of Cameron v. Frederick Thornton, III*, No. 00648, in which Mr. Thornton on August 22, 2000, pled guilty in the Cameron, Missouri, Municipal Court, and the Associate Circuit Court, Municipal Division, suspended the imposition of sentence (SIS) and placed him on a two-year probation.[1]

Mr. Thornton on October 27, 2007, pled guilty in DeKalb County Case No. 07K4-00429 to Driving While Intoxicated, RSMo. § 577.010, and his punishment was enhanced to that for a Class D Felony pursuant to RSMo. § 577.023 based on the allegation of two prior alcohol related driving offenses. On December 4, 2007, the trial court sentenced Mr. Thornton to imprisonment in the Missouri Department of Corrections for five years, and ordered execution of the sentence. Ex. ___. Thereafter, on February 8, 2008, the court pursuant to RSMo. § 559.115 entered a 120-Day Order of Probation, suspending the execution of the balance of Mr. Thornton's five-year sentence and placing him on probation for a period of five years. Ex. ___, p. ___. Mr. Thornton was not in prison and was unrepresented by

---

[1] Mr. Thornton does not deny that in *State of Missouri v. Frederick Thornton, III*, DeKalb County No. 06K4-CR00284-01, he pled guilty in Associate Circuit Court to the Class B misdemeanor of driving while intoxicated, and on October 10, 2006, was sentenced to six months, the execution of which was suspended.

2

Example—Petitioner's Statement, Brief and Argument (cont.)

counsel when in March of 2008 the Missouri Supreme Court decided *Turner v. State*, 245 S.W.3d 826 (Mo. banc 2008), which interpreted RSMo. § 577.023 to exclude from evidence for enhancement purposes a municipal court plea of guilty that resulted in a suspended imposition of sentence.

Nearly three years after being placed on probation, Mr. Thornton was charged in *State v. Thornton*, DeKalb County Case No. 11DK-CR00036-01, with driving while intoxicated and second degree murder in relation to a January 28, 2011, vehicle collision which resulted in the death of Laura Fisher in Cameron, Missouri. Ex. __. Based on his plea of guilty and conviction in that case, on November 21, 2011, Mr. Thornton's Class D felony probation in DeKalb County Case No. 07K4-CR00429 was revoked, and the five year sentence was executed and ordered to run consecutively to a twenty-five year sentence for murder and five year sentence for driving while intoxicated in the 2011 case.

Mr. Thornton's petition for writ of habeas corpus challenges the sentence in Case No. 07K4-CR00429 under *Turner v. State, supra.* Although RSMo. § 577.023.2(a) defined a persistent DWI offender as one "who has pleaded guilty to or has been found guilty of two or more intoxication-related traffic offenses," the statute forbade the use of municipal pleas of guilty resulting in a suspended imposition of sentence:

3

Example—Petitioner's Statement, Brief and Argument (cont.)

> Evidence of prior convictions shall be heard and determined by the trial court out of the hearing of the jury prior to the submission of the case to the jury, and shall include but not be limited to evidence of convictions received by a search of the records of the Missouri uniform law enforcement system maintained by the Missouri state highway patrol. After hearing the evidence, the court shall enter its findings thereon. *A conviction of a violation of a municipal or county ordinance in a county or municipal court for driving while intoxicated or a conviction or a plea of guilty or a finding of guilty followed by a suspended imposition of sentence, suspended execution of sentence, probation or parole or any combination thereof in a state court shall be treated as a prior conviction.*

Turner v. State, supra, p. 827, quoting RSMo. § 577.023.14 (Court's emphasis).

Mr. Thornton had only one prior conviction that would have qualified under *Turner* to enhance his sentence. Therefore, the trial court's sentencing jurisdiction would have been limited to the range of punishment for a Class A misdemeanor. RSMo. § 522.013.2. That would have made a considerable difference in the sentencing powers of the court. The trial court imposed a sentence of five years imprisonment for a Class D Felony, the maximum punishment authorized under RSMo. § 558.011.1(4). Under *Turner*, the court's power would have been limited

COURT'S ORDER TO SHOW CAUSE WHY WRIT SHOULD NOT BE GRANTED

Example—Petitioner's Statement, Brief and Argument (cont.)

to imprisonment for "a term not to exceed one year." RSMo. § 558.011.1(5). The trial court suspended the execution of Mr. Thornton's sentence after 120 days' imprisonment, and ordered a five-year period of probation, the maximum authorized for a felony conviction. RSMo. § 559.016.1(1). Under *Turner,* the court's power was limited to ordering probation for "[a] term not less than six months and not to exceed two years for a misdemeanor." RSMo. § 559.016.1(2). Therefore, under *Turner,* Mr. Thornton's probation should have expired on February 8, 2010, two years after he was placed on probation and eleven months prior to the events that formed the basis of his probation revocation.

This Court has accurately perceived the dispositive issues in the case and set them out in its Order to Show Cause of April 1, 2014. The first question addresses the universally accepted principal that habeas corpus will always lie to challenge a conviction and sentence imposed by a trial court that lacked the jurisdiction to do so. *See, State ex rel. Simmons v. White,* 866 S.W.2d 443 (Mo. banc 1993). The second and third questions address the issue of retroactivity of the *Turner* decision. Mr. Thornton will address them in order.

A. The *Turner* violation in Mr. Thornton's case presents a jurisdictional defect which may be raised in a petition for writ of habeas corpus, whether or not the issue could have been raised earlier, and without the necessity to establish "cause and prejudice."

COURT'S ORDER TO SHOW CAUSE WHY WRIT SHOULD NOT BE GRANTED

Example—Petitioner's Statement, Brief and Argument (cont.)

There are two instances in which the sentencing court entered orders that exceed his power under *Turner*. The first was on October 27, 2007, when the court sentenced Mr. Thornton to five years in the Missouri Department of Corrections. The second was on November 21, 2011, when it entered its order revoking Mr. Thornton's probation for an offense that occurred on January 28, 2011. As explained below, both orders exceeded the trial court's sentencing jurisdiction.

This Court posed its question about jurisdiction because of the universally understood principle that habeas corpus will always lie to challenge the jurisdiction of the sentencing court. The Supreme Court expressly held that habeas corpus is available "after an individual's failure to pursue appellate and post-conviction remedies *only* to raise jurisdictional issues or in circumstances so rare and exceptional that a manifest injustice results." *State ex rel. Simmons v. White, supra,*

6

Example—Petitioner's Statement, Brief and Argument (cont.)

at 446 (court's emphasis).[2] The power and duty of Missouri courts to entertain writs of habeas corpus raising jurisdictional defects in the prisoner's custody is indisputable. As this Court noted in its show cause order, it has already held that a sentence in excess of the statutory maximum raises a jurisdictional defect that can be challenged in habeas corpus. *State ex rel. Koster v. Jackson*, 301 S.W.3d 586, 590 (Mo. App. WD 2010), citing *State ex rel. Zinna v. Steele*, 301 S.W.3d 510 (Mo. banc 2010), and *Merriweather v. Grandison*, 904 S.W.2d 485, 486 (Mo. App. 1995).

The grounds that Mr. Thornton asserts for habeas corpus relief are also within the scope of Missouri statute, which authorizes habeas corpus relief

---

[2] Since there was no manifest injustice in *Simmons*, the court declined to further elaborate on what circumstances other than lack of jurisdiction would authorize a court to issue a writ of habeas corpus. Subsequently, the court incorporated by reference equitable federal habeas corpus doctrines of cause-and-prejudice and miscarriage of justice into Missouri's habeas corpus jurisprudence. *Clay v. Dormire*, 37 S.W.3d 214 (Mo. banc 2000). This Court has authorized or issued the writ in multiple cases upon finding cause for failing to raise prejudicial constitutional error. *See, e.g., State ex rel. Koster v. McElwain*, 340 S.W.3d 221 (Mo. App. WD 2011); *Ferguson v. Dormire*, 413 S.W.3d 40 (Mo. App. WD 2013).

7

Example—Petitioner's Statement, Brief and Argument (cont.)

"[w]here the jurisdiction of such court or officer has been exceeded, either as to matter, place, sum or person," or "[w]here, though the original imprisonment was lawful, yet, by some act, omission or event, which has taken place afterward, the party has become entitled to be discharged." RSMo. § 532.430(1) and (2). Given that "habeas corpus is, at its core, an equitable remedy," *State ex rel. Koster v. McElwain,* 340 S.W.3d 221 (Mo. App. WD 2011), quoting *Schlup v. Delo,* 513 U.S. 298, 319 (1995), it is difficult to identify any legitimate State interest in the incarceration of a prisoner beyond the term authorized by law.

   1. *The sentencing court lacked jurisdiction to impose a five-year sentence.*

As to the order imposing Mr. Thornton's five-year sentence in violation of *Turner*, this Court in *State ex rel Koster v. Jackson, supra,* properly perceived *Merriweather v. Grandison* as controlling. The Missouri Supreme Court stated, "On this point our cases are uniform and clear. A sentence which is in excess of that authorized by law is beyond the jurisdiction of the sentencing court." 904 S.W.2d at 486. Such a judgment is "not merely erroneous, but is absolutely void and subject to collateral attack on habeas corpus." *Id.,* quoting *State ex rel. Dutton v. Sevier,* 83 S.W.2d 581, 582 (Mo. 1935). Unlike the defendant in *State ex rel. Koster v. Jackson,* Merriweather could have filed a Rule 24.035 motion challenging her excessive sentence when the legislature reduced the range of punishment for her sentence. However, "where the prisoner, as in the present case,

COURT'S ORDER TO SHOW CAUSE WHY WRIT SHOULD NOT BE GRANTED

Example—Petitioner's Statement, Brief and Argument (cont.)

shows the court did not have jurisdiction to render the judgment it did render, and this defect is 'patent upon the face of the record,' then he need show no more to entitle him to relief. This view is in harmony with our usual rule that jurisdictional defects are not, and cannot, be waived." *Merriweather v. Grandison, supra,* at 489. Indeed, habeas corpus relief has always been available to vacate a sentence that exceeds the statutory maximum. *Ex parte Page*, 49 Mo. 291 (1872).

2. The sentencing court lacked jurisdiction to revoke Mr. Thornton's probation

Not only did Mr. Thornton's five-year sentence exceed the jurisdiction of the trial court, but the court also lacked jurisdiction to revoke his probation as well. As noted above, under *Turner,* the circuit court could not have imposed a period of probation longer than two years. RSMo. § 559.016.1(2). Since Mr. Thornton was placed on probation on February 8, 2008, there are no circumstances under which the trial court would have had the power to revoke his probation for a violation that occurred on January 28, 2011:

> The power of the court to revoke probation shall extend for the duration of the term of probation designated by the court and for any further period which is reasonably necessary for the adjudication of *matters arising before its expiration*, provided that some affirmative

9

Example—Petitioner's Statement, Brief and Argument (cont.)

manifestation of an intent to conduct a revocation hearing occurs prior to the expiration of the period and that every reasonable effort is made to notify the probationer and to conduct the hearing prior to the expiration of the period.

RSMo. § 559.036.8 (emphasis added). Thus, under *Turner,* the trial court lacked the power to impose a five-year sentence, and further lacked the power to revoke Mr. Thornton's probation and order execution of the five-year sentence.

The statutory maximum probationary period imposes a jurisdictional limit on the power of the court to revoke probation and order execution of the sentence. Once the probationary period lapses, the sentencing court "[does] not have jurisdiction over [the probationer] 'for any purpose, whether to cite him for probation violations, revoke probation, or order execution of the sentence previously imposed.'" *State ex rel. Limback v. Gum,* 895 S.W.2d 663, 664 (Mo. App. WD 1995), quoting *State ex rel. Musick v. Dickerson,* 813 S.W.2d 75, 77 (Mo. App. WD 1991). Where a court imposes a probationary term beyond that authorized by statute, "the court's jurisdiction over [the probationer] cease[s]" on the date that the probation should have expired. *Roach v. State,* 64 S.W.3d 884, 887 (Mo. App. SD 2002). Accord, *State ex rel. Moyer v. Calhoun,* 22 S.W.3d 250 (Mo. App. ED 2000). The limitation on the probationary term is unquestionably jurisdictional because it has been enforced through virtually every procedural vehicle available under Missouri law, including a motion for postconviction relief, *State v. Roach, supra; Norfolk v. State, supra;*, habeas corpus, *State ex rel. White v. Davis*, 174 S.W.3d 543 (Mo. App. WD 2005), and prohibition. *State ex rel. Limback v. Gum, supra; State ex rel. Musick v. Dickerson, supra; State ex rel. Heberlie v. Martinez*, 128 S.W.3d 616, 616 (Mo. App. 2004); *State ex rel. Moyer v. Calhoun*, 22 S.W.3d 250, 251 (Mo. App. ED 2000); *State ex rel. Brown v. Combs*, 994 S.W.2d 69, 70 (Mo. App. WD 1999); *State ex rel. Wright v. Dandurand*, 973 S.W.2d 161, 161 (Mo. App. WD 1998). In none of these cases was relief denied "merely because another extraordinary remedy ... was also available." *State ex rel. White v. Davis, supra,* at 548.

Contrary to Respondent's suggestion that this Court is powerless to remedy Mr. Thornton's unlawful five-year sentence, habeas corpus has long been the ordinary and appropriate vehicle to challenge a trial court's unlawful revocation of a prisoner's probation because it is "the duty of this and every other court to issue a writ of habeas corpus for any person...where there is evidence from judicial proceedings before it that a person is illegally confined." *Abel v. Wyrick*, 574 S.W.2d 411, 416 (Mo. banc 1978). This result flowed from the fact that an order revoking probation and imposing a sentence is historically unappealable under Missouri law, *id.,* and irregularities in the revocation of probation are generally not cognizable in postconviction proceedings. *Lane v. State*, 710 S.W.2d 354 (Mo.

Example—Petitioner's Statement, Brief and Argument (cont.)

App. ED 1986); *Solomon v. State,* 821 S.W.2d 133 (Mo. App. SD 1992).[3] Regardless of whether Mr. Thornton's claim could have been brought in a Rule 24.035 motion, it would be a relatively simple, straightforward and correct disposition for this Court simply to hold that the Great Writ is available to a Missouri prisoner whose probation is unlawfully revoked. Historically, that has always been true.

Thus, this Court has jurisdiction to issue the writ of habeas corpus discharging Mr. Thornton from his five-year sentence which was imposed when the trial court unlawfully revoked his probation.

B. ***Turner* applies to Mr. Thornton.**

---

[3] The only circumstance under which Rule 24.035 can be used to challenge an order revoking probation is if, as here, the sentencing court lacked jurisdiction to revoke probation. *See Norfolk v. State,* 200 S.W.3d 36 (Mo. App. WD 2006), authorizing relief in a timely Rule 24.035 motion where the sentencing court revoked Norfolk's probation after the expiration of the term of probation. Of course, habeas corpus is an equally viable remedy for challenging the order of a sentencing court that exceeds it jurisdiction. *Merriweather v. Grandison, supra.*

12

Example—Petitioner's Statement, Brief and Argument (cont.)

The remaining questions posed by this Court address the question of retroactivity. It makes sense to address the third question first, which asks the relevance of the Missouri Supreme Court's statement "in *State v. Severe*, 307 S.W.3d 640, 644 (Mo. banc 2010), that '*Turner* created no new law,'" because "[t]he state was on notice by the plain language of section 577.023.16 that a guilty plea followed by a suspended imposition of sentence in 'municipal court' was not to be treated as a prior conviction." Show Cause Order, April 1, 2014. If *Turner* created no new law, retroactivity is not even an issue because the outcome that Mr. Thornton seeks was the controlling law when his sentence was imposed.

It is easy to see from the plain text of the statute that a plea of guilty to an alcohol related driving offense followed by an SIS in state court would be sufficient evidence to trigger the repeat-offender enhanced punishment provisions of RSMo. § 577.023, while an SIS in city court would not. The Supreme Court rejected the State's attempt to resort to various rules of statutory construction to expand the scope of evidence admissible to enhance DWI offenses because "the legislature did not insert idle verbiage or superfluous language in a statute." *Turner, supra,* at 828, quoting *Civil Serv. Comm'n of St. Louis v. Members of Bd. of Aldermen of St. Louis*, 92 S.W.3d 785, 788 (Mo. banc 2003), and *Hyde Park Hous. P'ship v. Dir. of Revenue*, 850 S.W.2d 82, 84 (Mo. banc 1993). Therefore, a unanimous Missouri Supreme Court ruled that "the use of prior municipal offenses

Example—Petitioner's Statement, Brief and Argument (cont.)

resulting in an SIS cannot be used to enhance punishment under section 577.023." *Turner, supra,* 829.[4] Later, the Supreme Court observed that "[i]n Turner, this Court made no new law; it merely clarified the language of an existing statute." *State v. Severe,* 307 S.W.3d 640, 643 (Mo. banc 2010).[5]

Turner discussed the rule of lenity when it held that the statute should be interpreted in favor of the defendant, 245 S.W.3d at 829, but the Eastern District Court of Appeals observed, "Essentially, the Supreme Court decided *Turner* on the basis of *expressio unius est exclusio alterius*. The logic of the maxim underlies the Supreme Court's determination that certain dispositions, there a municipal-court SIS, were excluded by necessary implication from subsection 14, now subsection

---

[4] From a policy point of view, the result reached is not an absurd or anomalous reading of the statute. Municipal convictions are normally subject to *de novo* appeals under Missouri Rule 37.71; however, a judgment is not appealable unless a sentence is imposed. *State v. Williams,* 871 S.W.2d 450, 452 (Mo. banc 1994). It makes perfect sense to limit the collateral consequences of a judgment that cannot be reviewed on appeal.

[5] At the time of Mr. Thornton's plea, the only Missouri case interpreting RSMo. § 577.023.14 was *State v. Meggs,* 950 S.W.2d 608 (Mo.App. SD 1997), and that case essentially got it wrong.

Example—Petitioner's Statement, Brief and Argument (cont.)

16, because such dispositions were not listed therein." *State v. Carson,* 317 S.W.3d 136, 142 (Mo. App. ED 2010). Of course, the purpose of resort to any rule of statutory construction is to glean the intent of the legislature when the statute was enacted. In other words, when the Supreme Court "clarified" the arguable ambiguity in the statute, it was merely saying what the law meant when it was written. Because courts do not legislate, statutory interpretation should never produce a "new rule" that must trigger a retroactivity analysis. Compare *Desist v. United States,* 394 U.S. 244, 248 (1969) (a new rule is one that "constitutes "a clear break with the past"), and *Teague v. Lane,* 489 U.S. 288 (1989) (a new rule is one that is not "dictated by precedent"). *Turner* was a case of first impression and did not overrule any binding precedent; it is not "new" under either definition. If a rule is not "new," retroactivity concerns are not implicated. *McCoy v. North Carolina,* 494 U.S. 433 (1990). The clear implication of *Severe's* comment is that *Turner* applies to all defendants ever sentenced pursuant to RSMo. § 577.023.14.

Perhaps the most compelling evidence that *Turner* applies to sentences that are final under Missouri law is that *Turner* itself was a postconviction case. The issue of retroactivity does not apply during a direct appellate review of a conviction and sentence; it only arises with respect to postconviction challenges to a conviction. *State v. Whitfield,* 107 S.W.3d 253, 266 (Mo. banc 2003), citing *Griffith v. Kentucky,* 479 U.S. 314, 328 (1987). Turner plead guilty on April 18,

Example—Petitioner's Statement, Brief and Argument (cont.)

2005, and was sentenced to three years in prison. Since a guilty plea is not typically subject to appeal, his conviction was final. *State v. Onate,* 398 S.W.3d 102, 105 (Mo. App. W.D. 2013). Thereafter he filed a Rule 24.035 motion raising the municipal SIS enhancement issue. Thus, for Turner himself to get the benefit of his argument, the Missouri Supreme Court necessarily applied it to cases on collateral review.

The second question posed by this Court is "whether the appropriate standard for determining the retroactive application of the Turner decision is the three-part test announced in *Summers v. Summers*, 701 S.W. 2d 720, 724 (Mo. banc 1985), and applied in, e.g., *Trout v. State*, 231 S.W.3d 140 (Mo. Banc 2007), and *Trans UCU, Inc. v. Dir. Of Revenue*, 808 S.W.2d 374 (Mo. banc 1991)." In *State v. Whitfield,* 939 S.W.2d 361 (Mo. banc 1997), the Missouri Supreme Court answered this question in the affirmative, rejecting the more restrictive test for retroactivity of new rules adopted by the U.S. Supreme Court in *Teague v. Lane,* 489 U.S. 288 (1989). The *Teague* standard advances the policy that "federal habeas courts should generally not interfere with the state courts by applying new rules retroactively." *State v. Whitfield, supra,* at 267. However, a state's review of its own judgments are not concerned with the issues of comity and federalism at the heart of *Teague.* Therefore, Missouri rejects *Teague* as an appropriate test for retroactivity because it "essentially prevents state courts from achieving their goal

16

Example—Petitioner's Statement, Brief and Argument (cont.)

[of correcting injustice], for through its focus on the impropriety of disturbing a final conviction, it diverts attention from constitutional violations and prohibits relief except in the very rare case." *State v. Whitfield, supra,* at 268, n. 15, quoting Mary C. Hutton, *Retroactivity in the States: The Impact of Teague v. Lane on State Post-conviction Remedies*, 44 ALA. L. REV. 421, 449 (1993). Further, *Teague* is "unduly narrow as to what issues it will consider on collateral review." *Whitfield v. State, supra,* at 268, n. 16, quoting *Cowell v. Leapley*, 458 N.W.2d 514 (S.D. 1990). Therefore, the Missouri Supreme Court continues to require the three-part test set out in *Linkletter v. Walker*, 381 U.S. 618 (1965), and *Stovall v. Denno*, 388 U.S. 293 (1967):

> Applying the analysis set out in *Linkletter-Stovall* here, this Court must consider (1) the purpose to be served by the new rule, (2) the extent of reliance by law enforcement on the old rule, and (3) the effect on the administration of justice of retroactive application of the new standards.

COURT'S ORDER TO SHOW CAUSE WHY WRIT SHOULD NOT BE GRANTED

Example—Petitioner's Statement, Brief and Argument (cont.)

State v. Winfield, supra, at 268.[6] Missouri Courts apply *Linkletter* through a three-part analysis that requires the court to 1) determine whether the new rule is "a clear break with precedent," 2) "determine whether the purpose and effect of the newly announced rule will be enhanced or retarded by retrospective operation," and 3) "balance the interests of those who may be affected by the change in the law, weighing the degree to which parties may have relied upon the old rule and the hardship that might result to those parties from the retrospective operation of the new rule against the possible hardship to those parties who would be denied the benefit of the new rule." *Sumners*, supra, at 724.

The practical difference between the rejected *Teague* standard and the Missouri standard for retroactivity is that retroactivity is presumed in Missouri; the

---

[6] Mr. Thornton respectfully suggests that this discussion is academic since he would be entitled to relief even under the most restrictive standard of retroactivity. Under *Teague*, a defendant is entitled to the benefit of a new rule that would make him ineligible for the punishment imposed. Penry v. Lynaugh, 492 U.S. 302, 330 (1989). Also see *Atkins v. Virginia*, 536 U.S. 304 (2002), and *Roper v. Simmons*, 543 U.S. 551 (2005), retroactively applying bans on the execution of intellectually disabled persons and juveniles. Similarly, under *Turner*, Mr. Thornton was ineligible for penitentiary time or a term of probation beyond two years.

18

Example—Petitioner's Statement, Brief and Argument (cont.)

criteria for determining retroactivity are used to identify "exceptions to the general rule of retroactivity." *Sumners v. Sumners, supra*, at 723. "Solely prospective application of a decision is the exception not the norm..." *Trout v. State*, 231 S.W.3d 140, 148 (Mo. banc 2007) Application of *Turner* to Mr. Thornton is certainly supported under Missouri's retroactivity analysis. As discussed above, *Turner* does not represent a clear break with precedent. As to the second factor under *Sumner*, it is difficult to see how the purpose of a rule defining the sentencing power of a trial court would be enhanced by affirming sentences that exceed the statutory maximum. Refusing to apply the rule to Mr. Thornton would certainly defeat the purpose of RSMo. § 577.023 to fix the sentencing jurisdiction of the trial court within a defined range.

In resolving *Sumners'* third factor, "[a] court must balance the hardship imposed on those who may have relied on [the previous rule] against the hardship which may result for those who do not benefit from the application of a change in [the rule]." *Trout v. State, supra*, at 149, quoting *Sumners* at 723-24. This Court has identified three good examples of such analysis. In *Sumners*, a spouse purchased $154,000 in stock, and argued that because he purchased it through a partnership it was not part of the marital estate during dissolution of marriage proceedings. After the purchase, RSMo. Section 452.330 was amended to make clear that such funds are included in the marital estate in which both spouses are

19

Example—Petitioner's Statement, Brief and Argument (cont.)

entitled to share. Even though the new rule would deprive the husband of $77,000, the court reasoned that "By applying the source of funds rule prospectively-only, the non-owning spouse would be deprived of any benefit of the funds and effort of the marital community used to enhance the value of the asset." *Id.*, at 724. Because depriving a spouse of the proceeds of that investment would result in "exactly the injustice which led the Court to adopt the source of funds rule in [*Hoffmann v. Hoffmann*, 676 S.W.2d 817 (Mo. banc 1984)]," the court concluded that "the balance tips strongly in favor of retrospective operation of the *Hoffmann* rule." *Id.* In contrast, the court found that a Delaware corporation doing business in Missouri detrimentally relied on Missouri taxation statutes and decisions interpreting it when it relied on the advice of counsel to carefully structure the purchase and operation of a helicopter to minimize the tax consequences of the purchase. *Trans Ucu, Inc. v. Director of Revenue*, 808 S.W.2d 374 (Mo. banc 1991). The court concluded, "Missouri could have had no expectation of use tax benefit but the state now attempts to avail itself of this Court's unanticipated change of direction. It reasonably follows that the hardship of UCU having to pay $ 100,000 is greater than the disallowance of this State from collecting $ 100,000 the State did not reasonably anticipate until after the fact." *Id.*, at 378.[7] Finally, *Trout v. State*

---

[7] Justice Blackmar dissented from *Trans UCU's* prospective-only ruling because "the taxpayer is seeking a windfall in the form of tax avoidance, and this interest is

20

Example—Petitioner's Statement, Brief and Argument (cont.)

involved the retroactive application of state campaign finance law, and Trout lost because "[h]e has not suggested that he would experience injustice if the decision is applied retroactively to him." *Trout v. State, supra*, at 149.

These cases clearly point to the retroactive application of *Turner*. In order to prevail on his retroactivity argument, Respondent must do more than simply assert some vague finality interest to overcome Mr. Thornton's substantial liberty interest. The injustice and hardship of Mr. Thornton's illegal five years of incarceration is clear; it is difficult to imagine any hardship Respondent would suffer if forced to comply with *Turner* in Mr. Thornton's case.

CONCLUSION

Turner is retroactive to Mr. Thornton. Further, *Turner* was violated when Mr. Thonrton was sentenced to five years in prison, and violated again when his probation was revoked more than two years after the order placing him on probation. Since Mr. Thornton successfully completed the maximum term of probation, the appropriate remedy is for this Court to issue the writ of habeas

---

outweighed by the state's proper interest in protecting its revenue." *Trans UCU, Inc. v. Director of Revenue*, 808 S.W.2d 374, 379 (Mo. banc 1991) (Blackmar, J., dissenting).

Example—Petitioner's Statement, Brief and Argument (cont.)

corpus unconditionally discharging him from his five year sentence imposed in DeKalb County Case No. 07K4-00429.

Respectfully submitted,

/s/ Sean D. O'Brien
Sean D. O'Brien, MoBar # 30116
4920 N. Askew
Kansas City, MO 64119
Telephone (816) 235-6152
Facsimile (816) 235-5276
E-mail: obriensd@umkc.edu

CERTIFICATE OF SERVICE

I hereby certify that the foregoing document was served upon the parties by e-mail through this Court's eFiling system this 16th day of June, 2014, at the following addresses:

Andrew Bailey
Assistant Attorney General
andrew.bailey@ago.mo.gov

Stephen D. Hawke
Assistant Attorney General
stephen.hawke@ago.mo.gov

P.O. Box 899
Jefferson City, MO 65102

/s/ Sean D. O'Brien
Sean D. O'Brien

Example—Petitioner's Reply Brief

IN THE MISSOURI COURT OF APPEALS

WESTERN DISTRICT

Case No. WD77276

IN RE: FREDERICK W. THORNTON, III,

Petitioner,

v.

LARRY DENNNEY, Superintendent,
Crossroads Correctional Center

Respondent.

PETITIONER'S REPLY BRIEF

Respectfully submitted,

SEAN D. O'BRIEN #30116
4920 N. Askew
Kansas City, MO 64119
816/235-6152 • Fax 816/235-5276

Counsel for Petitioner

Example—Petitioner's Reply Brief (cont.)

TABLE OF CONTENTS

TABLE OF AUTHORITIES……………………………………………………ii

POINTS AND AUTHORITIES……………………………………………………1

I. **ARGUMENT I: MR. THORNTON IS ENTITLED TO HABEAS CORPUS RELIEF PURSUANT TO RULE 91 BECAUSE THE TRIAL COURT LACKED THE JURISDICTION TO IMPOSE A PUNISHMENT IN EXCESS OF THE STATUTORY MAXIMUM SENTENCE, AND *TURNER* IS RETROACTIVE**……………………2

CONCLUSION……………………………………………………………...12

CERTIFICATE OF SERVICE……………………………………………………13

CERTIFICATE OF COMPLIANCE……………………………………………………..14

Example—Petitioner's Reply Brief (cont.)

TABLE OF AUTHORITIES

CASES

Apprendi v. New Jersey, 530 U.S. 466 (2000)..................................10, 11

Clay v. Dormire, 37 S.W.3d 214 (Mo. banc 2000)..............................5

Martinez v. Ryan, 113 S. Ct. 1309 (2012)..6, 7, 8

State ex rel. Koster v. Jackson, 301 S.W.3d 586 (Mo. App. W.D. 2010)...........9

State ex rel. Nixon v. Jaynes, 63 S.W.3d 210, 214 (Mo. banc 2001)................8

State ex rel. Osowski v. Purkett, 908 S.W.2d 520 (Mo. banc 1995)..................5

State ex rel. Simmons v. White, 866 S.W.2d 443 (Mo. banc 1993).............3, 4, 5

State v. Reuscher, 887 S.W.2d 588 (Mo. banc 1994)..................................8

State v. Severe, 307 S.W.3d 640 (Mo. banc 2010)......................................9

State v. Shafer, 609 S.W.2d 153 (Mo. banc 1980)..................................9, 10

Turner v. State, 245 S.W.3d 826 (Mo. banc 2008)............................*passim*

STATUTES AND COURT RULES

Mo. Rule 24.035(d)...*passim*

Mo. Sup. Ct. R. Form 40..3

POINTS AND AUTHORITIES

POINT I

MR. THORNTON IS ENTITLED TO HABEAS CORPUS RELIEF PURSUANT TO RULE 91 BECAUSE THE TRIAL COURT LACKED THE JURISDICTION TO IMPOSE A PUNISHMENT IN EXCESS OF THE STATUTORY MAXIMUM SENTENCE, AND *TURNER V. STATE*, 245 S.W.3D 826 (MO. BANC 2008), IS RETROACTIVE.

Turner v. State, 245 S.W.3d 826 (Mo. banc 2008)

State v. Severe, 307 S.W.3d 640 (Mo. banc 2010)

State ex rel. Koster v. Jackson, 301 S.W.3d 586 (Mo. App. W.D. 2010)

ARGUMENT

I. **MR. THORNTON IS ENTITLED TO HABEAS CORPUS RELIEF PURSUANT TO RULE 91 BECAUSE THE TRIAL COURT LACKED THE JURISDICTION TO IMPOSE A PUNISHMENT IN EXCESS OF THE STATUTORY MAXIMUM SENTENCE, AND *TURNER V. STATE*, 245 S.W.3D 826 (MO. BANC 2008), IS RETROACTIVE.**

Mr. Thornton's opening brief explains that he is entitled to challenge his unlawful sentence in a petition for writ of habeas corpus pursuant to Rule 91 because the trial court lacked jurisdiction to impose a four-year sentence or to revoke his probation after the expiration of the maximum term of probation authorized under the statute. Respondent's brief offers little analysis on the jurisdictional issue,[1] and instead places primary reliance on Rule 24.035, but without citing the waiver clause, which provides:

---

[1] Respondent does not discuss the fact that the expiration of the maximum time in which Mr. Thornton's probation could be lawfully revoked prior to his new offense provides ample grounds for habeas corpus jurisdiction. See Petitioner's Statement, Brief and Argument, pp. 20-23.

2

Example—Petitioner's Reply Brief (cont.)

(d) Contents of Motion. The motion to vacate shall include every claim *known to the movant* for vacating, setting aside, or correcting the judgment or sentence. The movant shall declare in the motion that the movant has listed all claims for relief *known to the movant* and acknowledging the movant's understanding that the movant *waives any claim for relief known to the movant* that is not listed in the motion.

Rule 24.035(d) (emphasis added).[2] *See also State ex rel. Simmons v. White,* 866 S.W.2d 443, 446 (Mo. banc 1993), where the court stated that to proceed under Rule 91, "at a minimum, [Simmons] would have to establish that the grounds relied on were not 'known to him' while proceedings under Rule 24.035 were available."

---

[2] The scope of the waiver articulated in the rule is included in the mandatory acknowledgment that a movant must make in support of a Rule 24.035 motion:

> I have listed every claim *known to me* for vacating, setting aside or correcting the conviction and sentence attacked in this motion; and that I understand that I waive any claim for relief *known to me* that I have not listed in this motion.

Mo. Sup. Ct. R. Form 40 (emphasis added).

Example—Petitioner's Reply Brief (cont.)

Respondent's comparison of Mr. Thornton's case to *Simmons* misapprehends the circumstances in *Simmons*. Unlike Mr. Thornton, Mr. Simmons was in fact eligible for sentencing as a persistent offender. Although he initially pled guilty pursuant to an information that failed to properly allege his prior convictions, he was allowed to withdraw his plea, after which the prosecution was granted leave to amend the petition to properly charge him as a persistent offender. After consulting with counsel about his legal options, including appeal and Rule 24.035, Mr. Simmons again chose to plead guilty to the charge and was sentenced as a persistent offender. *See* 866 S.W.2d at 444-445, 446. Unquestionably, Mr. Simmons was eligible for sentencing as a prior offender under the evidence and the charging documents to which he pled guilty. In Mr. Thornton's case, the prosecution could *never* prove up a case that would establish

4

Example—Petitioner's Reply Brief (cont.)

his eligibility for a Class D felony sentence because the requisite prior convictions do not exist, never did, and never will.[3]

In Mr. Thornton's case, there are no additional convictions that could be alleged or proven to establish persistent offender status; at the time of his plea he could not have been eligible for sentencing as a persistent drunk driving offender under any set of circumstances. Unlike Mr. Thornton, Mr. Simmons *was* a persistent drunk driving offender. Unlike Mr. Thornton, Mr. Simmons was represented by counsel, and on advice of counsel he explicitly waived further challenges to his persistent offender status. The court in *Simmons* found that "[b]y deliberately bypassing appellate and post-conviction remedies in an attempt to gain a more favorable consideration of his request for probation, Simmons waived his rights to those remedies." *Id.,* at 447.

---

[3] For this same reason, *State ex rel. Osowski v. Purkett,* 908 S.W.2d 520, 522 (Mo. banc 1995), and *Clay v. Dormire,* 37 S.W.3d 214, 218 (Mo. banc 2000) do not apply to Mr. Thornton's circumstances. See Respondent's Brief, p. 14. While *Osowski, Clay* and *Simmons* can fairly be characterized as "evidentiary" issues, Respondent's Brief, p. 15, only a substantive expansion of the trial court's sentencing power would achieve the result that Respondent seeks in Mr. Thornton's case.

Example—Petitioner's Reply Brief (cont.)

It is impossible on this record to find that Mr. Thornton deliberately by-passed potential remedies under Rule 24.035. After his guilty plea on December 4, 2007, his public defender closed her file on Mr. Thornton's case. On the trial court's own motion, he was placed on probation on February 8, 2008, so that when the Supreme Court handed down *Turner* on March 6, 2008, Mr. Thornton was neither in custody nor represented by counsel. While this Court's briefing order did not ask the parties to discuss whether Mr. Thornton can meet the cause-and-prejudice standard to excuse his failure to file a Rule 24.035 motion, Respondent asserts that Mr. Thornton cannot proceed under Rule 91 "without showing cause and prejudice to excuse his default." Respondent's Brief, p. 12. The fact that Mr. Thornton was unrepresented by counsel enables him to make that showing; the Supreme Court recently held that in a proceeding that is the first available forum for asserting a claim, "'defendants pursuing first-tier review . . . are generally ill equipped to represent themselves' because they do not have a brief from counsel or an opinion of the court addressing their claim of error." *Martinez v. Ryan*, 113 S. Ct. 1309, 1317 (2012), quoting *Halbert v. Michigan*, 545 U. S. 605, 617 (2005). Because of the crucial role that counsel plays in the protection of individual rights, a prisoner satisfies the cause-and-prejudice gateway to the merits of his defaulted claims by showing that he was without competent legal representation when the default occurred:

6

COURT'S ORDER TO SHOW CAUSE WHY WRIT SHOULD NOT BE GRANTED

Example—Petitioner's Reply Brief (cont.)

Allowing a federal habeas court to hear a claim of ineffective assistance of trial counsel when an attorney's errors (or the absence of an attorney) caused a procedural default in an initial-review collateral proceeding acknowledges, as an equitable matter, that the initial-review collateral proceeding, if undertaken without counsel or with ineffective counsel, may not have been sufficient to ensure that proper consideration was given to a substantial claim. From this it follows that, when a State requires a prisoner to raise an ineffective-assistance-of-trial-counsel claim in a collateral proceeding, a prisoner may establish cause for a default of an ineffective-assistance claim in two circumstances. The first is where the state courts did not appoint counsel in the initial-review collateral proceeding for a claim of ineffective assistance at trial. The second is where appointed counsel in the initial-review collateral proceeding, where the claim should have been raised, was ineffective under the standards of *Strickland v. Washington,* 466 U. S. 668 (1984).

Martinez v. Ryan, supra, at 1318.[4] Thus, Respondent's heavy reliance on the absence of 24.035 litigation is misplaced. Again, this is yet another way in which Mr. Thornton's case is *not* like *Simmons*.

---

[4] Missouri courts have not yet explicitly applied *Martinez v. Ryan* in Rule 91, but the case for doing so is strong. In considering whether to adopt federal rules of procedural bar and equitable exceptions, the Missouri Supreme Court observed, "it is at least arguable that this Court should not defer habeas corpus jurisdiction to the federal courts." *State v. Reuscher,* 887 S.W.2d 588, 591 (Mo. banc 1994). Thereafter, the Missouri Supreme Court explicitly incorporated into Rule 91 procedural jurisprudence the federal equitable gateways of "cause and prejudice" and "miscarriage of justice" standards. *State ex rel. Nixon v. Jaynes,* 63 S.W.3d 210, 214 (Mo. banc 2001). Thus, applying *Martinez* would be consistent with Missouri's policy not to abdicate jurisdiction to federal courts. Further, *Martinez* is not limited to claims of ineffective assistance of trial counsel. "There is not a dime's worth of difference in principle between [ineffective assistance of counsel] cases and many other cases in which initial state habeas will be the first opportunity for a particular claim to be raised." *Martinez v. Ryan, supra,* at 1321 (Scalia, J., dissenting).

8

COURT'S ORDER TO SHOW CAUSE WHY WRIT SHOULD NOT BE GRANTED

Example—Petitioner's Reply Brief (cont.)

Curiously, Respondent alleges that "[t]here should be no dispute that the court's sentence in case 07K4-00429 was valid at least until March 4, 2008, the date the Missouri Supreme Court filed the *Turner* decision." Respondent's Brief, p. 14. To the contrary, that *is* the dispute on which this Court ordered briefing, and there is no room for mistake that Mr. Thornton disputes the power of the court to impose a felony sentence in the absence of the jurisdictional statutory factual premise for doing so. The Missouri Supreme Court would dispute Respondent's premise as well, which is clear from its observation that "*Turner* created no new law." *State v. Severe*, 307 S.W.3d 640, 644 (Mo. banc 2010). Thus, the law at the time of Mr. Thornton's charge, conviction and sentence made him ineligible for a conviction and sentence for a Class D felony in this case. Respondent's flawed premise and circular reasoning do not support his assertion that the trial court had jurisdiction to sentence Mr. Thornton to terms of imprisonment and probation in excess of the statutory maximum. *Id.* Respondent's position is further untenable in light of the fact that the Supreme Court and this Court have already applied *Turner* retroactively. *See, State v. Severe, supra; State ex rel. Koster v. Jackson*, 301 S.W.3d 586 (Mo. App. W.D. 2010). Respondent's argument should be rejected.

Finally, Respondent seeks to avoid the application of *Turner* by characterizing it as a rule of evidence. See Respondent's Brief, pp. 16-18, relying on *State v. Shafer*, 609 S.W.2d 153 (Mo. banc 1980). *Shafer* dealt with the

9

Example—Petitioner's Reply Brief (cont.)

application of an evidentiary statute that altered the spousal privilege in a way that permitted his wife's testimony to be used against him on charges of murder. The evidence neither altered the elements nor expanded the range of punishment for the underlying crime. The facts attested by Shafer's wife could conceivably be proven up by another witness or other means. The same is not true in Mr. Thornton's case; by specifying what evidence is admissible to establish persistent offender status under §577.023, the legislature limited the factual premises, i.e., the statutory elements, upon which a defendant could be eligible for an extended term. This fact cannot be avoided by characterizing the issue as a rule of evidence; "labels do not afford an acceptable answer." *Apprendi v. New Jersey,* 530 U.S. 466, 494 (2000). Justice Scalia explained the substantive effect of legislation providing for an enhanced range of punishment predicated upon proof of aggravating facts:

> "[I]f the legislature defines some core crime and then provides for increasing the punishment of that crime upon a finding of some aggravating fact -- of whatever sort, including the fact of a prior conviction -- the core crime and the aggravating fact together constitute an aggravated crime, just as much as grand larceny is an aggravated form of petit larceny. The aggravating fact is an element of the aggravated crime. Similarly, if the legislature, rather than creating

> grades of crimes, has provided for setting the punishment of a crime based on some fact -- such as a fine that is proportional to the value of stolen goods -- that fact is also an element. No multi-factor parsing of statutes, of the sort that we have attempted since *McMillan*, is necessary. One need only look to the kind, degree, or range of punishment to which the prosecution is by law entitled for a given set of facts. Each fact necessary for that entitlement is an element.

Apprendi v. New Jersey, supra, at 501 (Scalia, J., concurring). Thus, "when a statute increases punishment for some core crime based on the fact of a prior conviction, the core crime and the fact of the prior crime together create a new, aggravated crime." *Id.,* at 507-08. The substantive/procedural dichotomy proposed by Respondent does not exist in Mr. Thornton's situation. Under *Turner,* Mr. Thornton is not guilty of the Class D felony of driving under the influence of alcohol, and the State could never muster sufficient evidence to prove otherwise.

Example—Petitioner's Reply Brief (cont.)

CONCLUSION

For the foregoing reasons, this Court should issue the writ of habeas corpus discharging Mr. Thornton from his unlawful conviction and sentence in this matter.

Respectfully submitted,

/s/ Sean D. O'Brien
Sean D. O'Brien, MoBar # 30116
4920 N. Askew
Kansas City, MO 64119
Telephone (816) 235-6152
Facsimile (816) 235-5276
E-mail: obriensd@umkc.edu

Example—Petitioner's Reply Brief (cont.)

CERTIFICATE OF SERVICE

I hereby certify that the foregoing Reply Brief was served upon the parties by e-mail through this Court's eFiling system this 15th day of September, 2014, at the following addresses:

Andrew Bailey
Assistant Attorney General
andrew.bailey@ago.mo.gov

Stephen D. Hawke
Assistant Attorney General
stephen.hawke@ago.mo.gov

P.O. Box 899
Jefferson City, MO 65102

/s/ Sean D. O'Brien
Sean D. O'Brien

Example—Petitioner's Reply Brief (cont.)

CERTIFICATE OF COMPLIANCE

I hereby certify:

1. That the attached brief complies with the limitations contained in Missouri Supreme Court Rule 84.06 and contains 1991 words, excluding the cover and certification, as determined by Microsoft Word 2010 software; and

2. That the CD Rom filed with this brief, containing a copy of this brief, has been scanned for viruses and is virus-free; and

3. That two true and correct copies of the attached brief, and a CD containing a copy of this brief, were mailed this 15th day of September, 2014, to:

Andrew Bailey
Assistant Attorney General
andrew.bailey@ago.mo.gov

Stephen D. Hawke
Assistant Attorney General
stephen.hawke@ago.mo.gov

P.O. Box 899
Jefferson City, MO 65102

/s/ Sean D. O'Brien
Sean D. O'Brien

Example—Reply in Opposition to Respondent's Motion for Rehearing or Transfer

IN THE
MISSOURI COURT OF APEALS
WESTERN DISTRICT

IN RE: FREDERICK W. THORNTON, III,)
)
Petitioner,)
)
vs.) Case No. WD77276
)
LARRY DENNEY, Superintendent)
Crossroads Correctional Center,)
)
Respondent.)

**REPLY IN OPPOSITION TO RESPONDENT'S
MOTION FOR REHEARING OR TRANSFER**

Respondent's Motion for Rehearing or Transfer rests on the demonstrably false premise that "Central to this Court's analysis was its decision that Thornton's claim was a sentencing defect and therefore could not be procedurally defaulted." Motion for Rehearing or Transfer, p. 4. That is a gross mischaracterization of this Court's decision. To the contrary, this Court carefully examined and meticulously applied Missouri case law and statute in reaching its ultimate conclusion that "the circuit court was without jurisdiction to revoke Thornton's probation with respect to his 2007 conviction in November 2011, or execute any sentence previously imposed upon him." *State ex rel. Thornton v. Denney*, WD 77276, Slip op. p. 10 (Mar. 17, 2015).

Respondent argues that to warrant habeas corpus relief, "sentencing defects must be patent on the face of the record," Motion for Rehearing or Transfer, p. 4,

Example—Reply in Opposition to Respondent's Motion for Rehearing or Transfer (cont.)

but never suggests how the error in Mr. Thornton's case is not. The factual basis for Mr. Thornton's claim is established solely by certified documents of the DeKalb County Circuit Court; no extrinsic evidence or testimony was or could be offered to contradict the fact that he was not subject to a Class D felony sentence in *State v. Thornton,* DeKalb County Case No. 07K4-00429. Further, this Court had no need to engage in statutory interpretation, as Respondent alleged based on *dicta* from *Thomas v. Dormire,* 923 S.W.2d 533 (Mo. App. W.D. 1996), because that work had already been done by the Missouri Supreme Court's binding opinion in *Turner v. State*, 245 S.W.3d 826 (Mo. banc 2008). Respondent has not disputed any of the record-based facts supporting Mr. Thornton's claim. If it is indeed a requirement that Mr. Thornton's habeas claim be patent on the face of the record, it is amply met here.

Respondent further alleges that this Court's opinion is "contrary to *Thomas v. Dormire,* 923 S.W.2d 533 (Mo. App. W.D. 1996), *State v. Horn*, 384 S.W.3d 338 (Mo. App. E.D. 2012), and *State v. Logan*, 941 S.W.2d 728, 732 (Mo. App. E.D. 1997)." One would think that if these case were so helpful and pertinent that Respondent would have cited them in his brief. He did not, and for good reason. They have no bearing on the issue before this Court.[1]

---

[1] Respondent also suggests without explanation that this Court's decision is contrary to *In re Brooks v. Bowersox*, 2014 WL 5241645 (S.D. *en banc*), Motion for Rehearing or Transfer, p. 2. That case involves the retroactivity of *Miller v.*

Example—Reply in Opposition to Respondent's Motion for Rehearing or Transfer (cont.)

This Court in *Thomas* ordered habeas corpus relief to correct a sentence of 99 years for robbery because it exceeded the statutory maximum sentence, 923 S.W.2d at 934, which is perfectly consistent with the rationale supporting this Court's decision to grant habeas corpus relief to Mr. Thornton. Thomas was also sentenced to 99 years for forcible sodomy, and this Court rejected his argument that 99 years exceeded the statutory range of punishment for rape. This was simply an acknowledgment that Thomas failed to show conclusively, as Mr. Thornton was able to do, that his sentence exceeded that authorized by statute. The statute in question, section 565.030.2 authorized a life term or "a term of years not less than five years." Thomas relied on the opinion of the Eastern District Court of Appeals in *State v. Williams*, 828 S.W.2d 894 (Mo. App. 1992), which held that a sentence of 100 years for forcible sodomy exceeded the statutory maximum sentence. This Court in *Thomas* was correctly skeptical of the reasoning behind *Williams,* which was explicitly overruled by the Missouri Supreme Court, which explained, "The plain and ordinary meaning of this language in section 566.030.2 provides sentencing courts with two options: life imprisonment or an *unlimited* term of

---

Alabama, 132 S. Ct. 2455 (2012), finding that imposing a mandatory sentence of life without parole upon a juvenile offender violates the Eighth Amendment. *Brooks* concluded that *Miller* is not retroactive, and the Missouri Supreme Court has subsequently granted transfer. This Court correctly noted that "no issue of "retroactivity" is presented where a later judicial decision interprets the meaning of a pre-existing statute." *State ex rel. Thornton v. Denney*, WD 77276, Slip op. p. 10 (Mar. 17, 2015).

Example—Reply in Opposition to Respondent's Motion for Rehearing or Transfer (cont.)

years not less than five years." *State v. Hardin*, 429 S.W.3d 417, 420 (Mo. 2014) (emphasis added). In light of the plain language of section 566.030.2, the court found *Williams* "unpersuasive," and cautioned that it "should no longer be followed." *Id.*, at 420. Respondent's attempt to manufacture a conflict between the decision in Mr. Thornton's case and *Thomas* is quite a stretch; the two decisions are completely harmonious in all respects.

Respondent's second argument, that the defect in Mr. Thornton's case goes to his conviction rather than his sentence, is even more specious. There is no such dichotomy in the law of habeas corpus jurisdiction. *See, e.g., State ex rel. Verweire v. Moore*, 211 S.W.3d 89, 90 (Mo. 2006), finding that the petitioner was entitled to habeas corpus relief from his guilty plea and conviction, notwithstanding Verweire's failure to appeal or file a Rule 24.035 motion, because the record failed to establish a factual basis for his guilt of the charge to which he pled guilty. The cases relied upon in support of Respondent's attempt to characterize the unauthorized enhancement in Mr. Thornton's case as affecting his conviction rather than his sentence are simply not relevant. By specifying what evidence is admissible to establish persistent offender status under §577.023, the legislature limited the factual premises upon which a defendant could be eligible for an extended term. Therefore, it is apparent on the face of the record, which includes a charging document that relied on an unauthorized municipal court suspended imposition of sentence, that Mr. Thornton could not have been eligible for a Class D felony sentence.

This defect cannot be avoided by characterizing the error as something else; "labels do not afford an acceptable answer." *Apprendi v. New Jersey*, 530 U.S. 466, 494 (2000). As this Court aptly observed, "Whatever label is applied, . . . it is settled that the imposition of a sentence beyond that permitted by the applicable statute or rule may be raised by way of a writ of habeas corpus." Slip. Op., p. 5, citing *State ex rel. Zinna v. Steele*, 301 S.W.3d 510, 517 (Mo. banc 2010).

CONCLUSION

This Court's decision faithfully applies firmly established principles of Missouri law, including *Turner v. State*, 245 S.W.3d 826 (Mo. banc 2008), *State ex rel. Zinna v. Steele*, 301 S.W.3d 510, 513 (Mo. banc 2010), and *State ex rel. Koster v. Jackson*, 301 S.W.3d 586, 590 (Mo. App. W.D. 2010), to grant habeas corpus relief from Mr. Thornton's sentence which exceeds the punishment authorized by the law in effect at the time of his offense.

Example—Reply in Opposition to Respondent's Motion for Rehearing or Transfer (cont.)

WHEREFORE, for the foregoing reasons, counsel for Petitioner respectfully suggests that this Court deny Respondent's Motion for Rehearing or Transfer.

Respectfully submitted,

/s/ Sean D. O'Brien
Sean D. O'Brien, MoBar # 30116
4920 N. Askew
Kansas City, MO 64119
Telephone (816) 235-6152
Facsimile (816) 235-5276
E-mail: obriensd@umkc.edu

CERTIFICATE OF SERVICE

I hereby certify that the foregoing document was served upon the parties by e-mail through this Court's eFiling system this 2nd day of April, 2015, at the following addresses:

Gregory M. Goodwin
Assistant Attorney General
andrew.bailey@ago.mo.gov

P.O. Box 899
Jefferson City, MO 65102

/s/ Sean D. O'Brien
Sean D. O'Brien

COURT'S ORDER TO SHOW CAUSE WHY WRIT SHOULD NOT BE GRANTED

<7> DISCOVERY

Scope of Discovery

This chapter discusses the various methods that may be used to discover evidence—written interrogatories, oral or written depositions, production of documents or things, inspection of things and places, and requests for admissions.

Discovery rules are usually governed by each state's rules of civil procedure. Most states' discovery rules generally mirror the federal discovery rules, which allow a party (you or the respondent) to obtain discovery concerning any matter, not privileged, that is relevant to the subject matter involved in the habeas corpus proceeding, whether it relates to the claim(s) or defense(s) of the party seeking discovery or to the claim(s) or defense(s) of any other party, including the existence, description, nature, custody, condition and location of any books, documents or other tangible things, and the identity and locations of persons having knowledge of any discoverable matter.

Prior to conducting discovery, you should carefully research your state's civil rules of procedure for conducting discovery.

A party may not object, arguing that the information asked for will be inadmissible at the hearing, if the information appears reasonably calculated to lead to the discovery of admissible evidence. Upon an objection by the other party, the party requesting discovery will bear the burden of establishing the information's relevance.

Written Interrogatories

Written interrogatories (written questions that a party must answer or object to under oath) may be served upon the respondent, requesting the identity of any expert witness expected to be called at hearing, his or her name, address, occupation, place of employment and qualifications to give an opinion, the general nature of subjects on which the expert is expected to testify, and the expert's hourly deposition fee. Your written interrogatory may also request the location of documents and exhibits relevant to your claim(s), as well as what facts, exhibits, witnesses, and other evidence the respondent plans to use at the hearing. The respondent may also serve interrogatories upon you.

The number of interrogatories (questions) you or the respondent may serve is usually limited to twenty to twenty-five. Check your state's rules of civil procedure for conducting discovery, to determine the correct number.

Each interrogatory must be answered or objected to separately without thirty days after service, unless additional time is given. If you or the respondent objects to an interrogatory, the reason for the objection must answer everything else that isn't objectable. If an answer to an interrogatory isn't readily known, you or the respondent must make a reasonable attempt to find the information, by asking questions of others and reviewing reports, documents or other records. You and the respondent also have an obligation, under discovery rules, to supplement your answers to any previous interrogatory response if it is discovered that your response was incomplete or inaccurate.

An example set of interrogatories would look something like this:

[caption]

PETITIONER'S FIRST INTERROGATORIES

COMES NOW Petitioner, [name], pursuant to Rule [your state's rule] of the Rules of Civil Procedure, and requests that Respondent answer the following interrogatories:

1. Please identify names, addresses and telephone numbers of each individual likely to have discoverable information relevant to disputed facts alleged with particularity in Petitioner's petition.

2. Please describe by category and location all documents, data, compilations and tangible things in the possession, custody or control of Respondent that are relevant to disputed facts alleged with particularity in Petitioner's petition.

3. Please identify each and every person who has made to you sworn or unsworn statements or provided information for affidavits or statements that relate to the allegations made in Petitioner's petition.

4. Please identify each expert witness you conferred with concerning any aspect of the allegations made in Petitioner's petition, but not limited to, any opinions, written or oral, and any erroneous conclusions expert may have made in any other cases.

[signature]

[certificate of service]

Depositions—Oral and Written

You or the respondent may take the testimony of any person by deposition via orally or written questions. The attendance of witnesses may be compelled with a subpoena. However, if the person is incarcerated, leave of court must be obtained first.

Taking a deposition orally can be expensive if you use a stenographer to record the deposition. Of course, you may use a recording device if the respondent's attorney (usually the attorney general's office) agrees. In such instances, you may want to file a motion with the court, asking for suggestions as to how you can depose witnesses and audio- or video-record their testimony.

It may be more practical, for financial reasons, to take depositions via written questions. In such instances, you must send your questions to respondent, who then will prepare cross questions for the deponent. Upon receipt of these cross questions, you may prepare redirect questions then forward them to the respondent. Once the questions are prepared, they are submitted to the person being deposed. A stenographer will record the questions and the deponent's answers. Written depositions can be served upon a non-party, unlike interrogatories, which may only be served upon the respondent.

If you have thoroughly prepared for your hearing and know the essential facts of your case, the legal elements of your claim(s), and the evidence to present to meet your burden of proof, you may opt out of taking depositions. (How to prepare for a hearing will be discussed in the next chapter.)

Each state's civil rules of procedure provide specific information on taking oral or written depositions. Make sure to research these procedures before attempting to depose a potential witness.

If you are unsure of how to present the testimony of a witness, offer exhibits, or cross-examine a witness, read how these things were done in your trial transcripts and mimic that until you develop a style you are comfortable with. (See also the next chapter.)

Production of Documents and Things

You may make requests for the production of documents and things—police reports, lab reports, statements/interviews of witnesses, phone records, e-mails, investigative notes, crime scene diagrams, crime scene photographs, photographs of certain pieces of evidence/exhibits, autopsy photos & slides, identification photospreads, wound charts, criminal records of state witnesses, etc.

The respondent usually has thirty days to respond to a Request for the Production of Documents and Things.

An example Request for the Production of Documents and Things would look something like the following:

[caption]

*PETITIONER'S REQUEST FOR PRODUCTION
OF DOCUMENTS AND THINGS*

COMES NOW Petitioner, [name], pursuant to Rule [your state's rule] of the Rules of Civil Procedure, and requests Respondent to produce the following documents and/or things:

1. Any and all lab reports/expert opinions in [your case], Case No. [number], including but not limited to, any and all police reports, statements/interviews of witnesses, etc.

2. Any and all crime scene photographs, including but not limited to, autopsy photographs, crime scene diagrams, photographs of exhibits, etc.

[signature]

[certificate of service]

Inspection of Things and Places

If there is a dispute over a piece of evidence, you may want to inspect it to prove or disprove a certain aspect of the case, or have it examined by an expert. To do so, make a request to inspect the thing, stating what you want to inspect and when. If you are wanting to have an expert look at it, you would provide his/her name, qualifications, and address.

If you want access to a certain place or property to take measurements or photographs, do crime reconstruction, or take samples of dirt, as Conan Doyle did, you may have to request a court order, especially if the owner of the property objects. Most of this investigative fieldwork, however, is done by an attorney or a private investigator.

Requests for Admissions

You may serve requests for admissions, requiring the respondent to admit or deny statements or opinions of fact, or the application of law to fact, including the genuineness of any documents described in the request.

Any matter admitted by the respondent is conclusively established unless the court on motion permits withdrawal or amendment of the admission.

Requests for Admissions might resemble the following example:

[caption]

REQUESTS FOR ADMISSIONS

COMES NOW Petitioner, [name], and makes the following requests for admissions, pursuant to Rule [your state's rule] of Rules of Civil Procedure.

"A FAILURE TO TIMELY RESPOND TO REQUESTS FOR ADMISSIONS IN COMPLIANCE WITH RULE [number] SHALL RESULT IN EACH MATTER BEING ADMITTED BY YOU AND NOT SUBJECT TO FURTHER DISPUTE."

1. Admit or deny that Petitioner's Exhibit A is a genuine copy of "Affidavit of [name]."

2. Admit or deny that if a plea bargain has been offered, a defendant has the right to effective assistance of counsel in considering whether to accept it, and if that right is denied, prejudice is shown if loss of the plea opportunity led to trial resulting in a conviction on more serious charges and the imposition of a more severe sentence.

3. Admit or deny that the proper remedy for an attorney's error in failing to advise of plea is to re-offer the plea bargain and conduct further proceedings in the trial court.

4. Admit or deny that [attorney name] failed to advise [petitioner name] of a seventeen-year plea offer by the state.

[signature]

[certificate of service]

The respondent usually has thirty days to respond to requests for admissions. If the respondent does not respond in a timely manner, the admission is deemed admitted. You should check your state's rules of civil procedure for conducting discovery before requesting admissions.

Objections and Motions to Compel Discovery

Courts do not like to get involved in discovery disputes, expecting the parties to work them out without intervention. If this cannot be done, however, either you or the respondent may file a motion to compel. First, it must be shown that the parties made a good-faith effort to resolve the dispute. This is usually done by attaching an affidavit and copies of letters written to another party, asking for a response to requests for admissions, requests for production of documents, etc.

It is advisable to also use other methods to discover evidence to support your claim(s) without relying solely on the methods discussed in this chapter.

DISCOVERY

<8> EVIDENTIARY HEARING

Evidentiary Hearing

Although most habeas cases are summarily dismissed without an evidentiary hearing, the purpose of a hearing is for the petitioner to present evidence showing that his or her confinement is illegal.

As mentioned in Chapter 6, your petition, along with supporting exhibits, must show that you are entitled to relief. It is your burden to prove your claim(s) by a preponderance of evidence—that is, evidence that is more convincing than the evidence offered by the respondent.

Unless you hire an attorney or are appointed one by the court, you will be conducting the hearing yourself. Some courts appoint attorneys for pro se petitioners, some court do not. If you must present your own case at the hearing, this chapter will guide you along.

Writ of Habeas Corpus ad Testicandum

To secure your appearance at the hearing, once a date is set, you will need to prepare a writ of habeas corpus ad testicandum. The court may prefer to prepare its own, but you should submit a proposed writ as a matter of proper procedure. Doing so shows your understanding of the rules of civil procedure, leaving the court with the impression that you are ready and able to present your case. (See the example writ at the end of this chapter.)

Courtroom Appearance

As stated in *Smith's Guide to Executive Clemency*, we are judged on the basic and most fundamental things, one of these being our appearance. We automatically make a value assessment upon first seeing someone. For the purposes of representing yourself at the hearing, it is important that you make a good first impression.

Although being a prisoner will limit you somewhat, it is no excuse for not making use of what is available to look your best. There are a few small things you can do to make a big difference in how you appear to others. For example, if you are well-groomed, smile, and carry yourself with confidence, you will make good impressions. You may feel insecure about how you look, and think that there is nothing you can do to change, but this is not true.

If you are willing to make a few changes, you can make significant improvements to your appearance. One of the easiest and most fundamental things to affect a change is your hairstyle. For the purpose of your hearing debut, you want to look like an everyday average citizen, up to date but not flashy or flamboyant. The best example of this look is a hairstyle worn by one of the anchors from your local news channel, whose styles fit the time period and are inoffensive to residents of your region. If you have facial hair, consider shaving it off, as psychological studies have shown that many people feel it connotes untrustworthiness.

Whatever choices you make about your appearance, take extra care with your grooming to look your best for the hearing. Displaying a friendly smile when you walk into the courtroom will be disarming and convey openness, friendliness, and confidence.

Remember, you will be expected to be nervous. You will convey the opposite by having an I-just-bench-pressed-the-universe smile on your face, leaving the respondent to wonder what trick you have up your sleeve to feel so confident.

Presenting Yourself and Reading Others

We communicate every day with our words, with the tone of our voice, and with our body language. But before we even open our mouths, people form an impression of us based on our body language: postures, hand gestures, and facial expressions.

Posture

Poor posture is one sign people interpret as being indicative of low confidence. This can be corrected with a basic posture exercise known as the wall stance.

To do this exercise, find a wall and stand with your back against it. Your heels, buttocks, and shoulders need to be touching the wall. Slide your hand behind your back to verify that there isn't a lot of room between the small of your back and the wall. Place your hand back at your side and stay in this position for at least one minute.

Next, walk around while maintaining that posture. It will feel strange until you get used to it. Do this exercise daily, until the body posture becomes habitual, consciously checking yourself from time to time to make sure that your body is in alignment and that you are not slouching.

Erect posture will speak volumes about your level of confidence in your case at the hearing, before you even say one word out loud.

Tells

There is a simple way to read the body language of the judge, respondent, and witnesses, and to be aware of your own: the limbic system, a complex network in the brain, which controls our basic emotional responses. When we feel threatened—whether physically or psychologically—the limbic system alerts the nervous system to alleviate the threat. The body responds in one of three ways: freeze, flee, or fight. If you watch an animal respond to a potential threat, the first thing it will do is hold still, listening intently. Once the threat is fully realized, the animal either flees or turns to fight. These three responses can be perceived in human behavior, through nonverbal cues, also called *tells*.

For the purposes of this book, the flight-or-fight responses will be of the most interest. These responses are most apparent in avoidance, distancing, and pacifying behaviors.

When people feel anxious or psychologically threatened, the limbic system automatically triggers a need to pacify the discomfort or alleviate the threat. And since the face and neck are physical locations with many, many nerve endings, people are apt to touch or rub these areas in subconscious response to the limbic system's signal.

If you are paying attention, in real time, you will see these tells immediately proceeding something you say that makes a person uncomfortable. Through nonverbal cues, people will unconsciously indicate discomfort or disinterest with avoidance or distancing behavior, such as avoiding eye contact, turning or leaning away, crossing their arms, blocking or touching their eyes, and other tactics. Through verbal cues, people show discomfort by using pauses and being hesitant to answer questions, avoiding absolutes, and giving short noncommittal responses. Often times, people become argumentative, placing blame on the person questioning them or someone else.

As their discomfort increases, you will see a flurry of these tells, which will let you know you hit a nerve and should continue on that line of questioning, because it could help you reveal the truth or discredit the witness.

This intelligence is known to judges and attorneys. Now you know it too. Through practice, honing your observation skills to read tells, you will intuitively learn how to lead a witness, and how to present your argument to get the outcome you want.

Vocalization

Our voices are our identities. They tell people (literally and figuratively) who we are, how we feel about ourselves, and what we believe. Five of the most common problems people have when speaking with others are: talking in a low or soft voice, talking too fast, talking in a monotonous voice, using pausers, and talking in a manner that makes statements sound like questions. The following will help you identify which of these problems, if any, you have when talking with others, and suggest simple corrective exercises.

Low or Soft Voice
If you are soft-spoken, the problem you may have is that the volume of your voice sounds louder in your head than it actually is.

A thought exercise may correct this problem. Close your eyes and picture a large volume knob. Visualize turning the volume up a little over halfway. Now practice talking at this volume whenever you engage someone in conversation. If it's someone you talk to daily and they notice the change, you will know you have corrected the problem.

Talking too Fast
If you talk fast, you are probably hard to understand and give others the impression that you are nervous, lack confidence, and believe you must get everything out before people stop listening and ignore what you have to say.

To address this problem (and to make better impressions in the process), consciously slow down and speak in a calm, slow voice. To yourself, practice saying in an even-paced, commanding voice, "I am comfortable, confident, and command the attention of others when I speak."

Do this exercise daily until you get the desired results.

Monotone
If you speak in an unvarying tone, turn on your TV or radio and find someone who has a magnetic voice you like. Pay close attention to it—its volume, pitch, speed, rhythm, and inflections put on certain words.

Next, find a story or piece of writing, and practice reading it out loud while modeling the voice of that person whose voice you like. Practice this until you begin to develop a magnetic and compelling voice of your own, a voice that pulls people in and commands their attention.

Pausers
Is your speech littered with "um"s, "like"s, "you know"s, or other meaningless conversational filler? People use these pausers in an unconscious attempt to hold the attention of others while trying to think of what to say next, or to try to elicit understanding or agreement. Either purpose conveys insecurity.

To correct this problem, you will need to develop comfort with the momentary pauses that arise during conversation. Being consciously aware of the message of insecurity you are sending to others should be enough of a motivator for you to cut most pausers from your speech.

Statements That Sound Like Questions
Do you raise your voice at the end of declarative statements? If so, your statements sounds more like questions, a habit that makes you sound unsure of yourself and what you declare to be factual.

This problem can be corrected, in many cases, by taking a declarative statement and practice saying it with confidence, as if you believe every word without question. Through repetition and awareness of your speech patterns, this habit can be eliminated.

As you focus on your posture, body language, and voice, you will notice a day-to-day difference in the impressions you make on others, by seeing how they respond to you. And once you hone your observation skills to read others, you will level the playing field at the hearing, giving yourself a psychological boost and strategic leg-up.

Conducting Hearing and Introducing Evidence

Prior to representing yourself at the hearing, you must study the rules of civil procedure and any local rules for the court where the hearing will be held. These rules and procedures may vary from court to court, from state to state. The judge most likely will address the issue of how he or she wants the hearing to proceed, which will assure all parties that it will proceed in a timely and efficient manner.

Securing Attendance of Witnesses

To secure the attendance of witnesses at hearing, you will need to serve subpoenas. You can obtain subpoena forms from the court clerk. You may also need to file a motion with the court, listing all the witnesses you'll need served, and ask the court to appoint a process server to serve your subpoenas.

Do not rely on a witness's assurance that he or she will appear without being served with a subpoena. Better to be safe and serve a subpoena than to be sorry for not doing so.

Frames, Frame Control, and Reframing

Frames are the contexts in which one perceives people, things, or situations. Frames are ways of looking at the world. Controlling a frame means keeping the subject or point of view moving in a specific direction, during an interaction, to get a desired outcome. The person who controls the frame controls the interaction. This is what prosecutors and good defense attorneys do. The one with the strongest frame wins.

It is possible to change one's own frame, a frame set by someone else, or a frame that has been allowed to develop. This change is referred to as *reframing*, and it involves transforming the meaning of something by putting it into a different context—or frame—than it was originally in.

Understanding how to set a frame, how to control it, and how to reframe or, if necessary, take over another's frame, will be of great importance at your hearing. With such knowledge, you will be able to guide the presentation of evidence and its interpretation with frames that best serve you instead of the respondent.

You will see in a moment how to present the testimony of witnesses, introduce exhibits, make and respond to objections, and use frames, frame control, and reframing to your benefit.

Direct Examination of Witnesses

Prior to your hearing, you should carefully prepare an outline of what you must prove for each of your claims, the names of the witnesses whose testimony you will be relying on, and the exhibits you intend to introduce through each witness's testimony.

A witness can only testify about things he or she has firsthand personal knowledge of. otherwise, the witness's testimony is considered inadmissible hearsay. (This does not include testimony offered by expert witnesses, as long as he or she is qualified to testify as an expert. More on this later.)

Next, you should prepare a list of the questions you are going to ask each witness. (Note: never ask a question you do not know the answer to.) You can only ask non-leading questions during direct examination, usually questions that begin with interrogatory words: who, what, which, when, where, how, and why. To get a feel for how to question a witness, read trial transcripts. Even watching courtroom TV shows or movies, such as *Law and Order*, *The Lincoln Lawyer*, or *A Few Good Men*, can give you an idea of how witnesses can be questioned.

Of course, when you are eliciting background information from witnesses, you may use imperative sentences such as, "Please state your name and occupation." You may also use declarative sentences to control the subject matter being testified about, such as, "Now I want to direct your attention to October 31 of that year, and ask a few questions about the discovery you received from the prosecuting attorneys' office."

A leading question is a question that suggests the desired answer to the question asked. For example, "You did not provide John Pierson's statement in the discovery of *State v. Doe*, did you?" is a leading question. The only time leading questions will be permitted during direct examination is when the person being addressed is an adverse or hostile witness—one who does not want to testify on your behalf. Leading questions are usually only answerable with either a *yes* or a *no*.

Your own testimony may be the most important evidence you have, to prove certain elements of your claim(s). In such an instance, you should be permitted to give your testimony in a narrative, instead of in the usual direct examination format.

It would be prudent to prepare a written version of what you'll need to testify to, then rehearse it using the techniques you learned in Chapter 4. Practice how you will deliver it at your hearing. Use a mirror if you can. You *must* rehearse it out loud, over and over, focusing on your delivery, until it feels natural and is congruent with your body language, tone of voice, and facial expressions.

You will be cross-examined, so you should carefully consider the questions the respondent will likely ask you—what you did, how you did it, and why—before he or she has the chance to ask them at hearing. Anticipating these questions and your answers to them will allow you some control over the frames set, by predetermining what and how content is presented and interpreted.

It is inevitable that certain questions will be asked and, if not answered appropriately, will lead to a judgment in the respondent's favor. But if you can anticipate what these questions might be, you can devise a contingency plan.

Introducing Exhibits

During the testimony of certain witnesses, you will need to introduce exhibits into evidence. This is why requests for admissions are helpful. Then the exhibits are already in evidence and you can bring them up whenever you want to use them without laying a foundation first.

If you opt not to use requests for admissions, you will need to lay a foundation for each exhibit you intend to use. This is accomplished through the following four steps.

1. Prior to the start of the hearing, ask the court clerk to mark your exhibits for identification, assigning each exhibit its own number or letter label.

2. Hand the exhibit to the respondent for looking over.

3. Ask the court for permission to approach the witness, then say something like, "I am handing you Petitioner's Exhibit X. Can you identify it?" At that point, the witness should state what the exhibit is and how he or she is familiar with it. Sometimes additional questions are necessary to refresh the witness's recollection. You may even need to instruct the witness to read an exhibit before a foundation can be laid for the its admission.

4. Once the witness identifies the exhibit, you may offer it into evidence by simply stating that you offer Petitioner's Exhibit X into evidence. If the respondent doesn't object, it will be admitted into evidence. (Objections will be discussed later.)

When an exhibit is admitted into evidence, you may use it to ask the witness about its content and how it relates to certain facts, thereby establishing the factual and legal elements of your claim(s) and proving by a preponderance of evidence that you are entitled to relief.

Cross-Examination of Witnesses

When witnesses give direct testimony in a court proceeding, they may be subjected to cross-examination and questioned about any subject about which they testified to during their direct examination.

The purpose of cross-examination is to provide the parties with an opportunity to test the memory, the veracity, and the bias of any witness who has provided adverse or unfavorable testimony against either party.

It *is* permissible to ask leading questions during cross-examination, allowing you to set and control frames. This is done by asking short, unequivocal questions that cannot be reframed or misinterpreted, something an adverse witness will often attempt to do.

You can frame-control simply by beginning your questions with: "Isn't it true that...," "Isn't it a fact that...," "Isn't it correct that...," "Is it true that...,"etc. You can also use declarative statements and add a leading question at the end to maintain control of the frame—for example, "You never actually witnessed the shooting, only heard the gunshots, is that correct?"

The key to effective cross-examination is to set frames (using factual assertions) and compel witnesses to agree with them on the record. Setting frames and using frame control lets you act as a puppeteer: you hold the strings.

If a witness avoids your question and tries to set an unfavorable frame, you have to handle that. You can't allow the witness to keep talking. Instead, immediately object to the witness's non-responsive answer, then ask the court to strike the answer from the record and instruct the witness to answer only the questions asked.

If you are aggressive and argumentative with a witness, the witness will mirror your tone and demeanor. This will not be helpful. Your goal is to mine the witness for essential facts needed to prove your case or discredit the witness. Being combative or offensive will only give the respondent cause to object, which may lead the judge to limit your cross-examination.

Your strategy should be to approach each witness with a smile, maintaining a friendly frame. You are only after the facts necessary to establish your claim(s). Don't take anything a witness said or did in your case personally. Doing so will only cloud your judgment, limiting your objectivity.

You may impeach a witness with his or her felony conviction(s), with evidence of his or her interest in the outcome of the proceedings (such as a promise by the prosecution to assist with a plea bargain, sentence reduction, etc.), or with a prior inconsistent statement he or she made during direct examination, a written statement to police, deposition, or other legal proceeding. Impeaching a witness involves the following steps:

1. Using frame control, have the witness reaffirm what he or she testified to on direct.

2. Introduce the witness's prior statement and ask if he or she recalls making it. If the witness doesn't recall making it, show him or her the statement and ask the witness to read it.

3. Ask the witness if he or she remembers making the statement. If the witness continues to deny making it, you can call the person who heard or took down the witness's statement at the time that it was made.

Impeaching a witness with an inconsistent statement would go something like this:

Q: During your direct testimony, you testified that the shooter was wearing a black-hooded sweatshirt. Is that correct?

A: Yes.

Q: On August 5, 2013, you gave a statement to Detective Mark Jones. Do you remember giving a statement on that day?

A: Yes.

Q: I am handing you Respondent's Exhibit 101. Is that the statement you made to Detective Jones on August 5, 2013?

A: Yes.

Q: Please read over your statement to refresh your memory. Let me know when your finished.

A: I'm finished.

Q: Okay. Does that refresh your recollection of what you told Detective Jones on the night of the shooting?

A: Yes.

Q: Isn't it true that on August 5, 2013, you told Detective Jones that you did not see the actual shooting?

A: Yes.

Q: Isn't it also true that you told Detective Jones that you saw a man, wearing a black-hooded sweatshirt, walk down the street minutes after you heard the gunshots?

A: Yes.

Q: Isn't it also true that you said the man in the black-hooded sweatshirt had his hands in his pockets when you saw him?

A: Yes.

Q: Now, isn't it fair to say your memory would have been better on the night of the shooting than at your testimony today?

A: Yes.

Q: Thank you. Nothing further.

Expert Witnesses

It might be difficult to find an expert willing to work with, and provide testimony for, a pro se petitioner. The most obvious reason for this is the likely lack of compensation for time and expenses involved in appearing in court to give testimony. Another reason could be that an expert would rather work with an attorney.

Should your tenacity pay off and yield you an expert willing to testify on your behalf, presenting his or her testimony at the hearing will entail presenting testimony of: the expert's qualifications (background of witness's education and employment), the expert's forensic method, how he or she applied this method to evidence in your case, and what conclusions were reached (as well as why they were reached rather than others).

Let's look at these three steps in more detail.

Qualifications of Expert Witness

To meet the legal requirements and to establish the witness's credentials, you must ask questions that lay out the witness's education and employment in the field for which he or she is going to provide an expert opinion about. You may use as exhibits any scientific reports or books that the witness wrote and published about the forensic subject. A witness may be qualified as an expert as long as he or she has knowledge, skill, experience, training, or education about the scientific subject in question.

Expert's Forensic Method

Once the witness is qualified, you may present testimony about the general forensic method, showing how that method is used, step by step. Most judges will be familiar with forensic evidence and may make a comment to that effect. In such an instance, you should move on to step three.

Applying the Expert's Forensic Method

The last step is to present testimony of your expert's application of his or her forensic method to the evidence in your case. Here, the witness may identify exhibits he or she examined, explain how he or she applied the forensic method to the evidence in your case, and then give his or her expert conclusions about the evidence.

Frye and Daubert Tests

The United States Court of Appeals for the District of Columbia held, in *Frye v. United States, 293 F. 1013 (D.C.App. 1923)*, that lie-detector test results were inadmissible. The court found that polygraph examination had not gained "general acceptance in the particular field in which it belongs." In other words, the scientific community had not accepted lie-detector tests as scientifically sound, due to the tests' inherent unreliability.

In *Daubert v. Merrell Dow Pharmaceuticals, 113 S.Ct. 2786 (1993)*, the United States Supreme Court held that the Federal Rules of Evidence overruled the *Frye* test. However, the *Daubert* decision only applied to federal cases. Nonetheless, the state courts were free to adopt or reject the five factors laid out in *Daubert*, which are: 1) whether the method used can be, or has been, tested; 2) whether the theory or technique has been subjected to peer review and publication in the scientific community; 3) its known or potential rate of error; 4) whether there are standards controlling the technique's operation; and 5) whether the method has been generally accepted in the relevant scientific community.

When considering the use of an expert witness, it is good practice to search for case law and find out whether the scientific evidence you want to present has been accepted or rejected in other courts. If the case law is favorable, you may use it to convince the judge of the evidence's admissibility and reliability, should the respondent make an objection to your expert's testimony at the hearing.

Objections

To exclude improper evidence, whether it is extrinsic or testimonial, a party must make a timely objection. The objection must also be specific—that is, it must state what the party is objecting to and why.

Having a clear understanding of your state's rules of evidence will be essential to representing yourself at the hearing. The judge may grant you some leeway, but you shouldn't expect much. By thoroughly studying your state's rules of evidence, you'll know what evidence is objectionable and why.

When objecting to a question by the respondent or to an answer by a witness, you need only interrupt, saying, "Your Honor, I object to counsel's leading question during direct examination," or "Your Honor, I object to the witness's answer as non-responsive, and I ask that it be stricken from the record."

Below is a list of other possible objections you may need to make during a hearing. (Note: this list is not all-inclusive.)

"Your Honor, I object to counsel's question as being argumentative."

"Your Honor, I object to the witness's answer as hearsay, and I ask that it be stricken from the record."

"Your Honor, I object to counsel's question as it calls for hearsay."

"Your Honor, I object to counsel's question as it assumes facts not in evidence."

"Your Honor, I object to the admission of Respondent's Exhibit X because of a lack of proper foundation."

"Your Honor, I object to counsel's question because it asks for improper character evidence."

"Your Honor, I object to Respondent's Exhibit X because it has not been properly authenticated."

"Your Honor, I object to Respondent's Exhibit X because it is not best evidence."

When an objection is sustained as to the form of a question (e.g., leading, argumentative, etc.), you or the respondent may rephrase it. If the objection is to the admission of evidence, the rules of evidence will determine its admissibility. Of course, if a timely objection is not made, any error in admitting the evidence will not be preserved for a subsequent appeal (if your state allows for an appeal in a habeas case, most states require you to refile your petition in a higher court when your case is dismissed and disposed of in a lower court).

To be best prepared to make objections to improper questions or inadmissible evidence, you must thoroughly study your state's rules of evidence. By doing so, you will know when to object and what grounds to assert for your objection.

EVIDENTIARY HEARING

Example—Writ of Habeas Corpus ad Testificandum

IN THE CIRCUIT COURT OF JACKSON COUNTY, MISSOURI

ZACHARY A. SMITH, §
§
      Movant §
§
vs. § NO. 03CV20450
§
STATE OF MISSOURI § DIV. 12
§
      Respondent §

THE STATE OF MISSOURI TO:

SUPERINTENDENT
Crossroads Correctional Center
1115 E. Pence Rd.
Cameron, MO 64429

    The court having determined that the presence of the petitioner is necessary for a full and fair hearing in the above-entitled cause, **YOU ARE HEREBY COMMANDED** to deliver the person of Zachary Smith 521163, now in your custody, to the custody of the Jackson County Department of Corrections, at Kansas City, Missouri, not later than _____, 2004 so that the petitioner may be present at the time of the hearing scheduled in this cause at _____.m. on _____, 2004.

    Dated this _____.

                                                             Judge Presiding

I hereby certify that a copy of the foregoing Writ of Habeas Corpus ad Testificandum was served upon Superintendent, Crossroads Correctional Center; Elizabeth Unger Carlyle, Attorney for Petitioner; and Daniel Miller, Asst. Pros. Atty., on _____.

_____, Clerk

<9> CASE DISPOSITION AND APPELLATE REMEDIES

Case Disposition

A court may dispose of a habeas corpus case with an order summarily dismissing the petition, instead of issuing findings of fact and conclusions of law, which is the usual practice when an evidentiary hearing isn't held. (See examples at the end of this chapter.)

As mentioned at the end of Chapter 8, some states do not permit habeas cases to be appealed; rather, petitioners must refile their entire petitions in either a court of appeals or the state supreme court.

Habeas corpus proceedings are commonly governed by the civil and appellate rules for original writ proceedings. You should review these rules for your state to understand the proper procedure. You should be able to locate them in your prison law library. If not, write to the clerk of the appellate court of proper jurisdiction, and request a copy of these rules.

Appellate Remedies

Because each state has its own rules of appellate procedure that govern habeas petitions (original writs), some appellate courts allow the losing party to file post-opinion motions—motions for rehearing and motions for transfer to the State Supreme Court. However, most appellate court rules only permit post-opinion motions after a written decision has been issued in the case. An order summarily dismissing the case is not considered a written opinion.

You should thoroughly review your state appellate court's rules of appellate practice before proceeding with your petition. This is particularly important because of the time limits imposed for filing notices of appeal.

When briefs are filed and oral arguments heard, appellate courts write detailed findings of fact and conclusions of law when disposing of a case. (See the appellate court decisions at the end of this chapter.)

Remedies in Federal Court

If you exhaust all state remedies and do not receive any relief, you can petition the United States Supreme Court for a writ of certiorari, or file a petition for a writ of habeas corpus in federal district court under 28 U.S.C. §2254. (For detailed instructions on both, order a copy of *Smith's Guide to Habeas Corpus Relief for State Prisoners Under 28 U.S.C. §2254*.)

However, if you have already sought relief via 28 U.S.C. §2254, you must ask for permission from a United States court of appeals to file a second or successive habeas corpus application. (Due to the complexity of subject and page limitations, this remedy is not addressed in this book, but in *Smith's Guide™ to Second or Successive Federal Habeas Corpus Relief for State and Federal Prisoners*.)

Writ of Certiorari

United States Supreme Court Rule 10 governs the criteria for reviews on certiorari and states:

> Review on a writ of certiorari is not a matter of right, but of judicial discretion. A petition for a writ of certiorari will be granted only for compelling reasons. The following, although neither controlling nor fully measuring the Court's discretion, indicate the character of the reasons the Court considers:
>
> (a) a United States court of appeals has entered a decision in conflict with the decision of another United States court of appeals on the same important matter; has decided an important federal question in a way that conflicts with a decision by a state court of last resort; or has so far departed from the accepted and usual course of judicial proceedings, or sanctioned such a departure by a lower court, as to call for an exercise of this Court's supervisory power;
>
> (b) a state court of last resort has decided an important federal question in a way that conflicts with the decision of another state court of last resort or of a United states court of appeals;
>
> (c) a state court or a United states court of appeals has decided an important question of federal law that has not been, but should be, settled by this court, or has decided an important federal question in a way that conflicts with relevant decisions of this Court.

A petition for a writ of certiorari is rarely granted when the asserted error consists of erroneous factual findings or the misapplication of a properly stated rule of law.

For a writ of certiorari packet, you may write to:

Office of the Clerk
Supreme Court of the United States
Washington, DC 20543

Conclusion

Obtaining relief from a conviction is often a very long and arduous endeavor, requiring extreme patience and focused attention on the task until the desired results are achieved. So do not become discouraged when one court summarily dismisses your petition. Just proceed to the next court until either you obtain relief or there are no more courts to hear your petition. In such an event, take a break to clear your mind and think of other options you haven't considered to win your freedom. Never lose hope. Never give up.

Example Order—Smith v. Pash

```
                                                          FILED
                                                       <July 21, 2015>

          IN THE CIRCUIT COURT OF DEKALB COUNTY        JULIE WHITSELL
                    STATE OF MISSOURI                  CIRCUIT CLERK
                                                       DEKALB COUNTY, MO
```

Zachary A. Smith,   )   Plaintiff
)
v.   )   Case No. 15DK-CC00051
)
)
Ronda J. Pash,   )   Defendant.

<u>ORDER</u>

The Court, having reviewed the pleadings filed herein, finds Petitioner is not entitled to the relief requested. Petition for Writ of Habeas Corpus is denied.

Dismissal costs are taxed against the Petitioner.

Date: July 21, 2015

[signature: Tom Chapman]
Circuit Judge Thomas N. Chapman

COURT SEAL OF
DEKALB COUNTY

Example Order #2—Smith v. Pash

In the
Missouri Court of Appeals
Western District

IN RE: ZACHARY A. SMITH)) Petitioner,)) v.)) RONDA PASH, Warden,)) Respondent.)	WD78940

ORDER

The Petitioner's Petition for Writ of Habeas Corpus, filed on August 24, 2015, is taken up and considered. The Court, being fully informed, hereby denies Petitioner's Petition.

Dated this 25th day of August, 2015.

_____
Gary D. Witt
Presiding Judge, Writ Division

Karen King Mitchell, Judge, concurs.

cc: Zachary A. Smith, #521163
Crossroad Correctional Center
Petitioner Pro Se

Stephen D. Hawke, Esq.
Assistant Attorney General

CASE DISPOSITION AND APPELLATE REMEDIES

Example—Letter from Missouri Supreme Court (Smith v. Pash)

CLERK OF THE SUPREME COURT
STATE OF MISSOURI
POST OFFICE BOX 150
JEFFERSON CITY, MISSOURI
65102

BILL L. THOMPSON
CLERK

TELEPHONE
(573) 751-4144

September 17, 2015

Mr. Zachary A. Smith   via regular mail
No. 521163, H.U. 4C-152
Crossroads Correctional Center
1115 E. Pence Road
Cameron, MO 64429

In Re: State ex rel. Zachary A. Smith, Petitioner, vs. Ronda Pash, Respondent.
Missouri Supreme Court No. SC95256

Dear Mr. Smith:

This acknowledges receipt of petition for writ of habeas corpus, which was filed on this date in the above-entitled cause.

A receipt for the $70.00 filing fee is enclosed.

Please note that docket number **SC95256** has been assigned this case. This same number should appear on all correspondence and documents relating to this proceeding.

To follow the progress of your case on the Internet, use the Case.Net link on the Missouri Judiciary Homepage at http://www.courts.mo.gov. Other useful information may be found by using the Supreme Court link on the same homepage.

Very truly yours,

Bill L. Thompson

BILL L. THOMPSON

cc:
Attorney General   via e-mail and e-filing system

Example Opinion—*Thornton v. Denny*

IN THE MISSOURI COURT OF APPEALS
WESTERN DISTRICT

In re: FREDERICK W. THORNTON, III,
    Petitioner,

v.   WD77276

LARRY DENNEY, Warden, FILED: March 17, 2015
    Respondent.

Original Proceeding on Petition for Writ of Habeas Corpus

Before Writ Division: Alok Ahuja, C.J., and Joseph M. Ellis and Thomas H. Newton, JJ.

Frederick W. Thornton III pleaded guilty in October 2007 to driving while intoxicated (or "DWI"). The circuit court found Thornton to be a persistent offender because he had two prior convictions for driving while intoxicated. By finding that Thornton was a "persistent offender" with two prior DWI convictions, rather than a "prior offender" with one previous conviction, the circuit court enhanced Thornton's current offense from a Class A misdemeanor to a Class D felony. Thornton was given a sentence which exceeded the statutory punishment for a Class A misdemeanor. Thornton filed a petition for writ of habeas corpus, arguing that, as a result of the Missouri Supreme Court's decision in *Turner v. State*, 245 S.W.3d 826 (Mo. banc 2008), one of the convictions on which the circuit court relied to find him to be a persistent offender could not be used for enhancement purposes. We agree, and conclude that under *Turner*, Thornton could be classified only as a prior, rather than a persistent, offender. We accordingly grant Thornton's petition for writ of habeas corpus, vacate his 2007 conviction of a felony offense, and order that the record of Thornton's 2007 conviction be amended to reflect a conviction of Class A misdemeanor driving while intoxicated.

Factual Background

On October 2007, Thornton pleaded guilty in the Circuit Court of DeKalb County in Case No. 07K4-CR00429 to the charge of driving while intoxicated under § 577.010,[1] based on an incident which occurred on August 19, 2007. The State charged Thornton as a persistent offender, based on the fact that he had been convicted of driving while intoxicated on two prior occasions. Thornton's status as a persistent offender had the effect of enhancing the charge from a misdemeanor to a Class D felony. *See* § 577.023. The court sentenced Thornton to four years' imprisonment. Following Thornton's completion of an institutional treatment program, the court entered a 120-Day Order of Probation in February 2008, which suspended the execution of the balance of Thornton's sentence, and placed him on probation for five years.

On November 21, 2011, the court revoked Thornton's probation for the 2007 offense and executed his sentence, following his guilty plea to charges stemming from a January 28, 2011 accident in which another driver was killed. The court ordered that the sentences imposed in connection with the 2011 accident be served consecutively to Thornton's 2007 sentence.[2]

On January 14, 2013, Thornton petitioned the DeKalb County Circuit Court for habeas corpus relief with respect to his 2007 conviction, arguing that he did not qualify as a persistent offender under the Missouri Supreme Court's decision in *Turner*, because he had only one prior conviction that would qualify for enhancement. In response, the State argued that Thornton's

---

[1] Unless otherwise indicated, statutory citations refer to the 2000 edition of the Revised Statutes of Missouri, updated through the 2007 Cumulative Supplement.

[2] Thornton's motion for post-conviction relief in relation to the 2011 guilty plea was denied by the circuit court, and that ruling was affirmed by this Court. *Thornton v. State*, No. WD76734, 2014 WL 6781171 (Mo. App. W.D. Dec. 2, 2014), application for transfer filed Feb. 11, 2015, No. SC94786.

2

Example Opinion—*Thornton v. Denny (cont.)*

failure to file a timely post-conviction relief motion under Supreme Court Rule 24.035 barred him from seeking habeas relief. The circuit court denied Thornton's petition.

Thornton then filed a Petition for Writ of Habeas Corpus with this Court. We issued an order to show cause, and thereafter received briefing and heard oral argument.[3]

Analysis

"'Habeas corpus is the last judicial inquiry into the validity of a criminal conviction and serves as "a bulwark against convictions that violate fundamental fairness."'" *State ex rel. Taylor v. Steele*, 341 S.W.3d 634, 639 (Mo. banc 2011) (quoting *Amrine v. Roper*, 102 S.W.3d 541, 545 (Mo. banc 2003) (in turn quoting *Engle v. Isaac*, 456 U.S. 107, 126 (1982))). In determining whether or not to grant habeas relief, we are "limited to determining the facial validity of confinement, which is based on the record of the proceeding that resulted in the confinement." *State ex rel. Zinna v. Steele*, 301 S.W.3d 510, 513 (Mo. banc 2010), quoting *State ex rel. Nixon v. Jaynes*, 63 S.W.3d 210, 214 (Mo. banc 2001).

In 2007, the circuit court found Thornton to be a persistent offender based, in part, on his guilty plea on August 22, 2000 to driving while intoxicated in the Cameron Municipal Division of the Circuit Court of Clinton County.[4] It is undisputed that Thornton received a suspended imposition of sentence (or "SIS") in the 2000 case.

On March 4, 2008, the Missouri Supreme Court decided *Turner v. State*, 245 S.W.3d 826 (Mo. banc 2008), which held that "the use of prior municipal offenses resulting in an SIS cannot be used to enhance punishment under section 577.023." *Id.* at 829.

---

[3] The Court expresses its appreciation to attorney Sean D. O'Brien, who accepted this Court's appointment and represented Thornton on a *pro bono* basis.

[4] This guilty plea was identified in the charging document as occurring on August 22, 200<u>2</u>. The parties do not dispute that the charging document was intended to refer to Thornton's August 2000 guilty plea.

3

Example Opinion—*Thornton v. Denny (cont.)*

The State does not dispute that, if *Turner* is applicable to Thornton's 2007 conviction, there was no basis to find Thornton to be a persistent offender, and he should not have been convicted of a Class D felony. The State argues, however, that Thornton is not entitled to habeas corpus relief for two reasons: *first*, because he should have raised the *Turner* issue in a motion for post-conviction relief under Supreme Court Rule 24.035, which was required to be filed no later than May 2008; and *second*, because *Turner* should not be applied "retroactively" to Thornton's 2007 conviction, which is now final. We reject both of the State's arguments.

I.

Thornton could have raised his current claim in a motion for post-conviction relief under Rule 24.035. *Turner* was decided before the time for Thornton to file a post-conviction relief motion expired, and he therefore could have relied on that decision in a timely Rule 24.035 motion. We must first decide whether Thornton may raise his claim in this habeas corpus proceeding, despite his failure to raise it earlier in a timely-filed post-conviction relief motion.

Normally, a petitioner's failure to raise a claim in a direct appeal or in a post-conviction relief motion bars the petitioner from subsequently raising the claim in a petition for writ of habeas corpus. *State ex rel. Zinna v. Steele*, 301 S.W.3d 510, 516 (Mo. banc 2010).

> A defendant who fails to raise a challenge to his conviction on direct appeal or in a timely post-conviction proceeding is said to have procedurally defaulted on those claims. Procedurally defaulted claims cannot be raised in a petition for writ of habeas corpus unless: (1) the claim relates to a jurisdictional issue; or (2) the petitioner establishes a showing by the preponderance of the evidence of actual innocence, that would meet the manifest injustice standard for habeas relief under Missouri law, (a "gateway of innocence claim"); or (3) the petitioner establishes cause for failing to raise the claim in a timely manner and prejudice from the constitutional error asserted, (a "gateway cause and prejudice claim").

Ferguson v. Dormire, 413 S.W.3d 40, 52-53 (Mo. App. W.D. 2013) (citations and internal quotation marks omitted).

4

Example Opinion—Thornton v. Denny (cont.)

"Cases in which a person received a sentence greater than that permitted by law traditionally have been analyzed under the ['jurisdictional defect'] exception[ ]." *Zinna*, 310 S.W.3d at 517. Following the decision in *J.C.W. ex rel. Webb v. Wyciskalla*, 275 S.W.3d 249 (Mo. banc 2009), it is a misnomer to describe such unauthorized sentences as involving a "jurisdictional defect." *Zinna*, 310 S.W.3d at 517. *Zinna* emphasized, however, that "[w]hatever label is applied, . . . it is settled that the imposition of a sentence beyond that permitted by the applicable statute or rule may be raised by way of a writ of habeas corpus." *Id.*; *see also State ex rel. Koster v. Jackson*, 301 S.W.3d 586, 590 (Mo. App. W.D. 2010) ("Even if a habeas petitioner has failed to timely raise a claim in a Rule 24.035 motion, it is settled that the imposition of a sentence beyond that permitted by the applicable statute or rule may be raised by way of a writ of habeas corpus."; citing *Zinna* and *Merriweather v. Grandison*, 904 S.W.2d 485, 486 (Mo. App. W.D. 1995)).

We recently suggested that, because the unauthorized sentences subject to review in habeas corpus proceedings do not implicate the subject-matter jurisdiction of the sentencing court, such unauthorized sentences are more properly referred to as "sentencing defects," rather than "jurisdictional defects." *Branch v. Cassady*, No.WD77788, 2015 WL 160718, at *2 n.2 (Mo. App. W.D. Jan. 13, 2015). We use that terminology here.

In *State ex rel. Koster v. Jackson* we held that the exact same claim raised by Thornton in this case – that he did not qualify as a "persistent offender" in light of *Turner* – was a "sentencing defect" claim which could properly be raised in a habeas corpus proceeding, despite the petitioner's failure to raise the claim in a motion for post-conviction relief:

> In this case, Mitchell [(the habeas petitioner)] was sentenced as a persistent offender, supported, in part, by a guilty plea to a municipal charge of driving while intoxicated for which Mitchell received a suspended imposition of sentence. Following the interpretation of Section 577.023 provided in *Turner*,

5

Example Opinion—*Thornton v. Denny (cont.)*

>which held that a prior municipal offense resulting in a suspended imposition of sentence could not be used to enhance punishment, the State failed to demonstrate Mitchell was a persistent offender. Thus, the sentencing court exceeded its authority in sentencing Mitchell to five years of imprisonment as a persistent offender because the factual predicate necessary to place Mitchell in this enhanced statutory range of punishment was lacking.

Jackson, 301 S.W.3d at 590.

The State argues that *Jackson* is distinguishable, because *Turner* was decided after the time had expired for the habeas petitioner in *Jackson* to file a motion for post-conviction relief. Thus, the petitioner in *Jackson* could not have raised the *Turner* issue in a timely post-conviction relief motion. In this case, by contrast, Thornton had approximately two months following the decision in *Turner* within which to file a timely post-conviction relief motion raising the *Turner* issue.

The State's attempt to distinguish *Jackson* is unpersuasive. Under *Zinna*, a habeas corpus petitioner is entitled to raise a sentencing defect in a habeas corpus proceeding despite the fact that the petitioner could have raised the issue in a post-conviction relief motion; a petitioner raising a sentencing defect need not show that he had "cause" for failing to raise the issue at an earlier time. Indeed, in *Zinna*, the petitioner plainly could have raised his habeas claim in a timely direct appeal or post-conviction relief motion. The petitioner in *Zinna* argued that his sentence was unauthorized because the court's written judgment, which stated that his sentences would run consecutively, was inconsistent with the oral pronouncement of his sentences, which would be interpreted to impose concurrent sentences by virtue of Supreme Court Rule 29.09. The petitioner's argument in *Zinna* was based on Rule 29.09 (which has been in existence without amendment *since 1980*), and on caselaw which predated his conviction. In *Zinna*, therefore, the sentencing argument was available to the petitioner at a time when he could have appealed from the trial court's written judgment, or filed a timely post-conviction relief motion.

6

Example Opinion—*Thornton v. Denny (cont.)*

Yet the Supreme Court held that the claim could properly be raised in a habeas proceeding. Therefore, whether or not Thornton had the ability to raise the *Turner* issue in a timely post-conviction relief motion is irrelevant. *Jackson*'s holding that a claim like Thornton's involves a "sentencing defect" excuses Thornton's failure to raise the claim earlier.

The State also argues that Thornton is precluded from seeking habeas review under the Missouri Supreme Court's decision in *State ex rel. Simmons v. White*, 866 S.W.2d 443 (Mo. banc 1993). In *Simmons*, the petitioner sought to challenge a similar persistent offender finding, based on *State v. Stewart,* 832 S.W.2d 911 (Mo. banc 1992), which clarified the number of prior convictions necessary to establish "persistent offender" status. In *Simmons*, the petitioner initially pled guilty and admitted his status as a "persistent offender" under a charging document which alleged an insufficient number of prior convictions in light of the *Stewart* decision. *Simmons*, 866 S.W.2d at 444. (*Stewart* was decided ten days prior to Simmons' initial plea. *Id.*) The State later realized that the initial charging document was insufficient to establish "persistent offender" status under *Stewart*, and attempted to amend the charging document to allege additional prior convictions. *Id.* The sentencing court set aside the previous conviction and sentencing, and Simmons pleaded guilty to the amended charges, and received the same sentence as before. *Id.* at at 444-45.

Simmons later petitioned for habeas relief, alleging that his second guilty plea was invalid, and that the factual basis underlying his initial guilty plea failed to sufficiently establish "persistent offender" status under *Stewart*. 866 S.W.2d at 446. The Missouri Supreme Court determined that Simmons' second plea and sentencing were void. It held, however, that Simmons was not entitled to challenge his first conviction and sentence in a habeas corpus proceeding. The Court held that "[h]abeas corpus may be used to challenge a final judgment

7

after an individual's failure to pursue appellate and post-conviction remedies *only* to raise jurisdictional issues or in circumstances so rare and exceptional that a manifest injustice results."

Id. The Court held that Simmons had failed to satisfy this standard.

> We are convinced that petitioner's procedural defaults stemmed not from unawareness, but from a calculated, strategic decision to forego both appeal and post-conviction motions in the hope of receiving probation within 120 days. . . . [¶] . . . By deliberately bypassing appellate and post-conviction remedies in an attempt to gain a more favorable consideration of his request for probation, Simmons waived his rights to those remedies.

Id. at 446, 447.

Simmons does not control this case. First, to the extent *Simmons* suggests that proof of an insufficient number of prior convictions to support enhanced sentencing is not a "sentencing defect" reviewable in a habeas corpus proceeding, the decision has been superseded by *Zinna*. *Zinna* holds that "the imposition of a sentence beyond that permitted by the applicable statute or rule may be raised by way of a writ of habeas corpus." *Zinna*, 310 S.W.3d at 517. As we recognized in *Jackson*, in *Zinna* the trial court had the *statutory authority* to impose consecutive sentencing on the petitioner, but the trial court did so in a procedurally improper way – by referencing consecutive sentencing only in its written judgment, but not in its earlier oral pronouncement of sentence. *Jackson*, 301 S.W.3d at 590 n.5; *see also Taylor*, 341 S.W.3d at 639, and *State v. Whitfield*, 107 S.W.3d 253, 269 n.19 (Mo. banc 2003) (both cases holding that a defendant presented a "sentencing defect" claim reviewable in a habeas proceeding, where the defendant claimed that it was unconstitutional for a judge, rather than a jury, to decide whether statutory factors justified imposition of the death penalty). *Jackson* followed *Zinna* and held that the very same sentencing error alleged by Thornton in this case constitutes a "sentencing defect" subject to correction in a habeas corpus proceeding. To the extent *Simmons* applied a narrower understanding of the types of "sentencing defects" subject to review in a habeas corpus proceeding, it no longer accurately states the law.

More importantly, *Simmons*' refusal to allow the petitioner to pursue a habeas remedy was based on the fact that the petitioner in that case chose to plead guilty a second time, after the *Stewart* issue had become apparent. According to the Court, the petitioner's actions reflected "a calculated, strategic decision to forego both appeal and post-conviction motions," a "deliberate[] bypassing" of appellate and post-conviction remedies. *Simmons,* 866 S.W.2d at 447.[5] There is no evidence of such a "calculated, strategic decision," or "deliberate bypass," by Thornton in this case.

II.

Having established that this Court has the authority to hear Thornton's claim in this habeas corpus proceeding, we now turn to the State's alternative argument: that *Turner* should not be applied "retroactively" to Thornton's case.

Thornton is not seeking the "retroactive" application of *Turner*. Instead, Thornton's argument is that under § 577.023 (as interpreted in *Turner*), the State failed to prove the requisite number of prior convictions necessary to support a finding that Thornton was a "persistent offender." Section 577.023 was in effect at the time of Thornton's guilty plea – it is not being applied retroactively. Moreover, the Missouri Supreme Court has held that "[i]n *Turner,* this

---

[5] *Simmons*' reference to the petitioner's "deliberate bypass" of post-conviction remedies harkens back to the standard applied to procedural defaults in federal habeas proceedings by *Fay v. Noia,* 372 U.S. 391, 439 (1963) (overruled by *Coleman v. Thompson,* 501 U.S. 722 (1991)). This "deliberate bypass" standard required the petitioner to engage in "an intentional relinquishment or abandonment of a known right or privilege," reflecting "the considered choice of the petitioner." *Fay,* 372 U.S. at 439; *see also, e.g. Humphrey v. Cady,* 405 U.S. 504, 517 (1972) (stating that "deliberate bypass" standard requires "an understanding and knowing decision [to forego review] by the petitioner himself"; the petitioner must make "a deliberate strategic waiver of his claim").

9

Example Opinion—Thornton v. Denny (cont.)

Court made no new law; it merely clarified the language of an existing statute." *State v. Severe*, 307 S.W.3d 640, 642-43 (Mo. banc 2010). The Court held that – even before the *Turner* decision – "[t]he state was on notice by the plain language of section 577.023.16 that a guilty plea followed by a suspended imposition of sentence in 'municipal court' was not to be treated as a prior conviction." *Id.* at 644. The State itself argues in its Brief that "*Severe* makes plain that the *Turner* decision was based on statutory construction and not a new rule of law." State Br. at 19.

In these circumstances, where Thornton's petition relies on a judicial opinion interpreting a statute which was in effect at the time of his conviction, and that judicial opinion "created no new law," no retroactivity issue arises. Indeed, if the State were correct that *Turner*'s construction of § 577.023 cannot be applied "retroactively" to convictions which were final at the time *Turner* was decided, that would have prevented relief in *Turner* itself, since *Turner* was decided on a motion for *post-conviction* relief.

The Supreme Court of the United States has addressed a virtually identical issue, and held that no issue of "retroactivity" is presented where a later judicial decision interprets the meaning of a pre-existing statute. In *Fiore v. White*, 531 U.S. 225 (2001), the defendant Fiore was convicted of violating a Pennsylvania criminal statute. Although Fiore argued that the statute should not be interpreted to apply to his conduct, this argument was rejected by the intermediate Pennsylvania appellate courts, and the Pennsylvania Supreme Court refused to review his case. *Id.* at 227. After Fiore's conviction became final, the Pennsylvania Supreme Court determined – in a case involving Fiore's co-defendant Scarpone – that the criminal statute at issue could not be interpreted to apply to conduct like Fiore's. *Id.*

Example Opinion—*Thornton v. Denny (cont.)*

Fiore filed a petition for a writ of habeas corpus in the federal courts. In response to a certified question from the Supreme Court of the United States, the Pennsylvania Supreme Court explained that its decision in *Scarpone* "did not announce a new rule of law," but "merely clarified the plain language of the statute." *Id.* at 228. Given that the Pennsylvania Supreme Court's decision in *Scarpone* was merely intended to clarify the meaning of a pre-existing statute, the United States Supreme Court held that no retroactivity issue was presented by Fiore's request that *Scarpone*'s interpretation of the relevant statute be applied to his conviction:

> The Pennsylvania Supreme Court's reply [to the certified question] specifies that the interpretation of § 6018.401(a) set out in *Scarpone* "merely clarified" the statute and was the law of Pennsylvania – as properly interpreted – at the time of Fiore's conviction. Because *Scarpone* was not new law, this case presents no issue of retroactivity. Rather, the question is simply whether Pennsylvania can, consistently with the Federal Due Process Clause, convict Fiore for conduct that its criminal statute, as properly interpreted, does not prohibit.

Id. at 228. The Court held that Pennsylvania could not constitutionally punish Fiore for conduct which did not violate the relevant statute. *Id.* at 228-29. The Court applied the same analysis to a later judicial interpretation of a pre-existing statute in *Bunkley v. Florida*, 538 U.S. 835, 839-41 (2003).

In *Severe*, the Missouri Supreme Court characterized the decision in *Turner* in precisely the same way that the Pennsylvania Supreme Court characterized its decision in *Scarpone*: *Severe* holds that *Turner* "made no new law; it merely clarified the language of an existing statute." 307 S.W.3d at 642-43. Under *Fiore* and *Bunkley*, this case presents no "retroactivity" issue which can prevent the application of *Turner*'s interpretation of § 577.023 to Thornton's 2007 conviction.

III.

As noted at the outset of our analysis, the State has conceded that, if Thornton is entitled to raise his *Turner* claim in this habeas proceeding, and if we conclude that *Turner* applies to

11

Example Opinion—Thornton v. Denny (cont.)

Thornton's 2007 conviction, then that conviction violates *Turner*, because the State failed to prove that Thornton had two prior DWI convictions under § 577.023 as it existed at the time.

Thornton concedes that the State proved that he had *one* previous DWI conviction, and therefore that he qualified as a "prior offender" under § 577.023.1(6). Because Thornton was a "prior offender," under § 577.023.2 his violation of § 577.010 constituted a Class A misdemeanor (rather than a Class D felony). Because he could only properly be found guilty of a Class A misdemeanor, Thornton could be placed on probation for no more than two years. § 559.016.1(2).

The circuit court revoked Thornton's probation associated with the 2007 conviction in November 2011, almost four years after Thornton was placed on probation. This was well beyond the two-year maximum probationary period to which Thornton was subject on conviction of a Class A misdemeanor. Once the probationary period has expired, a court does "not have jurisdiction over [a probationer] 'for any purpose, whether to cite him for probation violations, revoke probation, or order execution of the sentence previously imposed.'" *State ex rel. Limback v. Gum*, 895 S.W.2d 663, 664 (Mo. App. W.D. 1995) (quoting *State ex rel. Musick v. Dickerson*, 813 S.W.2d 75, 77 (Mo. App. W.D. 1991)); *see also Roach v. State*, 64 S.W.3d 884, 887 (Mo. App. S.D. 2002). Therefore, the circuit court was without jurisdiction to revoke Thornton's probation with respect to his 2007 conviction in November 2011, or execute any sentence previously imposed upon him.

Conclusion

The circuit court lacked the authority to sentence Thornton for Class D felony driving while intoxicated in connection with his 2007 conviction, or to order the revocation of his probation and the execution of his sentence for the 2007 conviction in November 2011. We accordingly order that Thornton be discharged and relieved from his 2007 conviction of a Class

Example Opinion—*Thornton v. Denny (cont.)*

D felony, and from the execution of any sentence associated with that conviction. With respect to his 2007 DWI conviction, Thornton constituted a prior offender, not a persistent offender, and could be convicted only of a Class A misdemeanor, not a Class D felony. We order that the record of Thornton's conviction in Case No. 07K4-CR00429 in the Circuit Court of DeKalb County be amended to reflect Thornton's conviction of driving while intoxicated as a prior offender, a Class A misdemeanor.

Thornton's sentences for his separate 2011 convictions were ordered to run consecutively to the sentence on his 2007 conviction. At the time of his 2011 sentencing, however, there was no sentence associated with his 2007 conviction which could lawfully be executed. Therefore, no sentence associated with his 2007 conviction could delay the running of the sentences associated with Thornton's 2011 convictions.

[signature]
Alok Ahuja, Chief Judge

All concur.

CASE DISPOSITION AND APPELLATE REMEDIES

Example Order Denying Application to Transfer—Thornton v. Denney

Supreme Court of Missouri
en banc
SC94987
WD77276

May Session, 2015

In re: Frederick W. Thornton III,
      Petitioner,

vs. (TRANSFER)

Larry Denney, Warden,
      Respondent.

Now at this day, on consideration of the respondent's application to transfer the above-entitled cause from the Missouri Court of Appeals, Western District, it is ordered that the said application be, and the same is hereby denied.

STATE OF MISSOURI-Sct.

I, Bill L. Thompson, Clerk of the Supreme Court of the State of Missouri, certify that the foregoing is a full, true and complete transcript of the judgment of said Supreme Court, entered of record at the May Session, 2015, and on the 18th day of August, 2015, in the above-entitled cause.

Given under my hand and seal of said Court, at the City of Jefferson, this 18th day of August, 2015.

_Bill L. Thompson_____Clerk

_____Deputy Clerk

CASE DISPOSITION AND APPELLATE REMEDIES

Example Opinion—Engel v. Dormire

HOME   SEARCH   FEATURED DECISIONS   LEAGLE KONTACT   ABOUT US   CONTACT US

View Case   Cited Cases   Citing Case

STATE EX REL. ENGEL v. DORMIRE
NO. SC 90314.

304 S.W.3d 120 (2010)

STATE ex rel. Gary W. ENGEL, Petitioner,

v.

Dave DORMIRE, Superintendent, Respondent.

Supreme Court of Missouri, En Banc.
February 23, 2010.

Kent Gipson, Law Office of Kent Gipson, LLC, Kansas City, MO, for petitioner.
Chris Koster, Attorney General, Andrew W. Hassell, Assistant Attorney General, Office of Missouri Attorney General, for respondent.

MARY R. RUSSELL, Judge.

At issue in this case is whether habeas petitioner Gary Engel's convictions should be vacated because they are undermined by newly discovered evidence. This Court finds that material impeachment information was wrongly undisclosed to Engel during his trial, which violated his due process rights pursuant to *Brady v. Maryland*, 373 U.S. 83, 83 S.Ct. 1194, 10 L.Ed.2d 215 (1963). Accordingly, Engel's convictions are vacated.

I. PROCEDURAL BACKGROUND

Engel was arrested in July 1990 on charges stemming from a 1984 armed kidnapping. The State alleged that Engel, along with accomplices Steven Manning and Thomas McKillip, was hired by drug-dealer Anthony Mammolito to kidnap and rob Charles Ford, a competing drug dealer. The State alleged that the kidnappers, masquerading as drug enforcement agents, took Ford and his associate to a "safe house" and coerced payment of a ransom.

The crime was not investigated actively until 1989, when authorities interviewed Mammolito while he was in a federal prison on an unrelated matter. Based largely on Mammolito's testimony, Engel was convicted by a jury in June 1991 of two counts of kidnapping and two counts of armed criminal action. Consecutive sentences were entered against him for each count, resulting in a total sentence of 90 years imprisonment.[1] Engel's accomplice, Manning, also was convicted in the kidnapping and sentenced to two life sentences.

Engel appealed and moved for post-conviction relief, but his efforts at relief were unsuccessful, and his convictions were affirmed in 1993. *State v. Engel*, 859 S.W.2d 822 (Mo.App.1993). Acting pro se in 2003, Engel unsuccessfully sought habeas corpus relief in Missouri's courts and was denied discretionary review of his case by this Court. He also unsuccessfully sought habeas corpus relief in the federal courts.

Manning, however, did obtain federal habeas corpus relief from his kidnapping convictions after the federal court determined that his convictions were based on improper testimony from a jailhouse informant. *Manning v. Bowersox*, 310 F.3d 571, 575-77 (8th Cir.2002). Manning was released from Missouri's custody in 2004 after the prosecutor declined to retry him following the reversal of his kidnapping convictions.

Manning brought a federal civil suit against Chicago-based FBI Agent Robert Buchan and others whom Manning alleged had framed him in the kidnapping case and for an Illinois murder charge. *Manning v. Miller*, 355 F.3d 1028, 1029-30 (7th Cir.2004). He sought relief pursuant to the Federal Tort Claims Act (FTCA) and *Bivens v. Six Unknown Named Agents*, 403 U.S. 388, 91 S.Ct. 1999, 29 L.Ed.2d 619 (1971), which authorizes suits for damages based on Fourth Amendment violations by federal officials.[2] Manning asserted that Agent Buchan, the lead investigator in the 1984 kidnapping case, had manufactured false evidence, suborned the perjury of a witness, and secretly paid a witness to testify.

Discovery in Manning's proceedings unearthed important evidence calling into question the testimony Mammolito provided at Engel's and Manning's kidnapping trials. Newly discovered letters from Mammolito to the prosecutor and investigators hinted that Mammolito believed there was an "agreement" for him to be paid. Mammolito also wrote about investigators providing him reports before his trial testimony. Mammolito sent a letter to one of the investigators, Sergeant Quid, to request that he send the "agreement" money to Mammolito's mother. Another letter later was discovered from an investigator, Commander Del Re, to Mammolito's mother that indicated a check for $500 was enclosed and recognized "the help [Mammolito] provided in this very important case."

Other information revealed during the Manning proceedings evidenced the following: Mammolito made contradictory statements to the prosecution about who was involved in the kidnapping; Sergeant Quid made an undocumented visit to Mammolito; and Mammolito arranged for investigators to assist him in securing release from federal prison.

Following three weeks of testimony and a week of deliberations, the federal jury in Manning's civil trial issued a unanimous verdict in his favor and awarded him $6.5 million in damages. The jury found that Agent Buchan "knowingly induced or caused law enforcement officers to induce" Mammolito "to give false testimony and concealed information from prosecutors."[3] It also found that Agent Buchan had promised to pay Mammolito for his testimony.

In denying the defendants' motion for judgment as a matter of law or for a new trial, the district court found that Manning's evidence supported the jury's verdicts. *Manning v. Miller*, No. 02 C 372, 2005 WL 3078048, at *4 (N.D.Ill. Nov.14, 2005). The court found "[t]he evidence amply supported Manning's contention that Agent Buchan worked in concert with Quid to put together a case to support a prosecution of Manning for the Missouri kidnapping." *Id.* at *7. It noted that the investigators had a motive to succeed in prosecuting the kidnapping because they believed Manning was a dangerous criminal, but they lacked sufficient evidence to prosecute him for murders and other serious offenses. *Id.* The court also discussed that the jury reasonably determined that Agent Buchan's testimony was not credible. It noted that "[his] demeanor on the witness stand was among the worst this Court has seen in over [24] years as a lawyer and a judge." *Id.* at *8-9.

Ultimately, however, the jury's verdict was set aside because the court determined that the jury's *Bivens* verdict violated the court's determinations under the FTCA. *Manning v. U.S.*, 546 F.3d 430, 431, 438 (7th Cir.2008); *Manning v. U.S.*, No. 02 C 372, 2006 WL 3240112, at *37 (N.D.Ill. Sept.28, 2006). But although the district court found against Manning under the FTCA, it also opined that "[t]here is no question that a deal was made at some point before Mammolito testified at Manning's [Missouri] trials to pay him some amount of money," and it found that "[t]he deal to pay Mammolito was not disclosed to Manning's attorney in the Missouri case." *Manning*, 2006 WL 3240112, at *37. Nothing in the court's decision to set aside the jury's verdict negated the jury's findings that investigators in the kidnapping case had perjured their testimony.

Armed with the information from Manning's suits, Engel renewed his efforts to obtain habeas relief. The motion court denied Engel's new habeas petition in July 2007, and the court of appeals also denied him relief. Engel's plea for habeas relief is now before this Court, nearly 26 years after the alleged crimes for which he was convicted.

[304 S.W.3d 125]

II. ENGEL'S ARGUMENTS FOR HABEAS RELIEF

Engel asserts he is entitled to habeas relief from his convictions because the prosecution violated his due process rights pursuant to *Brady* when it failed to disclose to him material exculpatory and impeachment evidence at trial. He alleges the following information was developed during Manning's proceedings and supports his habeas claims:

1. Agent Buchan and Sergeant Quid conspired to frame Engel and Manning for the 1984 kidnapping.

2. Agent Buchan and Sergeant Quid failed to disclose the deal made with Mammolito in exchange for his testimony against Engel and Manning.

3. Agent Buchan and Sergeant Quid hid from the prosecutor that they had disseminated information to witnesses before their testimony to make them appear more credible.

4. Agent Buchan and Sergeant Quid produced false documentation of witness statements in an effort to persuade the prosecutor to pursue the 1984 kidnapping case.

5. New exculpatory and impeachment evidence was discovered during Manning's federal civil trial that was not disclosed to Manning or Engel during the defense of the kidnapping charges.

In addition to his *Brady* claims, Engel also argues he is entitled to relief from his convictions because the prosecution used perjured testimony during his trial. He further asserts that his armed criminal action convictions must be vacated because the armed criminal action charges were not filed timely.

III. STANDARDS FOR HABEAS RELIEF

"Habeas corpus is the last judicial inquiry into the validity of a criminal conviction and serves as 'a bulwark against convictions that violate fundamental fairness.'" *State ex rel. Amrine v. Roper*, 102 S.W.3d 541, 545 (Mo. banc 2003) (quoting *Engle v. Isaac*, 456 U.S. 107, 126, 102 S.Ct. 1558, 71 L.Ed.2d 783 (1982)). "[A] writ of habeas corpus may be issued when a person is restrained of his or her liberty in violation of the constitution or laws of the state or federal government." *Id.* Habeas proceedings, authorized under Rule 91, are limited to determining the facial validity of a petitioner's confinement. *State ex rel. Simmons v. White*, 866 S.W.2d 443, 445 (Mo. banc 1993). Engel, as the habeas corpus petitioner, has the burden of proof to show that he is entitled to habeas corpus relief. *State ex rel. Nixon v. Jaynes*, 73 S.W.3d 623, 624 (Mo. banc 2002).

Because Engel's arguments for habeas relief challenge the validity of his convictions and were cognizable in his direct appeal or post-conviction motion, he is afforded habeas review that is extremely limited in scope. *See Simmons*, 866 S.W.2d at 446 (explaining that prevention of "duplicative and unending challenges to the finality of a judgment" requires that habeas claims cognizable on direct appeal or in a post conviction motion be reviewed only if they present jurisdictional issues or "circumstances so rare and exceptional that a manifest injustice" will result if review is not taken). The procedural bar to raising a habeas claim can be overcome by showings of manifest injustice, cause and prejudice, or a jurisdictional defect. *See Amrine*, 102 S.W.3d at 546.

Engel seeks to overcome the procedural bar to his habeas claims by showing "cause and prejudice." Cause is established where there is a factor at issue external to the defense or beyond its responsibilities.

[304 S.W.3d 126]

Strickler v. Greene, 527 U.S. 263, 283 n. 24, 119 S.Ct. 1936, 144 L.Ed.2d 286 (1999) (noting that "cause for a procedural default must ordinarily turn on whether the prisoner can show that some objective factor external to the defense impeded counsel's efforts to comply with the State's procedural rule" (internal quotation omitted)). This Court will not undertake habeas review of Engel's claims unless he can "establish that the grounds relied on were not 'known to him'" during his direct appeal or post-conviction case. *Simmons*, 866 S.W.2d at 446.

CASE DISPOSITION AND APPELLATE REMEDIES

Example Opinion—Engel v. Dormire (cont.)

The State suggests that Engel's claims for habeas relief mirror the claims he raised in his prior pro se habeas petition, wherein he alleged that the prosecution had failed to disclose impeachment evidence related to Mammolito, including that Mammolito was paid for his testimony. Engel's current claims for habeas relief, however, are distinct from his previous claims because they rest on a collection of new evidence developed in Manning's cases and unknown or unavailable when Engel previously sought relief.

Justice requires that this Court consider all available evidence uncovered following Engel's trial that may impact his entitlement to habeas relief. *See Amrine,* 102 S.W.3d at 545 (noting that habeas review must assess the totality of all of the evidence uncovered over the years between various judicial reviews to determine if a habeas petitioner established a claim of innocence); *see also Kyles v. Whitley,* 514 U.S. 419, 436-37, 115 S.Ct. 1555, 131 L.Ed.2d 490 (1995) (discussing that courts must consider the cumulative effect of excluded evidence in determining if a *Brady* violation occurred). Engel has established the cause needed to overcome the procedural bar to review of his habeas claims by showing that his arguments are based on evidence and information that was not revealed until Manning's federal lawsuits.

Under the "cause and prejudice" standard, however, it is not enough that Engel's petition rests on newly discovered evidence. He also must establish that he is entitled to habeas review because this Court's failure to review his claims would prejudice him. In the context of whether Engel's *Brady* claims are barred procedurally from habeas review, prejudice is identical to this Court's assessment of prejudice undertaken in assessing Engel's *Brady* claims. Consequently, so long as Engel establishes the prejudice necessary to support his *Brady* claims, he will have shown the required prejudice to overcome the procedural bar for habeas relief.

IV. *BRADY* VIOLATIONS—MAMMOLITO EVIDENCE

Engel's principal argument for habeas relief is that the prosecution wrongly failed to disclose to him material impeachment evidence related to Mammolito, which he argues violated his due process rights under *Brady*. *Brady* holds that "'the suppression by the prosecution of evidence favorable to an accused upon request violates due process where the evidence is material either to guilt or to punishment, irrespective of the good faith or bad faith of the prosecution.'" *Merriweather v. State,* 294 S.W.3d 52, 54 (Mo. banc 2009) (quoting *Brady,* 373 U.S. at 87, 83 S.Ct. 1194).

To prevail in his *Brady* claims based on the Mammolito evidence, Engel must show each of the following: (1) the evidence at issue is favorable to him, either because it is exculpatory or because it is impeaching; (2) the evidence was suppressed by the State, either willfully or inadvertently; and (3) he was prejudiced. *Strickler,* 527 U.S. at 281-82, 119 S.Ct. 1936; *Merriweather,* 294 S.W.3d at 54.

A. THE EVIDENCE AT ISSUE IS FAVORABLE TO ENGEL

To prevail in his *Brady* claim that evidence related to Mammolito was wrongly not disclosed to him, Engel first must establish that the Mammolito evidence at issue was favorable to him. *Id.* The evidence developed in Manning's case related to Mammolito supports Engel's allegations that Mammolito was paid for his testimony against Engel and Manning. New evidence includes a letter to Mammolito's mother that enclosed a $500 payment and mentioned "the help [Mammolito] provided in this very important case." Other evidence supports Engel's allegations that investigators coached Mammolito to align his testimony with their testimony. And Engel now has letters evidencing that investigators sought leniency for Mammolito based on his cooperation in the kidnapping case. This Mammolito evidence is impeachment evidence favorable to Engel that proves the first prong of his *Brady* claim.

B. THE EVIDENCE AT ISSUE WAS SUPPRESSED

Engel next must prove his *Brady* claim as to the Mammolito evidence by showing that the State suppressed the evidence, either willfully or inadvertently. *Id.* There is no dispute that, during Engel's trial, he was not provided the Mammolito impeachment evidence that is the subject of his habeas claims.

The State contends, however, that Engel cannot show that the Mammolito evidence was suppressed for *Brady* purposes because it did not exist at the time of trial. It argues that the prosecutor cannot be faulted for failing to provide not-yet-existent documents about the alleged "deal" made between Mammolito and investigators. Documents memorializing the "deal," however, need not have existed at the time of trial; it is enough that the evidence shows that the "deal" itself already existed, even if had not yet been documented.

Under *Brady*, due process requires that the prosecution disclose to the defendant any evidence in its possession that is favorable to him and that is material to his guilt or punishment. *Id. Brady* provides that "the individual prosecutor has a duty to learn of any favorable evidence known to *the others acting on the government's behalf* in the case, including the police." *Kyles,* 514 U.S. at 437, 115 S.Ct. 1555 (emphasis added). It is irrelevant to Engel's *Brady* claim that the Mammolito evidence at issue in his habeas request involves non-Missouri investigators. These investigators were part of Missouri's prosecutorial team in the kidnapping cases against Engel and Manning, essentially acting as the prosecutor's agents during the investigation.

Similarly, it is no hindrance to Engel's *Brady* claim that the prosecutor did not have the same knowledge about his case as the investigators.[4] The prosecutor's lack of knowledge about information asserted in a *Brady* claim is not an impediment because the prosecutor is considered "'the representative not of an ordinary party to a controversy, but of a sovereignty whose obligation to govern impartially is as compelling as its obligation to govern at all; and whose interest, therefore, in a criminal prosecution is not that it shall win a case, but that justice shall be done.'" *Strickler,* 527 U.S. at 281, 119 S.Ct. 1936 (quoting *Berger v. United States,* 295 U.S. 78, 88, 55 S.Ct. 629, 79 L.Ed. 1314 (1935)).

Engel has satisfied the second prong for his *Brady* claim by showing that the Mammolito evidence that is the subject of his habeas petition was suppressed wrongly.

C. THE NONDISCLOSURE OF THE EVIDENCE PREJUDICED ENGEL

Having proved the first two prongs of his *Brady* claim, Engel also must show that he was prejudiced by the nondisclosure of the Mammolito evidence at issue. *See Merriweather,* 294 S.W.3d at 54. Before determining whether the evidence meets the test for *Brady* prejudice, this Court must assess whether the evidence at issue is material to Engel's case. *See Strickler,* 527 U.S. at 282, 119 S.Ct. 1936. Evidence is material if there is a reasonable probability that its disclosure to the defense would have caused a different result in the proceeding. *Strickler,* 527 U.S. at 280, 119 S.Ct. 1936. The materiality standard for *Brady* claims is established when "the favorable evidence could reasonably be taken to put the whole case in such a different light as to undermine confidence in the verdict." *Kyles,* 514 U.S. at 435, 115 S.Ct. 1555. "The question is not whether the defendant would more likely than not have received a different verdict with the evidence, but whether in its absence he received a fair trial, understood as a trial resulting in a verdict worthy of confidence." *Id.* at 434, 115 S.Ct. 1555.

The State suggests that the nondisclosure of the Mammolito impeachment evidence was not material or prejudicial to Engel because the defense offered other impeachment evidence related to Mammolito during the trial. Efforts to discredit Mammolito during the trial included attacking his character by highlighting his criminal history and work as a drug dealer, highlighting that he had testified in exchange for not being charged in the kidnapping, and noting inconsistencies in his pre-trial and

CASE DISPOSITION AND APPELLATE REMEDIES

Example Opinion—Engel v. Dormire (cont.)

trial testimonies. The State contends that any evidence that Mammolito had a "deal" with investigators "would have been overkill" and, therefore, was not material impeachment evidence.

Contrary to the State's assertions, it makes no difference to Engel's *Brady* claim that other Mammolito impeachment evidence was unpersuasive to the jury during the trial. *See Taylor v. State*, 262 S.W.3d 231, 244 (Mo. banc 2008) (noting "[t]he fact that a witness was impeached in other ways does not conclude the materiality inquiry required under *Brady*" because the witness's credibility is not a collateral issue). "In determining whether the suppressed impeachment evidence was material, the reviewing court must evaluate not only the ways that [the witness] *was* impeached, but also the ways that he was *not* impeached that would have been available had [the *Brady* claim] evidence been disclosed." *Id.*

If a witness is presenting false testimony, his testimony is not rendered truthful because he is cross-examined. *See Napue v. People of the State of Illinois*, 360 U.S. 264, 269-70, 79 S.Ct. 1173, 3 L.Ed.2d 1217 (1959) (noting that "a lie is a lie" (internal quotation omitted)). The unknown impeachment information, especially when coupled with the impeachment information presented at the time of trial, could have led the jury to a different assessment of Mammolito's credibility. *See Benn v. Lambert*, 283 F.3d 1040, 1056 (9th Cir. 2002). The defense's efforts to impeach Mammolito's credibility "were deprived of significant evidentiary force" by the prosecution's failure to disclose to Engel the evidence supporting his belief that investigators had encouraged Mammolito to testify

[304 S.W.3d 129]

falsely about Engel's role in the kidnapping. *Taylor*, 262 S.W.3d at 245.

The *Brady* materiality of the undisclosed Mammolito evidence is shown because (1) "knowledge of [the undisclosed] facts could have significantly undermined the legitimacy of [Mammolito's] testimony and involvement in the case in a way that no other impeachment presented was able to do" and (2) "[h]aving failed to disclose this impeachment evidence, the state was able to claim much greater credibility from [Mammolito's] testimony than the true facts would have warranted." *See id.*

Having determined that the undisclosed Mammolito evidence was material for purposes of *Brady*, this Court also considers whether the nondisclosure of this material evidence prejudiced Engel so as to warrant habeas relief based on a *Brady* violation. This assessment questions whether Engel's "trial result[ed] in a verdict worthy of confidence." *See Kyles*, 514 U.S. at 434, 115 S.Ct. 1555.

This Court finds that Engel has presented evidence showing that the verdict in his case is not "worthy of confidence." Nondisclosure of impeachment evidence related to Mammolito, who was a chief prosecution witness, caused Engel to suffer *Brady* prejudice because his defense hinged on undermining Mammolito's credibility. *Cf. Merriweather*, 294 S.W.3d at 57 (noting prejudice where impeachment evidence was nondisclosed wrongly and the defendant's credibility was pitted against the witness's credibility). The jury's verdict in Manning's federal civil case demonstrates that the nondisclosed Mammolito impeachment evidence would have aided Engel in discrediting Mammolito's testimony at trial.[5]

V. ENGEL IS ENTITLED TO HABEAS RELIEF

Engel has shown that his due process rights were violated because the prosecutor's failure to disclose the Mammolito impeachment evidence resulted in a *Brady* violation. Because he has shown that the nondisclosure of the Mammolito impeachment evidence was prejudicial for *Brady* purposes, he also has established the "cause and prejudice" necessary to overcome the procedural bar to granting him habeas relief. Accordingly, Engel's convictions are vacated.

Because the evidence was sufficient at the first trial to convict, there is no double jeopardy bar to retrial if the State believes it can produce enough evidence to bring Engel's case to a jury. *See Amrine*, 102 S.W.3d at 549. On retrial, however, Engel will have the opportunity to present the exculpatory and impeachment evidence discovered since his trial. Given this new evidence and the long delay since the original trial, during which time Engel has

[304 S.W.3d 130]

been imprisoned on convictions this Court herein sets aside, an expeditious and final resolution of this case is imperative. *See Amrine*, 102 S.W.3d at 549. This Court, therefore, orders Engel discharged from the State's custody 60 days from the date the mandate issues in this case, unless within that time the State files in the circuit court an election to retry him. If the State so elects, the new trial shall be held expeditiously.

All concur.

FOOTNOTES

1. He received a 30-year sentence for each kidnapping count and a 15-year sentence for each count of armed criminal action.

2. Manning also brought a federal civil suit against the Village of Buffalo Grove, Illinois, and two of its former officers, Sergeant Robert Quid and Commander Gary Del Re, for their roles in falsely convicting him in the Missouri kidnapping case. This suit was resolved in a confidential settlement.

3. The jury also found the agents had induced false testimony from witnesses Carolyn Heldenbrand and Sharon Dugan. Heldenbrand provided identification testimony in Manning's trial. She did not provide identification testimony against Engel, but he cites her discredited Manning testimony as representative of Agent Buchan's wrongful conduct. Dugan was formerly married to Engel. She testified at his trial about statements she said he had made about the kidnapping.

4. Engel does not allege that the prosecutor knew at trial of the "deal" between Mammolito and investigators.

5. The State argues that Mammolito's discredited testimony did not prejudice Engel because Sharon Dugan's testimony at trial provided sufficient evidence to convict him regardless of Mammolito's testimony. Sufficiency of the evidence excluding the discredited testimony, however, is not the correct test for determining *Brady* prejudice. *See Kyles*, 514 U.S. at 434-35, 115 S.Ct. 1555 ("A defendant need not demonstrate that after discounting the inculpatory evidence in light of the undisclosed evidence, there would not have been enough left to convict."). Regardless of the other evidence at trial, Engel successfully has demonstrated *Brady* prejudice by showing that undisclosed evidence puts his case in a "different light" and "undermine[s] confidence in the verdict." *See id.* at 434, 115 S.Ct. 1555. While exploration of Engel's *Brady* claim as to Dugan is not necessary, it is worth noting that Engel also has shown new impeachment evidence not available to him at trial evidencing that Agent Buchan induced Dugan to provide false testimony and that Dugan was compensated directly by the FBI for her trial-related travel expenses.

Example Opinion #2—Woodworth v. Denney

SUPREME COURT OF MISSOURI
en banc

STATE EX REL. MARK WOODWORTH,　　)
　　　　　　　　　　　　　　　　　　　　)
　　　　　　　Petitioner,　　　　　　　　)
　　　　　　　　　　　　　　　　　　　　)
vs.　　　　　　　　　　　　　　　　　　) No. SC91021
　　　　　　　　　　　　　　　　　　　　)
LARRY DENNEY, WARDEN,　　　　　　　)
　　　　　　　　　　　　　　　　　　　　)
　　　　　　　Respondent.　　　　　　　)

ORIGINAL PROCEEDING IN HABEAS CORPUS

Mark Woodworth was convicted of murder, assault, burglary and armed criminal action for the killing of Catherine Robertson and the serious assault of her husband, Lyndel Robertson. Mark[1] has now filed a petition for writ of habeas corpus, petitioning this Court to vacate his convictions and grant him a new trial because newly discovered evidence shows that the State violated *Brady v. Maryland, 373 U.S. 83 (1963),* by withholding material, favorable evidence and further shows that that the lack of disclosure of this *Brady* material was prejudicial and resulted in a verdict not worthy of confidence.

This Court appointed a special master under Rule 68.03 to take evidence and issue

---

[1] To avoid confusing Mark with his father Claude Woodworth, Mark and Claude will be referred to by their first names.

findings of fact and conclusions of law as to the allegations Mark made. After hearing numerous days of testimony, the master issued a report in which he found that the State had violated *Brady* in at least two important and material respects and that the State's failure to produce this *Brady* material, particularly when considered in light of other newly discovered exculpatory evidence, was prejudicial because it bolstered a key defense theory that another person had committed the crime and that the prosecution had focused improperly on Mark to the exclusion of pursuing the person Mark contends is the real perpetrator.

The judge had the opportunity to view and determine the credibility of witnesses and this Court affords his findings and conclusions the weight and deference given to the findings and conclusions entered by trial courts in court-tried cases. Here, substantial evidence supports the master's findings that *Brady* was violated and that the violations were prejudicial. Accordingly, this Court orders that Mark's convictions be vacated and orders him discharged from the custody of the department of corrections unless the State elects to retry him.

I. FACTUAL AND PROCEDURAL BACKGROUND

The following facts were adduced either at the first and second trials of Mark Woodworth or at the special master's hearings.

On the evening of November 13, 1990, Lyndel and Catherine Robertson were shot while sleeping in their rural Livingston County home. Mrs. Robertson was shot twice and died before paramedics arrived at the scene. Mr. Robertson survived three shots to the face and one to the shoulder. Investigators found no signs of forced entry, and there

Example Opinion #2—Woodworth v. Denney (cont.)

was no immediate indication at the scene as to who might have been the shooter.[2] The police did not find a murder weapon.

Claude Woodworth and his family lived across the street from the Robertsons. Claude and Mr. Robertson were farming partners and shared equipment space in a machine shed on the Robertson property. The Woodworths had a son, Mark, then 16 years old, a quiet boy who struggled in school, was considered "slow," and who lived at home with his parents and six younger siblings.

Investigators discovered a fingerprint on a partially full box of .22-caliber long rifle bullets allegedly located by Deputy David Miller on top of a workbench in the shed shared by the Woodworths and the Robertsons, but the print did not match any known prints on file at the time.[3] Ballistics tests revealed that the bullet fragments recovered from Mr. and Mrs. Robertson had the same type of brass wash coating as the .22-caliber Remington bullets found in the machine shed. Investigators also learned that Claude Woodworth owned a .22-caliber Ruger pistol that he kept in his bedroom and that Mr. Robertson kept an identical Ruger pistol in his pickup truck. The investigators sent the two pistols and the bullet fragments to the Missouri State Highway Patrol crime laboratory for testing. The bullets were so damaged and distorted that it was impossible

---

[2] A more complete factual background of the shooting and subsequent investigation can be found in *State v. Woodworth*, 941 S.W.2d 679 (Mo. App. 1997).

[3] At the hearing before the master, a Linn County sheriff's deputy testified that Deputy Paul Frey told him that he, not Deputy Miller, had lifted the fingerprints from the box of bullets. Deputy Miller denied at both trials and Deputy Frey denied at the hearing before the master that this was the case, testifying that it was Deputy Miller who recovered the prints.

3

Example Opinion #2—Woodworth v. Denney (cont.)

to conclude whether either gun fired the rounds.

The investigation then lay fairly dormant until July 1992, more than 18 months after the murder. At the master's hearing, evidence was presented showing that, as the months passed by without any arrests, Mr. Robertson became frustrated by the lack of progress in the investigation and hired a private investigator to conduct a separate examination of the case. This investigator, Terry Diester, had a prior relationship with the chief deputy in charge of the Robertson investigation. Mr. Diester, though not a member of law enforcement, was provided unfettered access to the sheriff's files regarding the Robertson case.

In private conversations with the chief deputy, Mr. Diester suggested that Claude Woodworth's son Mark should be a prime suspect in the case due to his familiarity with and proximity to the Robertson home and machine shed. Shortly thereafter, the sheriff's office brought Mark in for questioning. Mark denied any involvement in the shooting and agreed to provide his fingerprints. A thumbprint lifted from the .22-caliber shell-casing box on the workbench in the shed shared by the Robertsons and the Woodworths was found to match Mark's thumbprint.

At that point, investigators obtained a search warrant to reexamine Claude's pistol and, shortly thereafter, obtained a bullet fragment that just had been removed from Mr. Robertson's liver. Ballistics experts tested this fragment, as well as the fragments recovered from Mr. and Mrs. Robertson shortly after the shooting, and compared the fragments to the bullets found in the shed and to bullets test-fired from Claude's pistol. The experts found some similarities between the bullets test-fired from that pistol and the

4

Example Opinion #2—Woodworth v. Denney (cont.)

bullet fragments but concluded the evidence was insufficient to allow them to determine to a reasonable degree of certainty that the shooter used Claude's pistol to commit the crimes. Their tests did show, however, that his pistol was not excluded as the murder weapon, that three of the bullet fragments recovered from the Robertsons had individual characteristics that matched individual characteristics of bullets test-fired from Claude's pistol, and that one cartridge from the box of bullets the deputy said he found on the workbench had a mark consistent with a manufacturing defect that matched a similar manufacturing mark on the bullet fragment recovered from Mr. Robertson's liver.

Following the thumbprint match and the return of the ballistics tests that could not exclude the Woodworth gun as the murder weapon, Mr. Robertson began to lobby the Livingston County prosecutor to charge Mark with the Robertson crimes. He also presented the prosecutor with written reports that detailed the evidence Mr. Diester had compiled against Mark. When the prosecutor did not act on the evidence within the next two months, Mr. Robertson asked the circuit judge, Kenneth Lewis, to present the evidence against Mark to a grand jury. Judge Lewis did just that, stating later that Mr. Robertson's requests were what motivated him to convene a grand jury one month after Mr. Robertson's request and to appoint the attorney general's office to represent the State in the matter rather than the regular prosecutor, who withdrew when he learned that the judge and Mr. Robertson were insisting he proceed against Mark.

On October 29, 1993, nearly three years after the shooting, Mark was charged by indictment with second-degree murder of Catherine Robertson, first-degree burglary and first-degree assault of Lyndel Robertson, and two counts of armed criminal action.

Example Opinion #2—Woodworth v. Denney (cont.)

Although Mark was only 16 years old at the time of the shooting, the juvenile division certified Mark for trial as an adult based on the violent nature of the crimes and the fact that Mark was by that time 19 years old.

At trial, the evidence against Mark was entirely circumstantial. In addition to the matching thumbprint on the box of bullets and the bullet fragment evidence, investigators said Mark gave them conflicting information about how many times he had been in the shed, how often he shot his father's pistol and his feelings towards Mr. Robertson. Mark testified in his defense. He denied any involvement in the shooting and explained that his print may well have been on the ammunition box found in the shed shared by his family and the Robertsons because he and other farm employees used to target shoot using bullets from .22-caliber ammunition boxes in Mr. Robertson's truck. He also attempted to introduce evidence showing that another young man, Brandon Thomure, had motive and opportunity to commit the crime.

Mr. Thomure was the former boyfriend of the Robertsons' daughter, Rochelle.[4] The day after the shooting, police examined Mr. Thomure and found evidence of gunpowder residue on his hands. The police received reports that Mr. Thomure had abused Rochelle physically, that he impregnated Rochelle, that Rochelle terminated the pregnancy and that, not long before the shooting, Mr. and Mrs. Robertson offered to buy Rochelle a new car if she would break up with him. There was also evidence that while in the hospital Mr. Robertson told numerous people that it was "Brandon" who shot him

---

[4] For reasons that are not entirely clear, Mr. Thomure also goes by the name Brandon Hagan. For purposes of consistency, this Court will refer to him as Brandon Thomure.

CASE DISPOSITION AND APPELLATE REMEDIES

Example Opinion #2—Woodworth v. Denney (cont.)

or that he thought that it was "Brandon" who shot him. This made Mr. Thomure an early focus of investigation, but he claimed as an alibi that he was not in the area at the time of the shooting, and the police eventually stopped actively pursuing him as a suspect.

The trial court almost entirely excluded the evidence about Mr. Thomure and Rochelle and her family on the grounds that Mark could not show any direct evidence linking this young man with the crime. The jury only heard a single reference to Mr. Robertson's prior statement identifying Mr. Thomure. Mark, instead, based his defense on his belief that the evidence brought forth by the State against him was insufficient to establish guilt beyond a reasonable doubt.

The jury found Mark guilty on all counts, and he was sentenced to consecutive terms totaling 31 years. Mark appealed his convictions, arguing, among other things, that the prosecution failed to make a submissible case and that the trial court erred in excluding the evidence regarding Mr. Thomure.

In the first appeal, the appellate court held that the evidence was very "thin" yet minimally submissible. *State v. Woodworth, 941 S.W.2d 679, 690 (Mo. App. 1997)*. But the court agreed with Mark that trial court erred in excluding evidence pointing to Mr. Thomure as a suspect and held that in light of the weakness of the state's case, the exclusion of this evidence was prejudicial. The court noted that evidence of an alternative suspect is admissible so long as there is proof that the other person committed some act directly connecting him with the crime. *Id. at 690*. This standard was satisfied by the evidence that Mark had been precluded from introducing at trial, including statements by Mr. Robertson shortly after the attack accusing "Brandon" of being or

7

Example Opinion #2—Woodworth v. Denney (cont.)

probably being the shooter. The court said that this evidence should have been admitted both for purposes of impeaching Mr. Robertson and as direct evidence linking Mr. Thomure with the crime. *Id.* The court reversed and remanded for a new trial at which the defense could introduce evidence showing Mr. Thomure's opportunity and motive to commit the crimes. *Id. at 692.*

On remand, a jury again found Mr. Woodworth guilty on all counts. The trial judge, who presided over both trials, imposed four consecutive life sentences plus 15 additional consecutive years. The court of appeals affirmed. The trial and appellate courts denied post-conviction relief. The trial court and court of appeals subsequently denied Mark's petition for writ of habeas corpus under Rule 91.01.

Mark now seeks habeas relief in this Court, alleging serious violations of the State's duty under *Brady v. Maryland, 373 U.S. 83 (1963)*, to disclose potentially exculpatory evidence to the defense.

This Court issued a writ of habeas corpus and, on November 2, 2010, appointed Boone County Circuit Judge Gary M. Oxenhandler to serve as special master to take evidence and issue a master's report on the claims in the petition for writ. In particular, Mark alleges that he discovered through a reporter's investigation after the second trial that the State had failed to disclose a trio of letters (the "Lewis letters") involving an assistant attorney general, Judge Lewis – who originally had been assigned the case – and Mr. Robertson. He also alleges that the State did not disclose evidence that Rochelle Robertson reported to police several violations by Mr. Thomure of the ex parte order of protection she obtained against him after the murder of her mother. In addition, he alleges that the State concealed the testimony of two persons that discredited Mr. Thomure's alibi and so was material and favorable to his defense. Mark asserts that the State's failure to disclose this evidence violated *Brady* and that these violations, as well as substantial additional newly discovered evidence casting doubt on Mr. Thomure's alibi and on the sufficiency and impartiality of the sheriff's investigation, resulted in a "verdict not worthy of confidence."

The master conducted seven evidentiary hearings between November 2010 and November 2011 and filed his report with this Court on May 1, 2011. That report finds that the prosecution did violate its duty under *Brady* as alleged and that these violations resulted in prejudice to Mark of a degree that undermined the master's confidence in the verdict. The master strongly recommends to this Court that Mark's conviction be set aside and that the case be reviewed by an independent prosecutor before any decision is made as to retrial.

II. STANDARD OF REVIEW FOR MASTER'S REPORT

This Court affords the findings of fact, conclusions of law and recommendations made by a judge this Court has appointed as a master under Rule 68.03 the "weight and deference which would be given to a court-tried case by a reviewing court" in light of the master's unique ability to view and judge the credibility of witnesses. *State ex rel. Winfield v. Roper*, 292 S.W.3d 909, 910 (Mo. 2009). *Accord*, *State ex rel. Lyons v. Lombardi*, 303 S.W.3d 523 (Mo. banc 2010); *State ex rel. Busch by Whitson v. Busch*, 776 S.W.2d 374, 377 (Mo. banc 1989). As *Lyons* recently noted, in such cases, the master's findings and conclusions will be sustained by this Court unless there is no substantial evidence to support them. *Id. at 525-26*. This Court should exercise the power to set aside the findings and conclusions on the ground that they are against the weight of the evidence with caution and with a firm belief that the conclusions are wrong. *Id.*

III. STANDARD FOR HABEAS RELIEF

"Habeas corpus is the last judicial inquiry into the validity of a criminal conviction and serves as 'a bulwark against convictions that violate fundamental fairness.'" *State ex rel. Engel v. Dormire, 304 S.W.3d 120, 125 (Mo. banc 2010)* (quoting *State ex rel. Amrine v. Roper, 102 S.W.3d 541, 545 (Mo. banc 2003)*). It is the petitioner's burden to show that he or she is entitled to habeas corpus relief. *State ex rel. Nixon v. Jaynes, 73 S.W.3d 623, 624 (Mo. banc 2002)*. "[A] writ of habeas corpus may be issued when a person is restrained of his or her liberty in violation of the constitution or laws of the state or federal government." *Engel, 304 S.W.3d at 125*. Habeas review, however, is not meant to serve as a substitute for post-conviction relief claims cognizable on direct appeal or in Rule 29.15 motions. To avoid "duplicative and unending challenges to the finality of a judgment," habeas review of a challenge to the validity of a conviction requires that a petitioner show a jurisdictional defect, cause for failing to timely raise the ineffective assistance or other constitutional defect and prejudice resulting from the defect, or manifest injustice such as either a freestanding or a gateway claim of actual innocence. *Id.*; *Amrine v. Roper, 102 S.W.3d 541 (Mo. banc 2003)*.

Mark principally seeks to overcome the procedural bar to his habeas claims by showing "cause and prejudice." To demonstrate cause, the petitioner must show that an

Example Opinion #2—Woodworth v. Denney (cont.)

effort to comply with the State's procedural rules was hindered by some objective factor external to the defense. *Id. at 126.* In other words, "a showing that the factual or legal basis for a claim was not reasonably available to counsel, or that some interference by officials made compliance impracticable." *Murray v. Carrier, 477 U.S. 478, 488 (1986)* (citation omitted).[5]

Here, Mark alleges that the cause of the failure to raise this issue earlier was the State's failure to produce the exculpatory evidence on which he now relies in response to Mark's discovery requests prior to both trials for all exculpatory evidence and witness statements. Such a failure to disclose exculpatory evidence, if shown, constitutes adequate cause for failure to earlier raise the error. *See State ex rel. Griffin v. Denney, 347 S.W.3d 73, 77 (Mo. banc 2011)* (State's failure to disclose evidence that an inmate other than the defendant possessed a weapon at the time of victim's murder in jail yard constituted "cause" to overcome objection that defendant did not raise the issue at trial).

To establish "prejudice," Mark alleges that the State's failure to disclose

---

[5] Mark also argues that the additional evidence he now has discovered, some of it in regard to the alleged *Brady* violations and some of which is otherwise newly discovered evidence, shows by clear and convincing evidence that he is actually innocent. He is correct that a freestanding claim of actual innocence, if shown by a clear and convincing evidence, provides grounds for habeas relief without the need to prove any constitutional violation at trial, as is required under the "cause and prejudice" standard. *State ex rel. Amrine v. Roper, 102 S.W.3d 541 (Mo. banc 2003).* Alternatively, a showing of actual innocence by a preponderance of the evidence can substitute for "cause and prejudice," providing a "gateway" that entitles a habeas petitioner to review on the merits of the petitioner's otherwise defaulted constititutional claim. *Id. at 546.* Here, the master did not reach the claim of actual innocence, as he found cause and prejudice based on the *Brady* claims and had considered the newly discovered actual innocence evidence in regard to the prejudice prong of that claim, as discussed below. This Court does likewise.

Example Opinion #2—Woodworth v. Denney (cont.)

exculpatory information known to it undermined confidence in the verdict. The determination whether a constitutional violation is prejudicial under the cause and prejudice standard is identical to this Court's assessment of prejudice undertaken in assessing Mark's *Brady* claims. *Engel, 304 S.W.3d at 126*. This Court turns, therefore, to the *Brady* issue.

IV. BRADY VIOLATION ANALYSIS

To prevail in his *Brady* claims, Mark must satisfy three components: (1) The evidence at issue must be favorable to him, either because it is exculpatory or because it is impeaching of an adverse witness; (2) that evidence must have been suppressed by the State, whether willfully or inadvertently; and (3) he must have been prejudiced. *Strickler v. Greene, 527 U.S. 263, 281–82 (1999); Engel, 304 S.W.3d at 126*.

In determining prejudice, the United States Supreme Court has stated: "A showing of materiality does not require demonstration by a preponderance that disclosure of the suppressed evidence would have resulted ultimately in the defendant's acquittal." *Kyles v. Whitley, 514 U.S. 419, 434 (1995)*. Rather, to be entitled to a new trial under the *Brady* standard, a defendant must show "a 'reasonable probability' of a different result," *id.*, which means:

> The question is not whether the defendant would more likely than not have received a different verdict with the evidence, but whether in its absence he received a fair trial, understood as a trial resulting in a verdict worthy of confidence. A reasonable probability of a different result is accordingly shown when the government's evidentiary suppression undermines confidence in the outcome of the trial.

Id. (internal quotations omitted). *Accord, Griffin, 347 S.W.3d at 77*.

12

Example Opinion #2—Woodworth v. Denney (cont.)

The master found that both the Lewis letters and the police reports of the violations by Brandon Thomure of Rochelle Robertson's ex parte order of protection constituted evidence favorable to Mark, which should have been but was not produced by the State, and that suppression of it by the State, even if inadvertent, was prejudicial to the defense. The master also found substantial evidence to support Mark's allegation that the State suppressed testimony of two other persons who said they provided material and exculpatory evidence concerning Mr. Thomure to sheriff's deputies shortly after the shootings that, if accepted, cast considerable doubt on Mr. Thomure's alibi. The master did not address whether the failure to produce this additional testimony was a *Brady* violation but did set it out as matters he considered that supported his conclusion that Mark's verdict is not worthy of confidence. "When reviewing a habeas petition premised on an alleged *Brady* violation, this Court considers all available evidence uncovered following the trial." *Griffin, 347 S.W.3d at 77*. For the reasons discussed below, this Court concludes that the master's *Brady* violation findings are supported by substantial evidence and are not against the weight of the evidence.

A. Lewis Letters

Mark asserts that the State violated his due process rights pursuant to *Brady* when it failed to disclose the "Lewis letters" to the defense prior to his first and second trials. For Mark to prevail in his *Brady* claim that the Lewis letters were wrongly not disclosed to him, he was required to show that the Lewis letters constituted evidence favorable to him, that they were not revealed, and that their suppression was prejudicial. Mark presented evidence that the letters were not produced, were material exculpatory

13

Example Opinion #2—*Woodworth v. Denney (cont.)*

evidence, and their lack of production was prejudicial. The State presented evidence that it believed it gave Mark's defense attorneys access to the letters because the prosecutors had a policy of opening their file to the defense, that the letters do not contain material or exculpatory evidence, and that their lack of production, therefore, was not prejudicial. As set out below, after extensive hearings the master credited Mark's evidence that Mark's attorneys did not receive the letters prior to either trial and concluded that the letters were relevant impeachment evidence and that the State's failure to disclose them was "highly prejudicial" to Mark.

The Lewis letters are a series of letters exchanged between the original trial judge, Judge Kenneth Lewis; Kenny Hulshof, then a Missouri assistant attorney general appointed as special prosecutor; and one of the victims, Mr. Robertson. These letters were brought to the defense's attention by a reporter in 2009 following a review of the State's files long after the conclusion of the second trial.

Judge Lewis, a longtime resident of Livingston County, was the trial judge originally assigned to try Mark's case. He presided over many of the initial proceedings, called the grand jury that indicted Mark, and presided over the juvenile hearing that certified Mark as an adult. In a letter dated September 24, 1993 (Lewis letter #1), Mr. Robertson wrote Judge Lewis expressing frustration with Livingston County prosecuting attorney Douglas Roberts' handling of the "case" against Mark. His letter said he felt that the prosecutor was "not giving this case his full attention," and he pleaded with Judge Lewis to remove Mr. Roberts so that the case could be brought before a grand jury.

14

Example Opinion #2—Woodworth v. Denney (cont.)

When he learned of the letter, Mr. Roberts responded that he believed that "lack of enthusiasm" for a case was not sufficient grounds for disqualification, but in light of the case's importance to the community, he wrote to Judge Lewis on October 4 (Lewis letter #2), requesting that the judge appoint the attorney general's office to represent the State. The judge sought and obtained Mr. Hulshof's appointment as a special prosecutor in lieu of Mr. Roberts to prosecute Mark. In an October 7 letter addressed specifically to Mr. Hulshof (Lewis letter #3), Judge Lewis thanked the attorney general's office for agreeing to take on the case. In that letter, Judge Lewis enclosed a copy of Lewis letter #1 and stated that it was this letter that had "prompted [him] to bring about a grand jury inquiry."[6]

Testifying at one of the hearings before the master, Mr. Hulshof acknowledged that the Lewis letters were discovery materials that should have been disclosed. He also stated that he used a "Bates stamp" when providing discovery materials in a criminal case. The Bates stamp is used to number each page in sequence so that all disclosed materials can be tracked accurately. Mr. Hulshof agreed that none of the three Lewis letters was Bates-stamped and had not been produced in formal discovery.

The prosecutor for Mark's second trial, Rachel Smith, who was then an assistant

---

[6] Although Mr. Roberts had disqualified himself as prosecutor three days prior to the day the grand jury convened, Judge Lewis for unknown reasons also wrote: "To say that [Prosecutor] Roberts has been uncooperative would be a monumental understatement. He boycotted the grand jury proceedings this morning, which is simply unheard-of in my experience." The master's report describes evidence of Judge Lewis and Mr. Roberts being involved in a "quarrel" and "rift," but the report does not give further explanation of the origin of the problems between the two men.

Example Opinion #2—Woodworth v. Denney (cont.)

attorney general, also testified before the master. She admitted that she had prepared an inventory of prosecution file materials in response to a discovery request and that her inventory made no mention of the Lewis letters. She stated that she nonetheless believed that the letters had been made available to defense counsel when she had offered the defense the opportunity to look through that same prosecution file. But, on further questioning, she admitted to excluding documents from the files that she thought would be covered by attorney work product privilege. She also explained that although she assumed the Lewis letters were in the boxes of files that she allowed defense counsel to review – despite the fact that they were not in her inventory of the contents of the boxes and were not Bates-stamped – she could not recall whether defense counsel in fact found the Lewis letters during their review of the State's files.

Mark called his primary trial defense attorneys to testify before the master. They and the defense investigator testified that they did not learn about the Lewis letters or their contents until they were publicized by the news reporter, which did not occur until during the habeas proceeding investigation, well after both trials. Judge Lewis testified that he believed he had given the letters to Mark's juvenile certification proceeding attorney, Richard McFadin, although there was no written record of his so doing. The master found Judge Lewis' recollection regarding the letters was not accurate.

The master found that Mark had met all three elements of his *Brady* claim by showing that the Lewis letters were wrongly not disclosed to him; that they were material favorable impeachment evidence; and that their suppression, while not intentional, was prejudicial. This Court will defer to Judge Oxenhandler's findings as master as it would

Example Opinion #2—Woodworth v. Denney (cont.)

findings issued in a court-tried case, for in both instances he has the ability to view and judge the credibility of the witnesses. *Lyons*, 303 S.W.3d at 526; Winfield, 292 S.W.3d at 910.

(1) Failure to Produce Brady *Material.*

As noted, the master found that the State failed to produce the Lewis letters. In support, weighing all of the evidence, the master found that the letters were not made available to the defense. In so finding he noted the lack of a Bates stamp traditionally used by Mr. Hulshof to track disclosed material and the failure of Prosecutor Smith to list the letters in the inventory of the contents of the State's file that she made available for defense counsel's review. He did not credit Judge Lewis' testimony that the letters had been made available to defense counsel McFadin at the juvenile hearing, as there was no docket letter or cover letter memorializing such a delivery. The master also was not persuaded by Prosecutor Smith's testimony that the letters must have been in the file at the time defense counsel reviewed the non-privileged material in the file in 1999 prior to the second trial because they were in the file when she reviewed it prior to the special master's hearing.[7]

---

[7] As the State notes, *Williams v. State, 168 S.W.3d 433 (Mo. banc 2005),* recognizes that the State can meet its *Brady* obligation when it has produced its file to the defense in response to a request for particular records, so that the defense can view them. And, *Williams* and *State v. Salter, 250 S.W.3d 705 (Mo. banc 2008)*, recognize that *Brady* is not violated if defendant already was aware of the information that he says the State failed to disclose or if the information was not material. Here, however, the master noted that the Lewis letters were not Bates-stamped or included in the inventory of the records that were opened to defense counsel for inspection and that defense counsel was not aware of the Lewis letters prior to the discovery of the letters by the reporter during the habeas proceeding.

17

Example Opinion #2—Woodworth v. Denney (cont.)

The master did not find that the failure was willful, but under *Brady* it is irrelevant whether the failure to produce exculpatory evidence occurred willfully or inadvertently; if the evidence potentially is exculpatory, it must produced. *Engel, 304 S.W.3d at 126.*

The State says that this Court should set aside the master's finding that the prosecution did not produce this evidence. It admits that there is no written evidence that the defense had the letters, and that multiple defense counsel testified that they did not have the letters, and that this Court will defer to the special master's determination of credibility and will adopt the master's findings if supported by substantial evidence. *Lyon, 303 S.W.3d at 525-526.* But the State says this Court nonetheless should reject the special master's finding because the defense could have offered even more proof to support its claim by (1) offering to open their defense file to the prosecution and by (2) calling Mark's initial defense counsel, Mr. McFadin.

The State admits it has no authority for the extraordinary proposition that a *Brady* claimant must open his entire defense file to the State, waiving any privileged materials that might be contained therein, so that the State apparently can check the credibility of defense counsel's testimony that certain documents were not produced and are not a part of the defense file. Certainly this Court is aware of no case so holding. A duty to let the State see all defense evidence to bring a habeas action simply does not exist.

Similarly, Mark was not required to call every one of his defense counsel to claim that they had not seen the letters until the letters were discovered by a reporter long after Mark's trials. Of course, the master was free to consider the fact that Mr. McFadin was not called in determining the credibility of the evidence presented by Mark and by the

18

CASE DISPOSITION AND APPELLATE REMEDIES

Example Opinion #2—Woodworth v. Denney (cont.)

State, and the report shows that he did so. The master did not find the State's argument based on a failure to open the entire defense file persuasive, however, nor did he find the failure to call Mr. McFadin undermined the credibility of those witnesses who were called and testified that the letters were not in the defense file.

This Court defers to the master's determinations of credibility. The master found Mark's witnesses, and the lack of record evidence of production of the Lewis letters, more persuasive. His conclusion is supported by substantial evidence and is not against the weight of the evidence.[8] This Court adopts his findings as to this prong of *Brady*.

(2) Evidence Favorable to the Defense.

The master also found that Mark had presented substantial evidence that the Lewis letters were persuasive impeachment evidence that was favorable to the defense. The master believed the letters to be favorable to Mark because they diminished Mr. Robertson's credibility. In Lewis letter #2, Mr. Roberts indicated that Mr. Robertson at one point had been adamant that Mr. Thomure be charged for the shooting crimes. Yet in Lewis letter #3, Mr. Robertson declared to Judge Lewis that justice would not be served until the judge brought the evidence against Mark before a grand jury. These conflicting statements, in the master's opinion, would have aided in Mark's attempts at trial to impeach Mr. Robertson's credibility.

---

[8] The master did not reach the conclusion that the State intentionally concealed the letters. However, "the suppression by the prosecution of evidence favorable to an accused upon request violates due process … *irrespective of the good faith or bad faith of the prosecution.*" *Brady v. Maryland, 373 U.S. 83, 87 (1963)* (emphasis added).

19

Example Opinion #2—Woodworth v. Denney (cont.)

(3) Prejudice from Non-Disclosure.

Mark also argues that his defense was prejudiced by the State's failure to disclose the letters. In determining prejudice, as noted:

> The question is not whether the defendant would more likely than not have received a different verdict with the evidence, but whether in its absence he received a fair trial, understood as a trial resulting in a verdict worthy of confidence. A reasonable probability of a different result is accordingly shown when the government's evidentiary suppression "undermines confidence in the outcome of the trial."

Kyles, 514 U.S. at 534 (internal quotations omitted).

The master determined that during both trials without the use of the Lewis letters Mark's attempts to impeach key prosecution witnesses, such as Mr. Robertson and police investigators, "were deprived of substantial evidentiary force." Had Mark been in possession of these letters at trial, they would have bolstered his attempts to impeach key prosecution witnesses such as Mr. Robertson, would have assisted the defense in demonstrating that the State's investigation was not impartial and would have shown that the investigation improperly focused on him rather than on Mr. Thomure once Mr. Robertson put pressure on Judge Lewis.

In support of his finding of prejudice, the master further pointed to evidence contained in the Lewis letters that would have impeached the credibility of Mr. Robertson's testimony at both trials that he did not remember telling doctors and police officers that it was Brandon who shot him and to a deposition prior to the first trial in which Mr. Robertson claimed that he never had "pointed [his] finger at anybody" as

Example Opinion #2—Woodworth v. Denney (cont.)

being the shooter. The master believed the letters supported the defense claim that it was the persistence of Mr. Robertson and not a fair, thorough review of the case that "prompted" Judge Lewis to call the grand jury. This would have provided important support for the defense's argument that the investigation of Mark was one-sided and highlighted that the evidence against him was weak and circumstantial. This detriment, the master determined, prejudiced Mark because the circumstantial evidence was so slim that "the slightest bit of evidence eroding the force of the State's witnesses or bolstering the weight of the defense witnesses may have tipped the scales in favor of [Mark]."

The master concluded that the State's failure to disclose the Lewis letters was itself a sufficient showing of prejudice to entitle Mark to a new trial and recommends that this Court so hold considered alone or in combination with the *Brady* violation and additional evidence discussed below.

B. *Ex Parte Order of Protection*

The master found a second *Brady* violation stemmed from the State's failure to disclose Rochelle Robertson's reports to police of violations of an ex parte order of protection obtained by her against her ex-boyfriend, Brandon Thomure. Rochelle obtained the order in December 1990, the month after the murder, because Mr. Thomure had "tried to get a hold of [her] continuously after [her mother Catherine Robertson] died." The order required that Mr. Thomure not "abuse, threaten to abuse, molest or disturb the peace [of] Rochelle" or enter upon her apartment property.

(1) Failure to Produce Brady *Material.*

Only after both trials, during a deposition taken as part of discovery in this habeas

CASE DISPOSITION AND APPELLATE REMEDIES

Example Opinion #2—Woodworth v. Denney (cont.)

proceeding, did a Livingston County deputy reveal that Rochelle had made two complaints to police that Mr. Thomure violated the order of protection. Following the officer's testimony and pursuant to the master's order, the defense obtained files from the Livingston County circuit clerk that confirmed that Rochelle had reported to police after the murder, and long before Mark's trials, that Mr. Thomure had violated her order of protection against him.

The files revealed that in November 1991 Rochelle called the sheriff's office after she received two telephone calls from friends of Mr. Thomure. The callers asked if Rochelle would speak to him; she denied the request on both occasions. The office filed a case report detailing the order of protection violation. In May 1991, the sheriff's office filed a second offense report after Mr. Thomure went to Rochelle's place of work and accosted her for hanging up on him when he called, stating "he stated that he would get even with her new boyfriend … If he couldn't handle it, he would have some of his friends handle the job."

The now-sheriff of Livingston County testified that the reports should have been included in the Robertson shooting file because the violation complaints involved one of the prime suspects in the Robertson shooting. The State did not refute the sheriff's statement, and the master concluded that these reports fell within the scope of requested

22

CASE DISPOSITION AND APPELLATE REMEDIES

Example Opinion #2—Woodworth v. Denney (cont.)

discovery material.[9] The master found that the lack of a Bates stamp and lack of these items on Ms. Smith's inventory of discovery materials confirmed the sheriff's statement that these materials were not placed in the prosecution file and not produced to the defense.

(2) Evidence was Favorable to the Defense.

The master found that the violation reports were favorable to the defense because they could have been used by Mark to strengthen his argument that Mr. Thomure had motive and opportunity to commit the shooting and that they would have served to rebut the State's claim that Mr. Thomure had never threatened harm against Rochelle. The master also determined that Rochelle's failure to disclose the reports indicated her intent to protect Mr. Thomure from prosecution. The content of the reports provides substantial evidence to support the master's conclusion that the reports of the order of protection violations are favorable to Mark's defense.

(3) Prejudice from Nondisclosure.

Lastly, Mark must prove that that he was prejudiced by the nondisclosure. The State argues that, while Mark was not told of and did not know of the complaints to

---

[9] "It is no hindrance to ... [a] Brady claim that the prosecutor did not have the same knowledge about his case as the investigators. The prosecutor's lack of knowledge ... is not an impediment because the prosecutor is considered 'the representative ... of a sovereignty whose obligation to govern impartially is as compelling as its obligation to govern at all.'" *State ex rel. Engel v. Dormire, 304 S.W.3d 120, 127 (Mo. banc 2010)* (quoting *Strickler v. Greene, 527 U.S. 263, 281 (1999)*). *Brady* provides that "the individual prosecutor has a duty to learn of any favorable evidence known to the others acting on the government's behalf in the case, *including the police*." *Engel, 304 S.W.3d at 127* (quoting *Kyles, 514 U.S. at 437*) (emphasis added).

23

Example Opinion #2—Woodworth v. Denney (cont.)

police, he knew of the violations because Rochelle had testified to them at her deposition in 1994 and any failure to inform him of complaints to police could not have been prejudicial. The master rejected this argument, for it misses the issues on which a defendant would have used this evidence.

At her 1994 deposition, Rochelle testified that Mr. Thomure had called her in violation of the protective order, but she said that he never had made any threats and that she did not report the calls to police. She left the impression that the calls were unimportant and were not disturbing to her. This undercut the defense's ability to refute the State's evidence that Mr. Thomure never had threatened the Robertson family. The new evidence that indicated Rochelle in fact had reported Mr. Thomure's harassment to the police – harassment that threatened bodily harm – directly contradicted her 1994 deposition statements and supported the defense argument that Mr. Thomure had the motive to commit the shooting.

The master noted that the defense could argue that Rochelle's lack of candor about reporting the order of protection violations calls into question her overall credibility and raises critical questions regarding her willingness to shield Mr. Thomure, which the jury should have had a chance to consider. Lack of knowledge of the threats made by Mr. Thomure to Rochelle at her work, which indicate Mr. Thomure's willingness to resort to violence, prejudiced Mark's efforts to show that Mr. Thomure was a viable alternative perpetrator and that his willingness to commit violence against those who came between him and Rochelle – as Mr. and Mrs. Robertson had tried to do shortly before the murder – went so deep it even survived Rochelle's mother's murder.

24

Example Opinion #2—Woodworth v. Denney (cont.)

The master considered the prejudice caused by the failure to reveal this important evidence in light of what he, and the appellate court on the first appeal, noted to be a very thin and totally circumstantial case. Given the weakness of the case, the master concluded that the information about Rochelle's lies as to her complaints about violations of the ex parte order of protection may have tipped the scales in Mark's favor and the failure to disclose this evidence resulted in prejudice. Substantial evidence supports the master's determination of prejudice.

The master found this was itself a sufficient showing of prejudice to entitle Mark to a new trial and recommends that this Court so hold considered alone or in combination with the *Brady* violation discussed above and the additional evidence discussed below.

C. Additional Witness Testimony to Be Considered in Determining Prejudice

Some of the additional evidence considered by the master involved alleged additional *Brady* violations, but the master did not find it necessary to consider whether they reached that level in light of his finding of the two *Brady* violations just discussed. He nonetheless found them relevant to his determination whether the verdict in the second trial was worthy of confidence and found that it was not.

This Court need not determine whether it agrees that each *Brady* violation considered in isolation had a sufficiently prejudicial effect to entitle Mark to a new trial, for in *Griffin,* this Court noted that in deciding whether the prejudice shown by *Brady* violations is sufficient to determine that the prior verdict is not "worthy of confidence," the courts should consider the effect of all of the suppressed evidence along with the totality of the other evidence uncovered following the prior trial. *Griffin, 347 S.W.3d at*

25

Example Opinion #2—Woodworth v. Denney (cont.)

77. This Court, therefore, will consider the effect of the failure to disclose the Lewis letters along with the failure to disclose the police reports of Mr. Thomure's violations of the ex parte order of protection, both of which are *Brady* violations for the reasons found by the master, as well as the effect of the other pieces of recently discovered evidence considered by the master, in determining whether the prior verdict is no longer "worthy of confidence." *Id*.

The master found that, as might be expected in a small town, the habeas corpus proceeding created a great deal of publicity in Chillicothe, and a number of residents came forward with what they claimed to be direct knowledge of facts and circumstances regarding the shooting. Among those persons was June Cairns. Ms. Cairns testified at the hearing before the master that the morning after the shooting, she saw Mr. Thomure in her home visiting her son. Ms. Cairns found this odd because it was around 6:30 a.m. to 7:30 a.m., much earlier than when Mr. Thomure usually came to visit. If Mr. Thomure was indeed in Chillicothe at this time, it would contradict his trial testimony that he was nearly two hours away in Independence, Missouri, at the time of the Chillicothe murder.

Ms. Cairns stated that she reported this sighting of Mr. Thomure to the sheriff's office shortly after learning of the Robertson shooting. Ms. Cairns says she also recounted to the sheriff a telephone call that Mr. Thomure made from her home about two weeks prior to the shooting in which she heard him threaten to slit the listener's throat. Ms. Cairns presumed from the portion of the conversation that she overheard that the person on the other end of the line was the victim, Catherine Robertson, but she could not say for sure.

26

Example Opinion #2—Woodworth v. Denney (cont.)

The sheriff's report mentions only that Ms. Cairn's son stated he saw Mr. Thomure in Chillicothe the *afternoon* after the shooting. It did not mention her alleged report that she saw him in Chillicothe the morning after the shooting and it did not mention the telephone threat she heard Mr. Thomure make. No report of her statements is in the file. The defense was unaware of her evidence until this habeas proceeding, as apparently was the prosecution.

Another witness who came forward during the habeas proceeding was Connie Grell. Ms. Grell testified at the hearing that Rochelle had visited her hair salon approximately two weeks before the shooting. At that time, Ms. Grell says, Rochelle stated that there "was a lot of hate between her parents and [Mr. Thomure]" and that Mr. Thomure "wished they were dead or could kill them." Ms. Grell says she reported this statement to the sheriff after the shooting. Again, no report of her statement is contained in the sheriff's file, and none was turned over to the defense or prosecution.

Mark argues that these previously unreported statements constitute additional *Brady* violations by the State. Clearly they were exculpatory and greatly support the defense's theory that Mr. Thomure, not Mark, was involved in the shooting. Their failure to be disclosed would be a serious *Brady* violation and prejudicial in and of itself if known by an agent of the State such as a sheriff's deputy. *Engel, 304 S.W.3d at 127.*

The State claims, however, that these statements were not suppressed because the witnesses now are lying about what they told sheriff's deputies at the time of the murder. If not told to investigators and, therefore, not in the possession of an agent of the state, then, of course, the State would not have failed to reveal this evidence. The master

Example Opinion #2—Woodworth v. Denney (cont.)

detailed these witness statements in his report, but he made no determination as to whether the witnesses accurately recount now what they told sheriff's deputies at the time. Whether or not they constituted *Brady* violations, he found he could consider these witness statements as a part of the "totality of the circumstances" he reviewed to determine whether Mark had shown sufficient prejudice to be entitled to habeas relief.

The master additionally considered substantial other newly discovered evidence, including the testimony of numerous individuals who made statements regarding the case that either were not known at the time of the trials or were not properly recorded by the sheriff's office. For instance, a friend of Mr. Thomure testified that in 2007 Mr. Thomure threatened to kill him, stating that he "got away with one murder, what makes you think I can't do it again?" Another individual stated that he had seen Mr. Thomure at a Chillicothe bowling alley on the night of the shooting, contrary to Mr. Thomure's alibi.

Also contradicting Mr. Thomure's alibi was the former Chillicothe High School assistant principal who testified that he ran Mr. Thomure out of the school in Chillicothe the morning of the shooting. A high school student and Robertson neighbor supported the principal's sighting of Mr. Thomure at the school when she testified that Mr. Thomure pulled her out of class the morning after the shooting to ask whether she had seen anything at the time of the crimes.

None of this evidence was heard by the jury in either trial. The master found such evidence is very relevant to the question whether Mark is not guilty of the crime for which he was convicted. Clearly, if believed, this evidence would combine with the

28

CASE DISPOSITION AND APPELLATE REMEDIES

Example Opinion #2—Woodworth v. Denney (cont.)

detailed these witness statements in his report, but he made no determination as to whether the witnesses accurately recount now what they told sheriff's deputies at the time. Whether or not they constituted *Brady* violations, he found he could consider these witness statements as a part of the "totality of the circumstances" he reviewed to determine whether Mark had shown sufficient prejudice to be entitled to habeas relief.

The master additionally considered substantial other newly discovered evidence, including the testimony of numerous individuals who made statements regarding the case that either were not known at the time of the trials or were not properly recorded by the sheriff's office. For instance, a friend of Mr. Thomure testified that in 2007 Mr. Thomure threatened to kill him, stating that he "got away with one murder, what makes you think I can't do it again?" Another individual stated that he had seen Mr. Thomure at a Chillicothe bowling alley on the night of the shooting, contrary to Mr. Thomure's alibi.

Also contradicting Mr. Thomure's alibi was the former Chillicothe High School assistant principal who testified that he ran Mr. Thomure out of the school in Chillicothe the morning of the shooting. A high school student and Robertson neighbor supported the principal's sighting of Mr. Thomure at the school when she testified that Mr. Thomure pulled her out of class the morning after the shooting to ask whether she had seen anything at the time of the crimes.

None of this evidence was heard by the jury in either trial. The master found such evidence is very relevant to the question whether Mark is not guilty of the crime for which he was convicted. Clearly, if believed, this evidence would combine with the

Example Opinion #2—Woodworth v. Denney (cont.)

evidence presented at the second trial and with the *Brady* evidence discussed above to cast doubt on Mr. Thomure's alibi and on the thoroughness and lack of bias of the investigation. It would be up to the jury, of course, in any new trial to determine the reliability of these witness' memories, the propriety of the sheriff's deputies' actions, and the relevance of Mr. Thomure's alleged lies about his alibi in light of the multiple sightings of him in Chillicothe the morning of the murder.

In addition, the master expressed great upset and shock as to the extent of control that a private investigator, Mr. Diester, was permitted to exert over the investigation of the attack on the Robertsons. The master found that Mr. Diester, whom he specifically found not to be credible, "was clandestinely given access to the Sheriff's investigative file [including the Woodworth pistol and the bullet fragments][10] ... and, along with the Sheriff's deputies, disclosed and deep-sixed witness testimony as deemed necessary to keep tune with the theme of the investigation: [Mark] Woodworth did it." The master found that these actions constituted serious investigative misconduct and that "over time Diester morphed into the role of prosecutor," dismissing other leads and ensuring that Mark was charged with the crimes. The master found that this bias in the conduct of the investigation undermined the verdict and further supported his conclusion that the verdict

---

[10] The master did not reach Mark's additional claims that it first came to his attention only in the habeas proceeding that in addition to the sheriff's file, the sheriff's office also gave Mr. Diester control of the Woodworth pistol as well as the bullet fragments recovered from Mr. and Mrs. Robertson. The state admits that Mr. Diester had possession of the gun and bullet fragments but disputes whether this information was known earlier and says in any event chain of custody of these items was stipulated. The master did not address this issue and, as the stipulation issue presumably will not recur in any future retrial, there is no need for this Court to do so either.

29

Example Opinion #2—Woodworth v. Denney (cont.)

did not result in a "verdict worthy of confidence."

The master considered that this suppressed evidence along with the totality of the other evidence uncovered following Mark's last trial showed cause and prejudice and showed a violation of *Brady* that caused sufficient prejudice to undermine confidence in the outcome of the second trial and render the prior verdict no longer worthy of confidence. This determination is supported by substantial evidence, is not against the weight of the evidence, and does not erroneously declare or apply the law. This Court, therefore, adopts the master's recommendation and orders that Mark's convictions be vacated. The state has indicated an intent to retry Mark; therefore, on the date the mandate issues in this case, Mark shall be returned to the custody of the sheriff of Livingston County and be entitled to such release as the circuit court shall determine pursuant to Rule 33.

LAURA DENVIR STITH, JUDGE

Teitelman, C.J., Russell, Breckenridge, Fischer
and Draper, JJ., concur. Wilson, J., not participating.

31

ACKNOWLEDGMENTS

First, I want to thank Kristin Summers, my publisher at Redbat Books, for all the many talents she used to make this book a reality.

I want to thank my mother, Barbara Brister, for her continued support throughout the frustrating months when I wasn't able to get much writing done. Nonetheless, I drudged on and finished it.

I want to thank my cellmate, Ronnie Bolanos, for enduring countless hours of rat-a-tat-tat from my weapon of choice—my typewriter. (The pen is mightier than the sword.)

I want to give a special thanks to Frederick Thornton for letting me sift through his case file for examples to use in this book.

I also want to thank Sean O'Brien, Kent Gipson, and Robert Ramsey for being excellent. Each one of these attorneys inspired me to write this book in the hope that it will be an invaluable tool for those fighting day and night for their freedom.

APPENDIX

Alabama............300	Montana............425
Alaska............305	Nebraska............428
Arizona............308	Nevada............432
Arkansas............311	New Hampshire............440
California............323	New Jersey............444
Colorado............326	New Mexico............453
Connecticut............331	New York............459
Delaware............334	North Carolina............464
Florida............337	North Dakota............470
Georgia............339	Ohio............478
Hawaii............345	Oklahoma............483
Idaho............350	Oregon............486
Illinois............360	Pennsylvania............496
Indiana............366	Rhode Island............497
Iowa............370	South Carolina............503
Kansas............375	South Dakota............506
Kentucky............379	Tennessee............513
Louisiana............381	Texas............519
Maine............383	Utah............534
Maryland............389	Vermont............540
Massachusetts............398	Virginia............545
Michigan............404	Washington............554
Minnesota............409	West Virginia............557
Mississippi............416	Wisconsin............564
Missouri............421	Wyoming............570

ALABAMA

Code of Alabama
Title 15. Criminal Procedure
Chapter 21. Habeas Corpus

§15-21-1. Persons entitled to prosecute writ—Generally
Any person who is imprisoned or restrained of his liberty in the State of Alabama on any criminal charge or accusation or under any other pretense whatever, except persons committed or detained by virtue of process issued by a court of the United States or by a judge thereof in cases of which such courts have exclusive jurisdiction under the laws of the United States or have acquired exclusive jurisdiction by the commencement of actions in such courts, may prosecute a writ of habeas corpus according to the provisions of this chapter to inquire into the cause of such imprisonment or restraint.

§15-21-2. Persons entitled to prosecute writ—Person confined for failure to enter into undertaking to keep the peace
Any person confined in jail for failing to enter into an undertaking to keep the peace may prosecute a writ of habeas corpus as provided in this chapter; but such writ can be heard only by a judge of the circuit court, who may discharge the applicant, remand him to jail or reduce the amount of the undertaking as may seem right. If the amount of the undertaking is reduced, the sheriff must discharge the applicant upon the entering into the undertaking in the sum fixed by such judge.

§15-21-3. Persons entitled to prosecute writ—Persons confined as insane
Any person confined as insane may prosecute a writ of habeas corpus as provided in this chapter; and, if the judge or the jury, when the petitioner demands the issues arising to be tried by a jury, shall decide at the hearing that the person is insane, such decision does not bar a second application alleging that such person has been restored to sanity.

§15-21-4. Application to be made by petition; contents of petition
Application for a writ of habeas corpus must be made by petition, signed either by the party himself for whose benefit it is intended or by some other person in his behalf, must be verified by the oath of the applicant to the effect that the statements therein contained are true to the best of his knowledge, information and belief and must state, in substance, the name of the person on whose behalf the application is made, that he is imprisoned or restrained of his liberty in the county, the place of such imprisonment, if known, the name of the officer or person by whom he is so imprisoned and the cause or pretense of such imprisonment; and, if the imprisonment is by virtue of any warrant, writ or other process, a copy thereof must be annexed to the petition or the petition must allege that a copy thereof has been demanded and refused or must show some sufficient excuse for the failure to demand a copy.

§15-21-5. Description of party if name uncertain or unknown
If the name of the person on whose behalf an application for a writ of habeas corpus is made or the officer or person by whom he is imprisoned or detained is uncertain or unknown, he may be described in any way that is sufficient to identify him.

§15-21-6. To whom petition addressed
(a) When the person is confined in a county jail or any other place on a charge of felony or under a commitment or an indictment for felony, the petition for a writ of habeas corpus must be addressed to the nearest circuit court judge.

(b) When the person is confined in the penitentiary or under a sentence, judgment or order of the supreme court or the circuit court, other than an indictment for felony, the petition must be addressed to the nearest circuit court judge.

(c) In all other cases, it may be addressed to any one of them, and when the person is confined in any other place than the county jail or the penitentiary and on any other than a criminal charge, it may be addressed to any circuit court judge.

§15-21-7. When petition may be addressed to another judge; justifying proof required; ouster of jurisdiction of nearest judge

(a) When the petition for a writ of habeas corpus is required to be addressed to the nearest circuit court judge and such judge is absent, is incapable of acting, has refused to grant the writ, has refused to grant the writ returnable within five days or has granted the writ returnable in five days but has failed or refused to rule therein within five days from the return date, it may be addressed to any other circuit court judge. In such case, before the writ is granted, proof must be made, either by the oath of the applicant or other sufficient evidence, of the particular facts which justify such address.

(b) The jurisdiction of the nearest circuit court judge shall be ousted when the petition is filed with any other circuit court judge.

§15-21-8. Writ to be granted without delay; to whom writ returnable

(a) The judge to whom the application for a writ for habeas corpus is made must grant the same without delay, unless it appears from the petition itself or from the documents thereunto annexed that the person imprisoned or restrained is not entitled to the benefit of the writ under the provisions of this chapter.

(b) When the person is confined in the penitentiary, the writ must be made returnable before the circuit court of the county in which the convict is confined, but if the writ is granted more than 10 days before the time fixed for the holding of such court, it must be made returnable before the nearest circuit court judge. When a person is a patient or confined in any hospital in the state, the writ must be made returnable before the circuit court of the county in which the hospital is located in which he is so confined. In all other cases, the writ must be made returnable before the officer by whom it is granted.

§15-21-9. Form of writ

A writ of habeas corpus may be, in substance, as follows:

> The State of Alabama,   )
> .... county.   )
> To the sheriff of ... county, (or other person by whom the party is imprisoned or restrained): You are hereby commanded to have the body of A. B. alleged to be detained by you, by whatsoever name the said A. B. is called or charged, with the cause of such detention, before c. D., judge of the circuit court (or other officer, as required by *Section 15-21-8*), on .... at .... (specifying the time and place, or immediately after the receipt of this writ, as the case may be), to do and receive what shall then and there be considered concerning the said A. B.
> Dated this day of .... day of ...., [20 ..]
> (Signed by the officer, with his official title.)

§15-21-10. Writ not to be disobeyed for want of form or misdescription; writ presumed addressed to recipient

A writ of habeas corpus must not be disobeyed on account of any want of form or any misdescription of the person to whom it is addressed, and it must be presumed to have been addressed to the person on whom it is served, notwithstanding any mistake in the name or address.

§15-21-11. Repealed by Acts 1977, No. 607, p. 812, §9901, as amended, effective January 1, 1980

§15-21-12. Notice to any other person having interest required

If it appears from the petition for a writ of habeas corpus or from the documents thereunto annexed that the party is imprisoned or detained by virtue of any process under which any other person has an interest in continuing his imprisonment or restraint, the officer issuing the writ must endorse thereon an order requiring the applicant, or someone else for him, to give notice to such person, or to his attorney, of the issue of the writ and of the time and place at which it is returnable, in order that he may, if he thinks proper, appear and object to the discharge of the party who is imprisoned. If such notice is not given, when the party who is entitled to it is within SO miles of the place of examination, the party who is imprisoned must not be discharged.

§15-21-13. Notice to district attorney, prosecutor or arrestor required when criminal charge; bail without notice

If it appears from the petition for a writ of habeas corpus or from the documents thereunto annexed that the party is imprisoned and detained on any criminal charge or accusation, the officer issuing the writ must endorse thereon an order requiring the applicant, or someone else for him, to give notice to the district attorney of the circuit or to the prosecutor or principal agent in procuring the arrest of the issue of the writ and of the time and place at which it is returnable. If such notice is not given when the district attorney or other person entitled to it is within 50 miles of the place of examination, the party who is imprisoned must not be discharged. But, if the party is charged with an offense which is bailable and he waives an examination into the facts, the judge may fix the amount of bail, without notice to the district attorney or prosecutor, and in so doing, he must act on the presumption that the offense is of the highest grade.

§15-21-14. Issuance of precept; execution of precept by sheriff or constable

(a) At the time of issuing a writ of habeas corpus or at any time afterward before the hearing, the officer issuing the writ must, on a proper showing, issue a precept directed to any sheriff or constable of the state, commanding him to have the body of the person who is imprisoned or restrained produced before the officer before the writ is returnable at the time and place at which it is returnable.

(b) Such precept must be executed by any sheriff or constable into whose hands it may come according to its mandate.

(c) If the party is brought before the court or judge by virtue of a precept issued under the provisions of this section, the case must be heard and determined as if he had been produced in return to the writ.

§15-21-15. Subpoenas for witnesses

(a) On the application of either party, subpoenas for witnesses must be issued at any time before the hearing on a writ of habeas corpus by the clerk of the circuit court of the county to which the writ is returnable.

(b) Such subpoenas must be directed to the sheriff or any constable of the county in which the witness resides and must be executed and returned as in other cases.

§15-21-16. Service of writ

A writ of habeas corpus must be served by the sheriff, deputy sheriff or some constable of the county in which it is issued or in which the person on whose behalf it issued out is imprisoned or detained, by delivering a copy to the person to whom it is directed and showing the original, if demanded. If such person cannot be found, conceals himself or refuses admittance to the officer, the writ may be served by leaving a copy at the place where the party is confined with any person of full ago who, for the time being, has charge of the party or by posting it in a conspicuous place on the outside of the house or building in which the party is confined.

§15-21-17. When return to be made; form and contents of return

(a) After due service thereof, the person to whom a writ of habeas corpus is directed must make his return on the day therein specified if practicable; and, if no day is specified therein and the place to which the return is to be made is not more than 30 miles from the place where the party is imprisoned or detained, the return must be made within two days after service, but if more than 30 and less than 100 miles, within five days, and if over 100 miles, within eight days after service.

(b) The return must be signed by the person making it and be verified by his oath, unless he is a sworn public officer and makes the return in his official capacity, and it must state, plainly and unequivocally whether or not he has the party in his custody or power or under his restraint and, if so, by what authority and the cause thereof, setting out the same fully, together with a copy of the writ, warrant or other written authority, if any; and, if he has had the party in his custody or power or under his restraint at any time before or after the date of the writ but has transferred such custody or restraint to another, the return must state to whom, at what time, for what cause and by what authority such transfer was made.

§15-21-18. Person and original detaining warrant, writ, etc., to be produced with return; exception

At the time of making the return, one must also produce the person on whose behalf the writ of habeas corpus was sued out, according to the command of the writ, and the original warrant, writ or other written authority under which he was detained; but, if from sickness or infirmity the party cannot be produced without danger, that fact must be stated in the return, verified by oath and, if required, established by other sufficient evidence.

§15-21-19. Proceedings when person not produced on account of sickness or infirmity

When the party on whose behalf a writ of habeas corpus is sued out is not produced on account of sickness or infirmity, the court or judge before whom the writ is returnable may proceed to decide on the return as if the party had been produced if satisfied of such sickness of infirmity, may proceed to the place where he is imprisoned or detained and there make the examination or may adjourn the examination to another time.

§15-21-20. Contesting of return; examination into imprisonment or detention; disposition of detainee on adjournment of examination; forfeiture of bail

(a) The Party on whose behalf a writ of habeas corpus is sued out may deny any of the facts stated in the return and allege any other facts which may be material in the case.

(b) In a summary way, the court or judge may examine into the cause of the imprisonment or detention, may hear evidence adduced and adjourn the examination from time to time as the circumstances of the case may require and, in the meantime, remand the party or commit him to the custody of the sheriff of the county or place him under such other custody as his age or other circumstances may require, or, if the character of the charge authorizes it, take bail from him in a sufficient amount for his appearance from day to day until judgment is given.

(c) If the party fails to appear, as required by his undertaking, an entry of forfeiture must be endorsed thereon, signed by the judge and returned to the circuit court of the county in which the examination is had; and the same proceedings must be thereon had in such court as if the undertaking had been taken in such court, the endorsement of forfeiture being presumptive evidence of that fact.

§15-21-21. When party to be discharged or remanded
Upon hearing on a writ of habeas corpus, if no legal cause for the imprisonment or restraint of a party is shown, he must be discharged; but, if it appears that he is held or detained in custody by virtue of process issued by a court or judge of the United States in a case of which such court or judge has exclusive jurisdiction or by virtue of any legal engagement or enlistment in the army or navy of the United States or, being subject to the rules and articles of war is confined by anyone legally acting by authority thereof, or is in custody for any public offense committed in any other state or territory for which, by the Constitution and laws of the United States, he should be delivered up to the authority of such state or territory or that he is otherwise legally detained, he must be remanded.

§15-21-22. Admission to bail if charged with bailable offense; procedure when sufficient bail not offered; transmission of bail to clerk of court; forfeiture of bail
(a) Upon a hearing on a writ of habeas corpus, if it appears that the detained is charged with a public offense which is bailable, he must be admitted to bail on offering sufficient bail.

(b) If sufficient bail is not offered, the amount of bail required must be endorsed on the warrant, and the court to which he is required to appear, and the detained party may be afterwards discharged by the sheriff of the county on giving sufficient bail in the amount so required.

(c) All undertakings of bail taken by any judge or sheriff under the provisions of this section must be transmitted by him to the clerk of the court before which the party is bound to appear by the first day of the next succeeding session and may be forfeited, and the same proceedings thereon had, as against other bail in criminal cases.

§15-21-23. Judgment, etc., or contempt commitment not to be inquired into
On the return of a writ of habeas corpus, no court or judge has authority to inquire into the regularity or justice of any order, judgment, decree or process of any court legally constituted, nor into the justice or propriety of any commitment for contempt made by a court, officer or body according to law and charged in such commitment.

§15-21-24. Grounds for discharge of person in custody under process legally issued If it appears that the party is in custody by virtue of process from any court legally constituted or issued by any officer in the course of judicial proceedings before him authorized by law, he can only be discharged under a writ of habeas corpus where:

(1) The jurisdiction of such court has been exceeded, either as to matter, place, sum or person;
(2) Though the original imprisonment was lawful, the party has become entitled to his discharge by reason of some subsequent act, omission or event;
(3) The process is void in consequence of some defect in matter or substance required by law;
(4) The process, though in proper form, was issued in a case under circumstances not allowed by law;
(5) The process is not authorized by any judgment, order or decree nor by any provision of the law; or

(6) The person who has the custody of him under any order or process is not the person authorized by law to detain him.

Current through Act 2014-457 of the 2014 Regular Session.

ALASKA

Alaska Statutes
Title 12. Code of Criminal Procedure
Chapter 75. Habeas Corpus

§12.75.010. Persons entitled to prosecute writ
A person imprisoned or otherwise restrained of liberty under any pretense whatsoever, except in the cases specified in *AS 12.75.020*, may prosecute a writ of habeas corpus to inquire into the cause of the imprisonment or restraint, and, if illegal, to be released from custody or to be granted another remedy as law and justice require. Procedure may be as prescribed in the Rules of Civil Procedure.

§12.75.020. Person not entitled to prosecute writ
A person properly imprisoned or restrained by virtue of the legal judgment of a competent tribunal of civil or criminal jurisdiction, or by virtue of an execution regularly and lawfully issued upon that judgment or decree shall not be allowed to prosecute the writ.

§12.75.030. Offense not bailable
When it appears that the cause or offense for which the person prosecuting the writ is imprisoned or restrained is not bailable, the production of the party may be dispensed with and the writ issued accordingly.

§12.75.040. Production of body
The person on whom a writ is served shall bring the body of the person in custody or under restraint, according to the command of the writ, except in the cases provided in *AS 12.75.050*.

§12.75.050. Hearing without production of person
When, from the sickness or infirmity of the person directed to be produced, that person cannot without danger be brought before the court, the person in whose custody or power that person is may state that fact in the return to the writ. If the court is satisfied of the truth of the return and the return is otherwise sufficient, the court shall proceed to decide on the return and to dispose of the matter as if the party had been produced.

§12.75.060. Proceedings on disobedience of writ
If the person upon whom the writ is served refuses or neglects to obey it within the time required, and no sufficient excuse is shown, it is the duty of the court before whom the writ is returnable, upon due proof of service, to immediately apprehend and bring the person before the court. Upon that person being brought before the court, the court shall commit that person to custody until the person makes return to the writ and complies with any order that may be made.

§12.75.070. Precept to peace officer

A court that issues a writ without requiring the production of the person or that issues a warrant may also, at any time before final decision, issue a precept to the peace officer to whom the writ or warrant is directed commanding the officer to immediately bring the person for whose benefit the writ was allowed before the court. That person shall remain in the custody of the peace officer until discharged, remanded, or the matter is otherwise disposed of as law and justice required.

§12.75.080. Discharge of party

If no legal cause is shown for the imprisonment or restraint, or for its continuation, the court shall discharge the party from the custody or restraint under which the party is held or grant any other appropriate remedy.

§12.75.090. Remand of party legally detained

The court shall remand the party if it appears that the party is legally detained in custody.

§12.75.100. Remedy of person in custody by virtue of civil process

If it appears on the return of the writ that the prisoner is in custody by virtue of an order or civil process of a court legally constituted, or issued by an officer in the course of judicial proceedings before the officer, authorized by law, the prisoner shall be discharged or granted any other appropriate remedy in any of the following cases:

>   (1) when the jurisdiction of the court or officer has been exceeded, either as to matter, place, sum, or person;
>   (2) when, though the original imprisonment was lawful, yet by some act, omission, or event that has taken place afterwards, the party has become entitled to a discharge or other remedy;
>   (3) when the order or process is defective in some matter of substance required by law, rendering the process void;
>   (4) when the order or process, though in proper form, has been issued in a case not allowed by law;
>   (5) when the person having the custody of the prisoner under the order or process is not the person empowered by law to detain the prisoner; or
>   (6) when the order or process is not authorized by a judgment of a court or by a provision of law.

§12.75.110. Limitation on scope of court's inquiry

No court or judge, on the return of a writ of habeas corpus, may inquire into the legality or justice of any order, judgment, or process specified in *AS 12.75.020* or into the justice, propriety, or legality of a commitment for a contempt made by a court, officer, or body, according to law, and charged in the commitment, as provided by law.

§12.75.120. Proceedings where commitment irregular

If it appears by the testimony offered with the return, or upon the hearing that the party is probably guilty of a criminal offense, the court, although the commitment is irregular, shall immediately remand the party to the custody of the proper person.

§12.75.130. Custody of party pending judgment

Until judgment is given upon the return, the party may either be committed to the custody of a peace officer or placed in the officer's care or under such custody as the party's age or circumstances require.

§13-4123. Granting of writ; remand of prisoner
A. The writ of habeas corpus may be granted:

1. By the supreme court or any judge thereof. When so issued it may be made returnable before the court or any judge thereof, or before any superior court or any judge thereof.

2. By the superior court or a judge thereof, in their respective counties.

B. If the writ is granted by a superior court or judge, and after hearing thereof the prisoner has been remanded, he shall not be discharged from custody by the same or any other superior court or judge, unless upon some ground not existing at the time of issuing the prior writ, or unless upon some point of law not raised at the hearing upon the return of the prior writ.

§13-4124. Granting writ; time; bail
A. A court or judge authorized to grant a writ of habeas corpus, to whom a petition therefor is presented, if it appears that the writ ought to issue, shall grant it without delay.

B. If the person by or upon whose behalf the application for the writ is made is detained upon a criminal charge, the court or judge may admit him to bail if the offense is bailable, pending determination of the proceeding.

§13-4125. Direction of writ
The writ shall be directed to the person having custody of or restraining the person on whose behalf the petition is made, and shall command him to have the body of such person before the court or judge before whom the writ is returnable, at a time and place therein specified.

§13-4126. Delivery and service of writ
A. If the writ is directed to the sheriff or other officer of the court out of which the writ is issued, it shall be delivered by the clerk to such officer without delay, as other writs are delivered for service. If the writ is directed to any other officer or person, the writ shall be delivered to the sheriff, and shall be by him served upon such officer or person by delivering the writ to him without delay.

B. If the officer or person whom the writ is directed cannot be found, or refuses admittance of the officer or person serving or delivering the writ, the writ may be served or delivered by leaving it at the residence of the officer or person whom it is directed, or by affixing it on some conspicuous place on the outside either of his dwelling house or of the place where the party is confined or under restraint.

§13-4128. Return of writ
A. The person upon whom the writ is served shall state in his return, plainly and unequivocally whether or not he has the party in his custody or under his power or restraint and if so, by what authority, and the cause of such imprisonment or restraint, setting forth such authority and cause in detail.

B. If the party is restrained by virtue of any writ, warrant or other written authority, a copy thereof shall be annexed to the return, and the original shall be produced and exhibited to the court or judge on the hearing of the return.

C. If the person upon whom the writ is served has had the party in his custody or under his power or restraint any time prior or subsequent to the date of the writ of habeas corpus, but has transferred the custody or restraint to another, the return shall state particularly at what time and place, for what reason and by what authority the transfer was made.

D. The return shall be signed by the person making it, and, except when such person is a public officer who has taken the oath of off ice and makes the return in his official capacity, it shall be verified by his oath or affirmation.

§13-4129. Production of prisoner
A. The person upon whom the writ is served shall bring the body of the party in his custody or under his restraint before the court or judge according to the command of the writ.

B. When from sickness or infirmity of the person directed to be produced, the person cannot without danger be brought before the court or judge, the person in whose custody or power he is may state that fact in his return to the writ. If the court or judge is satisfied of the truth of the allegations of sickness or infirmity, and the return to the writ is otherwise sufficient the court or judge may decide the matter on such return and dispose of the matter as if the party had been produced on the writ, or the hearing thereof may be adjourned until the party can be produced.

§13-4130. Hearing on return
A. The court or judge to whom the writ is returned shall, immediately after the return thereof, hear and examine the return, and such other matters as may be properly submitted.

B. The petitioner may controvert the return, or object to the sufficiency thereof, or allege any fact to show either that his imprisonment or detention is unlawful or that he is entitled to discharge. The court or judge shall thereupon hear the evidence, and in a summary manner dispose of the party as justice may require.

§13-4131. Discharge of prisoner
A. If no legal cause is shown for the imprisonment or restraint, or for continuation thereof, the party shall be discharged from custody or restraint.

B. If the time during which the party may be legally detained in custody has not expired and he is detained in custody by virtue of process by any court, judge or agency of the United States, in an action where such court, judge or agency has exclusive jurisdiction, or by virtue of the final judgment or decree of any court of competent jurisdiction, or of any process issued upon such judgment or decree, the person shall not be discharged.

§13-4132. Discharge of prisoner held on process
If it appears, on the return of the writ, that the prisoner is in custody by virtue of process from any court of this state, or judge or officer thereof, the prisoner shall be discharged in any one of the following cases subject to the restrictions of §13-4131:
1. When the jurisdiction of the court or officer has been exceeded.

2. When the imprisonment was at first lawful, but by some act, omission or event, which has taken place afterward, the party has become entitled to be discharged.

3. When the process is defective in some matter of substance required by law rendering the process void.

4. When the process, though proper in form, has been issued in a proceeding not authorized by law.

5. When the person having custody of the prisoner is not the person authorized by law to detain him.

6. Where the process is not authorized by a judgment, order or decree of any court, nor by any provision of law.

7. Where a party has been committed on a criminal charge without reasonable or probable cause.

§13-4133. *Effect of defect in form*
If a person is committed or is in the custody of any officer on any charge by virtue of a warrant or commitment of a justice of the peace, such person shall not be discharged from imprisonment or custody on the ground of a mere defect of form in the warrant or commitment.

§13-4134. *Defective process or commitment; re-examination*
If it appears to the court or judge that the party is guilty of a criminal offense, or should not be discharged, the court or judge, although the charge is defectively set forth in the process or warrant of commitment, shall cause the witnesses to be subpoenaed to attend at the time ordered to testify before such court or judge. Upon the examination, the court shall discharge the prisoner, admit him to bail, if the offense is bailable, or recommit him to custody.

§13-4143. *Charging fee in habeas corpus prohibited*
No fee or compensation of any kind shall be charged or received by any officer for duties performed or services rendered in habeas corpus proceedings.

Current through the Second Regular and Second Special Sessions of the Fifty-first Legislature

ARKANSAS

Arkansas Code
Title 16. Practice, Procedure, and Courts
Chapter 112. Habeas Corpus
Subchapters 1 and 2. Procedure

§ 16-112-101. *Issuance—Service—Trial*
The writ of habeas corpus shall be issued, served, and tried in the manner prescribed in this chapter.

§16-112-102. *Power of issuance, determination*
(a)(1) The writ of habeas corpus shall be issued upon proper application by a Justice of the Supreme Court or a judge of the circuit court. The power of the Supreme Court and circuit court to issue writs of habeas corpus shall be coextensive with the state.

(2)(A) The county just shall have power coextensive with his or her county in the absence of the circuit judge therefrom to issue, hear, and determine writs of habeas corpus on proper application of parties entitled thereto, in all cases and with like powers, in which the circuit judge may issue and determine a writ of habeas corpus.

(B) However, no county judge shall have power to issue or hear any writ of habeas corpus in any case in which an indictment has been found by a grand jury.

(b) If any officer enumerated in subsection (a) of this section shall, when legally applied to, refuse to issue the writ of habeas corpus to the petitioner, he or she shall forfeit and pay to the petitioner five hundred dollar ($500).

§16-112-103. Application by petition

(a)(1) The writ of habeas corpus shall be granted forthwith by any of the officers enumerated in §16-112-102(a) to any person who shall apply for the writ by petition showing, by affidavit or other evidence, probable cause to believe he or she is detained without lawful authority, is imprisoned when by law he or she is entitled to bail, or who has alleged actual innocence of the offense or offenses for which the person was convicted.

(2) The procedures for persons who allege actual innocence shall be in accordance with §16-112-201 et seq.

(b)(1) The writ of habeas corpus shall be granted upon the application, and in the name of the father, mother, guardian, or next friend of any married woman or infant, against any person who shall unlawfully have or detain in custody or bondage any infant or married woman.

(2) Similar proceedings shall be had for hearing and determining the cause and affording the relief demanded as in other cases.

(c) Writs of habeas corpus shall issue upon the application of the husband, father, mother, guardian, or next friend of any married woman or infant detained by any religious or other association or by persons acting under the authority of the association. The prosecuting attorney, where the detention is made, shall prosecute the writ without fee, if required to do so.

(d) If the restraint or confinement is by virtue of any warrant, order, or process, a copy thereof must accompany the petition, or it must appear by affidavit annexed thereto, showing that by reason of the person being concealed before the application, a demand of the copy could not be made, or that the demand was made of the person by whom the prisoner is confined or restrained, and a copy refused.

§16-112-104. Bond—Required as security

(a) The officer granting the writ may previously require bond, with surety, in sufficient penalty, payable to the state or to the person against whom the writ is directed, conditioned that the person detained shall not escape by the way, and for the payment of such costs and charges as may be awarded against him or her.

(b) The bond shall be filed with the other proceedings in the court and may be sued on by the state for the benefit of any person injured by the breach of it.

§16-112-105. Writ—Format and manner

(a) Writs of habeas corpus may be granted without the seal of the officer but shall be signed by him or her.

(b)(1) The writ shall be directed to the person in whose custody the prisoner is detained, and made returnable as soon as may be, before the Supreme Court Justices, or before the circuit judges of the county in which it may be served, if either are within the county.

(2) The writ shall specify the time and place to which it shall be returned.

(c)(1) In a writ of habeas corpus the person having the custody of the prisoner may be designated either by his or her name of office, if he or she has any, or his or her own name. If both names are uncertain or unknown, he or she may be described by any assumed appellation.

(2) The person directed to be produced may be designated by his or her name. If his or her name is uncertain or unknown, he or she may be described in any other way so as to designate or identify the person intended.

(d) Writs of habeas corpus shall not be disobeyed for any defect of form. Anyone who shall be served therewith shall be deemed to be the person to whom it is directed, though it may be directed to him or her by a wrong name, or description, or to another person.

§16-112-106. Service of writ

(a) The writ shall be served by any qualified officer or by any private individual designated by the judge on the person to whom it is directed or, in his or her absence from the place where the petition is confined, on the person having him or her in immediate custody.

(b) If the person upon whom the writ ought to be served conceals himself or herself or refuses admittance to the person attempting the service, it may be served by affixing a copy of the writ in some conspicuous place on the outside either of the dwelling house or jail, or place where the party is confined.

(c) Anyone having in his or her custody or under his or her power any person for whose relief a writ of habeas corpus shall have been issued or who is entitled to a writ of habeas corpus to inquire into the cause of his or her detention who shall transfer the person to the custody of another or place the person under the control or power of another, conceal the person, or change the place of the person's confinement with the intent to elude the service of the writ shall be guilty of a Class A misdemeanor and shall pay the party injured five hundred dollars ($500).

§16-112-107. Removal within certain time

No person charged with a criminal offense shall be removed by a writ of habeas corpus out of the county in which he or she is confined at any time within fifteen (15) days next preceding the term of the court at which the prisoner ought to be tried, except to convey him or her into the county where the offense with which he or she is charged is properly cognizable.

§16-112-108. Requirements for return

(a) The writ shall be made returnable within three (3) days after it is served. However, if the person is to be brought more than twenty (20) miles, the writ shall be made returnable within so many days more as will be equal to one (1) day for every twenty (20) miles for the further distance. It shall be returned with the person of the petitioner, with the cause of his or her detention or his or her imprisonment stated in the return.

(b) The officer or other person serving the writ shall leave a copy with the person on whom it is served, upon which the cause of detention shall be stated, and return the original to the proper officer.

(c)(1) Every officer or other person upon whom a writ of habeas corpus shall be served shall state in his or her return plainly and unequivocally:

(A) Whether he or she has or has not the party in his or her custody or under his power or restraint;

(B) If he or she has the party in his or her custody or power or under his or her restraint, the authority and true cause of the imprisonment or restraint, setting forth the same at large;

(C) If the person making the return shall have had the party in his or her power or custody or under his or her restraint, at any time before the service of the writ, and has transferred the custody or possession to another, particularly to whom, at what time, for what cause, and by what authority the transfer took place.

(2) If the party is restrained, imprisoned, or detained by virtue of any writ, order, warrant, or other written authority, a copy thereof shall be annexed to the return. The original shall be exhibited on the return of the writ, to the court or judge to whom it is returnable.

(3) The return must be signed by the person making the return, and except where the person shall be a sworn officer and shall make his or her return in his or her official capacity, it shall be verified by his or her oath.

§16-112-109. *Information relating to commitment*
(a) When the party for whose relief a writ of habeas corpus has been issued shall stand committed for any criminal or supposed criminal matter, it shall be the duty of the officer or person upon whom the writ is served to bring with the writ all and every examination and information in his or her hands, possession custody, or charge, relating to the commitment.

(b) If no examination shall accompany the commitment nor be in the possession of the officer having the prisoner in custody, the officer shall exhibit the habeas corpus, when served on him or her, to the judge or magistrate by whom the prisoner was committed or the clerk of the court if the papers are in his or her office. It shall be the duty of the judge, magistrate, or clerk to deliver to the officer having the custody of the prisoner the examinations and proofs relating to the offense charged to be returned by the officer with the writ.

(c) If no examination has been filed with the commitment or in the office of the clerk and none is produced by the committing judge or magistrate upon the exhibition of the writ of habeas corpus to him or her, as provided in subsection (b) of this section, the judge or magistrate shall appear in person at the time and place to which the writ is returnable and, if he or she fails to do so, may be proceeded against by attachment.

§16-112-110. *Failure to bring prisoner*
If any person on whom a writ of habeas corpus is served fails to bring the body of the petitioner, with a return of the cause of his or her detention, at the time and place specified in the writ, he or she shall forfeit and pay the prisoner one thousand dollars ($1,000).

§16-112-111. *Order—Custody of applicant*
When the person who applies for a writ of habeas corpus shall not be in the custody of a jailer or other officer, the judge may, for good cause shown, direct the officer or person serving the writ to take the applicant into his or her custody and produce him or her on the return of the writ.

§16-112-112. Failure to produce—Sickness

(a) Whenever, for sickness of other infirmity of the person directed to be produced by a writ of habeas corpus, the person cannot, without danger, be brought before the court or judge before whom the writ is returnable, the person in whose custody he or she is may state the fact in his or her return, verifying the fact by his or her oath. The court or judge, if satisfied of the truth of the allegations, if the return is otherwise sufficient, shall proceed thereon to dispose of the matter in the same manner, as if the prisoner were brought before him, except as provided in subsection (b) of this section.

(b) If, in the case mentioned in subsection (a) of this section, it appears that the prisoner is legally imprisoned or restrained and not bailable, the judge shall proceed no further therein. If the prisoner ought to be held to answer for a bailable offense, an order shall be made accordingly. When it appears the prisoner is entitled to his or her discharge, the judge shall make an order to that effect.

§16-112-113. Denial—Allegations of fact

(a) The party brought before any court or judge, by virtue of any writ of habeas corpus, may deny the material facts set forth in the return, or allege any fact to show either that his or her detention or imprisonment is unlawful, or that he or she is entitled to his or her discharge. The allegations or denials shall be on oath.

(b) The return and the allegations made against it may be amended, by leave of the court or judge before whom the writ is returned at any time, that thereby material facts may be ascertained.

§16-112-114. Witnesses—Affidavits as evidence

(a) The officer issuing the writ in vacation or the officer before whom it may be returned for trial shall have the some power to compel the attendance of witnesses or to punish a contempt of his authority, as a court of record has. His or her judgment on the trial of the writ shall be considered and be enforced as if it were a judgment of the court.

(b) At the discretion of the judge before whom the writ is returned, the affidavits of witnesses taken by either party, on reasonable notice to his or her agent or attorney, may be read as evidence on the trial of the return. However, no county or circuit judge shall hear or permit any evidence on the hearing or examination before him or her, other than the return to the writ, if the process or commitment shall appear regular on its face.

§16-112-115. Judge's disposition of matter

The judge before whom the writ is returned, after hearing the matter, both upon the return and any other evidence, shall either discharge or remand the petitioner, admit the prisoner to bail, or make such order as may be proper. He or she shall adjudge the costs of the proceeding, including the charge for transporting the prisoner, to be paid as shall seem right. The payment may be enforced by attachment or otherwise by the court to which the proceedings are returned.

§16-112-116. Remand of prisoner—Conditions

It shall be the duty of the court or judge forthwith to remand the prisoner if it shall appear that he is held in custody, either:

(1) By virtue of any process issued by any court or judge of the United States in a cause where the court or judge has exclusive jurisdiction;

(2) By virtue of the final judgment or decree of any competent court of civil or criminal jurisdiction;

(3) For any contempt especially and plainly charged in the commitment by some court, judge, or body politic having authority by law to commit for contempt so charged; and,

(4) Where the time during which the party may be legally detained has not expired.

§16-112-117. *Defective proceedings against prisoners*
Upon the trial of a habeas corpus, if the judge shall be of the opinion that the prisoner has been guilty of a misdemeanor or felony, for which the prisoner may be liable to be tried and that the proceedings against him or her are so defective that he or she cannot be detained by them, the judge shall admit him or her to bail, if he or she is entitled to bail, to appear at the court having jurisdiction over the case, or remand him or her to the custody of the proper officer, to be conveyed to the proper county for new proceedings to be had against the prisoner.

§16-112-118. *Dischargement restrictions*
(a) No person shall be discharged under the provisions of this act:

(1) Who is in custody or held by virtue of any legal engagement or enlistment in the Army or Navy of the United States;

(2) Or who, being subject to the rules and articles of war, is confined by anyone legally acting under the authority thereof;

(3) Or who is held as a prisoner of war under the authority of the United States;

(4) Or who is in custody for any treason, felony, or other high misdemeanor committed in any other state or territory and who, by the Constitution and laws of the United States, ought to be delivered up to the legal authorities of the state or territory.

(b)(1) If it appears that the prisoner is in custody by virtue of process from any court legally constituted or issued by any officer in the exercise of judicial proceedings before him, the prisoner can be discharged in one (1) of the following cases:

(A) Where the jurisdiction of the court or officer has been exceeded, either as to matter, place, sum, or person;

(B) Where, though the original imprisonment was lawful, yet, by some act, omission, or event which has taken place afterward, the party has become entitled to his or her discharge;

(C) Where the process is defective is some matter or substance required by law, rendering the process void;

(D) Where the process, though in proper form, has been issued or executed by a person who is not authorized to issue or execute the process, or where the person having the custody of the prisoner, under the process, is not the person empowered by law to detain him or her;

(F) Where the process is not authorized by any judgment, order, decree, or by any provision of law.

(2) No court under this act shall in any other matter have power to inquire into the legality or justice of the process, judgment, decree, or order of any court, legally constituted, nor into the justice or propriety of any commitment for contempt made by any court, officer, or body corporate, according to law, and plainly charged in the commitment, as provided in this act.

(c) No person imprisoned on an indictment, found in any court of competent jurisdiction, or by virtue of any process or commitment to enforce an indictment, can be discharged under the provisions of this act. However, if the offense is bailable, he may be let to bail, and if the offense is not bailable, he or she be remanded forthwith.

(d) Where the imprisonment is for any criminal or supposed criminal matter, the court or judge before whom the prisoner shall be brought, under the provisions of this act, shall not discharge him or her for informality, insufficiency, or irregularity of the commitment. However, if from the examination taken and certified by the committing magistrate, or other evidence, it appears that there is sufficient legal cause for commitment, he or she shall proceed to take bail, if the offense is bailable and sufficient bail is offered, and if not, he or she shall recommit the prisoner to jail.

§16-112-119. Proceedings returned to clerk
The proceedings upon a writ of habeas corpus shall be returned to the clerk of the circuit court of the county in which the writ was heard or the court in which the prosecution, if any, is pending.

§16-112-120. Same offense—Commitment prohibition
A person released upon a writ of habeas corpus shall not again be imprisoned or committed for the same offense, except by the legal order or process of the court wherein he or she shall be bound by recognizance to appear or some other court having jurisdiction of the same cause.

§16-112-121. Proceedings under second writ
(a) If a prisoner remanded under the provisions of this act shall obtain a second writ of habeas corpus, it shall be the duty of the officer or other person on whom the writ shall be served to return therewith the order, remanding the prisoner. If it appears that the prisoner was remanded for an offense adjudged not bailable, the prisoner shall forthwith be remanded without further proceedings.

(b) It shall not be lawful for any court or judge, on a second writ of habeas corpus, to discharge the prisoner, if he or she is clearly and specifically charged in the order remanding him or her or in the warrant of commitment, with a criminal offense. However, the prisoner, on the return of the writ, shall be bail or remanded to prison, according to the circumstances of the case.

§16-112-122. Issuance upon evidence only
Whenever any court of record, any justice of the Supreme Court, or any judge of the circuit court or judge of the county court, shall have evidence, from any judicial proceedings had before them, that any person is illegally confined or restrained of his or her liberty within the jurisdiction of the court or judge, it shall be the duty of the court or judge to issue a writ of habeas corpus for his or her relief, although no application or petition is presented for writ.

§16-112-123. Illegal Imprisonment—Warrant
(a)(1) When it shall appear by satisfactory proof that any person is illegally imprisoned or restrained of his or her liberty and that there is good reason to believe that he or she will be carried out of the state,

or suffer some irreparable injury before he or she can be relieved by a writ of habeas corpus, any court or judge authorized to issue the writ may issue a warrant reciting the facts and directed to any sheriff, coroner, constable, or other person, commanding him or her to take the prisoner and to bring the prisoner forthwith before the court or judge, to be dealt with according to law.

(2) Where the proof shall also be sufficient to justify the arrest of the person having the prisoner in his or her custody, as for a criminal offense committed in the taking and detaining the prisoner, the warrant shall also contain an order for the arrest of the offender.

(b) The warrant shall be executed according to the command thereof, and, when the prisoner is brought before the court or judge, the person detaining the prisoner shall make a return in like manner, and the like proceedings shall be had as if a writ of habeas corpus had been issued in the first instance.

(c) If the person having the prisoner in custody is brought before a court or a judge as for a criminal offense, he or she shall be examined, committed, bailed, or discharged in the same manner as in other criminal cases of like nature.

Subchapter 2. Motions Based on Scientific Evidence.

§16-112-201. Writ of habeas corpus—New scientific evidence
(a) Except when direct appeal is available, a person convicted of a crime may commence a proceeding to secure relief by filing a petition in the court in which the conviction was entered to vacate and set aside the judgment and to discharge the petitioner or to resentence the petitioner or grant a new trial or correct the sentence or make other disposition as may be appropriate, if the person claims under penalty of perjury that:

(1) Scientific evidence not available at trial establishes the petitioner's actual innocence; or

(2) The scientific predicate for the claim could not have been previously discovered through the exercise of due diligence and the facts underlying the claim, if proven and viewed in light of the evidence as a whole, would be sufficient to establish by clear and convincing evidence that no reasonable fact-finder would find the petitioner guilty of the underlying offense.

(b) Nothing contained in this subchapter shall prevent the Arkansas Supreme Court or the Arkansas Court of Appeals, upon application by a party, from granting a stay of an appeal to allow an application to the trial court for an evidentiary hearing under this subchapter.

§16-112-202. Form of motion
Except when direct appeal is available, a person convicted of a crime may make a motion for the performance of fingerprinting, forensic deoxyribonucleic acid (DNA) testing, or other tests which may become available through advances in technology to demonstrate the person's actual innocence if:

(1) The specific evidence to be tested was secured as a result of the conviction of an offense's being challenged under §16-112-201;

(2) The specific evidence to be tested was not previously subjected to testing and the person making the motion under this section did not:

A) Knowingly and voluntarily waive the right to request testing of the evidence in a court proceeding commenced on or after August 12, 2005; or

(B) Knowingly fail to request testing of the evidence in a prior motion for post-conviction testing;

(3) The specific evidence was previously subjected to testing and the person making a motion under this section requests testing that uses a new method or technology that is substantially more probative than the prior testing;

(4) The specific evidence to be tested is in the possession of the state and has been subject to a chain of custody and retained under conditions sufficient to ensure that the evidence has not been substituted, contaminated, tempered with, replaced, or altered in any respect material to the proposed testing;

(5) The proposed testing is reasonable in scope, utilizes scientifically sound methods, and is consistent with accepted forensic practices;

(6) The person making a motion under this section identifies a theory of defense that:

(A) Is not inconsistent with an affirmative defense presented at the trial of the offense being challenged under ~16-112-201; and

(B) Would establish the actual innocence of the person in relation to the offense being challenged under §16-112-201;

(7) The identity of the perpetrator was at issue during the investigation or prosecution of the offense being challenge under §16-112-201;

(8) The proposed testing of the specific evidence may produce new material evidence that would:

(A) Support the theory of defense described in subdivision (6) of this section; and

(B) Raise a reasonable probability that the person making a motion under this section did not commit the offense;

(9) The person making a motion under this section certifies that he or she will provide a deoxyribonucleic acid (DNA) or other sample or a fingerprint for comparison; and

(10) The motion is made in a timely fashion subject to the following conditions:

(A) There shall be a rebuttable presumption of timeliness if the motion is made within thirty-six (36) months of the date of conviction. The presumption may be rebutted upon a showing:

(i) That the motion for testing under this section is based solely upon information used in a previously denied motion; or

(ii) Of clear and convincing evidence that the motion filed under this section was filed solely to cause delay or harassment; and

(B) There shall be a rebuttable presumption against timeliness for any motion not made within thirty-six (36) months of the date of conviction. The presumption may be rebutted upon a showing:

(i) That the person making a motion under this section was or is incompetent and the incompetence substantially contributed to the delay in the motion for a test;

(ii) That the evidence to be tested is newly discovered evidence;

(iii) That the motion is not based solely upon the person's own assertion of innocence and a denial of the motion would result in a manifest injustice;

(iv) That new method of technology that is substantially more probative than prior testing is available; or

(v) Of good cause.

§16-112-203. *Contents of motion*

(a) The petition filed under this subchapter shall be entitled in the name of the petitioner versus the State of Arkansas and shall contain:

(1)(A) A statement of the facts and the grounds upon which the petition is based and relief desired.

(B) All grounds for relief shall be stated in the petition or any amendment to the petition, unless the grounds could not reasonably have been set forth in the petition.

(C) The petition may contain argument or citation of authorities;

(2) An identification of the proceedings in which the petition was convicted, including the date of the entry of conviction and sentence or other disposition complained of;

(3) An identification of any previous proceeding, together with the grounds asserted in the previous proceeding, which sought to secure relief for the petitioner from the conviction and sentence or other disposition; and

(4)(A) The name and address of any attorney representing the petitioner; or

(B) If the petitioner is without counsel, the circuit clerk shall immediately transmit a copy of the petition to the judge and shall advise the petitioner of that referral.

(b) The filing of the petition and any related documents and any proceedings pursuant to the petition shall be without any costs or fees charged to the petitioner.

(c) The petition shall be:

(1)(A) Verified by the petitioner; or

(B) Signed by the petitioner's attorney; and

(2) Addressed to the court in which the conviction was entered.

(d) The circuit clerk shall deliver a copy of the petition to the prosecuting attorney and to the Attorney General.

§16-112-204. Other pleadings

(a) Within twenty (20) days after the filing of the petition, the prosecuting attorney or the Attorney General shall respond to the petition by answer or motion which shall be filed with the court and served on the petitioner if unrepresented or served on the petitioner's attorney.

(b)(1) No further pleadings are necessary except as the court may order.

(2) However, the court may at any time prior to its decision on the merits permit:

(A) A withdrawal of the petition;

(B) Amendments to the petition; and

(C) Amendments to the answer.

(3) The court shall examine the substance of the pleading and shall waive any irregularities or defects in form.

§16-112-205. Hearing

(a) Unless the petition and the files and records of the proceeding conclusively show that the petitioner is entitled to no relief, the court shall promptly set an early hearing on the petition and response, promptly determine the issues, make findings of fact and conclusions of law, and either deny the petition or enter an order granting the appropriate relief.

(b) Hearings on a petition filed pursuant to this subchapter shall be open and shall be held in the court in which the conviction was entered.

(c)(1) The court may order the petitioner to be present at the hearing.

(2) If the petitioner is represented by an attorney, the attorney shall be present at any hearing.

(3) A verbatim record of any hearing shall be made and kept.

(4) Unless otherwise ordered by the court, the petitioner shall bear the burden of proving the facts alleged in the petition by a preponderance of the evidence.

(5) The court may receive evidence in the form of affidavit, deposition, or oral testimony.

(d) The court may summarily deny a second or successive petition for similar relief on behalf of the same petitioner and may summarily deny a petition if the issues raised in it have previously been decided by the Arkansas Court of Appeals or the Arkansas Supreme Court in the same case.

§16-112-206. Appeals

(a) The appealing party, within thirty (30) calendar days after the entry of the order, shall file a notice of appeal if the party wishes to appeal.

(b)(1) If the appeal is by the petitioner, the service shall be on the prosecuting attorney and the Attorney General.

(2) If the appeal is by the state, the service shall be on the petitioner or the petitioner's attorney.

(c) No fees or bond for costs shall be required for the appeal.

§16-112-207. Appointment of counsel

(a)(1) A person financially unable to obtain counsel who desires to pursue the remedy provided in this subchapter may apply for representation by the Arkansas Public Defender Commission or appointed private attorneys.

(2) The trial public defenders or appointed private attorneys may represent indigent persons who apply for representation under this section.

(b)(1)(A) With the approval of the court, petitioners may use the services of the State Crime Laboratory for latent fingerprinting identification, deoxyribonucleic acid (DNA) testing, and other tests which may become available through advances in technology.

(B)(i) If approved by the court, the State Crime Laboratory shall provide the requested services.

(ii) Samples shall be of sufficient quantity to allow testing by both the prosecution and the defense.

(iii) Neither the prosecution nor the defense shall consume the entire sample in testing in the absence of a court order allowing the sample to be entirely consumed in testing.

(2) Subdivision (b)(1) of this section shall not apply to any tests before trial of a matter that will be governed by relevant constitutional provisions, statutory law, or court rules.

(c) The Executive Director and the State Crime Laboratory shall give priority to claims based on factors including:

(1) The opportunity for conclusive or near conclusive proof through scientific evidence that the person is actually innocent; and

(2) A lengthy sentence of imprisonment or a death sentence.

CALIFORNIA

California Rules of Court
Title 4. Criminal Rules
Chapter 3. Habeas Corpus

Rule 4.550. Habeas Corpus application and definitions

(a) Application

This chapter applies to habeas corpus proceedings in the superior court under *Penal Code section 1473 et seg* or any other provision of law authorizing relief from unlawful confinement or unlawful conditions of confinement.

(b) Definitions

In this chapter, the following definitions apply:

(1) A "petition for writ of habeas corpus" is the petitioner's initial filing that commences a proceeding.

(2) An "order to show cause" is an order directing the respondent to file a return. The order to show cause is issued if the petitioner has made a prima facie showing that he or she is entitled to relief; it does not grant the relief requested. An order to show cause may also be referred to as "granting the writ."

(3) The "return" is the respondent's statement of reasons that the court should not grant the relief requested by the petitioner.

(4) The "denial" is the petitioner's pleading in response to the return. The denial may be also referred to as the "traverse."

(5) an "evidentiary hearing" is a hearing held by the trial court to resolve contested factual issues.

(6) An "order on writ of habeas corpus" is the court's order granting or denying the relief sought by the petitioner.

Rule 4.551. Habeas corpus proceeding

(a) Petition; form and court ruling

(1) Except as provided in (2), the petition must be on the *Petition for Writ of Habeas Corpus (form MC-275)*.

(2) For good cause, a court may also accept for filing a petition that does not comply with (a)(1). A petition submitted by an attorney need not be on the Judicial Council form. However, a petition that is not on the judicial Council form must comply with *Penal Code section 1474* and must contain the pertinent information specified in the *Petition for Writ of Habeas Corpus (form MC-275)*, including the information required regarding other petitions, motions, or applications filed in any court with respect to the conviction, commitment, or issue.

(3)(A) On filing, the clerk of the court must immediately deliver the petition to the presiding judge or his or her designee. The court must rule on a petition for writ of habeas corpus within 60 days after the petition is filed.

(B) If the court fails to rule on the petition within 60 days of its filing, the petitioner may file a notice and request for ruling.

(i) The petitioner's notice and request for ruling must include a declaration stating the date the petition was filed and the date of the notice and request for ruling, and indicating that the petitioner has not received a ruling on the petition. A copy of the original petition must be attached to the notice and request for ruling.

(ii) If the presiding judge or his or her designee determines that the notice is complete and the court has failed to rule, the presiding judge or his or her designee must assign the petition to a judge and calendar the matter for a decision without appearances within 30 days of the filing of the notice and request for ruling. If the judge assigned by the presiding judge rules on the petition before the date the petition is calendared for decision, the matter may be taken off calendar.

(4) For the purposes of (a)(3), the court rules on the petition by:

(A) Issuing an order to show cause under (c);

(B) Denying the petition for writ of habeas corpus; or

(C) Requesting an informal response to the petition for writ of habeas corpus under (b). (5) The court must issue an order to show cause or deny the petition within 45 days after receipt of an informal response requested under (b).

(b) Informal response

(1) Before passing on the petition, the court may request an informal response from:

(A) The respondent or real party in interest; or

(B) The custodian of any record pertaining to the petitioner's case, directing the custodian to produce the record or a certified copy to be filed with the clerk of the court.

(2) A copy of the request must be sent to the petitioner. The informal response, if any, must be served on the petitioner by the party of whom the request is made. The informal response must be in writing and must be served and filed within 15 days. If any informal response is filed, the court must notify the petitioner that he or she may reply to the informal response within 15 days from the date of service of the response on the petitioner. If the informal response consists of records or copies of records, a copy of every record and document furnished to the court must be furnished to the petitioner.

(3) After receiving an informal response, the court may not deny the petition until the petitioner has filed a timely reply to the informal response or the 15-day period provided for a reply under (b)(2) has expired.

(c) Order to show cause

(1) The court must issue an order to show cause if the petitioner has made a prima facie showing that he or she is entitled to relief. In doing so, the court takes petitioner's factual allegations as true and makes a preliminary assessment regarding whether the petitioner would be entitled to relief if his or her factual allegations were proved. If so, the court must issue an order to show cause.

(2) On issuing an order to show cause, the court must appoint counsel for any unrepresented petitioner who desires but cannot afford counsel.

(3) An order to show cause is a determination that the petitioner has made a showing that he or she may be entitled to relief. If does not grant the relief sought in the petition.

(d) Return

If an order to show cause is issued as provided in (c), the respondent may, within 30 days thereafter, file a return. Any material allegation of the petition not controverted by the return is deemed admitted for purposes of the proceeding. The return must comply with *Penal Code section 1480* and must be served on the petitioner.

(e) Denial

Within 30 days after service and filing of a return, the petitioner may file a denial. Any material allegation of the return not denied is deemed admitted for purposes of the proceeding. Any denial must comply with *Penal Code section 1484* and must be served on the respondent.

(f) Evidentiary hearing; when required

Within 30 days after the filing of any denial or, if none is filed, after the expiration of the time for filing a denial, the court must either grant or deny the relief sought by the petition or order an evidentiary hearing. An evidentiary hearing is required if, after considering the verified petition, the return, any denial, any affidavits or declarations under penalty of perjury, and matters of which judicial notice may be taken, the court finds there is a reasonable likelihood that the petitioner may be entitled to relief and the petitioner's entitlement to relief depends on the resolution of an issue of fact. The petitioner must be produced at the evidentiary hearing unless the court, for good cause, directs otherwise.

(g) Reasons for denial of petition

Any order denying a petition for writ of habeas corpus must contain a brief statement of the reasons for the denial. An order only declaring the petition to be "denied" is insufficient.

(h) Extending or shortening time

On motion of any party or on the court's own motion, for good cause stated in the order, the court may shorten or extend the time for doing any act under this rule. A copy of the order must be mailed to each party.

Rule 4.552. Habeas corpus jurisdiction

(a) Proper court to hear petition

Except as stated in (b), the petition should be heard and resolved in the court in which it is filed.

(b) Transfer of petition

(1) The superior court in which the petition is filed must determine, based on the allegations of the petition, whether the matter should be heard by it or in the superior court of another county.

(2) If the superior court in which the petition is filed determines that the matter may be more properly heard by the superior court of another county, it may nonetheless retain jurisdiction in the matter or, without first determining whether a prima facie case for relief exists, order the matter transferred to the other county. Transfer may be ordered in the following circumstances:

    (A) If the petition challenges the terms of a judgment, the matter may be transferred to the county in which judgment was rendered.

    (B) If the petition challenges the conditions of an inmate's confinement, it may be transferred to the county in which the petitioner is confined. A change in the institution of confinement that effects a change in the conditions of confinement may constitute good cause to deny the petition.

    (C) If the petition challenges the denial of parole or the petitioner's suitability for parole and is filed in a superior court other than the court that rendered the underlying judgment, the court in which the petition is filed should transfer the petition to the superior court in which the underlying judgment was rendered.

(3) The transferring court must specify in the order of transfer the reason for the transfer.

(4) If the receiving court determines that the reason for transfer is inapplicable, the receiving court must, within 30 days of receipt of the case, order the case returned to the transferring court. The transferring court must retain and resolve the matter as provided by these rules.

(c) Single judge must decide petition

A petition for writ of habeas corpus filed in the superior court must be decided by a single judge; it must not be considered by the appellate division of the superior court.

Current with amendments received through 7/1/14

COLORADO

Colorado Revised statutes Annotated
Title 13. Courts and Court Procedure
Article 45. Habeas Corpus—General Provisions

§13-45-101. Petition for writ—criminal cases

(1) If any person is committed or detained for any criminal or supposed criminal matter, it is lawful for him to apply to the supreme or district courts for a writ of habeas corpus, which application shall be in writing and signed by the prisoner or some person on his behalf setting forth the facts concerning his imprisonment and in whose custody he is detained, and shall be accompanied by a copy of the warrant of commitment, or an affidavit that the said copy has been demanded of the person in whose custody the prisoner is detained, and by him refused or neglected to be given. The court to which the application is made shall forthwith award the writ of habeas corpus, unless it appears from the petition itself, or from the documents annexed, that the party can neither be discharged nor admitted to bail nor in any other manner relieved. Said writ, if issued by the court, shall be under the seal of the court, and directed to the person in whose custody the prisoner is detained, and made returnable forthwith.

(2) To the intent that no officer, sheriff, jailer, keeper, or other person to whom such writ is directed may pretend ignorance thereof, every writ shall be endorsed with the words "by the habeas corpus act". When the writ is served by any person upon the sheriff, jailer, or keeper, or other person to whom the same is directed, or brought to him, or left with any of his underofficers or deputies at the jail or place where the prisoner is detained, he or some of his underofficers or deputies, upon payment or tender of the charges of bringing the said prisoner, to be ascertained by the court awarding the said writ and endorsed thereon not exceeding fifteen cents per mile and upon sufficient security given to pay the charges of carrying him back if he is remanded, shall make return of the writ and bring, or cause to be brought, the body of the prisoner before the court which granted the writ and certify the true cause of his imprisonment within three days thereafter, unless the commitment of such person is in a place beyond the distance of twenty miles from the place where the writ is returnable; if it is beyond the distance of twenty miles and not above one hundred miles, the writ shall be returned within ten days and, if beyond the distance of one hundred miles, within twenty days after the delivery of the writ, and not longer.

§13-45-102. Petition for relief—civil cases

When any person not being committed or detained for any criminal or supposed criminal matter is confined or restrained of his liberty under any color or pretense whatever, he may proceed by appropriate action as prescribed by the Colorado rules of civil procedure in the nature of habeas corpus which petition shall be in writing, signed by the party or some person on his behalf, setting forth the facts concerning his imprisonment and wherein the illegality of such imprisonment consists, and in whose custody he is detained. The petition shall be verified by the oath or affirmation of the party applying or some other person on his behalf. If the confinement or restraint is by virtue of any judicial process or order, a copy thereof shall be annexed thereto or an affidavit made that the same has been demanded and refused. The same proceedings shall thereupon be had in all respects as are directed in *section 13-45-101*.

§13-45-103. Bearing—pleadings—discharge

(1) Upon the return of the writ of habeas corpus, a day shall be set for the hearing of the cause of imprisonment or detainer not exceeding five days thereafter, unless the prisoner requests a longer time. The prisoner may deny any of the material facts set forth in the return or may allege any fact to show either that the imprisonment or detention is unlawful or that he is then entitled to his discharge, which allegations or denials shall be made on oath. The return may be amended by leave of the court, before or after the same is filed as also may all suggestions made against it, that thereby all material facts may be ascertained. The court shall proceed in a summary way to settle the facts by hearing the testimony and arguments of all parties interested civilly, if there are any, as well as of the prisoner and the person who holds him in custody and shall dispose of the prisoner as the case may require.

(2) If it appears that the prisoner is in custody by virtue of process from any court legally constituted, he can be discharged only for some of the following causes:

(a) Where the court has exceeded the limit of its jurisdiction, either as to the matter, place, sum, or person;

(b) Where, though the original imprisonment was lawful, yet by some act, omission, or event which has subsequently taken place, the party has become entitled to his discharge;

(c) Where the process is defective in some substantial form required by law;

(d) Where the process, though in proper form, has been issued in a case or under circumstances where the law does not allow process or orders for imprisonment or arrest to issue;

(e) Where, although in proper form, the process has been issued or executed by a person either unauthorized to issue or execute the same or where the person having the custody of the prisoner under such process is not the person empowered by law to detain him;

(f) Where the process appears to have been obtained by false pretense or bribery;

(g) Where there is no general law, nor any judgment, order, or decree of a court to authorize the process, if in a civil suit, nor any conviction if in a criminal proceeding.

(3) No court on the return of a habeas corpus shall inquire into the legality or justice of a judgment or decree of a court legally constituted , i· n any other manner. In all cases where the imprisonment is for a criminal or supposed criminal matter, if it appears to the court that there is sufficient legal cause for the commitment of the prisoner although such commitment may have been informally made, or without due authority, or the process may have been executed by a person not authorized, the court shall make a new commitment, in proper form and directed to the proper officer, or admit the party to bail if the case is bailable.

§13-45-104. Witnesses—duty of sheriff
When a habeas corpus is issued to bring the body of any prisoner committed as aforesaid, unless the court issuing the same deems it wholly unnecessary and useless, the court shall issue a subpoena to the sheriff of the county where said person is confined, commanding him to summon the witnesses therein named to appear before the court at the time and place where such habeas corpus is returnable. It is the duty of the sheriff to serve such subpoena, if it is possible, in time to enable such witnesses to attend. It is the duty of the witnesses thus served with said subpoena to attend and give evidence before the court issuing the same on pain of being deemed guilty of a contempt of court and proceeded against accordingly by said court.

§13-45-105. Court to examine witnesses
On the hearing of any habeas corpus, it is the duty of the court who hears the same to examine the witnesses aforesaid, and such other witnesses as the prisoner may request, touching any offense named in the warrant of commitment whether or not said offense is technically set out in the commitment.

§13-45-106. Bail—recognizance—binding witness
(1) When any person is admitted to bail on habeas corpus, he shall enter into recognizance with one or more securities in such sum as the court directs, having regard to the circumstances of the prisoner and

the nature of the offense, conditioned upon his appearance at the district court held in and for the county where the offense was committed or where the same is to be tried. Where any court admits to bail or remands any prisoner brought before it on any writ of habeas corpus, it is the duty of the court to bind all such persons who declare anything material to prove the offense with which the prisoner is charged by recognizance to appear at the proper court having cognizance of the offense, upon a date certain, to give evidence touching the offense and not to depart the court without leave.

(2) The recognizance so taken, together with the recognizance entered into by the prisoner when he is admitted to bail, shall be certified and returned to the proper court. If any such witness neglects or refuses to enter into a recognizance when required, it is lawful for the court to commit him to jail until he enters into such recognizance or he is otherwise discharged by due course of law. If any judge neglects or refuses to bind any such witness or prisoner by recognizance when taken as aforesaid, he is guilty of a misdemeanor in office and shall be proceeded against accordingly.

§13-45-107. Remand—second writ—offenses not bailable

When any prisoner brought up on a habeas corpus is remanded to prison, it is the duty of the court remanding him to make out and deliver to the sheriff, or other person to whose custody he is remanded, an order in writing stating the cause of remanding him. If such prisoner obtains a second writ of habeas corpus, it is the duty of such sheriff or other person to whom the same is directed to return therewith the order aforesaid. If it appears that the prisoner was remanded for any offense not bailable, it shall be taken and received as conclusive, and the prisoner shall be remanded without further proceedings.

§13-45-108. Second writ—bailable offense

It is unlawful for any court, on a second writ of habeas corpus obtained by the prisoner to discharge the prisoner if he is clearly and specifically charged in the warrant of commitment with a criminal offense; but the court on the return of such second writ has power only to admit such prisoner to bail, where the offense is bailable by law, or remand him to prison where the offense is not bailable or where such prisoner fails to give the bail required.

§13-45-109. Once discharged—reimprisonment

(1) No person who has been discharged by order of a court on a habeas corpus shall be again imprisoned, restrained, or kept in custody for the same cause, unless he is afterwards indicted for the same offense or unless by the legal order or process of the court wherein he is bound by recognizance to appear.

(2) The following shall not be deemed to be the same cause:

(a) If, after a discharge for a defect of proof or on any material defect in the commitment in a criminal case, the prisoner is again arrested on sufficient proof and committed by legal process for the same offense;

(b) If, in a civil suit, the party has been discharged for any illegality in the judgment or process and is afterwards imprisoned by legal process for the same cause of action;

(c) Generally, when the discharge has been ordered on account of the nonobservance of any of the forms required by law, the party may be a second time imprisoned if the cause is legal and the forms required by law observed.

§13-45-110. Prisoner not to be removed—when

To prevent any person from avoiding or delaying his trial, it is unlawful to remove any prisoner on habeas corpus under this article out of the county in which he is confined within fifteen days next preceding the date certain set for trial except if it is to convey him into the county where the offense with which he stands charged is properly cognizable.

§13-45-111. Removal of prisoners—causes

Any person committed to any prison or in the custody of any officer, sheriff, jailer, keeper, or other person, or his underofficer or deputy, for any criminal or supposed criminal matter shall not be removed from the prison or custody into any other prison or custody, unless it is by habeas corpus or some other legal writ; or where the prisoner is delivered to some common jail; or is removed from one place to another within the county, in order to effect his discharge or trial in due course of law; or in case of sudden fire, infection, or other necessity; or where the sheriff commits such prisoner to the jail of an adjoining county for the want of a sufficient jail in his own county, as provided in *section 17-26-119, C.R.S.*; or where the prisoner, in pursuance of a law of the United States, is claimed or demanded by the executive of the United States or territories. If any person, after such commitment, makes out, signs, or countersigns any warrant for such removal except as before excepted, then he shall forfeit to the prisoner or aggrieved party a sum not exceeding three hundred dollars to be recovered by the prisoner or party aggrieved in the manner provided in *section 13-45-117*.

§13-45-112. Judge refusing or delaying writ—penalty

Any judge of a court empowered by this article to issue writs of habeas corpus who corruptly refuses to issue such writ when legally applied for in a case where such writ may lawfully issue or who, for the purpose of oppression, unreasonably delays the issuing of such writ shall for every such offense forfeit to the prisoner or party aggrieved a sum not exceeding five hundred dollars.

§13-45-113. Failure to obey writ—penalty

If any officer, sheriff, jailer, keeper, or other person to whom any such writ is directed neglects or refuses to make the returns or to bring the body of the prisoner according to the command of said writ within the time required by this article, such officer, sheriff, jailer, keeper, or other person is guilty of contempt of the court which issued said writ; whereupon the court shall issue an attachment against such officer, sheriff, jailer, keeper, or other person and cause him to be committed to the jail of the county, there to remain without bail, until he obeys the writ. Such officer, sheriff, jailer, keeper, or other person shall also forfeit to the prisoner or aggrieved party a sum not exceeding five hundred dollars and shall be incapable of holding or executing his said office.

§13-45-114. Avoiding writ—penalty

Anyone having a person in his or her custody or under his or her restraint, power, or control for whose relief a writ of habeas corpus is issued who, with the intent to avoid the effect of such writ, transfers such person to the custody, or places him or her under the control, of another or conceals him or her or changes the place of his or her confinement with intent to avoid the operation of such a writ or with intent to remove him or her out of this state commits a class 6 felony and shall be punished as provided in section 18-1.3-401, C.R.S. In any prosecution for the penalty incurred under this section, it shall not be necessary to show that the writ of habeas corpus had issued at the time of the removal, transfer, or concealment therein mentioned if it is proved that the acts therein forbidden were done with the intent to avoid the operation of such writ.

§13-45-116. Detention after release—penalty

Any person, knowing that another has been discharged by order of a competent tribunal on a habeas corpus, who, contrary to the provisions of this article, arrests or detains him again, for the same cause which was shown on the return of such writ, shall forfeit five hundred dollars for the first offense and one thousand dollars for every subsequent offense.

§13-45-117. Forfeitures go to use of prisoner
All pecuniary forfeitures under this article shall inure to the use of the party for whose benefit the writ of habeas corpus issued and shall be sued for and recovered, with costs, in the name of the state by every person aggrieved.

§13-45-118. Recovery of forfeiture not bar to civil suit
The recovery of the said penalties shall not be a bar to a civil suit for damages.

§13-45-119. Writ to testify or be surrendered—run to any county—copy—fees
The supreme and district courts within this state have power to issue writs of habeas corpus to bring the body of any person confined in any jail before them to testify or to be surrendered in discharged of bail. When a writ of habeas corpus is issued to bring into court any person to testify, or the principal to be surrendered in discharge of bail and such principal or witness is confined in any jail in this state out of the county in which such principal or witness is required to be surrendered or to testify, the writ may run into any county in this state and there be executed and returned by any officer to whom it is directed. The principal, after being surrendered or his bail discharged, or a person testifying as aforesaid shall be returned by the officer executing such writ by virtue of an order of the court for the purpose aforesaid, an attested copy of which, lodged with the jailer, exonerates such jailer of liability for an escape. The party praying out such writ of habeas corpus shall pay to the officer executing the same a reasonable sum for his services as adjudged by the courts respectively.

Current through the Second regular Session of the Sixty-Ninth General Assembly (2014).

CONNECTICUT

Connecticut General Statutes
Title 52. Civil Actions
Chapter 915. Habeas Corpus

§52-466. Application for writ of habeas corpus. Service. Return
(a)(1) An application for a writ of habeas corpus, other than an application pursuant to subdivision (2) of this subsection, shall be made to the superior court, or to a judge thereof, for the judicial district in which the person whose custody is in question is claimed to be illegally confined or deprived of such person's liberty.

(2) An application for a writ of habeas corpus claiming illegal confinement or deprivation of liberty, made by or on behalf of an inmate or prisoner confined in a correctional facility as a result of a conviction of a crime, shall be made to the superior court, or to a judge thereof, for the judicial district of Tolland.

(b) The application shall be verified by the affidavit of the applicant for the writ alleging that he truly believes that the person on whose account the writ is sought is illegally confined or deprived of his liberty.

(c) The writ shall be directed to some proper officer to serve and return, who shall serve the same by putting a true and attested copy of it into the hands of the person who has the custody of the body of the person who is directed to be presented upon the writ. If the officer fails to make immediate return of the writ, with his actions thereon, he shall pay fifty dollars to the person so held in custody.

(d) Any judge of the Superior Court to whom an application for a writ of habeas corpus is made may make the writ returnable before any other judge of the court, the consent of the other judge being first obtained; and the other judge shall thereupon proceed with the matter with the same authority as though the application had been originally presented to him.

(e) If the application is made to a judge, the judge may certify the proceedings into court and the case shall thereupon be entered upon the docket and proceeded with as though the application had originally been made to the court.

(f) A foster parent or an approved adoptive parent shall have standing to make application for a writ of habeas corpus regarding the custody of a child currently or recently in his care for a continuous period of not less than ninety days in the case of a child under three years of age at the time of such application and not less than one hundred eighty days in the case of any other child.

§52-467. Punishment for refusal to obey writ or accept copy
If any person having custody of the body of anyone directed to be presented to the court or to a judge by a writ of habeas corpus duly served fails to present the body according to the command in the writ, or refuses to accept the copy of the writ offered in service, or in any way fraudulently avoids presenting the body according to the command, or, having presented the body, does not make return of the cause of detaining the person in custody, he shall be guilty of a contempt of court and may be punished for contempt by the court or judge by commitment, and shall pay to the person so held in custody two hundred dollars.

§52-468. Commitment for contempt; application for discharge
The court may commit to prison, for any contempt of which the respondent has been guilty in this proceeding, for a period not exceeding sixty days; and the respondent may, at any time within such time of imprisonment, appear before the court which made the order of commitment, and apply for a discharge from imprisonment, which the court may, for sufficient cause shown, direct.

§52-469. Repealed. (1961, P.A. 517, §69.)

§52-470. Summary disposal of habeas corpus case. Determination of good cause for trial. Appeal by person convicted of crime
(a) The court or judge hearing any habeas corpus shall proceed in a summary way to determine the facts and issues of the case, by hearing the testimony and arguments in the case, and shall inquire fully into the cause of imprisonment and thereupon dispose of the case as law and justice require.

(b)(l) After the close of all pleadings in a habeas corpus proceeding, the court, upon the motion of any party or, on its own motion upon notice to the parties, shall determine whether there is good cause for trial for all or part of the petition.

(2) With respect to the determination of such good cause, each party may submit exhibits including, but not limited to, documentary evidence, affidavits and unsworn statements. Upon the motion of any party

and a finding by the court that such party would be prejudiced by the disclosure of the exhibits at that stage of the proceedings, the court may consider some or all of the exhibits in camera.

(3) In order to establish such good cause, the petition and exhibits must (A) allege the existence of specific facts which, if proven, would entitle the petitioner to relief under applicable law, and (B) provide a factual basis upon which the court can conclude that evidence in support of the alleged facts exists and will be presented at trial, provided the court makes no finding that such evidence is contradicted by judicially noticeable facts. If the petition and exhibits do not establish such good cause, the court shall hold a preliminary hearing to determine whether such good cause exists. If, after considering any evidence or argument by the parties at such preliminary hearing, the court finds there is not good cause for trial, the court shall dismiss all or part of the petition, as applicable.

(c) Except as provided in subsection (d) of this section, there shall be a rebuttable presumption that the filing of a petition challenging a judgment of conviction has been delayed without good cause if such petition is filed after the later of the following: (1) Five years after the date on which the judgment of conviction is deemed to be a final judgment due to the conclusion of appellate review or the expiration of the time for seeking such review; (2) October, 1, 2017; or (3) two years after the date on which the constitutional statutory right asserted in the petition was initially recognized and made retroactive pursuant to a decision of the Supreme Court or Appellate Court of this state or the Supreme Court of the United States or by the enactment of any public or special act. The time periods set forth in this subsection shall not be tolled during the pendency of any other petition challenging the same conviction.

(d) In the case of a petition filed subsequent to a judgment on a prior petition challenging the same conviction, there shall be a rebuttable presumption that the filing of the subsequent petition has been delayed without good cause if such petition is filed after the later of the following: (1) Two years after the date on which the judgment in the prior petition is deemed to be a final judgment due to the conclusion of appellate review or the expiration of the time for seeking such review; (2) October 1, 2014; or (3) two years after the date on which the constitutional or statutory right asserted in the petition was initially recognized and made retroactive pursuant to a decision of the Supreme Court or Appellate Court of this state or the Supreme Court of the United States or by the enactment of any public or special act. For the purposes of this section, the withdrawal of a prior petition challenging the same conviction shall not constitute a judgment. The time periods set forth in this subsection shall not be tolled during the pendency of any other petition challenging the same conviction. Nothing in this subsection shall create or enlarge the right of the petitioner to file a subsequent petition under applicable law.

(e) In a case in which the rebuttable presumption of delay under subsection (c) or (d) of this section applies, the court, upon the request of the respondent, shall issue an order to show cause why the petition should be permitted to proceed. The petitioner or, if applicable, the petitioner's counsel, shall have a meaningful opportunity to investigate the basis for the delay and respond to the order. If, after such opportunity, the court finds that the petitioner has not demonstrated good cause for the delay, the court shall dismiss the petition. For the purposes of this subsection, good cause includes, but not limited to, the discovery of new evidence which materially affects the merits of the case and which could not have been discovered by the exercise of due diligence in time to meet the requirements of subsection (c) or (d) of this section.

(f) Subsections (b) to (e), inclusive, of this section shall not apply to (1) a claim asserting actual innocence, (2) a petition filed to challenge the conditions of confinement, or (3) a petition filed to challenge a conviction for a capital felony for which a sentence of death is imposed under *section 53a-46a*.

(g) No appeal from the judgment rendered in a habeas corpus proceeding brought by or on behalf of a person who has been convicted of a crime in order to obtain such person's release may be taken unless the appellant, within ten days after the case is decided, petitions the judge before whom the case was tried or, if such judge is unavailable, a judge of the Superior Court designated by the Chief Court Administrator, to certify that a question is involved in the decision which ought to be reviewed by the court having jurisdiction and the judge so certifies.

Current with enactments of Public Acts of the 2014 February Regular Session of the Connecticut General Assembly effective on or before July 1, 2014.

DELAWARE

Delaware Code
Title 10. Courts and Judicial Procedure
Chapter 69. Habeas Corpus

§6901. Jurisdiction to grant writ
The writ of habeas corpus shall be awarded and issued by the Superior Court except in cases involving child support enforcement in which case the writ shall be awarded and issued by the Family Court. The writ may also be awarded and issued by the Family Court in other cases which are otherwise within its jurisdiction. A petition for the issuance of a writ of habeas corpus may be reviewed and decided by the judge issuing the order incarcerating the petitioner in the first instance.

§6902. Persons entitled to writs; exceptions
Every person imprisoned or restrained of liberty by any officer or person, for any cause or under any color or pretense, shall have remedy by the writ of habeas corpus, and may obtain relief, except:

(1) Persons committed or detained on a charge of treason or felony, the species whereof is plainly and fully set forth in the commitment;

(2) Persons convicted of, or charged with, treason, felony, or any offense in another state, who ought, by the Constitution of the United States, to be delivered to the executive of such state, subject to the provisions of §2510 of Title 11,; and

(3) Persons imprisoned by the authority of the United States.

§6903. Person committed for contempt; notice of hearing
(a) A person committed by any judge of this State, a justice of the peace, or by the mayor or any alderperson of any city or town, for a contempt, except a contempt issued by the Family Court in a case involving a child support order, shall be entitled to the writ of habeas corpus in the Superior Court. A person committed by the Family Court in a case involving a child support order shall be entitled to the writ of habeas corpus in the Family Court.

(b) Notice shall be given to the committing magistrate of the time and place of hearing. The prisoner may deny the alleged contempt, under oath. The court or judge may remand or discharge the party.

§6904. Custody of minor child
A writ of habeas corpus may be procured by 1 spouse living apart from the other, without being divorced, to determine the proper custody or charge of a minor child of the marriage, and orders may be made thereon, as provided by §705 of Title 13 [repealed].

6905. Application
Application for a writ of habeas corpus may be made by the party complaining, or anyone for such party, setting forth upon oath, where and by whom, and for what cause, to the best of his or her knowledge, such party is imprisoned or restrained of liberty, and exhibiting a copy of the commitment, if there be any, or showing why such copy could not be procured.

§6906. Award and service of writ
(a) The court or judge, to whom an application under this chapter is made, shall, without delay, under penalty of $1,000 to the party aggrieved, award and issue a writ of habeas corpus under seal of the court, directed to the officer or person in whose custody the prisoner is detained, returnable forthwith before such court or judge.

(b) The writ may be served by anyone who will do the service.

§6907. Method of service; return
(a) When the writ of habeas corpus is served on the person to whom it is directed, either personally or by being left with any deputy or agent of the person at the place where the prisoner is detained, such person shall, without delay and within 3 days thereafter, produce the body of the prisoner as therein commanded; and shall fully certify in writing and under oath, the true cause or causes of the prisoner's detainer, and a copy of all process under which the prisoner is detained.

(b) The return may be contradicted, and may also be amended.

§6908. Examination by court
The court or judge shall, upon the return of a writ of habeas corpus, without delay, proceed to examine the causes of imprisonment or restraint, giving notice to any party interested, and to the Attorney General of the Attorney General's deputy in cases of felony. The examination may be adjourned if necessary and the prisoner detained.

§6909. Discharge generally; defects in commitment
(a) If no legal cause be shown for the imprisonment or restraint, the court or judge shall discharge the party therefrom. Any order entered upon a petition for a writ of habeas corpus discharging the prisoner from custody or otherwise granting relief to the prisoner may be appealed by the State to the Delaware Supreme Court.

(b) No person shall be discharged for a mere defect in the commitment, if the evidence before the court or judge is sufficient to require that he or she should be committed, or bound for his or her appearance. In such case the committing magistrate shall be summoned, proper witnesses examined, and the accused committed properly.

§6910. Repealed

§6911. Discharge on bail

If the party is detained for any cause or offense for which the party is bailable, the party shall be discharged on becoming bound by recognizance, in a proper sum and with sufficient surety, for appearance at the court having cognizance of the matter. If the party does not give such security, the party shall be remanded with an order therefor expressing the sum in which the party is held to bail, and the court at which the party is required to appear. Any justice of the peace, court or other officer authorized by law to take bail, at any time before the sitting of the court, bail the party pursuant to such orders.

§6912. Reduction of excessive bail

If the party is committed on mesne process in a civil action for want of bail, and it appears that the sum required is excessive, the court or judge shall decide what bail is reasonable, and shall order that, on giving such bail, the party shall be discharged.

§6913. Remand

If the party is lawfully imprisoned or restrained and is not entitled to be discharged on giving bail, the party shall be remanded or otherwise properly committed.

§6914. Delivering copy of warrant or process; penalty

Any officer or such officer's deputy, neglecting for 6 hours after demand, to deliver a true copy of any warrant or process by which the officer detains a prisoner to any person who demands such copy and tenders a reasonable sum for copying the same, shall forfeit and pay to such prisoner $200.

§6915. Returning writ and producing body; violations and penalties; compelling production

(a) If any officer or person to whom the writ of habeas corpus is directed, or any deputy of such officer, or agent of such person, neglects to return the writ and produce the body as required by §6907 of this title, it shall be a contempt of the court under whose seal the writ issued and a forfeiture of office. Such officer, person, deputy, or agent shall forfeit and pay to the prisoner $500.

(b) Where the writ of habeas corpus is made returnable before the Superior Court, such contempt shall be punishable by the Court by both fine and imprisonment, or either, in its discretion; and the Court may, by attachment for contempt, compel the production before it, of the body of the person imprisoned or restrained of liberty.

§6916. Evasion of writ; penalty

Whoever, having in his or her custody or under his or her power, any person entitled to a writ of habeas corpus, whether any writ has been issued or not, with intent to elude the service of such writ, or to avoid the effect thereof, transfer the prisoner to the custody, or places the prisoner under the power or control of any other person, or conceals the prisoner, or changes the place of the prisoner's confinement, shall forfeit and pay to the party aggrieved $3,600.

§6917. Rearrest of discharged person for same offense; exceptions

No person who has been discharged on a habeas corpus shall be again imprisoned or restrained for the same cause, unless the person is indicted therefor, or convicted thereof, or committed for want of bail by some court having jurisdiction of the cause; or unless, after a discharge for defect of proof, or for some material defect in the commitment in a criminal case, the person is again arrested on sufficient proof, and committed by legal process for the same offense.

§6918. Costs and fees

The costs in any proceeding under this chapter may be ordered to be paid by the county or otherwise. If the commitment is insufficient, the justice or officer who made it shall have no compensation for attendance.

FLORIDA

Florida Statutes
Title VI. Civil Practice and Procedure
Chapter 79. Habeas Corpus

79.01. Application and writ

When any person detained in custody, whether charged with a criminal offense or not, applies to the Supreme Court or any justice thereof, or to any district court of appeal or any judge thereof or to any circuit court judge for a writ of habeas corpus and shows by affidavit or evidence probable cause to believe that he or she is detained without lawful authority, the court, justice, or judge to whom such application is made shall grant the writ forthwith, against the person in whose custody the applicant is detained and returnable immediately before any of the courts, justices, or judges as the writ directs.

79.02. Bond may be required

When it appears necessary, the court, justice, or judge granting the writ shall require bond with surety to be approved by the judge or clerk payable to the Governor executed in such manner and reasonable penalty as the court, justice, or judge prescribes; conditioned for the payment of the charges and costs awarded against the prisoner and that he or she will not escape by the way. The bond shall be filed and may be sued on in the name of the Governor for the benefit of any person interested therein. In the event of inability to give bond for the payment of charges and costs, he or she may be permitted, in the place thereof, to make deposit in such amount as the court, justice, or judge requires.

79.03. Service of writ

When issued, the writ shall be served by the sheriff of the county in which the petitioner is alleged to be detained on the officer or other person against whom it is issued, or in his or her absence from the place where the prisoner is confined, on the person having the immediate custody of the prisoner. When the sheriff of the county is the person holding the party detained, a delivery to or receipt of the writ by the sheriff is sufficient service.

79.04. Return to writ

(1) The person on whom the writ is served shall bring the body of the prisoner, or cause it to be brought, before the court, justice or judge before whom the writ is made returnable without delay and at the same time certify to the cause of the detention.

(2) When the writ is issued, the court shall set an early return date, at which time the formal return of the defendant shall be made. In the absence of a motion to quash or a motion for discharge notwithstanding the return, issue is joined when the return is filed and the action shall be ready for final disposition.

79.05. Compelling return and production of body
(1) Civil liability.—Any person failing to return to the writ served on him or her with the cause of the prisoner's detention, or to bring the body of the prisoner before the court, justice, or judge, according to the command of the writ for 3 days after the service shall forfeit and pay to the prisoner the sum of $300.

(2) By proceedings by the court.—A justice or judge in vacation may enforce obedience to any writ of habeas corpus and in cases pending before the Supreme Court, or any of the justices thereof, writs for the enforcement of obedience may be directed to the sheriff or other officer.

79.06. Effect of the return
(1) Generally.—The return made to the writ may be amended, and is not conclusive as to the facts stated therein, but the court, justice or judge before whom the return is made may examine into the cause of the imprisonment or detention, receive evidence in contradiction of the return, and determine it as the truth of the case requires.

(2) In cases of contempt.—On the return of the writ when the cause of detention appears to be a contempt, plainly and specifically charged in the commitment by some court officer or body having authority to commit for the contempt so charged and for the time stated, the court, justice or judge before whom the writ is returnable shall remand the prisoner forthwith if the time for detention for contempt has not expired.

79.07. Procurement of evidence
When it is inconvenient to procure the personal attendance of a witness, the witness's affidavit, taken upon reasonable notice to the adverse party, may be received in evidence.

9.071. Notice to prosecutor
If the validity of any statute, criminal law proceeding or conviction is attacked by habeas corpus in the circuit court, notice of the application for the writ shall be given to the prosecuting attorney of the court in which the statute under attack is being applied, the criminal law proceeding is being maintained or the conviction has occurred.

79.08. Hearing and judgment
The court, justice, or judge before whom the prisoner is brought shall inquire without delay into the cause of the prisoner's imprisonment, and shall either discharge the prisoner, admit him or her to bail or remand him or her to custody, as the law and evidence require; and shall either award against the prisoner the charges of his or her transportation, not exceeding 15 cents per mile and the costs of the proceedings, or shall award the costs in the prisoner's favor, or shall award no costs or charges against either party, as is right. The clerk of the court in which such action is pending shall issue execution for the costs and charges awarded.

79.09. Filing of papers
Before a circuit judge the petition and the papers shall be filed with the clerk of the circuit court of the county in which the prisoner is detained. Before the other courts, justices or judges, the papers shall be filed with the clerk of the court on which the justice or judge sits.

79.10. Effect of judgment
The judgment is conclusive until reversed and no person remanded by the judgment while it continues in force shall be at liberty to obtain another habeas corpus for the same cause or by any other proceeding

bring the same matter again in question except by an appeal or by action of false imprisonment; nor shall any person who is discharged from confinement by the judgment be afterward confined or imprisoned for the same cause except by order of a court of competent jurisdiction.

79.11. Repealed by Laws 1967, c. 67-254, §49

79.12. Trial of accused pending appeal
When in any criminal prosecution a writ of habeas corpus is applied for by any person charged with any criminal offense and the accused has been remanded to custody by the court to which such application is made, a supersedeas of the order made on appeal being taken to an appellate court shall not prevent the state from proceeding with the prosecution of the accused pending the decision by the appellate court in the habeas corpus, but the state may prosecute the accused as if appeal had not been taken in habeas corpus. If the accused is convicted of the charge, the court shall withhold imposition of sentence and final judgment until the appellate court has determined the issues presented in the habeas corpus.

Current through Ch. 254 (End) of the 2014 2nd Reg. Sess. of the Twenty-Third Legislature

GEORGIA

Code of Georgia Annotated
Title 9. Civil Practice
Chapter 14. Habeas Corpus
Article 1. General Provisions

§9-14-1. Who may sue out writ
(a) Any person restrained of his liberty under any pretext whatsoever, except under sentence of a state court of record, may seek a writ of habeas corpus to inquire into the legality of the restraint.

(b) Any person alleging that another person in whom for any cause he is interested is kept illegally from the custody of the applicant may seek a writ of habeas corpus to inquire into the legality of the restraint.

(c) Any person restrained of his liberty as a result of a sentence imposed by any state court of record may seek a writ of habeas corpus to inquire into the legality of the restraint.

§9-14-2. Detention of spouse or child
In all writs of habeas corpus sought on account of the detention of a spouse or child, the court on hearing all the facts may exercise its discretion as to whom the custody of the spouse or child shall be given and shall have the power to give the custody of a child to a third person.

§9-14-3. Application; how made and what to contain
The application for the writ of habeas corpus shall be by petition in writing, signed by the applicant, his attorney or agent, or some other person in his behalf, and shall state:

(1) The name or description of the person whose liberty is restrained;

(2) The person restraining, the mode of restraint, and the place of detention as nearly as practicable;

(3) The cause or pretense of the restraint. If the restraint is under the pretext of legal process, a copy of the process must be annexed to the petition if this is within the power of the applicant;

(4) A distinct averment of the alleged illegality in the restraint or of any other reason why the writ of habeas corpus is sought; and

(5) A prayer for the writ of habeas corpus.

§9-14-4. *Petition, how verified and to whom presented*
The petition for the writ of habeas corpus must be verified by the oath of the applicant or some other person in his behalf. It may be presented to the judge of the superior court of the circuit in which the illegal detention exists who may order the party restrained of his liberty to be brought before him from any county in his circuit, or it may be presented to the judge of the probate court of the county, except in cases of capital felonies or in which a person is held for extradition under warrant of the Governor.

§9-14-5. *When writ must be granted*
When upon examination of the petition for a writ of habeas corpus it appears to the judge that the restraint of liberty is illegal, he shall grant the writ, requiring the person restraining the liberty of another or illegally detaining such person in his custody to bring the person before him at a time and place to be specified in the writ for the purpose of an examination into the cause of the detention.

§9-14-6. *Form of writ*
The writ of habeas corpus may be substantially as follows:

—IN THE _____ COURT OF _____ COUNTY—
—STATE OF GEORGIA—

A.B.,)
Petitioner)
) Civil action
v.)
) File no. _____
C.D,)
Respondent)
)

—WRIT OF HABEAS CORPUS—

To C.D.,:

You are hereby commanded to produce the body of _____, alleged to be illegally detained by you, together with the cause of the detention, before me on the _____ day of _____, _____, at _____: _____ _____.M., then and there to be disposed of as the law directs. Given under my hand and official signature, this _____ day of _____, _____.

_____
Judge

§9-14-7. Return day of the writ
The return day of the writ of habeas corpus in civil cases shall always be within 20 days after the presentation of the petition therefor. The return day of the writ in criminal cases shall always be within eight days after the presentation of the petition therefor.

§9-14-8. How and by whom the writ shall be served
The writ of habeas corpus shall be served by delivery of a copy thereof by any officer authorized to make a return of any process or by any other citizen. The entry of the officer or the affidavit of the citizen serving the writ shall be sufficient evidence of the service. The person serving the writ shall exhibit the original if required to do so. If personal service cannot be effected, the writ may be served by leaving a copy at the house, jail, or other place in which the party in whose behalf the writ issues is detained.

§9-14-9. When and how the party detained may be arrested
If the affidavit of the applicant to the effect that he has reason to apprehend that the party detaining or holding another in custody will remove him beyond the limits of the county or conceal him from the officers of the law is filed with the petition, the judge granting the writ shall at the same time issue his warrant directed to the sheriff, deputy sheriff, coroner, or any lawful constable of the county requiring the officers to search for and arrest the body of the person detained and to bring him before the judge to be disposed of as he may direct.

§9-14-10. Within what time return to writ must be made
The return of the party served with the writ shall be made at the time and place specified by the court. Two days from the time of service shall be allowed for every 20 miles which the party has to travel from the place of detention to the place appointed for the hearing. If service has not been made a sufficient time before the hearing to cover the time allowed in this Code section to reach the place of hearing, the return shall be made within the time so allowed immediately after the service.

§9-14-11. Return to be under oath, and body produced
Every return to a writ of habeas corpus shall be under oath. If the custody or detention of the party on whose behalf the writ issues is admitted, his body shall be produced unless prevented by providential causes or prohibited by law.

§9-14-12. Transfer of custody must be stated in return
If the return denies the custody or detention of the person in question, it shall further state distinctly the latest date, if ever, at which custody was had and when and to whom custody was transferred. If it appears that a transfer of custody was made to avoid the writ of habeas corpus, the party making the return may be imprisoned, in the discretion of the judge hearing the case, until the body of the party kept or detained is produced.

§9-14-13. When process must be produced
In every case in which detention is justified under legal process, the legal process shall be produced and submitted to the judge at the hearing of the return.

§9-14-14. Trial of issue on the return
If the return denies any of the material facts stated in the petition or alleges other facts upon which issue is taken, the judge hearing the return may in a summary manner hear testimony as to the issue. To that end, he may compel the attendance of witnesses and the production of papers, may adjourn the

examination of the question, or may exercise any other power of a court which the principles of justice may require.

§9-14-15. Notice of the hearing
If the person who is the subject of a petition for the writ of habeas corpus is detained upon a criminal charge and the district attorney is in the county, he shall be notified of the hearing. If he is not, the notice shall be given to the prosecutor of the criminal charge.

§9-14-16. When party shall not be discharged
No person shall be discharged upon the hearing of a writ of habeas corpus in the following cases:

(1) When he is imprisoned under lawful process issued from a court or competent jurisdiction unless his case is one in which bail is allowed and proper bail is tendered;

(2) By reason of any irregularity in the warrant or commitment where the same substantially conforms to the requirements of law;

(3) For want of bond to prosecute;

(4) When the person is imprisoned under a bench warrant which is regular upon its face;

(5) By reason of any misnomer in the warrant or commitment when the court is satisfied that the person detained is the party charged with the offense;

(6) When the person is in custody for a contempt of court and the court has not exceeded its jurisdiction in the length of the imprisonment imposed; or

(7) In any other case in which it appears that the detention is authorized by law.

§9-14-17. No discharge for defect in proceedings
If the person in question is detained upon a criminal charge and it appears to the court that there is probable cause for his detention, he shall not be discharged for any defect in the affidavit, warrant, or commitment until a reasonable time has been given to the prosecutor to remedy the defect by a new proceeding.

§9-14-18. Offense committed in another state
If a person is arrested on suspicion of the commission of an offense in another state and the suspicion is reasonable, the person shall not be discharged until a sufficient time has been given for a demand to be made on the Governor for his rendition.

§9-14-19. Powers of court in other cases
In cases other than those specified in *Code Sections 9-14-16*, *9-14-17*, and *9-14-18*, the judge hearing the return shall discharge, remand, or admit the person in question to bail or shall deliver him to the custody of the officer or person entitled thereto, as the principles of law and justice may require.

§9-14-20. Proceedings must be recorded
In all habeas corpus cases, the proceedings shall be returned to the clerk of the superior court of the county the judge of which heard the same or to the probate court if the case was heard by the judge of the probate court and shall be recorded by such officer as are other cases. For such services, the officer shall receive the fees provided by *Code Section 15-6-77*.

§9-14-21. Costs; discretion; execution
The judge hearing the return to a writ of habeas corpus may in his discretion award the costs of the proceeding against either party and may order execution to issue therefor by the clerk.

§9-14-22. Practice as to appeals; hearing in habeas corpus cases.
(a) Appeals in habeas corpus cases shall be governed, in all respects where applicable, by the laws in reference to appeals in other cases regarding the practice in the lower courts and in the Supreme Court relating to the time and manner of signing, filing, serving, transmitting, and hearing.

(b) It shall be the duty of the Supreme Court to give a speedy hearing and determination in habeas corpus cases either under existing rules or under special rules to be formulated by the court for such purpose.

(c) If the judgment of the court below is affirmed by the Supreme Court, the clerk of the Supreme Court shall promptly transmit the remittitur to the clerk of the court from which the appeal was taken. Upon the receipt of the remittitur, the clerk shall notify the judge of the court who shall have full power to pass an order, sentence, or judgment necessary to carry into execution the judgment of the court.

§9-14-23. Disobedience of the writ, how punished
Any person disregarding the writ of habeas corpus in any manner whatever shall be liable to attachment for contempt, issued by the judge granting the writ, under which attachment the person may be imprisoned until he complies with the legal requirements of the writ.

Article 2. Procedure for Persons Under Sentence of State Court of Record

§9-14-40. Findings of General Assembly
(a) The General Assembly finds that:

(1) Expansion of the scope of habeas corpus in federal court by decisions of the United States Supreme Court together with other decisions of the court substantially curtailing the doctrine of waiver of constitutional rights by an accused and limiting the requirement of exhaustion of state remedies to those currently available have resulted in an increasingly large number of convictions of the courts of this state being collaterally attacked by federal habeas corpus based upon issues and contentions not previously presented to or passed upon by courts of this state;

(2) The increased reliance upon federal courts tends to weaken state courts as instruments for the vindication of constitutional rights with a resultant deterioration of the federal system and federal-state relations; and

(3) To alleviate such problems, it is necessary that the scope of state habeas corpus be expanded and the state doctrine of waiver of rights be modified.

(b) The General Assembly further finds that expansion of state habeas corpus to include many sharply contested issues of a factual nature requires that only the superior courts have jurisdiction of such cases.

§9-14-42. Denial of constitutional or other rights; waiver of objections
(a) Any person imprisoned by virtue of a sentence imposed by a state court of record who asserts that in the proceedings which resulted in his conviction there was a substantial denial of his rights under the Constitution of the United States or of this state may institute a proceeding under this article.

(b) The right to object to the composition of the grand or trial jury will be deemed waived under this Code section unless the person challenging the sentence shows in the petition and satisfies the court that cause exists for his being allowed to pursue the objection after the conviction and sentence have otherwise become final.

(c) Any action brought pursuant to this article shall be filed within one year in the case of a misdemeanor, except as otherwise provided in *Code Section 40-13-33*, or within four years in the case of a felony, other than one challenging a conviction for which a death sentence has been imposed or challenging a sentence of death, from:

(1) The judgment of conviction becoming final by the conclusion of direct review or the expiration of the time for seeking such review; provided, however, that any person whose conviction has become final as of July 1, 2004, regardless of the date of conviction, shall have until July 1, 2005, in the case of a misdemeanor or until July 1, 2008, in the case of a felony to bring an action pursuant to this Code section;

(2) The date on which an impediment to filing a petition which was created by state action in violation of the Constitution or laws of the United States or of this state is removed, if the petitioner was prevented from filing such state action;

(3) The date on which the right asserted was initially recognized by the Supreme Court of the United States or the Supreme Court of Georgia, if that right was newly recognized by said courts and made retroactively applicable to cases on collateral review; or

(4) The date on which the facts supporting the claims presented could have been discovered through the exercise of due diligence.

(d) At the time of sentencing, the court shall inform the defendant of the periods of limitation set forth in subsection (c) of this Code section.

§9-14-43. *Exclusive jurisdiction in superior court in county in which petitioner detained*
A petition brought under this article must be filed in the superior court of the county in which the petitioner is being detained. The superior courts of such counties shall have exclusive jurisdiction of habeas corpus actions arising under this article. If the petitioner is not in custody or is being detained under the authority of the United States, any of the several states other than Georgia, or any foreign state, the petition must be filed in the superior court of the county in which the conviction and sentence which is being challenged was imposed.

§9-14-44. *Contents and verification of petition*
A petition brought under this article shall identify the proceeding in which the petitioner was convicted, give the date of rendition of the final judgment complained of, clearly set forth the respects in which the petitioner's right were violated, and state with specificity which claims were raised at trial or on direct appeal, providing appropriate citations to the trial or appellate record. The petition shall have attached thereto affidavits, records, or other evidence supporting its allegations or shall state why the same are not attached. The petition shall identify any previous proceedings that the petitioner may have taken to secure relief from his or her conviction and, in the case of prior habeas corpus petitions, shall state which claims were previously raised. Argument and citations of authorities shall be omitted from the petition; however, a brief may be submitted in support of the petition setting forth any applicable argument. The petition must be verified by the oath of the applicant or of some other person in his or her behalf.

§9-14-45. Service of petition

Service of a petition brought under this article shall be made upon the person having custody of the petitioner. If the petitioner is being detained under the custody of the Department of Corrections, an additional copy of the petition shall be served on the Attorney General. If the petitioner is being detained under the custody of some authority other than the Department of Corrections, an additional copy of the petition shall be served upon the district attorney of the county in which the petition is filed. Service upon the Attorney General or the district attorney may be had by mailing a copy of the petition and a proper certificate of service.

§9-14-46. Custody, control and production of petitioner

Custody and control of the petitioner shall be retained by the Department of Corrections or other authority having custody of the petitioner. It shall be the duty of the department or authority to produce the petitioner at such times and places as the court may direct.

HAWAII

Hawaii Revised Statutes
Title 36. Civil Remedies and Defenses and Special Proceedings
Chapter 660. Habeas Corpus

§660-3. Issuable by whom

The supreme court, the justices thereof, and the circuit courts may issue writs of habeas corpus in cases in which persons are unlawfully restrained of their liberties; provided that persons committed or detained by order of the family court or under chapter 334 may, and if the jurisdiction of the family court is exclusive, shall, prosecute their application in the family court.

§660-4. For prisoners, for trial or testimony

Nothing in this chapter shall be construed to restrain the power of any court of record to issue a writ of habeas corpus ad respondendum, when necessary, to bring before it any prisoner for trial in any criminal cause, lawfully pending in the court, or a writ of habeas corpus ad testificandum, to bring in any prisoner to be examined as a witness in any action or proceeding, civil or criminal, pending in the court, when it thinks the personal attendance and examination of the witness is necessary for the attainment of justice. The writ may be issued for such purposes by any court of record in the exercise of a sound discretion, and with due regard to conflicting interests and liabilities, anything in this chapter to the contrary notwithstanding.

§660-5. Complaint

Application for the writ or an order to show cause shall be made to the court or judge authorized to issue the same, by complaint by writing, signed by the party for whose relief it is intended, or by some person in the party's behalf, setting forth:

> (1) The person by whom, and the place where, the party is imprisoned or restrained, naming the party and the person detaining the party, if their names are known, and describing them if they are not known;

(2) The cause or pretense of imprisonment or restraint, according to the knowledge and belief of the applicant;

(3) If the imprisonment or restraint is by virtue of any warrant or other process, an annexed copy thereof, unless it is made to appear that a sufficient reason exists for not annexing the same;

(4) That there has been no determination of the legality of the detention on a prior application for a petition for a writ of habeas corpus, or, if there has been a previous determination, the new grounds, if any, not presented and determined upon the previous application.

the facts alleged shall be verified by the oath of some credible person, to be administered by any person authorized to administer oaths.

§660-6. Form of writ
The court or judge to whom the complaint is made shall, without delay, award and issue the writ unless it appears from the application that the person detained is not entitled thereto or an order to show cause is issued under *section 660-7*. The writ of habeas corpus may be in the following form:

State of Hawaii.

To .... greeting.

We command you that immediately upon the receipt of this writ, you have and produce before .... at .... the body of .... who is unjustly imprisoned and restrained of his liberty, as it is said, to do and receive what shall then and there be considered concerning him in this behalf. And have you there this writ, with your doings thereon.

Witness the Honorable .... at .... this .... day of .... [20 ..]

[Seal]

§660-7. Order to show cause in lieu of writ
The court or judge to whom the complaint is made may issue an issue an order directing the person by whom the party is imprisoned or restrained, to appear and show cause for the imprisonment or restraint at such time as the court shall direct, but not later than five days from the date of the order to show cause; provided that whenever the record shows that there is a material issue of fact to be resolved by the taking of evidence the court shall order that the person detained be produced for the hearing.

§660-9. Sunday
Any writ of process authorized by this chapter may be issued or served on Sunday.

§660-12. By supreme court; to whom returnable
Whenever the writ or order to show cause is issued by the supreme court or a justice thereof, it may be made returnable before the supreme court or a circuit court.

§660-13. Issuance to person of known name
If the name of the person by whom the party is alleged to be restrained of the party's liberty is unknown

or uncertain, the person may be described by an assumed appellation. Whoever is served with writ or order to show cause, shall be deemed to be the person intended thereby.

§660-14. For person of unknown name
The person to be produced shall be designated by the person's name, if known, and if that is not known or is uncertain, the person may be designated in any other manner, so that it can be known who is the person intended.

§660-15. Costs
If the party is confined in any prison or is in the custody of any civil officer, the court or judge granting the writ shall certify thereon the sum to be paid for the expense of bringing the party from the place where the party is imprisoned or restrained. The officer to whom the same is directed shall not be bound to obey it, unless that sum is paid or tendered to the officer. This section is subject to section 607-3, pursuant to which prepayment of the expense may be waived, or the sum required may be reduced or remitted.

§660-16. Person held until writ issues, when
Whenever it appears by satisfactory proof, by affidavit or otherwise, to any court or judge authorized by law to issue writs habeas corpus, that anyone is illegally held in custody, confinement, or restraint and that there is good reason to believe that the person will be carried out of the jurisdiction of the court or judge or will suffer some irreparable injury before compliance with a writ of habeas corpus can be enforced, the court or judge may cause a warrant to be issued, reciting the facts and directed to the sheriff or the sheriff's deputy, or the chief of police of the city and county of Honolulu or the chief's deputies, or to any police officer in any other county, commanding such officer to take such person thus held in custody, confinement, or restraint and forthwith bring the person before the court or judge, and hold the person there until a writ of habeas corpus can be duly issued and served, after which the party alleged to be illegally restrained, shall be deemed to be before the court designated to hear the return in obedience to the writ.

§660-17. Return to be prompt
Any person to whom a writ of habeas corpus is directed, upon payment or tender of reasonable charges or expenses for its execution if ordered by the court, and any person to whom an order to show cause is directed, shall make return thereto with as much promptness as the nature of the case will permit.

§660-18. Contents
The person making the return shall state therein, in writing, plainly and unequivocally:

(1) Whether he has or has not the person designated in his custody or power, or in any manner under his restraint or control;

(2) If he has the person in his custody or power, or under his restraint or control, the authority, and the time, and whole cause of such imprisonment or restraint, with a copy of any process or warrant under which the person is detained;

(3) If he has had the person in his custody or power, or under his restraint or control, and has transferred such custody, restraint, or control to another, or if he has any knowledge or suspicion that any other person exercises or claims to exercise such custody, power, restraint, or control, all that he knows or suspects.

No return shall be adjudged sufficient when the respondent has once held the person in his custody or power, or under his restraint or control, unless it states fully all that the respondent knows or suspects, or alleges unequivocally that he neither knows nor suspects, nor has any cause to suspect anything as to the custody or restraint of the person alleged to be detained, up to the time of making the return.

§660-19. Signature, oath, evidence
The return shall be signed by the person making it, and sworn to be the person, unless the person is a sworn public officer making the return in the person's official capacity. The return shall be evidence in the case, but not conclusive.

§660-20. Body to be produced, except when
The person making the return to a writ of habeas corpus shall bring the body of the person, if in his custody or power, or under his restraint or control, according to the command in the writ, unless prevented by the sickness or infirmity of the person. This shall not prevent the person making the return, if a private person, from demanding in advance actual necessary expenses of travel and transportation.

§660-21. Procedure in case of sickness, etc.
When from sickness or infirmity of the person, the person cannot properly be brought to the place appointed for the return, that fact shall be set forth, and if verified by affidavit and established to the satisfaction of the court, the hearing may be adjourned to such other time or place or such order may be made as justice may require.

§660-22. Disobeying writ or order to show cause, penalties
Any person who neglects or ref uses promptly to perform any duty imposed upon such person by virtue of any writ of habeas corpus or order to show cause, conformably to this chapter, shall be responsible in a civil action to any person aggrieved for damages occasioned thereby, and may be fined not more than $5,000, or imprisoned at hard labor not more than ten years, or both.

§660-23. Evading service, penalties
The liabilities and penalties of section 660-22 shall also be imposed upon any person who, having in his custody or under his power any person entitled to a writ of habeas corpus, with intent to elude the service of the writ or to avoid the effect thereof, transfers such person to the custody or places him under the control or power of any other person, or conceals him or changes his place of confinement.

§660-24. Hearing without delay
Upon the return of the writ or order to show cause, the court shall proceed without delay to examine the causes of imprisonment or restraint. The examination may be adjourned from time to time as circumstances may reasonably require.

§660-25. Notice to other parties, when
If the person is detained on any process under which any other person has an interest in his detention, and the other person or his attorney is within the State and can be notified without unreasonable delay, the person detained shall not be discharged until the other person or his attorney has had an opportunity to be heard.

§660-26. Notice to attorney general, when
If the person is imprisoned on any criminal accusation, reasonable notice shall be given to the attorney general, or the attorney general's deputy, lawfully appointed, to appear and object if the attorney general or the attorney general's deputy thinks fit.

§660-27. Return, hearing

The person imprisoned or restrained may deny any of the facts set forth in the return and may allege other material facts, and the court shall proceed in a summary way to examine the causes of imprisonment or restraint and to hear evidence which may be offered by any person interested or authorized to appear either in support of the imprisonment or restraint or against it, and thereupon to dispose of the party as law and justice may require.

§660-28. Bail, etc., before judgment

Except as otherwise provided:

(1) Until judgment is given, the court may remand the party or accept bail for the party's appearance from day to day or may place the party under special care and custody, as circumstances may require; and

(2) After judgment is given, an order made by the court under paragraph (1) shall be continued in effect during a stay of enforcement of judgment, unless the trial court, the intermediate appellate court, or the supreme court after taking of the appeal, terminates the order or makes other provision in the circumstances.

§660-29. Discharge, when

If no legal cause for the imprisonment or restraint is shown the person shall be immediately discharged therefrom.

§660-30. Admitted to bail, when

If the person is detained for any cause or offense and admittance to bail is a matter of right, the person shall be admitted to bail, or bail may be dispensed with as provided by the State Constitution. If the person cannot furnish the bail ordered, then the person shall be remanded with an order of the court, expressing the sum in which the person is held to bail and the court at which the person is required to appear.

§660-31. Bail reduced, when

If the person is committed because the person cannot furnish the bail ordered, and the bail which is required appears to be excessive or unreasonable, the court shall decide what bail is reasonable, and shall order that upon furnishing such bail the person shall be discharged from custody.

§660-32. Remanded, when

If the person is lawfully imprisoned or restrained, and is not entitled to be admitted to bail, he shall be remanded to the person or officer having lawful authority to detain him.

§660-33. Discharge, effect of

No person who has been discharged upon a writ of habeas corpus shall be again imprisoned or restrained for the same cause, unless the person is indicated therefor, or convicted thereof, committed for want of bail, by some court of record, having jurisdiction of the cause, or unless after a discharge for default of proof, or for some material default in the commitment in a criminal case, the person is again arrested on sufficient proof, and committed by legal process, for the same offense.

APPENDIX—IDAHO

IDAHO

Idaho Code Annotated
Title 19. Criminal Procedure
Chapter 42. Habeas Corpus and Institutional Litigation Procedures Act

§19-4201. Short title
Sections 19-4201 through *19-4226, Idaho Code*, shall be known and may be cited as the "Idaho Habeas Corpus Institutional Litigation Procedures Act."

§19-4201A. Definitions
As used in this chapter:

(1) "Correctional facility" means a facility for the confinement of prisoners. Unless otherwise specifically provided, the term shall include a state, local or private correctional facility.

(2) "In-state prisoner" means a person who has been convicted of a crime in the state of Idaho and is either incarcerated in a correctional facility for that crime or is in custody for trial and sentencing.

(3) "Institution" or "state or county institution" means a place owned or operated by or under the control of the state or county in which a person other than a prisoner is restrained and with respect to which restraint the person may file a petition for a writ of habeas corpus under the provisions of this chapter.

(4) "Local correctional facility" means a facility for the confinement of prisoners operated by or under the control of a county or city. The term shall include any reference to "jail" or "county jail."

(5) "Out-of-state prisoner" means a person who has been convicted of and sentenced for a crime in a state other than the state of Idaho, or under the laws of the United States or other foreign jurisdiction, and who is being housed in any state, local or private correctional facility in the state of Idaho, or who is being transported in any manner within or through the state of Idaho.

(6) "Prisoner" includes an in-state or out-of-state prisoner, unless otherwise specifically provided or unless the context clearly indicates otherwise.

(7) "Private correctional facility" means a correctional facility owned or operated in the state of Idaho by a private prison contractor.

(8) "Private prison contractor" means any person, organization, partnership, joint venture, corporation or other business entity engaged in the site selection, design, design/building, acquisition, construction, construction/management, financing, maintenance, leasing, leasing/purchasing, management or operation of private correctional facilities or any combination of these services.

(9) "State correction facility" means a correctional facility owned or operated by or under the control of the state of Idaho.

§19-4202. Jurisdiction to consider petitions for writ of habeas corpus
The following courts of this state shall have original jurisdiction to consider a petition for writ of habeas corpus, grant the writ and/or order relief under this chapter:

(1) The supreme court; or

(2) The district court of the county in which the person is detained.

§19-4203. *Who may petition for a writ of habeas corpus*

(1) Any person, not a prisoner as defined in *section 19-4201A, Idaho Code*, who believes he is unlawfully restrained of his liberty in this state may file a petition for writ of habeas corpus to request that the court inquire into the cause and/or legality of the restraint.

(2) An in-state prisoner, as defined in *section 19-4201A, Idaho Code*, or a person who is restrained of his liberty while involved in parole revocation proceedings, or while held on an agent or commission warrant in this state, may file a petition for writ of habeas corpus to request that a court inquire into state or federal constitutional questions concerning:

   (a) The conditions of his confinement;

   (b) Revocation of parole;

   (c) Miscalculation of his sentence;

   (d) Loss of good time credits;

   (e) A detainer lodged against him.

(3) An out-of-state prisoner, as defined in *section 19-4201A, Idaho Code,* may file a petition for writ of habeas corpus only to request that an Idaho court inquire into a state or federal constitutional question concerning the conditions of his confinement. Habeas corpus relief shall not be available for an out-of-state prisoner to challenge:

   (a) Any issue concerning the legality of his out-of-state conviction or sentence;

   (b) Any issue concerning the legality of the fact or duration of his confinement in this state;

   (c) Any issue concerning the legality of the contract or agreement or any terms thereof pursuant to which he is housed in this state;

   (d) Any issue concerning the grant, denial or revocation of parole for his out-of-state conviction and sentence;

   (e) Miscalculation of his out-of-state sentence;

   (f) Loss of out-of-state good time credits or lack of (failure to grant) good time credits under the laws of the state of Idaho;

   (g) A detainer lodged against him.

(4) Habeas corpus shall not be used as a substitute for, or in addition to, a direct appeal of a criminal con-

viction or proceedings under *Idaho criminal rule 35* or the uniform post-conviction procedures act, chapter 49, title 19, Idaho Code, and the statutes of limitations imposed therein.

(5) Habeas corpus shall not be used as a substitute for or in addition to proceedings available in child custody matters and proceedings under the Idaho domestic violence crime prevention act, chapter 63, title 39, Idaho Code.

(6) Habeas corpus is an individual remedy only.

(7) For purposes of this chapter and any other civil challenges to conditions of confinement, the term "conditions of confinement" shall be defined as any civil proceeding with respect to a condition in any state or county institution, or state, local or private correctional facility, as those terms are defined in *section 19-4201A, Idaho Code,* arising under state or federal law pertaining to the conditions of confinement or the effects of actions by government officials or employees of a private prison contractor while employed at a private correctional facility in the state of Idaho on the life of a person confined in a state or county institution, or a state, local or private correctional facility.

§19-4204. Application for writ of habeas corpus by a person not a prisoner
(1) Application for a writ of habeas corpus by a person not a prisoner shall be made by filing a petition for writ of habeas corpus in the district court of the county in which the person in restrained.

(2) The petition must be verified by the oath or affirmation of the party applying for the writ and shall specify:

    (a) That the person is unlawfully restrained of his liberty;

    (b) The identity and address of the person restraining the subject of the petition;

    (c) The name and address of the place in which the person is restrained;

    (d) A description of the facts which make the restraint illegal; and

    (e) The theory of law upon which relief is sought, if known.

(3) Application under this section may be made by a guardian on behalf of a minor or by a guardian on behalf of an incapacitated person as defined in *section 15-5-101, Idaho Code.*

§19-4205. Application for writ of habeas corpus by a prisoner
(1) Application for a writ of habeas corpus by a prisoner shall be made by filing a petition for a writ of habeas corpus in the district court of the county in which the prisoner claims his confinement or aspects of his confinement violate provisions of the state or federal constitutions.

(2) With respect to a petition filed by an in-state prisoner, the petitioner must be verified by the oath or affirmation of the prisoner applying and shall specify that the prisoner is alleging state or federal constitutional violations concerning:

    (a) The conditions of his confinement;

(b) The revocation of his parole;

(c) Miscalculation of his sentence;

(d) Loss of good time credits; or

(e) A detainer lodged against him.

(3) With respect to a petition filed by an out-of-state prisoner, the petition must be verified by the oath or affirmation of the prisoner applying and shall specify that the prisoner is alleging state or federal constitutional violations concerning the conditions of his confinement, as provided in *section 19-4203(3), Idaho Code*.

(4) A petition filed by a prisoner under subsection (1), (2) or (3) of this section shall specify:

(a) The identity and address of the person or officer whom the prisoner believes is responsible for the alleged state or federal constitutional violations, and shall name the persons identified individually as respondents;

(b) The name, if any, and address of the place in which the prisoner is incarcerated;

(c) The name and address of the place in which the prisoner claims the constitutional violation occurred;

(d) A short and plain statement of the facts underlying the alleged state or federal constitutional violation; and

(e) Whether the petitioner is an out-of-state prisoner.

(5) Neither the state of Idaho, any of its political subdivisions, or any of its agencies, nor any private correctional facility shall be named as respondents in a prisoner petition for writ of habeas corpus.

§19-4206. *Prisoners required to exhaust administrative remedies in conditions of confinement cases*
(1) Unless a petitioner who is a prisoner establishes to the satisfaction of the court that he is in imminent danger of serious physical injury, no petition for writ of habeas corpus or any other civil action shall be brought by any person confined in a state or county institution, or in a state, local or private correctional facility, with respect to conditions of confinement until all available administrative remedies have been exhausted. If the institution, or state, local or private correctional facility does not have a system for administrative remedy, this requirement shall be waived.

(2) At the time of filing, the petitioner shall submit, together with the petition for writ of habeas corpus a true, correct and complete copy of any documentation which demonstrates that he has exhausted administrative remedies described in subsection (1) of this section.

(3) If at the time of filing the petition for writ of habeas corpus the petitioner fails to comply with this section, the court shall dismiss the petition with or without prejudice.

§19-4207. Application for writ of habeas corpus on behalf of another

A petition for writ of habeas corpus may only be filed by a person described in *section 19-4203, Idaho Code*, or his attorney, except that a petition may be filed on behalf of an aggrieved person who is a minor, or on behalf of a person who is incapacitated as defined by *section 15-5-101, Idaho Code*, by the aggrieved person's legal guardian.

§19-4208. General procedures governing habeas corpus proceedings

A habeas corpus proceeding in a civil action and is governed by the provisions of this chapter and the Idaho court rules to the extent that such rules are not inconsistent with this act.

§19-4209. Procedures governing prisoner habeas corpus proceedings

(1) The court may dismiss with prejudice a petition for writ of habeas corpus under this section, in whole or in part, prior to service of the petition on the respondent, if the court finds:

    (a) The petition is frivolous as defined in *section 12-122, Idaho Code*

    (b) The petition has been brought maliciously or solely to harass;

    (c) The petition fails to state a claim of constitutional violation upon which relief can be granted;

    (d) The alleged constitutional deprivation is de minimis in nature; or

    (e) The relief sought is monetary damages or the return of property.

(2) If the court finds that the petition should not be dismissed, then:

    (a) The court shall mail a copy of the petition and order of response to the respondent or the respondent's counsel, if known;

    (b) A response must be filed within thirty (30) days from the date the respondent or the respondent's counsel is served with the petition and order for response. If the court finds that exigent circumstances exist which warrant an earlier response, the court shall set forth those circumstances and the allowed time for response; and

    (c) If the court dismisses the petition in part, the court may specify which issues and/or allegations remain at issue for response.

(3) If the court orders a response to a petition for writ of habeas corpus under this section the respondent may file any responsive motion or pleading allowed by Idaho rules of civil procedure.

(4) Upon the filing of a responsive motion or pleading, a prisoner may file a reply to the response or the court may order a reply to the response on its own motion. The court should consider any reply filed only to the extent it is relevant to issues and allegations raised in the original petition for writ of habeas corpus.

(5) With respect to a petition filed by an in-state prisoner the court should not grant a writ of habeas corpus or order an evidentiary hearing under this section unless, after reviewing the petition for writ of habeas corpus, the response and the reply, if any, the court finds that the prisoner's state or federal constitutional rights may have been violated relative to:

(a) Conditions of confinement;

(b) Revocation of parole;

(c) Miscalculation of his sentence;

(d) Loss of good time credits; or

(e) A detainer lodged against him.

If, after review under this subsection, the court finds that the allegations do not state a state or federal constitutional claim, the court may dismiss the petition without a hearing.

(6) With respect to a petition filed by an out-of-state prisoner, the court should not grant a writ of habeas corpus or order an evidentiary hearing under this section unless, after reviewing the petition for writ of habeas corpus, the response and the reply, if any, the court finds that the out-of-state prisoner's state or federal constitutional rights may have been violated relative to the out-of-state prisoner's conditions of confinement. If, after review under this subsection, the court finds that the allegations do not state a state or federal constitutional claim, the court may dismiss the petition without a hearing.

(7) If the court issues a writ of habeas corpus and sets the matter for evidentiary hearing, the following shall apply:

(a) The hearing shall be set as expeditiously as possible and may be at a place convenient for the court and the parties, including the institution or the state, local or private correctional facility where the prisoner is confined;

(b) The burden of proof during an evidentiary hearing pursuant to a petition for writ of habeas corpus lies with the prisoner; and

(c) As soon as possible after the conclusion of the hearing, the court shall enter its findings of fact and conclusions of law, and either dismiss the dismiss the petition in part or in its entirety, or grant injunctive relief consistent with this act.

§19-4210. Discovery in habeas corpus proceedings
(1) Discovery shall not ordinarily be permitted in habeas corpus cases.

(2) No discovery shall be permitted if the issues raised by the petition, the response or reply are wholly legal in nature.

(3) If factual issues are raised by the pleadings, the court may, upon motion, grant leave for discovery in accordance with Idaho rules of civil procedure.

(a) The party must file a motion for leave to conduct discovery, attaching a copy of the discovery sought.

(b) If the court finds that discovery is necessary to protect or defend a substantive state or federal constitutional right at issue, it shall enter an order tailored to allowed discovery for that limited purpose.

§19-4211. Issuance of writ of habeas corpus

(1) Any court authorized under *section 19-4202, Idaho Code*, may grant a writ of habeas corpus pursuant to a petition filed by, or, pursuant to *section 19-4207, Idaho Code*, on behalf of a person not a prisoner if it finds that the restraint of the person's liberty is illegal.

(2) Any court authorized under *section 19-4202, Idaho Code*, may grant a writ of habeas corpus and order a hearing pursuant to a petition filed by a prisoner, or, pursuant to *section 19-4207, Idaho Code*, on behalf of a prisoner when:

(a) The court has considered the factual allegations contained in the petition together with any responsive pleading filed by the respondent, and a reply filed by the prisoner, if any;

(b) The court finds that the petitioner is likely to prevail on the merits of his state or federal constitutional challenge;

(c) The court finds that the petitioner will suffer irreparable injury if some relief is not granted;

(d) The court finds that the balance of potential harm to the petitioner substantially outweighs any legitimate governmental interest; and

(e) The court finds that equity favors granting relief to the petitioner.

(3) Any order granting the writ should issue without delay and a hearing should be scheduled. The court may provide a statement of the issues to be addressed, and whether evidence will be accepted.

(4) If a court issues an order granting the writ and setting the matter for hearing, the court may set the hearing at the state, local or private correctional facility or other appropriate place.

§19-4212. Injunctive relief available to a person not a prisoner
If a court finds that a person not a prisoner is being illegally restrained, the court may fashion appropriate injunctive relief to cure the illegality, including release.

§19-4213. Relief available for constitutional violations during the course of revocation of parole
(1) If a court finds that an in-state prisoner's constitutional rights have been violated during the course of revocation of his parole, the court may, upon specific findings of fact and conclusions of law, enter an order directing that the parole revocation proceedings be reconvened. The order shall identify the constitutional violation which occurred and direct that the violation be cured.

(2) The Idaho commission for pardons and parole has the exclusive authority to order release of an in-state prisoner on parole pursuant to *section 20-210 and 20-223, Idaho Code*.

§19-4214. Relief available for miscalculation of sentence
(1) If, upon findings of fact and conclusions of law, a court finds that an in-state prisoner's sentence has been miscalculated, the court may order the sentence to be recalculated consistent with the court's findings and conclusions.

(2) The court may order the prisoner released under this section only if the prisoner would be entitled to release due to expiration of his sentence correctly calculated.

§19-4215. Relief available for loss of good time credits

(1) If the court finds that an in-state prisoner has lost good time credits without constitutionally sufficient due process, the court may order a rehearing by the correctional facility authority.

(2) Any court order requiring rehearing shall specify:

    (a) How due process was constitutionally insufficient and direct that the insufficiency be cured; and

    (b) Provide that the officials of the correctional facility shall have not less than thirty (30) days in which to convene the rehearing.

(3) The correctional facility authority shall have the responsibility for the recalculation and restoration of good time credits. If good time credits are restored to the prisoner as a result of the rehearing, and restoration of good time credits entitles the prisoner to release, he shall be so released.

§19-4216. Relief available for detainers

(1) An in-state prisoner may petition for a writ of habeas corpus to challenge the legality of a detainer which has been lodged against him by another state under the interstate agreement on detainers, chapter 50, title 19, Idaho Code.

(2) The court may set a hearing on a petition for writ of habeas corpus to inquire into factual issues involving the legality of the detainer or the legality of delivery of the prisoner to the prosecuting state under the detainer. However, if the petition involves legal issues only, the court shall decide the matter without hearing consistent with *section 19-4209, Idaho Code.*

§19-4217. Injunctive relief available to prisoners and other institutionalized persons in conditions of confinement cases

(1) If the court finds that a prisoner's or other institutionalized person's constitutional rights have been violated involving conditions of confinement, the court may order injunctive relief consistent with and subject to the limitations set forth in this chapter.

(2) If the court concludes that injunctive relief is necessary to cure unconstitutional conditions of confinement, the court shall enter an order subject to the following limitations:

    (a) Any order for injunctive relief shall be accompanied by specific findings of fact and conclusions of law;

    (b) Injunctive relief shall be narrowly drawn and extend no further than necessary to correct the violation of the constitutional right;

    (c) Injunctive relief must be the least intrusive means necessary to correct the constitutional violation;

    (d) The court shall give substantial weight to any adverse impact on public safety;

    (e) The court shall give substantial deference to the discretion of administrators of the institution or the state, local or private correctional facility;

(f) The administrator of the institution, or of the state, local or private correctional facility shall be given all reasonable opportunities to correct state or federal constitutional errors made in the internal operations of the institution and shall be charged with the task of devising constitutionally sound modifications to their operations.

§19-4218. Termination of injunctive relief order or decree in conditions of confinement cases
In any civil action with respect to conditions of confinement in which prospective relief is ordered or obtained pursuant to consent decree, the relief order or decree shall be terminated upon the motion of any party or intervenor:

(1) Two (2) years after the date the court granted or approved the prospective relief;

(2) One (1) year after the date the court has entered an order or decree denying termination of prospective relief under this section; or

(3) In the case of an order issued on or before the date of enactment of this act, one (1) year after such date of enactment.

§19-4219. Immediate termination of order or decree for prospective relief in conditions of confinement cases
(1) In any civil action with respect to conditions of confinement, the administrator of the institution, or of the state, local or private correctional facility, or intervenor shall be entitled to the immediate termination of any prospective relief if the relief was approved or granted in the absence of an express finding by the court that the relief:

(a) Is narrowly drawn;

(b) Extends no further than necessary to correct the violation of the constitutional right; and

(c) Is the least intrusive means necessary to correct the violation of the constitutional right.

(2) Prospective relief shall not terminate if the court makes written findings based on the record that the prospective relief:

(a) Remains necessary to correct a current or ongoing violation of the constitutional right;

(b) Extends no further than necessary to correct the violation of the constitutional right;

(c) Is narrowly drawn; and

(d) Is the least intrusive means to correct the violation.

(3) Nothing in this section shall prevent the administrator of the institution, or of the state, local or private correctional facility, or intervenor from seeking modification or termination before the relief is terminable under subsection (1) or (2) of this section to the extent that modification or termination would otherwise be legally permissible.

§19-4220. Settlements and consent decrees in conditions of confinement cases

(1) In any civil action with respect to conditions of confinement, the court shall not enter or approve a settlement or consent decree unless it complies with the limitations on relief set forth in *section 19-4217, Idaho Code*.

(2) This section, together with sections 19-4217, 19-4218 and 19-4219, Idaho Code, applies to all settlements or consent decrees in effect at the time of passage of this act. Any settlement or consent decree entered into before enactment of this act shall not be construed as a waiver of the application of this section by any party to the settlement or consent decree, and may be terminated consistent with *sections 19-4218 and 19-4219, Idaho Code*.

§19-4221. Successive claims

In no event shall a prisoner bring a civil action or appeal a judgment in a civil action or proceeding if the prisoner has, on two (2) or more prior occasions, while incarcerated or detained in any state, local or private correctional facility, brought an action or appeal in a court of this state that was dismissed on any ground set forth in *section 19-4209(1)(a) through (d), Idaho Code*, unless:

(1) The prisoner first obtains leave from the district court having jurisdiction over the case; or

(2) The prisoner's action or petition is submitted for filing by an attorney licensed to practice law in the state of Idaho.

§19-4222. Prior showing of physical injury or mental illness required

No civil action may be brought by a prisoner confined in a state, local or private correctional facility for mental or emotional injury suffered while in custody without a prior showing either:

(1) Physical injury; or

(2) Diagnosed severe and disabling mental illness.

§19-4223. Right of access to court not expanded

Nothing in this chapter shall be construed to expand the right of access to courts for institutionalized persons under federal or state law.

§19-4224. Exclusive remedy

This chapter sets forth the exclusive procedures and remedies in habeas corpus actions.

§19-4225. Liberty interest not created

Nothing in this chapter shall be construed to create a liberty interest.

§19-4226. Severability

The provisions of this act are declared to be severable and if any provision of this act or the application of a provision to any person or circumstance is declared invalid for any reason, the declaration shall not affect the validity of the remaining portions of this act.

ILLINOIS

Illinois compiled Statutes Annotated
Chapter 735. Civil Procedure
Act 5. Code of Civil Procedure
Article X. Habeas Corpus

5/10-101. Action commenced by plaintiff
§10-101. Action commenced by plaintiff. In all proceedings commenced under Article X of this Act, the name of the person seeking the relief afforded by this Article shall be set out as plaintiff without the use of the phrase "People ex rel." or "People on the relation of".

5/10-102. Who may file
§10-102. Who may file. Every person imprisoned or otherwise restrained of his or her liberty, except as herein otherwise provided, may apply for habeas corpus in the manner provided in Article X of this Act, to obtain relief from such imprisonment or restraint, if it proved to be unlawful.

5/10-103. Application
§10-103. Application. Application for the relief shall be made to the Supreme Court or to the circuit court of the county in which the person in whose behalf the application is made, is imprisoned or restrained, or to the circuit court of the county from which such person was sentenced or committed. Application shall be made by complaint signed by the person for whose relief it is intended, or by some person in his or her behalf, and verified by affidavit. Application for relief under this Article may not be commenced on behalf of a person who has been sentenced to death without the written consent of that person, unless the person, because of a mental or physical condition, is incapable of asserting his or her own claim.

5/10-104. Substance of complaint
§10-104. Substance of complaint. The complaint shall state in substance:

1. That the person in whose behalf the relief is applied for is imprisoned or restrained of his or her liberty, and the place where—naming all the parties if they are known, or describing them if they are not known.

2. The cause or pretense of the restraint, according to the best knowledge and belief of the applicant, and that such person is not committed or detained by virtue of any process, or judgment, specified in Section 10-123 of this Act.

3. If the commitment or restraint is by virtue of any warrant or process, a copy thereof shall be annexed, or it shall be stated that by reason of such prisoner being removed or concealed before application, a demand of such copy could not be made, or that such demand was made, and the legal fees therefor tendered to the officer or person having such prisoner in his or her custody, and that such copy was refused.

5/10-105. Copy of process
§10-105. Copy of process. Any sheriff or other officer or person having custody of any prisoner committed on any civil or criminal process of any court who shall neglect to give such prisoner a copy of the process or order of commitment by which he or she is imprisoned within 6 hours after demand made by the prisoner, or anyone on behalf of the prisoner, shall forfeit to the prisoner or party affected not exceeding $500. This Section shall not apply to the Illinois Department of Corrections.

5/10-106. Grant of relief—penalty

§10-106. Grant of relief—penalty. Unless it shall appear from the complaint itself, or from the documents thereto annexed, that the party can neither be discharged, admitted to bail nor otherwise relieved, the court shall forthwith award relief by habeas corpus. Any judge empowered to grant relief by habeas corpus who shall corruptly ref use to grant the relief when legally applied for in a case where it may lawfully be granted, or who shall for the purpose of oppression unreasonably delay the granting of such relief shall, for every such offense, forfeit to the prisoner or party affected a sum not exceeding $1,000.

5/10-107. Form of orders

§10-107. Form of orders. If the relief is allowed by an order of a court it shall be certified by the clerk under the seal of the court; if by a judge, it shall be under the judge's signature, and shall be directed to the person in whose custody or under whose restraint the prisoner is, and may be substantially in the following form: The People of the State of Illinois, to the Sheriff of ... county (or, "to A B," as the case may be):

You are hereby commanded to have the body of c D, imprisoned and detained by you, together with the time and cause of such imprisonment and detention by whatsoever name C D is called or charged, before court of ... County (or before E F, judge of, etc.), at, etc., immediately after being served with a certified copy of this order, to be dealt with according to law; and you are to deliver a certified copy of this order with a return thereon of your performance in carrying out this order.

5/10-108. Indorsement

§10-108. Indorsement. With the intent that no officer or person to whom such order is directed may pretend ignorance thereof, every such order shall be indorsed with these words: "By the habeas corpus law. 11

5/10-109. Subpoena—service

§10-109. Subpoena—service. When the party has been committed upon a criminal charge, unless the court deems it unnecessary, a subpoena shall also be issued to summon the witnesses whose names have been endorsed upon the warrant of commitment, to appear before such court at the time and place when and where such order of habeas corpus is returnable, and it shall be the duty of the sheriff, or other officer to whom the subpoena is issued, to serve the same, if it is possible, in time to enable such witnesses to attend.

5/10-110. Service of order

§10-110. Service of order. The habeas corpus order may be served by the sheriff, coroner or any person appointed for that purpose by the court which entered the order; if served by a person not an officer, he or she shall have the same power, and be liable to the same penalty for non-performance of his or her duty, as though he or she were sheriff.

5/10-111. Manner of service

§10-111. Manner of service. Service shall be made by leaving a copy of the order with the person to whom it is directed, or with any of his or her under officers who may be at the place where the prisoner is detained; or if he or she can not be found, or has not the person imprisoned or restrained in custody, the service may be made upon any person who has the person in custody with the same effect as though he or she had been made a defendant therein.

5/10-112. Expense involved

§10-112. Expense involved. When the person confined or restrained is in the custody of a civil officer, the court entering the order shall certify thereon the sum to be paid for the expense of bringing the person from the place of imprisonment, not exceeding 10 cents per mile, and the office shall not be bound to obey it unless the sum so certified is paid or tendered to him or her, and security is given to pay the charges of carrying the party back if he or she should be remanded. If the court is satisfied that the party so confined or restrained is a poor person and unable to pay such expense, then the court shall so state in the order, and in such case no tender or payment of expenses need be made or security given but the officer shall be bound to obey such order.

5/10-113. Form of return
§10-113. Form of return. The officer or person upon whom such order is served shall state in his or her return, plainly and unequivocally:

1. Whether he or she has or has not the party in his or her custody or control, or under his or her restraint, and if he or she has not, whether he or she has had the party in his or her custody or control, or under his or her restraint, at any and what time prior or subsequent to the date of the order.

2. If he or she has the party in his or her custody or control, or under his or her restraint, the authority and true cause of such imprisonment or restraint, setting forth the same in detail.

3. If the party is detained by virtue of any order, warrant or other written authority, a copy thereof shall be attached to the return, and the original shall be produced and exhibited on the return of the order to the court before whom the same is returnable.

4. If the person upon whom the order is served has had the party in his or her custody or control or under his or her restraint, at any time prior or subsequent to the date of the order but has transferred such custody or restraint to another, the return shall state particularly to whom, at what time, for what cause and by what authority such transfer took place. The return shall be signed by the person what cause and by what authority such transfer took place. The return shall be signed by the person making the same, and except where such person is a sworn public officer and makes the return in his or her official capacity, it shall be verified by oath.

5/10-114. Bringing of body
§10-114. Bringing of body. The officer or person making the return, shall, at the same time, bring the body of the party, if in his or her custody or power or under his or her restraint, according to the command of the order unless prevented by the sickness or infirmity of the party.

5/10-115. Sickness or infirmity
§10-115. Sickness or infirmity. When, from the sickness or infirmity of the party, he or she cannot without danger, be brought to the place designated for the return of the order, that fact shall be stated in the return, and if it is proved to the satisfaction of the judge, he or she may proceed to the jail or other place where the party is confined, and there make an examination, or the judge may adjourn the same to such other time, or make such other order in the case as law and justice require.

5/10-116. Neglect to obey order
§10-116. Neglect to obey order. If the officer or person upon whom such order is served refuses or neglects to obey the same, by producing the party named in the order and making a full and explicit return thereto within the time required by Article X of this Act, and no sufficient excuse is shown for such refusal or neglect, the court before whom the order is returnable, upon proof of the service thereof, shall enforce

obedience by attachment as for contempt, and the officer or person so refusing or neglecting shall forfeit to the party a sum not exceeding $500, and be incapable of holding office.

5/10-117. Order in case of neglect
§10-117. Order in case of neglect. The court may also, at the same time or afterwards, enter an order to the sheriff or other person to whom such attachment is directed, commanding him or her to bring forthwith before the court the party for whose benefit the habeas corpus order was entered, who shall thereafter remain in the custody of such sheriff, or other person, until the party is discharged, bailed or remanded, as the court directs.

5/10-118. Proceedings in case of emergency
§10-118. Proceedings in case of emergency. Whenever it appears by the complaint, or by affidavit, that any one is illegally held in custody or restraint, and that there is good reason to believe that such person will be taken out of the jurisdiction of the court in which the application for a habeas corpus is made, or will suffer some irreparable injury before compliance with the order can be enforced, the court may enter an order directed to the sheriff or other proper officer, commanding him or her to take the prisoner thus held in custody or restraint, and forthwith bring him or her before the court to be dealt with according to law. The court may also, if it is deemed necessary, order the apprehension of the person charged with causing the illegal restraint. The officer shall execute the order by bringing the person therein named before the court, and the like return and proceedings shall be had as in other orders of habeas corpus.

5/10-119. Examination
§10-119. Examination. Upon the return of an order of habeas corpus, the court shall, without delay, proceed to examine the cause of the imprisonment or restraint, but the examination may be adjourned from time to time as circumstances require.

5/10-120. Denial of allegations in return
§10-120. Denial of allegations in return. The party imprisoned or restrained may file a reply to the return and deny any of the material facts set forth in the return, and may allege any other facts that may be material in the case, which denial or allegation shall be on oath; and the court shall proceed promptly to examine the cause of the imprisonment or restraint, hear the evidence produced by any person interested or authorized to appear, both in support of such imprisonment or restraint and against it, and thereupon shall determine the matter according to law.

5/10-121. Seeking wrong remedy not fatal
§10-121. Seeking wrong remedy not fatal. Where relief is sought under Article X of this Act and the court determines, on motion directed to the pleadings, or on motion for summary judgment or upon trial, that the plaintiff has pleaded or established facts which entitle the plaintiff to relief but that the plaintiff has sought the wrong remedy, the court shall permit the pleadings to be amended, on just and reasonable terms, and the court shall grant the relief to which the plaintiff is entitled on the amended pleadings or upon the evidence. In considering whether a proposed amendment is just and reasonable, the court shall consider the right of the defendant to assert additional defenses, to demand a trial by jury, to plead a counterclaim or third party complaint, and to order the plaintiff to take additional steps which were not required under the pleadings as previously filed.

5/10-122. Amendments
§10-122. Amendments. The return, as well as any denial or allegation, may be amended at any time by leave of the court. 5/10-123. When prisoner not entitled to discharge §10-123. When prisoner not entitled to discharge. No person shall be discharged under the provisions of this Act, if he or she is in custody:

1. By virtue of process of any court of the United States, in a case where such court has exclusive jurisdiction; or,

2. By virtue of a final judgment of any circuit court, or of any proceedings for the enforcement of such judgment, unless the time during which such party may be legally detained has expired; or,

3. For any treason, felony or other crime which committed in any other state or territory of the United States, for which such person ought, by the Constitution and laws of the United States, to be delivered to the executive power of such state or territory.

5/10-124. Causes for discharge when in custody on process of court
§10-124. Causes for discharge when in custody on process of court. If it appears that the prisoner is in custody by virtue of process from any court legally constituted, he or she may be discharged only for one or more of the following causes:
1. Where the court has exceeded the limit of its jurisdiction, either as to the matter, place, sum or person.

2. Where, though the original imprisonment was lawful, nevertheless, by some act, omission or event which has subsequently taken place, the party has become entitled to be discharged.

3. Where the process is defective in some substantial form required by law.

4. Where the process, though in proper form, has been issued in a case or under circumstances where the law does not allow process to issue or orders to be entered for imprisonment or arrest.

5. Where, although in proper form, the process has been issued in a case or under circumstances unauthorized to issue or execute the same, or where the person having the custody of the prisoner under such process is not the person empowered by law to detain him or her.

6. Where the process appears to have been obtained by false pretense or bribery.

7. Where there is no general law, nor any judgment or order of a court to authorize the process if in a civil action, nor any conviction if in a criminal proceeding. No court, on the return of a habeas corpus, shall, in any other matter, inquire into the legality of justice of a judgment of a court legally constituted.

5/10-125. New commitment
§10-125. New commitment. In all cases where the imprisonment is for a criminal, or supposed criminal matter, if it appears to the court that there is sufficient legal cause for the commitment of the prisoner, although such commitment may have been informally made, or without due authority, or the process may have been executed by a person not duly authorized, the court shall make a new commitment in proper form and direct it to the proper officer, or admit the party to bail if the case is bailable. The court shall also, when necessary, take the recognizances of all material witnesses against the prisoner, as in other cases. The recognizances shall be in the form provided by law, and returned as other recognizances. If any judge shall neglect or refuse to bind any such prisoner or witness by recognizance, or to return a recognizance when taken as hereinabove stated, he or she shall be guilty of a Class A misdemeanor in office, and be proceeded against accordingly.

5/10-126. Remand

§10-126. Remand. When any prisoner brought up on a habeas corpus is remanded to prison, it shall be the duty of the court remanding the prisoner to deliver to the sheriff, or other person to whose custody the prisoner is remanded, an order in writing, stating the cause of remanding the prisoner. If such prisoner obtains a second order of habeas corpus, it shall be the duty of such sheriff, or other person to whom the same is directed, to return therewith the order above stated; and if it appears that the prisoner was remanded for an offense adjudged not bailable, it shall be taken and received as conclusive, and the prisoner shall be remanded without further proceedings.

5/10-127. Grant of habeas corpus

§10-127. Grant of habeas corpus. It is not lawful for any court, on a second order of habeas corpus obtained by such prisoner, to discharge the prisoner, if he or she is clearly and specifically charged in the warrant of commitment with a criminal offense; but the court shall, on the return of such second order, have power only to admit such prisoner to bail where the offense is bailable by law, or remand him or her to prison where the offense is not bailable, or being bailable, where such prisoner fails to give the bail required.

5/10-128. Person discharged again imprisoned

§10-128. Person discharged again imprisoned. No person who has been discharged by order of the court on a habeas corpus, shall be again imprisoned, restrained or kept in custody for the same cause, unless he or she is afterwards indicted for the same offense, nor unless by the legal order or process of the court wherein he or she is bound by recognizance to appear. The following shall not be deemed to be the same cause:

1. If, after a discharge for a defect of proof, or any material defect in the commitment, in a criminal case, the prisoner is again arrested on sufficient proof, and committed by legal process for the same offense.

2. If, in a civil, the party has been discharged for any illegality in the judgment or process, and is afterwards imprisoned by legal process for the same cause of action.

3. Generally, whenever the discharge is ordered on account of the nonobservance of any of the forms required by law, the party may be a second time imprisoned if the cause is legal and the forms required by law observed.

5/10-129. Penalty for rearrest of person discharged

§10-129. Penalty for rearrest of person discharged. Any person who, knowing that another has been discharged by order of a competent court on a habeas corpus, shall, contrary to the provisions of Article X of this Act, arrest or detain him or her again for the same cause which was shown on the return to such order, shall forfeit $500 for the first offense, and $1,000 for every subsequent offense.

5/10-130. Prisoner not to be removed from county

§10-130. Prisoner not to be removed from county. To prevent any person from avoiding or delaying his or her trial, it shall not be lawful to remove any prisoner on habeas corpus under Article X of this Act out of the county in which he or she is confined, within 15 days next preceding the first day of the calendar month in which such person ought to be tried unless it is done to convey him or her into the county where the offense with which he or she stands charged is properly cognizable.

INDIANA

Annotated Indiana Code
Title 34. Civil Procedure
Article 25.5. Special Proceedings: Habeas Corpus

34-25.5-1-1 Prosecution of writ; delivery from restraint
Sec. 1. Every person whose liberty is restrained, under any pretense whatever, may prosecute a writ of habeas corpus to inquire into the cause of the restraint, and shall be delivered from the restraint if the restraint is illegal.

34-25.5-2-1 Persons entitled to make; contents Sec. 1. (a) Application for the writ must be made by complaint, signed and verified either by:

(1) the applicant; or

(2) Some person on the applicant's behalf.

(b) The complaint must specify the following:

(1) Who is restraining the applicant's liberty, the place where the applicant is being held, and the names of all the parties, if they are known, or descriptions of them if they are not known.

(2) The cause or pretense of the restraint, according to the best of the knowledge and belief of the applicant.

(3) If the restraint is alleged to be illegal, the nature of the illegality.

34-25.5-2-2 Courts and judges authorized to grant writ
Sec. 2. (a) Writs of habeas corpus may be granted by:

(1) the circuit or superior courts of the county in which the person applying for the writ may be restrained of his or her liberty, or by the judges of those courts; or

(2) if the judges described in subdivision (1) are:

(A) Absent from their circuits; or

(B) by reason of sickness or other cause, unable or incompetent to hear and determine the application for the writ;

then by any judge of an adjoining circuit.

(b) Upon application, a writ granted under subsection (a) shall be granted without delay.

34-25.5-2-3 Criminal circuit judges authorized to grant writ
Sec. 3. The criminal circuit judges in Indiana may:

(1) issue writs of habeas corpus within their respective counties;

(2) hear and determine writs of habeas corpus in favor of all persons arrested and held upon any charge in violation of Indiana criminal laws; and

(3) admit to bail, or discharge the prisoner;

in the same manner, to the same extent, and under the same rules and regulations as judges of the circuit courts are authorized by law to do.

34-25.5-2-4 Contents of writ
Sec. 4. The writ shall be directed to the office or party restraining the applicant, commanding the party to have the applicant before the court or judge, at the time and place the court or judge directs, to do and receive the court's order concerning the applicant.

34-25.5-3-1 Writ directed and delivered to sheriff
Sec. 1. If the writ is directed to the sheriff, the clerk shall deliver it to the sheriff without delay. 34-25.5-3-2 Writ directed to other person; delivery to and service by sheriff Sec. 2. If the writ is directed to any other person, the writ shall be delivered to the sheriff. The sheriff shall serve the writ by delivering the writ to the person without delay.

34-25.5-3-3 Service by leaving at residence or affixing in conspicuous place
Sec. 3. If the person to whom a writ is directed cannot be found or refuses admittance to the sheriff, the writ may be served by:

(1) leaving the writ at the residence of the person to whom the writ is directed; or

(2) affixing the writ on some conspicuous place, either at the person's dwelling house or where the party is confined or under restraint.

34-25.5-3-4 Return; required
Sec. 4. The sheriff or other person to whom the writ is directed shall return the writ immediately and if the person to whom the writ is directed refuses after due service to return the writ, the court shall enforce obedience by attachment.

34-25.5-3-5 Return; requisites
Sec. 5. The return must be signed and verified by the person making it, who shall state the following:

(1) The authority or cause of the restraint of the applicant in the custody of the person to whom the writ is directed.

(2) If the authority is in writing, the person to whom the writ is directed shall return a copy and produce the original at the hearing.

(3) If the person to whom the writ is directed has had the applicant in custody or under restraint, and has transferred the applicant to another, the person to whom the writ is directed shall state to whom, the time, place, and cause of the applicant's transfer.

The person to whom the writ is directed shall produce the applicant at the hearing unless prevented by sickness or infirmity, which must be shown in the return.

34-25.5-3-6 Issuance of writ or process by clerk of court; service and return
Sec. 6. (a) All writs and other process authorized under this article shall be issued by the clerk of the court, and, except summonses, sealed with the seal of the court.

(b) Documents described in subsection (a) shall be served and returned immediately unless the court or judge specifies a particular time for the return.

34-25.5-3-7 Immaterial defects in writ or process
Sec. 7. A writ or other process shall not be disregarded for any defect if enough is shown to notify the officer or person to whom the writ is directed of the purpose of the process.

34-25.5-3-8 Amendments to writ; temporary commitments
Sec. 8. The court may allow amendments to a writ, and temporary commitments, when necessary.

34-25.5-4-1 Sickness or infirmity of applicant; procedure
Sec. 1. The court or judge, if satisfied of the truth of the allegation of sickness or infirmity under *IC 34-25.5-3-5*, may:

(1) proceed to decide on the return; or

(2) adjoin the hearing:

(A) until the party can be produced; or

(B) for other good cause.

34-25.5-4-2 Return of writ; proceedings and pleadings
Sec. 2. The applicant may:

(1) except to the sufficiency of, or controvert the return, or any part of the return; or
(2) allege any new matter in avoidance.

The new matter must be verified except in cases of commitment on a criminal charge. The return and pleadings may be amended without causing any delay.

34-25.5 4-3 Summary hearing and determination; discharge of applicant
Sec. 3. The court or judge shall proceed in a summary way to hear and determine the cause. If no legal cause is shown for the restraint or for the continuation of the restraint, the court shall discharge the applicant.

34-25.5-4-4 Powers of court or judge
Sec. 4. The court or judge may require and compel the attendance of witnesses and do all other acts necessary to determine the case.

34-25.5-5-1 Limitation on questioning legality of judgment or process
Sec. 1. (a) Except as provided in subsection (b), the court or judge shall not inquire into the legality of any judgment or process by which the party is in custody, or discharge the party when the term of commitment has not expired in any of the following cases:

(1) Upon process issued by any court or judge of the United States where the court or judge had exclusive jurisdiction.

(2) Upon any process issued on a final judgment of a court of competent jurisdiction.

(3) For any contempt of any court, officer, or body with authority to commit.

(4) Upon a warrant issued from the circuit court upon an indictment or information.

(b) Subsection (a)(1), (a)(2), and (a)(3) do not include an order of commitment, as for contempt, upon proceedings to enforce the remedy of a party.

34-25.5-5-2 When persons not to be discharged from order of commitment
Sec. 2. (a) A person shall not be discharged from an order of commitment issued by any judicial or peace officer:

(1) for want of bail, or in cases not bailable, on account of a defect in the charge or process; or

(2) for alleged want of probable cause.

(b) In cases described in subsection (a), the court or judge shall:

(1) summon the prosecuting witnesses;

(2) investigate the criminal charge;

(3) discharge, let to bail, or recommit the prisoner, as may be just and legal; and

(4) recognize witnesses when proper.

34-25.5-5-3 Letting prisoner to bail
Sec. 3. The writ may be used for the purpose of letting a prisoner to bail in civil and criminal actions.
34-25.5-5-4 Notice of discharge of prisoner
Sec. 4. When any person has an interest in the detention, the prisoner shall not be discharged until the person having an interest in the detention is notified.

34-25.5-5-5 Immunity of officer obeying writ or order of discharge
Sec. 5. A sheriff or other officer shall not be liable to a civil action for obeying a writ of habeas corpus or an order of discharge made pursuant to a writ of habeas corpus.

34-25.5-6-1 Warrant for appearance of illegally held person
Sec. 1. Whenever it appears by affidavit that a person is illegally held in custody or restraint and there is good reason to believe that the applicant:

(1) will be carried out of the jurisdiction of the court or judge before whom the application is made; or

(2) will suffer some irreparable injury before compliance with the writ can be enforced;

the court or judge may cause a warrant to be issued, reciting the facts and directed to the sheriff or any constable of the county, commanding the sheriff or constable to take the restrained person and immediately bring the person before the court or judge, to be dealt with according to law.

34-25-6-2 Apprehension of person causing illegal restraint
Sec. 2. The court or judge may also, if considered necessary, insert in the warrant a command for the apprehension of the person charged with causing the illegal restraint.

34-25.5-6-3 Execution
Sec. 3. The officer shall execute the warrant by bringing the person named in the warrant before the court or judge, and the same return and proceedings shall be required as in case of writs of habeas corpus.

34-25.5-6-4 Issuance and service of writ on Sunday; temporary orders; changing custody of restrained person
Sec. 4. (a) Any writ or process authorized by this article may be issued and served on Sunday in cases of emergency.

(b) The court or judge may make any temporary orders in the cause or disposition of the party, during the progress of the proceedings, that justice may require. The custody of any party restrained may be changed from one (1) person to another by order of the court or judge.

IOWA

Iowa Code
Title XV. Judicial Branch and Judicial Procedures
Subtitle 5. Special Actions
Chapter 663. Habeas Corpus

663.1. Petition
The petition for the writ of habeas corpus must state:

1. That the person in whose behalf it is sought is restrained of the person's liberty, and the person by whom and the place where the person is so restrained, mentioning the names of the parties, if known, and if unknown describing them with as much particularity as practicable.

2. The cause or pretense of such restraint, according to the best information of the applicant; and if by virtue of any legal process, a copy thereof must be annexed, or a satisfactory reason given for its absence.

3. That the restraint is illegal, and wherein.

4. That the legality of the restraint has not already been adjudged upon a prior proceeding of the same character, to the best knowledge and belief of the applicant.

5. Whether application for the writ has been before made to and refused by any court or judge, and if so, a copy of the petition in that case must be attached, with the reasons for the refusal, or satisfactory reasons given for the failure to do so.

663.2. Verification—presentation to court
The petition must be sworn to by the person confined, or by someone in the confined person's behalf, and presented to some court or officer authorized to allow the writ.

663.3. Writ allowed—service
The writ may be allowed by the supreme or district court, or by a supreme court judge or district judge, and may be served in any part of the state.

663.4. Application—to whom made
Application for the writ must be made to the court or judge most convenient in point of distance to the applicant, and the more remote court or judge, if applied to therefor, may refuse the same unless a sufficient reason be stated in the petition for not making the application to the more convenient court or a judge thereof.

663.5. Inmates of state or federal institutions
When the applicant is confined in a state or federal institution, other than a penal institution, the provisions of *section 663.4* relating to the court to which or the judge to whom applications must be made are mandatory, and the convenience or preference of an attorney or witness or other person interested in the release of the applicant shall not be a sufficient reason to authorize a more remote court or judge to assume jurisdiction.

663.6. Writ refused
If, from the showing of the petitioner, the plaintiff would not be entitled to any relief, the court or judge must refuse to allow the writ.

663.7. Reasons endorsed
If the writ is disallowed, the court or judge shall cause the reasons thereof to be appended to the petition and returned to the person applying for the writ.

663.8. Form of writ
If the petition is in accordance with the foregoing requirements and states sufficient grounds for the allowance of the writ, it shall issue, and may be substantially as follows:

> The State of Iowa,
>
> To ......:
>
> You are hereby commanded to have the body of .... , by you unlawfully detained, as is alleged, before the court (or before me, or before .... judge, etc., as the case may be), at .... , on .... (or immediately after being served with this writ), to be dealt with according to law, and have you then and there this writ, with a return thereon of your doings in the premises.

663.9. How issued
When the writ is allowed by a court, it must be issued by the clerk, but when by a judge, the judge must issue it personally, subscribing the judge's name thereto.

663.10. Penalty for refusing
Any judge, whether acting individually or as a member of the court, who wrongfully and willfully refuses the allowance of the writ when properly applied for, shall forfeit to the party aggrieved the sum of one thousand dollars.

663.11. Issuance on judge's own motion
When any court or judge authorized to grant the writ has evidence, from a judicial proceeding before the court or judge, that any person within the jurisdiction of such court or officer is illegally restrained of the person's liberty, such court or judge shall issue the writ or cause it to be issued, on the court's or judge's own motion.

663.12. County attorney notified
The court or officer allowing the writ must cause the county attorney of the proper county to be informed thereof, and of the time and place where and when it is made returnable.

663.13. Service of writ
The writ may be served by the sheriff, or by any other person appointed in writing for that purpose by the court or judge by whom it is issued or allowed. If served by any other than the sheriff, the person appointed possesses the same power, and is liable to the same penalty for a nonperformance of the duty, as though the person were the sheriff.

663.14. Mode
The services shall be made by leaving the original writ with the defendant, and preserving a copy thereof on which to make the return of service, but a failure in this respect shall not be held material.

663.15. Defendant not found
If the defendant cannot be found, or if the defendant has not the plaintiff in custody, the service may be made upon any person who has, in the same manner and with the same effect as though the person had been made defendant therein.

663.16. Power of officer
If the defendant hides, or refuses admittance to the person attempting to serve the writ, or if the defendant attempts wrongfully to carry the plaintiff out of the county or the state after the service of the writ, the sheriff, or the person who is attempting to serve or who has served it, is authorized to arrest the defendant and bring the defendant, together with the plaintiff, forthwith before the officer or court before whom the writ is made returnable.

663.17. Arrest
In order to make the arrest, the sheriff or other person having the writ possesses the same power as is given to a sheriff for the arrest of a person charged with a felony.

663.18. Repealed by acts 1970 (63 G.A.) ch. 1276, § 16

663.19. Defects in writ
The writ must not be disobeyed for any defects of form or misdescription of the plaintiff or defendant, provided enough is stated to show the meaning and intent thereof.

663.20. Penalty for eluding writ
If the defendant attempts to elude the service of the writ, or to avoid the effect thereof by transferring the plaintiff to another, or by concealing the plaintiff, the defendant shall be guilty of a serious misdemeanor, and any person knowingly aiding or abetting in any such act shall be subject to like punishment.

663.21. Refusal to give copy of process
An officer refusing to deliver a copy of any legal process by which the officer detains the plaintiff in custody to any person who demands it and tenders the fees thereof, shall forfeit two hundred dollars to the person who demands it.

663.22. Preliminary writ
The court or judge to whom the application for the writ is made, if satisfied that the plaintiff would suffer any irreparable injury before the plaintiff could be relieved by the proceedings above authorized, may issue an order to the sheriff, or any other person selected instead, commanding the sheriff or other person to bring the plaintiff forthwith before such court or judge.

663.23. Arrest of defendant
If the evidence is sufficient to justify the arrest of the defendant for a criminal offense committed in connection with the illegal detention of the plaintiff, the order must also direct the arrest of the defendant.

663.24. Execution of writ—return
The officer or person to whom the order is directed must execute the same by bringing the defendant, and also the plaintiff if required, before the court or judge issuing it, and the defendant must make return to the writ in the same manner as if the ordinary course had been pursued.

663.25. Examination
The defendant may also be examined and committed, or bailed, or discharged, according to the nature of the case.

663.26. Informalities
Any person served with the writ is to be presumed to be the person to whom it is directed, although it may be directed to the person served by a wrong name or description, or to another person.

663.27. Appearance—answer
Service being made in any of the modes herein provided, the defendant must appear at the proper time and answer the petition, but no verification shall be required to the answer.

663.28. Body to be produced
The defendant must also produce the body of the plaintiff, or show good cause for not doing so.

663.29. Penalty—contempt
A willful failure to comply with the above requirements will render the defendant liable to be attached for contempt, and to be imprisoned till the defendant complies, and shall subject the defendant to the forfeiture of one thousand dollars to the party thereby aggrieved.

663.30. Attachment
Such attachment may be served by the sheriff or any other person authorized by the court or judge, who shall also be empowered to produce the body of the plaintiff forthwith, and has, for this purpose, the same powers as are above conferred in similar cases.

663.31. Answer
The defendant in the answer must state whether the defendant then has, or at any time has had, the plaintiff under the defendant's control and restraint, and if so the cause thereof.

663.32. Transfer of plaintiff
If the defendant has transferred the plaintiff to another person, the defendant must state that fact, and to whom, and the time thereof, as well as the reason or authority therefor.

663.33. Copy of process
If the defendant holds the plaintiff by virtue of a legal process or written authority, a copy thereof must be annexed.

663.34. Demurrer or reply—trial
The plaintiff may demur or reply to the defendant's answer, but not verification shall be required to the reply, and all issues joined therein shall be tried by the judge or court.

663.35. Commitment questioned
The reply may deny the sufficiency of the testimony to justify the action of the committing magistrate, on the trial of which issue all written testimony before such magistrate may be given in evidence before the court or judge, in connection with any other testimony which may then be produced.

663.36. Nonpermissible issues
It is not permissible to question the correctness of the action of a court or judge when lawfully acting within the scope of their authority.

663.37. Discharge
If no sufficient legal cause of confinement is shown, the plaintiff must be discharged

663.38. Plaintiff held
Although the commitment of the plaintiff may have been irregular, if the court or judge is satisfied from the evidence that the plaintiff ought to be held or committed, the order may be made accordingly.

663.39. Repealed

663.40. Plaintiff retained in custody
Until the sufficiency of the cause of restraint is determined, the defendant may retain the plaintiff in the defendant's custody, and may use all necessary and proper means for that purpose.

663.41. Right to be present waived
The plaintiff may, in writing, or by attorney, waive the right to be present at the trial, in which case the proceedings may be had in the plaintiff's absence. The writ will in such cases be modified accordingly.

663.42. Disobedience of order

Disobedience to any order of discharge will subject the defendant to attachment for contempt, and also to the forfeiture of one thousand dollars to the party aggrieved, besides all damages sustained by the plaintiff in consequence thereof.

663.43. Papers filed with clerk

When the proceedings are before a judge, except when the writ is refused, all the papers in the case, including the judge's final order, shall be filed with the clerk of the district court of the county wherein the final proceedings were had, and a memorandum thereof shall be entered by the clerk upon the judgment docket.

663.44. Costs

1. If the plaintiff is discharged, the costs shall be assessed to the defendant, unless the defendant is an officer holding the plaintiff in custody under a commitment, or under other legal process, in which case the costs shall be assessed to the county. If the plaintiff's application is refused, the costs shall be assessed against the plaintiff, and, in the discretion of the court, against the person who filed the petition in the plaintiff's behalf.

2. Notwithstanding subsection 1, if the plaintiff is confined in any state institution and is discharged in habeas corpus proceedings, or if the habeas corpus proceedings fail, and costs and fees cannot be collected from the person liable to pay costs and fees, the costs and fees shall be paid by the county in which such state institution is located. The facts of such payment and the proceedings on which it is based, with a statement of the amount of fees or costs incurred, with approval in writing by the presiding judge appended to the statement or endorsed on the statement, shall be certified by the clerk of the district court under the seal of office to the state executive council. The executive council shall review the proceedings and authorize reimbursement for all such fees and costs or such part of the fees and costs as the executive council finds justified, and shall notify the director of the department of administrative services to draw a warrant to such county treasurer for the amount authorized. There is appropriated from moneys in the general fund not otherwise appropriated an amount necessary to pay the reimbursement authorized by the executive council. The costs and fees referred to above shall include any award of fees made to a court appointed attorney representing an indigent party bringing the habeas corpus action.

Current with legislation form the 2014 Reg.Sess.

KANSAS

Kansas Statutes
Chapter 60. Procedure, Civil
Article 15. Habeas Corpus

60-1501. Jurisdiction and right to writ; time limitations

(a) Subject to the provisions of *K.S.A. 60-1507*, and amendments thereto, any person in this state who is detained, confined or restrained of liberty on any pretense whatsoever, and any parent, guardian, or next friend for the protection of infants or allegedly incapacitated or incompetent persons, physically present in this state may prosecute a writ of habeas corpus in the supreme court, court of appeals or the district court of the county in which such restraint is taking place. No docket fee shall be required, as long as the petitioner complies with the provisions of subsection (b) of K.S.A. 60-2001, and amendments thereto.

(b) Except as provided in K.S.A. 60-1507, and amendments thereto, an inmate in the custody of the secretary of corrections shall file a petition for writ pursuant to subsection (a) within 30 days from the date the action was final, but such time is extended during the pendency of the inmate's timely attempts to exhaust such inmate's administrative remedies.

(c) Except as provided in K.S.A. 60-1507, and amendments thereto, a patient in the custody of the secretary of social and rehabilitation services pursuant to K.S.A. 59-29a et seq., and amendments thereto, shall file a petition for writ pursuant to subsection (a) within 30 days from the date the action was final, but such time is extended during the pendency of the patient's timely attempts to exhaust such patient's administrative remedies.

60-1502. Petition
The petition shall be verified and state: (1) The place where the person is restrained and by whom; (2) the cause or pretense of the restraint to the best of plaintiff's knowledge and belief; and (3) why the restraint is wrongful. Individuals in the custody of the secretary of corrections must also include a list of all civil actions, including habeas corpus actions, the inmate has filed, or participated in, in any state court within the last five years.

60-1503. The writ
(a) **Issuance**. The petition shall be presented promptly to a judge in the district court in accordance with the procedure of the court for the assignment of court business. The petition shall be examined promptly by the judge to whom it is assigned. If it plainly appears from the face of the petition and any exhibits attached thereto that the plaintiff is not entitled to relief in the district court, the petition shall be dissolved at the cost of the plaintiff. If the judge finds that the plaintiff may be entitled to relief, the judge shall issue the writ and order the person to whom the writ is directed to file an answer within the period of time fixed by the court or to take such other action as the judge deems appropriate.

(b) **Form**. The writ shall be directed to the party having the person under restraint and shall command such person to have the restrained person before the judge at the time and place specified in the writ.

(c) **Service**. The writ shall be served without delay. If directed to the sheriff it shall be served by the clerk. If directed to any other person it shall be served by the sheriff or some other person designated by the judge. If the person to whom it is directed cannot be found or shall refuse admittance, the writ may be served by leaving it at such person's residence or affixing it at some conspicuous place where the party is confined or restrained.

(d) **Sundays, holidays and accessibility**. The writ may be issued and served at any time, including Sundays, holidays, and days on which the office of the clerk of the court is not accessible.

60-1504. Answer
(a) **Time**. Except as provided in subsection (b), the person to whom the writ is directed shall file an answer thereto within 72 hours after the writ is served or at such other time as shall be specified in the writ.

(b) **Time; exceptions**. If the petition for writ challenges a denial of parole or a prison disciplinary action, the person to whom the writ is directed shall file an answer thereto within 30 days after the writ is served or at such other time as specified in the writ.

(c) **Contents**. The answer must be verified by the person making it and shall contain: (1) a statement of the authority or reasons for the restraint, (2) a copy of the written authority for the restraint, if any, (3) if the custody of the party has been transferred, a statement as to whom, the time, place, and reason for the transfer, and (4) if it is claimed that the party cannot be produced for any reason, a statement as to the reasons why the party cannot be produced.

(d) **Truth of contents**. The contents of the answer, if not controverted by the plaintiff, shall be accepted as true except as to the extent that the judge finds from the evidence that the contents are not true.

60-1505. Hearing

(a) **Summary proceedings**. The judge shall proceed in a summary way to hear and determine the cause and may do so regardless of whether the person restrained is present. If the plaintiff is an inmate in the custody of the secretary of corrections and the motion and the files and records of the case conclusively show that the inmate is entitled to no relief, the writ shall be dissolved at the cost of the inmate.

(b) **Infectious diseases**. When any person is restrained because of an alleged infectious or communicable disease, the judge may appoint at least one competent physician to make an examination of such person and report findings to the judge.

(c) **Temporary orders**. The judge may make an order for the temporary custody of the party and any other temporary orders during the pendency of the proceeding that justice may require.

(d) **Judgment**. If the court determines that the restraint is not wrongful, the writ shall be dissolved at the cost of the plaintiff. If the restraint is found to be wrongful, the judgment shall be either that the person shall be released, or that custody shall be transferred to some other person rightfully entitled thereto, and the court may make such other orders as justice and equity or the welfare of a minor physically present in the state may require. In cases in which the person restrained is a minor, or other incompetent or incapacitated, at the time of rendering judgment at the request of any person adversely affected thereby, the judge shall stay the enforcement of the judgment for a period of not to exceed 48 hours to permit the filing of an appeal, and the judge may provide for the temporary custody of the person during such stay in such manner as the judge sees fit. Enforcement of the judgment after the taking of any appeal may be stayed on such terms and conditions, including such provisions for custody during pendency of the appeal, as the judge shall prescribe. If the state, in open court, announces its intention to appeal from an order discharging a prisoner, the judge shall stay the enforcement of the judgment for a period not more than 24 hours to permit the filing of an appeal.

(e)(1) **The record**. In habeas corpus proceedings involving extradition to another state, when written notice of appeal from a judgment or an order is filed, the transcript shall be prepared within 21 days after the notice of appeal is filed and sent to the appellate court for review. The appellate court may shorten or extend the time for filing the record if there is a reasonable explanation for the need for such action. When the record is received by the appellate court, the court shall set the time for filing of briefs, if briefs are desired, and shall set the appeal for submission.

(2) **Hearing**. Such cases, taken to the court of appeals by appeal, shall be heard at the earliest practicable time. The appellant need not be personally present, and such appeal shall be heard and determined upon the law and the facts arising upon record. No incidental question which may have arisen on the hearing of the application before the court shall be reviewed.

(3) **Orders on appeal**. In such cases, the appellate court shall render such judgment and make such orders as the law and the nature of the case may require, and may make such orders relative to the costs in the case as may seem right, allowing costs and fixing the amount, or allowing no cost at all.

60-1506. Warrant in aid of writ

(a) Issuance. If it be made to appear by affidavit that a person may be carried out of the jurisdiction or suffer irreparable injury before compliance with the writ can be enforced, the judge may cause a warrant to be issued commanding such person to be brought before him or her forthwith.

(b) **Person causing restraint**. The judge may also insert in the warrant a command for the apprehension of the person charged with causing the illegal restraint.

(c) **Procedure**. The officer shall execute the writ by bringing the person therein named before the judge, and the answer and proceedings shall be the same as in cases of writs of habeas corpus.

60-1507. Prisoner in custody under sentence

(a) **Motion attacking sentence**. A prisoner in custody under sentence of a court of general jurisdiction claiming the right to be released upon the ground that the sentence was imposed in violation of the constitution or laws of the United States, or the constitution or laws of the state of Kansas, or that the court was without jurisdiction to impose sentence, or that the sentence was in excess of the maximum authorized by law, or is otherwise subject to collateral attack, may, pursuant to the time limitations imposed by subsection (f), move the court which imposed the sentence to vacate, set aside or correct the sentence.

(b) **Hearing and judgment**. Unless the motion and the files and records of the case conclusively show that the prisoner is entitled to no relief, the court shall cause notice thereof to be served upon the county attorney, grant a prompt hearing thereon, determine the issues and make findings of fact and conclusions of law with respect thereto. The court may entertain and determine such motion without requiring the production of the prisoner at the hearing. If the court finds that the judgment was rendered without jurisdiction, or that the sentence imposed was not authorized by law or is otherwise open to collateral attack, or that there has been such a denial or infringement of the constitutional rights of the prisoner as to render the judgment vulnerable to collateral attack, the court shall vacate and set the judgment aside and shall discharge the prisoner or resentence said prisoner or grant a new trial or correct the sentence as may appear appropriate.

(c) **Successive motions**. The sentencing court shall not be required to entertain a second or successive motion for similar relief on behalf of the same prisoner.

(d) **Appeal**. An appeal may be taken to the appellate court as provided by law from the order entered on the motion as from a final judgment on application for a writ of habeas corpus.

(e) **Exclusiveness of remedy**. An application for a writ of habeas corpus in behalf of a prisoner who is authorized to apply for relief by motion pursuant to this section, shall not be entertained if it appears that the applicant has failed to apply for relief, by motion, to the court which sentenced said applicant, or that such court has denied said applicant relief, unless it also appears that the remedy by motion is inadequate or ineffective to test the legality of said applicant's detention.

(f) **Time limitations**. (1) Any action under this section must be brought within one year of: (i) The final order of the last appellate court in this state to exercise jurisdiction on a direct appeal or the termination of such appellate jurisdiction; or (ii) the denial of a petition for writ of certiorari to the United States Supreme Court or issuance of such court's final order following granting such petition.

(2) The time limitation herein may be extended by the court only to prevent a manifest injustice.

Statutes are current through laws effective July 1, 2014, including Chapters 4, 23, 27, 60, 73, 74, 75, 87, 91, 93, 98, 100, 103, 122, 127, 131 and 142 of the 2014 Regular Session of the Kansas Legislature.

KENTUCKY

Kentucky Revised Statutes
Title XXXVII. Special Proceedings
Chapter 419. Habeas Corpus

419.020 Issuance of writs
The writ of habeas corpus shall be issued upon petition on behalf of anyone showing by affidavit probable cause that he is being detained without lawful authority or is being imprisoned when by law he is entitled to bail. The writ may be issued by any Circuit Judge on any day at any time and his power to issue such writs shall be coextensive with the Commonwealth.

419.030 Signatures; production of person; return of writ
The writ must be signed by the judge issuing it and command the person having custody of or restraining the person in whose behalf it is issued to bring him personally before the Circuit Judge of the county in which the person is being detained at the time therein specified. The writ must be made returnable as soon as possible.

419.040 Bond
The judge granting the writ may require bond conditioned that the person detained shall not escape by the way, and for the payment of costs. The bond shall be filed with the record of the proceedings, and shall be sued on by the Commonwealth for the benefit of anyone injured by the breach of it.

419.050 Accused not in custody
When the person on whose behalf the writ is granted is not in the custody of a public officer, the judge issuing it, for good cause shown, may direct the person serving it to take the person detained into his custody and produce him on the return of the writ.

419.060 Service of writ; on concealed person
(1) Service shall be made by delivering a copy of the writ personally to the person to be served, or if acceptance is refused, by offering personal delivery to such person.

(2) If the person to be served is absent from the place of detention, service shall be made by delivering a copy of the writ personally to the person having the person detained in immediate custody.

(3) If the person to be served conceals himself, or refuses admittance to the party attempting to serve the writ, it may be served by affixing a copy of it on some conspicuous place on the outside of his place of abode, or of the place where the party is confined or detained.

(4) The writ may be served at any time on any day. The return of the officer or person serving shall be proof of the time and manner of service.

419.070 Response to writ
(1) The person commanded by the writ may file a response in which he shall state whether he has the party in his custody, or under his power of restraint.

(2) If he has the party in his custody or under his power of restraint, he shall state the authority for and cause of such custody or restraint. If the detention is by virtue of a legal process, a copy thereof must be annexed to the response.

(3) If he had the party in his custody or under his power of restraint at any time prior or subsequent to the date of the writ, but has transferred such custody or restraint to another, the response must state particularly to whom, at what time and place, for what cause and by what authority such transfer took place.

(4) The response must be signed by the party making it or his attorney in accordance with the Rules of Civil Procedure governing the signing of pleadings.

419.080 Production of person; exception for infirmity or illness
The person commanded by the writ shall bring the detained person according to the command of the writ unless it is made to appear by affidavit that because of sickness or infirmity such person cannot be brought before the judge without danger to his health. If the judge is satisfied of the truth of the affidavit he may proceed and dispose of the case as if the part had been produced, or the hearing may be postponed until the party can be present.

419.090 Refusal to obey writ
If the person commanded by the writ refuses to obey, he shall be adjudged in contempt of court.

419.100 Production of evidence; depositions
Evidence may be produced and compelled as in civil actions. Depositions taken in accordance with the provisions of the Rules of Civil Procedure may be read as evidence at the hearing on the writ.

419.110 Trial and judgment
(1) The hearing on the writ shall be summary in nature.

(2) The judgment shall fix the costs of the proceeding, including the charge for transportation of the prisoner or party detained.

(3) Where the person detained is a party to a prosecution pending in another court, a copy of the judgment shall be forwarded to the clerk of that court.

419.120 Removal of person to another state
If the evidence at the hearing shows probable cause that the detained person is guilty of an offense that is within the exclusive jurisdiction of another court, or that was committed in another county, the court

shall order that he be taken immediately before the court having jurisdiction or remand him to the custody of an officer to be taken to the proper county for new proceedings against him.

419.130 Appeal; supersedeas

(1) Any party to a hearing on a writ may appeal to the Court of Appeals by filing with the clerk of the court, within thirty (30) days after the entry of the judgment, the original record and a transcript of the evidence, together with a notice of appeal, which notice shall be served on the other parties at least two (2) days before the appeal is filed. Upon the filing of the appeal the clerk shall immediately deliver the papers to the Chief Judge.

(2) If the judgment in a habeas corpus proceeding orders the release of the person detained, any party may have the judgment stayed until the appeal is filed by notifying the judge rendering the judgment that he intends to appeal and upon complying with such terms as to bond or otherwise as the judge deems proper for the security of the person detained. The Court of Appeals may continue, modify or set aside the stay pending the appeal. The appellant may be required to give security for costs.

Current through the end of the 2014 legislation

LOUISIANA

Louisiana Statutes
Louisiana Code of Civil Procedure
Title III. Extraordinary Remedies
Chapter 2. Habeas Corpus

Art. 3821. Definition

Habeas corpus is a writ commanding a person who has another in his custody to produce him before the court and to state the authority for the custody.

Custody, as used in this Chapter, includes detention and confinement.

A petition for a writ of habeas corpus may be filed by the person in custody or by any other person in his behalf.

Art. 3822. Venue

Habeas corpus proceedings may be brought in the parish in which the defendant is domiciled or the parish in which the person detained is in custody.

Art. 3823. Persons authorized to make service; proof of service

A writ of habeas-corpus may be served by any person over the age of twenty-one who is capable of testifying.

If the writ is served by someone other than a sheriff, the affidavit of the person who served it shall be prima facie proof of such service.

Art. 3824. Method of service
A writ of habeas corpus shall be served upon the party to whom it is addressed or who has the person in custody in the manner provided by Article 1232 and 1233. If personal service cannot be made, service may be made by attaching the writ to an entrance door of the residence of the party to be served or to a door of the place where the person is in custody.

Art. 3825. Answer; production of person in custody
The person upon whom the writ has been served, whether it is directed to him or not, shall file an answer stating whether he has custody of the person named in the writ. If the person is in his custody, he shall produce him and state in his answer by what authority he holds the person detained.

Art. 3826. Transfer of custody; answer
If the person upon whom the writ of habeas corpus is served has transferred the custody of the person detained prior to service of the writ, he shall state in his answer the name and address of the person to whom custody was transferred, the time of and the authority for the transfer, and the place where the person detained is then in custody.

Art. 3827. Inability to produce person in custody
If the person in custody cannot be brought before the court, the reasons therefor shall be stated in the answer. The hearing may proceed as if he had been produced.

Art. 3828. Custody pendente lite
If judgment cannot be rendered immediately, the court may award the custody to a proper person until rendition of the judgment.

Art. 3829. Notice of hearing
When a person is in custody by virtue of a prior court order, or at the request of any person, reasonable written notice of the hearing shall be given to the person who provoked the prior court order or requested the custody.

Art. 3830. Judgment
The judgment may order the person released or placed in the custody of a proper person.

Art. 3831. Appeal not to suspend execution of judgment; delay
An appeal from a judgment ordering the release of a person from custody or placing him in the custody of another person shall not suspend the execution of the judgment.

Such an appeal shall be taken only within thirty days from the applicable dates provided in Article 2087(A).

Current through the 2014 Regular Session with Acts effective on or before December 31, 2014.

MAINE

Maine Revised Statutes Annotated
Title 14. Court Procedure—Civil
Chapter 609. Habeas Corpus

§5501. Right to writ
Every person unlawfully deprived of his person liberty by the act of another, except in the cases mentioned, shall of right have a writ of habeas corpus according to the provisions herein contained.

§5509. Minors in armed forces entitled to writ
A minor enlisted within the State into the Army or Navy of the United States without the written consent of his parent or guardian shall have all the benefits of this chapter on the application of himself, parent or guardian.

§5510. Parent or guardian of minor may have writ
The parent or guardian of any minor imprisoned or restrained of his liberty shall be entitled to the writ of habeas corpus for him, if he would be entitled to it on his own application.

§5511. Application for writ on behalf of another
The Supreme Judicial Court or the Superior Court or any justice of either of said courts, on application of any person, may issue the writ of habeas corpus to bring before them any party alleged to be imprisoned or restrained of his liberty but not convicted and sentenced, who would be entitled to it on his own application, when from any cause he is incapable of making it.

§5512. Writ not available
The following persons shall not of right have such writ:

1. Persons committed to jail for certain offenses. Persons committed to or confined in prison or jail on suspicion of treason, felony or accessories before the fact to a felony, when the same is plainly and specifically expressed in the warrant of commitment;

2. Persons committed on civil process. Persons committed in execution of civil process or on mesne process on any civil action on which they are liable to be arrested or imprisoned.

§5513. Application
Application for such writ by any person shall be made to any Justice of the Supreme Judicial Court or Superior Court, regardless whether or not the Supreme Judicial Court or Superior Court is in session. It shall be made returnable before such justice to whom application is made. If the writ is denied and an appeal taken to the law court, the person restrained may be admitted to bail within the discretion of the justice rendering judgment thereon, pending such appeal.

§5514. Where writ returnable; entry of judgment
When awarded by a Justice of the Supreme Judicial Court or of the Superior Court, such writ may issue, under his hand and seal or upon his order from any clerk's office in vacation as if issued by the court, and run throughout the state, and may be returnable before the court or before himself or any other justice thereof, and shall be entered upon the docket of the court in the county where returnable, and the judgment shall there be recorded by the clerk.

§5515. Application; denial of writ
The application shall be in writing, signed and sworn to by the person I making it, stating the place where and the person by whom the restraint is made. The applicant shall produce to the court or justice a copy of the precept by which the person is so restrained, attested by the officer holding it. If, on inspection, it appears to the court or justice that such person is thereby lawfully imprisoned or restrained of his liberty, a writ shall not be granted, unless from examination of the whole case, the court or justice is of opinion that it ought to issue.

§5516. Excessive bail
If it appears that he is imprisoned on mesne process for want of bail and the court or justice thinks that excessive bail is demanded, reasonable bail shall be fixed, and on giving it to the plaintiff, he shall be discharged.

§5517. Refusal of copy of precept; writ granted
If the prison keeper or other officer having custody of such person refuses or unreasonably delays to deliver to the applicant an attested copy of the precept by which he restrains him on demand therefor, the court or justice, on proof of such demand and refusal, shall forthwith issue the writ as prayed for.

§5518. Form of writ
When such writ is issued on an application in behalf of any person described in section 5512, it shall be substantially as follows:

> "STATE OF MAINE.
>
> "c. ......, ss. To A.B., of ......;
>
> [L.S.]
>
> Greeting.
>
> "We command you, that you have the body of c.o., in our prison, at ...., under your custody," (or by you imprisoned and restrained of his liberty, as the case may be,) "as it is said, together with the day and cause of his taking and detaining, by whatever name he is called or charged, before our Supreme Judicial" (or Superior) "Court, held at ...., within and for the County of ...., immediately after the receipt of this writ, to do and receive what our said court shall then and there consider concerning him in this behalf, and have you there this writ.
>
> "Witness ...., Esquire, our ...., this .... day of ...., in the year [20 ..)
>
> ...., Clerk."

The like form shall be used by any justice of said court, changing what should be changed, when such writ is awarded by him.

§5519. Time of service, return and tender of fees
When such writ is offered to the officer to whom it is directed, he shall receive it. On payment or tender of such sum as the court or justice thereof directs, he shall make due return thereof within 3 days if the

place of return is within 20 miles of the place of imprisonment; if over 20 and less than 100 miles, within 7 days; and if more than 100 miles, within 14 days. If such writ was issued against such officer, on his refusal or neglect to deliver, on demand, to the applicant a copy of the precept by which he restrained the person of his liberty, in whose behalf application was made, then the officer shall obey the writ without payment or tender of expenses.

§5520. *Production of body of restrained person; sickness*
The person making the return shall, at the same time, bring the body of the party, as commanded in the writ, if in his custody or power or under his restraint, unless prevented by sickness or infirmity of such party. In such case that fact shall be stated in the return. If proved to the satisfaction of the court or justice, a justice of the court may proceed to the place where the party is confined and there make his examination or may adjourn it to another time or make such other in the case as law and justice require.

§5521. *Examination of causes of restraint*
On return of the writ, the court or justice, without delay, shall proceed to examine the causes of imprisonment or restraint, and may adjourn such examination from time to time.

§5522. *Notice to interested persons before discharge*
When it appears that the party is detained on any process under which any other person has an interest in continuing such imprisonment or restraint, the party shall not be discharged until notice has been given to such other person or his attorney, if within the State or within 30 miles of the place of examination, to appear and object, if he sees cause. If imprisoned on any criminal accusation, he shall not be discharged until sufficient notice has been given to the Attorney General or other attorney for the State that he may appear and object, if he thinks fit.

§5523. *Proceedings in court*
The party imprisoned or restrained may deny allegations of fact in the return or statement and may allege other material facts. The court or justice may, in a summary way, examine the cause of imprisonment or restraint, hear evidence produced on either side, and if no legal cause is shown for such imprisonment or restraint, the court or justice shall discharge him, except as provided in section 5516.

§5525. *Form of writ if restraint not by officer*
In cases of imprisonment or restraint of personal liberty by any person not a sheriff, deputy sheriff, constable, jailer or marshal, deputy marshal or other officer of the courts of the United States, the writ shall be in the following form, viz:

"STATE OF MAINE.

[L.S.] "To the sheriffs of our several counties and their respective deputies,

Greeting.

"We command you, that you take the body of C.D., of ...., imprisoned and restrained of his liberty, as it is said, by A.B., of ...., and have him before our Supreme Judicial" (or Superior) "court, held at ...., within and for our County of ...., immediately after receipt of this writ, to do and receive what our court shall then and there consider concerning him in this behalf; and summon the said A.B. then and there to appear before our said court, to show cause for taking and detaining said C.D., and have you there this writ with your doings thereon.

"Witness, ... , Esquire, our ...., at ...., this .... day of ...., in the year (20 ..] ...., Clerk."

§5526. Issuance and service of writ
The writ described in section 5525 may be issued by the Supreme Judicial Court or Superior Court sitting in any county in which the person in whose behalf application is made is restrained or by any justice thereof, the form to be varied so far as necessary when issued by a justice of the court, and may be served in any county in the State.

§5527. Designation of unknown person; restraining person
The person having custody of the prisoner may be designated by the name of his office, if he has any, or by his own name; or if both are unknown or uncertain, he may be described by an assumed name. Anyone served with the writ shall be deemed the person thereby intended.

§5528.—restrained person
The person restrained shall be described by his name, if known; if unknown or uncertain, in any other way so as to make known who is intended.

§5529 Form of return
In cases under section 5518, the person who makes the return, and in cases under section 5525, the person in whose custody the prisoner is found, shall state in writing to the court or justice before whom the process is returned, plainly and unequivocally:

1. Whether party in custody. Whether he has or has not the party in his custody or power, or under restraint;

2. If so, authority and cause. If he has, he shall state, at large, the authority and true and whole cause of such imprisonment or restraint upon which the party is detained; and,

3. If transferred to another. If he has had the party in his custody or power or under his restraint and has transferred him to another, he shall state particularly to whom, at what time, for what cause and by what authority such transfer was made.

§5530. Verification of returns
Such return or statement shall be signed and sworn to by the person making it, unless he is a sworn public officer and makes and signs his return in his official capacity.

§5531. Custody of party
The party may be bailed to appear from day to day until judgment is rendered or remanded or committed to the sheriff or placed in custody, as the case requires.

§5532. Neglect of officer to deliver copy of precept
An officer forfeits $200 to a prisoner if the officer refuses or neglects, within the time period provided in subsection 1 or 2, to deliver a true and attested copy of the warrant or process by which the officer detains a prisoner to any person who demands it and tenders the fee for the copy.

1. Sentenced prisoners. In the case of sentenced prisoners, the copy of the warrant or process must be delivered within 3 business days of the demand. As used in this subsection, "business day" has the same meaning as found in Title 21-A, section 1, subsection 4.

2. Other prisoners. In the case of any prisoner other than a sentenced prisoner, the copy of the warrant or process, which need not be a true and attested copy, must be delivered within 4 hours of the demand.

§5533. Failure to serve writ; contempt
If any person or officer to whom such writ is directed refuses to receive it or neglects to obey and execute it as required, and no sufficient cause is shown therefor, he forfeits to the aggrieved party $400. The court or justice before whom the writ was returnable shall proceed forthwith by attachment as for a contempt, to compel obedience to the writ and to punish for the contempt.

§5534. Attachment against sheriff; service
If such attachment is issued against a sheriff or his deputy, it may be directed to any person therein designated, who shall thereby have power to execute it, and the sheriff or his deputy may be committed to jail on such process in any county but his own.

§5535. Refusal to obey writ
If the person to whom the writ is directed refuses to obey and execute it, the court or justice may issue a precept to any officer or other person therein named, commanding his to bring the person for whose benefit the writ was issued before such court or justice. The prisoner shall thereupon be discharged, bailed or remanded as if brought in on habeas corpus.

§5536. No rearrest after discharge
No person discharged by post-conviction review, except as provided in Title 15, chapter 305-A, [FN 1] shall be again imprisoned or restrained for the same cause, unless indicted therefor, convicted thereof or committed for want of bail; or unless, after a discharge for defect of proof or some material defect in the commitment in a criminal case, he is arrested on sufficient proof and committed by legal process for the same offense.

[FN 1] *15 M.R.S.A. §2121 et seq.*

§5537. Transfer of prisoner with intent to elude service; penalty
A person ordered to be committed to prison on a criminal charge shall be carried to such prison as soon as may be and shall not be delivered from one officer to another except for easy and speedy conveyance; nor removed without his consent from one county to another unless by habeas corpus. If anyone having in his custody or under his power a person entitled to a writ of habeas corpus, whether issued or not, transfers him to the custody of another or changes his place of confinement with intent to elude the service of such writ, he forfeit $400 to the party aggrieved.

§5538. Penalty no bar to action
No penalty established by this chapter shall bar any action at common law for damages for false imprisonment.

§5539. Third person may appear by stipulating for costs
When a person is unlawfully carried out of the state or is imprisoned in a secret place, any other person

may appear for him in an action therefor in his name, who shall stipulate for the payment of costs as the court orders.

§5543. Surety bonds authorized in criminal cases
In any criminal proceeding or mesne process or other process where a bail bond recognizance or personal sureties or other obligation is required, or whenever any person is arrested and is required or permitted to recognize with sureties for his appearance in court, the court official or other authority authorized by law to accept and approve the same shall accept and approve in lieu thereof, when offered, a good and sufficient surety bond duly executed by a surety company authorized to do business in this State.

§5545. Habeas corpus for prisoner as witness
A court may issue a writ of habeas corpus, when necessary, to bring before it a prisoner for trial in a cause pending in such court, or to testify as a witness when his personal attendance is deemed necessary for the attainment of justice.

Whenever, under this section or under any other section in this chapter, [FN 1] a court issues a writ of habeas corpus ordering before it a prisoner confined in any penal or correctional institution under the control of the Department of Health and Human Services or the Department of Corrections, or confined in any county jail, its order as to the transportation of the prisoner to and from the court must be directed to the sheriff of the county in which the court is located. It is the responsibility of the sheriff or any one or more of the sheriff's authorized deputies pursuant to any such order to safely transport a prisoner to and from the court and to provide safe and secure custody of the prisoner during the proceedings, as directed by the court. At the time of removal of a prisoner from an institution, the transporting officer shall leave with the head of the institution an attested copy of the order of the court, and upon return of the prisoner shall note that return on the copy. This paragraph as it relates to the responsibility for transportation is applicable to transfers from the county jail to any other county jail or to a state correctional facility under *Title 34-A, section 1405*.

Any prisoner who escapes from custody of the sheriff or any of his deputies or any other law enforcement officer following removal for appearance in court, from a penal or correctional institution or from a county jail, and prior to return thereof, shall be chargeable with escape from the penal or correctional institution or county jail from which he was removed, and shall be punished in accordance with *Title 17-A, section 755*.

[FN 1] *14 M.R.S.A. §§5501 to 5547.*

§5546. Habeas corpus for mentally ill person
When a mentally ill person is arrested or imprisoned on mesne process or execution in a civil action, a Justice of the Supreme Judicial court or of the Superior Court or the judge of probate within his county, on application, may inquire into the case; issue a writ of habeas corpus; cause such person to be brought before him for examination; and after notice to the creditor or his attorney, if either is living in the State, and a hearing, if it is proved to the satisfaction of said justice or judge that the person is mentally ill, he may discharge him from arrest or imprisonment; and the creditor may make a new arrest on the same demand when the debtor becomes of sound mind. If he is arrested on the same demand a 2nd time before he becomes of sound mind and is again discharged for that reason, he is forever after exempt from arrest for the same cause.

Current with legislation through the 2013 Second Regular Session of the 126th Legislature. The Second Regular Session convened January 8, 2014 and adjourned May 2, 2014. The general effective date is August 1, 2014.

MARYLAND

Annotated Code of Maryland
Maryland Rules
Title 15. Other Special Proceedings
Chapter 300. Habeas Corpus

RULE 15-301. HABEAS CORPUS—APPLICABILITY
The rules in this Chapter apply to all habeas corpus proceedings challenging the legality of the confinement or restraint of an individual.

RULE 15-302. PETITION
(a) Generally. A petition for a writ of habeas corpus shall be supported by affidavit of the petitioner and shall include:

(1) a statement that the individual by or on behalf of whom the writ is sought is unlawfully confined or restrained;

(2) the place where the individual is confined or restrained, if known;

(3) the name and any official capacity of the person by whom the individual is confined or restrained or, if not known, a description sufficient to enable that person to be identified;

(4) the circumstances and the cause of the confinement; and

(5) if the confinement is pursuant to a judgment or order of a court, the name of the court, the date of the judgment or order, and the case number, if known.

(b) Certain Confinements. If a petition is filed by or on behalf of an individual confined as a result of a sentence for a criminal offense, of an order in a juvenile proceeding, or of a judgment of contempt of court, the petition, in addition to complying with the provisions of section (a) of this Rule, shall state, to the best of the petitioner's knowledge, information, and belief:

(1) whether any previous petition for habeas corpus or other post conviction relief: (A) the court or judge to whom the petition was directed, (B) all grounds of the petition, (C) the determination made on the petition, (D) whether any appeal or application for leave to appeal was filed from any order on the petition, and (E) any determination made on the appeal or application for leave to appeal; and

(3) all grounds for the issuance of the writ that were not asserted in any previous petition for habeas corpus or other post conviction relief.

RULE 15-303. PROCEDURE ON PETITION

<Section effective until further Order of the Court. See, also, section effective after further Order of the Court.>

(a) Generally. Upon receiving a petition for a writ of habeas corpus, the judge immediately shall refer it as provided in section (c) of this Rule or act on the petition as provided in section (d) or (e) of this Rule, except that if the petition seeks a writ habeas corpus for the purpose of determining admission to bail or the appropriateness of any bail set, the judge may proceed in accordance with section (b) of this Rule.

(b) Bail.

(1) Pretrial. If a petition by or on behalf of an individual who is confined prior to or during trial seeks a writ of habeas corpus for the purpose of determining admission to bail or the appropriateness of any bail set, the judge to whom the petition is directed may deny the petition without a hearing if a judge has previously determined the individual's eligibility for pretrial release or the conditions for such release pursuant to Rule 4-216 or 4-216.1 and the petition raises no grounds sufficient to warrant issuance of the writ other than grounds that were raised when the earlier pretrial release determination was made.

(2) After Conviction.

(A) Except as otherwise provided in subsection (2)(B) of this section, if a petition by or on behalf of an individual confined as a result of a conviction pending sentencing or exhaustion of appellate review seeks a writ of habeas corpus for the purpose of determining admission to bail or the appropriateness of any bail set, the judge to whom the petition is directed may deny the writ and order that the petition be treated as a motion for release or for amendment of an order of release pursuant to Rule 4-349. Upon entry of the order, the judge shall transmit the petition, a certified copy of the order, and any other pertinent papers to the trial judge who presided at the proceeding as a result of which the individual was confined. Upon receiving of the transmittal, the trial judge shall proceed in accordance with Rule 4-349.

(B) If a petition directed to a circuit court judge is filed by or on behalf of an individual confined as a result of a conviction in the District Court that has been appealed to a circuit court, the circuit court judge shall act on the petition and may not transmit or refer the petition to a District Court judge.

(c) Referral. If the petition is made by or on behalf of an individual confined or restrained as the result of a prior judicial proceeding, a judge to whom the petition has been made may refer the petition, without taking other action, to the administrative judge of the court in which the prior proceeding was held. In exercising the discretion to refer the petition, the judge to whom the petition has been directed shall consider the interests and convenience of the parties and the State. Upon receiving the referral, the administrative judge shall assign the petition to a judge in accordance with the assignment procedures of that court, except that, without the written consent of the individual confined or restrained, the petition shall not be assigned to any judge who sat at the proceeding as a result of which the individual was confined or restrained. The judge to whom the petition has been assigned may not further refer the petition and shall act on it immediately pursuant to section (d) or (e) of this Rule.

(d) Show Cause Order.

APPENDIX—MARYLAND

(1) Entry; Contents. If the individual is confined as a result of a sentence in a criminal case, including a proceeding for criminal contempt other than a direct criminal contempt summarily punished, or as a result of a disposition or post-dispositional order following an adjudication of delinquency in a juvenile proceeding, the judge, prior to taking any further action, may enter an order directed to the person having custody of the individual to show cause why the writ should not issue. The show cause order may be entered regardless of whether the petition complies with *Rule 15-302*. The show cause order shall:

(A) state a date by which the order must be served upon the person having custody of the individual;

(B) state a date by which the person having custody may file a response and a date by which a copy of any response must be served on the petitioner in accordance with subsection (4) of this section;

(C) state that the petitioner may file a reply to the response within 30 days after service of the response; and

(D) require the petitioner to serve a copy of any reply on the person having custody by first-class mail, postage prepaid.

(2) Service of Show Cause Order. The show cause order, together with a copy of the petition, shall be served by certified mail on the person having custody of the individual confined. The show cause order shall be served by first-class mail, postage prepaid, on the petitioner.

(3) Notice in Response. A response to the show cause order shall include notice to the petitioner in substantially the following form:

NOTICE TO _____, (Name of Petitioner) PETITIONER

This response alleges your petition for a writ of habeas corpus should be denied because (check all that apply):

[] There is no good reason why new grounds now raised by the petition were not raised in previous proceedings.

[] There has been unjustified delay in filing the petition and that delay has prejudiced the ability of _____

_____

(Name of person having custody of the individual confined) to respond to the petition.

[] Other reasons for denial (specify):

You may file a reply to this response. Any reply must be filed with the court by_____ [Calendar Date] and you must mail a copy of your reply to _____*

_____*
(Name of person having custody)

If you do not file a reply by that date or if your reply does not show the court a good reason why the allegations in this response are wrong, the court may deny your petition.

Committee note: The calendar date for a reply shall be 30 days after personal service is made or 33 days after served by mail is mailed.

(4) Service of Response. The person having custody shall serve a copy of the response on the petitioner or the petitioner's attorney by first-class mail, postage prepaid, or by hand-delivery. The response shall be accompanied by a certificate of service showing the date and manner of making service and, if service is by hand-delivery, the name of the individual making service.

(5) If Show Cause Order or Response Not Timely served. If (A) the show cause order was not timely served upon the person having custody and the person having custody has not filed a response or (B) the response was not timely served upon the petitioner and the petitioner has not filed a reply, the judge shall either reissue the show cause order or set the matter in for a hearing.

(e) Action on Petition.

(1) Preliminary Determination. Unless the judge refers the petition pursuant to section (c) of this Rule, the judge shall first determine whether the petition complies with the provisions of *Rule 15-302*, except that if a show cause order was entered in accordance with section (d) of this Rule, the judge may defer making this determination until the time for a reply has expired. In determining whether the writ should be granted or denied, a judge shall consider any response or reply filed pursuant to a show cause order entered under section (d) of this Rule and may examine public records.

(2) Noncompliance with *Rule 15-302*. If the petition fails to comply with the provisions of *Rule 15-302*, the judge may (A) deny the petition; (B) permit the petition to be amended or supplemented; or (C) grant the writ if there is a sufficient showing of probable illegal confinement or restraint.

(3) Compliance with *Rule 15-302*. If the petitioner complies with the provisions of *Rule 15-302*, the judge shall grant the writ unless:

> (A) the judge finds from the petition, any response, reply, document filed with the petition or with a response or reply, or public record that the individual confined or restrained is not entitled to any relief;
>
> (B) the petition is made by or on behalf of an individual confined as a result of a sentence for a criminal offense, of an order in a juvenile proceeding, or of a judgment of contempt of court, the legality of the confinement was determined in a prior habeas corpus or other post conviction proceeding, and no new ground is shown sufficient to warrant issuance of the writ;
>
> (C) there is no good reason why new grounds now raised by the petitioner were not raised in previous proceedings; or
>
> (D) there has been an unjustified delay in filing the petition that has prejudiced the ability of the person having custody of the individual confined or restrained to respond to the petition.

(4) Exception; Notice, Reply. The judge may not deny the writ on a ground set forth in subsection (e)(3)(C) or (e)(C)(D) of this Rule unless the petitioner has been given notice of that ground and has had an opportunity to reply, either in accordance with section (d) of this Rule or as otherwise directed by the court.

RULE 15-303. PROCEDURE ON PETITION

<Section affective upon further Order of the Court. The Court of Appeals of Maryland amended this rule on November 6, 2013, "it shall take effect upon further Order of the Court and apply to all actions commenced on or after the date specified in such Order and, insofar as practicable, to all actions then pending".>

(a) Generally. Upon receiving a petition for a writ of habeas corpus, the judge immediately shall refer it as provided in section (c) of this Rule or act on the petition as provided in section (d) or (e) of this Rule, except that if the petition seeks a writ of habeas corpus for the purpose of determining admission to bail or the appropriateness of any bail set, the judge may proceed in accordance with section (b) of this Rule.

(b) Bail.

(1) Pretrial. If a petition by or on behalf of an individual who is confined prior to or during trial seeks a writ of habeas corpus for the purpose of determining admission to bail or the appropriateness of any bail set, the judge to whom the petition is directed may deny the petition without a hearing if a judge has previously determined the individual's eligibility for pretrial release or the conditions for such release pursuant to Rule 4-216, 4-216.1., or 4-216.2 and the petition raises no grounds sufficient to warrant issuance of the writ other than grounds that were raised when the earlier pretrial release determination was made.

(2) After Conviction.

(A) Except as otherwise provided in subsection (2)(B) of this section, if a petition by or on behalf of an individual confined as a result of a conviction pending sentencing or exhaustion of appellate review seeks a writ of habeas corpus for the purpose of determining admission to bail or the appropriateness of any bail set, the judge to whom the petition is directed may deny the writ and order that the petition be treated as a motion for release or for amendment of an order of release pursuant to Rule 4-349. Upon entry of the order, the judge shall transmit the petition, a certified copy of the order, and any other pertinent papers to the trial judge who presided at the proceeding as a result of which the individual was confined. Upon receiving of the transmittal, the judge shall proceed in accordance with Rule 4-349.

(B) If a petition directed to a circuit court judge is filed by or on behalf of an individual confined as a result of a conviction in the District Court that has been appealed to a circuit court, the circuit court judge shall act on the petition and may not transmit or refer the petition to a District Court judge.

(c) Referral. If the petition is made by or on behalf of an individual confined or restrained as the result of a prior judicial proceeding, a judge to whom the petition has been made may refer the petition, without taking other action, to the administrative judge of the court in which the prior proceedings was held. In exercising the discretion to refer the petition, the judge to whom the petition has been directed shall consider the interests and convenience of the parties and the State. Upon receiving the referral, the administrative judge shall assign the petition to a judge in accordance with the assignment procedures of that court, except that, without the written consent of the individual confined or restrained, the petition shall not be assigned to any judge who sat at the proceeding as a result of which the individual was confined or restrained. The judge to whom the petition has been assigned may not further refer the petition and shall act on it immediately pursuant to section (d) or (e) of this Rule.

APPENDIX—MARYLAND

(d) Show cause Order.

(1) Entry; Contents. If the individual is confined as a result of a sentence in a criminal case, including a proceeding for criminal contempt other than a direct criminal contempt summarily punished, or as a result of a disposition or post-dispositional order following an adjudication of delinquency in a juvenile proceeding, the judge, prior to taking any further action, may enter an order directed to the person having custody of the individual to show cause why the writ should not issue. The show cause order may be entered regardless of whether the petition complies with *Rule 15-302*. The show cause order shall:

(A) state a date by which the order must be served upon the person having custody of the individual;

(B) state a date by which the person having custody may file a response and a date by which a copy of any response must be served on the petitioner in accordance with subsection (4) of this section;

(C) state that the petitioner may file a reply to the response within 30 days after service of the response; and

(D) require the petitioner to serve a copy of any reply on the person having custody by first-class mail, postage prepaid.

(2) Service of Show cause Order. The show cause order, together with a copy of the petition, shall be served by certified mail on the person having custody of the individual confined. The show cause order shall be served by first-class mail, postage prepaid, on the petitioner.

(3) Notice in Response. A response to the show cause order shall include notice to the petitioner in substantially the following form:

NOTICE TO _____, (Name of Petitioner) PETITIONER

This response alleges your petition for a writ of habeas corpus should be denied because (check all that apply):

[] There is no good reason why new grounds now raised by the petition were not raised in previous proceedings.

[] There has been unjustified delay in filing the petition and that delay has prejudiced the ability of _____

(Name of person having custody of the individual confined) to respond to the petition.

[] Other reasons for denial (specify):

You may file a reply to this response. Any reply must be filed with the court by _____ [Calendar Date] and you must mail a copy of your reply to _____.

(Name of person having custody)

If you do not file a reply by that date or if your reply does not show the court a good reason why the allegations in this response are wrong, the court may deny your petition.

Committee note: The calendar date for a reply shall be 30 days after personal service is made or 33 days after service by mail is mailed.

(4) Service of Response. The person having custody shall serve a copy of the response on the petitioner or the petitioner's attorney by first-class mail, postage prepaid, or by hand-delivery. The response shall be accompanied by a certificate of service showing the date and manner of making service and, if service is by hand-delivery, the name of the individual making service.

(5) If Show cause Order or Response Not Timely Served. If (A) the show cause order was not timely served upon the person having custody and the person having custody has not filed a response or (B) the response was not timely served upon the petitioner and the petitioner has not filed a reply, the judge shall either reissue the show cause order or set the matter in for a hearing.

(e) Action on Petition.

(1) Preliminary Determination. Unless the judge refers the petition pursuant to section (c) of this Rule, the judge shall first determine whether the petition complies with the provisions of *Rule 15-302*, except that if a show cause order was entered in accordance with section (d) of this Rule, the judge may defer making this determination until the time for a reply has expired. In determining whether the writ should be granted or denied, a judge shall consider any response or reply filed pursuant to a show cause order entered under section (d) of this Rule and may examine public records.

(2) Noncompliance with *Rule 15-302*. If the petition fails to comply with the provisions of *Rule 15-302*, the judge may (A) deny the petition; (B) permit the petition to be amended or supplemented; or (C) grant the writ if there is a sufficient showing of probable illegal confinement or restraint.

(3) Compliance with *Rule 15-302*. If the petition complies with the provisions of *Rule 15-302*, the judge shall grant the writ unless:

> (A) the judge finds from the petition, any response, reply, document filed with the petition or with a response or reply, or public record that the individual confined or restrained is not entitled to any relief;

> (B) the petition is made by or on behalf of an individual confined as a result of a sentence for a criminal offense, of an order in a juvenile proceeding, or of a judgment of contempt of court, the legality of the confinement was determined in a prior habeas corpus or other post conviction proceeding, and no new ground is shown sufficient to warrant issuance of the writ;

> (C) there is no good reason why new grounds now raised by the petitioner were not raised in previous proceedings; or

> (D) there has been an unjustified delay in filing the petition that has prejudiced the ability of the person having custody of the individual confined or restrained to respond to the petition.

(4) Exception; Notice, Reply. The judge may not deny the writ on a ground set forth in subsection (e)(3)(C) or (e)(3)(D) of this Rule unless the petitioner has been given notice of that ground and has had an opportunity to reply, either in accordance with section (d) of this Rule or as otherwise directed by the court.

RULE 15-304. ALTERNATE REMEDY—POST CONVICTION PROCEDURE ACT
When a petition for a writ of habeas corpus is filed by or on behalf of an individual confined as a result of a sentence for a criminal offense, including a criminal contempt, or a commitment order in a juvenile delinquency proceeding, the judge may order that the petition be treated as a petition under the Post Conviction Procedure Act if the individual confined consents in writing or on the record and the judge is satisfied that the post conviction proceeding is adequate to test the legality of the confinement. Upon entry of the order, the judge shall transmit the petition, a certified copy of the order, and any other pertinent papers to the court in which the sentence or judgment was entered. Subsequent procedure shall be as in a post conviction proceeding.

RULE 15-305. TO WHOM WRIT DIRECTED—BEFORE WHOM RETURNABLE
A writ of habeas corpus shall be directed to the person having custody of the individual confined or restrained. The writ shall be returnable before the judge granting it or, in the discretion of that judge, before some other judge designated in the writ except that without the written consent of the individual confined or restrained, the judge designated in the writ shall not be a judge who sat at the proceeding as a result of which the individual was confined or restrained. In exercising the discretion granted by this Rule, the judge granting the writ shall consider the interests and convenience of the parties and the State.

RULE 15-306. SERVICE OF WRIT; APPEARANCE BY INDIVIDUAL; AFFIDAVIT
(a) Service. Except as provided in section (c) of this Rule, a writ of habeas corpus and a copy of the petition shall be served by delivering them to the person to whom the writ is directed or by mailing them by first class mail, postage prepaid, as ordered by the court.

(b) Production of Individual. At the time stated in the writ, which, unless the court orders otherwise, shall not be later than three days after service of the writ, the person to whom the writ is directed shall cause the individual confined or restrained to be taken before the judge designated in the writ. If the petition is by or behalf of an individual confined or restrained pursuant to an isolation or quarantine directive or order issued under any federal, State, or local public health law or public emergency law, production of the individual may be by means of a telephonic conference call, live closed circuit television, live internet or satellite video conference transmission, or other available means of communication that reasonably permit the individual to participate in the proceedings.

(c) Immediate Appearance. Subject to section (b) of this Rule, if the judge finds probable cause to believe that the person having custody of the individual or would evade or disobey the writ, the judge shall include in the writ an order directing the person immediately to appear, together with the individual confined or restrained, before the judge designated in the writ. The sheriff to whom the writ is delivered shall serve the writ immediately, together with a copy of the petition, on the person having custody of the individual confined or restrained and shall bring that person, together with the individual confined or restrained, before the judge designated in the writ.

RULE 15-307. ABSENCE OF JUDGE—RETURN TO ANOTHER COURT OR JUDGE
If the judge designated in the writ is unavailable when the individual confined or restrained is produced, the individual shall be taken before another judge of the same judicial circuit. If the individual is confined or restrained as a result of a sentence for a criminal offense, including a criminal contempt, or

as a result of an order in a juvenile proceeding, the individual shall not be taken before a judge who sat at any proceeding as a result of which the individual was confined or restrained unless the individual consents in writing.

RULE 15-308. NOTICE TO STATE'S ATTORNEY AND ATTORNEY GENERAL

If a judge grants a writ with respect to an individual confined as a result of a sentence for a criminal offense, including a criminal contempt, or as a result of an order in a juvenile proceeding, the judge shall instruct the clerk to give notice of the time and place of the hearing to the State's Attorney for the county in which the sentence or order was entered. If the petition presents an issue of illegal confinement in the Division of Correction unrelated to the underlying conviction or order, notice shall also be directed to the Attorney General.

RULE 15-309. HEARING

(a) Generally. Upon the production of the individual confined or restrained, the judge shall conduct a hearing immediately to inquire into the legality and propriety of the individual's confinement or restraint. The individual confined or restrained for whom the writ is issued may offer evidence to prove the lack of legal justification for the confinement or restraint, and evidence may be offered on behalf of the person having custody to refute the claim.

(b) Conduct of Hearing If Isolation or Quarantine. If, pursuant to an isolation or quarantine directive or order issued under any federal, State, or local public health law or public emergency law, one or more of the parties, their counsel, or witnesses are unable to appear personally at the hearing, and the fair and effective adjudication of the proceedings permits, the court may:

(1) admit documentary evidence submitted or proffered by courtier, facsimile, or other electronic means;

(2) If feasible, conduct the proceedings by means of a telephonic conference call, live closed circuit television, live internet or satellite video conference transmission, or other available means of communication that reasonably permits the parties or their authorized representatives to participate in the proceedings; and

(3) decline to require strict application of the rules of evidence other than those relating to the competency of witnesses and lawful privileges.

RULE 15-310. DISPOSITION

(a) Appropriate Remedy. If the judge determines that the individual is confined or restrained without legal warrant or authority, the judge shall order that the individual be released or discharged immediately, or shall enter such other order as justice may require. If the judge determines that the confinement or restraint is lawful and proper, the individual shall be remanded to custody or admitted to bail pending trial or retrial.

(b) Errors on Face of Commitment—Correction. The judge to whom the writ is returned shall not discharge the individual confined or restrained merely because of errors, omissions, or irregularities on the face of the warrant or other written authority for commitment. The judge may direct that the warrant or other written authority be sent for correction to the court or judicial officer who issued it and that, after correction, it be redelivered to the person having custody of the individual.

RULE 15-311. MEMORANDUM BY JUDGE
The judge to whom the petition is made or referred shall prepare and file or dictate into the record a memorandum setting forth the grounds of the petition, the questions involved, and the reasons for the action taken. A copy of the memorandum or a transcription of the dictation shall be sent to the petitioner and the person having custody of the individual confined or restrained.

RULE 15-312. DISCHARGE ON GROUND OF UNCONSTITUTIONALITY—REVIEW
When an individual is released or discharged under a writ of habeas corpus on the ground that all or part of the statute or law under which the individual was convicted is unconstitutional, the memorandum or the transcription required by *Rule 15-311* shall be filed by the judge within five days after the judge orders the release or discharge. The clerk shall promptly transmit the record to the Clerk of the Court of Special Appeals for further proceedings.

Current with amendments received through 2/1/14.

MASSACHUSETTS

Massachusetts General Laws
Titled IV. Certain Writs and Proceedings in Special Cases
Chapter 248. Habeas Corpus and Personal Liberty

§1. Persons entitled to writ; exceptions
Whoever is imprisoned or restrained of his liberty may, as of right and of course, prosecute a writ of habeas corpus, according to this chapter, to obtain release from such imprisonment or restraint, if it proves to be unlawful, unless—

First, He has been committed for treason or felony, or on suspicion thereof, or as accessory before the fact to felony, and the cause has been plainly expressed in the warrant of commitment.

Second, He has been convicted or is in execution upon legal process, civil or criminal.

Third, He has been committed on mesne process in a civil action in which he was liable to arrest and imprisonment, unless excessive and unreasonable bail was required.

§2. By whom issued
The writ may be issued, irrespective of the county in which the person is imprisoned or restrained, by the supreme judicial or the superior court, by a probate or a district court or by a judge of any of said courts.

§3. Petition for writ; annexed papers
The petition for the writ shall be in writing, signed and sworn to by the person for whose release it is intended, or by a person in his behalf, and shall state by whom and where the person is imprisoned or restrained, the name of the prisoner and of the person detaining him, if their names are known, or a description of them, if their names are not known, and the cause or pretense of such imprisonment or restraint, according to the knowledge and belief of the petitioner.

If the imprisonment or restraint is by virtue of a warrant or other process, a copy thereof shall be annexed, unless it appears that such copy has been demanded and refused or that, for a sufficient reason, a demand therefor could not be made.

§4. Issuance of writ; return
The court or magistrate to whom the petition is presented shall, without delay, issue a writ of habeas corpus, substantially in the form heretofore established and used in the commonwealth, and returnable forthwith to the supreme judicial court, or a justice thereof, at such place as shall be designated in the writ.

§5. Form of writ
If the imprisonment or restraint is not by a sheriff, deputy sheriff or jailer, the writ shall be in the following form:

> COMMONWEALTH OF MASSACHUSETTS.
> (SEAL.) To the sheriffs of our several counties and to their respective deputies,
>
> We command you that the body of, of
>
> , by, of,
> imprisoned and restrained of his liberty, as it is said, you take and have before a justice of our supreme judicial court at immediately after the receipt of this writ, to do and receive what our said justice shall then and there consider concerning him in this behalf; and summon said then and there to appear before our said justice to show the cause of the taking and detaining of said; and have you there this writ with your doings thereon.
>
> Witness at this day
> of in the year.

§6. Signature of magistrate or clerk; service
If the writ is issued by the court when sitting for the transaction of business, it shall be signed by the clerk, otherwise by the magistrate issuing it, and may be served in any county by any sheriff or deputy sheriff.

§7. Designation of custodian of prisoner
The person who has the custody of the prisoner may be designated by his office or by his own name, or, if they are known or uncertain, he may be described by a fictitious name and the person upon whom the writ is served shall be held to be the person intended.

§8. Designation of prisoner
The person restrained shall be designated by name, if known; otherwise, he may be so described as to identify him.

§9. Expense of transporting prisoner; advance payment
If the person restrained is confined in jail or is in the custody of a civil officer, the court or magistrate granting the writ shall certify thereon the amount to be paid for the expense of transporting him from the place of imprisonment, and the officer shall not be bound to obey the writ unless that amount is paid or tendered to him.

§10. Return of writ
Any person to whom the writ is directed shall receive it, and, upon payment or tender of the charges de-

mandable for its execution, shall make due return thereof within five days after receiving it.

§11. Contents of return
The person in whose custody the prisoner is found shall state in writing, plainly and unequivocally, to the court or justice before whom the writ is returnable—

First, Whether the prisoner is in his custody or power or under his restraint.

Second, If the prisoner is in his custody or power or under his restraint, his specific authority for and the true and whole cause of such imprisonment or restraint, with a copy of the writ, warrant or other process, if any, upon which the prisoner is detained.

Third, If the prisoner has been in his custody or power or under his restraint, and has been transferred to that of another, particularly to whom, when, why and by what authority such transfer was made.

The statement shall be signed by him and, unless he is a sworn public officer and makes the statement in his official capacity, shall be sworn to by him.

§12. Production of prisoner
The person who makes the statement shall at the same time produce the prisoner, if in his custody or power or under his restraint, according to the command of the writ, unless prevented by the illness or infirmity of the prisoner.

§13. Illness preventing production of prisoner
If by reason of the illness or infirmity of the prisoner he cannot without danger be taken to the place appointed for the return of the writ, that fact shall be stated in the statement and, if proved, the judge may proceed to the place where the prisoner is confined and there made his examination; or he may postpone the examination or may make such other order in the case as law and justice require.

§14. Return before justice of court
If the court to which the writ is returnable is not sitting for the transaction of business when the writ is returned, the return shall be made before a justice thereof. If the writ is returned before a justice when the court is sitting for the transaction of business, be may adjourn the case into the court, to be there heard and determined.

§15. Causes of imprisonment; examination
After the writ has been returned, the prisoner may deny any of the facts set forth in the statement and may allege any other material facts; and the court or justice shall examine summarily and without delay the causes of the imprisonment or restraint, hear the evidence produced by any persons interested or authorized to appear and dispose of the prisoner as law and justice require, and may adjourn the examination from time to time.

§16. Notice to persons interested in continuing imprisonment
If it appears from the return of the writ or otherwise that the prisoner is detained on a process under which another person has an interest in continuing his imprisonment or restraint, he shall not be discharged until notice has been given to such other person or his attorney, if within the commonwealth. If such person or his attorney is not within the commonwealth the court may order notice to be given to him.

§17. Notice; prisoners held for crimes
If it appears from the return of the writ or otherwise that the prisoner is imprisoned on a criminal accusation, he shall not be discharged until notice has been given to the attorney general or other attorney for the commonwealth.

§18. Custody of prisoner pending examination
Until judgment is given, the court or justice may remand the prisoner, bail him to appear from day to day, commit him to the sheriff of the county, or place him under such other care and custody as the circumstances of the case require.

§19. Bail
If the prisoner is detained for a cause or crime for which he is bailable, he shall be admitted to bail if sufficient bail is offered; and if not, he shall be remanded with an order of the court or justice expressing the amount in which he shall be held to bail and the court at which he shall be required to appear; and any magistrate authorized to admit to bail may, at any time before the sitting of said court, bail the prisoner pursuant to such order.

§20. Prisoners committed in civil actions for want of bail; bail
If the prisoner has been committed on mesne process in a civil action for want of bail, and it appears that the amount for which bail was required is excessive and unreasonable, the court or justice shall decide how much bail is reasonable, and shall order that on giving such bail the prisoner shall be discharged.

§21. Prisoners committed on criminal charges; bail
If a person is committed to jail on a criminal accusation for want of bail, a justice of the superior court or of a district court or a trial justice may issue a writ of habeas corpus and cause the prisoner to be brought before him, when it is necessary for the purpose of admitting him to bail pursuant to chapter two hundred and seventy-six.

§22. Remanding prisoner
If the prisoner is lawfully imprisoned or restrained and is not entitled to be admitted to bail, he shall be remanded to the person from whose custody he was taken or any other person or officer authorized by law to detain him.

§23. Discharging prisoner
If no legal cause is shown for the imprisonment or restraint, the court or justice shall discharge the prisoner.

§24. Imprisonment after discharge
No person who has been discharged upon a habeas corpus shall be again imprisoned or restrained for the same cause, unless indicted therefor, convicted thereof, or committed for want of bail by a court of record having jurisdiction of the cause; or unless, after a discharge for defect of proof or for some material defect in the commitment in a criminal case, he is again arrested on sufficient proof and committed by legal process.

§25. Scope of chapter
This chapter shall not affect the power of the supreme judicial court, or the superior court, or a justice thereof, to issue a writ of habeas corpus in its discretion, and thereupon grant bail to a person for whatever cause he has been committed or restrained, or to discharge him as law and justice require. The court shall have no power to issue a writ of habeas corpus, at its discretion for—a person who has been committed by the governor and council, the senate, or the house of representatives in the manner and for the

causes mentioned in the constitution, or a person who is imprisoned or restrained of his liberty pursuant to a criminal conviction.

This chapter shall not affect the power of any court or magistrate to issue a writ of habeas corpus, when necessary to bring before it a prisoner for trial in a pending criminal case; or to bring a prisoner to be examined as a witness in a suit or proceeding, civil or criminal, pending before the court, if the personal attendance and examination of the witness is necessary for the attainment of justice.

§26. Refusal of officer to deliver copy of warrant; penalty
An officer who refuses or neglects for six hours to deliver a printed copy of the warrant contained in the warrant management system or process by which he detains a prisoner to any person who demands such copy and tenders the fees therefor shall forfeit two hundred dollars to such prisoner.

§27. Refusal to obey writ; attachment
If a person to whom a writ of habeas corpus is directed refuses to receive it, or neglects to execute it according to the provisions of this chapter and no sufficient excuse is shown therefor, the court or justice before whom the writ was returnable shall forthwith by process of attachment, as for a contempt, compel obedience to the writ, and punish the person guilty of the contempt.

§28. Attachment; executing officers
If such attachment is issued against a sheriff or his deputy, it may be directed to a special sheriff or to some other person designated therein, who shall have full power to execute it; and if the sheriff or his deputy is to be committed upon such process, he may be committed to the jail of any county other than his own.

§29. Refusal to obey writ; precept commanding production of prisoner
Upon the refusal or neglect of the person to whom the writ of habeas corpus is directed to receive and execute it, the court or justice may issue a precept to any officer or other person designated therein, commanding him to bring the prisoner forthwith before such court or justice, who shall thereupon discharge, bail or remand the prisoner as if he had been brought in upon the writ of habeas corpus.

§30. Refusal to obey writ; penalty
Whoever refuses or neglects to receive and execute a writ of habeas corpus shall forfeit four hundred dollars to the party aggrieved thereby.

§31. Resistance or disobedience of writ; attachment
Whoever resists the service of the writ of habeas corpus, or disobeys it when served, shall be liable to attachment as for a contempt of the court or justice before whom the writ is returnable.

§32. Removing or concealing prisoner; penalty
Whoever, having in his custody or power a person entitled to a writ of habeas corpus, transfers him to the custody, or places him under the power or control, of another person, conceals him or changes thereof, whether the writ has been issued or not, shall forfeit four hundred dollars to the party aggrieved thereby.

§33. Recovery of penalties; effect on actions by aggrieved parties
The recovery of penalty imposed by the foregoing provisions of this chapter shall not bar an action at common law for false imprisonment, or for a false return to the writ of habeas corpus, or for any other injury or damage sustained by the aggrieved party.

§34. Persons in custody of United States marshal

This chapter shall not authorize the taking of a person by writ of habeas corpus out of the custody of the United States marshal, or his deputy, who holds him by legal and sufficient process issued by any court or magistrate of competent jurisdiction; but this section shall not affect the authority of the supreme judicial court or of its justices, in accordance with the provisions of the constitution of the United States and of the commonwealth, to investigate and determine the validity and legal effect of any process which may be relied on to defect the writ, or any other matter properly arising.

§35. Person liberty; how secured

No person shall be deprived of his liberty or held in custody by any person or in any place against his will or, if he is a minor, against the will of his patents, guardian or other person entitled to his custody, except by due process of law; but this section shall not apply to persons who have been legally convicted of crime and are serving sentence therefor.

§36. Petition to obtain personal liberty

Whoever has reason to believe that another person is deprived of his liberty or held in custody in violation of the preceding section may file a petition, on the oath of the petitioner, in the probate court for the county where such person is believed to be detained, stating his name, age and general description, where, when and under what circumstances he was deprived of his liberty, where he is believed to be detained, the name of the person so depriving him of his liberty, if known, the name of his supposed custodian and any other material facts and circumstances.

§37. Notice to custodians, etc

Upon the filing of such petition, the court shall cause notice to be served upon all the supposed custodians or persons alleged to be detaining or holding in custody said person, as stated in said petition, or as otherwise known, ordering them to appear before said court at a time and place named therein, to be examined as said court shall order; and may cause said person to be brought before it for examination as to his desire to be released and as to any other relevant matters.

§38. Examination of witnesses

The court may examine the witnesses separately and may permit the petition, parent, guardian or other person entitled to the custody of a person deprived of his liberty, in person or by counsel, to examine publicly his alleged custodian as to the condition of such person and the place where he is detained or held in custody; and may also examine separately and apart, or publicly, such person, and may make orders for his release or permitting correspondence or personal interviews between him and his friends or relatives, and may modify its orders upon notice to the parties.

§39. Conducting examinations; assistance from district attorneys

The probate court may request the district attorney for the district where it is held to attend the examination under the preceding section, and to conduct or assist in conducting the examination. If the court is unable to obtain satisfactory information, or to satisfactorily determine the questions involved or to furnish proper relief, it shall notify the district attorney, who may institute proceedings under sections one to thirty-four, inclusive, or such other proceedings as the case may require. The provisions of said sections shall apply to all proceedings under the four preceding sections so far as appropriate.

§40. Payment of fees

The fees for the service of process and notices and for summoning witnesses shall, upon the approval of the court or district attorney, be paid by the commonwealth if the petitioner is not able to pay them.

MICHIGAN

Michigan Complied Laws Annotated
Chapter 600. Revised Judicature Act of 1961
Chapter 43. Habeas Corpus

600.4301. Habeas corpus; application of provisions of chapter
Sec. 4301. The provisions of sections 4301 to 4379 [FN 1] shall be construed to apply to every writ of habeas corpus authorized to be issued under any statute of this state, insofar as they are consistent with the statute granting the right to habeas corpus.

[FN 1] M.C.L.A. §§ 600.4301 to 600.4379.

600.4304. Power to issue writ
Sec. 4304. The writ of habeas corpus to inquire into the cause of detention, or an order to show cause why the writ should not issue, may be issued by the following:

(1) The supreme court, or a justice thereof.

(2) The court of appeals, or a judge thereof.

(3) The circuit courts, or a judge thereof.

(4) The municipal courts of record, including but not limited to the recorder's court of the city of Detroit, common pleas court, or a judge thereof.

(5) The district courts, or a judge thereof.

600.4307. Right to bring action
Sec. 4307. An action for habeas corpus to inquire into the cause of detention may be brought by or on the behalf of any person restrained of his liberty within this state under any pretense whatsoever, except as specified in section 4310. [FN 1]

[FN 1] M.C.L.A. § 600.4310.

600.4310. Persons not entitled to writ
Sec. 4310. An action for habeas corpus to inquire into the cause of detention may not be brought by or on behalf of the following persons:

(1) Persons detained by virtue of any process issued by any court of the United States, or any judge thereof, in cases where such courts or judges have exclusive jurisdiction under the laws of the United States, or have acquired exclusive jurisdiction by the commencement of suits in such courts;

(2) Persons committed for treason or felony, or for suspicion thereof, or as accessories before the fact to a felony, where the cause is plainly and specially expressed in the warrant of commitment;

(3) Persons convicted, or in execution, upon legal process, civil or criminal;

(4) Persons committed on original process in any civil action on which they were liable to be arrested and imprisoned, unless excessive and unreasonable bail is required.

600.4313. Habeas corpus; refusal to consider; malfeasance of judge
Sec. 4313. Any judge who willfully or corruptly refuses or neglects to consider an application, action, or motion for habeas corpus, is guilty of malfeasance in office.

600.4316. Habeas corpus; granting the writ
Sec. 4316. Any court or judge empowered to grant the writ of habeas corpus shall, upon proper application, grant the preliminary writ (or an order to show cause) without delay, unless the party applying therefor is not entitled to the writ.

600.4322. Habeas corpus; prisoner defined
Sec. 4322. The term "prisoner"" as used in connection with habeas corpus, means the person on whose behalf the writ is issued, such as an inmate of a penal or mental institution, the child whose custody is sought, and other persons alleged to be restrained of their liberty.

600.4325. Habeas corpus; body of prisoner brought up
Sec. 4325. If a writ of habeas corpus is issued, the person on whom it is served shall bring the body of the person in his custody according to the command of the writ, except as provided in section 4328. [FN 1]

[FN 1] M.C.L.A. § 600.4328.

600.4328. Habeas corpus; sickness or infirmity of prisoner
Sec. 4328. If, from the sickness or infirmity of the prisoner directed to be produced by any writ of habeas corpus, the prisoner cannot, without danger, be brought before the court or judge, the party having custody of the prisoner may state that fact in his answer. The court or judge, if satisfied of the truth of the allegation, and if the answer is otherwise sufficient, shall proceed to dispose of the matter on the record.

600.4331. Habeas corpus; disobedience, arrest; production of prisoner; aid in execution, power of county
Sec. 4331.
(1) Arrest for disobedience. If the person upon whom the writ of habeas corpus was duly served refuses or neglects to obey the writ without sufficient excuse, the court or judge before whom the writ was to be answered, upon due proof of the service thereof, shall direct the arrest of such person.

(2) Close custody of arrested person. The sheriff of any county within this state, or other officer, who is directed to make the arrest, shall apprehend such person, and bring him before the court or judge. The person shall be committed to close custody in the jail of the county in which the court or judge is, without being allowed the liberties thereof, until the person complies with the writ.

(3) Proceeding against sheriff; commitment. If the person ordered arrested is the sheriff of any county, the order may be directed to any coroner or other person, to be designated therein, who has thereby full power to arrest the sheriff. Such sheriff upon being brought up may be committed to the jail of any county other than his own.

(4) Prisoner to be produced. The person directed to make the arrest shall also bring the prisoner named in the writ of habeas corpus before the court or judge which issued the writ.

(5) Aid in execution, power of county. In making the arrest the sheriff or other person so directed may call to his aid the power of the county as in other cases.

600.4334. Arrest in support of writ
Sec. 4334. If any person attempts wrongfully to carry the prisoner out of the county or state after service of a writ of habeas corpus or order to show cause, the person serving the writ or order to show cause, or other officer, shall arrest the person so resisting, and bring him together with the prisoner before the court or judge issuing the writ or order to show cause.

600.4337. Warrant for prisoner in lieu of habeas corpus; issuance
Sec. 4337. Whenever it appears by satisfactory proof, that anyone is held in illegal confinement or custody, and that there is good reason to believe that he will be carried out of the state, or suffer some irreparable injury, before he can be relieved by the issuing of a writ of habeas corpus, any court or judge authorized to issue such writs may issue a warrant, reciting the facts, and directed to any sheriff, constable or other person, and commanding the officer or person to take the prisoner, and forthwith to bring him before the court or judge, to be dealt with according to law.

600.4340. Arrest of person having custody of prisoner; warrant
Sec. 4340. When the proof mentioned in section 4337 [FN 1] is sufficient to justify an arrest of the person having the prisoner in his custody, as for a criminal offense committed in the taking or detaining of the prisoner, the warrant shall also contain an order for the arrest of such person for that offense.

[FN 1] *M.C.L.A. § 600.4337.*

600.4343. Arrest of person having custody of prisoner; execution of warrant, answer
Sec. 4343. Any officer or person to whom the warrant is directed shall execute the warrant by bringing the prisoner therein named, and the person who detains him, if so commanded by the warrant, before the court or judge issuing the warrant. The person detaining the prisoner shall make answer as if a writ of habeas corpus had been issued in the first instance.

600.4346. Arrest of person having custody of prisoner; procedure
Sec. 4346. If the person having the prisoner in his custody is brought before the court or judge, as for a criminal offense, he shall be examined, committed, bailed or discharged by the court or judge in the like manner as in other criminal cases of like nature.

600.4349. Custody of prisoner
Sec. 4349. The court or judge issuing the writ of habeas corpus may commit the prisoner to the custody of such individual or individuals as the court or judge considers proper.

600.4352. Discharge of prisoner; enforcement of order; obedience by sheriff or other custodian
Sec. 4352. (1) If no legal cause is shown for the restraint, or for the continuation thereof, the court or judge shall discharge the person restrained from the restraint under which he is held.

(2) Obedience to any order for the discharge of any prisoner may be enforced by the court or judge granting such order, by arrest in the same manner as is herein provided for disobedience to a writ of habeas corpus, and with like effect in all respects. The person guilty of disobedience to an order for the discharge of any prisoner is liable to the party aggrieved in the sum of $1,000.00 damages, in addition to any special damages the party may have sustained.

(3) No sheriff or other officer is liable to any civil action for obeying any such order of discharge.

600.4355. remanding of prisoner
Sec. 4355. The court or judge shall forthwith remand the person restrained if the person restrained is detained in custody, either:

(1) By virtue of process issued by any court or judge of the United States, in a case where such court or judge has exclusive jurisdiction; or

(2) By virtue of the final judgment or decree of any competent court of civil or criminal jurisdiction, or of any execution issued upon such judgment or decree; or

(3) For any contempt specially and plainly charged in the commitment by some court, officer or body having authority to commit for the contempt so charged; and

(4) The time during which such party may be legally detained has not expired.

600.4358. Discharge of prisoner in civil cases
Sec. 4358. If the prisoner is in custody by virtue of civil process from any court legally constituted, or issued by any officer in the course of judicial proceedings before him, authorized by law, the prisoner shall be discharged only if 1 of the following situations exists:

(1) Where the jurisdiction of the court or officer has been exceeded, either as to matter, place, sum or person;

(2) Where, though the original imprisonment was lawful, the party is entitled to be discharged;

(3) Where the process is void;

(4) Where the process, though in proper form, has been issued in a case not allowed by law;

(5) Where the person having the custody of the prisoner is not the person empowered by law to detain him; or

(6) Where the process is not authorized by any judgment, order or decree of any court, nor by any provision of law.

600.4361. Remanding or commitment of prisoner
Sec. 4361. If the prisoner is not entitled to his discharge, and is not bailed, the court or judge shall place him under the restraint from which he was taken, if the person under whose restraint he was is legally entitled thereto. If not so entitled, the court or judge shall commit the prisoner to the custody of such officer or person as by law is entitled thereto.

600.4364. Recommitment of prisoner; causes
Sec. 4364. No person who has been discharged by the order of any court or judge upon habeas corpus shall be again restrained for the same cause. It is not the same cause if:

(1) He was discharged from a commitment on a criminal charge, and is afterwards committed for the same offense, by the legal order or process of the court wherein he is bound by recognizance to appear, or in which he is indicted or convicted for the same offense; or

(2) After a discharge for defect of proof, or for any material defect in the commitment, in a criminal case, the prisoner is again arrested on sufficient proof, and committed by legal process for the same offense; or

(3) In a civil suit the party was discharged for any illegality in the judgment or process and is afterwards imprisoned by legal process for the same cause of action; or

(4) In any civil suit in which process may lawfully issue against the body, he was discharged from commitment on original process, and is afterwards committed on execution in the same cause, or on original process in any other suit, after such first suit was discontinued.

600.4367. Recommitment of prisoner; violation; penalty
Sec. 4367. If any person knowingly:

(1) violates section 4364, [FN 1] or

(2) causes section 4364 to be violated, or

(3) aids or assists in the violation of section 4364; he is guilty of a misdemeanor, and is liable to the party aggrieved in the sum of $1,000.00 damages.

[FN 1] *M.C.L.A. § 600.4364.*

600.4370. Concealment of prisoner; misdemeanor
Sec. 4370. Any one having under his power any person who would be entitled to a writ of habeas corpus to inquire into the cause of his detention, or for whose relief any such writ, warrant, or order to show cause was issued, who shall, with intent to elude the service of the writ, or to avoid the effect thereof, place any such prisoner under the power of another, or conceal him, or change the place of his confinement, is guilty of a misdemeanor.

600.4373. Concealment of prisoner; aiding, misdemeanor
Sec. 4373. Every person who knowingly aids or assists in the violation of section 4370 [FN 1] is guilty of a misdemeanor.

[FN 1] *MC.L.A. § 600.4370.*

600.4376. Concealment of prisoner; misdemeanor; penalty
Sec. 4376. Every person convicted of any of the misdemeanors specified in sections 4367, 4370 and 4373 [FN 1] shall be punished by a fine not exceeding $1,000.00, or by imprisonment in the county jail not exceeding 6 months, or by both such fine and imprisonment, in the discretion of the court.

[FN 1] *M.C.L.A. §§ 600.4367, 600.4370 and 600.4373.*

600.4379. Refusal to deliver copy of authority for detention of prisoner; civil liability
Sec. 4379. Any officer or other person who refuses or neglects for 6 hours to deliver a copy of any order,

warrant, process or other authority by which he detains any person, to any one who demands such copy and tenders the lawful fees therefor, is liable to the person so detained in the sum of $200.00 damages.

600.4385. Habeas corpus for witness; issuance, transfer of prisoner

Sec. 4385. (1) The judges of every court of record have the power to issue a writ of habeas corpus for the purpose of bringing before that court, or another court or body authorized to examine witnesses, any prisoner who may be detained in any jail or prison within this state, to be examined as a witness.

(2) The judge may order in the writ that the prisoner be placed in the custody of a designated officer for transportation to the place of examination and return, instead of requiring the person having custody of the prisoner to produce the prisoner at the place of examination.

600.4387. Habeas corpus for witness; liability of officer for disobedience to writ

Sec. 4387. Whenever any writ of habeas corpus is issued pursuant to section 4385, [FN 1] the officer on whom the writ is served shall obey the writ in the manner and within the time prescribed by statute or court rule. Every officer who neglects or refuses so to do, is liable in the sum of $500.00 to:

(1) the people of this state, if the writ was issued upon the application of the attorney general, or a prosecuting attorney; or

(2) the party upon whose application the writ was issued.

> [FN 1] *M.C.L.A. § 600.4385.*

The statutes are current through P.A.2014, No. 249, 251-280, of the 2014 Regular Session, 97th Legislature.

MINNESOTA

Minnesota Statutes Annotated
Remedies Controlling Personal Action
Chapter 589. Habeas Corpus

589.01. Writ of habeas corpus; who may apply

A person imprisoned or otherwise restrained of liberty, except persons committed or detained by virtue of the final judgment of a competent tribunal of civil or criminal jurisdiction, or by virtue of an execution issued upon the judgment, may apply for a writ of habeas corpus to obtain relief from imprisonment or restraint. For purposes of this section, an order of commitment for an alleged contempt or an order upon proceedings as for contempt to enforce the rights or remedies of a party is not a judgment, nor does attachment or other process issued upon these types of orders constitute an execution.

589.011. Definitions

Subdivision 1. Scope. In this chapter, the words listed in this section have the meanings or inclusions given them here.

Subd. 2. Detaining authority. "Detaining authority" includes a state or local correctional agency or officer or employee of that agency or any other public or private agency or person that is alleged in the writ of habeas corpus to have restrained or imprisoned the petitioner.

Subd. 3. Petitioner. "Petitioner" means a person who is imprisoned or otherwise restrained of liberty and who applies for a writ of habeas corpus to obtain release. 589.02. Petition; to whom and how made A person may apply for a writ of habeas corpus by petition addressed to the Supreme Court, Court of Appeals, or to the district court of the county where the petitioner is detained. The petition must be signed and verified by the petitioner or some person applying on the petitioner's behalf. If there is within the county a judge of the court to which the petition is addressed, that judge may grant the writ. If there is no judge within the county capable of acting and willing to grant the writ, it may be granted by a judge in an adjoining county.

589.03. Application for writ in another county; proof required
When application for a writ of habeas corpus is made to a judge whose chambers are not located within the county where the prisoner is detained, that judge shall require proof, by the oath of the applicant or other evidence:

(1) that there is no judge in the detaining county authorized to grant the writ;

(2) that judges authorized to grant the writ are absent from the detaining county;

(3) that judges in the detaining county for reasons specified are incapable of acting; or

(4) that judges in the detaining county have refused to grant the writ.

If the proof required by this section is not produced, the application must be denied.

589.04. Statements in petition
A petition for a writ of habeas corpus must contain information set forth in paragraphs (a) to (e):

(a) It must state that the person on whose behalf the writ is applied for is imprisoned or restrained of liberty, the name of the officer or person by whom the person is imprisoned or restrained, and the place where that person is imprisoned or restrained.

(b) It must name the restrained and the restraining person if their names are known, or describe them if they are not.

(c) It must state that the restrained person is not committed or detained under process, judgment, decree, or execution, as specified in *section 589.01*.

(d) It must state the basis of the confinement or restraint, according to the knowledge or belief of the party verifying the petition.

(e) If the confinement or restraint is under warrant, order, or process, the petitioner shall attach a copy of the document authorizing the confinement or restraint to the petition. The petitioner shall also attach copies of all papers which are attached to or accompany the warrant, order, or process to the petition. If the confinement results from conviction of a crime and sentence, the petitioner shall include a transcript of the proceedings taken at the time of arraignment and sentence in the court which imposed the sentence. If the petitioner is unable to attach the documents required by this paragraph, the petitioner shall state the reasons for not doing so. Documentation is not required when:

(1) the petitioner is removed or concealed before application for a writ was made; or

(2) a demand for documentation was made but the person to whom the demand was made refused to supply the document requested.

(f) If the imprisonment is alleged to be illegal, the petition shall state in what the illegality consists.

If the imprisonment which claimed to be illegal is under a district court judgment or sentence, the judge before whom the petition is pending may examine the official files and records of the court issuing the warrant of commitment, including any official transcript of the proceedings taken at the time of the arraignment and sentence. A judge before whom a petition is pending may take judicial notice of official records or transcripts to determine the sufficiency of the petition or the propriety of issuing the writ of habeas corpus.

589.05. Form of writ; requirements
A writ of habeas corpus must be under the seal of the court, and substantially in the following form:

> "The State of Minnesota, to the Sheriff of, etc. (or to A.B.):
>
> You are commanded to bring C.D., who is imprisoned and detained by you, by whatever named C.D. is called or charged, before E.F., judge of the ………. court, at ………., on ………. (or immediately after the receipt of this writ), to receive the court's judgment on the legality of the detention. Bring this writ to the hearing and be prepared to tell the court the time and cause of imprisonment and detention.
>
> Witness, etc."

589.06. Contents of writ; when sufficient
The writ may not be disobeyed because of any defect of form. A writ is sufficient if the petitioner and the person to whom the writ is directed are designated in it with reasonable certainty, by name, description, or otherwise. Either the petitioner or the person to whom the writ is directed may be designated by an assumed name if the true name is unknown or uncertain. The person served with the writ is considered to be the person to whom it is directed, although the name or description is wrong, or is that of another person.

589.07. Refusal to grant; penalty
If a judge authorized to grant writs of habeas corpus willfully refuses to grant the writ when legally applied for, the judge shall forfeit to the party aggrieved $1,000 for each offense.

589.08. Return to writ; content requirements
The detaining authority upon whom a writ of habeas corpus is duly served shall state in the return, plainly and unequivocally, the information specified in paragraphs (a) to (c):
(a) The return shall state whether the detaining authority is detaining or has at any time in the past detained the petitioner. If the petitioner was detained before or after the writ was issued, the detaining authority shall indicate the date and time of detention.

(b) If the petitioner is being detained, the detaining authority shall state the reason for detention and authority under which the person is being detained.

(c) If the detaining authority has detained the petitioner at any time before or after the date of the writ, but has transferred custody to another, the return must state particularly to whom, at what time, for what cause, and by what authority, the transfer took place.

If the petitioner is detained under writ, warrant, or other written authority, a copy of the document authorizing detention must be attached to the return. On the return of the writ to the judge before whom the writ is returnable, a copy of the original documents authorizing detention must be produced and exhibited.

The person making the return must sign it and except where the person is a sworn public officer, and makes the return in an official capacity, verify it by oath.

589.09. *Producing person required except when sick*
The person on whom the writ is served shall bring the person being detained, according to the command of the writ, to the judge named on the writ except when the detained person is sick, as provided in *section 589.20*.

589.10. *Enforcing the writ*
If the person upon whom the writ is served refuses or neglects to produce the person named in it and make a full return of the writ at the time and place required and does not give sufficient excuse, the judge before whom the writ is returnable, upon proof of service of it, shall immediately issue an attachment against the person, directed to the sheriff or coroner of any county. The attachment must direct the sheriff or coroner to apprehend the person upon whom the writ is served as soon as possible and bring that person before the judge before whom the writ is returnable. The judge before whom the writ is returnable shall commit the person apprehended under the attachment to the county jail until that person makes the return and compiles with all other orders made by the judge.

589.11. *Petitioner held in custody by sheriff*
The judge who issues an attachment under section 589.10 may also, at the same t i me or afterward, issue an order to the sheriff or other person to whom the attachment was directed, commanding the bringing of the petitioner before that judge immediately. After that, the petitioner must remain in the custody of the sheriff or other person until discharged, bailed, or remanded, as the judge may direct.

589.12. *Proceedings on return of writ*
Immediately after the return of the writ, the judge before whom the petitioner is brought shall examine the facts set forth in the return, the cause of the imprisonment or restraint, and whether the cause was upon commitment for a criminal charge or not.

589.13. *Discharging petitioner*
If the judge, under *section 589.12*, finds no legal cause to support imprisonment or restraint of the petitioner, the judge shall discharge the petitioner.

589.14. *Sending petitioner back to custody*
The judge shall immediately send the petitioner back to the detaining authority if it appears that the petitioner is detained in custody;

(1) under process issued by a court or judge of the United States, in a case where the court or judge has exclusive jurisdiction;

(2) under final judgment of a competent court of civil or criminal jurisdiction, or under an execution issued upon a judgment of either of those courts; or

(3) for contempt of court, specially and plainly charged in the commitment, by a court having authority to commit for the contempt so charged.

The judge shall also immediately send the petitioner back to the detaining authority if it appears that the time during which the person may be legally detained has not expired.

589.15. Discharging petitioner held under civil process
If it appears on the return that the petitioner is in custody under a valid civil process of a court, the petitioner can be discharged only in the following cases:

(1) if the jurisdiction of the court has been exceeded, either as to matter, place, sum or person;

(2) if, though the original imprisonment was lawful, yet, by some act, omission, or event which has taken place afterward, the person is entitled to be discharged;

(3) if the process is defective in some matter of substance required by law, rendering it void;

(4) if the process, though in proper form, has been issued in a case not allowed by law;

(5) if the person having the custody of the petitioner under the process is not the person empowered by law to detain the petitioner; or

(6) if the process is not authorized by a judgment or order of a court, or by a provision of law.

589.16. When bail or remand or discharge allowed
If the petitioner has been legally committed for a criminal offense, or if upon hearing it appears by the testimony offered with the return that the petitioner is guilty of the offense, although the commitment is irregular, the judge before whom the petitioner is brought shall allow release on bail, if good bail is offered, or, if not, the judge shall immediately send that petitioner back to the detaining authority. In other cases the petitioner must be placed in the custody of the person legally entitled to custody, or, if no one is so entitled, the petitioner must be discharged.

589.17. Requiring petitioner to be held in custody until judgment
Until judgment is given upon the return, the judge before whom the petitioner is brought may either commit the petitioner to the custody of the sheriff of the county, or place the petitioner in other custody as the petitioner's age and other circumstances require.

589.18. Notice must be given to county attorney or attorney general
In criminal cases, if the petitioner is confined in a county jail or other local correctional facility, notice of the time and place at which the writ is returnable must be given to the county attorney of the county from which the petitioner was committed, if the county attorney is within the petitioner's county. If the petitioner is confined in a state correctional facility, the notice of the time and place

at which the writ is returnable must be given to the attorney general, and the attorney general shall appear for the person named as respondent in the writ. In other cases, notice of the time and place at which the writ is returnable must be given to any person interested in continuing the custody or restraint of the petitioner.

589.19. Denial of return; new matter
At the hearing on the return of the writ, the petitioner may, on oath, deny any of the material facts alleged in the return, or allege any fact to show either that the imprisonment or detention is unlawful, or that the petitioner is entitled to discharge. The judge shall proceed, in a summary way, to hear allegations and admit relevant evidence in support or against imprisonment or detention and, at the conclusion of the hearing, dispose of the petitioner in accordance with law.

589.20. Proceedings in case of sickness of petitioner
When the petitioner is so sick or infirm that the petitioner would be endangered if brought before the judge before whom the writ is returnable, the person having the petitioner in custody may state that fact in the return. If the judge finds that the statement is true, and the return is otherwise sufficient, the judge shall decide upon the return and dispose of the matter in accordance with law. The petitioner under this section may appear by attorney and plead to the return as if present. If the petitioner is illegally imprisoned or restrained of liberty, the judge shall order those having custody to immediately discharge the petitioner. If the petitioner is legally imprisoned or restrained and is not entitled to be released on bail, the judge shall dismiss the proceedings.

589.21. Enforcing order of discharge
The judge may enforce obedience to an order for the discharge of the petitioner by attachment, as provided in *section 589.10*, directed to the person disobeying the order. If a person disobeys an order, that person shall forfeit to the petitioner $1,000 in addition to any special damages sustained by the petitioner.

589.22. Conditions under which discharged petitioner may be incarcerated
A petitioner who has been discharged upon a writ of habeas corpus may be incarcerated again for the same conduct only under the following circumstances:

(1) if, after discharge for defect of proof or for a material defect in the commitment in a criminal case, the petitioner is arrested again on probable cause and detained in accordance with law;

(2) if the petitioner fails to post bond;

(3) if the petitioner is indicted for the conduct and detained pending criminal proceedings; or

(4) if the petitioner is convicted and sentenced for the conduct.

589.23. Transferring or concealing person; forfeiture
A person who has custody of a petitioner entitled to a writ of habeas corpus and who, with intent to elude the service of the writ or to avoid its effect, (1) transfers the petitioner to the custody or places the petitioner under the power or control of another person, (2) conceals the petitioner, or (3) changes the place of confinement, shall forfeit $400 to the petitioner, recoverable in a civil action .

589.24. Refusing to furnish copy of document authorizing detention
An officer or another who detains a person and refuses to deliver a copy of an order, warrant, process, or

other authority by which the person is detained to any one who requests the copy and who offers to pay the reproduction costs, shall forfeit $200 to the person detained.

589.25. Person serving writ; bond
The writ can be served only by a legal voter of the state. The judge granting it may require a bond to the state in a sum not more than $1,000, conditioned for the payment of all costs and expenses of the proceeding, and the reasonable charges of restoring the petitioner, if sent back to custody, to the person from whose custody the petitioner was taken. The bond must be approved by the judge issuing the writ, and be filed with the court administrator.

589.26. Manner of service of writ
The writ of habeas corpus may be served by delivering it to the person to whom it is directed, or, if that person cannot be found, by leaving it at the jail or other place in which the petitioner is confined, with any correctional officer or other person of proper age having charge of the petitioner. If the person upon whom the writ should be served hides, or refuses admittance to the party attempting to serve the writ, it may be served by affixing the writ in some conspicuous place on the outside either of the dwelling house, or of the place where the party is confined.

589.27. When return to writ must be made
If the writ is returnable on a certain day, the person to whom the writ is directed shall make the return and produce the petitioner at the time and place specified in the writ. If the writ is returnable immediately, and the place of return is within 20 miles of the place of service, the return must be made and the petitioner produced within 24 hours. Twenty-four additional hours are allowed for return for each additional 20 miles of distance between the place of return and the place of service.

589.28. Power of court not restrained
Nothing in *section 589.01* to *589.30* is to be construed to prevent a court from issuing a writ of habeas corpus necessary or proper to bring an inmate before it or an inferior court for trial, an omnibus hearing, arraignment, appearance, or to be examined as a witness in a civil or criminal action or proceeding.

589.29. Appeals
A party aggrieved by the final order in proceedings upon a writ of habeas corpus may appeal to the Court of Appeals as in other civil cases, except that no bond is required of the appellant. Upon filing notice of appeal with the court administrator of the district court, and payment of filing fees, the court administrator shall make, certify, and return to the clerk of the appellate courts copies of the petition, writ, return of respondent, answer, if any, of the relator, and the order appealed from.

589.30. Hearing on appeal; costs; papers
Either party in a proceeding upon a writ of habeas corpus may appeal a final order by applying to the Court of Appeals. The clerk of appellate courts shall serve the order fixing the time of hearing on the adverse party at least five days before the date fixed for the hearing. The hearing must be held not less than six nor more than 15 days from the date of application. No costs or disbursement may be allowed any party to the appeal, nor may any of the papers used on the hearing be required to be printed.

589.35. Release of institutionalized persons for judicial purposes
Subdivision 1. Order. Except as provided in this chapter and chapter 590, a court requiring the appearance of a person confined in a state correctional facility, hospital for persons with mental illnesses, or other institution after criminal conviction, civil commitment, or under court order, may order the con-

fining institution to release the person into the temporary custody of the court. The order must specify:

(1) the reason for the person's appearance;

(2) to whom the confined person may be released; and

(3) the date and time of the release.

Subd. 2 . Costs . The court shall, without any cost to the releasing institution, determine and implement a cost-effective and convenient method for obtaining the person's appearance, including requiring the parties to the proceedings to pay all or a part of the costs as otherwise provided by law.

Subd. 3. Compliance. Upon receipt of a court order for release under this section, the chief executive officer of the confining institution shall take appropriate steps to comply with the order in a manner which is consistent with public safety.

Current with legislation of the 2014 Regular Session effective through July 31, 2014.

MISSISSIPPI

Annotated Mississippi Code
Title 11. Civil Practice and Procedure
Chapter 43. Habeas Corpus

§11-43-1. Cases where relief available
The writ of habeas corpus shall extend to all cases of illegal confinement or detention by which any person is deprived of his liberty, or by which the rightful custody of any person is withheld from the person entitled thereto, except in the cases expressly excepted .

§11-43-3. Cases where relief not available
Nothing in this chapter shall authorize the discharge of any person convicted of an offense, or charged with an offense committed in any other part of the United States, and who, agreeably to the Constitution of the United States or the laws of the state, ought to be delivered up to the executive power of the state or territory where the offense is charged to have been committed; nor of any person suffering imprisonment under lawful judgment.

This chapter shall not apply to any collateral relief sought by any person following his conviction of a crime. Such relief shall be governed by the procedures prescribed in the Mississippi Uniform Post-Conviction Collateral Relief Act.

Provided, in any suit filed seeking the release of any person being held for extradition to any other part of the United States, its territories or foreign countries or any suit filed hereunder seeking the release of any person ordered extradited, a copy of the petition and writ shall be served upon the attorney general not less than three (3) days before the date and time set for hearing thereon.

§11-43-5. Invalid proceedings, crime relator not necessarily discharged
If it appear on the trial of any habeas corpus that the relator is held by virtue of proceedings against him for crime which are invalid, the judge shall not discharge the relator because thereof, but shall investigate the facts; and if it be found that he ought to be held for any crime alleged against him, the judge shall not discharge him, but shall commit him or require bail, according to the nature of the case.

§11-43-7. Authority to grant writ
The writ of habeas corpus may be granted by a judge of the Supreme Court, or a judge of the circuit or chancery court, in term time or in vacation, returnable before himself or another judge.

§11-43-9. Procedure for obtaining writ
Application for a writ of habeas corpus shall be by petition, in writing, sworn to by the person for whose relief it is intended, or by someone in his behalf, describing where and by whom he is deprived of liberty, and the facts and circumstances of the restraint, with the ground relied on for relief; and the application shall be made to the judge or chancellor of the district in which the relator is imprisoned, unless good cause be shown in the petition to the contrary. However, any petition filed by an inmate of any training school or hospital attacking his commitment for a claimed denial of a fundamental constitutional right under the Constitution of the State of Mississippi or of the United States which would affect his commitment shall be filed in a court of the county from which he was committed. And, if filed in any other court, the judge of that court shall, if he grants the writ, make it returnable to a court of the county from which relator was committed; and in the case of a person committed by a youth court, not less than five (5) days' notice prior to hearing shall be given to the county attorney or district attorney of the county of commitment.

§11-43-11. Denial of relief
If from the showing made by the petition for habeas corpus it be manifest that the person by whom, or on whose behalf, it is presented is not entitled to any relief thereby, the judge or chancellor may refuse to grant the writ, indorsing on the application his reason therefor.

§11-43-13. Bail may be required
Where the application is by or on behalf of one detained on a criminal charge, the judge or chancellor, on granting the writ, may, in his discretion, require a bail bond by or on behalf of the person detained, conditioned that he shall not escape by the way. The judge or chancellor may fix the amount of such bail, and direct who shall approve the bond; but such bail bond shall not operate to discharge the relator from custody. Such bond shall be deposited by the judge or chancellor in the clerk's office of the court in which the case is triable. If the condition of the bond be broken, the proceedings thereon shall be as in case of other forfeited bonds or recognizances.

§11-43-15. Order to issue writ
The judge granting the writ may order it to be issued by the Clerk of the Supreme Court, or of any circuit or chancery court, who shall immediately issue it on receiving the order; or, when not convenient to a clerk, the judge himself shall issue the writ. Any judge or chancellor who shall willfully refuse or neglect to grant, or to issue and try, the writ of habeas corpus, when required by law to do so, shall be guilty of a high misdemeanor in office, and any clerk who shall not, when ordered, immediately issue the writ, and other process, shall be liable, on conviction thereof, to be removed from office; and the judge or clerk shall, in case of such neglect or refusal, be liable, civilly, to the party aggrieved.

§11-43-17. *Form of writ*
The writ may be in substance, as follows, to wit:

"The State of Mississippi, to _____ :

"We command you to have the body of _____ , by you detained, as it is said, before _____ , a judge of our _____ court, at _____ , forthwith (or on a given day), to do and receive what may be then and there considered concerning him Witness my hand," etc.

And it may be served by such person as the judge granting it may direct, or by the sheriff or any constable, and it shall be served by the delivery of a true copy thereof to the person to whom it is directed, if to be found. And if it be directed to a sheriff or other officer who cannot be found, it may be served by leaving a copy with any deputy or servant of the officer to whom it is directed, at the place where the prisoner or other person is detained; and it shall be returned with an indorsement of service as in other cases.

§11-43-19. *Taking of person*
When it shall be shown to the judge to whom application is made for the writ, that there is reasonable ground to apprehend that the person in whose behalf the writ is applied for will be concealed or removed so as not to be brought up with the writ, it shall be the duty of the judge to order or issue the writ directed to the sheriff or other officer or person designated to execute it, commanding him to take the body of the person to be relieved by the writ, and bring him forthwith before the judge, and to summon the person alleged to have illegally detained him; in which case the form of the writ shall be, in substance, as follows, to wit:

"The State of Mississippi.

"To the sheriff of any lawful officer of _____ county:

"We command you to take and have the body of _____ restrained of his liberty, it is said, by _____ , before _____ , a judge of our _____ court, at _____ , forthwith, to do and receive what shall then be considered; and do you summon the said _____ to appear, then and there to show the cause of detaining said _____ ; and have you then and there this writ, with your proceedings indorsed thereon. Witness my hand," etc.

The writ shall be executed according to its tenor and effect, and returned as other writs.

§11-43-21. *Service on Sunday*
All writs of habeas corpus may be issued or served on Sunday in case of emergency.

§11-43-23. *Where returnable*
The writ of habeas corpus shall be returnable forthwith, or on a particular day within a reasonable time, and at a place to be named by the judge granting the writ. But when granted by a circuit judge or chancellor, on the application of any person in custody, before conviction upon a criminal charge under the laws of this state, the judge or chancellor shall cause the writ to be made returnable at a convenient place in the county in which the offense is alleged to have been committed, unless so doing will interfere with his holding of a term of court.

§11-43-25. *Unlawfully detaining another, criminal liability*
Whenever the judge or chancellor, on issuing a writ of habeas corpus, shall be satisfied, by affidavit or

otherwise, that the person unlawfully depriving another of his liberty has committed a crime in connection with such unlawful act, he may embody in the writ a warrant for the arrest of such person and have him brought up for examination at the hearing of the habeas corpus; and being satisfied, on the trial and examination, of the guilty of such person, the judge or chancellor shall commit him or order his release on bail, to appear before the proper court to answer the charge.

§11-43-27. Producing person before judge
Whenever any writ of habeas corpus shall be served upon the sheriff or any other person to whom the same may be directed, or who may be ordered summoned thereby, he shall bring, or permit the officer executing the writ to bring, the body of the prisoner or person detained in custody before the judge who is to try the same, at the time and place designated in the writ, or, in case of the absence of such judge, then before any other judge and to make return or answer to said writ.

§11-43-29. Contents of answer
The officer or other person upon whom a writ of habeas corpus shall be served shall state in his return or answer:

First.—Whether he have or have not the party in his custody or under his power or restraint.

Second.—If he have the party in his custody or power, or under his restraint, he shall state the authority and cause of imprisonment or restraint, setting forth the same at large.

Third.—If the party be restrained by virtue of any writ, warrant, or other written authority, a copy thereof shall be annexed to the return or answer, and the original shall be produced on the hearing.

Fourth.—If the officer or person upon whom the writ is served shall have had the party in his power or custody, or under his restraint, at any time prior or subsequent to the date of the writ of habeas corpus, but such person has escaped, or such officer or person has transferred the custody or restraint to another, the return or answer shall state the facts particularly, and, in case of transfer, set forth the time and place, for what cause, and by what authority the transfer took place.

Fifth.—The return must be signed by the officer or person making it, and, except when a sworn public officer shall make return in his official capacity, it shall be verified by his oath.

§11-43-31. Disobedience of writ, penalty
Any person who is duly served with a writ of habeas corpus commanding him to produce the body of any other person in his custody, who shall fail to produce the body of the person before the judge, according to the command of the writ, shall forfeit and pay to the party not so produced the sum of one thousand dollars, to be recovered before any court having jurisdiction, the right to recover which shall not cease by the death of either party. The judge before whom the writ was made returnable may also punish the person failing to obey the command thereof or to perform the duties prescribed, or to obey such order as the judge may make, as for a contempt, and compel obedience by process of attachment or otherwise. Any officer from whom the custody of any person is taken by writ of habeas corpus who shall fail to return the cause of commitment of any prisoner or other person as prescribed, may be punished in like manner.

§11-43-33. Judicial orders
The judge or chancellor before whom the prisoner or other person may be brought, shall inquire into the cause of imprisonment or detention, and shall either discharge, commit, admit to bail, or remand the pris-

oner, or award the custody to the party entitled thereto, as the law and the evidence shall require; and may also award costs and charges, for or against either party, as may seem right. And the clerk of the court in whose office the proceedings may be filed, shall issue execution for the costs and charges so awarded, against the party bound therefor. But the judge may continue the trial from day to day as the case may require.

§11-43-37. Answer not conclusive of facts
The return or answer made to a writ of habeas corpus shall not be conclusive as to the facts therein stated, but evidence may be received to contradict the same.

§11-43-39. Subpoena of witnesses
The judge or chancellor may issue or order subpoenas for witnesses and compel their attendance, as a circuit court could in term time, and fine witnesses or others for contempt. Whenever the personal attendance of a witness cannot be procured, his affidavit, taken on reasonable notice to the adverse party, may be received in evidence.

§11-43-41. Record required
The proceedings and judgment shall in all cases be entered of record. If the trial be in vacation, the proceedings shall be written out and signed by the judge or chancellor and deposited with the clerk of the circuit court of the county in which the habeas corpus is tried, unless the judge shall direct it to be deposited with such clerk of some other county. If either party require it, the evidence shall be made a party of the record by bill of exceptions, as in other cases.

§11-43-43. Judgment conclusive
The judgment rendered on the trial of any writ of habeas corpus shall be conclusive until reversed, and, whilst so in force, shall be a bar to another habeas corpus in the same cause, or to any other proceedings, to bring the same matter again in question, except by appeal or by action for false imprisonment; nor shall any person so discharged be afterward confined for the same cause, except by a court of competent jurisdiction.

§11-43-45. Attendance by sheriff
The sheriff, when required by the judge or chancellor, shall attend in person, or by deputy, upon the trial of a habeas corpus in his county, to keep order and execute the mandates of the judge or chancellor, and shall be subject to the orders of the judge or chancellor during the trial in vacation in the same manner as in term time. The judge or chancellor trying a habeas corpus in vacation shall have the same power to fine and imprison for contempt as in term time.

§11-43-47. Costs
When the application for a writ of habeas corpus is in the nature of a civil action between parties, the law providing for security for costs shall be applicable; and in such cases persons who may produce the body of another, or render other services, may be allowed the same fees as allowed by law to officers for the same services, the costs to be taxed and collected as in other cases.

§11-43-49. Witness disobedience of subpoena
If a witness shall not obey the subpoena served on him in case of habeas corpus, the judge or chancellor may not only issue, or cause the clerk to issue, an attachment for the witness, but shall indorse on the subpoena the default of the witness and a fine therefor, and file it with the other papers in the clerk's office of the proper circuit court. Scire facias shall issue for the witness, returnable before the court, and proceedings shall be had as provided in case of a defaulting witness in the circuit court.

§11-43-51. Witness penalties and privileges

Witnesses in a habeas corpus case shall be subject to the same penalties, and be entitled to the same privileges and compensation, and be paid in the same way, as in other cases. They may prove their attendance before the clerk in whose office the record of the proceeding is filed, and obtain from him a certificate of their attendance and of the compensation to which they are entitled, as in cases in the circuit courts; or the judge trying the case may give the witnesses certificates of their attendance and the compensation to which they are entitled, which shall have the same effect as such certificates in a like case by the clerk.

§11-43-53. Appeal

Any party aggrieved by the judgment on the trial of a habeas corpus, shall have an appeal to the Supreme Court. If any person held in service by this state, or by the United States should be discharged by any judge in vacation, or any court, on habeas corpus, the Attorney General or any district attorney, or any attorney duly authorized by the United States, may in like manner obtain an appeal to reverse the judgment by which such person was discharged.

§11-43-55. Appeal procedure

An appeal from a judgment on the trial of a writ of habeas corpus may be had by or in behalf of the person deprived of his liberty on the same terms and conditions as are provided for in criminal cases; but such appeal shall not entitle a party to be discharged on bail in any case held not to be one in which the party is entitled to bail. In all other cases, an appeal from a judgment on trial of a writ of habeas corpus may be had on their terms prescribed for appeals in civil cases, where a supersedeas is not desired.

Current through 2014 Regular (End) and First and Second Extraordinary (End) Sessions.

MISSOURI

Missouri Supreme Court Rules
Rules of Civil Procedure
Rule 91. Habeas Corpus

91.01. Habeas Corpus—General—Who may petition for—Form of action

(a) Proceedings in habeas corpus in a circuit court shall be as prescribed in this Rule 91 and in this Court or the court of appeals shall be as prescribed in *Rule 84.22* to *84.26*, inclusive, and this Rule 91. In all particulars not provided for by the foregoing provisions, proceedings in habeas corpus shall be governed by and conform to the rules of civil procedure and the existing rules of general law upon the subject. The court may, by order, direct the form of such further details of procedure as may be necessary to the orderly course of the action to give effect to the remedy.

(b) Any person restrained of liberty within this state may petition for a writ of habeas corpus to inquire into the cause of such restraint. Custody of a child may be the subject of a proceeding in habeas corpus.

(c) A habeas corpus proceeding shall be a civil action in which the person seeking relief is petitioner and the person against whom such relief is sought is respondent. If appropriate, there may be multiple petitioners or multiple respondents.

91.02. Petition to what court first made

(a) Except as provided in subdivision (b) of this Rule 91.02, when a person who is held in custody on a charge of crime seeks the benefit of this Rule 91, the petition in the first instance shall be to a circuit or associate circuit judge for the county in which the person is held in custody if at the time of the petition such judge is in the county, unless good cause is shown for filing the petition in a higher court. The petitioner shall give reasonable notice of the time and place of filing the petition to the prosecuting attorney for the county in which the petition is to be filed, if at the time thereof the attorney is in the county. Upon such notice, the attorney shall attend the hearing of the petition on behalf of the state.

(b) If a person is held in custody pursuant to a conviction for a capital crime and a sentence of death and this Court has affirmed the conviction and sentence, any petition seeking the benefit of this Rule 91 may be filed in this court in the first instance. The petitioner shall give reasonable notice of the time and place of filing the petition to the attorney general of this state, who shall represent the state in the matter. Any such petition filed in a state court other than this Court shall be deemed to have been filed in this court. Any clerk filing such a petition shall give notice for the filing of the petition to the clerk of this Court by telephone or by other expeditious means and shall forward the petition to this Court immediately.

91.03. Petition—By whom made

The petition for a writ of habeas corpus shall be signed by the person for whose relief it is intended or by some person acting in such person's behalf.

91.04. Petition—Contents—Attachments

(a) Contents. The petition shall state:

(1) The name or description of the person who is restraining the person's liberty;

(2) The place where the person is detained;

(3) Facts showing that the restraint is illegal or improper; and

(4) That no petition for the relief sought has been made to any higher court to the one to which the petition is presented or that the higher court denied the writ without prejudice to proceeding in a lower court.

(b) Attachment to Petition. If the restraint is by virtue of any warrant, order, or process, a copy thereof must accompany the petition, unless reasons are set forth in the petition constituting good cause for failure to do so.

91.05. Writ or show cause order to be granted without delay

A court to which a petition for a writ of habeas corpus is presented shall forthwith grant the writ or issue an order directing the respondent to show cause why the writ should not be granted, unless it appears from the petition that the person restrained is not entitled thereto.

91.06. Writ shall issue without petition—When

Whenever any court of record, or any judge thereof, shall have evidence from any judicial proceedings had before such court or judge that any person is illegally confined or restrained of liberty within the jurisdiction of such court or judge, it shall be the duty of the court or judge to issue a writ of habeas corpus for the person's relief, although no petition be presented for such writ.

91.07. Form of writ or order—To whom directed

Every writ shall be captioned with the style of the case, shall be entitled "Writ of Habeas Corpus," and shall be issued in the name of the State of Missouri. All such writs or orders to show cause shall be issued under the seal of the court, unless issued by a judge out of court in which event the writ or order shall be signed by the judge. The writ or order shall be directed to the person having custody of the person restrained and shall designate a time for filing an answer to the petition, which shall not be later than three days after service. For good cause additional time may be allowed.

91.08. Service of writ or order

(a) By Delivery. The writ of habeas corpus or the order to show cause may be served by delivering the same to the person to whom it is directed or to any other person having custody of the person restrained.

(b) By offer of Delivery and Refusal. When the person to be served refuses to receive service of the writ or order to show cause, the offer of the server to deliver the same and such refusal, when these facts are shown on the server's return, shall be service.

(c) By Posting. When service of the writ or order to show cause cannot be made pursuant to paragraph (a) or (b), service may be made by affixing the writ or order in a conspicuous place on the dwelling house of the person to be served or the place where the person is restrained.

91.09. Answer—Time for—Contents—Attachments

(a) Time. The person served shall file an answer at the time designated in the writ or order.

(b) Contents. The answer shall be directed to the petition and shall also contain:

(1) A statement whether the person who is allegedly restrained is being restrained by respondent and, if so, the circumstances and authority for such restraint;

(2) If the person filing the answer shall have had the person under restraint at any time before service of the writ or order and has transferred the person to another, a statement to whom, at what time, for what cause, and by what authority such transfer took place.

(c) Attachment to Answer. If the person is restrained by virtue of any writ, order, warrant, or other written authority, a copy shall be attached to the answer.

91.10. Pleadings—Amendments and supplementation

Any pleading may be amended or supplemented as provided in *Rule 55.33*.

91.11. Person restrained to be produced with answer to petition—Exception—Custody pending judgment

If a person filing an answer has the custody of the person for whose benefit the writ was issued, he shall produce such person before the court according to the command of the writ unless the writ directs otherwise. Pending determination of the issues, the court may either commit the restrained person to the custody of the sheriff or make such other orders pertaining to the care or custody as circumstances may require. The person filing an answer may state facts showing that because of sickness or other infirmity the restrained person cannot be brought before the court. Upon making such finding the court may proceed in the absence of such person.

91.12. Reply to answer
By written reply the petitioner or person restrained may deny any facts set forth in the answer and allege any other material facts.

91.13. Disobedience of writ—Further proceedings
The person served shall comply with the writ or order to show cause even though direct ed to him by the wrong name or description or to another person.

Unless a sufficient excuse is shown, failure to comply with the writ shall authorize the court to order the incarceration of the delinquent until he complies.

The court may make any other orders necessary to bring before the court the person for whose benefit the writ of habeas corpus is issued.

91.14. Condition of release
If the person for whose relief a writ of habeas corpus has been issued is charged with a bailable offense, the court in which the answer is to be filed shall set conditions of release pursuant to *Rule 33*.

91.15. Time of hearing
When the answer is filed, the court may proceed with the hearing not more than five days after filing of the answer unless the person being restrained requests a longer time or for good cause additional time is allowed.

91.16. Production of restrained person a t hearing
The person upon whom the writ is served shall produce the restrained person at the hearing unless the court otherwise orders.

91.17. Duty of court on final hearing
The court shall forthwith hear and determine the matter.

91.18. Order of discharge
If no legal cause is shown for the restraint, the court shall forthwith order the person discharged.

91.19. Order of discharge—How enforced
Any order of discharge may be enforced by incarceration in the same manner as provided in *Rule 91.13* or by contempt or by any other proper order of the court.

91.20. Order of remand or other disposition
If legal cause is shown for the restraint, the person shall be returned to the restraint from which he was taken or committed to such other restraint as may be proper.

91.21. Warrant in lieu of writ
When the court finds that any person is illegally restrained of liberty and that there is good cause to believe that the person will be removed from the state or suffer some irreparable injury before the person can be relieved by a writ of habeas corpus, any court authorized to issue such writs may issue a warrant reciting the facts directed to any officer or other person commanding the officer or person to take the person so restrained and bring that person forthwith before the court to be dealt with according to law.

A copy of the warrant shall be served on the restraining person together with an order directing the restraining person to file an answer as provided by *Rule 91.09*.

Proceedings thereafter shall be as if a writ of habeas corpus had been originally issued .

91.22. Second writ not to issue by lower court
When a petition for a writ of habeas corpus has been denied by a higher court, a lower court shall not issue the writ unless the order in the higher court denying the writ is without prejudice to proceeding in a lower court.

91.23. Certain persons not entitled to discharge
No person shall be discharged under the provisions of this Rule 91 who is in custody or held by virtue of any legal engagement or enlistment in the armed services of the United States or who, being subject to the rules and articles of war, is confined by one legally acting under the authority thereof or who is held as a prisoner of war under the authority of the United States or who is in custody for any treason, felony or other high misdemeanor committed in any other state or territory of the United State and, by the Constitution and laws of the United States, ought to be delivered up to such state of territory.

MONTANA

Montana Code
Title 46. Criminal Procedure
Chapter 22. Habeas Corpus

46-22-101. Applicability of writ of habeas corpus
(1) Except as provided in subsection (2), every person imprisoned or otherwise restrained of liberty within this state may prosecute a writ of habeas corpus to inquire into the cause of imprisonment or restraint and, if illegal, to be delivered from the imprisonment or restraint.

(2) The writ of habeas corpus is not available to attack the validity of the conviction or sentence of a person who has been adjudged guilty of an offense in a court of record and has exhausted the remedy of appeal. The relief under this chapter is not available to attack the legality of an order revoking a suspended or deferred sentence.

46-22-102. No release for technical defects
A person may not be released on a writ of habeas corpus due to any technical defect in commitment not affecting the person's substantial rights.

46-22-103. Writ for purpose of bail
When a person is imprisoned or detained in custody on any criminal charge for want of bail, the person is entitled to a writ of habeas corpus for the purpose of giving bail upon averring that fact in the person's petition, without alleging that the person is illegally confined.

Part 2. Issuance of Writ

46-22-201. Application for writ of habeas corpus

(1) Application for a writ of habeas corpus is made by petition signed either by the party for whose relief it is intended or by some person on the petitioner's behalf. It must specify:

    (a) that the petitioner is unlawfully imprisoned or restrained of liberty;

    (b) why the imprisonment or restraint is unlawful; and

    (c) where and by whom the petitioner is confined or restrained.

(2) All parties must be named if they are known or otherwise described so that they may be identified.

(3) The petition must be verified by the oath or affirmation of the party making the application.

46 22 202. Granting writ of habeas corpus

(1) A writ of habeas corpus may be granted by any justice of the supreme court or by any district court judge upon petition by or on behalf of any person restrained of liberty within the justice's or judge's jurisdiction.

(2) When a writ of habeas corpus is issued, it may be made returnable before the issuing court.

46-22-203. Writ granted without delay

Any justice or judge authorized to grant a writ of habeas corpus shall grant the writ without delay if it appears that a writ ought to issue.

46-22-204. Writ and process may issue at any time

The writ of habeas corpus or any associated process may be issued and served on any day or at any time.

46-22-205. Form of writ

(1) The writ of habeas corpus must be directed to the person having custody of or restraining the person on whose behalf the application is made and must command that person to have the petitioner before the judge before whom the writ is returnable at a time and place specified.

(2) The issue or issues to be determined upon return of the writ may be stated either in the writ or in an order attached to the writ. If the issues to be determined are not stated in the writ or in an attached order, then a copy of the petition must be attached to the writ.

46-22-206. Service of writ

(1) The writ of habeas corpus must be served upon the person to whom it is directed. If the writ is directed to a state institution, a copy of the writ must be served upon the attorney general. If the writ is directed to a county facility, a copy of the writ must be served upon the county attorney.

(2) The writ must be served by the clerk of court, the sheriff, or any other person directed to do so by the court.

(3) The writ must be served in the same manner as a summons in civil actions, except when otherwise expressly directed by the judge.

Part 3. Return of Writ, Hearing, Appeal

46-22-301. Return of service
(1) The person upon whom the writ is served shall make a return and state in that return:

 (a)(i) whether the petitioner is in that person's custody or under that person's power or restraint; and

  (ii) if the petitioner is in custody or otherwise restrained, the authority for and cause of the custody or restraint; or

 (b) if the petitioner has been transferred to the custody of or otherwise restrained by another, to whom the party was transferred, the time and place of transfer, the reason for the transfer, and the authority under which the transfer took place.

(2) The return must be signed and verified by oath unless the person making the return is a sworn public officer making a return in an official capacity.

46-22-302. Appearance of petitioner
(1) The person commanded by the writ shall bring the petitioner before the court as required by the writ unless the petitioner cannot be brought before the court without danger to the petitioner's health. Sickness or infirmity must be confirmed in an affidavit by the person having custody of the petitioner.

(2) If the court is satisfied with the truth of the affidavit, the court may proceed and dispose of the case as if the petitioner were present or the hearing may be postponed until the petitioner is present.

46-22-303. Refusal to obey writ—Contempt
If the person commanded by the writ refuses to obey, that person must be adjudged in contempt of court.

46-22-304. Hearing on return
The court before whom the writ is returned shall immediately proceed to hear and examine the return. The hearing may be summary in nature.

46-22-305. Production of evidence
Evidence may be produced and compelled in preparation of a hearing as provided in Title 46, chapter 22.

46-22-306. Disposition of petitioner
(1) If the court finds in favor of the petitioner, an appropriate order must be entered with respect to the judgment or sentence in the former proceeding and any supplementary orders as to reassignment, retrial, custody, bail, or discharge as may be necessary and proper.

(2) If the court finds for the prosecution, the petitioner must be returned to the custody of the person to whom the writ was directed.

NEBRASKA

Revised Statutes of Nebraska Annotated
Chapter 29. Criminal Procedure
Article 28. Habeas Corpus

29-2801. Habeas corpus; writ; when allowed
If any person, except persons convicted of some crime or offense for which they stand committed, or persons committed for treason or felony, the punishment whereof is capital, plainly and specially expressed in the warrant of commitment, now is or shall be confined in any jail of this state, or shall be unlawfully deprived of his or her liberty, and shall make application, either by him or herself or by any person on his or her behalf, to any one of the judges of the district court, or to any county judge, and does at the same time produce to such judge a copy of the commitment or cause of detention of such person, or if the person so imprisoned or detained is imprisoned or detained without any legal authority, upon making the same appear to such judge, by oath or affirmation, it shall be his duty forthwith to allow a writ of habeas corpus, which writ shall be issued forthwith by the clerk of the district court, or by the county judge, as the case may require, under the seal of the court whereof the person allowing such writ is a judge, directed to the proper officer, person or persons who detains such prisoner.

29-2802. Writ; application; to be taken before judge; return
It shall be the duty of the officer or person to whom such writ shall be directed to convey the person or persons so imprisoned or detained and named in such writ, before the judge allowing the same, or in case of his absence or disability, before some other judge of the same court, on the day specified in such writ, and to make due return of the writ, together with the day and cause of caption and detention of such person, according to the command thereof.

29-2803. Habeas corpus; applicant; subpoena for witnesses
Whenever a habeas corpus shall be issued to bring the body of any prisoner committed as aforesaid, unless the court or judge issuing the same shall deem it wholly unnecessary and useless, the court or judge shall issue a subpoena to the sheriff of the county where such person shall be confined, commanding him to summon the witness or witnesses therein named to appear before such judge or court, at the time and place when and where such habeas corpus shall be returnable. It shall be the duty of such sheriff to serve the subpoena, if possible, in time to enable such witness or witnesses to attend.

29-2804. Subpoena; duty of witness; noncompliance; penalty
It shall be the duty of the witness or witnesses thus served with subpoena to attend and give evidence before the judge or court issuing the same, on pain of being guilty of a contempt, in which event he or they shall be proceeded against accordingly by the judge or court.

29-2805. Habeas corpus; hearing by court or judge; procedure
On the hearing of any habeas corpus issued as aforesaid, it shall be the duty of the judge or court who shall hear the same to examine the witness or witnesses aforesaid, and such other witnesses as the prisoner may request, touching any offense mentioned in the warrant of commitment, whether the offense be technically set out in the commitment or not. Upon the hearing the judge or court may either recommit, bail or discharge the prisoner, according to the facts of the case.

29-2806. Habeas corpus; disposition of cause
When the judge shall have examined into the cause of the capture and detention of the person so brought

before him, and shall be satisfied that the person is unlawfully imprisoned or detained, he shall forthwith discharge such prisoner from confinement. In case the person or persons applying for such writ shall be confined or detained in a legal manner, on a charge of having committed any crime or offense, the judge shall, at his discretion, commit, discharge or let to bail such person or persons, and if the judge shall deem the offense bailable, on the principles of law, he shall cause the person charged as aforesaid to enter into recognizance, with one or more sufficient securities, in such sum as the judge shall think reasonable, the circumstances of the prisoner and the nature of the offense charged considered, conditioned for his appearance at the next court where the offense is cognizable. The judge shall certify his proceedings, together with the recognizance, forthwith, to the proper court; and if the person or persons charged as aforesaid shall fail to enter into such recognizance, he or they shall be committed to prison by such judge.

29-2807. Writ; failure to obey; penalty
If any person to whom writ of habeas corpus shall be directed as aforesaid, shall neglect or refuse to obey or make return of the same according to the command thereof, or shall make a false return of the writ, or upon demand made by the prisoner, or any person in his or her behalf, shall refuse to deliver to the person demanding, within six hours after the demand therefor, a true copy of the warrant or commitment or detainer of such prisoner, every person so offending shall, for the first offense, forfeit to the party aggrieved the sum of two hundred dollars, and for the second offense, the sum of four hundred dollars, and shall, if an officer, be incapable to hold his office.

29-2808. Writ; failure to issue; penalty
If any clerk of the district court shall refuse to issue such writ after allowance and demand made as aforesaid, he shall forfeit to the party aggrieved the sum of five hundred dollars.

29-2809. Applicant discharged; rearrest for same offense prohibited; penalty; exceptions
Any person who shall be set at large upon any habeas corpus, shall not be again imprisoned for the same offense, unless by the legal order or process of the court wherein he or she shall be bound by recognizance to appear, or other court having jurisdiction of the cause or offense. If any person shall knowingly, contrary to *sections 29-2801* to *29-2824*, recommit or imprison, or cause to be recommitted or imprisoned for the same offense or pretended offense, any person so set at large, or shall knowingly aid or assist therein, he shall forfeit to the party aggrieved five hundred dollars, any colorable pretense or variation in the warrant or commitment notwithstanding.

29-2810. Person in custody of officer; delivery to another officer prohibited; penalty; exceptions
If any person of this state shall be committed to prison, or be in custody of any officer for any criminal matter, such prisoner shall not be removed therefrom into the custody of any other officer, unless by legal process, or when the prisoner shall be delivered to some inferior officer to carry to jail, or shall, by order of the proper court, be removed from one place to another within the state for trial, or in case of fire, infection or other necessity; and if any person, after such commitment, shall make out or sign or countersign any warrant for such removal, contrary to this section, he or she shall for every such offense forfeit to the party aggrieved five hundred dollars .

29-2811. Accessories before the fact in capital cases; not bailable
When any person shall appear to be committed by any judge or magistrate, and charged as accessory before the fact to any felony, the punishment whereof is capital, which felony shall be plainly and especially charged in the warrant of commitment, such person shall not be removed or bailed by virtue of *sections 29-2801* to *29 2824*, or in any other manner than as if said section had not been enacted.

29-2812. Extradition of citizens of Nebraska for prosecution in sister state; imprisonment for; general prohibition; penalty; exception

No citizen of this state, being an inhabitant or resident of the same, shall be sent a prisoner to any place whatever out of the state, for any crime or offense committed within this state, except in cases specially authorized by law, and every such imprisonment is hereby declared to be illegal. If any such citizen shall be so imprisoned, he may for every such imprisonment maintain an action of false imprisonment, in any court having cognizance thereof, against the person or persons by whom he shall be so imprisoned or transported contrary to law, and against any person who shall contrive, write, seal, sign or countersign any writing for such imprisonment or transportation, or shall be aiding and assisting in the same or any of them, and shall recover triple costs besides damages, which damages, so to be given, shall not be less than five hundred dollars; and every person knowingly concerned in any manner as aforesaid in such illegal imprisonment or transportation, contrary to this section, and being thereof lawfully convicted, shall be disabled from henceforth to bear any office of trust or profit within this state; Provided, if any citizen of this state, or any person or persons at any time resident in the same, shall have committed or shall be charged with having committed any treason, felony or misdemeanor in any other part of the United States or territories where he or she ought to be tried for such offense, he, she or they may be sent to the state or territory having jurisdiction of the offense as provided by the Uniform Criminal Extradition Act of this state.

29-2813. False imprisonment; penalties; action for; limitation

The penalties recoverable pursuant to sections 29-2801 to 29-2824 shall be recovered by the party aggrieved, his or her executors or administrators, by civil action in any court having cognizance of the same; Provided, no person shall be sued or molested for any offense against the provisions of said sections, unless within two years after the time when such offense shall have been committed; but if the party aggrieved shall then be in prison, then within two years after the decease of the person imprisoned, or his or her delivery out of prison. In every such action it shall be lawful for the defendant to plead the general issue, and give the special matter in evidence.

29-2814. Warrant or commitment; defects; when harmless

If any person shall be committed to prison, or be in custody of any officer for any criminal matter, by virtue of any warrant or commitment of any magistrate of this state having jurisdiction of such criminal matter, such person shall not be discharged from such imprisonment or custody by reason of any informality or defect of such warrant or commitment; Provided, such warrant or commitment shall show substantially a criminal matter for which such magistrate had jurisdiction so to arrest or commit.

29-2815. Applicant in custody of person not an officer; form of writ

In case of confinement, imprisonment, or detention by any person not a sheriff, deputy sheriff, coroner, jailer, or marshal of this state, nor a marshal or other like officer of the court of the United states, the writ of habeas corpus shall be in the form following:

    The State of Nebraska,

    ss

    .... County,

    The People of the State of Nebraska to the Sheriff of such county, greeting:

We command you, that the body of .... , of .... , by .... of .... , imprisoned and restrained of his or her liberty, as it is said, you take and have before .... , a judge of our .... court .... , or, in case of his or her absence or disability, before some other judge of the same court at .... , to do and receive what our judge shall then and there consider .... concerning him or her in his or her behalf, and summon .... then and there to appear before our judge to show the cause of the taking and detaining .... ; and have you there this writ, with your doings thereon.

Witness .... , at .... , this .... day of .... , in the year ....

29-2816. Writ; service and return
Such writ may be served in any county by any sheriff of the same or of any other county. When such writ shall be issued by a court in session, if such court shall have adjourned when the same is returned, it shall be returned before any judge of the same court, and if such writ is returned before one judge at a time when the court is in session, he may adjourn the case into the court, there to be heard and determined.

29-2817. Writ; return by person detaining; contents
In every case in which a writ of habeas corpus has been allowed, the person to whom the writ is directed shall file a return in which he shall plainly and unequivocally state the following: (1) Whether he has or has not the party in his custody or power, or under restraint; (2) if he has the party in his custody or power, or under restraint, he shall set forth at large the authority and the true and whole cause of such imprisonment and restraint, with a copy of the writ, warrant, or other process, if any, upon which the party is detained; and (3) if he has had the party in his custody or power, or under restraint, and has transferred such custody or restraint to another, he shall state particularly to whom, at what time, for what cause and by what authority such transfer was made.

29-2818. Writ; return by person detaining; signature and verification
The return or statement shall be signed by the person making it, and it shall be sworn to by him, unless he is a public officer and makes the return in his official capacity.

29-2819. Writ; return of person detaining; prima facie evidence of cause of detention, when; order for costs
Upon the return of any writ of habeas corpus, issued as aforesaid, if it shall appear that the person detained or imprisoned is in custody under any warrant or commitment in pursuance of law, the return shall be considered as prima facie evidence of the cause of detention; but if the person so imprisoned or detained is restrained of liberty by any alleged private authority, the return of the writ shall be considered only as a plea of the facts therein set forth, and the party claiming the custody shall be held to make proof of such facts. Upon the final disposition of any case arising upon a writ of habeas corpus, the court or judge determining the same shall make such order as to costs as t he case may require.

29-2820. Writ; person detaining; how designated
The person having the custody of the prisoner may, in all writs of habeas corpus issued under sections 29-2801 to 29-2824, be designated by his name of office, if he has any, or by his own name; or if both such names are unknown or uncertain , he may be described by an assumed appellation, and any person who is served with the writ shall be deemed the person intended thereby.

29-2821. Writ; person detained; how designated
The person t o be produced shall be designated by his name, if known, and if that is unknown or uncertain, he may be described in any other way so as to make known who i s intended .

29-2822. Writ; order for safekeeping of person detained
When any writ of habeas corpus shall have been allowed, the court or judge to which the same shall be returned, or into which it shall be adjourned, shall, for good cause shown, continue the cause and shall make order for the safekeeping of the person imprisoned, or detain him, as the nature of the case may require.

29 2823. Habeas corpus proceedings; review; procedure; bail pending appeal
The proceedings upon any writ of habeas corpus shall be recorded by the clerk and judges respectively, and may be reviewed as provided by law for appeal in civil cases. If the state shall appeal from a final order of a district court made upon the return of a writ of habeas corpus discharging a defendant in a criminal case, the defendant shall not be discharged from custody pending final decision upon appeal; Provided, said defendant may be admitted to bail pending disposition of said appeal as is otherwise provided by law.

29-2824. Habeas corpus proceedings; fees; taxation as costs; payment by county; payment in advance not demandable
The county judge shall be allowed the sum of five dollars for every allowance of the writ of habeas corpus and the hearing and determining of the case upon the return of the writ, which sum, together with the fees of the clerk, sheriff, and witnesses in the case, shall be taxed by the judge on his or her return of proceedings on the writ, and the same shall be taxed and collected as part of the original costs in the case whenever the person brought before the judge on the writ was in custody by virtue of the proceedings in any case in which such person is charged or attempted to be charged with the commission of any criminal offense, and when such person shall either be held to bail, or shall be remanded to custody by the judge, but when such person shall be wholly discharged by the judge the costs shall be taxed to the state, and paid out of the county treasury of the proper county, upon the order of the county board; Provided, no person or officer shall have the right to demand the payment in advance of any fees which such person or officer may be entitled to by virtue of such proceedings on habeas corpus, when the writ shall have been issued or demanded for the discharge from custody of any person confined under color of proceedings in any criminal case.

NEVADA

Nevada Revised Statutes Annotated
Titled 3. Remedies; Special Actions and Proceedings
Chapter 34. Habeas Corpus

34.360. Persons who may prosecute writ
Every person unlawfully committed, detained, confined or restrained of his or her liberty, under any pretense whatever, may prosecute a writ of habeas corpus to inquire into the cause of such imprisonment or restraint.

34.370. Application for writ; verification required; contents; supporting documents
1. A petition for a writ of habeas corpus must be verified by the petitioner or the petitioner's counsel. If the petition is verified by counsel, counsel shall also verify that the petitioner personally authorized counsel to commence the action.

2. A verified petition for issuance of a writ of habeas corpus must specify that the petitioner is imprisoned or restrained of the petitioner's liberty, the officer or other person by whom the petitioner is confined or restrained, and the place where the petitioner is confined, naming all the parties if they are known, or describing them if they are not known.

3. If the petitioner claims that the imprisonment is illegal, the petitioner must state facts which show that the restraint or detention is illegal.

4. If the petition requests relief from a judgment of conviction or sentence in a criminal case, the petition must identify the proceedings in which the petitioner was convicted, give the date of entry of the final judgment and set forth which constitutional rights of the petitioner were violated and the acts constituting violations of those rights. Affidavits, records or other evidence supporting the allegations in the petition must be attached unless the petition recites the cause or failure to attach these materials. The petition must identify any previous proceeding in state or federal court initiated by the petitioner to secure relief from the petitioner's conviction or sentence. Argument, citations and other supporting documents are unnecessary.

34.390. Judge to grant writ without delay; exceptions; effect of writ

1. Any judge empowered to grant a writ of habeas corpus applied for pursuant to this chapter, if it appears that the writ ought to issue, shall grant the writ without delay, except as otherwise provided in NRS 34.720 to 34.830, inclusive.

2. A writ of habeas corpus does not entitle a petitioner to be discharged from the custody or restraint under which the petitioner is held. The writ requires only the production of the petitioner to determine the legality of the petitioner's custody or restraint.

34.400. Contents of writ

> <Amendments to this section contingent upon approval of Senate Joint Resolution No. 14 at the general election on Nov. 4, 2014.>

The writ must be directed to the person who has the petitioner in custody or under restraint, commanding the person to have the body of the petitioner produced before the district court or Supreme Court at a time which the judge or justice directs.

34.410. Service of writ

1. If the writ be directed to the sheriff or other ministerial officer, it shall be delivered to such officer without delay by the clerk of the court presided over by the judge issuing the writ.

2. If the writ be directed to any other person, it shall be delivered to the sheriff or the sheriff's deputy, and shall be served by the sheriff or the sheriff's deputy without delay upon such person by delivering the same to the person.

3. If the officer or person to whom the writ is directed cannot be found, or shall refuse admittance to the officer or person serving or delivering the writ, it may be served or delivered by leaving it at the residence of the officer or person to whom it is directed or by affixing the same on some conspicuous place on the outside of the officer's or person's dwelling house, or of the place where the party is confined or under restraint.

4. Service of the writ is made by serving a copy and exhibiting the original, and where posting is required, by posting a copy.

34.420. Proceedings upon disobedience of writ
If the officer or person to whom such writ is directed refuse, after service, to obey the same, the judge shall, upon affidavit, issue an attachment against such person, directed to the sheriff, or, if the sheriff be the defendant, to an elisor, appointed for the purpose by the judge, commanding the sheriff or elisor forthwith to apprehend such person and bring the person immediately before such judge; and upon being so brought the person shall be committed to the jail of the county until the person makes due return to such writ, or be otherwise legally discharged.

34.430. Return and answer; service and filing; contents; signature and verification
1. Except as otherwise provided in subsection 1 of NRS 34.745, the respondent shall serve upon the petitioner and file with the court a return and an answer that must respond to the allegations of the petition within 45 days or a longer period fixed by the judge or justice.

2. The return must state plainly and unequivocally whether the respondent has the party in custody, or under the respondent's power or restraint. If the respondent has the petitioner in the respondent's custody or power, or under the respondent's restraint, the respondent shall state the authority and cause of the imprisonment or restraint, setting forth with specificity the basis for custody.

3. If the petitioner is detained by virtue of any judgment, writ, warrant or other written authority, a certified or exemplified copy must be annexed to the return.

4. If the respondent has the petitioner in the respondent's power or custody or under the respondent's restraint before or after the date of the writ of habeas corpus but has transferred custody or restraint to another, the return must state particularly to whom, at what time and place, for what cause, and by what authority the transfer took place.

5. The return must be signed by the respondent and, unless the respondent is a sworn public officer who makes the return in the respondent's official capacity, verified under oath or affirmation.

34.440. Person served must bring body of person in custody; exceptions
If the writ of habeas corpus be served, the person or officer to whom the same is directed shall also bring the body of the party in the person's or officer's custody or under the person's or officer's restraint, according to the command of the writ, except in the cases specified in NRS 34.450.

34.450. Sickness or infirmity of party restrained; hearing may proceed or be adjourned
1. Whenever, from sickness or infirmity of the party directed to be produced by any writ of habeas corpus, the party cannot, without danger be brought before the judge, the officer or person in whose custody or power the party is may state that fact in the officer's or person's return to the writ, verifying the same by affidavit.

2. If the judge be satisfied of the truth of such allegation of sickness or infirmity, and the return to the writ is otherwise sufficient, the judge may proceed to decide on such return and to dispose of the matter as if such party had been produced on the writ, or the hearing thereof may be adjourned until such party can be produced.

34.470. Answer to return; summary proceeding; attendance of witnesses

1. The petitioner brought before the judge on the return of the writ may deny or controvert any of the material facts or matters set forth in the return or answer, deny the sufficiency thereof, or allege any fact to show either that the petitioner's imprisonment or detention is unlawful or that the petitioner is entitled to discharge.

2. The judge shall thereupon proceed in a summary way to hear such allegation and proof as may be produced against or in favor of such imprisonment or detention, and to dispose of the case as justice may require.

3. The judge may compel the attendance of witnesses by process of subpoena and attachment and perform all other acts necessary to a full and fair hearing and determination of the case.

34.480. If no legal cause shown; judge shall discharge person from custody

If no legal cause be shown for such imprisonment or restraint, or for the continuation thereof, such judge shall discharge such party from the custody or restraint under which the party is held.

34.500. Grounds for discharge in certain cases

If it appears on the return of the writ of habeas corpus that the petitioner is in custody by virtue of process from any court of this State, or judge or officer thereof, the petitioner may be discharged in any one of the following cases;

1. When the jurisdiction of the court or officer has been exceeded.

2. When the imprisonment was at first lawful, yet by some act, omission or event, which has taken place afterwards, the petitioner has become entitled to be discharged.

3. When the process is defective in some matter of substance required by law, rendering it void.

4. When the process, though proper in form, has been issued in a case not allowed by law.

5. When the person having the custody of the petitioner is not the person allowed by law to detain the petitioner.

6. Where the process is not authorized by any judgment, order or decree of any court, nor by any provision of law.

7. Where the petitioner has been committed or indicted on a criminal charge, including a misdemeanor, except misdemeanor violations of chapters 484A to 484E, inclusive, of NRS or any ordinance adopted by a city or county to regulate traffic, without reasonable or probable cause.

8. Where the petitioner has been committed or indicted on any criminal charge under a statute or ordinance that is unconstitutional, or if constitutional on its face is unconstitutional in its application.

9. Where the court finds that there has been a specific denial of the petitioner's constitutional rights with respect to the petitioner's conviction or sentence in a criminal case.

34.510. Defect of form in warrant or commitment not ground for discharge

If any person be committed to prison, or be in custody of any officer on any criminal charge, by virtue of any warrant or commitment of a justice of the peace, such person shall not be discharged from such imprisonment or custody on the ground of any defect or form in such warrant or commitment.

34.520. If charge defectively set forth in process or warrant, judge shall examine witnesses and discharge or recommit person

If it shall appear to the judge, by affidavit, or upon hearing of the matter, or otherwise, or upon the inspection of the process or warrant of commitment, and such other papers in the proceedings as may be shown to the judge, that the party is guilty of a criminal offense, or ought not to be discharged, the judge, although the charge is defectively or unsubstantially set forth in such process or warrant of commitment, shall cause the complainant, or other necessary witnesses, to be subpoenaed to attend at such time as ordered, to testify before the judge; and upon the examination, the judge shall discharge such prisoner, let the prisoner to bail, if the offense be bailable, or recommit the prisoner to custody, as may be just and legal.

34.530. Writ for purpose of bail

Any person who is imprisoned or detained in custody on any criminal charge before conviction for want of bail may file a petition for a writ of habeas corpus for the purpose of giving bail, upon averring that fact in the person's petition, without alleging that the person is illegally confined.

34.540. Bail in habeas corpus proceedings

<Amendments to this section contingent upon approval of Senate Joint Resolution No. 14 at the general election on Nov. 4, 2014.>

Any Supreme Court justice or judge, before whom any person who has been committed on a criminal charge before conviction is brought on a writ of habeas corpus, if that person is bailable, may take a recognizance from that person, as in other cases, and shall file the same in the proper court without delay. In no case where the applicant for a writ of habeas corpus has been admitted to bail and failed to appear before the Supreme Court justice, the judge or presiding judge of the court wherein the bail was fixed may the proceedings for a writ of habeas corpus be dismissed, except upon good cause shown. Upon the failure of that person to appear, the justice, district judge or presiding judge shall cause a bench warrant to be issued and that person arrested and brought before the justice, judge or court as upon contempt.

34.550. Judge to remand to custody if party not entitled to discharge or is not bailed

If a party brought before the judge on the return of the writ is not entitled to discharge, and is not bailed where such bail is allowable, the judge shall remand the party to custody or place the party under the restraint from which the party was taken, if the person under whose custody or restraint the party was is legally entitled thereto.

34.560. Judge may order change of custody; enforcement of commitment order stayed; appeal to Supreme Court

<Amendments to this section contingent upon approval of Senate Joint Resolution No. 14 at the general election on Nov. 4, 2014.>

1. In cases where any party is held under illegal restraint or custody, or any other person is entitled to the restraint or custody of such party, the judge may order such party to be committed to the restraint or custody of such person as is by law entitled thereto.

2. If a party is ordered committed to the restraint or custody of an officer from a jurisdiction outside the State of Nevada, the district judge ordering such commitment shall stay the enforcement thereof for 5 days, during which time an aggrieved party may file a notice of appeal therefrom to the Supreme Court.

3. Upon the filing of a notice of appeal as provided in subsection 2, the enforcement of such order of commitment shall be stay during the pendency of the appeal.

4. During any period of stay as provided in this section, the local officer having custody of such party shall retain custody thereof.

34.570. Pending judgment on proceedings, judge may commit or place in custody
Until judgment is given on a petition, the judge before whom any party may be brought on the petition may:

1. Commit the party to the custody of the sheriff of the county; or

2. Place the party in such case or under such custody as the party's age or circumstances may require.

34.575. Appeal from order of district court granting or denying writ
<Amendments to this section contingent upon approval of Senate Joint Resolution No. 14 at the general election on Nov. 4, 2014.>

1. An applicant who, after conviction or while no criminal action is pending against the applicant, has petitioned the district court for a writ of habeas corpus and whose application for the writ is denied, may appeal to the Supreme Court from the order and judgment of the district court, but the appeal must be made within 30 days after service by the court of written notice of entry of the order or judgment.

2. The State of Nevada is an interested party in proceedings for a writ of habeas corpus. If the district court grants the writ and orders the discharge or a change in custody of the petitioner, the district attorney of the county in which the application for the writ was made, or the city attorney of a city which is situated in the county in which the application for the writ was made, or the Attorney General on behalf of the State, may appeal to the Supreme Court from the order of the district judge within 30 days after the service of the court of written notice of entry of the order.

3. Whenever an appeal is taken from an order of the district court discharging a petitioner or committing a petitioner to the custody of another person after granting a pretrial petition for habeas corpus based on alleged want of probable cause, or otherwise challenging the court's right or jurisdiction to proceed to trial of a criminal charge, the clerk of the district court shall forthwith certify and transmit to the Supreme Court, as the record on appeal, the original papers on which the petition was heard in the district court and, if the appellant or respondent demands it, a transcript of any evidentiary proceedings had in the district court. The district court shall require its court reporter to expedite the preparation of the transcript in preference to any request for a transcript in a civil matter. When the appeal is docketed in the Supreme Court, it stands submitted without further briefs or oral argument unless the Supreme Court otherwise orders.

34.580. Defect of form in writ immaterial
No writ of habeas corpus shall be disobeyed for defect of form if it sufficiently appear therefrom in whose

custody or under whose restraint the party imprisoned or restrained is, the officer or person detaining the party, and the judge before whom the party is to be brought.

34.590. Cases where imprisonment after discharge is permitted
No person who has been discharged by the order of the judge upon habeas corpus issued pursuant to the provisions of this chapter shall be again imprisoned, restrained or kept in custody for the same cause, except in the following cases:

1. If the person shall have been discharged from custody on a criminal charge and be afterwards committed for the same offense by legal order or process.

2. If after a discharge for defect of proof, or for any defect of the process, warrant or commitment in a criminal case, the person be again arrested on sufficient proof and committed by legal process for the same offense.

34.600. In certain cases warrant may issue instead of writ
Whenever it shall appear by satisfactory proof, by affidavit, to any judge authorized by law to grant a writ of habeas corpus, that anyone illegally held in custody, confinement or restraint, and that there is good reason to believe that such person will be carried out of the jurisdiction of such judge before whom the application is made, or will suffer some irreparable injury before compliance with the writ of habeas corpus can be enforced, the judge may cause a warrant to be issued, reciting the facts, and directed to the sheriff or any constable of the county, commanding such officer to take such person thus held in custody, confinement or restraint and forthwith bring him or her before such judge, to be dealt with according to law.

34.610. Judge may include in warrant order for arrest of person charged with illegal detention
The judge may also, if the same be deemed necessary, insert in such warrant a command for the apprehension of the person charged with such illegal detention and restraint.

34.620. Execution of warrant
The officer to whom such warrant is delivered shall execute the same by bringing the person or persons therein named before the judge who may have directed the issuing of such warrant.

34.630. Return, answer and hearing on warrant
The person alleged to have such party under illegal confinement or restraint may make return to such warrant, as in the case of a writ of habeas corpus, and the same may be denied, and like allegations, proofs and trial shall be thereon had as upon the return to a writ of habeas corpus.

34.640. Party may be discharged or remanded
If such party be held under illegal restraint or custody, the party shall be discharged, and if not, the party shall be restored to the custody of the person entitled thereto, or left at liberty, as the case may require.

34.650. Writ of process may issue on Sunday or nonjudicial day
Any writ of process authorized by NRS 34.360 to 34.830, inclusive, may be issued and served on Sunday or any other nonjudicial day.

34.660. Clerk to issue writs, warrants, processes and subpoenas; when returnable
All writ of process authorized by the provisions of NRS 34.360 to 34.830, inclusive, shall be issued by

34.670. Damages recoverable for failure to issue or obey writ

If any judge, after a proper application is made, shall refuse to grant an order for a writ of habeas corpus, or if the officer or person to whom such writ may be directed shall refuse obedience to the command thereof, the judge, officer or person shall forfeit and pay to the person aggrieved a sum not exceeding $5,000, to be recovered by action in any court of competent jurisdiction.

34.680. Penalties for custodian or accessory disobeying or avoiding writ

1. Any person having in his or her custody or under his or her restraint or power any person for whose relief a writ of habeas corpus shall have been duly issued pursuant to the provisions of this chapter, who, with the intent to elude the service of such writ or to avoid the effect thereof, shall transfer such person to the custody of another, or shall place the person under the power or control of another or shall conceal or exchange the place of the person's confinement or restraint, or shall remove the person without the jurisdiction of such judge, shall be deemed guilty of a gross misdemeanor.

2. Every person who shall knowingly aid or assist in the commission of any offense specified in subsection 1 shall be punished as in subsection 1 mentioned.

34.700. Time for filing; waiver and consent of accused respecting date of trial

1. Except as provided in subsection 3, a pretrial petition for a writ of habeas corpus based on alleged lack of probable cause or otherwise challenging the court's right or jurisdiction to proceed to the trial of a criminal charge may not be considered unless:

(a) The petition and all supporting documents are filed within 21 days after the first appearance of the accused in the district court; and

(b) The petition contains a statement that the accused:

    (1) Waives the 60-day limitation for bringing an accused to trial; or

    (2) If the petition is not decided within 15 days before the date set for trial, consents that the court may, without notice or hearing, continue the trial indefinitely or to a date designated by the court.

2. The arraignment and entry of a plea by the accused must not be continued to avoid the requirement that a pretrial petition be filed within the period specified in subsection 1.

3. The court may extend, for good cause, the time to file a petition. Good cause shall be deemed to exist if the transcript of the preliminary hearing or of the proceedings before the grand jury is not available within 14 days after the accused's initial appearance and the court shall grant an ex parte application to extend the time for filing a petition. All other applications may be made only after appropriate notice has been given to the prosecuting attorney.

34.710. Limitations on submission and consideration of pretrial petition

    <Amendments to this section contingent upon approval of Senate Joint Resolution No. 14 at the general election on Nov. 4, 2014.>

1. A district court shall not consider any pretrial petition for habeas corpus:

(a) Based on alleged lack of probable cause or otherwise challenging the court's right or jurisdiction to proceed to the trial of a criminal charge unless a petition is filed in accordance with NRS 34.700.

(b) Based on a ground which the petitioner could have included as a ground for relief in any prior petition for habeas corpus or other petition for extraordinary relief.

2. If an application is made to a justice of the Supreme Court for a writ of habeas corpus and the application is entertained by the justice or the Supreme Court, and thereafter denied, the person making the application may not submit thereafter an application to the district judge of the district in which the applicant is held in custody, not to any other district judge in any other judicial district of the State, premised upon the illegality of the same charge upon which the applicant is held in custody.

NEW HAMPSHIRE

Revised Statutes of New Hampshire
Title LV. Proceedings in Special Cases
Chapter 534. Habeas Corpus

534:1. Right
A person imprisoned or otherwise restrained of his personal liberty, by an officer or other person, except in the cases mentioned in the following section, is entitled of right to a writ of habeas corpus according to the provisions of this chapter.

534:2. Limitation on
Persons imprisoned upon legal process, civil or criminal, in which the cause of the imprisonment is distinctly expressed, and persons committed by a court or judge of the United States, and where no judge of a court of this state has authority to discharge or to commit to bail, are not entitled of right to such writ.

534:3. Application
Application for the writ shall be made to the superior court in the county in which the person is imprisoned, by a person so imprisoned or restrained, or by some person in his behalf.

534:4. Form
The application shall be in writing, signed by the applicant, and under oath, and shall state the place where the person is supposed to be imprisoned or restrained of his liberty, and by whom; and a copy of the warrant or precept, if any, under which he is confined shall be annexed to the application.

534:5. Denial
If by such copy it appears that the person is lawfully imprisoned or restrained of his liberty by virtue thereof, a writ of habeas corpus shall not be granted.

534:6. Excessive bail

If by such copy it appears that the person imprisoned on criminal process before a magistrate for want of recognizance, and that excessive bail or recognizance is required, the court or justice shall decide what bail is reasonable, and he shall, on giving such bail, be discharged.

534:7. Copy of precept

If an officer having the custody of any such person by virtue of a precept refuses or delays unnecessarily to deliver to the applicant an attested copy of the precept, on demand, the court or justice, on proof by affidavit of the applicant or other credible witness of the demand and refusal or of unnecessary delay, shall forthwith issue the writ of habeas corpus as prayed for.

534:8. Writ

The form of writ may be substantially as follows:

THE STATE OF NEW HAMPSHIRE

............ss. To: ....

[L. S.] We command you that the body of ...., in our prison, under your custody detained [or, by you imprisoned and restrained of his liberty, as the case may be], as is said, together with the day and cause of the taking and detaining of the said .... by whatever name the said .... may be called, or charged, you have before our justice of our superior court, holden at .... , within and for our county of .... , immediately after the receipt of this writ, to undergo and receive what our said justices shall then and there consider of him in this behalf; and have you then and there this writ.

Witness .... at .... , this .... day of .... , in the year ....

All necessary alterations in the form shall be made to adapt the writ to the circumstances of the application.

534:9. Attestation

The writ, when awarded by the court, shall be under the seal of the court, shall bear teste of the chief or senior justice who is not a party, and shall be signed by the clerk; when awarded by a justice of the court it shall be under his hand and seal.

534:10. How returnable

The writ, when issued by the court, may be made returnable to the court or a justice thereof in any county immediately, or at a time and place therein directed.

534:11. When issued by justice

If the writ is issued by a justice of the court it may be made returnable before himself, the court or any justice thereof at a place certain, immediately or at other time therein directed.

534:12. Mode of return

In all cases the writ shall be made returnable in such mode as to secure to the applicant the enjoyment of it in the most free, easy, cheap and expeditious manner.

534:13. Security; expenses

The court or justice awarding the writ may, in his discretion, require the applicant to give satisfactory security to the person to whom the writ is directed, for the payment of all charges incurred by reason of the process, and that the person imprisoned shall not escape by the way. The court or justice may also fix and cause to be indorsed upon the writ the expense of producing the person imprisoned or restrained, according to the precept, and may require it to be paid or tendered when the writ is served.

534:14. Service

The service of the writ may be made by any person, by delivering the original to the person to whom it is directed, or, if the person for whom application is made is in prison, by leaving it with the jailer or deputy keeper at the prison, and paying or tendering the sum indorsed on the writ, if any.

534:15. Return of service

The person making the service shall keep a copy of the writ, and shall make his return or affidavit of service and of the payment or tender of fees thereon as in other cases, and shall deliver it to the court or justice before whom the writ is returnable, on or before the time of hearing therein designated.

534:16. Return of writ

The person to whom the writ is directed shall receive it when offered, and, upon payment of tender of the sum indorsed on the writ, if any, shall yield obedience to the command thereof; shall make return thereof to the court or justice, at the time and place therein mentioned; and shall state every cause of taking and detaining the person imprisoned or restrained; all of which shall be made under oath; and he shall also have present the body of such person, unless imprisoned or restrained for some one or more of the causes specified in *RSA 534:2*.

534:17. Time

If no time is specified for the return, but the writ is returnable immediately, the return shall be made within three days after the service, unless the prisoner is to be brought more than twenty miles, in which case the return shall be made within so many days more as will be equal to one day for every ten miles of such further distance.

534:18. Place

If the court is not in session when any such writ is made returnable it shall be returned to any justice of the court as if it were issued by and returnable to him.

534:19. Adjourning to court

A justice of the court to whom any such writ is returned may certify and return it, with all things pertaining thereto, to the court, if then sitting; and, at any time before the prisoner is discharged, bailed or remanded, he may adjourn further proceedings on the writ to the court, if then in session, or to the next term thereof if to begin within three months next afterward. The court, in any such case, shall proceed therein as if the writ had been, by the tenor thereof, returnable thereto.

534:20. Orders

The court or justice may require and take security by recognizance, with sufficient sureties if necessary, for the appearance of any party at the time and place of hearing on any such writ, and to abide the order of court thereon; and may made all decrees necessary to insure the attainment of the object of the writ and enforce it upon the principles of equity.

534:21. Hearing

Whenever any person is brought before a court or any justice thereof as aforesaid the court or justice shall, within three days thereafter, examine the causes of detention.

534:22. Judgment

If the person imprisoned or restrained is so imprisoned or restrained without sufficient cause or due order of law, he shall be discharged; but if otherwise he shall be remanded.

534:23. Bail, crimes

If the person is committed for a bailable offense the court or justice may bail him by ordering him to recognize, with sufficient surety or sureties, in a reasonable sum, for his appearance at the court having cognizance of the offense, and shall certify the recognizance into the court.

534:24. Bail, civil actions

[repealed 1971, 227:18, eff. Aug. 17, 1971.]

534:25. Contempt

If the person is imprisoned or restrained by order of a justice, or of any court or authority other than the supreme or superior court or a justice thereof, for contempt, the proceedings in the order and the cause thereof may be revised, and the order affirmed, modified or reversed by the superior court or a justice thereof.

534:26. Copy of process

If an officer having the custody of a prisoner, on payment or tender of his fees therefor, shall not, within 12 business hours after demand made, deliver to the prisoner a true copy of the warrant or process by which he is holden in custody he shall forfeit to the party aggrieved the sum of two hundred dollars.

534:27. Disobeying writ

If a person to whom a writ of habeas corpus is directed refuses to receive it, or conceals himself or avoids, so that the writ cannot be delivered to him, or, after the receipt thereof, and payment or tender of expenses when required as aforesaid, he refuses or neglects to yield obedience thereto, unless prevented by the sickness of the person detained or other necessity, he shall forfeit for every such offense, to the person aggrieved, the sum of five hundred dollars.

534:28. False return

If a person makes a false return to any such writ he shall be liable to the action of the party aggrieved, and also to any action at common law for false imprisonment or unlawful restraint.

534:29. Enforcement

The court or justice awarding any such writ, or to whom it is returned, may punish every disobedience to the order thereof as for a contempt, and may compel obedience thereto by process of attachment.

534:30. Reimbursement

No person enlarged by habeas corpus shall again be imprisoned or restrained of his liberty for the same cause, unless he shall be indicted therefor, or convicted thereof, or shall neglect to appear according to his recognizance, or to find bail required thereto; and if an officer or other person shall willfully again imprison or restrain the person so discharged, except as aforesaid, he shall forfeit to the party aggrieved eight hundred dollars.

534:31. Limitation of actions and prosecutions

All actions and prosecutions for any offense against the provisions of this chapter shall be begun within two years next after the commission of the offense, saving to all persons in prison the right to sue or prosecute at any time within two years after such impediment is removed.

534:32. Survival of right of action

The right of action in any such case shall not cease by the death of either party, but shall survive for and against the personal representatives of the deceased.

NEW JERSEY

New Jersey statutes Annotated
Title 2A. Administration of Civil And Criminal Justice
Chapter 67. Habeas Corpus; Illegal Confinement
Article 1. General Provisions, Including Certain Civil Rights

2A:67-1. Construction of chapter

This chapter shall be liberally construed so as to secure, as far as possible, the liberty of the citizen.

2A:67-2. Chapter not generally applicable to habeas corpus ad testificandum

No provision of this chapter shall apply to the writ of habeas corpus when used to bring a prisoner before a court as a witness, unless it is expressly made applicable thereto.

2A:67-3. Issuance of writ without application

When the superior court shall have evidence from any judicial proceeding had before it that a person within this state is illegally confined of his liberty, such court shall issue a writ of habeas corpus for his relief, although no application be made for such writ. If the writ is granted by the court on its own motion, no fee shall be allowed.

2A:67-4. Prisoner not to be removed except in certain cases

No person committed to a prison or in the custody of an officer or other person for a criminal or supposed criminal matter shall be removed from such prison or custody into the custody of any other officer or person, except:

a. By habeas corpus or other legal writ or process; or

b. Where he is delivered to a constable or other inferior officer in accordance with law; or

c. Where he is sent by order of a court, judge or magistrate to a workhouse or house of correction; or

d. Where he is removed to another place, within the county, for his trial or discharge in due course of law; or

e. In case of sudden fire or infection or other necessity.

APPENDIX— NEW JERSEY

2A:67-5. Penalty for signing and executing warrant for removal contrary to chapter
If, after such commitment mentioned in *section 2A:67-4* of this title, a person shall make out, sign or countersign a warrant for the removal of any person, so committed, contrary to this chapter, he and the officer or person obeying or executing the same shall, for every such offense, forfeit to the person aggrieved the sum of $500 to be recovered in a civil action.

2A:67-6. Sending citizen as prisoner out of state for offense committed within state; action for damages; punishment; disqualification; exceptions
For preventing illegal imprisonment of citizens of this State in prisons out of this State, no citizen of this state who is an inhabitant or resident thereof, shall be sent as a prisoner to any place whatsoever out of this State, for any crime or offense committed within this state, and every such imprisonment is hereby declared to be illegal unless such transfer of such person to a place of confinement outside the State is accomplished pursuant to the provisions of any interstate compact approved by the Legislature for such purpose and to which the state is signatory.

If any such citizen shall be so imprisoned, except as provided for herein by compact, he may, for every such imprisonment, maintain, by virtue of this chapter, an action at law in the Superior Court for the damages sustained thereby, against the person by whom he shall be so committed, detained, imprisoned, sent prisoner or transported contrary to the true intent and meaning of this chapter, and against any person who shall frame, contrive, write, seal, sign, or countersign any warrant or writing for such commitment, detainer, imprisonment or transportation, or who shall advise, aid or assist in the same or any of them. In such action the plaintiff may recover penal as well as compensatory damages but in any case the damages shall not be less than $1,500.00.

Any person who shall knowingly frame, contrive, write, seal, sign or countersign any warrant for such commitment, detainer, or transportation, or shall so commit, detain, imprison or transport any person contrary to this chapter, or advise, aid or assist therein, shall be fined or imprisoned at hard labor, or both, at the discretion of the court before which the conviction shall be had and shall in addition thereto, from thenceforth be disqualified from holding any office or trust or profit under this State.

Nothing contained in this chapter shall be construed to prevent the sending of a citizen of this State or person at any time resident therein, who has committed any treason, felony or misdemeanor in another state of the United States or in any foreign country, to such other state or foreign country having jurisdiction of such offense, for the purpose of being tried therefor.

2A:67-7. Discharge on criminal charge not extended to discharge on civil process
Nothing in this chapter shall extend to discharge out of prison any person in custody by virtue of a judgment, order or process in any civil cause unless by virtue of the proceedings had for that purpose under authority of this chapter. A discharge, under this chapter, from imprisonment under a criminal charge shall not have the effect or discharging from prison a person imprisoned by virtue of any civil judgment, order or process but the person so discharged shall be kept in custody in such civil cause until discharged by proceedings had for that purpose.

2A:67-8. Warrant in lieu of writ; arrest of person having custody of person detained
A judge of the superior court may, when it shall appear by satisfactory proof that anyone is held in illegal confinement or custody and there is good reason to believe that he will be taken out of the state or suffer some irreparable injury before he can be relieved by the issuance of a habeas corpus, issue a warrant under his hand and seal reciting the facts and directed to any sheriff, constable or other person, commanding him to take the prisoner and forthwith bring him before the court to be dealt with according to law.

If the proof shall also be sufficient to justify an arrest of the person having the prisoner in his custody, as for a criminal offense committed in the taking or detaining of the prisoner, the warrant may also contain an order for the arrest of such person for such offense.

2A:67-9. Service of warrant; return
Any officer or person to whom the warrant mentioned in *section 2A:67-8* of this title shall be directed shall execute the same by bringing the prisoner named therein, and the person who detains him, if so commanded by the warrant, before the court or judge issuing the same.

Thereupon the person detaining such prisoner shall make a return in like manner and the like proceedings shall be had as if a writ of habeas corpus had been issued in the first instance.

2A:67-10. Proceedings against person detaining prisoner
If the person having the prisoner in his custody shall be brought before the superior court, as for a criminal offense, he shall be examined, committed, bailed or discharged in like manner as in other criminal cases like nature.

2A:67-11. Limitation of action for offenses against chapter
No person shall be liable to an action for any offense against this chapter unless the action is commenced against such person so offending within 2 years after the offense is committed; but if the person aggrieved shall be in prison, by reason of such wrongful act, then within 2 years after the decease of such party while in prison or his deliverance out of prison whichever shall happen first.

2A:67-12. Witnesses, production of prisoners or inmates as
Upon the issuance of a writ by any court of competent jurisdiction of the United States or of another state, requiring the production before it of any prisoner or inmate of a penal or correctional institution in the state of New Jersey, as a witness in a criminal case or for prosecution as a defendant charged with crime, the keeper or person in charge of such institution, with the consent and approval of the attorney general, upon such conditions as the attorney general shall prescribe, shall produce or cause to be produced the inmate or prisoner according to the requirements of said writ. The attorney general shall require the return of the prisoner or inmate to the institution from which taken, immediately upon the conclusion of such prosecution or testimony, and shall require the authorities of the demanding jurisdiction to pay or indemnify the keeper or person in charge of such institution for all expenses incurred. He shall decline to honor such writs when in his opinion the same would not be in the furtherance of justice.

Article 2. Persons Entitled to Writ

2A:67-13. Who may prosecute writ
Except as provided in *N.J.S. 2A:67-14*, a person may prosecute a writ of habeas corpus, in accordance with this chapter, to inquire into the cause of the person's imprisonment or restraint, if the person is:

a. committed, detained, confined, or restrained of liberty, within this state, for a criminal or supposed criminal matter;

b. in custody by virtue of civil process issued out of a court in this State;

c. committed, detained, confined, or restrained of liberty, within the State, under any pretense;

d. in confinement on a charge of a criminal offense, which is of a bailable nature, for the purpose of posting bail; or

e. confined in a psychiatric facility, for the purpose of determining whether the person is in need of commitment to treatment.

f. (Deleted by amendment, P.L. 2013, c. 103)

g. (Deleted by amendment, P.L. 2013, c. 103)

h. (Deleted by amendment, P.L. 2013, c. 103)

If sufficient cause appears, the complaint may be filed and the writ may be prosecuted by another on behalf of the person entitled to prosecute the writ.

2A:67-14. Who may not prosecute writ
The persons hereinafter specified shall not be entitled to prosecute writ of habeas corpus:

a. Any person committed or restrained of his liberty by virtue of any process issued by any court of the United States, or any judge thereof, in cases where such court or judge has or shall have acquired exclusive jurisdiction.

b. Any person committed or restrained of his liberty by virtue of a final judgment of a competent tribunal of civil or criminal jurisdiction or by virtue of any process issued pursuant thereto, but no order of commitment for an alleged contempt, or upon contempt proceedings, to enforce the rights or remedies of a party or any process issued upon such order shall be deemed a final judgment or a process issued pursuant to a final judgment within the meaning of this section.

c. Any person in custody or restrained of his liberty for any capital crime plainly and specially expressed in the warrant or commitment, unless the judge to whom the application is made, as an act of discretion, shall direct the issuance of the writ.

d. Any person in custody or restrained of his liberty on any civil process who does not show either that he has, prior to applying for the writ, exhausted the other remedies available to him in the courts of this state to secure his release or that such remedies are or will be ineffective to protect his rights.

Article 3. Application for Writ; Issuance; Service

2A:67-15. Power and authority to issue writ
The power and authority to issue writs of habeas corpus shall be and reside in:

a. The superior court and each judge thereof.

b. Each county judge, who shall have concurrent jurisdiction in his county with the judges of the superior court to grant such writ in all criminal cases where a person may be confined in prison or detained in custody, and to hear and determine the same in like manner as though the application had been made before a judge of the superior court.

2A:67-16. Application by complaint; contempts; verification

Application for the writ shall be made, by complaint, either by the party for whose relief it is intended or by some person in his behalf, and shall be duly verified. The complaint shall allege (a) the facts concerning the commitment, confinement or restraint of the person for whose relief the action has been instituted; (b) the place of such confinement or restraint; (c) the name of the person who has custody over him or by whom he is confined or restrained; (d) the cause or pretense of such confinement or restraint, if known; and (e) if the confinement or restraint is alleged to be illegal, in what the alleged illegality consists.

2A:67-17. Issuance of writ; contents

The judge to whom the application is made shall grant such writ without delay or issue an order directing the defendant named in the complaint to show cause why the writ should not be granted, unless it appears from the complaint or otherwise that the applicant or person confined or restrained is not entitled thereto.

The writ or order to show cause shall be directed to the person by whom such party is confined or restrained in his liberty. It shall be returned within 3 days unless for good cause additional time, not exceeding 20 days, is allowed.

If the judge shall have reason to believe that the person confined or restrained may be removed from the state, or otherwise suffer irreparable injury, he may direct that the writ be made returnable and the person, confined or restrained, produced before the court forthwith.

If the prisoner shall be in the custody of a public officer, the judge may require that a bond be given in such amount as the judge may fix with sufficient surety and conditioned that the prisoner will not escape either in going to or returning from the place to which he is to be taken pursuant to the writ.

Except in proceedings under subsection g. of *section 2A:67-13*, the writ shall require the defendant to produce, in court, the party detained either upon the return to the writ or at the hearing after notice of the time and place thereof, unless the applicant, in writing, waives such production, or the only questions presented are issues of law; and may require such production in any case.

2A:67-18. Defect of form not cause for disobedience of writ

Writs of habeas corpus shall not be disobeyed for any defect of form.

2A:67-19. Service of writ

A writ of habeas corpus issued under this chapter may be served by delivering it to the person to whom it is directed, together with a copy of the complaint.

If the person to whom the writ is directed cannot be found, then the writ may be served by leaving it, together with a copy of the complaint, at the jail or other place in which the prisoner may be confined, with an under officer or other person having charge of the prisoner at the time.

If the person to whom the writ is directed conceals himself or refuses admittance, then the writ may be served by affixing it, together with a copy of the complaint, in some conspicuous place on the outside, either of his dwelling house or of the place where the party is confined.

Except when the writ is issued on application of the attorney general, county prosecutor or on the court's own motion, no service of a writ requiring the production of the person confined or restrained with the return shall be valid upon a sheriff, keeper of the jail or other public officer, unless the party serving the writ shall pay or tender to the officer, in whose custody the prisoner shall be, his fees and charges, allowed by law, for bringing the prisoner to and returning him from the place to which he is to be taken pursuant to the writ, and shall also deliver to the officer such bond, if any, as the court may have directed when authorizing the issuance of the writ. If the prisoner shall be discharged, the officer shall repay the money so paid to him for the charges of carrying back such prisoner.

No service on any other person shall be valid unless the party serving the writ shall pay or tender to such person the charges, if any, required by the court or judge issuing the writ and set forth therein.

Article 4. Return of Writ and Proceedings Thereunder

2A:67-20. Return
Every public officer upon whom the writ shall be duly served, whether the writ be directed to him or not, and every other person to whom the writ shall be directed and upon whom it shall be duly served, shall make a return to the writ as required thereby. The return to the writ may be made without producing in court the person detained or restrained, unless the writ requires such production.

2A:67-21. Excuse for failure to produce person detained as required
The defendant shall be excused for failure to comply with a command in the writ to produce the person detained, and the hearing may proceed without such production, if (a) the applicant, in writing, has waived such production, or (b) the court shall be satisfied that the person detained cannot be brought into court without danger to himself because of sickness or infirmity.

2A:67-22. Contents of return; verification
The return shall set forth, fully and explicitly, whether the defendant has or has not the party in his power or custody or under his restraint and, if he has, the authority and true cause of the confinement or restraint.

If a party is detained by virtue of any writ, warrant or other written authority, a copy thereof shall be annexed to the return.

If the party, upon whom the writ shall have been served, shall have had the party in his power or custody or under his restraint, but shall have transferred such custody or restraint to another, the return shall set forth fully the facts relating thereto.

The return shall be verified unless the same is made by a public officer in his official capacity.

2A:67-23. Effect of return; answer thereto
The allegations of the return, if not controverted, shall be accepted as true except to the extent that the judge finds from the evidence that they are not true.

At or before the time of hearing, the plaintiff or any other party in interest may file an answer to the return, which shall be verified, denying any of the facts set forth in the return or alleging any other material facts.

2A:67-24. Arrest for failure to produce prisoner or make return; commitment
If the person upon whom the writ shall have been duly served refuses or neglects to produce the person

named in the writ, or to make a full and explicit return to the writ, as required, and no sufficient cause is shown for such refusal or neglect, the court or judge before whom the writ has been made returnable, upon due proof of the service of the writ, shall forthwith initiate contempt proceedings against such person by issuing an order of arrest against him directed to the sheriff of any county commanding him forthwith to apprehend such person and bring him before such court or judge. Such person shall be committed to the county jail until he shall make return and comply with any order that may be made by the court or judge relative to the party confined or restrained. If the order of arrest is against the sheriff, it may be directed to any other person to be designated therein who shall have full power to execute the same, and the sheriff, when brought before the court or judge, may be committed to the jail of any county other than his own.

2A:67-25. Order to enforce production of prisoner
When an order of arrest is issued against a defendant and the person named in the writ or order has not been produced as required, the court or judge issuing such order of arrest may also issue an order to the sheriff or other person designated therein, commanding him to bring forthwith before such court or judge the person named in the writ for production.

2A:67-26. Custody pending determination
When a person is produced before the court in habeas corpus proceedings, the judge may, until judgment is given, commit such person to the custody of the sheriff or place him in such care or under such custody as the circumstances of the case may require.

Article 5. Hearing Judgment

2A:67-27. Time of hearing; notice
When the writ is returned, the court may hold the hearing immediately, unless the validity of a detention on any civil process, or the mental capacity of the party is to be determined, and may, in any case, set a date for the hearing, which shall be not more than five days after the return of the writ unless for good cause additional time is allowed.

Notice of the time and place set for a later hearing shall be served at least two days before the hearing or earlier, as the court may order, by the applicant upon the defendant, and (a) if the party is in custody on any criminal matter, upon the county prosecutor of the county in which the alleged offense was committed, or (b) if the party is in custody on any civil process, upon each person having as interest in continuing the confinement or restraint or upon the party's attorney, or (c) if the party is in custody of any psychiatric facility or other institution, upon the person or persons whose application was the basis for commitment to the facility or institution, and upon the medical director or other head officer of the facility or institution.

2A:67-28. Hearing; jury
In all cases in which the mental capacity of the party is to be determined, the testimony shall be taken orally and the judge may hear the matter without a jury or may direct that the action be tried by a jury called from the general panel or, if not available, by a jury specially summoned as in other actions.

In all other cases, the judge may hear the matter summarily on the complaint, return and answer to the return, or require that testimony be offered orally and, on its own motion, may summon witnesses and require any person to produce documents, records, or other writings.

In a proceeding under subsection d. of N.J.S. 2A:67-13, the judge may take testimony concerning the truth of affidavits and proofs upon which the order for process was made and process issued.

2A:67-29. Judgment

In any proceeding under subsection a., b., or c. of N.J.S. 2A:67-13, if no cause is shown for the imprisonment or restraint or for the continuation thereof, the judge shall discharge the party from the confinement or restraint. If the party is not entitled to a discharge and is not bailed, the party shall be remanded by the judge to the custody or placed under the restraint from which the party was taken, so long as custody or restraint is lawful. If the custody or restraint is not lawful, the judge shall commit the party to the custody of the officer or person lawfully entitled thereto.

In any proceedings under subsection a., b., c., or d., of N.J.S. 2A:67-13, if it appears that the person is entitled to be bailed, the judge shall discharge the person immediately, upon taking a secured or bonded recognizance in an amount as the judge may approve for the person's appearance, as the circumstances may require, and the judge shall then certify the writ with the return and the recognizance to the court where the appearance is to be made.

In any proceeding under subsection d. of N.J.S. 2A:67-13, the judge shall discharge the party in custody if the process was improperly or improvidently issued.

In any proceeding under subsection e. of N.J.S. 2A:67-13, the person shall not be discharged unless found not to be dangerous to self or dangerous to others or to property, either by the judge, if the hearing is held without a jury, or by unanimous verdict of the jury.

No person shall be entitled to a discharge because of any informality or insufficiency in the original arrest or commitment.

2A:67-30. Enforcement of court's order

Article 6. Effect of Discharge; Penalties for Offenses in Connection with Writ

2A:67-31. Reimprisonment for same cause of person discharged upon writ; exceptions

No person who has been discharged by the order of such court or judge upon a writ of habeas corpus issued pursuant to the provisions of this chapter shall again be imprisoned, restrained or kept in custody for the same cause, but it shall not be deemed the same cause:

a. If he shall have been discharged from a commitment on a criminal charge and is afterwards committed for the same offense by the legal order or process of the court wherein he shall be bound by recognizance to appear or in which he shall be indicted or convicted for the same offense; or,

b. If after a discharge for defect of proof or for any material defect in the commitment, in a criminal case, the prisoner is again arrested on sufficient proof, and committed by legal process for the same offense; or

c. If, in a civil action, the party has been discharged for any illegality in the judgment or process hereinbefore specified, and is afterwards imprisoned by legal process for the same cause of action; or

d. If, in a civil action, he shall have been discharged from commitment on mesne process and shall afterwards be committed on execution in the same cause or on mesne process in any other cause, after such first suit shall have been discontinued.

2A:67-32. Penalty for reimprisoning; aiding or assisting; misdemeanor

Any person, either solely or as a member of any court, or in the execution of any order, judgment or process, who shall knowingly recommit, imprison or restrain of his liberty, or cause to be recommitted, imprisoned or restrained of his liberty, for the same cause, except as provided by *section 2A:67-31* of this title, any person so discharged or who shall knowingly aid or assist therein shall forfeit to the party aggrieved the sum of $1400, to be recovered in an action at law in the superior court and shall be guilty of a misdemeanor.

2A:67-33. Eluding writ by removing or transferring prisoner to other custody; misdemeanor

Any person having in his custody or under his power any party for whose relief a writ of habeas corpus shall have been duly issued pursuant to the provisions of this chapter and who with intent to elude the service of such writ or to avoid the effect thereof shall transfer the prisoner to the custody or place him under the power or control of another or conceal him or change the place of his confinement or who shall knowingly aid or assist therein, shall be deemed guilty of a misdemeanor.

2A:67-34. Neglect or refusal to obey writ; forfeiture; misdemeanor

If any officer or other person shall neglect or refuse to make the required returns or to produce the prisoner according to the command of the writ, every such officer and person so neglecting shall forfeit and pay to the party aggrieved the sum of $500 and shall be guilty of a misdemeanor.

2A:67-35. Misdemeanor; punishment

Every person convicted of a misdemeanor under *section 2A:67-32, 2A:67-33* or *2A:67-34* of this title, shall be punished by fine or imprisonment, or both, at the discretion of the court in which he shall be convicted but such fine shall not exceed $1,000 nor such imprisonment 6 months.

Article 7. Appeals

2A:67-36. Appeal to appellate division of superior court

In all proceedings involving the writ of habeas corpus before a judge of the superior court, the prisoner may, after final decision by such judge, appeal therefrom to the appellate division of the superior court, if the imprisonment is for an alleged crime, and the decision is against the right of the prisoner to a discharge, and in any other case either party may so appeal.

If a discharge, which is appealable, has been awarded, and an appeal is taken the discharge shall not be stayed on such appeal.

Current with laws effective through L.2014, c. 22 and J.R. No. 3.

NEW MEXICO

New Mexico Statutes Annotated
Chapter 44. Miscellaneous Civil Law Matters
Article 1. Habeas Corpus

§44-1-1. Who may obtain writ
Every person imprisoned or otherwise restrained of his liberty, except in the cases in the following section specified, may prosecute a writ of habeas corpus, according to the provisions of this chapter, to obtain relief from such imprisonment or restraint, if it proves to be unlawful.

§44-1-2. Detention under judgment or execution; contempt
The following persons are not entitled to prosecute such writ: persons committed or detained by virtue of the final judgment, conviction or decree of any competent tribunal or by virtue of an execution issued upon such judgment or decree; but no order of commitment for any alleged contempt, or upon proceedings as for contempt, to enforce the rights or remedies of any party shall be deemed a judgment, conviction or decree within the meaning of this section; nor shall any attachment or other process issued upon any such order be deemed an execution within the meaning of this section.

§44-1-3. Application for writ; to whom made; petition; signature; verification
Application for such writ shall be made by petition to any judge of the supreme court, signed and verified either by the party for whose relief it is intended, or by some person in his behalf, as follows: to the supreme or district court or to any judge thereof, being within the district where the prisoner is detained; or if there is no such officer within such district, or if he be absent or from any cause is incapable of acting, or has refused to grant such writ, then to some officer having such authority residing in any other district.

§44-1-4. Application to officer residing outside district of detention; jurisdictional proof required
Whenever application for any such writ is made to any officer not residing within the district where the prisoner is detained, he shall require proof by oath of the party applying, or by other sufficient evidence, that there is no officer in such district authorized to grant the writ; or if there is one, that he is absent or has refused to grant such writ; or for some cause, to be specially set forth, is incapable of acting, and if such proof is not produced, the application shall be denied.

§44-1-5. Petition for writ; allegations; exhibits
The petition shall state in substance:

A. that the person in whose behalf the writ is applied for is imprisoned or restrained of his liberty, the officer or person by whom he is so confined or restrained and the place where, naming both parties, if their names are known, or describing them if they are not,

B. that such person is not committed or detained by virtue of any process, judgment, decree or execution, specified in *Section 44-1-2 NMSA* 1978;

C. the cause or pretense of such confinement or restraint, according to the knowledge or belief of the party verifying the petition;

D. if the confinement or restraint is by virtue of any warrant, or order, or process, a copy thereof shall be annexed, or it shall be averred that by reason of such prisoner being removed or concealed before application, a demand of such copy could not be made, or that such demand was made, and the legal fees therefor tendered to the officer or person having such prisoner in his custody, and that such copy was refused;

E. if the imprisonment is alleged to be illegal, the petition shall state in what the illegality consists.

§44-1-6. Form of writ
Every writ of habeas corpus issued under the provisions of this chapter shall be substantially in the following form:

> The state of New Mexico to the sheriff of, etc., or to A.B.:
>
> You are hereby commanded to have the body of C.D., by you imprisoned and detained, as it is said, together with the time and cause of such imprisonment and detention, by whatever name the said C.D. shall be called or charged, before E.F., judge of the district court, as etc. (or immediately after the receipt of this writ), to do, and receive what shall then and there be considered concerning the said C.D., and have you then and there this writ.
>
> Witness, etc.

44-1-7. Defects of form· names of prisoner and custodian
Such writ of habeas corpus shall not be disobeyed for any defect of form. It is sufficient:

A. if the person having the custody of the prisoner is designated either by his name or office, if he has any, or by his own name, or if both such names are unknown or uncertain, he may be described by any assumed appellation, and anyone who may be served with the writ, shall be deemed to be the person to whom it is directed, although it is directed to him by a wrong name or description, or to another person;

B. if the person who is directed to be produced is designated by name, or if his name is uncertain or unknown, he may be described in any other way so as to designate the person intended.

§44-1-8. Wrongful refusal of writ; forfeiture
If any officer herein authorized to grant writs of habeas corpus willfully refuses to grant such writ when legally applied for, he shall forfeit for any such offense, to the party aggrieved, one thousand dollars ($1,000).

§44-1-9. Return; contents; exhibits; signature; verification
The person upon whom such writ is duly served shall state in his return plainly and unequivocally:

A. Whether he has or has not the party in his custody, or control, or under his restraint, and, if he has not, whether he has had the party in his custody, or under his control or restraint, at any and what time prior or subsequent to the date of the writ;

B. if he has the party in his custody or control, or under his restraint, the authority and true cause of such imprisonment or restraint, setting forth the same at large;

c. if the party is detained by virtue of any writ, warrant or other written authority, a copy thereof shall be annexed to the return, and the original shall be produced and exhibited on the return of the writ to the officer before whom the same is returnable;

D. if the person upon whom such writ is served has had the party in his control or custody, or under his restraint, at any time prior or subsequent to the date of the writ, but has transferred such custody or restraint to another, the return shall state particularly to whom, at what time, for what cause and by what authority such transfer took place. The return shall be signed by the person making the same, and except where such person is a sworn public officer and makes his return in his official capacity, it shall be verified by oath.

§44-1-10. Petitioner to be produced; exception
The person or officer on whom the writ is served shall bring the body of the person in his custody, according to the command of such writ, except in the case of the sickness of such person, as hereinafter provided in this chapter.

§44-1-11. Attachment for disobedience of writ; issuance; to whom directed; proceedings
If the person upon whom such writ is duly served refuses or neglects to obey the same, by producing the party named in such writ, and making a full and explicit return to every such writ within the time required by the provisions of this chapter, and no sufficient excuse is shown for such refusal or neglect, the officer before whom such writ is returnable, upon due proof of the service thereof, shall forthwith issue an attachment against such person, directed to the sheriff of any county in this state, and commanding him forthwith to apprehend such person and to bring him immediately before such officer, and on such person being so brought he shall be committed to close custody in the jail of the county in which such officer is, until he makes return to such writ and complies with any order that may be made by such officer in relation to the person for whose relief such writ was issued.

§44-1-12. Attachment against sheriff; place of detention
If a sheriff neglects to return such writ the attachment may be directed to any person designated therein, who shall have full power to execute the same, and such sheriff upon being brought up may be committed to the jail of any county other than his own.

§44-1-13. Precept for production of petitioner by officer executing attachment
The officer by whom any such attachment is issued may also at the same time or afterward issue a precept to the sheriff, or other person to whom such attachment was directed, commanding him to bring forthwith before such officers the party for whose benefit such writ was allowed, who shall thereafter remain in the custody of such sheriff or person until he is discharged, bailed or remanded, as such officer directs.

§44-1-14. Bearing
The officer before whom such party is brought on such writ shall immediately after the return thereof, proceed to examine into the facts contained in such return, and into the cause of the confinement or restraint of such party, whether the same was before commitment for any criminal charge or not.

§44-1-15. When petitioner will be discharged
If no legal cause is shown for such imprisonment or restraint, or for the continuation thereof, such officer shall discharge such party from the custody or restraint under which he is held.

§44-1-16. When petitioner will be remanded to custody
The officer shall forthwith remand such party, if it appears that he is detained in custody, either:

A. by virtue of process issued by any court or judge of the United States in a case where such court or judge has exclusive jurisdiction; or

B. by virtue of the final judgment or decree of any competent court, or of any execution issued upon such judgment or decree; or

C. for any contempt, specially and plainly charged in the commitment by some court, officer or body having authority to commit for the contempt so charged; and

D. that the time during which such party may be legally detained has not expired.

§44-1-17. Causes for discharge of petitioner in custody under civil process
If it appears on the return that the prisoner is in custody by virtue of civil process of any court legally constituted, or issued by an officer in the course of judicial proceedings before him, authorized by law, such prisoner can only be discharged in one of the following cases:

A. when the jurisdiction of such court or officer has been exceeded either as to matter, place, sum or person;

B. where, though the original imprisonment was lawful, yet by some act, omission or event which has taken place afterward, the party is entitled to be discharged;

C. where the process is defective in some matter of substance required by law rendering such process void;

D. where the process, though in proper form, has been issued in a case not allowed by law;

E. where the person having the custody of the prisoner under such process is not the person empowered by law to detain him; or

F. where the process is not authorized by any judgment, order or decree of any court, nor by any provision of law.

§44-1-18. Legality or justice of judgment or execution
But no officer on the return of any habeas corpus can inquire into the legality or justice of any judgment, decree or execution specified in *Section 44-1-16 NMSA* 1978.

§44-1-19. Petitioner legally committed or guilty of offense; release on bail
If it appears that the party has been legally committed for any criminal offense, or if he appears, by the testimony offered with the return upon the hearing thereof, to be guilty of such an offense, although the commitment is irregular, the officer before whom such party is brought shall proceed to let such party to bail, if the case be bailable and good bail is offered, or if not, shall forthwith remand such party.

§44-1-20. Decision in other cases
In other cases the party shall be placed in custody of the person legally entitled thereto, or if no one is so entitled, he shall be discharged.

§44-1-21. Custody of petitioner pending decision
Until judgment is given upon the action, the officer before whom such party is brought may either commit such party to the custody of the sheriff of the county in which such officer is, or place him in such care or under such custody as his age and other circumstances require.

§44-1-22. Notice of hearing
In criminal cases, notice of the time and place at which the writ is made returnable shall be given to the district attorney, if he is within the county; in other cases like notice shall be given to any person interested in continuing the custody or restraint of the party seeking the aid of said writ.

§44-1-23. Bail proceedings; authorization of habeas corpus; committing magistrate's proceedings to be reviewed
Hereafter all persons to whom bail has been denied or who are confined for failure to give bail, may have the benefit of a writ of habeas corpus for the purpose of being admitted to bail or having the bail reduced, and the court or judge shall, upon habeas corpus, review the proceedings or action of a committing magistrate.

§44-1-24. Certiorari to committing magistrate; transcript; examination of case de novo; decision
When an application is made before any authority authorized by law to issue such writs of habeas corpus it shall be the duty of such officers to issue a writ of certiorari commanding the committing magistrate forthwith to send to said officers a full and complete transcript of all his proceedings had thereof, and the said officer upon the return of such writ shall proceed to examine the case de novo and either commit to jail, discharge or recognize such person to appear before the district court as the case may require.

§44-1-25. Pleading by petitioner after return; summary hearing
The party brought before any such officer on the return of any writ of habeas corpus, may deny any of the material facts set forth in the return, or allege any fact to show, either that his imprisonment or detention is unlawful, or that he is entitled to his discharge, which allegations or denials shall be on oath; and thereupon such officer shall proceed in a summary way to hear such allegations and proofs as are legally produced in support of such imprisonment or detention or against the same, and to dispose of such party as justice requires.

§44-1-26. Procedure when petitioner is sick or infirm
Whenever from the sickness or infirmity of the person directed to be produced by any writ of habeas corpus such person cannot, without danger, be brought before the officer before whom the suit is made returnable, the party in whose custody he is may state the fact in his return to the writ, verifying the same by his oath; and if such officer is satisfied of the truth of such allegation and the return is otherwise sufficient, he shall proceed to decide upon such return and to dispose of the matter; and if it appears that the person detained is illegally imprisoned, confined or restrained of his liberty, the officer shall order those having such person in their custody to discharge him forthwith; and if it appears that such person is legally detained, imprisoned and confined, and is not entitled to be bailed, such officer shall dismiss the proceedings.

§44-1-27. Disobedience of order for discharge; attachment; damages recoverable
Obedience to any order for the discharge of any prisoner, granted pursuant to the provisions of this chapter, may be enforced by the officer issuing such writ or granting such order, by attachment, in the same manner as herein provided for a neglect to make a return to a writ of habeas corpus, and the person guilty of such disobedience shall forfeit to the party aggrieved, one thousand dollars [($1,000)] in addition to any special damages such party may have sustained.

§44-1-28. Detention for same offense after discharge on habeas corpus prohibited; when permissible
No person who has been discharged upon a habeas corpus shall be again imprisoned or restrained for the same cause, unless indicted therefor, convicted thereof or committed for want of bail by some court of

record having jurisdiction of the cause; or unless after a discharge for a defect of proof or for some material defect in the commitment in a criminal case, he is again arrested on sufficient proof and committed by legal process.

§44-1-29. Concealment or transfer of prisoner to avoid writ; forfeiture
If anyone, who has in his custody, or under his control, a person entitled to a writ of habeas corpus, whether a writ has been issued or not, transfers such prisoner to the custody, or places him under the power or control of another person, or conceals him, or changes the place of his confinement, with intent to elude the service of such writ, or to avoid the effect thereof, the person so offending shall forfeit to the party aggrieved thereby the sum of four hundred dollars [($400)], to be recovered in a civil action.

§44-1-30. Detention officer refusing to furnish copies; forfeiture
Any officer, or other person, refusing to deliver a copy of any order, warrant, process or other authority, by which he detains any person, to anyone who demands such copy and tenders the fees thereof, shall forfeit two hundred dollars [($200)] to the person so detained.

§44-1-31. When writ returnable; seal
Every writ of habeas corpus may be made returnable at a day certain, or forthwith, as the case may require, and shall be under the seal of the court.

§44-1-32. Who may serve writ; tender of fees; bond for costs and restoration of prisoner
It can only be served by an elector of this state, and the service thereof shall not be deemed complete unless the party serving the same tenders to the person in whose custody the prisoner is, if such person is a sheriff, constable or marshal, the fees allowed by law for bringing up such prisoner. The officer granting the writ may, in his discretion, require a bond in a penalty not exceeding one thousand dollars [($1,000)], with sufficient sureties, conditioned that the obligators will pay all costs and expenses of the proceeding, and the reasonable charges of restoring the prisoner to the person from whose custody he was taken, if he is remanded. Such bond shall run to the sheriff of the county and be filed in the office of the clerk of the court from which the writ issues.

§44-1-33. Service by delivery to custodian or person to whom writ is directed
Every writ of habeas corpus issued pursuant to this chapter may be served by delivering the same to the person to whom it is directed. If he cannot be found, it may be served by being left at the jail or other place in which the prisoner is confined, with any under officer or other person of proper age having charge for the time of such prisoner.

§44-1-34. Service by posting
If the person on whom the writ ought to be served, conceals himself, or refuses admittance to the party attempting to serve the same, it may be served by affixing the same in some conspicuous place on the outside, either of his dwelling house or of the place where the party is confined.

§44-1-35. Time allowed for making return and producing prisoner
If the writ is returnable at a certain day, such return shall be made, and such prisoner produced at the time and place specified therein; if he is returnable forthwith, and the place is within twenty miles of the place of service, such return shall be made and such prisoner produced within twenty-four hours, and the like time shall be allowed for every additional twenty miles.

§44-1-36. Compelling attendance of prisoner for trial or as witness
Nothing contained in this chapter shall be construed to restrain the power of any court to issue a writ of habeas corpus when necessary to bring before them any prisoner for trial, in any criminal case lawfully pending in the same court, or to bring any prisoner to be examined as a witness in any action or proceeding, civil or criminal, pending in such court, when they think the personal attendance and examination of the witness necessary for the attainment of justice.

§44-1-37. Sheriff's fees for producing prisoner
The sheriff or person who shall be required to bring up a person on habeas corpus, if the person be held by virtue of any legal process directed to such person as an officer, shall be entitled to the same fees and allowances as are allowed to sheriffs for removing prisoners in other cases.

§44-1-38. Federal court proceedings; payment of costs, fees and expenses by state
If the petition for the writ is filed in any federal court, all the reasonably necessary costs, fees and expenses incurred or paid by the respondent shall be paid by the penitentiary of New Mexico. The budget of the penitentiary shall include an item for the anticipated expenses of habeas corpus proceedings. If budgeted funds shall not be sufficient to pay the costs and expenses that will arise, an emergency allowance from the state court fund shall be allowed upon application of the warden of the penitentiary to the state board of finance.

Current through laws of the 2nd
Regular Session of the 51st Legislature (2014), effective May 21, 2014.

NEW YORK

Civil Practice Law and Rules
Chapter Eight. Of the Consolidated Laws
Article 70. Habeas Corpus

§7001. Application of article; special proceeding
Except as otherwise prescribed by statute, the provisions of this article are applicable to common law or statutory writs of habeas corpus and common law writs of certiorari to inquire into detention. A proceeding under this article is a special proceeding.

§7002. Petition
(a) By whom made. A person illegally imprisoned or otherwise restrained in his liberty within the state, or one acting on his behalf or a party in a child abuse proceeding subsequent to an order of the family court, may petition without notice for a writ of habeas corpus to inquire into the cause of such detention and for deliverance. A judge authorized to issue writs of habeas corpus having evidence, in a judicial proceeding before him, that any person is so detained shall, on his own initiative, issue a writ of habeas corpus for the relief of that person.

(b) To whom made. Except as provided in paragraph five of this subdivision, a petition for the writ shall be made to:

1. the supreme court in the judicial district in which the person is detained; or

2. the appellate division in the department in which the person is detained; or

3. any justice of the supreme court; or

4. a county judge being or residing within the county in which the person is detained; where there is no judge within the county capable of issuing the writ, or if all within the county capable of doing so have refused, the petition may be made to a county judge being or residing within an adjoining county.

5. in a city having a population of one million or more inhabitants, a person held as a trial inmate in a city detention institution shall petition for a writ to the supreme court in the county in which the charge for which the inmate is being detained is pending. Such inmate may also petition for a writ to the appellate division in the department in which he is detained or to any justice of the supreme court provided that the writ shall be made returnable before a justice of the supreme court held in the county in which the charge for which the inmate is being detained is pending.

(c) Content. The petition shall be verified and shall state, or shall be accompanied by an affidavit which shall state,

1. that the person in whose behalf the petition is made is detained, naming the person by whom he is detained and the place of detention if they are known, or describing them if they are not known; where the detention is by virtue of a mandate, a copy of it shall be annexed to the petition, or sufficient reason why a copy could not be obtained shall be stated;

2. the cause or pretense of the detention, according to the best knowledge and belief of the petitioner;

3. that a court or judge of the United States does not have exclusive jurisdiction to order him released;

4. if the writ is sought because of an illegal detention, the nature of the illegally;

5. whether any appeal has been taken from any order by virtue of which the person is detained, and, if so, the result;

6. the date, and the court or judge to whom made, of every previous application for the writ, the disposition of each such application and of any appeal taken, and the new facts, if any, presented in the petition that were not presented in any previous application; and

7. if the petition is made to a county judge outside the county in which the person is detained, the facts which authorize such judge to act.

§7003. *When the writ shall be issued*
(a) Generally. The court to whom the petition is made shall issue the writ without delay on any day, or, where the petitioner does not demand production of the person detained or it is clear that there is no disputable issue of fact, order the respondent to show cause why the person detained should not be released. If it appears from the petition or the documents annexed thereto that the person is not illegally detained or that a court or judge of the United States has exclusive jurisdiction to order him released, the petition shall be denied.

(b) Successive petitions for writ. A court is not required to issue a writ of habeas corpus if the legality of the detention has been determined by a court of the state on a prior proceedings for a writ of habeas corpus and the petition presents no ground not theretofore presented and determined and the court is satisfied that the ends of justice will not be served by granting it.

(c) Penalty for violation. For violation of this section in refusing to issue the writ, a judge, or, if the petition was made to a court, each member of the court who assents to the violation, forfeits to the person detained one thousand dollars, to be recovered by an action in his name or in the name of the petitioner to his use.

§7004. Content of writ
(a) For whom issued. The writ shall be issued on behalf of the state, and where issued upon the petition of a private person, it shall show that it was issued upon his relation.

(b) To whom directed. The writ shall be directed to, and the respondent shall be, the person having custody of the person detained.

(c) Before whom returnable. A writ to secure the discharge of a person from a state institution shall be made returnable before a justice of the supreme court or a county judge being or residing within the county in which the person is detained; if there is no such judge it shall be made returnable before the nearest accessible supreme court justice or county judge. In all other cases, the writ shall be made returnable in the county where it was issued, except that where the petition was made to the supreme court or justice may make the writ returnable before any judge authorized to issue it in the county of detention.

(d) When returnable. The writ may be made returnable forthwith or on any day or time certain, as the case requires.

(e) Expenses; undertaking. A court issuing a writ directed to any person other than a public officer may require the petitioner to pay the charges of bringing up the person detained and to deliver an undertaking to the person having him in custody, in an amount fixed by the court, to pay the charges for taking back the person detained if he should be remanded. Service of the writ shall not be complete until such charge is paid or tendered and such undertaking is delivered.

§7005. Service of the writ
A writ of habeas corpus may be served on any day. Service shall be made by delivering the writ and a copy of the petition to the person to whom it is directed. If he cannot with due diligence be found, the writ may be served by leaving it and a copy of the petition with any person who has custody of the person detained at the time. Where the person to whom the writ is directed conceals himself or refuses admittance, the writ may be served by affixing it and a copy of the petition in a conspicuous place on the outside either of his dwelling or of the place where the person is detained and mailing a copy of the writ and the petition to him at such dwelling or place, unless the court which issues the writ determines, for good cause shown, that such mailing shall be dispensed with, or directs service in some other manner which it finds reasonably calculated to give notice to such person of the proceeding. If the person detained is in the custody of a person other than the one to whom the writ is directed, a copy of the writ may be served upon the person having such custody with the same effect as if the writ had been directed to him.

§7006. Obedience to the writ
(a) Generally; defects in form. A person upon whom the writ or a copy thereof is served, whether it is

directed to him or not, shall make a return to it and, if required by it, produce the body of the person detained at the time and place specified, unless the person detained is too sick or infirm to make the required trip. A writ of habeas corpus shall not be disobeyed for defect of form so long as the identity of the person detained may be derived from its contents.

(b) Compelling obedience. If the person upon whom the writ or a copy thereof is served refuses or neglects fully to obey it, without showing sufficient cause, the court before whom the writ is returnable, upon proof of its service, shall forthwith issue a warrant of attachment against him directed to the sheriff in any county in which such person may be found requiring him to be brought before the court issuing the warrant; he may be ordered committed in close custody to the county jail until he complies with the order of the court. Where such person is a sheriff, the warrant shall be directed to a person specifically designated to execute it. Such person shall have power to call to his aid the same assistance as the sheriff in executing the warrant; a sheriff shall be committed to a jail in a county other than his own.

(c) Precept to bring up person detained. A court issuing a warrant of attachment as prescribed in subdivision (b) may at the same time, or thereafter, issue a precept to the person to whom the warrant is directed ordering him immediately to bring before the court the person detained.

§7007. Warrant preceding or accompanying writ
A court authorized to issue a writ of habeas corpus, upon satisfactory proof that a person is wrongfully detained and will be removed from the state or suffer irreparable injury before he can be relieved by habeas corpus, shall issue a warrant of attachment directed to an appropriate officer requiring him immediately to bring the person detained before the court. A writ of habeas corpus directed to the person having custody of the person detained shall also be issued. Where it appears that the detention constitutes a criminal offense, the warrant may order the apprehension of the person responsible for the detention, who shall then be brought before the court issuing the warrant and examined as in a criminal case.

§7008. Return
(a) When filed and served. The return shall consist of an affidavit to be served in the same manner as an answer in a special proceeding and filed at the time and place specified in the writ, or, where the writ is returnable forthwith, within twenty-four hours after its service.

(b) Content. The affidavit shall fully and explicitly state whether the person detained is or has been in the custody of the person to whom the writ is directed, the authority and cause of the detention, whether custody has been transferred to another, and the facts of and authority for any such transfer. A copy of any mandate by virtue of which the person is detained shall be annexed to the affidavit, and the original mandate shall be produced at the hearing; where the mandate has been delivered to the person to whom the person detained was transferred, or a copy of it cannot be obtained, the reason for failure to produce it and the substance of the mandate shall be stated in the affidavit.

7009. Hearing
(a) Notice before hearing. Where the detention is by virtue of a mandate, the court shall not adjudicate the issues in the proceeding until written notice of the time and place of the hearing has been served either personally eight days prior to the hearing, or in any other manner or time as the court may order,

1. where the mandate was issued in a civil cause, upon the person interested in continuing the detention or upon his attorney; or,

2. where a person is detained by order of the family court, or by order of any court while a proceeding affecting him or her is pending in the family court, upon the judge who made the order. In all such proceedings, the court shall be represented by the attorney-general; or,

3. in any other case, upon the district attorney of the county in which the person was detained when the writ was served and upon the district attorney of the county from which he was committed.

(b) Reply to return. The petitioner or the person detained may deny under oath, orally or in writing, any material allegation of the answering affidavits or allege any fact showing that the person detained is entitled to be discharged.

(c) Hearing to be summary. The court shall proceed in a summary manner to hear the evidence produced in support of and against the detention and to dispose of the proceeding as justice requires.

(d) Sickness or infirmity of person detained. Where it is proved to the satisfaction of the court that the person detained is too sick or infirm to be brought to the appointed place, the hearing may be held without his presence, may be adjourned, or may be held at the place where the prisoner is detained.

(e) Custody during proceeding. Pending final disposition, the court may place the person detained in custody or parole him or admit him to bail as justice requires.

§7010. Determination of proceeding
(a) Discharge. If the person is illegally detained a final judgment shall be directed discharging him forthwith. No person detained shall be discharged for a defect in the form of the commitment, or because the person detaining him is not entitled to do so if another person is so entitled. A final judgment to discharge a person may be enforced by the court issuing the order by attachment in the manner prescribed in *subdivision (b) of section 7006*.

(b) Bail. If the person detained has been admitted to bail but the amount fixed is so excessive as to constitute an abuse of discretion, and he is not ordered discharged, the court shall direct a final judgment reducing bail to a proper amount. If the person detained has been denied bail, and he is not ordered discharged, the court shall direct a final judgment admitting him to bail forthwith, if he is entitled to be admitted to bail as a matter of right, or if it appears that the denial of bail constituted an abuse of discretion. Such judgment must fix the amount of bail, specify the time and place at which the person detained is required to appear, and order his release upon bail being given in accordance with the criminal procedure law.

(c) Remand. If the person detained is not ordered discharged and not admitted to bail, a final judgment shall be directed dismissing the proceeding, and, if he was actually produced in court, remanding him to the detention from which he was taken, unless the person then detaining him was not entitled to do so, in which case he shall be remanded to proper detention.

§7011. Appeal
An appeal may be taken from a judgment refusing to grant a writ of habeas corpus or refusing an order to show cause issued under *subdivision (a) of section 7003*, or from a judgment made upon the return of such a writ or order to show cause. A person to whom notice is given pursuant to *subdivision (a) of section 7009* is a party for purposes of appeal. The attorney-general may appeal in the name of the state in any case where a district attorney might do so. Where an appeal from a judgment admitting a person to bail is taken by the state, his release shall not be stayed thereby.

§7012. Redetention after discharge
A person discharged upon the return of a writ of habeas corpus shall not be detained from the same cause, except by virtue of a subsequent lawful mandate. Current through L.2014, chapters 1 to 327.

NORTH CAROLINA

North Carolina General Statutes Annotated
Chapter 17. Habeas Corpus
Article 1. Constitutional Provisions

§17-1. Remedy without delay for restraint of liberty
Every person restrained of his liberty is entitled to a remedy to inquire into the lawfulness thereof, and to remove the same, if unlawful; and such remedy ought not be denied or delayed.

§17-2. Habeas corpus not to be suspended
The privileges of the writ of habeas corpus shall not be suspended.

§17-3. Who may prosecute writ
Every person imprisoned or restrained of his liberty within this State, for any criminal or supposed criminal matter, or on any pretense whatsoever, except in cases specified in *G.S. 17-4*, may prosecute a writ of habeas corpus, according to the provisions of this Chapter, to inquire into the cause of such imprisonment or restraint, and, if illegal, to be delivered therefrom.

§17-4. When application denied
Application to prosecute the writ shall be denied in the following cases:

(1) Where the persons are committed or detained by virtue of process issued by a court of the United States, or a judge thereof, in cases where such courts or judges have exclusive jurisdiction under the laws of the United States, or have acquired exclusive jurisdiction by the commencement of suits or decree.

(2) Where persons are committed or detained by virtue of the final order, judgment or decree of a competent tribunal of civil or criminal jurisdiction, or by virtue of an execution issued upon such final order, judgment or decree.

(3) Where any person has willfully neglected, for the space of two whole sessions after his imprisonment, to apply for the writ to the superior court of the county in which he may be imprisoned, such person shall not have a habeas corpus in vacation time for his enlargement.

(4) Where no probable ground for relief is shown in the application.

§17-5. By whom application is made
Application for the writ may be made either by the party for whose relief it is intended or by any person in his behalf.

§17-6. To judge of appellate division or superior court in writing
Application for the writ shall be made in writing, signed by the applicant—

(1) To any one of the justices or judges of the appellate division.

(2) To any one of the superior court judges, either during a session or in vacation.

§17-7. Contents of application
The application must state, in substance, as follows:

(1) That the party, in whose behalf the writ is applied for, is imprisoned or restrained of his liberty, the place where, and the officer or person by whom he is imprisoned or restrained, naming both parties, if their names are known, or describing them if they are not known.

(2) The cause or pretense of such imprisonment or restraint, according to the knowledge or belief of the applicant.

(3) If the imprisonment is by virtue of any warrant or other process, a copy thereof shall be annexed, or it shall be made to appear that a copy thereof has been demanded and refused, or that for some sufficient reason a demand for such copy could not be made.

(4) If the imprisonment or restraint is alleged to be illegal, the application must state in what the alleged illegality consists; and that the legality of the imprisonment or restraint has not been already adjudged, upon a prior writ of habeas corpus, to the knowledge or belief of the applicant.

(5) The facts set forth in the application must be verified by the oath of the applicant, or by that of some other credible witness, which oath may be administered by any person authorized by law to take affidavits.

§17-8. Issuance of writ without application
When the appellate division or superior court division, or any judge of either division, has evidence from any judicial proceeding before such court or judge that any person within this State is illegally imprisoned or restrained of his liberty, it is the duty of said court or judge to issue a writ of habeas corpus for his relief, although no application be made for such writ.

§17-9. Writ granted without delay
Any court or judge empowered to grant the writ, to whom such applications may be presented, shall grant the writ without delay, unless it appear from the application itself or from the documents annexed that the person applying or for whose benefit it is intended is, by this Chapter, prohibited from prosecuting the writ.

§17-10. Penalty for refusal to grant
If any judge authorized by this Chapter to grant writs of habeas corpus refuses to grant such writ when legally applied for, every such judge shall forfeit to the party aggrieved two thousand five hundred dollars ($2,500).

§17-11. Sufficiency of writ; defects of form immaterial
No writ of habeas corpus shall be disobeyed on account of any defect of form. It shall be sufficient—

(1) If the person having the custody of the party imprisoned or restrained be designated either by his name of office, if he have any, or by his own name, or, if both such names be unknown or uncertain, he may be described by an assumed appellation, and anyone who may be served with the writ shall be deemed the person to whom it is directed, although it may be directed to him by a wrong name, or description, or to another person.

(2) If the person who is directed to be produced be designated by name, or if his name be uncertain or unknown, he may be described by an assumed appellation or in any other way, so as to designate the person intended.

§17-12. Service of writ
The writ of habeas corpus may be served by any qualified elector of this State thereto authorized by the court or judge allowing the same. It may be served by delivering the writ, or a copy thereof, to the person to whom it is directed; or, if such person cannot be found, by leaving it, or a copy, at the jail, or other place in which the party for whose relief it is intended is confined, with some under officer or other person of proper age; or, if none such can be found, or if the person attempting to serve the writ be refused admittance, by affixing a copy thereof in some conspicuous place on the outside, either of the dwelling house of the party to whom the writ is directed or of the place where the party is confined for whose relief it is sued out.

§17-13. When writ returnable
Writs of habeas corpus may be made returnable at a certain time, or forthwith, as the case may require. If the writ be returnable at a certain time, such return shall be made and the party shall be produced at the time and place specified therein.

§17-14. Contents of return; verification
The person or officer on whom the writ is served must make a return thereto in writing, and, except where such person is a sworn public officer and makes his return in his official capacity, it must be verified by his oath. The return must state plainly and unequivocally—

(1) Whether he has or has not the party in his custody or under his power or restraint.

(2) If he has the party in his custody or power, or under his restraint, the authority and the cause of such imprisonment or restraint, setting forth the same at large.

(3) If the party is detained by virtue of any writ, warrant, or other written authority, a copy thereof shall be annexed to the return; and the original shall be produced and exhibited on the return of the writ to the court or judge before whom the same is returnable.

(4) If the person or officer upon whom such writ is served has had the party in his power or custody, or under his restraint, at any time prior or subsequent to the date of the writ, but has transferred such custody or restraint to another, the return shall state particularly to whom, at what time, for what cause and by what authority such transfer took place.

§17-15. Production of body if required
If the writ requires it, the officer or person on whom the same has been served shall also produce the body of the party in his custody or power, according to the command of the writ, except in the case of the sickness of such party, as hereinafter provided.

§17-16. Attachment for failure to obey

If the person or officer on whom any writ of habeas corpus has been duly served refuses or neglects to obey the same, by producing the body of the party named or described therein, and by making a full and explicit return thereto, within the time required, and no sufficient excuse is shown for such refusal or neglect, it is the duty of the court or judge before whom the writ has been made returnable, upon due proof of the service thereof, forthwith to issue an attachment against such person or officer, directed to the sheriff of any county within this State, and commanding him forthwith to apprehend such person or officer and bring him immediately before such court or judge. On being so brought such person or officer shall be committed to close custody in the jail of the county where such court or judge may be, without being allowed the liberties thereof, until such person or officer make return to such writ and comply with any order that may be made by such court or judge in relation to the party for whose relief the writ has been issued.

§17-17. Liability of judge refusing attachment

If any judge willfully refuses to grant the writ of attachment, as provided for in G.S. 17-16, he shall be liable to impeachment, and moreover shall forfeit to the party aggrieved twenty-five hundred dollars ($2,500).

§17-18. Attachment against sheriff to be directed to coroner; procedure

If a sheriff has neglected to return the writ agreeably to the command thereof, the attachment against him may be directed to the coroner or to any other person to be designated therein, who shall have power to execute the same, and such sheriff, upon being brought up, may be committed to the jail of any county other than his own.

§17-19. Precept to bring up party detained

The court or judge by whom any such attachment may be issued may also at the same time, or afterwards, direct a precept to any sheriff, coroner, or other person to be designated therein, commanding him to bring forthwith before such court or judge the party, wherever to be found, for whose benefit the writ of habeas corpus has been granted.

§17-20. Liability of judge refusing precept

If any judge refuses to grant the precept provided for in G.S. 17-19, he shall be liable to impeachment, and moreover shall forfeit to the party aggrieved twenty-five hundred dollars ($2,500).

§17-21. Liability of judge conniving at insufficient return

If any judge grants the attachment, or the precept, and gives the officer or other person charged with the execution of the same verbal or written instructions not to execute the same, or to make any evasive or insufficient return, or any return other than that provided by law; or shall connive at the failing to make any return or any evasive or insufficient return, or any return other than that provided by law, he shall be liable to impeachment, and moreover shall forfeit to the party aggrieved twenty-five hundred dollars ($2,500).

§17-22. Power of county to aid service

In the execution of any such attachment, precept or writ, the sheriff, coroner, or other person to whom it may be directed, may call to his aid the power of the county, as in other cases.

§17-23. Obedience to order of discharge compelled

Obedience to a judgment or order for the discharge of a prisoner or person restrained of his liberty, pursuant to the provisions of this Chapter, may be enforced by the court or judge by attachment in the same manner and with the same effect as for a neglect to make return to a writ of habeas corpus; and the person found guilty of such disobedience shall forfeit to the party aggrieved two thousand five hundred dollars ($2,500), besides any special damages which such party may have sustained.

§17-24. No civil liability for obedience
No officer or other person shall be liable to any civil action for obeying a judgment or order of discharge upon writ of habeas corpus.

§17-25. Recommittal after discharge; penalty
If any person shall knowingly again imprison or detain one who has been set at large upon any writ of habeas corpus, for the same cause, other than by the legal process or order of the court wherein he is bound by recognizance to appear, or of any other court having jurisdiction in the case, he shall be guilty of a Class 1 misdemeanor.

§17-26. Disobedience to writ or refusing copy of process; penalty
If any person to whom a writ of habeas corpus is directed shall neglect or refuse to make due return thereto, or to bring the body of the party detained according to the command of the writ without delay, or shall not, within six hours after demand made therefor, deliver a copy of the commitment or cause of detainer, such person shall, upon conviction on indictment, be fined one thousand dollars ($1,000), or imprisoned not exceeding 12 months, and if such person be an officer, shall moreover be removed from office.

§17-27. Penalty for false return
If any person shall make a false return to a writ of habeas corpus, he shall be guilty of a Class 1 misdemeanor.

§17-28. Penalty for concealing party entitled to writ
If anyone having in his custody, or under his power, any party who, by law, would be entitled to a writ of habeas corpus, or for whose relief such writ shall have been issued, shall, with intent to elude the service of such writ, or to avoid the effect thereof, transfer the party to the custody, or put him under the power or control, of another, or shall conceal or change the place of his confinement, or shall knowingly aid or abet another in so doing, he shall be guilty of a Class 1 misdemeanor.

§17-29. Notice to interested parties
When it appears from the return to the writ that the party named therein is in custody on any process, or by reason of any claim of right, under which any other person has an interest in continuing his imprisonment or restraint, no order shall be made for his discharge until it appears that the person so interested, or his attorney, if he have one, has had reasonable notice of the time and place at which such writ is returnable.

§17-30. Notice to district attorney
When it appears from the return that such party is detained upon any criminal accusation, the court or judge may, if he thinks proper, make no order for the discharge of such party until sufficient notice of the time and place at which the writ has been returned, or is made returnable, is given to the district attorney of the district in which the person prosecuting the writ is detained.

§17-31. Subpoenas to witnesses
Any party to a proceeding on a writ of habeas corpus may procure the attendance of witnesses at the hearing, by subpoena, to be issued by the clerk of any superior court, under the same rules, regulations and penalties prescribed by law in other cases.

§17-32. *Proceedings on return; facts examined; summary hearing of issues*

The court or judge before whom the party is brought on a writ of habeas corpus shall, immediately after the return thereof, examine into the facts contained in such return, and into the cause of the confinement or restraint of such party, whether the same has been upon commitment for any criminal or supposed criminal matter or not; and if issue be taken upon the material facts in the return, or other facts are alleged to show that the imprisonment or detention is illegal, or that the party imprisoned is entitled to his discharge, the court or judge shall proceed, in a summary way, to hear the allegations and proofs on both sides, and to do what to justice appertains in delivering, bailing or remanding such party.

§17-33. *When party discharged*

If no legal cause is shown for such imprisonment or restraint, or for the continuance thereof, the court or judge shall discharge the party from the custody or restraint under which he is held. But if it appears on the return to the writ that the party is in custody by virtue of civil process from any court legally constituted, or issued by any officer in the course of judicial proceedings before him, authorized by law, such party can be discharged only in one of the following cases:

(1) Where the jurisdiction of such court or officer has been exceeded, either as to matter, place, sum or person.

(2) Where, though the original imprisonment was lawful, yet by some act, omission or event, which has taken place afterwards, the party has become entitled to be discharged.

(3) Where the process is defective in some matter of substance required by law, rendering such process void.

(4) Where the process, though in proper form, has been issued in a case not allowed by law.

(5) Where the person, having the custody of the party under such process, is not the person empowered by law to detain him.

(6) Where the process is not authorized by any judgment, order or decree of any court, nor by any provision of law.

§17-34. *When party remanded*

It is the duty of the court or judge forthwith to remand the party, if it appears that he is detained in custody, either—

(1) By virtue of process issued by any court or judge of the United States, in a case where such court or judge has exclusive jurisdiction.

(2) By virtue of the final judgment or decree of any competent court of civil or criminal jurisdiction, or of an execution issued upon such judgment or decree.

(3) For any contempt specially and plainly charged in the commitment by some court, officer or body having authority to commit for the contempt so charged.

(4) That the time during which such party may be legally detained has not expired.

§17-35. When the party bailed or remanded

If it appears that the party has been legally committed for any criminal offense, or if it appears by the testimony offered with the return of the writ, or upon the hearing thereof, that the party is guilty of such an offense, although the commitment is irregular, the court or judge shall proceed to let such party to bail, if the case is bailable and good bail is offered; if not, the court or judge shall forthwith remand such party to the custody or place him under the restraint from which he was taken, if the person or officer, under whose custody or restraint he was, legally entitled thereto; if not so entitled, the court or judge shall commit such party to the custody of the officer or person legally entitled thereto.

§17-36. Party held in execution not to be discharged

When a writ of habeas corpus cum causa issues and the sheriff or other officer to whom it is directed returns upon the same that the prisoner is condemned, by judgment given against him, and held in custody by virtue of an execution issued against him, the prisoner shall not be let to bail out but shall be presently remanded, where he shall remain until discharged in due course of law.

§17-37. When party ill, cause determined in his absence

When, from the illness or infirmity of the person directed to be produced by a writ of habeas corpus, such person cannot, without danger, be brought before the court or judge where the writ is made returnable, the party in whose custody he is may state the fact in his return to the writ; and if the court or judge is satisfied of the truth of the allegation, and the return is otherwise sufficient, the court or judge shall proceed to decide on such return and to dispose of the matter in the same manner as if the body had been produced.

§17-38. No second committal after discharge; penalty

No person who has been set at large upon any writ of habeas corpus shall be again imprisoned or detained for the same cause by any person whatsoever other than by the legal order or process of the court wherein he shall be bound by recognizance to appear or of any other court having jurisdiction in the case, under the penalty of two thousand five hundred dollars ($2,500) to the party aggrieved thereby.

The statutes and Constitution are current through Chapters 1-74 of the 2014 Regular Session of the General Assembly.

NORTH DAKOTA

North Dakota Century Annotated
Title 32. Judicial Remedies
Chapter 32-22. Habeas Corpus

§32-22-01. Persons restrained may prosecute the writ

Every person imprisoned or restrained of the person's liberty under any pretense whatever may prosecute a writ of habeas corpus to inquire into the cause of such imprisonment or restraint and thereby, except in the cases specified in *section 32-22-02*, obtain relief from such imprisonment or restraint if it is unlawful.

§32-22-02. Who not entitled to relief

The person in whose behalf the application is made is not entitled to relief from imprisonment or restraint under a writ of habeas corpus, if the time during which such person may be detained legally in custody has not expired, whenever it appears:

1. That the person is detained in custody by virtue of process issued by any court or judge of the United States in a case where such court or judge has exclusive jurisdiction; or

2. Except as provided in *section 32-22-17*, that the person is detained in custody by virtue of the final order or judgment of any competent court of criminal jurisdiction or of any process issued upon such order or judgment.

§32-22-03. Application for writ—contents—verification

Application for the writ must be made by petition signed either by the person for whose relief it is intended or by some person in that person's behalf, and must specify:

1. That the person in whose behalf the writ is applied for is imprisoned or restrained of the person's liberty, the officer or person by whom the person is so confined or restrained, and the place where, naming all the parties if they are known, or describing them if they are not known.

2. The cause or pretense of such confinement or restraint according to the knowledge or belief of the party verifying the petition.

3. If the confinement or restraint is by virtue of any warrant, order, or process, a copy thereof shall be annexed, or it shall be averred because such person was removed or concealed before application, a demand of such copy could not be made, or that such demand was made and the legal fees therefor tendered to the officer or person having such in custody, and that such copy was refused.

4. If the imprisonment is alleged to be illegal, the petition shall state in what the illegality consists.

The petition must be verified by the oath or affirmation of the person making the application.

§32-22-04. By what court application granted

The writ of habeas corpus must be granted, issued, and made returnable as hereinafter stated:

1. The writ must be granted by the supreme court, or any judge thereof, upon petition by or on behalf of any person restrained of the person's liberty within this state. When granted by the court, it, in all cases, shall be issued out of and under the seal of the supreme court, and may be made returnable, either before the supreme court, or before the district court or any judge of the district court; or

2. The writ may be granted, issued, and determined by the district courts and the judges thereof upon petition by or on behalf of any person restrained of the person's liberty in their respective districts. When application is made to the supreme court, or to a judge thereof, proof by the oath of the person applying or other sufficient evidence shall be required that the judge of the district court having jurisdiction by the provisions of subsection 2 is absent from the judge's district or has refused to grant such writ, or for some cause to be specially set forth, is incapable of acting, and if such proof is not produced the application shall be denied.

§32-22-05. When court must grant the writ
The court authorized to grant the writ to whom a petition therefor is presented, if it appears that the writ ought to issue, must grant the same without delay, and the writ shall not be denied for any informality in the petition or for any want of matters of substance, if the same can be supplied, and the court to whom application is made, must point out the matters wanting and direct the manner of supplying the same.

§32-22-06. Application to supreme court for writ of habeas corpus
When, upon application to the supreme court for a writ of habeas corpus, it is apparent that no necessity exists for its immediate issuance, and a district court has entertained an application for the writ, and, upon hearing, quashed it, the supreme court will require all the papers, including the application and supporting affidavits, the return and supporting affidavits, and the order of such lower court, to accompany the application made to said court. In emergency cases, the foregoing requirement may be waived.

§32-22-07. Direction of writ
The writ must be directed to the person having custody of or restraining the person on whose behalf the application is made, and must command that person to have the person in custody or restraint personally appear before the court before whom the writ is returnable, at a place therein specified, immediately or at some specified time, regard being had to the circumstances and the distance to be traveled.

§32-22-08. Writ of habeas corpus—form
Every writ of habeas corpus issued under the provisions of this chapter shall be in substantially the following form:

    State of North Dakota   )

)   ss.

    County of _____   )

    The state of North Dakota to the sheriff of _____ etc. (or to _____) :

You are hereby commanded to have _____ by you imprisoned and detained, as is alleged, together with the time and cause of such imprisonment and detention, by whatever name the said shall be called or charged, before , judge of the district court, (or before the district or supreme court, as the case may be), at (naming the place), on (naming the date), (or immediately upon the receipt of this writ), to do and receive what shall then and there be considered concerning the said _____ Witness, etc., and have you then and there this writ.

Such writ must be endorsed "By the Habeas Corpus Act," and if issued by the court, it shall be under the seal of the court, and if by the judge, it shall be under the judge's hand.

§32-22-09. Manner of serving the writ
Whenever the writ is directed to the sheriff or other ministerial officer of the court out of which it is issued, it must be delivered by the clerk or by such person as it may be entrusted to, without delay, as other writs are delivered to such sheriff or other officer for service, or it may be left with the jailer, keeper, or other person under such sheriff or other officer in charge of and at the jail or place where the person seeking the writ may be imprisoned or restrained. If it is directed to any other person, it may be delivered to

the sheriff or sheriff's deputy and be by the sheriff or sheriff's deputy served upon such person by delivering the same to such person without delay. If the person to whom the writ is directed cannot be found or refuses admittance to the officer or person serving or delivering such writ, it may be served or delivered by leaving it at the residence of the person to whom it is directed, or by affixing it to some conspicuous place on the outside either of that person's dwelling house or of the place where the party is confined or under restraint. In any case the court issuing the writ, at its discretion, may authorize any person to serve and deliver it by an entry signed by the judge thereon to the following effect: "I hereby authorize _____ to serve the within writ," and service made by such person in the manner designated in this section shall be due and lawful service.

§32-22-10. Penalty if officer refuses to execute and return writ
If the person to whom the writ is directed refuses, after service, to obey the same, the court, upon affidavit stating such facts, must issue an attachment against such person, directed to the sheriff or coroner, commanding the sheriff or coroner forthwith to arrest such person and bring such person immediately before such court, and upon being so brought that person must be committed to the jail of the county until that person makes due return to such writ or is otherwise legally discharged. The person disobeying such writ also shall forfeit to the person imprisoned or restrained a sum not exceeding five hundred dollars to be recovered in a civil action by the person restrained. If the person disobeying the writ is an officer, that officer shall be incapable of holding or executing that office.

§32-22-11. What the return must set forth
The person upon whom the writ is served must state in the person's return, plainly and unequivocally:

1. Whether that person has or has not the party in custody or under power or restraint.

2. If that person has the party in custody or power or under restraint, that person must state the authority and cause of such imprisonment or restraint.

3. If the party is detained by virtue of any writ, warrant, or other written authority, a copy thereof must be annexed to the return and the original produced and exhibited to the court on the hearing of such return.

4. If the person upon whom the writ is served had the party in the person's custody or power or under the person's restraint, at any time prior or subsequent to the date of the writ of habeas corpus, but has transferred such custody or restraint to another, the return must state particularly to whom, at what time and place, for what cause, and by what authority such transfer took place.

5. The return must be signed by the person making the same, and, except when such person is a sworn public officer and makes such return in an official capacity, it must be verified by the officer's oath or affirmation.

§32-22-12. Party restrained must be brought into court—exception
The person to whom the writ is directed, if it is served, must bring the party in custody or under restraint, according to the command of the writ, except in cases specified in *section 32-22-13*.

§32-22-13. When party need not be brought
When from sickness or infirmity of the person directed to be produced such person cannot be brought before the court without danger, the person in whose power or custody such person is may state that

fact in the return to the writ, verifying the same by affidavit. If the court is satisfied of the truth of such return and the return to the writ is otherwise sufficient, the court may proceed to decide on such return and to dispose of the matter as if such party had been produced on the writ, or the hearing thereof may be adjourned until such party can be produced.

§32-22-14. When hearing must be had
The court before whom the writ is returned, immediately after the return or within five days thereafter, must proceed to hear and examine the return, and such other matters as may be properly submitted for its consideration.

§32-22-15. Return may be controverted—proofs
The party brought before the court on the return of the writ may deny or controvert any of the material facts or matters set forth in the return, or except to the sufficiency thereof, or allege any fact to show either that the imprisonment or detention is unlawful or that the party is entitled to be discharged. The court thereupon must proceed in a summary way to hear such proof as may be produced against such imprisonment or detention, or in favor of the same, and to dispose of such party as the justice of the case may require, and has full power and authority to require and compel the attendance of witnesses, by process of subpoena and attachment, and to do and perform all other acts and things necessary to a full and fair hearing and determination of the case. The court may allow the return to be amended according to the facts of the case, whenever it may be deemed necessary.

§32-22-16. When person restrained must be discharged
If no legal cause is shown for the imprisonment or restraint or for the continuation thereof, the court must discharge the party from the custody or restraint under which the party is held.

§32-22-17. Causes for discharge of person restrained
If it appears on the return of the writ that the party is in custody by virtue of process from any court of this state, or any judge or officer thereof, such person may be discharged in any of the following cases, subject to the restrictions of *section 32-22-02*;

1. When the jurisdiction of such court or officer has been exceeded.

2. When the imprisonment was at first lawful, but by some act, omission, or event which has taken place afterward, the party has become entitled to a discharge.

3. When the process is defective in some matter of substance required by law rendering such process void.

4. When the process, though regular in form, has been issued in a case not allowed by law.

5. When the person having the custody of the party is not the person allowed by law to detain the party.

6. When the process is not authorized by any order or judgment of any court nor by any provisions of law.

7. When a party has been committed on a criminal charge without reasonable or probable cause.

8. When the process appears to have been obtained by false pretense or bribery.

§32-22-18. Informal commitment from district judge

If the person is committed to prison, or is in custody of an officer on a criminal charge, by virtue of a warrant of commitment of a district judge, the person must not be discharged on the ground of any mere defect of form in the warrant of commitment.

§32-22-19. Procedure when person appears to be guilty

If it appears to the court, by affidavit or otherwise, or upon inspection of the process or warrant of commitment and proceedings as may be shown to the court, that the party is guilty of a criminal offense or ought not to be discharged, such court, although the charge is defectively or not substantially set forth in such process or warrant of commitment, must cause the complainant or other necessary witness to be subpoenaed to attend at such time as ordered, to testify before the court, and upon the examination the judge may discharge such party, admit the party to bail if the offense is bailable, or recommit the party to custody, as may be just and legal.

§32-22-20. Habeas corpus to give bail

Whenever a person is imprisoned or detained in custody on a criminal charge, for want of bail, such person is entitled to a writ of habeas corpus for the purpose of giving bail, upon averring that fact in such person's petition, without alleging that the person is confined illegally. Any judge in or out of the court in which the judge is authorized to act may take an undertaking of bail from any person who has been committed on a criminal charge, when brought before the judge on a writ of habeas corpus, as in other cases, if the offense is bailable, and file the undertaking in the proper court.

§32-22-21. Procedure when person not entitled to discharge

If a party brought before the court on the return of the writ is not entitled to a discharge, and is not admitted to bail or bailed when allowable, the court must remand the party to custody, or place the party under the restraint from which the party was taken, if the person under whose custody or restraint the party was is legally entitled thereto.

§32-22-22. Prisoner may be ordered to custody of proper officer

In cases in which any party is held under illegal restraint or custody, and any other person is entitled to the custody or restraint of such party, the court may order such party to be committed to the custody or restraint of such person as by law is entitled thereto.

§32-22-23. Bow person disposed of before judgment

Until judgment is given on the return, the court before whom any party may be brought on such writ may commit the party to the sheriff of the county or place the party in such care or under such custody as the party's age or circumstances may require.

§32-22-24. When notice of hearing must be given state's attorney

When it appears that the person in whose behalf a writ of habeas corpus is issued is held upon a criminal charge of any kind, notice of the time and place of the hearing upon the return shall be given to the state's attorney of the county where the offense arose if the person is within the state's attorney's county. In other cases, like notice shall be given to any person interested in continuing the custody or restraint of the party asking aid of such writ.

§32-22-25. Person taken out of county—expenses

Whenever the officer or person to whom a writ of habeas corpus is directed and delivered is required thereby to make return and take the person in whose behalf the writ is issued into a county other than the county in which such person is imprisoned or restrained, the court awarding the writ, at the court's discretion, may ascertain, and by an entry thereon specifying the amount, but not exceeding fifteen cents per mile, may require the payment or tender, at the time of delivering the writ, of the charges of obeying the same. However, in no case when an entry is not made can the payment or tender of such charges be demanded before the return of the writ in accordance with its direction.

§32-22-26. Writ must not be disobeyed
No writ of habeas corpus can be disobeyed for defect of form, if it sufficiently appears therefrom in whose restraint the party imprisoned or restrained is, the officer or person detaining the party, and the court before whom the party is to be brought.

§32-22-27. When person discharged may be arrested again
No person who has been discharged by the order of the court upon habeas corpus can be imprisoned again or kept in custody for the same cause, except in any of the following cases:
1. If the person has been discharged from custody on a criminal charge and is committed afterwards for the same offense, by legal order or process.

2. If, after a discharge for defect of proof, or for any defect of the process, warrant, or commitment in a criminal action, the accused is arrested again on sufficient proof and committed by legal process for the same offense.

3. If in a civil action the party has been discharged for any illegality in the order, judgment, or process and afterwards is imprisoned by legal process for the same claim for relief.

32-22-28. Bow obedience to order of discharge enforced
Obedience to an order for the discharge of any person, granted pursuant to the provisions of this chapter, may be enforced by the court or judge issuing such writ, or granting such order, by attachment, in the same manner as hereinbefore provided for a neglect to make a return to a writ of habeas corpus, and the person guilty of such disobedience shall forfeit to the party aggrieved five hundred dollars, in addition to any special damages such party may have sustained.

§32-22-29. Person restrained in danger of being taken out of jurisdiction—warrant
When it appears to any court authorized by law to issue the writ of habeas corpus that anyone is illegally held in custody, confinement, or restraint, and that there is reason to believe that the person will be carried out of the jurisdiction of the court, or will suffer some irreparable injury before compliance with the writ of habeas corpus can be enforced, the court may cause a warrant to be issued reciting the facts and directed to the sheriff or coroner of the county, commanding the officer to take the person thus held in custody, confinement, or restraint, and forthwith bring that person before the court to be dealt with according to law. The court also may insert in the warrant a command for the arrest of the person charged with the illegal detention and restraint.

§32-22-30. Execution of warrant
The officer to whom such warrant is delivered must execute it by bringing the person therein named before the court who directed the issuing of such warrant, but if such warrant is issued by the supreme court or a judge thereof, upon the return of the warrant, the hearing and decision of the matter may be ordered by such court or judge to be had before the district court of the proper county or the judge thereof.

§32-22-31. Return to warrant—procedure
The person alleged to have such party under illegal confinement or restraint may make return to such warrant, as in case of a writ of habeas corpus, and the same may be denied, and like allegations, proofs, and trial thereupon may be had as upon a return to a writ of habeas corpus.

§32-22-32. When person must be discharged
If the party is held under illegal custody or restraint, the party must be discharged or be restored to the care or custody of the person entitled thereto.

§32-22-33. When writ may be served
Any writ or process authorized by this chapter may be issued and served on any day or at any time.

§32-22-34. Accused liberated for want of prosecution
If any person shall be committed for a criminal or supposed criminal matter and not admitted to bail, and shall not be tried on or before the second term of the court having jurisdiction of the offense, the prisoner shall be set at liberty by the court, unless the delay shall happen on the application of the prisoner. If such court at the second term shall be satisfied that due exertions have been made to procure the evidence for and on behalf of the state, and that there are reasonable grounds to believe that such evidence may be procured at the third term, it shall have power to continue such case until the third term. If any such prisoner shall have been admitted to bail for a crime other than a capital offense, the court may continue the trial of said cause to a third term, if it shall appear by oath or affirmation that the witnesses for the state are absent, such witnesses being mentioned by name, and the court shown wherein their testimony is material.

§32-22-35. Writ not allowed to delay trial
To prevent any person from avoiding or delaying that person's trial, it shall not be lawful to remove any prisoner on habeas corpus under this chapter out of the county in which the prisoner is confined, within fifteen days next preceding the term of the court at which such person ought to be tried, unless it is to convey the prisoner into the county where the offense with which the prisoner stands charged properly is cognizable.

§32-22-36. Repealed by S.L. 1997, ch. 114, §8, eff. Aug. 1, 1997

§32-22-37. Penalty if judge refuses or delays writ
Any judge empowered by this chapter to issue writs of habeas corpus, who corruptly shall refuse to issue such writ when legally applied to, in a case in which such writ may issue lawfully, or who, for the purpose of oppression, shall delay unreasonably the issuing of such writ, shall forfeit to the prisoner or party aggrieved a sum not exceeding five hundred dollars for every such offense. §32-22-38. Removing or concealing prisoner to avoid writ—penalty Anyone having a person in custody or under restraint, power, or control, for whose relief a writ of habeas corpus is issued, who, with intent to avoid the effect of such writ, shall transfer such person to the custody, or place such person under control of another, or shall conceal such person or change the place of such person's confinement with intent to avoid the operation of such writ, or with intent to remove such person out of this state, shall be guilty of a class c felony. In any prosecution under this section, it shall not be necessary to show that the writ of habeas corpus had issued at the time of the removal, transfer, or concealment therein mentioned, if it is proven that the acts therein forbidden were done with the intent to avoid the operation of such writ.

§32-22-39. Repealed

§32-22-40. Penalty for rearresting on same charge
Any person who, knowing that another has been discharged by order of a competent judge or tribunal on a writ of habeas corpus, shall arrest or detain that person again, contrary to the provisions of this chapter, for the same cause which was shown on the return of such writ, shall forfeit five hundred dollars for the first offense, and one thousand dollars for every subsequent offense.

§32-22-41. All penalties inure to use of party aggrieved
All the pecuniary forfeitures under this chapter shall inure to the use of the party for whose benefit the writ of habeas corpus issued, and shall be sued for and recovered with costs, in the name of the state, by any person aggrieved.

§32-22-42. Recovery of penalties no bar to civil action
The recovery of the penalties prescribed by this chapter shall be no bar to a civil suit for damages.

§32-22-43. Writ may issue for witness or for surrender of principal in discharge of bail—liability of jailer—costs
The supreme court or any district court within this state, or any judge of any such court, may issue a writ of habeas corpus to bring the body of any person confined in any jail in the state before such court or judge to testify or to be surrendered in discharge of bail. Where a writ is issued for any such purpose and the witness or principal sought is confined in any jail in a county other than the county in which such person is to be surrendered, or to which such person is to be removed, and where such writ is executed and returned by an officer to whom it is directed, the jailer from whose custody such person is taken shall be exonerated from liability for an escape if:

1. The court or judge issuing the writ shall make an order directing the return of such person to the custody of such jailer.

2. An attested copy of such order is delivered to the said jailer.

3. The officer to whom the writ was directed shall return such person pursuant to the said order after the execution of the writ.

The party praying out such writ of habeas corpus shall pay to the officer executing the same such reasonable sum for the officer's services as shall be adjudged by the court.

Current through the 2013 Regular Session of the 63rd Legislative Assembly.

OHIO

Ohio Revised Code
Title XXVII. Courts—General Provisions—Special Remedies
Chapter 2725. Habeas Corpus

2725.01. Persons entitled to writ of habeas corpus
Whoever is unlawfully restrained of his liberty, or entitled to the custody of another, of which custody

such person is unlawfully deprived, may prosecute a writ of habeas corpus, to inquire into the cause of such imprisonment, restraint, or deprivation.

2725.02. Courts authorized to grant writ
The writ of habeas corpus may be granted by the supreme court, court of appeals, court of common pleas, probate court, or by a judge of any such court.

2725.03. Jurisdiction for production or discharge of inmate of institution
If a person restrained of his liberty is an inmate of a state benevolent or correctional institution, the location of which is fixed by statute and at the time is in the custody of the officers of the institution, no court or judge other than the courts or judges of the county in which the institution is located has jurisdiction to issue or determine a writ of habeas corpus for his production or discharge. Any writ issued by a court or judge of another county to an officer or person in charge at the state institution to compel the production or discharge of an inmate thereof is void.

2725.04. Application for writ
Application for the writ of habeas corpus shall be by petition, signed and verified either by the party for whose relief it is intended, or by some person for him, and shall specify:

(A) That the person in whose behalf the application is made is imprisoned, or restrained of his liberty;

(B) The officer, or name of the person by whom the prisoner is so confined or restrained; or, if both are unknown or uncertain, such officer or person may be described by an assumed appellation and the person who is served with the writ is deemed the person intended;

(C) The place where the prisoner is so imprisoned or restrained, if known;

(D) A copy of the commitment or cause of detention of such person shall be exhibited, if it can be procured without impairing the efficiency of the remedy; or, if the imprisonment or detention is without legal authority, such fact must appear.

2725.05. Writ not allowed
If it appears that a person alleged to be restrained of his liberty is in the custody of an officer under process issued by a court or magistrate, or by virtue of the judgment or order of a court of record, and that the court or magistrate had jurisdiction to issue the process, render the judgment, or make the order, the writ of habeas corpus shall not be allowed. If the jurisdiction appears after the writ is allowed, the person shall not be discharged by reason of any informality or defect in the process, judgment, or order.

2725.06. Writ must be granted
When a petition for a writ of habeas corpus is presented, if it appears that the writ ought to issue, a court or judge authorized to grant the writ must grant it forthwith.

2725.07. Clerk shall issue writ
When a writ of habeas corpus is granted, the clerk of the court which granted the writ shall forthwith issue said writ under the seal of such court. In case of emergency, the judge who allowed the writ may issue it under his own hand, and depute any officer or other person to serve it.

2725.08. Designation of prisoner
The person to be produced upon a writ of habeas corpus shall be designated by his name, if known, and

if his name is not known, or is uncertain, such person may be described in any other way so as to make known who is intended.

2725.09. Requisites of writ

In case of confinement, imprisonment, or detention of a person by an officer, a writ of habeas corpus shall be directed to him, and command him to have such person before the court or judge designated in the writ, at a time and place therein specified.

2725.10. Form of writ when prisoner not in custody of an officer

In case of confinement, imprisonment, or detention by a person not an officer, the writ of habeas corpus shall be in the following form:

The State of Ohio, _____County, ss.: To the sheriff of our several counties, greeting:

We command you that the body of _____ of _____ , by _____ , of _____, imprisoned and restrained of his liberty, as it is said, you take and have before _____ , a judge of our _____ court, or, in case of his absence or disability, before some other judge of the same court, at _____ , forthwith to do and receive what our said judge shall then and there consider _____ concerning him in his behalf; and summon the said _____ then and there to appear before our said judge, to show the cause of the taking and detention of the said

(Seal) Witness _____ , at _____, this _____ day of _____ , in the year _____ .

2725.11. Service of writ

The writ of habeas corpus may be served in any county by the sheriff of that or any other county or by a person deputed by the court or judge issuing the writ.

2725.12. Execution and return of writ

The officer or person to whom a writ of habeas corpus is directed shall convey the person imprisoned or detained, and named in the writ, before the judge granting the writ, or, in case of his absence or disability, before some other judge of the same court, on the day specified in the writ. Said officer or person shall make due return of the writ, together with the day and cause of the caption and detention of such person, according to its command.

2725.13. Return of writ to another judge

When a writ of habeas corpus is issued by a court in session, if the court has adjourned when the writ is returned, it shall be returned before any judge of the same court. When the writ is returned before one judge, at a time when the court is in session, he may adjourn the case into the court, there to be heard and determined.

2725.14. Contents of the return

When the person to be produced under a writ of habeas corpus is imprisoned or restrained by an officer, the person who makes the return shall state therein, and in other cases the person in whose custody the prisoner is found shall state, in writing, to the court or judge before whom the writ is returnable, plainly and unequivocally:

(A) Whether or not he has the prisoner in his custody or power or under restraint.

(B) If the prisoner is in his custody or power or under restraint, he shall set forth, at large, the authority, and the true and whole cause, of such imprisonment and restraint, with a copy of the writ, warrant, or other process upon which the prisoner is detained.

(C) If such prisoner was in his custody or power or under restraint, and such custody or restraint was transferred to another, he shall state particularly to whom, at what time, for what case, and by what authority such transfer was made.

2725.15. Return must be signed and sworn to
The return or statement referred to in *section 2725.14 of the Revised Code* shall be signed by the person who makes it, and shall be sworn to by him, unless he is a sworn public officer and makes the return in his official capacity.

2725.16. Continuance of cause
The court or judge to whom a writ of habeas corpus is returned, or the court into which it is adjourned, for good cause shown, may continue the cause, and, in that event, shall make such order for the safekeeping of the person imprisoned or detained as the nature of the case requires.

2725.17. Discharge of prisoner
When the judge has examined the cause of caption and detention of a person brought before him as provided in *section 2725.12 of the Revised Code* and is satisfied that such person is unlawfully imprisoned or detained, he shall forthwith discharge such person from confinement. On such examination, the judge may disregard matters of form or technicalities in any mittimus or order of commitment by a court or officer authorized by law to commit.

2725.18. Prisoner may be committed or let to bail
When the person brought before a judge under *section 2725.12 of the Revised Code* is confined or detained in a legal manner on a charge of having committed a crime or offense which is bailable, the judge may recommit him or let him to bail. If such person is let to bail, the judge shall require him to enter into a recognizance, with sufficient surety, in such sum as the judge finds reasonable, after considering the circumstances of the prisoner and the nature of the offense charged, and conditioned for his appearance at the court where the offense is properly cognizable. The judge forthwith shall certify his proceedings, together with any recognizance, to the proper court. If the person charged fails to give such recognizance, he shall be committed to prison by the judge.

2725.19. Mandatory commitment for capital offense
If a prisoner brought before a judge under *section 2725.12 of the Revised Code* was committed by a judge, and is plainly and specifically charged in the warrant of commitment with a felony the punishment for which is capital, he shall not be removed, discharged, or let to bail.

2725.20. Return as evidence or plea
If a prisoner brought before a judge under *section 2725.12 of the Revised Code* is in custody under a warrant or commitment in pursuance of law, the return of the writ of habeas corpus is prima-facie evidence of the cause of detention. If such prisoner is restrained of his liberty by alleged private authority, the return is only a plea of the facts therein set forth, and the party claiming the custody shall be held to make proof of such facts. Upon the final disposition of a case, the court or judge shall make such order as to costs as it requires.

2725.21. Forfeiture by clerk for refusal to issue writ
A clerk of a court who refuses to issue a writ of habeas corpus, after an allowance of such writ and a demand therefor, shall forfeit to the party aggrieved the sum of five hundred dollars.

2725.22. Failure to obey writ
No person to whom a writ of habeas corpus is directed shall neglect or refuse to obey or make return of it according to the command thereof, or make a false return, or upon demand made by the prisoner, or by any person on his behalf, refuse to deliver to the person demanding, within six hours after demand therefor, a true copy of the warrant of commitment and detainer of the prisoner.

Whoever violates this section shall forfeit to the party aggrieved two hundred dollars for a first offense; for a second offense such person shall forfeit four hundred dollars, and, if an officer shall be incapable of holding his office.

2725.23. Persons at large upon writ not to be again imprisoned
A person who is set at large upon a writ of habeas corpus shall not be imprisoned again for the same offense, unless by the legal order or process of the court in which he is bound by recognizance to appear, or other court having jurisdiction of the cause or offense.

No person shall knowingly, contrary to *section 2725.01 to 2725.28, inclusive, of the Revised Code*, recommit, imprison, or cause to be recommitted or imprisoned, for the same offense, or pretended offense, a person so set at large, or knowingly aid or assist therein.

Whoever violates this section shall forfeit to the party aggrieved five hundred dollars, notwithstanding any colorable pretense or variation in the warrant or commitment.

2725.24. Prisoner shall not be removed from custody of one officer to another
A person committed to prison, or in the custody of an officer for a criminal matter, shall not be removed therefrom into the custody of another officer, unless by legal process, or unless the prisoner is delivered to an inferior officer to be taken to jail, or, by order of the proper court, is removed from one place to another within this state for trial, or in case of fire, infection, or other necessity. A person who, after such commitment, makes, signs, or countersigns a warrant for such removal contrary to this section shall forfeit to the party aggrieved five hundred dollars.

2725.25. No prisoner to be sent out of state—repealed

2725.26. Record of writs
The proceedings upon a writ of habeas corpus must be recorded by the clerk of the court in which such proceedings were had, and may be reviewed on appeal as in other cases.

2725.27. Recovery of forfeiture; limitations
The forfeitures mentioned in *sections 2725.21 to 2725.24 of the Revised Code* may be recovered by the party aggrieved or the executors or administrators of the party aggrieved against the offender or the offender•s executors or administrators by civil action in a court having cognizance thereof. Actions for violations of *sections 2725.21 to 2725.24 of the Revised Code* shall be brought within two years after the offense is committed, except in cases of imprisonment of the party aggrieved, when action may be brought within two years after the delivery of the part aggrieved out of prison, or after death if the party aggrieved dies in prison.

2725.28. Fees and costs

The fees of officers and witnesses shall be taxed by the judge, on return of the proceedings on a writ of habeas corpus, and corrected as a part of the original costs in the case. When the prisoner is discharged, the costs shall be taxed to the state, and paid out of the county treasury, upon the warrant of the county auditor. No officer or person shall demand payment in advance for any fees to which he is entitled by virtue of the proceedings, when the writ is demanded or issued for the discharge from custody of a person confined under color of proceedings in a criminal case. When a person in custody by virtue or under color of proceedings in a civil case is discharged, costs shall be taxed against the party at whose instance he was so in custody. If he is remanded to custody, costs shall be taxed against him.

Current through Files 1 to 140 and Statewide Issue 1 of the 130th GA (2013-2014).

OKLAHOMA

Oklahoma Statutes
Title 12. Civil Procedure
Chapter 23. Habeas Corpus

§1331. Persons who may prosecute writ

Every person restrained of his liberty, under any pretense whatever, may prosecute a writ of habeas corpus to inquire into the cause of the restraint, and shall be delivered therefrom when illegal.

§1332. Application—How made—Contents

Application for the writ shall be made by petition, signed and verified either by the plaintiff or by some person in his behalf, and shall specify:

First, By whom the person in whose behalf the writ is applied for is restrained of his liberty, and the place where, naming all the parties, if they are known, or describing them, if they are not known.

Second. The cause or pretense of the restraint, according to the best of the knowledge and belief of the applicant.

Third. If the restraint be alleged to be illegal, in what the illegality consists.

§1333. Court which may grant writ—Grant without delay

Writs of habeas corpus may be granted by any court of record in term time, or by a judge of any such court, either in term or vacation; and upon application the writ shall be granted without delay.

§1334. Direction and command of writ

The writ shall be directed to the officer or party having the person under restraint, commanding him to have such person before the court, or judge, at such time and place as the court or judge shall direct, to do and receive what shall be ordered concerning him and have then and there the writ.

§1335. Delivery to sheriff

If the writ be directed to the sheriff, it shall be delivered by the clerk to him without delay.

§1336. Service on party other than sheriff
If the writ be directed to any other person, it shall be delivered to the sheriff and shall be by him served by delivering to such person without delay.

§1337. Service when person not found or refuses admittance
If the person to whom such writ is directed cannot be found, or shall refuse admittance to the sheriff, the same may be served by leaving it at the residence of the person to whom it is directed, or by affixing the same on some conspicuous place, either of his dwelling house or where the party is confined under restraint.

§1338. Return of writ—Enforcing obedience
The sheriff or other person to whom the writ is directed shall make immediate return thereof, and if he neglect or refuse, after due service, to make return, or shall refuse or neglect to obey the writ by producing the party named therein, and no sufficient excuse be shown for such neglect or refusal, the court shall enforce obedience by attachment.

§1339. Return—Signature and verification—Contents—Production of party
The return must be signed and verified by the person making it, who shall state:

First. The authority of cause of restraint of the party in his custody.

Second. If the authority be in writing, he shall return a copy and produce the original on the hearing.

Third. If he has had the party in his custody or under his restraint, and has transferred him to another, he shall state to whom, the time, place and cause of the transfer.

He shall produce the party on the hearing, unless prevented by sickness or infirmity, which must be shown in the return.

§1340. Proceedings in case of allegation of sickness or infirmity—Exceptions to return—Controverting—New matter—Amendments
The court or judge, if satisfied with the truth of the allegation of sickness or infirmity, may proceed to decide on the return, or the hearing may be adjourned until the party can be produced, or for other good cause. The plaintiff may except to the sufficiency of, or controvert the return or any part thereof, or allege any new matter in avoidance; the new matter shall be verified, except in cases of commitment on a criminal charge; the return and pleadings may be amended without causing any delay.

§1341. Hearing and discharge
The court or judge shall thereupon proceed in a summary way to hear and determine the cause, and if no legal cause be shown for the restraint or for the continuance thereof, shall discharge the party.

§1342. Inquiry into legality of judgment or process—Limitations
No court or judge shall inquire into the legality of any judgment or process, whereby the party is in custody, or discharge him when the term of commitment has not expired in either of the cases following:

First. Upon process issued by any court or judge of the United States, or where such court or judge has exclusive jurisdiction; or

Second. Upon any process issued on any final judgment of a court of competent jurisdiction; or,

APPENDIX—OKLAHOMA

Third. For any contempt of any court, officer or body having authority to commit; but an order of commitment as for a contempt, upon proceedings to enforce the remedy of a party, is not included in any of the foregoing specifications;

Fourth. Upon a warrant or commitment issued from the district court, or any other court of competent jurisdiction, upon an indictment or information.

§1343. Procedure when person committed for want of bail—Defects in charge or process—Want of probable cause
No person shall be discharged from an order of commitment issued by any judicial or peace officer for want of bail, or in cases not bailable, on account of any defect in the charge or process, or for alleged want of probable cause; but in all such cases, the court or judge shall summon the prosecuting witnesses, investigate the criminal charge, and discharge, let to bail or recommit the prisoner, as may be just and legal, and recognize witnesses when proper.

§1344. Writ may issue to admit to bail
The writ may be had for the purpose of letting a prisoner to bail in civil and criminal actions.

§1345. Notice to interested persons before discharge
When any person has an interest in the detention, the prisoner shall not be discharged until the person having such interest is notified.

§1346. Power of court—Attendance of witnesses
The court or judge shall have power to require and compel the attendance of witnesses and to do all other acts necessary to determine the case.

§1347. Officers not liable for obeying orders
No sheriff or other officer shall be liable to a civil action for obeying any writ of habeas corpus or order of discharge made thereon.

§1348. Issuance of warrant to prevent removal from jurisdiction
Whenever it shall appear by affidavit that anyone is illegally held in custody or restraint, and that there is good reason to believe that such person will be carried out of the jurisdiction of the court or judge before whom the application is made, or will suffer some irreparable injury before compliance with the writ can be enforced, such court or judge may cause a warrant to be issued, reciting the facts, and directed to the sheriff or any constable of the county, commanding him to take the person thus held in custody or restraint, and forthwith bring him before the court or judge, to be dealt with according to law.

§1349. Arrest of party causing restraint
The court or judge may also, if the same be deemed necessary, insert in the warrant a command for the apprehension of the person charged with causing the illegal restraint.

§1350. Execution of writ—Return and proceedings
The officer shall execute the writ by bringing the person therein named before the court or judge; and the like return and proceedings shall be required and had as in case of writs of habeas corpus.

§1351. Temporary orders—Change of custody
The court or judge may make any temporary orders in the cause or disposition of the party during the

progress of the proceedings, that justice may require. The custody of any party restrained may be changed from one person to another, by order of the court or judge.

§1352. Writs and processes—Issuance and service on Sunday
Any writ or process authorized by this article [FN1] may be issued and served, in case of emergency, on Sunday.

[FN1] R.L.1910, c. 60, art. 11, Title 12, §1331 et seq.

§1353. Issue, service and amendment of process
All writs and other process, authorized by the provisions of this article, [FN1] shall be issued by the clerk of the court, and except summons, sealed with the seal of such court, and shall be served and returned forthwith, unless the court or judge shall specify a particular time for any such return. And no writ or other process shall be disregarded for any defect therein, if enough is shown to notify the officer or person of the purport of the process. Amendments may be allowed, and temporary commitments, when necessary.

[FN1] R.L.1910, c. 60, art. 11, Title 12, §1331 et seq.

§1354. Grant of writ to parents, etc.—Protection of infants and insane persons—Proceedings
Writ of habeas corpus shall be granted in favor of parents, guardians, masters, husbands and wives; and to enforce the rights and for the protection of infants and insane persons; and the proceedings shall, in all such cases, conform to the provisions of this article. [FN1]

[FN1] R.L.1910, c. 60, art. 11, Title 12, §1331 et seq.

§1355. Deposit or security for costs
No deposit or security for costs shall be required of an applicant for the initial application for a writ of habeas corpus. An applicant for a writ of habeas corpus shall be required to pay court costs pursuant to the procedures provided in Section 566.3 of Title 57 of the Oklahoma Statutes.

Current with chapters of the Second Regular Session of the 54th Legislature (2014) effective September 1, 2014.

OREGON

Oregon Revised Statutes Annotated
Title 3. Remedies and Special Actions and Proceedings
Chapter 34. Writs

34.310. Purpose of writ; standing to prosecute
The writ of habeas corpus ad subjiciendum is the writ designated in ORS 34.310 to 34.730, and every other writ of habeas corpus is abolished. Every person imprisoned or otherwise restrained of liberty, within this state, except in the cases specified in ORS 34.330, may prosecute a writ of habeas corpus to inquire into the cause of such imprisonment or restraint, and if illegal, to be delivered therefrom.

34.320. Jurisdiction; transfer of proceedings

The circuit court of the judicial district wherein the party is imprisoned or restrained, and, if vested with power to exercise judicial functions, the county court and county judge of the county wherein the party is imprisoned or restrained, shall have concurrent jurisdiction of proceedings by habeas corpus, and said courts and judges may issue, hear and decide all questions arising upon habeas corpus. If a plaintiff has filed a petition in a court with jurisdiction over the proceedings, and the plaintiff is thereafter transferred to a place that is outside of the jurisdiction of that court, the court shall transfer the proceedings to the circuit court for the judicial district in which the party is imprisoned or restrained. If the court in which the petition was filed determines that by reason of the plaintiff's transfer the claims of the plaintiff do not require immediate judicial scrutiny, or are otherwise subject to dismissal, the court shall dismiss the petition.

34.330. Entitlement to prosecute writ

A person may not prosecute a writ of habeas corpus if:

(1) The person is imprisoned or restrained by virtue of process issued by a court of the United States, or a judge, commissioner or other officer thereof, in cases where such courts, or judges or officers thereof, have exclusive jurisdiction under the laws of the United States, or have acquired exclusive jurisdiction by the commencement of actions, suits or other proceedings in such court, or before such commissioner or other officer.

(2) The person is imprisoned or restrained by virtue of the judgment of a competent tribunal of civil or criminal jurisdiction, or by virtue of an execution issued upon such judgment.

(3) Except as provided in ORS 138.530, the person is eligible to obtain post-conviction relief pursuant to ORS 138.510 to 138.680.

(4) The person is eligible to seek judicial review of a final order of the State Board of Parole and Post-Prison Supervision under ORS 144.335 but the person fails to seek judicial review of the order in a timely manner.

(5) The person seeks judicial review of a final order of the board under ORS 144.335 but the court of Appeals:

>(a) summarily affirms the order of the board on the grounds that the person failed to present a substantial question of law;

>(b) otherwise disposes of the judicial review on the merits of the petitioner's issues on judicial review; or

>(c) Dismisses the judicial review because of a procedural defect.

34.340. Petition; standing to apply; fee

The writ shall be allowed by the court or judge thereof upon the petition of the party for whose relief it is intended, or of some other person in behalf of the party, signed and verified by the oath of the plaintiff, to the effect that the plaintiff believes it to be true. The petition must be accompanied by the filing fee established under ORS 21.135.

34.350. Application by district attorney

Whenever a writ of habeas corpus is required in any action, suit or proceeding, civil or criminal, to which the state is a party, the application therefor may be made by the district attorney having charge thereof, and whenever so issued the court or judge shall state in the order of allowance that it was issued on such application.

34.355. Appointment of counsel; compensation and costs

If counsel is appointed by a court to represent, in an initial proceeding by habeas corpus or on appeal as provided in ORS 34.710, a person who is imprisoned or otherwise restrained of liberty by virtue of a charge or conviction of crime and who is determined to be financially eligible for appointed counsel at state expense, the public defense services executive director shall determine compensation for counsel and expenses of the person in an initial proceeding or in a circuit court on appeal shall be determined and paid as provided in ORS 135.055. Compensation for counsel and costs and expenses of the person on appeal to the Court of Appeals or on review by the Supreme Court shall be determined and paid as provided in ORS 138.500. The compensation and expenses so allowed in an initial proceeding in a county court shall be paid by the county in which the person was charged or convicted of crime.

34.360. Petition when person challenges authority for confinement

If the challenge is to the authority for confinement, the petition shall state, in substance:

(1) That the party in whose behalf the writ is petitioned is imprisoned or restrained of liberty, the place where, and officer or person by whom the party is imprisoned or restrained, naming both parties if their names are known, or describing them if not known.

(2) That such person is not imprisoned or restrained by virtue of any order, judgment or process specified in ORS 34.330.

(3) The cause or pretense of the imprisonment or restraint, according to the best knowledge or belief of the plaintiff.

(4) If the original imprisonment or restraint is by virtue of any order, warrant or process, a copy thereof shall be annexed to the petition, or it must be alleged that, by reason of the removal or concealment of the party before the application, a demand of such copy could not be made, or that the demand was made, and the legal fees therefor tendered to the person having the party in custody, and that a copy was refused.

(5) That the claim has not already been adjudged upon a prior writ of habeas corpus, to the knowledge or belief of the plaintiff.

34.362. Petition when person challenges conditions of confinement or deprivation of rights while confined

If the person is imprisoned or restrained by virtue of any order, judgment or process specified in ORS 34.330 and the person challenges the conditions of confinement or complains of a deprivation of rights while confined, the petition shall:

(1) Comply with requirements of ORS 34.360 (1), (3), (4), and (5); and

(2) State facts in support of a claim that the person is deprived of a constitutional right that requires immediate judicial attention and for which no other timely remedy is practicably available to the plaintiff.

34.365. Prisoner petition; filing without payment of filing fees; fee as charge against trust account
(1) Any court of the State of Oregon may authorize the filing of a petition for a writ of habeas corpus by or on behalf of any person imprisoned or otherwise restrained of liberty by virtue of a charge or conviction of crime without payment of the filing fees therefor, if such person presents to the court or judge thereof satisfactory proof, by affidavit and as otherwise required by such judge, that the person is unable to pay such fees.

(2) Notwithstanding the fact that a court has authorized the filing of a petition without payment of the filing fee required by ORS 34.340, the fee may be drawn from, or charged against, the plaintiff's trust account if the plaintiff is an inmate in a correctional facility.

34.370 Order to show cause; time for ruling; attorney fees; entry of judgment or issuance of writ; effect
(1) Except as provided in subsection (6) of this section, the judge to whom the petition for a writ of habeas corpus is presented shall, without delay, issue an order directing the defendant to show cause why the writ should not be allowed.

(2) Upon the issuance of a show cause order under subsection (1) of this section, the following shall apply:

(a) The judge shall order that the defendant appear in writing in opposition to the issuance of the writ as soon as is practicable and not more than 14 days from the date that the show cause order issues.

(b) The judge shall rule on the show cause order within seven days after either the defendant files a written appearance in opposition or the appearance period expires, whichever comes first. Upon making a ruling, the judge shall do one of the following, as appropriate:

(A) If the petition is a meritless petition, issue a judgment denying the petition and ordering the plaintiff to pay the cost of attorney fees incurred by the defendant. In no case shall the award of attorney fees exceed $100. The fees may be drawn from, or charged against, the inmate's trust account.

(B) Issue a judgment granting appropriate habeas corpus relief.

(C) Issue a writ of habeas corpus requiring that a return be made.

(3) Entry of a judgment under subsection (2)(b)(A) or subsection (6) of this section shall be without prejudice. The judgment shall explain to the parties the reason for the denial.

(4) If the court has issued a writ of habeas corpus requiring a return under subsection (2)(b)(C) of this section, the parties may stipulate to a hearing as described in ORS 34.670 without the necessity of a return or a replication. If the court accepts the stipulation, it shall set the matter for hearing in an expedited manner.

(5) Issuance of the writ under subsection (2) of this section shall not bind the court with respect to any subsequent rulings related to the pleadings of the parties or the ultimate disposition of the proceeding.

(6) The court may, on its own motion, enter a judgment denying a meritless petition brought under ORS 34.310 to 34.730.

(7) As used in this section, "meritless petition" means one which, when liberally construed, fails to state a claim upon which habeas corpus relief may be granted.

34.380. Warrant in lieu of writ
Whenever it appears by satisfactory evidence that any person is illegally imprisoned or restrained and there is good reason to believe that the person will be carried out of the state or suffer irreparable injury before the person can be relieved by the issuing of a habeas corpus, any court or judge authorized to issue such writ may issue a warrant reciting the facts, directed to any sheriff or other person therein designated, commanding the sheriff or other person to take such illegally imprisoned or restrained person and forthwith bring the person before such court or judge, to be dealt with according to law.

34.390. Order for arrest of custodian
When the proof mentioned in ORS 34.380 is also sufficient to justify an arrest of the person having the party in custody, as for a criminal offense committed in the taking or detaining of such party, the warrant may also contain an order for the arrest of such person for such offense.

34.400. Execution of warrant; return and proceedings
Any officer or person to whom a warrant issued under ORS 34.380 is directed shall execute the same by bringing the party therein named and the person who detains the party, if so commanded by the warrant, before the court or judge issuing the warrant; and thereupon the person detaining such party shall make a return in like manner, and the like proceedings shall be had thereon, as if a writ of habeas corpus had been issued in the first instance.

34.410. Criminal offense by custodian
If the person having such party in custody is brought before the court or judge as for a criminal offense, the person shall be examined, committed, released or discharged by the court or judge in like manner as in other criminal cases of like nature.

34.420. Repealed

34.421. Contents of writ
The writ shall require the defendant to file a return, at a specified time and place, that states the time and cause of plaintiff's imprisonment or restraint. The writ shall not command the defendant to produce the plaintiff before the court or judge issuing the writ, unless the court, in its discretion, so orders. The court shall consider an allegation of lack of authority, brought only under ORS 34.360, as a factor weighing in favor of requiring the defendant to produce the plaintiff at the time of the return.

34.430. Defect of form; designation of persons
The writ shall not be disobeyed for any defect of form. It is sufficient:

(1) If the officer or person having the custody of the person imprisoned or restrained is designated either by name of office, if the officer or person has any, or by the own name of the officer or person, or if both such names are unknown or uncertain, the officer or person may be described by an assumed appellation; and anyone who may be served with the writ is to be deemed the officer or person to whom it was directed, although it may be directed to the officer or person by a wrong name or description, or to another person.

(2) If the person who is directed to be produced is designated by name, or if the name of the person is uncertain or unknown, the person may be described in any other way, so as to designate the person intended.

34.440 Persons qualified to serve writ; tender of fees and undertaking when service is on sheriff or other officer

(1) A writ of habeas corpus may be served by any sheriff within the county of the sheriff, or by any other person designated in the writ in any county within the state. The service of the writ shall be deemed complete, so as to require the prisoner to be brought up before the court or judge issuing the writ under the provisions of ORS 34.370, only if:

> (a) The party serving the writ tenders to the person in whose custody the prisoner may be, if such person is a sheriff or other officer, the fees allowed by law for bringing up such prisoner; and

> (b) The party also enters into an undertaking to such sheriff or other officer, in a penalty double the sum for which the prisoner is detained, if the prisoner is detained for any specific sum of money, and if not, then in such a sum as the judge granting the writ directs, not exceeding $1,000, to the effect that such person shall pay the charges for carrying back the prisoner if the prisoner is remanded, and that the prisoner will not escape, either in going to or returning from the place to which the prisoner is to be taken.

(2) If such fees are not paid, or such security is not tendered, the officer to whom the writ is directed shall make a return, in the manner required by ORS 34.540, and shall state in the return the reason why the prisoner is not produced, and thereupon the court or judge granting the writ may proceed as if the prisoner was produced. This section, except for the first sentence, does not apply to a case wherein the writ is issued on the application of the district attorney.

34.450. Payment of charges when service is on person other than sheriff or officer

Every court or judge allowing a writ of habeas corpus, directed to a person other than a sheriff or other officer, may require, in order to render the service effectual, that the charges of producing the party be paid by the applicant; and in such case the court or judge shall, in the order allowing the writ, specify the amount of such charges, which shall not exceed the fees allowed by law to sheriffs for similar services.

34.460. Manner of service

The writ of habeas corpus may be served by delivery of the original to the officer or person to whom it is directed, or if the officer or person cannot be found, by leaving it at the jail or other place in which the party is imprisoned or restrained, with any under officer or other person having charge for the time of such party.

34.470. Service where party hides or refuses admittance

If the officer or person on whom the writ ought to be served hides from the person attempting to make service, or refuses admittance to the person attempting to make service, it may be served by affixing it in some conspicuous place on the outside, either of the dwelling house of the officer or person or the jail or other place where the party is confined.

34.480. Proof of service

The proof of service of the writ shall be the same as in the service of a summons, except that the same shall be indorsed upon a copy of the writ made by the officer or person serving it, and returned to the clerk who issued the writ.

34.490. Obedience to writ

It is the duty of every sheriff or other officer upon whom a writ of habeas corpus is served, whether such writ is directed to the sheriff or officer or not, upon payment or tender of the fees allowed by law, and the delivery or tender of the undertaking described in ORS 34.440, to obey and return the writ according to the exigency thereof; and it is the duty of every other person upon whom the writ is served, having the custody of the person for whose benefit it is issued, to obey and return it in like manner, without requiring the payment of any fees, unless the payment of such fees has been required by the court or judge allowing such writ.

34.500. Time for return of writ

If the writ is returnable at a certain time, the return shall be made at the time and place specified therein; if it is returnable forthwith, and the place of return is within 20 miles of the place of service, the return must be made within 24 hours, and the same time is allowed for every additional 20 miles.

34.510. Repealed

34.520. Sickness of person to be produced

Whenever, from the sickness or infirmity of the party, the party cannot, without danger, be produced, the officer or person in whose custody the party is may state that fact in the return to the writ, and if satisfied of the truth of the allegation, and the return is otherwise sufficient, the court or judge shall proceed to decide on the return, and to dispose of the matter, the same as if the party had been produced.

34.530. Return and production of party by order

At any time after the allowance of a writ of habeas corpus, the plaintiff therein, or the person applying therefor on behalf of the plaintiff, may give notice to the judge issuing the writ, and thereupon, if necessary to avoid delay, the judge shall by order require that the return be made and the party produced before the judge at such time and place, within the county or district, as may be convenient.

34.540. Contents of return

(1) The officer or person upon whom the writ was duly served shall state in the return, plainly and unequivocally:

> (a) Whether the officer or person has the party in custody or power or under restraint, and if the officer or person has not, whether the officer or person has had the party in custody or under power or restraint at any and what time prior or subsequent to the date of the writ.

> (b) If the officer or person has the party in custody or power or under restraint, the authority and true cause of such imprisonment or restraint, setting forth the same at large.

(2) If the party is detained by virtue of any writ, warrant or other written authority, a copy thereof shall be annexed to the return, and the original shall be produced, and exhibited on the return of the writ, to the court or judge before whom the writ is returnable.

(3) If the person upon whom the writ was served has had the party in power or custody or under restraint at any time prior or subsequent to the date of the writ, but has transferred such custody or restraint to another, the return shall state particularly to whom, at what time, for what cause, and by what authority the transfer took place.

(4) The return shall be signed by the person making the same, and except where the person is a sworn public officer, and makes the return in official capacity, it shall be verified by oath.

34.550. Warrant upon refusal or neglect to obey writ
If the person upon whom the writ was duly served refuses or neglects to obey the same by producing the party named in the writ and making a full and explicit return thereto within the time required, and no sufficient excuse is shown therefor, the court or judge before whom the writ was made returnable shall, upon due proof of the service thereof, forthwith issue a warrant against such person, directed to any sheriff in this state, commanding the sheriff forthwith to apprehend such person and bring the person immediately before such court or judge; and on the person being so brought, the person shall be committed to close custody in the jail of the county in which such judge shall be until the person makes return to the writ and complies with any order made in relation to the party for whose relief the writ was issued.

34.560. Failure of sheriff to return writ
If a sheriff neglects to return the writ, the warrant may be directed to any other person to be designated therein, who shall have full power to execute the same, and such sheriff, upon being brought up, may be committed to the jail of any county other than the county over which the sheriff has jurisdiction.

34.570. Precept commanding bringing of party in custody
The court or judge issuing the warrant may also, at the same time or afterwards, issue a precept to the person to whom the warrant is directed, commanding the person to bring forthwith before such court or judge the party for whose benefit the writ was allowed, who shall thereafter remain in the custody of such person until discharged or remanded.

34.580. Inquiry into cause of imprisonment
The court or judge before whom the party is brought on the writ shall, immediately after the return thereof, proceed to examine into the facts contained in the return, and into the cause of the imprisonment or restraint of such party.

34.590. Discharge where no legal cause for restraint
If no legal cause is shown for the imprisonment or restraint, or for the continuation thereof, the court or judge shall discharge such party from the custody or restraint under which the person is held.

34.600. Remand of party
It shall be the duty of the court or judge forthwith to remand such party if it appears that the party is legally detained in custody, either:

(1) By virtue of process issued by any court, or judge or commissioner or any other officer thereof, of the United states, in a case where such court, or judge or officer thereof, has exclusive jurisdiction; or,

(2) By virtue of the judgment of any court, or of any execution issued upon such judgment; or,

(3) For any contempt, specially and plainly charged in the commitment, by some court, officer or body having authority to commit for the contempt so charged; and,

(4) That the time during which such party may legally be detained has not expired.

34.610. Grounds for discharge of prisoner in custody under order or civil process

If it appears on the return that the prisoner is in custody by virtue of an order or civil process of any court legally constituted, or issued by an officer in the course of judicial proceedings before the officer, authorized by law, such prisoner shall be discharged only if one of the following cases exists:

(1) The jurisdiction of the court or officer has been exceeded, either as to matter, place, sum or person.

(2) The original imprisonment was lawful, yet by some act, omission or event which has taken place afterwards, the party has become entitled to be discharged.

(3) The order or process is defective in some matter of substance required by law, rendering the same void.

(4) The order or process, though in proper form, has been issued in a case not allowed by law.

(5) The person having the custody of the prisoner under such order or process is not the person empowered by law to detain the prisoner.

(6) The order or process is not authorized by any judgment of any court, nor by any provision of law.

34.620. Limitation upon inquiry into legality of certain judgments and process

No court or judge, on the return of a writ of habeas corpus, has power to inquire into the legality or justice of any order, judgment or process specified in ORS 34.330, nor into the justice, propriety or legality of any commitment for a contempt made by a court, officer or body, according to law, and charged in such commitment, as provided by law.

34.630. Proceedings where commitment for criminal offense is legal or party probably is guilty

If it appears that the party has legally been committed for a criminal offense, or if the party appears by the testimony offered with the return, or upon the hearing thereof, probably to be guilty of such offense, although the commitment is irregular, the party shall forthwith be remanded to the custody or placed under the restraint from which the party was taken, if the officer or person under whose custody or restraint the party was, is legally entitled thereto; if not so entitled, the party shall be committed to the custody of the officer or person so entitled.

34.640. Custody of party pending proceedings

Until judgment is given upon the return, the party may either be committed to the custody of the sheriff of the county, or placed in such care or custody as age and other circumstances may require.

34.650. Notice to third persons

When it appears from the return that the party named therein is in custody on an order or process under which another person has an interest in continuing imprisonment or restraint of the party, no order shall be made for discharge of the party until it shall appear that the party so interested, or the attorney of the party so interested has had notice of the time and place at which the writ has been made returnable.

34.660. Notice to district attorney

When it appears from the return that the party is imprisoned or restrained on a criminal accusation, the court or judge shall make no order for the discharge of the party until notice of the return is given to the district attorney of the county where the party is imprisoned or restrained.

34.670. Replication after return; hearing
The plaintiff in the proceeding, on the return of the writ, may, by replication, signed as in an action, controvert any of the material facts set forth in the return, or the plaintiff may allege therein any fact to show, either that imprisonment or restraint of the plaintiff is unlawful, or that the plaintiff is entitled to discharge. Thereupon the court or judge shall proceed in a summary way to hear such evidence as may be produced in support of or against the imprisonment or restraint, and to dispose of the party as the law and justice of the case may require.

34.680. Motion to deny petition; motion to strike; controverting replication; time to plead
(1) The defendant may, before the writ issues, move to deny the petition on the grounds that the petition fails to state a claim for habeas corpus relief. The defendant may, at any time after the writ issues, move to dismiss the writ on the grounds that the pleadings, including the petition, the return, the replication, if any, and any supporting evidence, demonstrate that plaintiff has failed to state or establish a claim for habeas corpus relief.

(2) The plaintiff may move to strike the return or any allegation or defense in the return. The defendant may move to strike the replication or any new matter in the replication, or by proof controvert the same, as upon a direct denial or avoidance.

(3) The return and replication shall be made within such time as the court or judge shall direct, and the petition, return and replication shall be construed and have the same effect as in an action.

34.690. Requirement for production of person after writ issued
The court or judge before whom the writ is returnable may, before final decision, issue a precept to the officer or other person to whom the writ is directed, requiring the production of the person.

34.695. Conduct of hearing
If the matter proceeds to an evidentiary hearing, as described in ORS 34.670, the court shall decide the issues raised in the pleadings and may receive proof by affidavits, depositions, oral testimony or other competent evidence.

34.700. Judgment; obedience to judgment; attorney fees
(1) If it appears that the party detained is imprisoned or restrained illegally, judgment shall be given that the party be discharged forthwith; otherwise, judgment shall be given that the proceeding be dismissed and the party remanded. No officer or other person is liable to any action or proceeding for obeying such judgment of discharge.

(2) The court shall include in the judgment an order that the defendant pay the attorney fees incurred by the petition, not to exceed $100, if:

(a) The court enters a judgment requiring that the plaintiff be discharged; and

(b) The court finds that the allegations or defenses in the return were frivolous.

34.710. Appeal; conclusiveness of judgment
Any party to a proceeding by habeas corpus, including the state when the district attorney appears therein, may appeal from the judgment of the court refusing to allow such writ or any judgment therein, either in term time or vacation, in like manner and with like effect as in an action. No question once finally determined upon a proceeding by habeas corpus shall be reexamined upon another proceeding of the same kind.

34.712. Summary affirmation of judgment on appeal
In reviewing the judgment of any court under ORS 34.310 to 34.730, the Court of Appeals, on its own motion or on the motion of the defendant, may summarily affirm, without oral argument, the judgment after submission of the appellant's brief and without submission of the defendant's brief if the court finds that no substantial question of law is presented by the appeal. Notwithstanding ORS 2.570, the Chief Judge of the Court of Appeals may deny or, if the plaintiff does not oppose the motion, grant a defendant's motion for summary affirmation. A dismissal of appeal under this section constitutes a decision upon the merits of the appeal.

34.720. Imprisonment after discharge
A person who has been finally discharged upon a proceeding by habeas corpus may not again be imprisoned, restrained or kept in custody for the same cause. A person is not deemed to be imprisoned, restrained or kept in custody for the same cause if:

(1) The person has been discharged from a commitment on a criminal charge, and afterwards is committed for the same offense by the legal order or process of the court wherein the person is bound by a release agreement or has deposited security, or in which the person is indicted or convicted for the same offense;

(2) After a judgment of discharge for a defect of evidence or for a material defect in the commitment, in a criminal case, the party again is arrested on sufficient evidence, and committed by legal process for the same offense;

(3) In a civil action or suit, the party has been discharged for illegality in the judgment or process, and afterwards is imprisoned for the same cause of action or suit; or

(4) In a civil action or suit, the person has been discharged from commitment on a writ of arrest, and afterwards is committed on execution, in the same action or suit, or on a writ of arrest in another action or suit, after the dismissal of the first one.

34.730 Forfeiture for refusing copy of order or process
Any officer or other person refusing to deliver a copy of any order, warrant, process or other authority by which the officer or person detains any person, to anyone who demands a copy, and tenders the fees therefor, shall forfeit $200 to the person so detained.

PENNSYLVANIA

Pennsylvania Statutes
Title 42 Pa.C.S.A. Judiciary and Judiciary Procedure
Chapter 65. Habeas Corpus

§6501. Writ not to be suspended
The privilege of the writ of habeas corpus shall not be suspended, unless when in the case of rebellion or invasion the public safety may require it.

§6502. Power to issue writ
(a) General rule.—Any judge of a court of record may issue the writ of habeas corpus to inquire into the cause of detention of any person or for any other lawful purpose.

(b) Venue.—The venue of matters brought under this chapter shall be as prescribed by general rule.

§6503. Right to apply for writ
(a) General rule.—Except as provided in subsection (b), an application for habeas corpus to inquire into the cause of detention may be brought by or on behalf of any person restrained of his liberty within this Commonwealth under any pretense whatsoever.

(b) Exception.—Where a person is restrained by virtue of sentence after conviction for a criminal offense, the writ of habeas corpus shall not be available if a remedy may be had by post-conviction hearing proceedings authorized by law.

§6504. Return on writ
The writ, or the order to show cause why the writ should not issue, shall be directed to the person having custody of the person detained. It shall be returned within three days unless for good cause additional time, not exceeding 20 days, is allowed. The person to whom the writ or the order is directed shall make a return certifying the true cause of the detention and, except as otherwise prescribed by general rules or by rule or order of court, shall produce at the hearing the body of the person detained.

§6505. Interference with writ prohibited
Any person who shall fail or refuse to respond to a writ or to an order issued under this chapter, or who shall change the place of detention of any person for the purpose of defeating the writ, or shall, without express authorization from a judge of a court of record, recommit on substantially the same facts and circumstances any person set at large upon a habeas corpus, or shall do any act for the purpose of defecting the writ or the order, commits a misdemeanor of the second degree.

Current through 2014 Regular Session Acts 1 to 130

RHODE ISLAND

General Laws of Rhode Island
Title 10. Courts and Civil Procedure—Procedure in Particular Actions
Chapter 9. Habeas Corpus

§10-9-1. General right to writ
Every person imprisoned in any correctional institution or otherwise restrained of his or her liberty, other than persons imprisoned or restrained pursuant to a final judgment entered in a criminal proceeding, may prosecute a writ of habeas corpus, according to the provisions of this chapter, to obtain relief from the imprisonment or restraint, if it shall prove to be unlawful.

§10-9-3. Application for writ—contents
Application for such a writ shall be made to the supreme or superior or family court, or to any justice of

those courts, by complaint in writing, signed by the party for whose relief it is intended, or by some person in his or her behalf, setting forth:

(1) The person by whom and the place where the party is imprisoned or restrained, naming the prisoner and the person detaining him or her if their names are known, and describing them if they are not known.

(2) The cause or pretense of the imprisonment or restraint, according to the knowledge and belief of the person applying. If the imprisonment or restraint is by virtue of any warrant or other process a copy thereof shall be annexed or it shall be made to appear that a copy thereof has been demanded and refused, or that for some sufficient reason a demand of a copy could not be made. The facts set forth in the complaint shall be verified by the oath of the person making the application or by that of some other credible witness, which oath may be administered by the court or justice to whom the application is made, or by any justice of the peace or notary public.

§10-9-4. Issuance of writ—forms

(a) The court or justice to whom the complaint shall be made shall, without delay, award and issue a writ of habeas corpus; if against any sheriff or deputy sheriff of this state, or against the warden of any correctional institution in this state, or against any marshal or deputy marshal of the United states, it shall be substantially in the following form:

The State of Rhode Island and Providence Plantations.

SC.

(SEAL) _____ to _____ Greeting:

We command you, that the body of _____ of _____ , in your custody (or, by you imprisoned or restrained of his or her liberty, as the case may be), as it is said, together with the day and cause of his or her taking and detaining by whatsoever name the said _____ shall be called or charged, you have before our supreme (or superior as the case may be) court, held at _____ immediately after the receipt of this writ, to do and receive what our court shall then and there consider concerning him or her in this behalf, and have there this writ.

Witness, the seal of the _____ court at _____ this day of _____ , in the year ____ .

Or, witness my hand this _____ day of _____ in the year ____ .

Justice of the _____ court.

(b) And if not against an officer as described in subsection (a), it shall be substantially in the following form:

The State of Rhode Island and Providence Plantations.

SC.

To the sheriffs of our several counties and their deputies,

APPENDIX—RHODE ISLAND

(SEAL) _____ Greeting:

We command you, that the body of _____ of _____ by _____ of _____ imprisoned or restrained of his or her liberty, as it is said, you take and have before our supreme (or superior, as the case may be) court, held at _____ immediately after the receipt of this writ, to do and receive whatever the court shall then consider concerning him or her in this behalf, and summon the said _____ then and there to appear before our said court to show the cause of the taking and detaining of the said and have you there this writ with your doings thereon.

Witness, the seal of the _____ court at _____ this _____ day of _____ in the year ____ .

Or, witness my hand this _____ day of _____ in the year ____ .

Justice of the _____ court.

§10-9-5. Court to which writ returnable
Any justice issuing a writ under this chapter shall make the writ returnable to the court of which he or she is a justice.

§10-9-6. Return to Providence superior court when other courts not in session
If the writ is returnable to the supreme court and the court is not in session upon the return of the writ, it shall be returned to, and action on the writ be had by the superior court at Providence. If returnable to the superior court for either Newport, Kent, or Washington county, and the court is not in session upon its return, it shall be returned to the superior court at Providence.

§10-9-7. Receipt and return of writ
Any person to whom the writ is directed shall receive it, and upon payment or tender of charges, if any be demandable for the execution of it, he or she shall make due return of the writ.

§10-9-8. Return or statement by person to whom writ directed
The person to whom the writ is directed shall state in his or her return on the writ:

(1) Whether he or she has or has not the party in his or her custody or power or under restraint;

(2) If he or she has the party in his or her custody or power or under restraint, he or she shall set forth at large the authority, and the true and whole cause of the imprisonment or restraint, with a copy of the writ, warrant, or other process, if any, upon which the party is detained; and

(3) If he or she has had the party in his or her custody or power or under restraint and has transferred custody or restraint to another, he or she shall state particularly to whom, at what time, for what cause, and by what authority the transfer was made.

§10-9-9. Signature and oath to return or statement
The return or statement shall be signed by the person making it, and it shall also be sworn to by him or her, unless he or she be a sworn public officer and shall make the return in his or her official capacity.

§10-9-10. Body brought with return or statement
The person who makes the return or statement shall, at the same time, bring the body of the party, if in

his or her custody or power or under his or her restraint, according to the command of the writ, unless prevented by the sickness or infirmity of the party.

§10-9-11. Illness of person confined
Whenever, from the sickness or infirmity of the party, he or she cannot, without danger, be brought to the place appointed for the return of the writ, that fact shall be stated in the return, and if it is proved to the satisfaction of the court, the court may proceed to the institution or other place where the party is confined and there make the examination, or may adjourn the court to another time or may make such other order in the case as law and justice shall require.

§10-9-12. Remand, bail, or commitment pending judgment
Until judgment is given, the court may remand the party, or may bail him or her to appear from day to day, or may commit him or her to a member of the division of sheriffs, or place him or her under such other care and custody as the circumstances of the case may require.

§10-9-13. Failure of officer to deliver copy of process by which prisoner held
Every officer who shall refuse or neglect, for six (6) hours, to deliver a true copy of the warrant or process, by which he or she detains any prisoner, to any person who shall demand such copy and tender the fees therefor, shall forfeit and pay to the prisoner the sum of one hundred dollars ($100).

§10-9-14. Examination of cause of restraint—adjournment
When the writ of habeas corpus is returned, the court shall, without delay, proceed to examine the causes of the imprisonment or restraint, but the examination may be adjourned from time to time, as circumstances may require.

§10-9-15. Notice to party on whose process restraint based
Whenever it appears, from the return of the writ, or otherwise, that the party is detained on any process under which any other person has an interest in continuing his or her imprisonment or restraint, the party shall not be discharged until sufficient notice shall have been given to the interested person or his or her attorney, if within the state or within thirty (30) miles of the place of examination, to appear and object to the discharge, if he or she think fit, which notice shall be given by the party imprisoned, in the manner prescribed by the court, or, in default thereof, he or she shall be remanded to the custody of the person against whom the writ of habeas corpus issued.

§10-9-16. Notice to attorney general or complainant in criminal cases
Whenever it appears from the return of the writ, or otherwise, that the party is imprisoned on any criminal accusation, he or she shall not be discharged until sufficient notice shall have been given to the attorney general, or to the complainant in the matter, that he or she may appear and object to the discharge, if he or she think fit, which notice shall be given by the party imprisoned, in the manner prescribed by the court, or, in default thereof, he or she shall be remanded to the custody of the person against whom the writ of habeas corpus issued.

§10-9-17. Denial of facts in return or statement—hearing of evidence
The party imprisoned or restrained may deny any of the facts set forth in the return or statement and may allege any other facts that may be material in the case, and the court shall proceed in a summary way to examine the causes of imprisonment or restraint and to hear the evidence that may be produced by any person interested and authorized to appear, both in support of the imprisonment or restraint and against it, and thereupon to dispose of the party as law and justice shall require.

§10-9-18. Discharge on failure to show cause for restraint
If no legal cause be shown for the imprisonment or restraint, the court shall discharge the party therefrom.

§10-9-19. Admission to bail
If the party is detained for any cause or offense for which he or she is bailable of right, he or she shall be admitted to bail if sufficient bail be offered, and if not, he or she shall be remanded with an order of the court expressing the sum in which he or she shall be held to bail, and the court at which he or she shall be required to appear, and any person authorized thereto may, at any time before the sitting of the court, bail the party pursuant to the order.

§10-9-20. Order as to bail when person held on civil mesne process
If the party is committed on mesne process in any civil action for want of bail and if it shall appear that the sum for which bail is required is excessive and unreasonable, the court shall decide what bail is reasonable and shall order that on giving reasonable bail the party shall be discharged.

§10-9-21. Remand to custody
If the party is lawfully imprisoned or restrained and is not entitled to be enlarged on giving bail, he or she shall be remanded to the person from whose custody he or she was taken or to such other person or officer as is by law authorized to detain him or her.

§10-9-22. Appeals and exceptions barred—subsequent application to supreme court allowed
No appeal or exception shall lie to the judgment of the superior court in habeas corpus; but if the superior court shall remand the person imprisoned or restrained, the superior court's judgment shall not bar an application to the supreme court, or a justice thereof, for another writ upon the same facts.

§10-9-23. Enforcement of writ by attachment as for contempt
If any person to whom a writ of habeas corpus shall be directed shall refuse to receive the writ or shall neglect to obey and execute it according to the provisions of this chapter and no sufficient excuse shall be shown for his or her refusal or neglect, the court before which the writ is returnable shall proceed immediately, by process of attachment as for a contempt, to compel obedience to the writ and to punish the person guilty of the contempt.

§10-9-24. Attachment and commitment of a member of the division of sheriffs
If an attachment shall be issued against any deputy sheriff, it may be directed to the commissioner of public safety and the superintendent of the Rhode Island state police, who shall have full power to execute the attachment; and if the deputy sheriff or deputy should be committed upon such process, he or she may be committed to the adult correctional institutions.

§10-9-25. Forfeiture for failure to receive and execute writ
Every person guilty of such a refusal or neglect to receive and execute a writ of habeas corpus shall also forfeit and pay to the party aggrieved by the refusal or neglect one thousand dollars ($1,000).

§10-9-26. Precept after disobedience of writ
Upon the refusal or neglect of the person to whom the writ of habeas corpus is directed, the court may also issue a precept to any officer, or other person designated in the writ, commanding him or her to bring immediately before the court the person for whose benefit the writ of habeas corpus was issued, and

the prisoner shall be thereupon discharged, bailed or remanded, in like manner as if he or she had been brought in upon the writ of habeas corpus.

§10-9-27. Transfer or concealment of prisoner with intent to avoid
Every person who shall have in custody or under his or her power any person entitled to any writ of habeas corpus, whether any writ has issued or not, and who shall, with intent to elude the service of a writ habeas corpus or to avoid the effect of a writ of habeas corpus, transfer the prisoner to the custody, or place him or her under the power or control, of any other person, or conceal him or her, or change the place of his or her confinement, shall forfeit and pay to the party aggrieved thereby one thousand dollars ($1,000).

§10-9-28. Common law remedies not barred by penalties
The recovery of any penalty imposed by this chapter shall not bar any action at the common law for false imprisonment, or for false return to the writ of habeas corpus, or for any other injury or damage sustained by the aggrieved party.

§10-9-29. Rearrest of discharged person
No person who has been discharged upon a writ of habeas corpus shall be again imprisoned or restrained for the same cause, unless he or she is indicted or charged by information therefor or convicted thereof, or committed for want of bail, by some court of record having jurisdiction of the cause, or unless, after a discharge for defect of proof or for some material in the commitment in a criminal case, he or she shall be again arrested on sufficient proof, and committed by legal process, for the same offense.

§10-9-30. Judicial powers not restrained
Nothing contained in this chapter shall be so construed as to restrain the power of the supreme or superior court, or any one of the justices thereof, to issue a writ of habeas corpus at their discretion, and thereupon to bail any person for whatsoever cause he or she may be committed or restrained, or to discharge him or her, as law and justice shall require.

§10-9-31. Power of justices to admit to bail
Whenever any person is committed to a correctional institution on any criminal accusation for want of bail, any justice of the supreme or superior court, or any person specially appointed by either of the courts, may admit him or her to bail in like manner as might have been done by the court or magistrate who committed him or her, and the supreme or superior court justices respectively shall have power to issue a writ of habeas corpus and to cause the prisoner to be brought before them, whenever it shall be necessary for the purpose expressed in this section.

§10-9-32. Judicial power to bring criminal defendants and witnesses
Nothing contained in this chapter shall be so construed as to restrain the power of any court to issue a writ of habeas corpus, whenever necessary to bring before them any prisoner for trial, in any criminal case lawfully pending in the same court, or to bring in any prisoner to be examined as a witness in any suit or proceeding, civil or criminal, pending in the court, whenever they shall think the personal attendance and examination of the witness necessary for the attainment of justice.

The Statutes and Constitution are current through Chapter 104 of the January 2014 session.

SOUTH CAROLINA

Code of Laws of South Carolina
Title 17. Criminal Procedure
Chapter 17. Habeas Corpus

§17-17-10. Persons entitled to writ of habeas corpus
If any person shall be or stand committed or detained for any crime, unless (a) for felony the punishment of which is death or treason, plainly expressed in the warrant of commitment, (b) charged as accessory before the fact to treason or felony the punishment of which is death or (c) charged with suspicion of treason or felony which is punishable with death, which shall be plainly expressed in the warrant of commitment, he shall be entitled to the writ of habeas corpus.

§17-17-20. Forfeiture of entitlement in certain cases
If any person shall have willfully neglected by the space of two whole terms after his imprisonment to pray a habeas corpus for his enlargement such person, so willfully neglecting, shall not have any habeas corpus to be granted in vacation time in pursuance of this chapter.

§17-17-30. Authority of judges to grant writs of habeas corpus
Any of the judges of this State, in vacation time and out of term, upon view of the copy of the warrant of commitment and detainer or otherwise and upon oath made that such copy was denied to be given by the person in whose custody the prisoner is detained, shall, upon request made in writing by such person as is committed as aforesaid or any on his behalf, attested and subscribed by two witnesses who were present at the delivery of the request, award and grant a writ of habeas corpus, under the seal of such court, whereof he shall be one of the judges.

§17-17-40. Authority of any two magistrates to grant writs of habeas corpus
Any two magistrates shall grant the writ of habeas corpus as fully, effectually and lawfully as may any judge of the court of common pleas and general sessions or justice of the Supreme Court of this State, except in cases of felony the punishment for which is death or imprisonment for life and except in changing the custody of any child, in which cases magistrates shall have no jurisdiction in applications for habeas corpus.

§17-17-50. Persons to whom writ shall be directed
Such writ shall be directed to the officer in whose custody the party so committed or detained shall be and shall be returned immediately before the judge issuing it.

§17-17-60. Service of writ
The writ shall be served upon the officer or left at the jail or prison with any of the underofficers, underkeepers or deputies of any such officer or keeper.

§17-17-70. Handling of prisoner after service of writ; payment of charges; return of writ
Such officer or his underofficer, underkeeper or deputy shall, within three days after the service thereof and upon:

(1) Payment or tender of charges, not exceeding ten cents per mile, of bringing the prisoner, to be ascertained by the judge or court that awarded the writ and endorsed thereon; and

(2) Security given by his own bond (a) to pay the charges of carrying back the prisoner, if he shall be remanded by the court or judge to which he shall be brought and (b) that he will not make any escape by the way;

Make return of such writ and bring or cause to be brought the body of the person so committed or restrained unto or before the judge or court from whence the writ shall issue or unto and before such other person before whom the writ is made returnable, according to the command thereof, and shall then certify the true cause of his detainer or imprisonment; provided, however, that:

(1) If any prisoner be not able to pay such charges they shall be paid by the county wherein he is confined; and

(2) If such prisoner shall be acquitted of the charge against him or finally discharged on habeas corpus by the judge or court hearing the habeas corpus proceedings the expenses of the proceeding in habeas corpus shall be paid by the county in which the case is situated.

§17-17-80. Time within which prisoners must be brought before court
If the place of imprisonment of the person be beyond the distance of twenty miles from the place where such court is held and not above one hundred miles he shall be brought before the court or the person before whom the writ is returnable within the space of ten days and if beyond the distance of one hundred miles then within the space of twenty days after the delivery of such writ and not longer.

§17-17-90. Granting of writ during term of court
During the term of the circuit court for the county in which any prisoner is detained no person shall be removed from the common jail upon any writ of habeas corpus granted in pursuance of this chapter but, upon any such writ, shall be brought before the circuit judge, in open court, who is thereupon to do what to justice shall appertain.

§17-17-100. Transfer of matter for hearing to judge of court in county where prisoner was convicted
Any judge before whom a petition for a writ of habeas corpus is made by any person confined by the State Board of Corrections in any of its places of confinement who has been tried and convicted by a court of competent jurisdiction, shall upon issuance of the writ of habeas corpus transfer the matter for hearing to any judge of any court of competent jurisdiction in the county where the person was convicted.

§17-17-110. Granting of writ after adjournment
After the circuit court adjourns any person detained may have a writ of habeas corpus, according to the direction and intention of this chapter.

§17-17-120. Discharge only after notice given to Attorney General, Circuit Solicitor, or attorney acting for State
When it appears from the return of the writ or otherwise that the person is imprisoned on a criminal accusation he shall not be discharged until sufficient notice has been given to the Attorney General or circuit solicitor or other attorney acting for the State, that he may appear and object to such discharge, if he thinks fit.

§17-17-130. Discharge of prisoner after hearing; recognizance in judge's discretion, appearance in the following term of court
If, upon a hearing, the prisoner shall be entitled to his discharge then the judge before whom he is brought

shall within two days after the prisoner shall be brought before him discharge the prisoner from his imprisonment, taking his recognizance, with one or more surety or sureties, in any sum according to the judge's discretion, having regard to the nature of the offense, for his appearance the term following in the court of general sessions for the county in which the offense is alleged to have been committed or in the court of such other county in which the alleged offense is properly cognizable, as the case shall require. And the judge shall then certify the writ, with the return thereof, and the recognizance into the court in which such appearance is to be made. But if no legal cause be shown for the imprisonment or restraint the prisoner shall be discharged therefrom.

§17-17-140. Right to appeal from decision on writ
An appeal from all final decisions rendered on applications for writs of habeas corpus shall be allowed as is provided by law in civil actions.

§17-17-150. Person discharged shall not be rearrested or committed for same offense
No person who shall be delivered or set at large upon any writ of habeas corpus shall, at any time, be again imprisoned or committed for the same offense by any person whatsoever, other than by the legal order and process of such court wherein he shall be bound by recognizance to appear or other court having jurisdiction of the cause. If any other person shall knowingly, contrary to this chapter, recommit or imprison or knowingly procure or cause to be recommitted or imprisoned for the same offense or pretended offense any person delivered or set at large, as aforesaid, or be knowingly aiding or assisting therein, then he shall forfeit to the prisoner or person grieved the sum of two thousand five hundred dollars, any colorable pretense or variation in the warrant of commitment notwithstanding, to be recovered as provided in §17-17-180.

§17-17-160. Officers shall execute writ
Every sheriff, deputy sheriff or jailer shall give due obedience to the execution of every writ of habeas corpus made or signed by any person by law empowered to grant the writ and shall do and perform any matter or thing which by the writ he may be required to do. And if he shall willfully neglect, refuse or omit to obey or perform the writ when legally requested and demanded in such case, for each such neglect, refusal, or omission, he shall forfeit the sum of five hundred dollars, to be recovered by indictment.

§17-17-170. Penalty for officers neglecting their duty
Every person whatsoever to whom any power is given, either judicial or ministerial, by this chapter which, by virtue hereof, he is required and commanded to exercise who shall willfully neglect, refuse or omit to exercise the power when such exercise shall be legally requested and demanded, according to the directions herein, and when the person so requesting and demanding such exercise is legally entitled so to request or demand by the provisions of this chapter, for each such offense shall forfeit the sum of five hundred dollars and shall be thereafter incapable of holding or executing his office.

§17-17-180. Recovery of penalties
Such penalties may be recovered by the prisoner or party grieved, his executors and administrators, against such offender, his executors or administrators, by action in any court of competent jurisdiction wherein no protection, rebellion or any unlawful obstruction of the laws, as set forth in §25-1-1850, the Governor in his judgment shall deem the public safety to require it, he may suspend the privilege of the writ of habeas corpus in any case throughout the State or any part thereof.

§17-17-200. Effect of suspension of writ
Whenever the privilege of the writ of habeas corpus shall be suspended, as aforesaid, no military or other of-

ficer shall be compelled in answer to any writ of habeas corpus to return the body of any person detained by him by authority of the Governor. But upon certificate under oath of the officer having charge of anyone so detained that such person is detained by him as a prisoner under the authority of the Governor further proceedings under the writ of habeas corpus shall be suspended by the judge or court having issued the writ so long as such suspension by the Governor shall remain in force and the cause for such suspension continue.

Current through End of 2013 Reg. Sess.

SOUTH DAKOTA

South Dakota Codified Laws
Title 21. Judicial Remedies
Chapter 21-27. Habeas Corpus

21-27-1. *Right of person detained or imprisoned to apply for writ*
Any person committed or detained, imprisoned or restrained of his liberty, under any color or pretense whatever, civil or criminal, except as provided herein, may apply to the Supreme or circuit court, or any justice or judge thereof, for a writ of habeas corpus.

21-27-1.1. *Penal institution disciplinary sanctions—writ not available remedy*
A writ of habeas corpus is not a remedy available to an applicant who is incarcerated or detained under a lawful order, or judgment and sentence to seek relief from sanctions imposed upon an applicant or administrative decisions made with regard to such application arising out of disciplinary or administrative actions of the penal institution where the applicant is being confined.

21-27-2. *Inquiry into delay in bringing criminal prosecution to trial—powers of court on return of writ*
Any person committed for a criminal offense and not brought to trial, as provided by the provisions of this code, is entitled to have the delay inquired into upon a writ of habeas corpus, and the court or judge, upon the return of such writ, shall have power to remand or discharge the applicant or to admit him to bail, with or without sureties as the case may be.

21-27-3. *Contents of application for writ—documentary authority for commitment attached—identification of prior applications*
An application for a writ of habeas corpus shall be in writing and signed by the applicant or some person on his behalf, setting forth the facts concerning his detention and in whose custody he is detained, and shall be accompanied by a copy of the warrant of commitment or other documentary authority, if any, or by an affidavit that such copy has been demanded of the person in whose custody he is detained and by him refused or not given. The application shall identify any previous applications made pursuant to this chapter, together with the grounds therein asserted.

21-27-3.1. *Time for application*
Proceedings under this chapter cannot be maintained while an appeal from the applicant's conviction and sentence is pending or during the time within which such appeal may be perfected.

21-27-3.2. repealed by SL 2012, ch 118, §2

21-27-3.3. Two-year statute of limitation
A two-year statute of limitation applies to all applications for relief under this chapter. This limitation period shall run from the latest of:

(1) The date on which the judgment became final by the conclusion of direct review or the expiration of the time for seeking such review;

(2) The date on which the impediment to filing an application created by state action in violation of the constitution or laws of the United States or of this state is removed, if such impediment prevented the applicant from filing;

(3) The date on which the constitutional right asserted in the application was initially recognized by the Supreme Court of the United States or the Supreme court of this state if the right has both been newly recognized and is retroactively applicable to cases on collateral review; or

(4) The date on which the factual predicate of the claim or claims presented could have been discovered through the exercise of due diligence.

21-27-4. Counsel appointed for indigent applicant—counsel fees—ineffective assistance of counsel
If a person has been committed, detained, imprisoned, or restrained of liberty, under any color or pretense whatever, civil or criminal, and if upon application made in good faith to the court or judge thereof, having jurisdiction, for a writ of habeas corpus, it is satisfactorily shown that the person is without means to prosecute the proceedings, the court or judge shall, if the judge finds that such appointment is necessary to ensure a full, fair, and impartial proceeding, appoint counsel for the indigent person pursuant to chapter 23A-40. Such counsel fees or expenses shall be a charge against and be paid by the county from which the person was committed, or for which the person is held as determined by the court. Payment of all such fees or expenses shall be made only upon written order of the court or judge issuing the writ. The ineffectiveness or incompetence of counsel, whether retained or appointed, during any collateral post-conviction proceeding is not grounds for relief under this chapter.

21-27-5. Writ awarded unless application shows no right to relief
The court or judge to whom the application for a writ of habeas corpus is made, shall forthwith award the writ, unless it shall appear from the application itself or from any document annexed thereto, that the applicant can neither be discharged nor admitted to bail, nor in any other manner relieved.

21-27-5.1. Second or subsequent application for writ—leave to file—dismissal
A claim presented in a second or subsequent habeas corpus application under this chapter that was presented in a prior application under this chapter or otherwise to the courts of this state by the same applicant shall be dismissed.

Before a second or subsequent application for a writ of habeas corpus may be filed, the applicant shall move in the circuit court of appropriate jurisdiction for an order authorizing the applicant to file the application.

The assigned judge shall enter an order denying leave to file a second or successive application for a writ of habeas corpus unless:

(1) The applicant identifies newly discovered evidence that, if proven and viewed in light of the evidence as a whole, would be sufficient to establish by clear and convincing evidence that no reasonable fact finder would have found the applicant guilty of the underlying offense; or

(2) The application raises a new rule of constitutional law, made retroactive to cases on collateral review by the United States Supreme Court and the South Dakota Supreme Court, that was previously unavailable. The grant or denial of an authorization by the circuit court to file a second or subsequent application shall not be appealable.

21-27-6. *Forfeiture by judge for refusal or delay in issuing writ—liability for damages unimpaired*
Any judge empowered by this chapter to issue writs of habeas corpus, who shall corruptly refuse to issue such writ, when legally applied to, in a case where such writ may lawfully issue, or who shall, for the purpose of oppression, unreasonably delay the issuing of such writ, shall, for every such offense, forfeit to the prisoner or person aggrieved a sum not exceeding five hundred dollars. Recovery of the penalty provided therein shall be no bar to a civil suit for damages.

21-27-7. *Writ used to produce prisoners for testimony in criminal proceedings*
The Supreme and circuit courts and the judges thereof shall have power to issue writs of habeas corpus for the purpose of bringing any person imprisoned in any prison before any court or magistrate, to testify in any criminal action or proceeding in any county of the state, and returning such person to such prison.

21-27-8. *Signature and direction of writ—endorsement by Habeas Corpus Act*
The writ of habeas corpus, if issued by the court, shall be under the seal of the court, or if by a judge, under his hand; and shall be directed to the person in whose custody the applicant is detained. To the end that no officer, sheriff, jailer, keeper, or other person to whom such writ is directed may pretend ignorance thereof, every such writ shall be endorsed with these words, By the Habeas Corpus Act.

21-27-9. *Repealed by SL 1983, ch 169, §7*

21-27-9.1. *Server of writ—eligibility—power—liability—manner of service—persons served*
The writ of habeas corpus may be served by the sheriff, coroner, or any person appointed for that purpose by the court or judge by whom the writ is entered; if served by a person not an officer, he has the same power, and is liable to the same penalty for nonperformance of his duty, as though he were sheriff. Service shall be made by leaving a copy of the order with the person to whom it is directed, or with l; 'J I any of his subordinates who may be at the place where the applicant is detained. If the respondent does not have the applicant imprisoned or restrained in custody, the service may be made upon any person who has the applicant in custody with the same effect as though he had been made a respondent. Concurrent service of the writ of habeas corpus shall be made upon the state's attorney of the county in which the application is made.

21-27-9.2. *Production of applicant—payment of expenses—applicant in state hospital or penitentiary*
The officer or person upon whom the writ of habeas corpus is served shall produce the body of the applicant before the court at the hearing of the cause of imprisonment or detainer. If the applicant is in the custody of a civil officer, the court or judge who granted the writ shall determine the expense of bringing the applicant to court, which shall be paid prior to the hearing. Security shall be given to pay the charges for carrying him back, if he is remanded. If the applicant is confined in the state penitentiary or state hospital, an order shall be issued commanding the sheriff of the county in which the

application is made to take custody of the applicant during the pendency of any proceedings before the court and to transport the applicant from and return the applicant to the state penitentiary or state hospital if he is not released.

21-27-9.3. *Return to writ—time for filing—content*
The state's attorney of the county in which the writ of habeas corpus was issued shall file a return to the writ within fifteen days unless for good cause additional or less time, is granted. The return shall state the true cause or authority for the detention.

21-27-10. *Contempt and forfeiture by sheriff or jailer for failure to return writ and produce applicant—liability for damages unaffected*
If any officer, sheriff, jailer, keeper, or other person to whom any writ of habeas corpus is directed shall neglect or refuse to make the return, or to bring the body of the applicant according to the command of such writ, he shall be punished as for contempt and shall also forfeit to the prisoner or person aggrieved a sum not exceeding five hundred dollars. Recovery of the penalties provided herein shall be no bar to a civil suit for damages.

21-27-11. *Transfer or concealment of applicant to avoid writ as felony*
Anyone having a person in his custody or under his restraint, power, or control for whose relief a writ of habeas corpus is issued who, with intent to avoid the effect of such writ, shall transfer such person to the custody, or place him or her under the control of another, or shall conceal him or her, or change the place of his or her confinement, with intent to avoid the operation of such writ, or with intent to remove him or her out of this state, is guilty of a Class 5 felony.

21-27-12. *Day set for hearing of cause*
Upon the return of the writ of habeas corpus, a day shall be set for the hearing of the cause of imprisonment or detainer, not exceeding thirty days thereafter, unless for good cause additional or less time is allowed.

21-27-13. *Denials and new allegations in applicant's answer to return of writ—amendment of return and suggestions against return*
The applicant for a writ of habeas corpus may deny any of the material facts set forth in the return or may allege any fact to show, either that the imprisonment or detention is unlawful or that he is then entitled to his discharge, which allegations or denials shall be made on oath. The return may be amended by leave of the court or judge, before or after the same is filed, as also may all suggestions made against it, in order that all material facts may be ascertained.

21-27-14. *Hearing and disposition of cause by judge*
The court or judge shall proceed in a summary way to settle the facts by hearing the evidence and arguments, as well of all persons interested civilly, if any there be, as of the applicant and the person who holds him in custody, and shall dispose of the applicant as the case may require.

21-27-14.1. *Judge to hear application*
The application shall be heard before any judge of the court in which the conviction took place. A record of the proceedings shall be made and kept. There may be no proceedings on an application by a judge who imposed sentence on the applicant or who otherwise denied him relief concerning the subject matter involved in the application.

21-27-15. Judgment not inquired into on writ

No court or judge, on the return of a writ of habeas corpus, shall in any other manner inquire into the legality or justice of a judgment or decree of a court legally constituted.

21 27-16. Causes for discharge of applicant committed on judicial process

If it appears on the return of a writ of habeas corpus that the applicant is in custody by virtue of process from any court legally constituted, he can be discharged only for one or more of the following causes:

(1) When the court has exceeded the limit of its jurisdiction, either as to the matter, place, sum, or person;

(2) Where, though the original imprisonment was lawful, yet by some act, omission, or event, which has subsequently taken place, the party has become entitled to his discharge;

(3) Where the process is defective in some substantial form required by law;

(4) Where the process, though in proper form, has been issued in a case or under circumstances where the laws do not allow process or orders for imprisonment or arrest to issue;

(5) When, although in proper form, the process has been issued or executed by a person either unauthorized to issue or execute the same, or where the person having the custody of the applicant, under the process, is not the person empowered by law to detain him;

(6) Where the process appears to have been obtained by fraud, false pretense, or bribery;

(7) Where there is no general law nor any judgment, order, or decree of a court to authorize the process, if in a civil suit, nor any conviction, if in a criminal proceeding.

21-27-17. New commitment in criminal case to remedy defects in previous commitment—admission of applicant to bail

In all cases where the imprisonment is in a criminal, or supposed criminal matter, if it shall appear to the court or judge that there is sufficient legal cause for the commitment of the applicant, although such commitment may have been informally made or without due authority, or the process may have been executed by a person not authorized, the court or judge shall make a new commitment in proper form, directed to the proper officer, or shall admit the applicant to bail, if the case be bailable, as upon a preliminary examination.

21-27-18. Admission to bail of applicant in custody under judicial process

Sections 21-27-19 to 21-27-24, inclusive, shall control the admission to bail where the application for the writ of habeas corpus is by or in behalf of a person in custody under judicial process.

21-27-18.1. Review by Supreme Court—certificate of probable cause required—motion for issuance of certificate—appeal

A final judgment or order entered under this chapter may not be reviewed by the Supreme Court of this state on appeal unless the circuit judge who renders the judgment or a justice of the Supreme Court issues a certificate of probable cause that an appealable issue exists. A motion seeking issuance of a certificate of probable cause shall be filed within thirty days from the date the final judgment or order is entered. The issuance or refusal to issue a certificate of probable cause is not appealable. However, a party may, upon the circuit court judge's refusal to issue a certificate of probable cause, file a separate motion for issuance of a certificate of probable cause with the Supreme Court within twenty days of the entry of the circuit judge's refusal. Any party filing a motion with the Supreme Court shall serve a copy of the motion upon the opposing party, who shall have ten days to respond. The applying party shall then have five days to reply to such response. If a certificate of probable cause is issued the appeal may be brought by an applicant or the state within thirty days after entry of the certificate of probable cause.

Service of either a motion for a certificate of probable cause or of an appeal must be made upon both the attorney general and the appropriate state's attorney when the motion is made or the appeal is taken by the party seeking the habeas corpus relief.

21-27-19. Admission to bail on grant of writ
When the writ of habeas corpus is granted, the court or judge granting the writ may, within its discretion, admit the prisoner to bail, pending further order of the court.

21-27-20. Supreme Court order required for admission to bail pending application for writ or pending appellate review
The prisoner shall not be admitted to bail pending application for the writ of habeas corpus, or pending appellate review of an order refusing the writ, except by order of the Supreme Court or one of the judges thereof.

21-27-21. Remand to custody or admission to bail pending review of order discharging writ
Pending appellate review of an order discharging a writ of habeas corpus after it has been issued, the prisoner may be remanded to the custody from which he was taken by the writ, or detained in other appropriate custody, or admitted to bail, as to the court or judge rendering the decision may appear fitting in the circumstances of the particular case.

21-27-22. Bail without surety pending review of order discharging prisoner
Pending appellate review of an order discharging a prisoner on habeas corpus, he shall be admitted to bail without surety.

21-27-23. Admission to bail by Supreme Court pending review
Where the writ of habeas corpus is refused, or where the writ is discharged after having been issued, and the prisoner has been denied bail, he may be admitted to bail by the Supreme Court or one of the judge thereof, pending appellate review.

21-27-24. Terms of bond given on admission to bail—surety
When the prisoner is admitted to bail, he shall furnish a bond in such sum as the court directs, conditioned that he shall render himself amenable to all orders and process of the court or judge and that he will forthwith comply with any order directing his return to custody. Except as to the bond of a prisoner whose discharge has been ordered, the bond must be with the same surety as required on a bail bond of a defendant in a criminal action.

21-27-25. Order for temporary custody of person not held under judicial process—security required of person granted custody
Where a writ of habeas corpus is granted in proceedings involving the custody of a person not held under judicial process, the court shall have discretion to make a proper order concerning the temporary custody of such person pending final determination of the proceeding or pending appeal and may, as a condition of such order, require from the person granted such custody security, through bond or otherwise, for the

production of such person at such time and place as the court orders, and for the safety and well-being of such person during such temporary custody.

21-27-26. Order remanding applicant to custody—conclusive on second application for writ

When any person shall be remanded in any habeas corpus proceeding, it shall be the duty of the court or judge remanding him to make out and deliver to the sheriff or other person to whose custody he shall be remanded an order in writing stating the cause or causes of remanding him. If such person shall obtain a second writ of habeas corpus, it shall be the duty of such sheriff, or other person to whom the same shall be directed, to return therewith the order aforesaid, and if it shall appear that such person was remanded for any offense adjudged not bailable, it shall be taken and received as conclusive and the applicant shall be remanded without further proceedings.

21-27-27. Discharge on second writ unlawful where crime charged—admission to bail or remand to custody

It shall not be lawful for any court or judge, on a second writ of habeas corpus, to discharge any person, if he is clearly and specifically charged in the warrant of commitment with a criminal offense; but the court or judge shall, on the return of such second writ, have power only to admit such person to bail, where the offense is bailable by law, or remand him to prison where the offense is not bailable, or where such person shall fail to give the bail required.

21-27-28. Second imprisonment on same cause prohibited after discharge on writ—circumstances justifying second imprisonment

No person who has been discharged by order of a court or judge upon a writ of habeas corpus shall be again imprisoned, restrained, or kept in custody for the same cause, unless he be afterward prosecuted for the same offense; nor unless by the legal order or process of the court wherein he is bound by recognizance to appear. The following shall not be deemed to be the same cause:

(1) If after a discharge for a defect of proof, or on any material defect in the commitment in a criminal case, such person should be again arrested on sufficient proof, and committed by legal process for the same offense;

(2) If in a civil suit such person has been discharged for any illegality in the judgment or process, and is afterward imprisoned by legal process for the same cause of action;

(3) Generally, whenever the discharge has been ordered on account of the nonobservance of any of the forms required by law, such person may be a second time imprisoned, if the cause be legal, and the forms required by law observed.

21-27-29. Forfeiture for new arrest or detention after discharge on writ—liability for damages unaffected

Any person who, knowing that another has been discharged by order of a competent judge or tribunal on a writ of a habeas corpus, shall, contrary to the provisions of this chapter, arrest or detain him again for the same cause which was shown on the return of such writ, shall forfeit to the prisoner or person aggrieved five hundred dollars for the first offense and one thousand dollars for every subsequent offense. Recovery of the penalties provided herein shall be no bar to a civil suit for damages.

Current through the 2014 Regular Session and Supreme Court Rule 14-10.

TENNESSEE

Tennessee Code Annotated
Title 29. Remedies and Special Proceedings
Chapter 21. Habeas Corpus

§29-21-101. Grounds

(a) Any person imprisoned or restrained of liberty, under any pretense whatsoever, except in cases specified in subsection (b) and in cases specified in §29-21-102, may prosecute a writ of habeas corpus, to inquire into the cause of such imprisonment and restraint.

(b) Persons restrained of their liberty pursuant to a guilty plea and negotiated sentence are not entitled to the benefits of this writ on any claim that:

(1) The petitioner received concurrent sentencing where there was a statutory requirement for consecutive sentencing;

(2) The petitioner's sentence included a release eligibility percentage where the petitioner was not entitled to any early release; or

(3) The petitioner's sentence included a lower release eligibility percentage than the petitioner was entitled to under statutory requirements.

§29-21-102. Federal prisoners

Persons committed or detained by virtue of process issued by a court of the United states, or a judge thereof, in cases where such judges or court have exclusive jurisdiction under the laws of the United states, or have acquired exclusive jurisdiction by the commencement of suits in such courts, are not entitled to the benefits of this writ.

§29-21-103. Authority

The writ may be granted by any judge of the circuit or criminal courts, or by any chancellor in cases of equitable cognizance.

§29-21-104. Issuance; no application

Whenever any court or judge, authorized to grant this writ, has evidence, from a judicial proceeding, that any person within the jurisdiction of such court or officer is illegally imprisoned or restrained of liberty, it is the duty of such court or judge to issue, or cause to be issued, the writ as aforementioned, although no application be made therefor.

§29-21-105. Application; place

The application should be made to the court or judge most convenient in point of distance to the applicant, unless a sufficient reason be given in the petition for not applying to such court or judge.

§29-21-106. Jurisdiction

(a) The judges of the municipal courts or corporation courts and/or the judges of the courts of general sessions of the state of Tennessee are hereby vested with the jurisdiction to grant the writ of habeas corpus in all cases wherein any person is being unreasonably held or detained by any municipal official or authority without a warrant of arrest having been issued prior to such detention and against whom no formal charges have been made or placed and who has not been taken before a committing magistrate.

(b) The petition for such writ of habeas corpus shall be sworn to and shall recite generally that the petitioner is presently being detained without charges; that the petitioner is being held by municipal authorities and/or officials; that petitioner was arrested without a warrant and has not been docketed or charged with any offenses and has not been brought before a committing magistrate.

(c) It is the expressed intention of the general assembly to confer on the municipal or corporation courts and general sessions courts of this state, and the judges thereof, the jurisdiction to inquire into the detention of any person being held by municipal authorities and/or officials wherein no warrant for arrest has been issued or any formal charges have been made.

(d) No application for habeas corpus made under this section shall be required to be brought pursuant to *§29-21-105*, it being the legislative intent that habeas corpus petitions pursuant to this section shall not be required to be brought before the general sessions or municipal courts but that such petitions may be permitted to be brought before such courts.

§29-21-107. Application; petition
(a) Application for the writ shall be made by petition, signed either by the party for whose benefit it is intended, or some person on the petitioner's behalf, and verified by affidavit.

(b) The petition shall state:

(1) That the person in whose behalf the writ is sought, is illegally restrained of liberty, and the person by whom and place where restrained, mentioning the name of such person, if known, and, if unknown, describing the person with as much particularity as practicable;

(2) The cause or pretense of such restraint according to the best information of the applicant, and if it be by virtue of any legal process, a copy thereof shall be annexed, or a satisfactory reason given for its absence;

(3) That the legality of the restraint has not already been adjudged upon a prior proceeding of the same character, to the best of the applicant's knowledge and belief; and

(4) That it is first application for the writ, or, if a previous application has been made, a copy of the petition and proceedings thereon shall be produced, or satisfactory reasons be given for the failure so to do.

§29-21-108. Duty of court; wrongful refusal; fines and penalties
(a) It is the duty of the court or judge to act upon such applications instanter.

(b) A wrongful and willful refusal to grant the writ, when properly applied for, is a misdemeanor in office, besides subjecting the judge to damages at the suit of the party aggrieved.

§29-21-109. Refusal
If, from the showing of the petitioner, the plaintiff would not be entitled to any relief, the writ may be refused, the reasons for such refusal being briefly endorsed upon the petition, or appended thereto.

§29-21-110. Writ.
(a) If the petition show a sufficient ground for relief, the writ shall be forthwith allowed, and may be substantially as follows:

APPENDIX—TENNESSEE

State of Tennessee,   )   To the sheriff, etc. [or to
)   A B, as the case may be]:
_____ County.   )

You are hereby commanded to have the body of C B, who is alleged to be unlawfully detained by you, before the _____ court, [or before me, or before EE, Judge, etc., as the case may be], at _____ , on _____ [or immediately after being served with this writ], to be dealt with according to law, and have you then and there this writ, with a return thereon of your doings in the premises.

This _____ day of _____ , 20__ . G H, Judge, etc.

(b) The writ of habeas corpus shall not be disobeyed for any defect of form, or misdescription of the plaintiff or defendant, provided enough is stated to show the meaning and intent of the writ.

(c) When the writ is allowed by a court in term, it is issued by the clerk, but in other cases the judge or chancellor issues the writ, signing it officially.

§29-21-111. Service; officers and employees
(a) The writ may be served by the sheriff, coroner, or constable, or any other person appointed for that purpose by the court or judge by whom it is issued or allowed.

(b) If served by any other person than the sheriff, that person possesses the same power, and is liable to the same penalty for nonperformance the duty performed by that person, as though the person were the sheriff.

§29-21-112. Service; mode
(a) The proper mode of service is by leaving a copy of the original writ with the defendant, and making the return upon the original.

(b) Any person served with the writ is presumed to be the person for whom it is intended, although it may be directed to the person by a wrong name or description, or to another person.

(c) If the defendant cannot be found, or, if the defendant have not the plaintiff in custody, the service may be made upon any person having the plaintiff in custody, in the same manner and with the same effect as though that person had been made a defendant therein.

§29-21-113. Evading service; arrest
If the defendant refuses admittance to the person attempting to serve the writ, hides, or attempts wrongfully to carry the plaintiff out of the county or state, the defendant may be arrested by the person having the writ, and brought, together with the plaintiff, immediately before the officer or court before whom the writ is returnable. In order to make such arrest, the sheriff, or other person having the writ, has the same power as is given to a sheriff for the arrest of a person charged with a felony.

§29-21-114. Plaintiff; custody
If the person in whose name the application is made can be found, and no one appears to have the charge or custody of the plaintiff, the person having the writ may take the plaintiff into custody, and make return

accordingly, and, to get possession of the plaintiff's person in such case, the person possesses the same power as is given by §29-21-113 for the arrest of the defendant.

§29-21-115. Precept
(a) The court or judge to whom the application for the writ is made, if satisfied that the plaintiff is likely to suffer irreparable injury before the plaintiff could be relieved by the proceedings as authorized in §§29-21-112—29-21-114, may issue a precept to the sheriff, or other person selected, commanding the sheriff or other person to bring the plaintiff forthwith before such judge or court.

(b) When the evidence is further sufficient to justify the arrest of the defendant, for a criminal offense committed in connection with the illegal detention of the plaintiff, the precept shall also contain an order for the arrest of the defendant.

(c) The officer or person to whom the precept is directed shall execute the same by bringing the defendant, and also the plaintiff, if required, before the court or judge issuing it, and thereupon the defendant shall make return to the writ of habeas corpus in the same manner as if the ordinary course had been pursued. The defendant may also be examined and committed, bailed or discharged, according to the nature of the case.

§29-21-116. Defendants; appearance and return
(a) Service being made in any of the modes provided for in this part, the defendant shall appear at the proper time, and make due return of the writ, and answer the petition, if required.

(b) The person served with the writ shall state in the return, plainly and unequivocally:

(1) Whether the person then has, or at any time has had, the plaintiff in the person's control or restraint, and, if so, the authority and cause thereof, setting out the same fully;

(2) If the party is detained under a writ, warrant, or other written authority, a copy thereof shall be annexed to the return, and the original shall be produced and exhibited to the court or judge, if required; and

(3) If the person on whom the writ has been served, has had the plaintiff in the person's custody or power or under the person's restraint, at any time before or after the date of the writ, but has transferred the plaintiff to another person, that person shall state the facts explicitly, and to whom, at what time, for what cause, and by what authority such transfer was made.

(c) The return shall be signed by the person making it, and verified by the oath; unless the person is a sworn public officer, and makes the return in an official capacity.

§29-21-117. Production of plaintiff
(a) At the time of making the return, the person on whom the same has been served shall also produce the body of the person detained according to the command of the writ, or show good cause for not doing so.

(b) If the cause shown for not producing such person be sickness or infirmity, the fact shall be verified by affidavit, and other evidence if required.

(c) The court may thereupon proceed as if the party were produced, or adjourn to the place where such party then is, or to some other time and place, according to circumstances.

§29-21-118. Plaintiffs; presence at examination; waiver
The plaintiff, in writing, or the plaintiff's attorney, may waive the right to be present at the examination, in which case the proceedings may be had in the plaintiff's absence.

§29-21-119. Return by defendant; subsequent proceedings
The plaintiff may demur or reply to the return, and all issues shall be tried by the court or judge in a summary way, the examination being adjourned from time to time, if necessary to the proper administration of justice, and all such orders being made for the custody of the plaintiff, in the meantime, as the nature of the case requires.

§29-21-120. Bail
The plaintiff may also, in any case, be committed, let to bail, or the plaintiff's bail diminished or increased, as justice may require.

§29-21-121. Witnesses; Subpoena
(a) Subpoena for witnesses in all proceedings under this chapter may be issued by the court or judge granting the writ, or before whom the same is returnable, or by any general sessions judge.

(b) Witnesses thus summoned are subject to the same penalties and entitled to the same privileges and fees as other witnesses.

(c) Upon failure of the witness to attend, the fact shall be noted by the officer before whom the subpoena is returned, on the back thereof, and transmitted to the clerk of the circuit court of the county, who shall issue scire facias, as in other cases.

§29-21-122. Plaintiff; discharge or detention
(a) If no sufficient legal cause of detention is shown, the plaintiff shall be discharged.

(b) The party detained shall be remanded to custody;

(1) If it appears the party is detained by virtue of process issued by a court or judge of the United States, in a case where such court or judge has exclusive jurisdiction;

(2) Where the time during which such party may be legally detained has not expired; or

(3) In every case in which the detention is authorized by law.

§29-21-123. Commitment, irregularities
Although the commitment of the person detained may have been irregular, still, if the court or judge is satisfied, from the examination, that the person ought to be held to bail, or committed, either for the offense charged, or any other, the order shall be made accordingly.

§29-21-124. Records; costs
The proceedings under a writ of habeas corpus, including all the papers in the cause, and the final order, shall be returned by the judge to the nearest court served by the judge, to be filed there by the clerk, as other records, a brief memorandum thereof, duly indexed, being made upon the judgment or execution docket, and such taxing the costs and issuing execution therefor, as in other cases.

§29-21-125. Costs
The costs of proceedings under this chapter, except when otherwise expressly provided, shall be adjudged as the court or judge may think right, and taxed and collected as in other cases.

§29-21-126. Costs; discharge of defendant
(a) Where the defendant in a criminal prosecution is brought before any circuit or criminal judge on a writ of habeas corpus, and discharged by the judge, the costs shall be paid as in other state cases, when the defendant is tried and acquitted by a jury.

(b)(1) When the defendant in the cases provided for in this section is charged with a felony, the judge shall make out and certify the bill of costs, and deliver the same to the clerk of the circuit court before which the defendant is bound to appear, by whom the costs shall be collected and paid out as in other cases.

(2) If the defendant is charged with a misdemeanor, the judge shall deliver the bill of costs, made out and certified as before, to the court of general sessions of the county in which the defendant was charged with committing the offense, by whom the same shall be allowed as in other cases.

§29-21-127. Appeal and review
(a) Any party, either relator or defendant, in any habeas corpus case shall have the right of appeal to the proper appellate court from any judgment or decree rendered against such party by an inferior court.

(b) The party so appealing shall give bond and security for the costs of such appeal except where the relator or defendant is under confinement and serving a prison sentence on final judgment.

(c) This section shall not apply to parties held in custody in criminal cases.

§29-21-128. Disobedience; fines and penalties
Disobedience of the original writ, or any subsequent order thereon, subjects the defendant to commitment for contempt, and also to a forfeiture of one thousand dollars ($1,000) to the party aggrieved, besides rendering the defendant liable for all damages sustained in consequence of such disobedience.

§29-21-129. Evasion of service; crimes and offenses
The attempt to elude the service of the writ of habeas corpus, or to avoid the effect thereof by transferring the plaintiff out of the jurisdiction or to another person, or by concealing the plaintiff, or the place of the plaintiff's confinement, is a Class C misdemeanor.

§29-21-130. Delivery of process; refusal; fines and penalties
Any officer refusing to deliver a copy of any legal process by which the officer retains a party in custody to a person who demands such copy, and tenders the fees therefor, forfeits two hundred dollars ($200) to the person so detained.

Current with laws from the 2014 Second Reg. Sess., eff. through June 20, 2014.

APPENDIX—TEXAS

TEXAS

Texas Statutes and Codes Annotated
Title 1. Code of Criminal Procedure of 1965 Habeas Corpus
Chapter Eleven. Habeas Corpus

Art. 11.01. [113] [160-161] *What writ is*
The writ of habeas corpus is the remedy to be used when any person is restrained in his liberty. It is an order issued by a court or judge of competent jurisdiction, directed to any one having a person in his custody, or under his restraint, commanding him to produce such person, at a time and place named in the writ, and show why he is held in custody or under restraint.

Art. 11.02. [114] [162] [152] *To whom directed*
The writ runs in the name of "The State of Texas." It is addressed to a person having another under restraint, or in his custody, describing, as near as may be, the name of the office, if any, of the person to whom it is directed, and the name of the person said to be detained. It shall fix the time and place of return, and be signed by the judge, or by the clerk with his seal, where issued by a court.

Art. 11.03. [115] [163] [153] *Want of form*
The writ of habeas corpus is not invalid, nor shall it be disobeyed for any want of form, if it substantially appear that it is issued by competent authority, and the writ sufficiently show the object of its issuance.

Art. 11.04. [116] [164] [154] *Construction*
Every provision relating to the writ of habeas corpus shall be most favorably construed in order to give effect to the remedy, and protect the rights of the person seeking relief under it.

Art. 11.05. [117] [69-84-92-100-165] *By whom writ may be granted*
The Court of Criminal Appeals, the District Courts, the County Courts, or any Judge of said Courts, have power to issue the writ of habeas corpus; and it is their duty, upon proper motion, to grant the writ under the rules prescribed by law.

Art. 11.051. *Filing fee prohibited*
Notwithstanding any other law, a clerk of a court may not require a filing fee from an individual who files an application or petition for a writ of habeas corpus.

Art. 11.06. [118] [166] [156] *Returnable to any county*
Before indictment found, the writ may be made returnable to any county in the State.

Art. 11.07. [119] [167] [157] *Procedure after conviction without death penalty*
Sec. 1. This article establishes the procedures for an application for writ of habeas corpus in which the applicant seeks relief from a felony judgment imposing a penalty other than death.

Sec. 2. After indictment found in any felony case, other than a case in which the death penalty is imposed, and before conviction, the writ must be made returnable in the county where the offense has been committed.

Sec. 3. (a) After final conviction in any felony case, the writ must be made returnable to the Court of Criminal Appeals of Texas at Austin, Texas.

(b) An application for writ of habeas corpus filed after final conviction in a felony case, other than a case in which the death penalty is imposed, must be filed with the clerk of the court in which the conviction being challenged was obtained, and the clerk shall assign the application to that court. When the application is received by that court, a writ of habeas corpus, returnable to the Court of Criminal Appeals, shall issue by operation of law. The clerk of that court shall make appropriate notation thereof, assign to the case a file number (ancillary to that of the conviction being challenged), and forward a copy of the application by certified mail, return receipt requested, by secure electronic mail, or by personal service to the attorney representing the state in that court, who shall answer the application not later than the 15th day after the date the copy of the application is received. Matters alleged in the application not admitted by the state are deemed denied.

(c) Within 20 days of the expiration of the time in which the state is allowed to answer, it shall be the duty of the convicting court to decide whether there are controverted, previously unresolved facts material to the legality of the applicant's confinement. Confinement means confinement for any offense or any collateral consequence resulting from the conviction that is the basis of the instant habeas corpus. If the convicting court decides that there are no such issues, the clerk shall immediately transmit to the Court of Criminal Appeals a copy of the application, any answers filed, and a certificate reciting the date upon which that finding was made. Failure of the court to act within the allowed 20 days shall constitute such a finding.

(d) If the convicting court decides that there are controverted, previously unresolved facts which are material to the legality of the applicant's confinement, it shall enter an order within 20 days of the expiration of the time allowed for the state to reply, designating the issues of fact to be resolved. To resolve those issues the court may order affidavits, depositions, interrogatories, additional forensic testing, and hearings, as well as using personal recollection. The state shall pay the cost of additional forensic testing ordered under this subsection, except that the applicant shall pay the cost of the testing if the applicant retains counsel for purposes of filing an application under this article. The convicting court may appoint an attorney or a magistrate to hold a hearing and make findings of fact. An attorney so appointed shall be compensated as provided in *Article 26.05* of this code. It shall be the duty of the reporter who is designated to transcribe a hearing held pursuant to this article to prepare a transcript within 15 days of its conclusion. on completion of the transcript, the reporter shall immediately transmit the transcript to the clerk of the convicting court. After the convicting court makes findings of fact or approves the findings of the person designated to make them, the clerk of the convicting court shall immediately transmit to the Court of Criminal Appeals, under one cover, the application, any answers filed, any motions filed, transcripts of all depositions and hearings, any affidavits, and any other matters such as official records used by the court in resolving issues of fact.

(e) For the purposes of Subsection (d), "additional forensic testing" does not include forensic DNA testing as provided for in Chapter 64.

Sec. 4. (a) If a subsequent application for writ of habeas corpus is filed after final disposition of an initial application challenging the same conviction, a court may not consider the merits of or grant relief based on the subsequent application unless the application contains sufficient specific facts establishing that:

(1) the current claims and issues have not been and could not have been presented previously in an original application or in a previously considered application filed under this article because the factual or legal basis for the claim was unavailable on the date the applicant filed the previous application; or

(2) by a preponderance of the evidence, but for a violation of the United States Constitution no rational juror could have found the applicant guilty beyond a reasonable doubt.

(b) For purposes of Subsection (a)(1), a legal basis of a claim is unavailable on or before a date described by Subsection (a)(1) if the unavailable legal basis was not recognized by and could not have been reasonably formulated from a final decision of the United States Supreme Court, a court of appeals of the United states, or a court of appellate jurisdiction of this state on or before that date.

(c) For purposes of subsection (a)(1), a factual basis of a claim is unavailable on or before a date described by Subsection (a)(1) if the factual basis was not ascertainable through the exercise of reasonable diligence on or before that date.

Sec. 5. The Court of Criminal Appeals may deny relief upon the findings and conclusions of the hearing judge without docketing the cause, or may direct that the cause be docketed and heard as through originally presented to said court or as an appeal. Upon reviewing the record the court shall enter its judgment remanding the applicant to custody or ordering his release, as the law and facts may justify. The mandate of the court shall issue to the court issuing the writ, as in other criminal cases. After conviction the procedure outlined in this Act shall be exclusive and any other proceeding shall be void and of no force and effect in discharging the prisoner.

Sec. 6. Upon any hearing by a district judge by virtue of this Act, the attorney for applicant, and the state, shall be given at least seven full days' notice before such hearing is held.

Sec. 7. When the attorney for the state files an answer, motion, or other pleading relating to an application for a writ of habeas corpus or the court issues an order relating to an application for a writ of habeas corpus, the clerk of the court shall mail or deliver to the applicant a copy of the answer, motion, pleading, or order.

Art. 11.071. *Procedures in death penalty cases*
Application to Death Penalty case

Sec. 1. Notwithstanding any other provision of this chapter, this article establishes the procedures for an application for a writ of habeas corpus in which the applicant seeks relief from a judgment imposing a penalty of death.

Representation by Counsel

Sec. 2. (a) An applicant shall be represented by competent counsel unless the applicant has elected to proceed pro se and the convicting trial court finds, after a hearing on the record, that the applicant's election is intelligent and voluntary.

(b) If a defendant is sentenced to death the convicting court, immediately after judgment is entered under *Article 42.01*, shall determine if the defendant is indigent and, if so, whether the defendant desires appointment of counsel for the purpose of a writ of habeas corpus. If the defendant desires appointment of counsel for the purpose of a writ of habeas corpus, the court shall appoint the office of capital writs to represent the defendant as provided by Subsection (c).

(c) At the earliest practical time, but in no event later than 30 days, after the convicting court makes the findings required under Subsection (a) and (b), the convicting court shall appoint the office of capital writs or, if the office of capital writs does not accept or is prohibited from accepting an appointment under *Section 78.054, Government Code*, other competent counsel under Subsection (f), unless the applicant elects to proceed pro se or is represented by retained counsel. On appointing counsel under this section, the convicting court shall immediately notify the court of criminal appeals of the appointment, including in the notice a copy of the judgment and the name, address, and telephone number of the appointed counsel.

(d) Repealed by *Acts 2009, 81st Leg., ch. 781, §11*.

(e) If the court of criminal appeals denies an applicant relief under this article, an attorney appointed under this section to represent the applicant shall, not later than the 15th day after the date the court of criminal appeals denies relief or, if the case is filed and set for submission, the 15th day after the date the court of criminal appeals issues a mandate on the initial application for a writ of habeas corpus under this article, move for the appointment of counsel in federal habeas review under *18 U.S.C. Section 3599*. The attorney shall immediately file a copy of the motion with the court of criminal appeals, and if the attorney fails to do so, the court may take any action to ensure that the applicant's right to federal habeas review is protected, including initiating contempt proceedings against the attorney.

(f) If the office of capital writs does not accept or is prohibited from accepting an appointment under *Section 78.054, Government Code*, the convicting court shall appoint counsel from a list of competent counsel maintained by the presiding judge of the administrative judicial regions under *Section 78.056, Government Code*. The convicting court shall reasonably compensate as provided by Section 2A an attorney appointed under this section, other than an attorney employed by the office of capital writs, regardless of whether the attorney is appointed by the convicting court or was appointed by the court of criminal appeals under prior law. An attorney appointed under this section who is employed by the office of capital writs shall be compensated in accordance with Subchapter B, Chapter 78, Government Code.

State Reimbursement; County Obligation

Sec. 2A. (a) The state shall reimburse a county for compensation of counsel under Section 2, other than for compensation of counsel employed by the office of capital writs, and for payment of expenses under Section 3, regardless of whether counsel is employed by the office of capital writs. The total amount of reimbursement to which a county is entitled under this section for an application under this article may not exceed $25,000. Compensation and expenses in excess of the $25,000 reimbursement provided by the state are the obligation of the county.

(b) A convicting court seeking reimbursement for a county shall certify to the comptroller of public accounts the amount of compensation that the county is entitled to receive under this section. The comptroller of public accounts shall issue a warrant to the county in the amount certified by the convicting court, not to exceed $25,000.

(c) The limitation imposed by this section on the reimbursement by the state to a county for compensation of counsel and payment of reasonable expenses does not prohibit a county from compensating counsel and reimbursing expenses in an amount that is in excess of the amount the county receives from the state as reimbursement, and a county is specifically granted discretion by this Subsection to make payments in excess of the state reimbursement.

(d) The comptroller shall reimburse a county for the compensation and payment of expenses of an attorney appointed by the court of criminal appeals under prior law. A convicting court seeking reimbursement for a county as permitted by this subsection shall certify the amount the county is entitled to receive under this subsection for an application filed under this article, not to exceed a total amount of $25,000.

Investigation of Grounds for Application

Sec. 3. (a) on appointment, counsel shall investigate expeditiously, before and after the appellate record is filed in the court of criminal appeals, the factual and legal grounds for the filing of an application) for a writ of habeas corpus.

(b) Not later than the 30th day before the date the application for a writ of habeas corpus is filed with the convicting court, counsel may file with the convicting court an ex parte, verified, and confidential request for prepayment of expenses, including expert fees, to investigate and present potential habeas corpus claims. The request for expenses must state:

(1) the claims of the application to be investigated;

(2) specific facts that suggest that a claim of possible merit may exist; and

(3) an itemized list of anticipated expenses for each claim.

(c) The court shall grant a request for expenses in whole or in part if the request for expenses is timely and reasonable. If the court denies in whole or in part the request for expenses, the court shall briefly state the reasons for the denial in a written order provided to the applicant.

(d) Counsel may incur expenses for habeas corpus investigation, including expenses for experts, without prior approval by the convicting court or the court of criminal appeals. On presentation of a claims for reimbursement, which may be presented ex parte, the convicting court shall order reimbursement of counsel for expenses, if the expenses are reasonably necessary and reasonably incurred. If the convicting court denies in whole or in part the request for expenses, the court shall briefly state the reasons for the denial in a written order provided to the applicant. The applicant may request reconsideration of the denial for reimbursement by the convicting court.

(e) Materials submitted to the court under this section are a part of the court's record .

(f) This section applies to counsel's investigation of the factual and legal grounds for the filing of an application for a writ of habeas corpus, regardless of whether counsel is employed by the office of capital writs.

Filing of Application

Section 4. (a) An application for a writ of habeas corpus, returnable to the court of criminal appeals, must be filed in the convicting court not later than the 180th day after the date the convicting court appoints counsel under Section 2 or not later than the 45th day after the date the state's original brief is filed on direct appeal with the court of criminal appeals, whichever date is later.

(b) The convicting court, before the filing date that is applicable to the applicant under Subsection (a), may for good cause shown and after notice and an opportunity to be heard by the attorney representing the state grant one 90-day extension that begins on the filing date applicable to the defendant under Subsection (a). Either party may request that the court hold a hearing on the request. If the convicting court finds that the applicant cannot establish good cause justifying the requested extension, the court shall make a finding stating that fact and deny the request for the extension.

(c) An application filed after the filing date that is applicable to the applicant under Subsection (a) or (b) is untimely.

(d) If the convicting court receives an untimely application or determines that after the filing date that is applicable to the applicant under Subsection (a) or (b) no application has been filed, the convicting court immediately, but in any event within 10 days, shall send to the court of criminal appeals and to the attorney representing the state:

(1) a copy of the untimely application, with a statement of the convicting court that the application is untimely, or a statement of the convicting court that no application has been filed within the time periods required by Subsections (a) and (b); and

(2) any order the judge of the convicting court determines should be attached to an untimely application or statement under Subsection (1).

(e) A failure to file an application before the filing date applicable to the applicant under Subsection (a) or (b) constitutes a waiver of all grounds for relief that were available to the applicant before the last date on which an application could be timely filed, except as provided by Section 4A.

Untimely Application; Application Not Filed

Sec. 4A. (a) on command of the court of criminal appeals, a counsel who files an untimely application or fails to file an application before the filing date applicable under Section 4(a) or (b) shall show cause as to why the application was untimely filed or not filed before the filing date.

(b) At the conclusion of the counsel's presentation to the court of criminal appeals, the court may:

(1) find that good cause has not been shown and dismiss the application;

(2) permit the counsel to continue representation of the applicant and establish a new filing date for the application, which may be not more than 180 days from the date the court permits the counsel to continue representation; or

(3) appoint new counsel to represent the applicant and establish a new filing date for the application, which may be not more than 270 days after the date the court appoints new counsel.

(c) The court of criminal appeals may hold in contempt counsel who files an untimely application or fails to file an application before the date required by Section 4(a) or (b). The court of criminal appeals may punish as a separate instance of contempt each day after the first day on which the counsel fails to timely file the application. In addition to or in lieu of holding counsel in contempt, the court of criminal appeals may enter an order denying counsel compensation under Section 2A.

(d) If the court of criminal appeals establishes a new filing date for the application, the court of criminal appeals shall notify the convicting court of that fact and the convicting court shall proceed under this article.

(e) Sections 2A and 3 apply to compensation and reimbursement of counsel appointed under Subsection (b)(3) in the same manner as if counsel had been appointed by the convicting court, unless the attorney is employed by the office of capital writs, in which case the compensation of that attorney is governed by Subchapter B, Chapter 78, Government Code.

(f) Notwithstanding any other provision of this article, the court of criminal appeals shall appoint counsel and establish a new filing date for application, which may be no later than the 270th day after the date on which counsel is appointed, for each applicant who before September 1, 1999, filed an untimely application or failed to file an application before the date required by Section 4(a) or (b). Section 2A applies to the compensation and payment of expenses of counsel appointed by the court of criminal appeals under this subsection, unless the attorney is employed by the office of capital writs, in which case the compensation of that attorney is governed by Subchapter B, Chapter 78, Government Code.

Subsequent Application

Sec. 5. (a) If a subsequent application for a writ of habeas corpus is filed after filing an initial application, a court may not consider the merits of or grant relief based on the subsequent application unless the application contains sufficient specific facts establishing that:

(1) the current claims and issues have not been and could not have been presented previously in a timely initial application or in a previously considered application filed under this article or *Article 11.07* because the factual or legal basis for the claim was unavailable on the date the applicant filed the previous application;

(2) by a preponderance of the evidence, but for a violation of the United States Constitution no rational juror could have found the applicant guilty beyond a reasonable doubt; or

(3) by clear and convincing evidence, but for a violation of the United States Constitution no rational juror would have answered in the state's favor one or more of the special issues that were submitted to the jury in the applicant's trial under *Article 37.071, 37.0711,* or *37.072.*

(b) If the convicting court receives a subsequent application, the clerk of the court shall:

(1) attach a notation that the application is a subsequent application;

(2) assign to the case a file number that is ancillary to that of the conviction being challenged; and

(3) immediately send to the court of criminal appeals a copy of:

(A) the application;

(B) the notation;

(C) the order scheduling the applicant's execution, if scheduled; and

(D) any order the judge of the convicting court directs to be attached to the application.

(c) On receipt of the copies of the documents from the clerk, the court of criminal appeals shall determine whether the requirements of Subsection (a) have been satisfied. The convicting court may not take further action on the application before the court of criminal appeals issues an order finding that the requirements have been satisfied. If the court of criminal appeals determines that the requirements have not been satisfied, the court shall issue an order dismissing the application as an abuse of the writ under this section.

(d) For purposes of Subsection (a)(1), a legal basis of a claim is unavailable on or before a date described by Subsection (a)(1) if the legal basis was not recognized by or could not have been reasonably formulated from a final decision of the United States Supreme Court, a court of appeals of the United States, or a court of appellate jurisdiction of this state on or before that date.

(e) For purposes of Subsection (a)(1), a factual basis of a claim is unavailable on or before a date described by Subsection (a)(1) if the factual basis was not ascertainable through the exercise of reasonable diligence on or before that date.

(f) If an amended or supplemental application is not filed within the time specified under Section 4(a) or (b), the court shall treat the application as a subsequent application under this section.

Issuance of Writ

Sec. 6. (a) If a timely application for a writ of habeas corpus is filed in the convicting court, a writ of habeas corpus, returnable to the court of criminal appeals, shall issue by operation of law.

(b) If the convicting court receives notice that the requirements of Section 5 for consideration of a subsequent application have been met, a writ of habeas corpus, returnable to the court of criminal appeals, shall issue by operation of law.

(b-1) If the convicting court receives notice that the requirements of Section 5(a) for consideration of a subsequent application have been met and if the applicant has not elected to proceed pro se and is not represented by retained counsel, the convicting court shall appoint, in order of priority:

(1) the attorney who represented the applicant in the proceedings under Section 5, if the attorney seeks the appointment;

(2) the office of capital writs, if the office represented the applicant in the proceedings under Section 5 or otherwise accepts the appointment; or

(3) counsel from a list of competent counsel maintained by the presiding judges of the administrative judicial regions under *Section 78.056, Government Code*, if the office of capital writs:

(A) did not represent the applicant as described by Subdivision (2); or

(B) does not accept or is prohibited from accepting the appointment under *Section 78.054, Government Code*.

(b-2) Regardless of whether the subsequent application is ultimately dismissed, compensation and reimbursement of expenses for counsel appointed under Subsection (b-1) shall be provided as described by Section 2, 2A, or 3, including compensation for time previously spent and reimbursement of expenses previously incurred with respect to the subsequent application.

(c) The clerk of the convicting court shall:

(1) make an appropriate notation that a writ of habeas corpus was issued;

(2) assign to the case a file number that is ancillary to that of the conviction being challenged; and

(3) send a copy of the application by certified mail, return receipt requested, or by secure electronic mail to the attorney representing the state in that court.

(d) The clerk of the convicting court shall promptly deliver copies of documents submitted to the clerk under this article to the applicant and the attorney representing the state.

Answer to Application

Section 7. (a) The state shall file an answer to the application for a writ of habeas corpus not later than the 120th day after the date the state receives notice of issuance of the writ. The state shall serve the answer on counsel for the applicant or, if the applicant is proceeding pro se, on the applicant. The state may request from the convicting court an extension of time in which to answer the application by showing particularized justifying circumstances for the extension, but in no event may the court permit the state to file an answer later than the 180th day after the date the state receives notice of issuance of the writ.

(b) Matters alleged in the application not admitted by the state are deemed denied.

Findings of Fact Without Evidentiary Hearing

Section 8. (a) Not later than the 20th day after the last date the state answers the application, the convicting court shall determine whether controverted, previously unresolved factual issues material to the legality of the applicant's confinement exist and shall issue a written order of the determination.

(b) If the convicting court determines the issues do not exist, the parties shall file proposed findings of fact and conclusions of law for the court to consider on or before a date set by the court that is not later than the 30th day after the date the order is issued.

(c) After argument of counsel, if requested by the court, the convicting court shall make appropriate written findings of fact and conclusions of law not later than the 15th day after the date the parties filed proposed findings or not later than the 45th day after the date the court's determination is made under Subsection (a), whichever occurs first.

(d) The clerk of the court shall immediately send to:

(1) the court of criminal appeals a copy of the:

(A) application;

(B) answer;

(C) orders entered by the convicting court;

(D) proposed findings of fact and conclusions of law; and

(E) findings of fact and conclusions of law entered by the court; and

(2) counsel for the applicant or, if the applicant is proceeding pro se, to the applicant, a copy of:

(A) orders entered by the convicting court;

(B) proposed findings of fact and conclusions of law; and

(C) findings of fact and conclusions of law entered by the court.

Hearing

Sec. 9. (a) If the convicting court determines that controverted, previously unresolved factual issues material to the legality of the applicant's confinement exist, the court shall enter an order, not later than the 20th day after the last date the state answers the application, designing the issues of fact to be resolved and the manner in which the issues shall be resolved. To resolve the issues, the court may require affidavits, depositions, interrogatories, and evidentiary hearings and may use personal recollection.

(b) The convicting court shall hold the evidentiary hearing not later than the 30th day after the date on which the court enters the order designating issues under Subsection (a). The convicting court may grant a motion to postpone the hearing, but not for more than 30 days, and only if the court states, on the record, good cause for delay.

(c) The presiding judge of the convicting court shall conduct a hearing held under this section unless another judge presided over the original capital felony trial, in which event that judge, if qualified for assignment under *Section 74.054 or 74.055, Government Code*, may preside over the hearing.

(d) The court reporter shall prepare a transcript of the hearing not later than the 30th day after the date the hearing ends and file the transcript with the clerk of the convicting court.

(e) The parties shall file proposed findings of fact of conclusions of law for the convicting court to consider on or before a date set by the court that is not later than the 30th day after the date the transcript is filed. If the court requests argument of counsel, after argument the court shall make written findings of fact that are necessary to resolve the previously unresolved facts and make conclusions of law not later than the 15th day after the date the parties file proposed findings or not later than the 45th day after the date the court reporter files the transcript, whichever occurs first.

(f) The clerk of the convicting court shall immediately transmit to:

(1) the court of criminal appeals a copy of:

(A) the application;

(B) the answers and motions filed;

(C) the court reporter's transcript;

(D) the documentary exhibits introduced into evidence;

(E) the proposed findings of fact and conclusions of law;

(F) the findings of fact and conclusions of law entered by the court;

(G) the sealed materials such as a confidential request for investigative expenses; and

(H) any other matters used by the convicting court in resolving issues of fact; and

(2) counsel for the applicant or, if the applicant is proceeding pro se, to the applicant, a copy of:

(A) orders entered by the convicting court;

(B) proposed findings of fact and conclusions of law; and

(C) findings of fact and conclusions of law entered by the court.

(g) The clerk of the convicting court shall forward an exhibit that is not documentary to the court of criminal appeals on request of the court.

Rules of Evidence

Sec. 10. The Texas Rules of Criminal Evidence apply to a hearing held under this article.

Review by Court of Criminal Appeals

Sec. 11. The court of criminal appeals shall expeditiously review all applications for a writ of habeas corpus submitted under this article. The court may set the cause for oral argument and may request further briefing of the issues by the applicant or the state. After reviewing the record, the court shall enter its judgment remanding the applicant to custody or ordering the applicant's release, as the law and facts may justify.

Art. 11.072. Procedure in community supervision case

Sec. 1. This articles establishes the procedures for an application for a writ of habeas corpus in a felony or misdemeanor case i n which the applicant seeks relief from an order or a judgment of conviction ordering community supervision.

Sec. 2. (a) An application for a writ of habeas corpus under this article must be filed with the clerk of the court in which community supervision was imposed.

(b) At the time the application is filed, the applicant must be, or have been, on community supervision, and the application must challenge the legal validity of:

(1) the conviction for which or order in which community supervision was imposed; or

(2) the conditions of community supervision.

Sec. 3. (a) An application may not be filed under this article if the applicant could obtain the requested relief by means of an appeal under *Article 44.02* and *Rule 25.2, Texas Rules of Appellate Procedure*.

(b) An applicant seeking to challenge a particular condition of community supervision but not the legality of the conviction for which or the order in which community supervision was imposed must first attempt to gain relief by filing a motion to amend the conditions of community supervision.

(c) An applicant may challenge a condition of community supervision under this article only on constitutional grounds.

Sec. 4. (a) When an application is filed under this article, a writ of habeas corpus issues by operation of law.

(b) At the time the application is filed, the clerk of the court shall assign the case a file number ancillary to that of the judgment of conviction or order being challenged.

Sec. 5 (a) Immediately on filing an application, the applicant shall serve a copy of the application on the attorney representing the state, by either certified mail, return receipt requested, or personal service.

(b) The state may file an answer within the period established by Subsection (c), but is not required to file an answer.

(c) The state may not file an answer after the 30th day after the date of service, except that for good cause the convicting court may grant the state one 30-day extension.

(d) Any answer, motion, or other document filed by the state must be served on the applicant by certified mail, return receipt requested, or by personal service.

(e) Matters alleged in the application not admitted by the state are considered to have been denied.

Sec. 6 (a) Not later than the 60th day after the day on which the state's answer is filed, the trial court shall enter a written order granting or denying the relief sought in the application.

(b) In making its determination, the court may order affidavits, depositions, interrogatories, or a hearing, and may rely on the court's personal recollection.

(c) If a hearing is ordered, the hearing may not be held before the eighth day after the day on which the applicant and the state are provided notice of the hearing.

(d) The court may appoint an attorney or magistrate to hold a hearing ordered under this section and make findings of fact. An attorney appointed under this subsection is entitled to compensation as provided by *Article 26.05*.

Sec. 7 (a) If the court determines from the face of an application or documents attached to the application that the applicant is manifestly entitled to no relief, the court shall enter a written order denying the application as frivolous. In any other case, the court shall enter a written order including findings of fact and conclusions of law. The court may require the prevailing party to submit a proposed order.

(b) At the time an order is entered under this section, the clerk of the court shall immediately, by certified mail, return receipt requested, or by secure electronic mail, send a copy of the order to the applicant and to the state.

Sec. 8. If the application is denied in whole or in part, the applicant may appeal under *Article 44.02* and Rule 31, Texas Rules of Appellate Procedure. If the application is granted in whole or in part, the state may appeal under *Article 44 . 01* and Rule 31, Texas Rules of Appellate Procedure.

Sec. 9. (a) If a subsequent application for a writ of habeas corpus is filed after final disposition of an initial application under this article, a court may not consider the merits of or grant relief based on the subsequent application unless the application contains sufficient specific facts establishing that the current claims and issues have not been and could not have been presented previously in an original application or in a previously considered application filed under this article because the factual or legal basis for the claim was unavailable on the date the applicant filed the previous application.

(b) For purposes of Subsection (a), a legal basis of a claim is unavailable on or before a date described by that subsection if the legal basis was not recognized by and could not have been reasonably formulated from a final decision of the United States Supreme Court, a court of appeals of the United states, or a court of appellate jurisdiction of this state on or before that date.

Art. 11.073. *Procedure related to certain scientific evidence*

(a) This article applies to relevant scientific evidence that:

(1) was not available to be offered by a convicted person at the convicted person's trial; or

(2) contradicts scientific evidence relied on by the state at trial.

(b) A court may grant a convicted person relief on an application for a writ of habeas corpus if:

(1) the convicted person files an application, in the manner provided by *Article 11.07, 11.071,* or *11.072*, containing specific facts indicating that:

(A) relevant scientific evidence is currently available and was not available at the time of the convicted person's trial because the evidence was not ascertainable through the exercise of reasonable diligence by the convicted person before the date of or during the convicted person's trial; and

(B) the scientific evidence would be admissible under the Texas Rules of Evidence at a trial held on the date of the application; and

(2) the court makes the findings described by Subdivisions (1)(A) and (B) and also finds that, had the scientific evidence been presented at trial, on the preponderance of the evidence the person would not have been convicted.

(c) For purposes of Section 4(a)(1), *Article 11.07, Section 5(a)(1), Article 11.071,* and Section 9(a), *Article 11.072,* a claim or issue could not have been presented previously in an original application or in a previously considered application if the claim or issue is based on relevant scientific evidence that was not ascertainable through the exercise of reasonable diligence by the convicted person on or before the date on which the original application or previously considered application, as applicable, was filed.

(d) in making a finding as to whether relevant scientific evidence was not ascertainable through the exercise of reasonable diligence on or before a specific date, the court shall consider whether the scientific knowledge or method on which the relevant scientific evidence is based has changed since:

(1) the applicable trial date or dates, for a determination made with respect to an original application; or

(2) the date on which the original application or a previously considered application, as applicable, was filed, for a determination made with respect to a subsequent application.

Art. 11.08. [120] [168] [158] *Applicant charged with felony*
If a person is confined after indictment on a charge of felony, he may apply to the judge of the court in which he is indicted; or i f there be no judge within the district, then to the judge of any d i strict whose residence is nearest to the court house of the county in which the applicant is held in custody.

Art. 11.09. [121] [169] [159] *Applicant charged with misdemeanor*
If a person is confined on a charge of misdemeanor, he may apply to the county judge of the county in which the misdemeanor is charged to have been committed, or if there be no county judge in said county, then to the county judge whose residence is nearest to the courthouse of the county in which the applicant is held in custody.

Art. 11.10. [122] [170] [160] *Proceedings under the writ*
When motion has been made to a judge under the circumstances set forth in the two preceding Articles, he shall appoint a time when he will examine the cause of the applicant, and issue the writ returnable at that time, in the county where the offense is charged in the indictment or information to have been committed. He shall also specify some place in the county where he will hear the motion.

Art. 11.11. [123] [171] [161] *Early hearing*
The time so appointed shall be the earliest day which the judge can devote to hearing the cause of the applicant .

Art. 11.12. [124] [172] [162] *Who may present petition*
Either the party for whose relief the writ is intended, or any person for him, may present a petition to the proper authority for the purpose of obtaining relief .

Art. 11.13. [125] [173] [163] *Applicant*
The word applicant, as used in this Chapter, refers to the person for whose relief the writ i s asked, though the petition may be signed and presented by any other person.

Art. 11.14. [126] [174] [164] *Requisites of petition*
The petition must state substantially:

1. That the person for whose benefit the application is made is illegally restrained in his liberty, and by whom, naming both parties, if their names are known, or if unknown, designating and describing them;

2. When the party is confined or restrained by virtue of any writ, order or process, or under color of either, a copy shall be annexed to the petition, or it shall be stated that a copy cannot be obtained;

3. When the confinement or restraint is not by virtue of any writ, order or process, the petition may state only that the party is illegally confined or restrained in his liberty;

4. There must be a prayer in the petition for the writ of habeas corpus; and

5. Oath must be made that the allegations of the petition are true, according to the belief of the petitioner.

Art. 11.15. [127] [175] [165] Writ granted without delay
The writ of habeas corpus shall be granted without delay by the judge or court receiving the petition, unless it be manifest from the petition itself, or some documents annexed to it, that the party is entitled to no relief whatever .

Art. 11.16. [128] [176] [166] Writ may issue without motion
A judge of the district or county court who has knowledge that any person is illegally confined or restrained in his liberty within his district or county may, if the case be one within his jurisdiction, issue the writ of habeas corpus, without any motion being made for the same.

Art. 11.17. [129] [177] [167] Judge may issue warrant of arrest
Whenever it appears by satisfactory evidence to any judge authorized to issue such writ that any one is held in illegal confinement or custody, and there is good reason to believe that he will be carried out of the State, or suffer some irreparable injury before he can obtain relief in the usual course of law, or whenever the writ of habeas corpus has been issued and disregarded, the said judge may issue a warrant to any peace officer, or to any person specially named by said judge, directing him to take and bring such person before such judge, to be dealt with according to law.

Art. 11.18. [130] [178] [168] May arrest detainer
Where it appears by the proof offered, under circumstances mentioned in the preceding Article, that the person charged with having illegal custody of the prisoner is, by such act, guilty of an offense against the law, the judge may, in the warrant, order that he be arrested and brought before him; and upon examination, he may be committed, discharged, or held to bail, as the law and the nature of the case may require.

Art. 11.19. [131] [179] [169] Proceedings under the warrant
The officer charged with the execution of the warrant shall bring the persons therein mentioned before the judge or court issuing the same, who shall inquire into the cause of the imprisonment or restraint, and make an order thereon, as in cases of habeas corpus, either remanding into custody, discharging or admitting to bail the party so imprisoned or restrained.

Art. 11.20. [132] [180] [170] Officer executing warrant
The same power may be exercised by the officer executing the warrant in cases arising under the foregoing Articles as is exercised in the execution of warrants of arrest.

Art. 11.21. [133] [181] [171] Constructive custody
The words "confined", "imprisoned", "in custody", "confinement", "imprisonment", refer not only to the actual, corporeal and forcible detention of a person, but likewise to any coercive measures by threats, menaces or the fear of injury, whereby one person exercises a control over the person of another, and detains him within certain limits.

Art. 11.22. [134] [182] [172] Restraint
By "restraint" is meant the kind of control which one person exercises over another, not to confine him within certain limits, but to subject him to the general authority and power of the person claiming such right.

Art. 11.23. [135] [183] [173] Scope of writ
The writ of habeas corpus is intended to be applicable to all such cases of confinement and restraint, where there is no lawful right in the person exercising the power, or where, though the power in fact exists, it is exercised in a manner or degree not sanctioned by law.

Art. 11.24. [136] [184] [174] One committed in default of bail
Where a person has been committed to custody for failing to enter into bond, he is entitled to the writ of habeas corpus, if it be stated in the petition that there was no sufficient cause for requiring bail, or that the bail required is excessive. If the proof sustains the petition, it will entitle the party to be discharged, or have the bail reduced.

Art. 11.25. [137] [185] [175] Person afflicted with disease
When a judge or court authorized to grant writs of habeas corpus shall be satisfied, upon investigation, that a person in legal custody is afflicted with a disease which will render a removal necessary for the preservation of life, an order may be made for the removal of the prisoner t o some other place where his health will not be likely to suffer; or he may be admitted to bail when it appears that any species of confinement will endanger his life.

Art. 11. 26. [138] [186] [176] Who may serve writ
The service of the writ may be made by any person competent to testify.

UTAH

State Court Rules
Utah Rules of Civil Procedure
Part VIII . Provisional and Final Remedies and Special Proceedings

Rule 65B. Extraordinary Relief
(a) Availability of Remedy. Where no other plain, speedy and adequate remedy is available, a person may petition the court for extraordinary relief on any of the grounds set forth in paragraph (b) (involving wrongful restraint on personal liberty), paragraph (c) (involving the wrongful use of pubic or corporate authority) or paragraph (d) (involving the wrongful use of judicial authority, the failure to exercise such

authority, and actions by the Board of Pardons and Parole). There shall be no special form of writ. Except for instances governed by Rule 65C, the procedures in this rule shall govern proceedings on all petitions for extraordinary relief. To the extent that this rule does not provide special procedures, proceedings on petitions for extraordinary relief shall be governed by the procedures set forth elsewhere in these rules.

(b) Wrongful Restraints on Personal Liberty.

(b)(1) *Scope*. Except for instances governed by Rule 65C, this paragraph shall govern all petitions claiming that a person has been wrongfully restrained of personal liberty, and the court may grant relief appropriate under this paragraph.

(b)(2) *Commencement*. The proceeding shall be commenced by filing a petition with the clerk of the court in the district in which the petitioner is restrained or the respondent resides or in which the alleged restraint is occurring.

(b)(3) *Contents of the Petition and Attachments*. The petition shall contain a short, plain statement of the facts on the basis of which the petitioner seeks relief. It shall identify the respondent and the place where the person is restrained. It shall state the cause or pretense of the restraint, if known by the petitioner. It shall state whether the legality of the restraint has already been adjudicated in a prior proceeding and, if so, the reasons for the denial of relief in the prior proceeding. The petitioner shall attach to the petition any legal process available to the petitioner that resulted in restraint. The petitioner shall also attach to the petition a copy of the pleadings filed by the petitioner in any prior proceeding that adjudicated the legality of the restraint.

(b)(4) *Memorandum of Authorities*. The petitioner shall not set forth argument or citations or discuss authorities in the petition, but these may be set out in a separate memorandum, two copies of which shall be filed with the petition.

(b)(5) *Dismissal of Frivolous Claims*. On review of the petition, if it is apparent to the court that the legality of the restraint has already been adjudicated in a prior proceeding, or if for any other reason any claim in the petition shall appear frivolous on its face, the court shall forthwith issue an order dismissing the claim, stating that the claim is frivolous on its face and the reasons for this conclusion. The order need not state findings of fact or conclusions of law. The order shall be sent by mail to the petitioner. Proceedings on the claim shall terminate with the entry of the order of dismissal.

(b)(6) *Responsive Pleadings*. If the petition is not dismissed as being frivolous on its face, the court shall direct the clerk of the court to serve a copy of the petition and a copy of any memorandum upon the respondent by mail. At the same time, the court may issue an order directing the respondent to answer or otherwise respond to the petition, specifying a time within which the respondent must comply. If the circumstances require, the court may also issue an order directing the respondent to appear before the court for a hearing on the legality of the restraint. An answer to a petition shall state plainly whether the respondent has restrained the person alleged to have been restrained, whether the person so restrained has been transferred to any other person, and if so, the identity of the transferee, the date of the transfer, and the reason or authority for the transfer. Nothing in this paragraph shall be construed to prohibit the court from ruling upon the petition based upon a dispositive motion.

(b)(7) *Temporary Relief*. If it appears that the person alleged to be restrained will be removed from the court's jurisdiction or will suffer irreparable injury before compliance with the hearing order can be enforced, the court shall issue a warrant directing the sheriff to bring the respondent before the court to be dealt with according to law. Pending a determination of the petition, the court may place the person alleged to have been restrained in the custody of such other persons as may be appropriate.

(b)(8) *Alternative Service of the Hearing Order.* If the respondent cannot be found, or if it appears that a person other than the respondent has custody of the person alleged to be restrained, the hearing order and any other process issued by the court may be served on the person having custody in the manner and with the same effect as if that person had been named as respondent in the action.

(b)(9) *Avoidance of Service by Respondent.* If anyone having custody of the person alleged to be restrained avoids service of the hearing order or attempts wrongfully to remove the person from the court's jurisdiction, the sheriff shall immediately arrest the responsible person . The sheriff shall forthwith bring the person arrested before the court to be dealt with according to law.

(b)(10) *Hearing or Other Proceedings.* In the event that the court orders a hearing, the court shall hear the matter in a summary fashion and shall render judgment accordingly. The respondent or other person having custody shall appear with the person alleged to be restrained or shall state the reasons for failing to do so. The court may nevertheless direct the respondent to bring before it the person alleged to be restrained. If the petitioner waives the right to be present at the hearing, the court shall modify the hearing order accordingly. The hearing order shall not be disobeyed for any defect of form or any misdescription in the order or the petition, if enough is stated to impart the meaning and intent of the proceeding to the respondent.

(c) Wrongful Use of or Failure to Exercise Public Authority.

(c)(1) *Who May Petition the Court; Security.* The attorney general may, and when directed to do so by the governor shall, petition the court for relief on the grounds enumerated in this paragraph. Any person who is not required to be represented by the attorney general and who is aggrieved or threatened by one of the acts enumerated in subparagraph (2) of this paragraph may petition the court under this paragraph if (A) the person claims to be entitled to an office unlawfully held by another or (B) if the attorney general fails to file a petition under this paragraph after receiving notice of the person's claim. A petition filed by a person other than the attorney general under this paragraph shall be brought in the name of the petitioner, and the petition shall be accompanied by an undertaking with sufficient sureties to pay any judgment for costs and damages that may be recovered against the petitioner in the proceeding. The sureties shall be in the form for bonds on appeal provided for in Rule 73.

(c)(2) *Grounds for Relief.* Appropriate relief may be granted: (A) where a person usurps, intrudes into, or unlawfully holds or exercises a public office, whether civil or military, a franchise, or an office in a corporation created by the authority of the state of Utah; (B) where a public officer does or permits any act that results in a forfeiture of the office; (C) where persons acts as a corporation in the state of Utah without being legally incorporated; (D) where any corporation has violated the laws of the state of Utah relating to the creation, alteration or renewal of corporations; or (E) where any corporation has forfeited or misused its corporate rights, privileges or franchises.

(c)(3) *Proceedings on the Petition.* On the filing of a petition, the court may require that notice be given to adverse parties before issuing a hearing order, or may issue a hearing order requiring the adverse party to appear at the hearing on the merits. The court may also grant temporary relief in accordance with the terms of Rule 65A .

(d) Wrongful Use of Judicial Authority or Failure to Comply With Duty; Actions by Board of Pardons and Parole .

(d)(1) *Who May Petition*. A person aggrieved or whose interests are threatened by any of the acts enumerated in this paragraph may petition the court for relief.

(d)(2) *Grounds for Relief*. Appropriate relief may be granted: (A) where an inferior court, administrative agency, or officer exercising judicial functions has exceeded its jurisdiction or abused its discretion; (B) where an inferior court, administrative agency, corporation or person has failed to perform an act required by law as a duty of office, trust or station; (C) where an inferior court, administrative agency, corporation or person has refused the petitioner the use or enjoyment of a right or office to which the petitioner is entitled; or (D) where the Board of Pardons and Parole has exceeded its jurisdiction or failed to perform an act required by constitutional or statutory law.

(d)(3) *Proceedings on the Petition*. On the filing of a petition, the court may require that notice be given to adverse parties before issuing a hearing order, or may issue a hearing order requiring the adverse party to appear at the hearing on the merits. The court may direct the inferior court, administrative agency, officer, corporation or other person named as respondent to deliver to the court a transcript or other record of the proceedings. The court may also grant temporary relief in accordance with the terms of rule 65A.

(d)(4) *Scope of Relief*. Where the challenged proceedings are judicial in nature, the court's review shall not extend further then to determine whether the respondent has regularly pursued its authority.

RULE 65C. POST-CONVICTION RELIEF

(a) Scope. This rule governs proceedings in all petitions for post- conviction relief filed under the Post-Conviction Remedies Act, Utah Code Title 78B, Chapter 9 . The Act set forth the manner and extent to which a person may challenge the legality of a criminal conviction and sentence after the conviction and sentence have been affirmed in a direct appeal under *Article I, Section 12 of the Utah Constitution*, or the time to file such an appeal has expired.

(b) Procedural defenses and merits review. Except as provided in paragraph (h), if the court comments on the merits of a post-conviction claim, it shall first clearly and expressly determine whether that claim is independently precluded under *Section 78B-9-106*.

(c) Commencement and venue. The proceeding shall be commenced by filing a petition with the clerk of the district court in the county in which the judgment of conviction was entered. The petition should be filed on forms provided by the court. The court may order a change of venue on its own motion if the petition is filed in the wrong county. The court may order a change of venue on motion of a party for the convenience of the parties or witnesses.

(d) Contents of the petition. The petition shall set forth all claims that the petitioner has in relation to the legality of the conviction or sentence. The petition shall state:

(d)(1) whether the petitioner is incarcerated and, if so, the place of incarceration;

(d)(2) the name of the court in which the petitioner was convicted and sentenced and the dates of proceedings in which the conviction was entered, together with the court's case number for those proceedings, if known by the petitioner;

(d)(3) in plain and concise terms, all of the facts that form the basis of the petitioner's claim to relief;

(d)(4) whether the judgment of conviction, the sentence, or the commitment for violation of probation has been reviewed on appeal, and, if so, the number and title of the appellate proceeding, the issues raised on appeal, and the results of the appeal;

(d)(S) whether the legality of the conviction or sentence has been adjudicated in any prior post- conviction or other civil proceeding, and, if so, the case number and title of those proceedings, the issues raised in the petition, and the results of the prior proceeding; and

(d)(6) if the petitioner claims entitlement to relief due to newly discovered evidence, the reasons why the evidence could not have been discovered i n time for the claim to be addressed in the trial, the appeal, or any previous post- conviction petition.

(e) Attachments to the petition. If available to the petitioner, the petitioner shall attach to the petition:

(e)(1) affidavits, copies of records and other evidence in support of the allegations;

(e)(2) a copy of or a citation to any opinion issued by an appellate court regarding the direct appeal of the petitioner's case;

(e)(3) a copy of the pleadings filed by the petitioner in any prior post- conviction or other civil proceeding that adjudicated the legality of the conviction of sentence; and

(e)(4) a copy of all relevant orders and memoranda of the court.

(f) Memorandum of authorities. The petitioner shall not set forth argument or citations or discuss authorities in the petition, by these may be set out in a separate memorandum, two copies of which shall be filed with the petition.

(g) Assignment. On the filing of the petition, the clerk shall promptly assign and deliver it to the judge who sentenced the petitioner. If the judge who sentenced the petitioner is not available, the clerk shall assign the case in the normal course.

(h)(l) Summary dismissal of claim. The assigned judge shall review the petition, and, if it is apparent to the court that any claim has been adjudicated in a prior proceeding, or if any claim in the petition appears frivolous on its face, the court shall forthwith issue an order dismissing the claim, stating either that the claim has been adjudicated or that the claim is frivolous on its face. The order shall be sent by mail to the petitioner. Proceedings on the claim shall terminate with the entry of the order of dismissal. The order of dismissal need not recite findings of fact or conclusions of law.

(h)(2) A claim is frivolous on its face when, based solely on the allegations contained in the pleadings and attachments, it appears that:

(h)(2)(A) the facts alleged do not support a claim for relief as a matter of law;

(h)(2)(B) the claim has no arguable basis in fact; or

(h)(2)(C) the claim challenges the sentence only and the sentences has expired prior to the filing of the petition.

(h)(3) If a claim is not frivolous on its face but is deficient due to a pleading error or failure to comply with the requirements of this rule, the court shall return a copy of the petition with leave to amend within 21 days. The court may grant one additional 21-day period to amend for good cause shown.

(h)(4) The court shall not review for summary dismissal the initial post- conviction petition in a case where the petitioner is sentenced to death .

(i) Service of petitions. If, on review of the petition, the court concludes that all or part of the petition should not be summarily dismissed, the court shall designate the portions of the petition that are not dismissed and direct the clerk to serve a copy of the petition, attachments and memorandum by mail upon the respondent. If the petition is a challenge to a felony conviction or sentence, the respondent is the state of Utah represented by the Attorney General . In all other cases, the respondent is the governmental entity that prosecuted the petitioner.

(j) Appointment of pro bono counsel. If any portion of the petition is not summarily dismissed, the court may, upon the request of an indigent petitioner, appoint counsel on a pro bono basis to represent the petitioner in the post conviction court or on post-conviction appeal. In determining whether to appoint counsel the court shall consider whether the petition or the appeal contains factual allegations that will require an evidentiary hearing and whether the petition involves complicated issues of law or fact that require the assistance of counsel for proper adjudication.

(k) Answer or other response. Within 30 days after service of a copy of the petition upon the respondent, or within such other period of time as the court may allow, the respondent shall answer or otherwise respond to the portions of the petition that have not been dismissed and shall serve the answer or other response upon the petitioner in accordance with Rule 5(b). Within 30 days (plus time allowed for service by mail) after service of any motion to dismiss or for summary judgment, the petitioner may respond by memorandum to the motion . No further pleadings or amendments will be permitted unless ordered by the court.

(L) Hearings. After pleadings are closed, the court shall promptly set the proceeding for a hearing or otherwise dispose of the case. The court may also order a prehearing conference, but the conference shall not be set so as to delay unreasonably the hearing on the merits of the petition. At the prehearing conference, the court may:

(i)(1) consider the formation and simplification of issues;

(i)(2) require the parties to identify witnesses and documents; and

(i)(3) require the parties to establish the admissibility of evidence expected to be presented at the evidentiary hearing.

(m) Presence of the petitioner at hearings. The petitioner shall be present at the prehearing conference if the petitioner is not represented by counsel. The prehearing conference may be conducted by means of telephone or video conferencing. The petitioner shall be present before the court at hearings on dispositive issues but need not otherwise be present in court during the proceeding. The court may conduct any hearing at the correctional facility where the petitioner is confined.

(n) Discovery; records. Discovery under Rule 26 through 37 shall be allowed by the court upon motion of a party and a determination that there is good cause to believe that discovery is necessary to provide a party with evidence that is likely to be admissible at an evidentiary hearing. The court may order either the petitioner or the respondent to obtain any relevant transcript or court records.

(o) Orders; stay.

(o)(1) If the court vacates the original conviction or sentence, it shall enter findings of fact and conclusions of law and an appropriate order. If the petitioner is serving a sentence for a felony conviction, the order shall be stayed for 7 days. Within the stay period, the respondent shall give written notice to the court and the petitioner that the respondent will pursue a new trial, pursue a new sentence, appeal the order, or take no action. Thereafter the stay of the order is governed by these rules and by the Rules of Appellate Procedure.

(o)(2) If the respondent fails to provide notice or gives notice that no action will be taken, the stay shall expire and the court deliver forthwith to the custodian of the petitioner the order to release the petitioner.

(o)(3) If the respondent gives notice that the petitioner will be retried or resentenced, the trial court may enter any supplementary orders as to arraignment, trial, sentencing, custody, bail, discharge, or other matters that may be necessary and proper.

(p) Costs. The court may assign the costs of the proceedings, as allowed under Rule 54(d), to any party as it deems appropriate. If the petitioner is indigent, the court may direct the costs to be paid by the governmental entity that prosecuted the petitioner. If the petitioner is in the custody of the Department of Corrections, Utah Code Title 78A, Chapter 2, Part 3 governs the manner and procedure by which the trial court shall determine the amount, if any, to charge for fees and costs.

(q) Appeal. Any final judgment or order entered upon the petition may be appealed and reviewed by the Court of Appeals or the Supreme Court 9 of Utah in accord with the statutes governing appeals to those courts.

VERMONT

Vermont Statutes Annotated
Title Twelve. Court Procedure
Part 8. Extraordinary Writs
Chapter 143. Habeas Corpus

§3951. Unlawful restraint
A person shall not be restrained or imprisoned unless by authority of law.

§3952. Prisoners entitled to writ of habeas corpus
A person imprisoned in a common jail, or the liberties thereof, or otherwise restrained of his liberty by an officer or other person, may prosecute a writ of habeas corpus to inquire into the cause of such imprisonment or restraint, and obtain relief therefrom if it is unlawful.

§3953. Authority to grant writ; complaint
Such writ may be granted by a superior judge, or by superior court during its sitting, in the county where such person is imprisoned, on application by complaint in writing signed by the party for whose relief it is intended or by some person in his behalf, stating the person by whom and the place where the party is imprisoned or restrained, naming the prisoner and the person detaining him, if their names are known, and describing them, if they are not known, and stating also the cause or pretense of such imprisonment or restraint, according to the knowledge and belief of the person applying. The petitioner or the state may appeal from the decision on the petition to the supreme court under chapter 102 of this title.

§3954. Copy of process annexed to complaint
When the imprisonment or restraint is by virtue of a warrant or other process, a copy thereof shall be annexed to the complaint, or it shall appear that copy thereof has been demanded and refused, or that for sufficient reason a demand of such could not be made.

§3955. Complaint to be sworn to
The facts set forth in the complaint shall be verified by the oath of the person making the application or by that of some credible witness. Such oath may be administered by the court or magistrate to whom the application is made, or a district judge.

§3956. Issue and return of writ
Without delay, such court or magistrate shall award and issue a writ of habeas corpus, which shall be made returnable forthwith.

§3957. Signing of writ
When the writ is issued by the superior court, it shall be signed by the clerk, otherwise by the magistrate issuing the same.

§3958. Return after court adjourns; procedure
When the court to which the writ is returnable adjourns before it is returned, the return shall be made before one of the justices of the supreme court. If the writ is in any case returned before one justice or judge when the court is in session, he may adjourn the case into the court, to be there heard and determined as if the writ had been returned into the same court.

§3959. Designation of person to be served
The person having the custody of the prisoner may be designated by his official title, if he has any, or by his name. If such title or name is unknown or uncertain, he may be described by an assumed appellation. Any one upon whom the writ is served, shall be deemed the person intended thereby.

§3960. Designation of prisoner
The prisoner to be produced shall be designated by his name, if known, and if that is unknown or uncertain, he may be otherwise described so as to make known who is intended.

§3961. Pay for transporting prisoner

When the prisoner is confined in a common jail, or in the custody of a civil officer, the court or magistrate issuing the writ shall certify thereon the sum to be paid for bringing him from the place of imprisonment. The officer to whom the writ is directed shall not be bound to obey it, unless such sum is paid or tendered to him.

§3962. When a person to be served is not an officer

In cases of imprisonment by a person not an officer of the state or of the courts of the United States, the writ shall be directed to a sheriff or his deputy, commanding him to take and have the person imprisoned before the court or magistrate granting the writ, immediately after the receipt thereof, and summon the person by whom such prisoner is restrained to appear before such court or magistrate and show the cause for taking and detaining such prisoner.

§3963. Receipt and return of writ; notice to state's attorney or attorney general

A person to whom the writ is directed shall receive the same and, upon payment or tender of the charges demandable for its execution, shall make return thereof forthwith. In case a person is restrained of his liberty by reason of a court sentence to a penal institution the judge may, in his discretion, order such other or further notice be given to the state's attorney of the county in which the prisoner was convicted or to the attorney general as he deems reasonable.

§3964. Return of statement as to custody and authority

In cases other than those provided for in *section 3962* of this title, the person who makes the return shall state therein, and, in the cases provided for in such section, the person in whose custody the prisoner is found shall state, in writing, to such court or magistrate, plainly and unequivocally, whether he has or has not the prisoner in his custody or power or under restraint. If he has him in his custody or power or under restraint, he shall set forth at large the authority and the true and whole cause of such imprisonment or restraint, with a copy of the writ, warrant or other process, if any, upon which he is detained. If he has had him in his custody or power or under restraint and has transferred such custody or restraint to another, he shall state particularly to whom, at what time, for what cause and by what authority such transfer was made.

§3965. Return to be signed and sworn to; exception

The return or statement shall be signed by the person making it, and shall be sworn to by him unless he is a sworn public officer and makes the return in his official capacity.

§3966. Prisoner brought unless sick

The person who makes the return or statement, at the same time, shall bring the prisoner, if in his custody or power or under his restraint, according to the command of the writ, unless prevented by the sickness or infirmity of such prisoner.

§3967. Examination in case of sick prisoner

When the prisoner cannot be brought to the place appointed for the return of the writ, without danger, because of his sickness or infirmity, that fact shall be stated in the return. When such fact is provided to the satisfaction of such court or magistrate, he may proceed to the jail or other place where the prisoner is confined and there make an examination or adjourn the hearing to another time or make such order in the case as law and justice require.

§3968. Examination; time; adjournment
When the writ is returned, such court or magistrate, without delay, shall examine the causes of imprisonment or restraint; but the examination may be adjourned from time to time.

§3969. Notice of examination
When it appears that the prisoner is detained on a process under which another person has an interest in continuing his imprisonment or restraint, he shall not be discharged until sufficient notice has been given to such other person, or his attorney, if within the state, to appear and object to such discharge.

§3970. Prisoner charged with crime, notice to state's attorney
When it appears that the prisoner is imprisoned on a criminal accusation, he shall not be discharged until sufficient notice is given to the state's attorney, whose duty it is to prosecute for such offense, to appear and object to such discharge.

§3971. Pleading; bearing
The prisoner may deny any of the facts set forth in the return or statement and may allege other material facts. Such court or magistrate may examine the causes of the imprisonment or restraint in a summary manner and hear the evidence produced by any person interested or authorized to appear, in support of or against such imprisonment or restraint.

§3972. Discharge; decision and record
When legal cause is not shown for the imprisonment or restraint, such court or magistrate shall discharge the person therefrom. The petition for a writ of habeas corpus heard by a court or magistrate, together with the decision thereon in writing, shall be returned for record to the office of the county clerk of the county in which the person is alleged to be restrained or confined, or, if restrained upon process issuing from a court, into the clerk's office in the county where such court is held. Such proceedings shall be docketed and properly indexed, and the same, together with the decision thereon, recorded in the same manner as other judgments of such court.

§3973. Bail
When the prisoner is detained for a bailable cause or offense, such court or magistrate shall admit him to bail, if a sufficient amount thereof is offered, and if not, shall remand him with an order fixing the sum in which he shall be held to bail, and the court at which he shall be required to appear. A judge of the superior court in the county where such prisoner is confined may admit him to bail pursuant to such order before the sitting of such court.

§3974. Remand of prisoner
When the prisoner is lawfully imprisoned or restrained or is not entitled to be released on bail, he shall be remanded to the person from whose custody he was taken or to such other person or officer as by law is authorized to detain him.

§3975. Custody pending judgment
Until the judgment is given, such court or magistrate may remand the prisoner, admit him to bail to appear from day to day, commit him to the custody of the sheriff of the county or place him under such other care and custody as the circumstances of the case require.

§3976. Refusal to receive or obey and execute writ—contempt proceedings
When a person to whom a writ of habeas corpus is directed refuses to receive the same, or does not obey and

execute it, unless sufficient excuse therefor is shown, such court or magistrate shall compel obedience to the writ and punish the person guilty of the contempt forthwith, by process of attachment as for contempt.

§3977. Precept to another officer or person
Upon such refusal or neglect, such court or magistrate may also issue a precept to an officer or other person, to be designated therein, commanding him to bring forthwith before such court or magistrate the person for whose benefit the writ of habeas corpus was issued. The prisoner shall be thereupon discharged, bailed or remanded, in like manner as if he had been brought in on habeas corpus.

§3978. Penalty for not executing writ
A person neglecting or refusing to receive and execute a writ of habeas corpus shall forfeit to the person aggrieved $400.00, to be recovered in an action of tort on this statute.

§3979. Confinement for contempt—issuance and return of writ
When a person disobeys the order, decree, judgment or process of a court or a magistrate thereof, or is guilty of a contempt of such court or magistrate, and in consequence is imprisoned or confined by the order or judgment of such court or magistrate, such person shall be entitled to his writ of habeas corpus, returnable to the supreme court.

§3980. Discharge of person confined for contempt
When it appears on the hearing upon such writ that such disobedience or contempt was committed through ignorance, mistake or misapprehension, or by acting in good faith under the advice of counsel, and that relief may be granted without impairing the rights of the parties concerned or the due administration of law, the supreme court may discharge such person from such imprisonment or confinement upon such terms as seem just.

§3981. Bond
The supreme court may order the person bringing such writ to file a bond with the clerk of the court, in such sum and with such sureties and conditions as it directs, to be given to the clerk of the court or to such person as the court designates in the order, and may further order that, upon filing such bond, the person may go at large. The bond may be prosecuted for the benefit of any party interested.

§3982. Penalty for attempting to elude service
Whether a writ has been issued or not, a person who has in his custody or under his power a prisoner entitled to a writ of habeas corpus, and who, with intent to elude the service of such writ or to avoid the effect thereof, transfers such prisoner to the custody, or places him under the power or control of another person, or conceals him or changes the place of his confinement, shall forfeit to the person aggrieved $400.00, to be recovered in an action of tort of this statute.

§3983. Recovery of penalty not bar to further suit
The recovery of a penalty imposed by this chapter shall not be a bar to an action for false imprisonment or for a false return to the writ of habeas corpus or for damages.

§3984. Imprisonment for same cause after discharge
A person who has been discharged upon habeas corpus shall not be imprisoned or restrained again for the same cause, unless he is indicted therefor or convicted thereof, or does not find bail as ordered by a court of record or unless, after a discharge for a defect of proof or for material defect in the commitment in a criminal cause, he is again arrested on sufficient proof and committed for the same offense.

§3985. Habeas corpus to bring respondent or witness into court
Nothing in this chapter shall prevent a court from issuing a writ of habeas corpus, when necessary, to bring before it a prisoner for trial in a criminal cause pending in the court, or to be surrendered in discharge of bail, or examined as a witness in any action or proceeding, civil or criminal, pending in such court, when the personal attendance and examination of the witness is necessary in the administration of justice.

The statutes are current through laws No. 90 to 101, 103, 107, 108, 110, 111, 116, and 192 of the Adjourned Session of the 2013-2014 Vermont General Assembly (2014).

VIRGINIA

Annotated Code of Virginia
Title 8.01. Civil Remedies and Procedure
Chapter 25. Extraordinary Writs
Article 3. Habeas Corpus

§8.01 654. When and by whom writ granted; what petition to contain
A. 1. The writ of habeas corpus ad subjiciendum shall be granted forthwith by the Supreme Court or any circuit court, to any person who shall apply for the same by petition, showing by affidavits or other evidence probable cause to believe that he is detained without lawful authority.

2. A petition for writ of habeas corpus ad subjiciendum, other than a petition challenging a criminal conviction or sentence, shall be brought within one year after the cause of action accrues. A habeas corpus petition attacking a criminal conviction or sentence, except as provided in §8.01-654.1 for cases in which a death sentence has been imposed, shall be filed within two years from the date of final judgment in the trial court or within one year from either final disposition of the direct appeal in state court or the time for filing such appeal has expired, whichever is later.

B. 1. With respect to any such petition filed by a petitioner held under criminal process, and subject to the provisions of subsection C of this section and of §17.1-310, only the circuit court which entered the original judgment order of conviction or convictions complained of in the petition shall have authority to issue writs of habeas corpus. If a district court entered the original judgment order of conviction or convictions complained of in the petition, only the circuit court for the city or county wherein the district court sits shall have authority to issue writs of habeas corpus. Hearings on such petition, where granted in the circuit court, may be held at any circuit court within the same circuit as the circuit court in which the petition was filed, as designated by the judge thereof.

2. Such petition shall contain all allegations the facts of which are known to petitioner at the time of filing and such petition shall enumerate all previous applications and their disposition. No writ shall be granted on the basis of any allegation the facts of which petitioner had knowledge at the time of filing any previous petition. The provisions of this section shall not apply to a petitioner's first petition for a writ of habeas corpus when the sole allegation of such petition is that the petitioner was deprived of the right to

pursue an appeal from a final judgment of conviction or probation revocation, except that such petition shall contain all facts pertinent to the denial of appeal that are known to the petitioner at the time of the filing, and such petition shall certify that the petitioner has filed no prior habeas corpus petitions attacking the conviction or probation revocation.

3. Such petition may allege detention without lawful authority through challenge to a conviction although the sentence imposed for such conviction is suspended or is to be served subsequently to the sentence currently being served by petitioner.

4. In the event the allegations of illegality of the petitioner's detention can be fully determined on the basis of recorded matters, the court may make its determination whether such writ should issue on the basis of the record.

5. The court shall give findings of fact and conclusions of law following a determination on the record or after hearing, to be made a part of the record and transcribed.

6. If petitioner alleges as a ground for illegality of his detention the inadequacy of counsel, he shall be deemed to waive his privilege with respect to communications between such counsel and himself to the extent necessary to permit a full and fair hearing for the alleged ground.

C. 1. With respect to any such petition filed by a petitioner held under the sentence of death, and subject to the provisions of this subsection, the Supreme Court shall have exclusive jurisdiction to consider and award writs of habeas corpus. The circuit court which entered the judgment order setting the sentence of death shall have authority to conduct an evidentiary hearing on such a petition only if directed to do so by order of the Supreme Court.

2. Hearings conducted in a circuit court pursuant to an order issued under the provisions of subdivision 1 of this subsection shall be limited in subject matter to the issues enumerated in the order.

3. The circuit court shall conduct such a hearing within 90 days after the order of the Supreme Court has been received and shall report its findings of fact and recommend conclusions of law to the Supreme Court within 60 days after the conclusion of the hearing. Any objection to the report of the circuit court must be filed in the Supreme court within 30 days after the report is filed.

§8.01-654.1. Limitation on consideration of petition filed by prisoner sentenced to death

No petition for a writ of habeas corpus filed by a prisoner held under a sentence of death shall be considered unless it is filed within 60 days after the earliest of: (i) denial by the United State Supreme Court of a petition for a writ of certiorari to the judge of the Supreme Court of Virginia on direct appeal, (ii) a decision by the United States Supreme Court affirming imposition of the sentence of death when such decision is in a case resulting from a granted writ of certiorari to the judgment of the Supreme Court of Virginia on direct appeal, or (iii) the expiration of the period for filing a timely petition for certiorari without a petition being filed.

However, notwithstanding the time restrictions otherwise applicable to the filing of a petition for a writ of habeas corpus, an indigent prisoner may file such a petition within 120 days following appointment, made under *§19.2-163.7*, of counsel to represent him.

APPENDIX—VIRGINIA

§8.01-654.2. Presentation of claim of mental retardation by person sentenced to death before April 29, 2003

Notwithstanding any other provision of law, any person under sentence of death whose sentence became final in the circuit court before April 29, 2003, and who desires to have a claim of his mental retardation presented to the Supreme Court, shall do so by one of the following methods: (i) if the person has not commenced a direct appeal, he shall present his claim of mental retardation by assignment of error and in his brief in that appeal, or if his direct appeal is pending in the Supreme Court, he shall file a supplemental assignment of error and brief containing his claim of mental retardation, or (ii) if the the person has not filed a petition for a writ of habeas corpus under *section C of §8.01-654*, he shall present his claim of mental retardation in a petition for a writ of habeas corpus under such subsection, or if such a petition is pending in the Supreme Court, he shall file an amended petition containing his claim of mental retardation. A person proceeding under this section shall allege the factual basis for his claim of mental retardation. The Supreme Court shall consider a claim raised under this section and if it determines that the claim is not frivolous, it shall remand the claim to the circuit court for a determination of mental retardation; otherwise the Supreme Court shall dismiss the petition. The provisions of *§§19.2-264.3:1.1* and *19.2-264.3:1.2* shall govern a determination of mental retardation made pursuant to this section. If the claim is before the Supreme Court on direct appeal and is remanded to the circuit court and the case wherein the sentence of death was imposed was tried by a jury, the circuit court shall empanel a new jury for the sole purpose of making a determination of mental retardation.

If the person has completed both a direct appeal and a habeas corpus proceeding under *section C of §8.01-654*, he shall not be entitled to file any further habeas petitions in the Supreme Court and his sole remedy shall lie in federal court.

§8.01-655. Form and contents of petition filed by prisoner

A. Every petition filed by a prisoner seeking a writ of habeas corpus must be filed on the form set forth in subsection B. The failure to use such form and to comply substantially with such form shall entitle the court to which such petition is directed to return such petition to the prisoner pending the use of and substantial compliance with such form. The petitioner shall be responsible for all statements contained in the petition and any false statement contained therein, if the same be knowingly or willfully made, shall be a ground for prosecution and conviction of perjury as provided for in §18.2-434.

B. Every petition filed by a prisoner seeking a writ of habeas corpus shall be filed on a form to be approved and provided by the office of Attorney General, the contents of which shall be substantially as follows:

IN THE .... COURT

Full name and prisoner number (if any) of Petitioner -vs-	Case No. (To be supplied by the Clerk of the Court)

Name and Title of Respondent

PETITION FOR WRIT OF HABEAS CORPUS

Instructions—Read Carefully

APPENDIX—VIRGINIA

In order for this petition to receive consideration by the Court, it must be legibly handwritten or typewritten, signed by the petitioner and verified before a notary or other officer authorized to administer oaths. It must set forth in concise form the answers to each applicable question. If necessary, petitioner may finish his answer to a particular question on an additional page. Petitioner must make it clear to which question any such continued answer refers. The petitioner may also submit exhibits.

Since every petition for habeas corpus must be sworn to under oath, any false statement of a material fact therein may serve as the basis of prosecution and conviction for perjury under §18.2-434. Petitioner's should, therefore, exercise care to assure that all answers are true and correct.

When the petition is completed, the original and two copies (total of three) should be mailed to the clerk of the court. The petitioner shall keep one copy.

NOTICE

The granting of a writ of habeas corpus does not entitle the petitioner to dismissal of the charges for conviction of which he is being detained, but may gain him no more than a new trial.

....

Place of detention: ....

A. Criminal Trial

1. Name and location of court which imposed the sentence which you seek relief:

2. The offense or offenses for which sentence was imposed (include indictment number or numbers if known):

a.

b.

c.

3. The date upon which sentence was imposed and the terms of the sentence:

a.

b.

c.

4. Check which plea you made and whether trial by jury: Plea of guilty: ...; Plea of not guilty: ...; Trial by jury: ...; Trial by judge without jury: ...

5. The name and address of each attorney, if any, who represented you at your criminal trial:

6. Did you appeal the conviction?

7. If you answered "yes" to 6, state: the result and the date in your appeal or petition for certiorari:

a.

b.

citations of the appellate court opinions or orders:

a.

b.

8. List the name and address of each attorney, if any, who represented you on your appeal:

B. Habeas corpus

9. Before this petition did you file with respect to this conviction any other petition for habeas corpus in either a State or federal court?

10. If you answered "yes" to 9, list with respect to each petition: the name and location of the court in which each was filed:

a.

b.

the disposition and the date:

a.

b.

the name and address of each attorney, if any, who represented you on your habeas corpus:

a.

b.

11. Did you appeal form the disposition of your petition for habeas corpus?

12. If you answered "yes" to 11, state: the result and the date of each petition:

a.

b. citations of court opinions or orders on your habeas corpus petition:

a.

b.

the name and address of each attorney, if any, who represented you on appeal of your habeas corpus:

a.

b.

C. Other Petitions, Motions or Applications

13. List all other petitions, motions or applications filed with any court following a final order of conviction and not set out in A or B. Include the nature of the motion, the name and location of the court, the result, the date, and citations to opinions or orders. Give the name and address of each attorney, if any, who represented you.
a.

b.

c.

D. Present Petition

14. State the grounds which make your detention unlawful, including the facts on which you intend to rely:

a.

b.

c.

15. List each ground set forth in 14, which has been presented in any other proceeding:

a.

b.

c.

List the proceedings in which each ground was raised:

a.

APPENDIX—VIRGINIA

b.

c.

16. If any ground set forth in 14 has not been presented to a court, list each ground and the reason why it was not:

a.

b.

c.

_____
Signature of Petitioner
Address of Petitioner

STATE OF VIRGINIA
CITY/COUNTY OF

The Petitioner being first duly sworn, says:

1. He signed the foregoing petition;

2. The facts stated in the petition are true to the best of his information and belief.

_____
Signature of Petitioner

Subscribed and sworn to before me

This .... day of ...., 20..

_____
Notary Public

My commission expires: ....

The petition will not be filed without payment of court costs unless the petitioner is entitled to proceed in forma pauperis and has executed the affidavit in forma pauperis.

The petitioner who proceeds in forma pauperis shall be furnished, without cost, certified copies of the arrest warrants, indictment and order of his conviction at his criminal trial in order to comply with the instructions of this petition.

APPENDIX—VIRGINIA

AFFIDAVIT IN FORMA PAUPERIS

STATE OF VIRGINIA
CITY/COUNTY OF ....

The petitioner being first duly sworn, says:

1. He is unable to pay the costs of this action or give security therefor;

2. His assets amount to a total of $ ....

_____
Signature of Petitioner

Subscribed and sworn to before me

This .... day of .... , 20..

_____
Notary Public

My commission expires: ....

§8.01-656. *Bond may be required of petitioner*
Before granting the writ, the court may require the petitioner to give bond with surety in a reasonable amount for the payment of such costs and charges as may be awarded against him.

Such bond shall be made payable to the person to whom the writ is directed, with condition that the petitioner will not escape, and shall be filed with the other proceedings on the writ, and may be sued on for the benefit of any person injured by the breach of its condition.

§8.01-657. *How directed and returnable*
The writ shall be directed to the person in whose custody the petitioner is detained and shall be made returnable as soon as may be before the court ordering the same, or any other of such courts.

Provided that in the event the allegations of illegality of the petitioner's detention present a case for the determination of unrecorded matters of fact relating to any previous judicial proceeding, such writ shall be made returnable before the court in which such judicial proceeding occurred.

§8.01-658. *How writ served*
The writ shall be served on the person to whom it is directed, or, in his absence from the place where the petitioner is confined, on the person having the immediate custody of him.

§8.01-659. *Penalty for disobeying it*
If the person on whom such writ is served shall, in disobedience to the writ, fail to bring the petitioner, with a return of the cause of his detention, before a court before which the writ is returnable, he shall forfeit to the petitioner $300.

§8.01-660. When affidavits may be read

In the discretion of the court or judge before whom the petitioner is brought, the affidavits of witnesses taken by either party, on reasonable notice to the other, may be read as evidence.

§8.01-661. Facts proved may be made part of record

All the material facts proved shall, when it is required by either party, be made a part of the proceedings and entered by the clerk among the records of the court.

§8.01-662. Judgment of court or judge trying it; payment of costs and expenses when petition denied

After hearing the matter both upon the return and any other evidence, the court before whom the petitioner is brought shall either discharge or remand him, or admit him to bail and adjudge the cost of the proceeding, including the charge for transporting the prisoner.

Provided, however, that if the petition is denied, the costs and expenses of the proceeding and the attorney's fees of any attorney appointed to represent the petitioner shall be assessed against the petitioner. If such cost, expenses and fees are collected, they shall be paid to the Commonwealth.

§8.01-663. Judgment conclusive

Any such judgment entered of record shall be conclusive, unless the same be reversed, except that the petitioner shall not be precluded from bringing the same matter in question in an action for false imprisonment.

§8.01-664. How and when Supreme Court summoned to try appeal therefrom

If, during the recess of the Supreme Court, the Governor or the Chief Justice of the Court should think the immediate revision of any such judgment to be proper, he may summon the Court for that purpose, to meet on any day to be fixed by him.

§8.01-665. When execution of judgment suspended; when prisoner admitted to bail

When the prisoner is remanded, the execution of the judgment shall not be suspended by a petition for appeal or by a writ of error, or for the purpose of applying for such writ. When he is ordered to be discharged, and the execution of the judgment is suspended for the purpose of petitioning for appeal to the Court of Appeals or applying for a writ of error from the Supreme Court, the court making such suspending order may admit the prisoner to bail until the expiration of the time allowed for filing a petition for appeal or applying for the writ of error, or, in case the petition for appeal is filed or the writ of error is allowed, until the decision of the Court of Appeals or the Supreme Court thereon is duly certified.

§8.01-666. When and by whom writs of habeas corpus ad testificandum granted

Writs of habeas corpus ad testificandum may be granted by any circuit court in the same manner and under the same conditions and provisions as are prescribed by this chapter as to granting the writ of habeas corpus ad subjiciendum so far as the same are applicable.

§8.01-667. Transmission of records to federal court

Whenever any habeas corpus case is pending in a federal court, upon written request of the Attorney General or any assistant attorney general, a court of this Commonwealth shall transmit to such federal court such records as may be requested.

§8.01-668. Writ de homine abolished

The writ de homine replegiando is abolished.

Current through the End of the 2014 Reg. Sess. and the End of the 2014 Sp. S. I.

WASHINGTON

Revised Code of Washington
Title 7. Special Proceedings and Actions
Chapter 7.36. Habeas Corpus

7.36.010. Who may prosecute writ

Every person restrained of his or her liberty under any pretense whatever, may prosecute a writ of habeas corpus to inquire into the cause of the restraint, and shall be delivered therefrom when illegal.

7.36.020. Parents, guardians, etc., may act for persons under disability

Writs of habeas corpus shall be granted in favor of parents, guardians, limited guardians where appropriate, spouses or domestic partners, and next of kin, and to enforce the rights, and for the protection of infants and incompetent or disabled persons within the meaning of *RCW 11.88.010*; and the proceedings shall in all cases conform to the provisions of this chapter.

7.36.030. Petition—Contents

Application for the writ shall be made by petition, signed and verified either by the plaintiff or by some person in his or her behalf, and shall specify:

(1) By whom the petitioner is restrained of his or her liberty, and the place where, (naming the parties if they are known, or describing them if they are not known).

(2) The cause or pretense of the restraint according to the best of the knowledge and belief of the applicant.

(3) If the restraint be alleged to be illegal, in what the illegally consists.

7.36.040. Who may grant writ

Writs of habeas corpus may be granted by the supreme court, the court of appeals, or superior court, or by any judge of such courts, and upon application the writ shall be granted without delay.

7.36.050. To whom directed—Contents

The writ shall be directed to the officer or party having the person under restraint, commanding him or her to have such person before the court or judge at such time and place as the court or judge shall direct to do and receive what shall be ordered concerning him or her, and have then and there the writ.

7.36.060. Delivery to sheriff if to him or her directed

If the writ be directed to the sheriff, it shall be delivered by the clerk to him or her without delay.

7.36.070. Service by sheriff if directed to another

If the writ be directed to any other person, it shall be delivered to the sheriff and shall be by him or her served by delivering the same to such person without delay.

7.36.080. Service when person not found

If the person to whom such writ is directed cannot be found or shall refuse admittance to the sheriff, the same may be served by leaving it at the residence of the person to whom it is directed, or by posting the same in some conspicuous place, either on his or her dwelling house or where the party is confined or under restraint.

7.36.090. Return—Attachment for refusal

The sheriff or other person to whom the writ is directed shall make immediate return thereof, and if he or she refuse after due service to make return, the court shall enforce obedience by attachment.

7.36.100. Form of return—Production of person

The return must be signed and verified by the person making it, who shall state:

(1) The authority or cause of the restraint of the party in his or her custody.

(2) If the authority shall be in writing, he or she shall return a copy and produce the original on the hearing.

(3) If he or she has had the party in his or her custody or under his or her restraint, and has transferred him or her to another, he or she shall state to whom, the time, place, and cause of the transfer. He or she shall produce the party at the hearing unless prevented by sickness or infirmity, which must be shown in the return.

7.36.110. Procedure—Pleadings—Amendment

The court or judge, if satisfied of the truth of the allegation of sickness or infirmity, may proceed to decide on the return, or the hearing may be adjourned until the party can be produced, or for other good cause. The plaintiff may except to the sufficiency of, or controvert the return or any part thereof, or allege any new matter in evidence. The new matter shall be verified, except in cases of commitment on a criminal charge. The return and pleadings may be amended without causing a delay.

7.36.120. Hearing—Determination

The court or judge shall thereupon proceed in a summary way to hear and determine the cause, and if no legal cause be shown for the restraint or for the continuation thereof, shall discharge the party.

7.36.130. Limitation upon inquiry

No court or judge shall inquire into the legality of any judgment or process whereby the party is in custody, or discharge the party when the term of commitment has not expired, in either of the cases following:

(1) Upon any process issued on any final judgment of a court of competent jurisdiction except where it is alleged in the petition that rights guaranteed the petitioner by the Constitution of the state of Washington or of the United States have been violated and the petition is filed within the time allowed by *RCW 10.73.090* and *10.73.100*.

(2) For any contempt of any court, officer or body having authority in the premises to commit; but an order of commitment, as for a contempt upon proceedings to enforce the remedy of a party, is not included in any of the foregoing specifications.

(3) Upon a warrant issued from the superior court upon an indictment or information.

7.36.140. Duty of courts when federal question is raised

In the consideration of any petition for a writ of habeas corpus by the supreme court or the court of appeals, whether in an original proceeding or upon an appeal, if any federal question shall be presented by the pleadings, it shall be the duty of the supreme court to determine in its opinion whether or not the petitioner has been denied a right guaranteed by the Constitution of the United States.

7.36.150. Admission to bail or discharge—Duty of court
No person shall be discharged from an order of commitment issued by any judicial or peace officer for want of bail, or in cases not bailable on account of any defect in the charge or process, or for alleged want of probable cause; but in all cases the court or judge shall summon the prosecuting witnesses, investigate the criminal charge, and discharge, admit to bail or recommit the prisoner, as may be just and legal, and recognize witnesses when proper.

7.36.160. Writ to admit prisoner to bail
The writ may be had for the purpose of admitting a prisoner to bail in civil and criminal actions. When any person has an interest in the detention, and the prisoner shall not be discharged until the person having such interest is notified.

7.36.170. Compelling attendance of witnesses
The court or judge shall have power to require and compel the attendance of witnesses, and to do all other acts necessary to determine the case.

7.36.180. Officers protected from civil liability
No sheriff or other officer shall be liable to a civil action for obeying any writ of habeas corpus or order of discharge made thereon.

7.36.190. Warrant to prevent removal
Whenever it shall appear by affidavit that any one is illegally held in custody or restraint, and that there is good reason to believe that such person will be carried out of the jurisdiction of the court or judge before whom the application is made, or will suffer some irreparable injury before compliance with the writ can be enforced, such court or judge may cause a warrant to be issued reciting the facts, and directed to the sheriff or any constable of the county, commanding him or her to take the person thus held in custody or restraint, and forthwith bring him or her before the court or judge to be dealt with according to the law.

7.36.200. Warrant may call for apprehension of offending party
The court or judge may also, if the same be deemed necessary, insert in the warrant a command for the apprehension of the person charged with causing the illegal restraint.

7.36.210. Execution of warrant
The officer shall execute the writ [warrant] by bringing the person therein named before the court or judge, and the like return of proceedings shall be required and had as in case of writs of habeas corpus.

7.36.220. Temporary orders
The court or judge may make any temporary orders in the cause or disposition of the party during the progress of the proceedings that justice may require. The custody of any party restrained may be changed from one person to another, by order of the court or judge.

7.36.230. Emergency acts on Sunday authorized
Any writ or process authorized by this chapter may be issued and served, in cases of emergency, on Sunday.

7.36.240. Writs and process—Issuance—Service—Defects—Amendments
All writs and other process authorized by this chapter shall be issued by the clerk of the court, and sealed with the seal of such court, and shall be served and returned forthwith, unless the court or judge shall specify a particular time for such return. And no writ or other process shall be disregarded for any defect

7.36.250. Proceeding in forma pauperis

Any person entitled to prosecute a writ of habeas corpus who, by reason of poverty is unable to pay the costs of such proceeding or give security therefor, may file in the court having original jurisdiction of the proceeding an affidavit setting forth such facts and that he or she believes himself or herself to be entitled to the redress sought. Upon the filing of such an affidavit the court may, if satisfied that the proceeding or appeal is instituted or taken in good faith, order that such proceeding, including appeal, may be prosecuted without prepayment of fees or costs or the giving of security therefor. This section also applies to filing fees assessed under *RCW 36.18.016*.

Current with 2014 Legislation effective on June 12, 2014, the General Effective Date for the 2014 Regular Session, and other 2014 Legislation effective through October 1, 2014.

WEST VIRGINIA

Annotated Code of West Virginia
Chapter 53. Extraordinary Remedies
Article 4A. Post-Conviction Habeas Corpus

§53-4A-1. Right to habeas corpus for post-conviction review; jurisdiction; when contention deemed finally adjudicated or waived; effect upon other remedies

(a) Any person convicted of a crime and incarcerated under sentence of imprisonment therefor who contends that there was such a denial or infringement of his rights as to render the conviction or sentence void under the Constitution of the United states or the Constitution of this State, or both, or that the court was without jurisdiction to impose the sentence, or that the sentence exceeds the maximum authorized by law, or that the conviction or sentence is otherwise subject to collateral attack upon any ground of alleged error heretofore available under the common law or any statutory provision of this State, may without paying a filing fee, file a petition for a writ of habeas corpus ad subjiciendum, and prosecute the same, seeking release from such illegal imprisonment, correction of the sentence, the setting aside of the plea, conviction and sentence, or other relief, if and only if such contention or contentions and the grounds in fact or law relied upon in support thereof have not been previously and finally adjudicated or waived in the proceedings which resulted in the conviction and sentence, or in a proceeding or proceedings on a prior petition or petitions filed under the provisions of this article, or in any other proceeding or proceedings which the petitioner has instituted to secure relief from such conviction or sentence. Any such petition shall be filed with the clerk of the supreme court of appeals, or the clerk of any circuit court, said supreme court of appeals and all circuit courts of this State having been granted original jurisdiction in habeas corpus cases by the Constitution of this State, or with the clerk of any court of record of limited jurisdiction having criminal jurisdiction in this State. Jurisdiction is hereby conferred upon each and every such court of record of limited jurisdiction having criminal jurisdiction (hereinafter for convenience of reference referred to simply as a "statutory court") to refuse or grant writs of habeas corpus ad subjiciendum in accordance with the provisions of this article and to hear and determine any contention or contentions and to pass upon all grounds in fact or law relief upon in support thereof in any proceeding on any such writ made returnable thereto in accordance with the provisions of this article. All proceedings in accordance with this article shall be civil in character and shall under no circumstances be regarded as criminal proceedings or a criminal case.

(b) For the purposes of this article, a contention or contentions and the grounds in fact or law relied upon in support thereof shall be deemed to have been previously and finally adjudicated only when at some point in the proceedings which resulted in the conviction and sentence, or in a proceeding or proceedings on a prior petition or petitions filed under the provisions of this article, or in any other proceeding or proceedings instituted by the petitioner to secure relief from his conviction or sentence, there was a decision on the merits thereof after a full and fair hearing thereon and the time for the taking of an appeal with respect to such decision has not expired or has expired, as the case may be, or the right of appeal with respect to such decision has been exhausted, unless said decision upon the merits is clearly wrong.

(c) For the purposes of this article, a contention or contentions and the grounds in fact or law relied upon in support thereof shall be deemed to have been waived when the petitioner could have advanced, but intelligently and knowingly failed to advance, such contention or contentions and grounds before trial, at trial, or on direct appeal (whether or not said petitioner actually took an appeal), or in a proceeding or proceedings on a prior petition or petitions filed under the provisions of this article, or in any other proceeding or proceedings instituted by the petitioner to secure relief from his conviction or sentence, unless such contention or contentions and grounds are such that, under the Constitution of the United States or the Constitution of this state, they cannot be waived under the circumstances giving rise to the alleged waiver. When any such contention or contentions and grounds could have been advanced by the petitioner before trial, at trial, or on direct appeal (whether or not said petitioner actually took an appeal), or in a proceeding or proceedings on a prior petition or petitions filed under the provisions of this article, or in any other proceeding or proceedings instituted by the petitioner to secure relief from his conviction or sentence, but were not in fact so advanced, there shall be a rebuttable presumption that the petitioner intelligently and knowingly failed to advance such contention or contentions and grounds.

(d) For the purposes of this article, and notwithstanding any other provisions of this article, no such contention or contentions and grounds shall be deemed to have been previously and finally adjudicated or to have been waived where, subsequent to any decision upon the merits thereof or subsequent to any proceeding or proceedings in which said question otherwise may have been waived, any court whose decisions are binding upon the lower courts of this state holds that the Constitution of the United States or the Constitution of West Virginia, or both, impose upon state criminal proceedings a procedural or substantive standard not theretofore recognized, if and only if such standard is intended to be applied retroactively and would thereby affect the validity of the petitioner's conviction or sentence.

(e) The writ of habeas corpus as subjiciendum provided for in this article is not a substitute for nor does it affect any remedies which are incident to the criminal proceedings in the trial court or any remedy of direct review of the conviction or sentence, but such writ comprehends and takes the place of all other common law and statutory remedies, including, but not limited to, the writ of habeas corpus ad subjiciendum provided for in article four of this chapter, which have heretofore been available for challenging the validity of a conviction or sentence and shall be used exclusively in lieu thereof: Provided, that nothing contained in this article shall operate to bar any proceeding or proceedings in which a writ of habeas corpus ad subjiciendum is sought for any purpose other than to challenge the legality of a criminal conviction or sentence of imprisonment therefor. A petition for a writ of habeas corpus ad subjiciendum in accordance with the provisions of this article may be filed at any time after the conviction and sentence in the criminal proceedings have been rendered and imposed and the time for the taking of an appeal with respect thereto has expired or the right of appeal with respect thereto has been exhausted.

§53-4A-2. Petition; contents thereof; supreme court may prescribe form of petition, verification and writ; duties of clerk

A petition seeking a writ of a habeas corpus ad subjiciendum in accordance with the provisions of this article shall identify the proceedings in which the petitioner was convicted and sentenced, give the date of the entry of the judgment and sentence complained of, specifically set forth the contention or contentions and grounds in fact or law in support thereof upon which the petition is based, and clearly state the relief desired. Affidavits, exhibits, records or other documentary evidence supporting the allegations of the petition shall be attached to the petition unless there is a recital therein as to why they are not attached. All facts within the personal knowledge of the petitioner shall be set forth separately from other allegations, and such facts and the authenticity of all affidavits, exhibits, records or other documentary evidence attached to the petition must be sworn to affirmatively as true and correct. The petition must also identify any previous proceeding or proceedings on a petition or petitions filed under the provisions of this article, or any other previous proceeding or proceedings which the petitioner instituted to secure relief from his conviction or sentence and must set forth the type or types of such previous proceeding or proceedings, the contention or contentions there advanced, the grounds in fact or law assigned therein for the relief there sought, the date thereof, the forum in which instituted and the result thereof. Argument, citations and discussion of authorities shall be omitted from the petition, but may be filed as a separate document or documents. The supreme court of appeals may by rule prescribe the form of the petition, verification and the writ itself. The clerk of the court in which the petition is filed shall docket the petition upon its receipt, and shall bring the petition and any affidavits, exhibits, records and other documentary evidence attached thereto the attention of the court.

§53-4A-3. Refusal of writ; granting of writ; direction of writ; how writ made returnable; duties of clerk, attorney general and prosecuting attorney

(a) If the petition, affidavits, exhibits, records and other documentary evidence attached thereto, or the record in the proceedings which resulted in the conviction and sentence, or the record or records in a proceeding or proceedings on a prior petition or petitions filed under the provisions of this article, or the record or records in any other proceeding or proceedings instituted by the petitioner to secure relief from his conviction or sentence (if any such record or records are part of the official court files of the court with whose clerk the petition is filed or are part of the official court files of any other court within the same judicial circuit as the court with whose clerk such petition is filed and are thus available for examination and review by such court) show to the satisfaction of the court that the petitioner is entitled to no relief, or that the contention or contentions and grounds (in fact or law) advanced have been previously and finally adjudicated or waived, the court shall by order entered of record refuse to grant a writ, and such refusal shall constitute a final judgment. If it appears to such court from said petition, affidavits, exhibits, records and other documentary evidence, or any such available record or records referred to above, that there is probable cause to believe that the petitioner may be entitled to some relief, and that the contention or contentions and grounds (in fact or law) advanced have not been previously and finally adjudicated or waived, the court shall forthwith grant a writ, directed to and returnable as provided in subsection (b) hereof. If any such record or records referred to above are not a part of the official court files of the court with whose clerk the petition is filed or are not part of the official court files of any other court within the same judicial circuit as the court with whose clerk such petition is filed and are thus not available for examination and review by such court, the determination as to whether to refuse or grant the writ shall be made on the basis of the petition, affidavits, exhibits, records and other documentary evidence attached thereto.

(b) Any writ granted in accordance with the provisions of this article shall be directed to the person under whose supervision the petitioner is incarcerated. Whether the writ is granted by the supreme court of appeals, a circuit court, or any statutory court in this State, it shall, in the discretion of the court, be returnable before (i) the court granting it, (ii) the circuit court, or a statutory court, of the county wherein the petitioner is incarcerated, or (iii) the circuit court, or the statutory court, in which, as the case may be, the petitioner was convicted and sentenced.

(c) The clerk of the court to which a writ granted in accordance with the provisions of this article is made returnable shall promptly bring the petition and any affidavits, exhibits, records and other documentary evidence attached thereto, and the writ to the attention of the court if the writ was granted by some other court, and in every case deliver a copy of such petition and any affidavits, exhibits, records and other documentary evidence attached thereto and the writ to the prosecuting attorney of the county, or the attorney general if the writ is returnable before the supreme court of appeals. The prosecuting attorney or the attorney general, as the case may be, shall represent the State in all cases arising under the provisions of this article.

§53-4A-4. Inability to pay costs, etc.; appointment of counsel; obtaining copies of record or records in criminal proceedings or in a previous proceeding or proceedings to secure relief; payment of all costs and expenses; adjudging of costs

(a) A petition filed under the provisions of this article may allege facts to show that the petitioner is unable to pay the costs of the proceeding or to employ counsel, may request permission to proceed in forma pauperis and may request the appointment of counsel. If the court to which the writ is returnable (hereinafter for convenience of reference referred to simply as "the court," unless the context in which used clearly indicates that some other court is intended) is satisfied that the facts alleged in this regard are true, and that the petition was filed in good faith, and has merit or is not frivolous, the court shall order that the petitioner proceed in forma pauperis, and the court shall appoint counsel for the petitioner. If it shall appear to the court that the record in the proceedings which resulted in the conviction and sentence, including, but not limited to, a transcript of the testimony therein, or the record or records in a proceeding or proceedings on a prior petition or petitions filed under the provisions of this article, or the record or records in any other proceeding or petitions filed under the provisions of this article, or the record or records in any other proceeding or proceedings instituted by the petitioner to secure relief from his conviction or sentence, or all of such records, or any part or parts thereof, are necessary for a proper determination of the contention or contentions and grounds (in fact or law) advanced in the petition, the court shall, by order entered of record, direct the State to make arrangements for copies of any such record or records, or all of such records, or such part or parts thereof as may be sufficient, to be obtained for examination and review by the court, the State and the petitioner. The State may on its own initiative obtain copies of any record or records, or all of the records, or such part or parts thereof as may be sufficient, as aforesaid, for its use and for examination and review by the court and the petitioner. If, after judgment is entered under the provisions of this article, an appeal or writ of error is sought by the petitioner in accordance with the provisions of section nine of this article, and the court which rendered the judgment is of opinion that the review is being sought in good faith and the grounds assigned therefor have merit or are not frivolous, and such court finds that the petitioner is unable to pay the costs incident thereto or to employ counsel, the court shall, upon the petitioner's request, order that the petitioner proceed in forma pauperis and shall appoint counsel for the petitioner. If an appeal or writ of error is allowed, whether upon application of the petitioner or the State, the reviewing court shall, upon the requisite showing the request as aforesaid, order that the petitioner proceed in forma pauperis and shall appoint counsel for petitioner. If it is determined that the petitioner has the financial means with which to pay the costs incident to any proceedings hereunder and to employ counsel, or that the petition was filed in bad faith or is without merit or is frivolous, or that review is being sought or prosecuted in bad faith or the grounds assigned therefor are without merit or are frivolous, the request to proceed in forma pauperis and for the appointment of counsel shall be denied and the court making such determination shall enter an order setting forth the findings pertaining thereto and such order shall be final.

(b) Whenever it is determined that a petitioner shall proceed in forma pauperis, all necessary costs and expenses incident to proceedings hereunder, originally, or on appeal pursuant to section nine of this article, or both, including, but not limited to, all court costs, and the cost of furnishing transcripts, shall, upon certification by the court to the state auditor, be paid out of the treasury of the state from the appropriation for criminal charges. Any attorney appointed in accordance with the provisions of this section shall be paid for his services and expenses in accordance with the provisions of article twenty-one, chapter twenty-nine of the Code. All costs and expenses incurred incident to obtaining copies of any record or records, or all of the records, or such part or parts thereof as may be where the petitioner is proceeding in forma pauperis, and the court orders the state to make arrangements for the obtaining of same or the State obtains the same on its own initiative, be paid out of the treasury of the state, upon certification by the court to the state auditor, from the appropriation for criminal charges. All such costs, expenses and fees shall be paid as provided in this subsection (b) notwithstanding the fact that all proceedings under the provisions of this article are civil and not criminal in character. In the event a petitioner who is proceeding in forma pauperis does not substantially prevail, all such costs, expenses and fees shall be and constitute a judgment of the court against the petitioner to be recovered as any other judgment for costs.

{c) In the event a petitioner who is not proceeding in forma pauperis does not substantially prevail, all costs and expenses incurred incident to obtaining copies of any record or records, or all of the records, or such part or parts thereof as may be sufficient, as aforesaid, for examination and review by the court, the State and the petitioner, shall, where the court orders the State to make arrangements for the obtaining of same or the State obtains the same on its own initiative, be and constitute a judgment of the court against the petitioner to be recovered as any other judgment for costs. In any case where the petitioner does not proceed in forma pauperis, the court shall adjudge all costs and expenses to be paid as shall seem to the court to be right, consistent with the immediately preceding sentence of this subsection (c) and with the provisions of chapter fifty-nine of this Code, as amended.

§53-4A-5. Service of writ
Any writ granted in accordance with the provisions of this article shall be served upon the person to whom it is directed, or, in his absence from the place where the petitioner is incarcerated, upon the person having the immediate custody of the petitioner.

§53-4A-6. Return; pleadings; amendments
Within such time as may be specified in the writ or as the court may fix, the State shall make its return. No other or further pleadings shall be filed except as the court may order. At any time prior to entry of judgment on the writ in accordance with the provisions of this article, the court may permit the petitioner to withdraw his petition. The court may make such orders as to amendment of the petition or return or other pleading, as to pleading over, or filing other or further pleadings, or extending the time for the making of the return or the filing of other pleadings, as shall seem to the court to be appropriate, meet and reasonable. In considering the petition, the return or other pleading, or any amendment thereof, substance and not form shall control.

§53-4A-7. *Denial of relief; hearings; evidence; record; judgment*

(a) If the petition, affidavits, exhibits, records and other documentary evidence attached thereto, or the return or other pleadings, or the record in the proceedings which resulted in the conviction and sentence, or the record or records in a proceeding or proceedings on a prior petition or petitions filed under the provisions of this article, or the record or records in any other proceeding or proceedings instituted by the petitioner to secure relief from his conviction or sentence, show to the satisfaction of the court that the petitioner is entitled to no relief, or that the contention or contentions and grounds (in fact or law) advanced have been previously and finally adjudicated or waived, the court shall enter an order denying the relief sought. If it appears to the court from said petition, affidavits, exhibits, records and other documentary evidence attached thereto, or the return or other pleadings, or any such record or records referred to above, that there is probable cause to believe that the petitioner may be entitled to some relief and that the contention or contentions and grounds (in fact or law) advanced have not been previously and finally adjudicated or waived, the court shall promptly hold a hearing and/or take evidence on the contention or contentions and grounds (in fact or law) advanced, and the court shall pass upon all issues of fact without a jury. The court may also provide for one or more hearings to be held and/or evidence to be taken in any other county or counties in the state.

(b) A record of all proceedings under this article and all hearings and evidence shall be made and kept. The evidentiary deposition of witnesses taken by either the petitioner or the state, on reasonable notice to the other, may be read as evidence. The court may receive proof by proper oral testimony or other proper evidence. All of the evidence shall be made a part of the record. When a hearing is held and/or evidence is taken by a judge of a circuit court or statutory court in vacation, a transcript of the proceedings shall be signed by the judge and certified to the clerk of the court in which the judgment is to be rendered, and be entered by him among the records of that court. A record of all proceedings in the Supreme Court of Appeals shall be entered among the records of such court.

(c) When the court determines to deny or grant relief, as the case may be, the court shall enter an appropriate order with respect to the conviction or sentence in the former criminal proceedings and such supplementary matters as are deemed necessary and proper to the findings in the case, including, but not limited to, remand, the vacating or setting aside of the plea, conviction and sentence, rearraignment, retrial, custody, bail, discharge, correction of sentence and resentencing, or other matters which may be necessary and proper. In any order entered in accordance with the provisions of this section, the court shall make specific findings of fact and conclusions of law relating to each contention or contentions and grounds (in fact or law) advanced, shall clearly state the grounds upon which the matter was determined, and shall state whether a federal and/or state right was presented and decided. Any order entered in accordance with the provisions of this section shall constitute a final judgment, and, unless reversed, shall be conclusive.

(d) Notwithstanding any provision of law to the contrary, whenever a conviction from a crime of violence is reversed or a sentence of incarceration for such an offense is vacated pursuant to the provisions of this article, the prosecuting attorney of the county of prosecution shall, prior to a retrial or entering into any plea negotiations or sentence negotiations to resolve the matter, notify the victim or if the offense was a homicide, the next of kin of the victim, by United states mail sent to the last known address of said person, if his or her name and address has previously been provided to the prosecuting attorney.

§53-4A-8. *Powers of judges or judge in vacation*

A writ may be granted or refused in accordance with the provisions of this article by any three concurring judges of the supreme court of appeals, or a judge of any circuit court or any statutory court, in vacation as well as by any such court in term, and any such writ may be made returnable, consistent with the provisions of subsection (b) of section three of this article, to the supreme court of appeals in term, or to a judge of a circuit court or any statutory court in vacation as well as to such court in term. Although a writ granted in accordance with the provisions of this article is returnable to a circuit court in term or a statutory court in term, the contention or contentions and grounds (in fact of law) advanced, and any incidental matters related thereto, may be heard and/or determined or passed upon by a judge of the court in vacation. Any judge of the supreme court of appeals (where at least three judges of such court concur therein), or of a circuit court or a statutory court, in vacation shall have the same power to enforce obedience to the writ, to compel the attendance of witnesses, or to punish contempt of their or his authority, as a court has; and the judgment of a judge of a circuit court or a statutory court in vacation when entered of record shall be considered and be enforced as if it were a judgment of the court among whose records it is entered.

§53-4A-9. Judicial review; disposition of petitioner pending appeal
(a) A final judgment entered under the provisions of this article by a statutory court may be appealed by the petitioner or the State to the circuit court of the county upon application for an appeal or writ of error in the manner and within the time provided in article four, chapter fifty-eight of this Code, as amended. A final judgment entered under the provisions of this article by a circuit court or a final judgment entered by the circuit court after an appeal or writ of error was granted by such circuit court with respect to the judgment of a statutory court entered under the provisions of this article, as well as an order by a circuit court rejecting an appeal from or writ of error to the judgment of a statutory court entered under the provisions of this article, may be appealed by the petitioner or the state to the supreme court of appeals upon application for an appeal or writ of error in the manner and within the time provided by law for civil appeals generally. When an application for an appeal or writ of error is rejected by the circuit court (and the order of rejection is not appealed to the supreme court of appeals), or the supreme court of appeals, as the case may be, or both, the order sought to be reviewed shall thereby become final to the same extent and with like effect as if said order had been affirmed on appeal.

(b) When the petitioner is remanded, execution of the judgment entered under the provisions of this article shall not be suspended by the granting of an appeal or writ of error, or suspended while the petitioner is applying for an appeal or writ of error. When the petitioner is ordered to be discharged, and execution of the judgment entered under the provisions of this article is ordered suspended to permit the State to apply for an appeal or writ of error, the court making such suspending order may, in its discretion, admit the petitioner to bail until expiration of the time allowed for making application for an appeal or writ of error, or, in case the appeal or writ of error is allowed, until the decision of the appellate court thereon is duly certified.

§53-4A-10. Construction; repeal
All other pertinent provisions of this Code shall be construed so as to conform to and be consistent with the provisions of this article. In the event that there are pertinent provisions in this Code so inconsistent with the provisions of this article as to preclude such construction, such other provisions shall be considered as having been repealed to the extent of such inconsistency by the enactment of this article. The provisions of this article shall be liberally construed so as to effectuate its purposes.

§53-4A-11. Severability
If any provision of this article or the application thereof to any person or circumstances is held invalid, such invalidity shall not affect other provisions or applications of the article which can be given effect without the invalid provision or application, and to this end the provisions of this article are hereby de-

clared to be serverable. The legislature does hereby further declare that it would have enacted this article even if it had known at the time of enactment that such provision or application thereof would he held to be invalid.

Current with laws of the 2014 Second Extraordinary Session.

WISCONSIN

Wisconsin Statutes Annotated
Actions and Proceedings in Special Cases
Chapter 782. Habeas Corpus

782.01. *Habeas corpus, who to have; definitions*
(1) Every person restrained of personal liberty may prosecute a writ of habeas corpus to obtain relief from such restraint subject to *ss. 782.02* and *974.06*.

(2) Any person confined in any hospital or institution as mentally ill or committed for treatment of alcoholism under *s. 51.45(13)* may prosecute such writ, and the question of mental illness or need for treatment shall be determined by the court or judge issuing the same. If such court or judge decides that the person is mentally ill or in need of treatment such decision shall not bar the prosecution of such writ a 2nd time if it is claimed that such person has been restored to reason or is no longer in need of treatment.

(3) In this Chapter, unless the context requires otherwise, judge includes the supreme court, the court of appeals and circuit courts and each justice and judge thereof and circuit and supplemental court commissioners; and prisoner includes every person restrained of personal liberty; and imprisoned includes every such restraint, and "respondent" means the person on whom the writ is to be served.

782.02. *Who not entitled to*
No person shall be entitled to prosecute such writ who shall have been committed or detained by virtue of the final judgment or order of any competent tribunal of civil or criminal jurisdiction or by virtue of any execution issued upon such order or judgment; but no order of commitment for any alleged contempt or upon proceedings as for contempt to enforce the rights or remedies of any party shall be deemed a judgment or order within the meaning of this section; nor shall any attachment or other process issued upon any such order be deemed an execution within the meaning of this section.

782.03. *Petition for writ*
Application for the writ shall be by petition, signed either by the prisoner or by some person in his or her behalf, and may be made to the supreme court, the court of appeals or the circuit court of the county, or to any justice or judge of the supreme court, court of appeals or circuit court or to any circuit or supplemental court commissioner, within the county where the prisoner is detained; or if there is no judge within the county, or for any cause he or she is incapable of acting, or has refused to grant the writ, then to some judge residing in an adjoining county; but every application, made by or on behalf of a person sentenced to the state prisons, must contain a copy of any motion made under *s. 974.06* and shall indicate

the disposition of the motion and the court in which the disposition was made. If no motion was made, the petition shall so state.

782.04. Petition; contents

Such petition must be verified and must state in substance:

(1) That the person in whose behalf the writ is applied for is restrained of personal liberty, the person by whom imprisoned and the place where, naming both parties, if their names are known, or describing them if they are not.

(2) That such person is not imprisoned by virtue of any judgment, order or execution specified in s. 782.02.

(3) The cause or pretense of such imprisonment according to the best of petitioner's knowledge and belief.

(4) If the imprisonment is by virtue of any order or process a copy thereof must be annexed, or it must be averred that, by reason of such prisoner being removed or concealed a demand of such copy could not be made or that such demand was made and a fee of $1 therefor tendered to the person having such prisoner in custody, and that such copy was refused.

(5) In what the illegality of the imprisonment consists.

782.05. Application to officer in another county

Whenever application for any such writ is made to any officer not residing within the county where the prisoner is detained the officer shall require proof, by oath of the party appearing or by other sufficient evidence, that there is no officer in such county authorized to grant the writ or if there is one that the officer is absent or has refused to grant such writ, or for some cause, to be specifically set forth, is incapable of acting; and if such proof is not produced the application shall be denied.

782.06. Writ granted without delay

The court or judge to whom such petition shall be properly presented shall grant the same without delay unless it shall appear from the petition or from the documents annexed that the party applying therefor is prohibited from prosecuting the same.

782.07. Form of writ

(1) Such writ shall be substantially in the following form:

> The state of Wisconsin: To the sheriff, etc. (or A.B.):
>
> You are hereby commanded to have C.D., by you imprisoned and detained, as it is said, together with the time and cause of such imprisonment, (by whatever name the said C.D. shall be called or charged), before [here name the court or judge], at, etc. (or immediately after the receipt of the writ), to do and receive what shall then and there be considered concerning the said C.D.
>
> Witness, etc.

(2) Every such writ shall be made returnable forthwith or at a day certain, as the case may require; when not issued by the court shall be endorsed with a certificate that the same has been allowed, with the date of such allowance, signed by the judge allowing the same.

782.08. Writ, when sufficient
Such writ shall not be disobeyed for any defect in form. It shall be sufficient:

(1) If the person having the custody of the prisoner is designated, either by name of office, if any, or by the person's name, or if both names are unknown or uncertain the person may be described by an assumed name or title. Anyone who is served with the writ is considered the person to whom it is directed, although it is directed to the person by a wrong name or description or to any other person.

(2) If the person who is directed to be produced be designated by name, or if the person's name be uncertain or unknown, he or she may be described in any other way so as to designate the person intended.

782.09. Refusal of writ
Any judge who refuses to grant a writ of habeas corpus, when legally applied for, is liable to the prisoner in the sum of $1,000.

782.10. Writ, who may serve
Such writ can only be served by an elector of the state and shall be served as follows:

(1) By delivering a copy of the same to the person to whom it is directed.

(2) If such person cannot be found, by being left at the jail or other place in which the prisoner may be confined, with any underofficer or other person of proper age having charge of such prisoner.

(3) If the person on whom the writ ought to be served hides or refuses admittance to the party attempting to serve the writ, by affixing the copy, in some conspicuous place on the outside of the house or other place where the prisoner is confined.

(4) The person serving the writ shall make due and prompt return thereof with proof of service.

782.11. Petitioner, when to pay charges
When such writ is directed to any person other than an officer, it may require as a duty to be performed, in order to render the service thereof effectual, that the charges of bringing up such prisoner shall be paid by the petitioner, and in such case the writ shall specify the amount of such charges so to be paid, which shall not exceed the fees allowed by law to sheriffs for similar services.

782.12. Service of writ, when complete
Except where service is made under s. 782.10(3), the service of a writ of habeas corpus is not complete until the party serving the writ tenders to the custodian of the prisoner, if an officer, the fees allowed for bringing up the prisoner, nor unless, when required by the officer, the party shall also give the officer a bond in double the sum for which the prisoner is detained, if detained for a specific sum of money, and if not, then in the sum of $1,000, conditioned that the obligor will pay the charges of carrying back the prisoner if remanded and that the prisoner will not escape, either going to or returning from the place to which taken, and if the prisoner is not in the custody of an officer, and the writ requires that the charges of bringing up the prisoner shall be paid by the petitioner, then until the charges having been tendered to the respondent.

782.13. Return to writ
Whenever a complete service of such writ shall have been made, the person upon whom it was served,

having the custody of the prisoner, whether such writ be directed to the person or not, shall obey and make return to such writ and such prisoner shall be produced at the time and place specified therein.

782.14. Return, what to state
The respondent shall state in the return:

(1) Whether the prisoner is in the respondent's custody or power.

(2) If the prisoner is in the respondent's custody or power the authority and true cause of such imprisonment, setting forth the same at large.

(3) If the prisoner be detained by virtue of any written authority a copy thereof shall be annexed to the return and the original shall be produced to the court or judge before whom the same is returnable.

(4) If the respondent shall have had the prisoner in the respondent's power or custody at any time, but has transferred such custody to another, the return shall state particularly to whom, at what time, for what cause and by what authority such transfer took place. The return must be signed by the person making it and shall be verified by oath.

782.15. Prisoner produced, exception
The respondent shall being the prisoner, according to the command of such writ, except in the case of sickness as provided in s. 782.29.

782.16. Obedience to writ compelled
If any person upon whom such writ shall have been duly served shall refuse or neglect to obey the same, within the time required, and no sufficient excuse shall be shown for such refusal or neglect the court or judge before whom such writ is returnable shall, upon proof of such service, forthwith issue an attachment against such person, directed to the sheriff of any county, commanding the sheriff forthwith to apprehend such person and to bring the person before such court or judge. The person so brought shall be committed to the county jail until making return to such writ and comply with any order that may be made in relation to the prisoner.

782.17. Attachment of sheriff
If a sheriff neglects to make return to such writ the attachment may be directed to any coroner or other person to be designated therein, who shall execute the same; and such sheriff may be committed to the jail of any county other than the sheriff's own.

782.18. Attachment may issue
In case of attachment an order may be issued to the officer or other person to whom such attachment is directed, commanding the officer or person to bring, forthwith, before the court or judge, the party for whose benefit such writ was allowed, who shall thereafter remain in the custody of such officer or other person, until discharged, bailed or remanded. In the execution of such attachment or order, the person executing it may call to the person's aid the power of the county.

782.19. Return may be traversed
The prisoner may move to strike the return or may deny any of the material facts set forth in the return to the writ or allege any fact to show either that the imprisonment is unlawful or that the prisoner is entitled to a discharge, which allegations and denials shall be verified by oath; and the court or judge shall proceed

in a summary way to examine into the facts contained in the return and to hear the allegations and proofs of the parties in support of such imprisonment or against the same.

782.20. When party discharged
If no legal cause be shown for such imprisonment or restraint or for the continuance thereof the court or judge shall make a final order discharging such party from the custody or restraint.

782.21. When remanded
The court or judge must make a final order to remand the prisoner if it shall appear that the prisoner is detained in custody either:

(1) By virtue of process issued by any court or judge of the United States, in a case where such court or judge has exclusive jurisdiction; or

(2) By virtue of the final judgment or order of any competent court of civil or criminal jurisdiction or of any execution issued upon such judgment or order; or

(3) For any contempt, specially and plainly charged in the commitment by some court, officer or body having authority to commit for the contempt so charged; and

(4) That the time during which such party may be legally detained has not expired.

782.22. Discharge if in custody under process
(1) If it appear that the prisoner is in custody by virtue of civil process of any court or issued by any officer in the course of judicial proceedings before the officer such prisoner can be discharged in the following cases only:

(a) Where the jurisdiction of such court or officer has been exceeded, either as to matter, place, law or person.

(b) Where, although the original imprisonment was lawful, yet by some act, omission or event which has taken place afterward the prisoner is entitled to be discharged.

(c) Where the process is void.

(d) When the process was issued in a case not allowed by law.

(e) Where the person having the custody of the prisoner is not empowered by law to detain the prisoner; or

(f) Where the process is not authorized by any judgment or order of any court nor by any provision of law.

(2) But no court or judge, on the return of such writ, shall inquire into the legality or justice of any judgment, order or execution specified in s. 782.21.

782.23. Prisoner, when bailed
If it appear that the prisoner has been legally committed for crime or if the prisoner appears, by the testimony offered with the return the hearing thereof, to be guilty of crime, although the commitment is irregular, the court or judge before whom the prisoner is brought shall release the prisoner on bail, if bailable and good bail be offered, or shall remand the prisoner.

782.24. Prisoner, when remanded
If the prisoner is not entitled to discharge and is not bailed the court or judge shall remand the prisoner to the custody from which taken, if the person who had custody is legally entitled to custody; if not so entitled, the prisoner shall be committed to his or her legal custodian.

782.25. Custody of prisoner pending proceedings
Until judgment be given upon the return the court or judge before whom the prisoner is brought may either commit the prisoner to the custody of the sheriff or place the prisoner in such care or under such custody as age and other circumstances may require.

782.26. Interested person notified
When it appears from the return to such writ that the prisoner is in custody on any process under which any other person has an interest in continuing imprisonment no order shall be made for discharge until it shall appear that the interested person or attorney, if the person has one, if to be found within the county, shall have sufficient notice of the time and place at which writ is returnable.

782.27. Notice to district attorney
When the prisoner is detained upon any criminal accusation no order or discharge shall be made until sufficient notice of the time and place at which such writ shall have been returned or shall be made returnable shall be given to the district attorney of the county, if to be found within the county.

782.28. Transfer from circuit court commissioner
If the writ is returnable before a circuit court commissioner, either party may make a request for transfer to the court in which the matter is filed. Upon receipt of such request the circuit court commissioner shall forthwith transmit all papers and records in the proceedings to the court.

782.29. Proceedings in absence of prisoner; appearance by attorney
When from sickness or infirmity the prisoner cannot without danger be brought before the court or judge before whom the writ is made returnable the respondent may state that fact in the return, verifying the same by oath. If satisfied of the truth of such allegation and the return is otherwise sufficient, the court or judge shall proceed to dispose of the matter. The prisoner may appear by attorney and plead to the return. If it appears that the prisoner is illegally imprisoned the court or judge shall order discharge forthwith; but if it appears that the person is legally imprisoned and is not entitled to bail all further proceedings thereon shall cease.

782.30. Order of discharge, how enforced, action for damages
Obedience to any final order discharging or directing the discharge of any prisoner may be enforced by the court making the order by attachment, in the manner provided for a neglect to make a return to a writ of habeas corpus and with the like effect in all respects. The person who is guilty of disobedience of the order shall be liable to the prisoner in the sum of $1,250 for damages, in addition to any special damages that the prisoner may have sustained.

WYOMING

Wyoming Statutes
Title 1. Code of civil Procedure
Chapter 27. Habeas Corpus

§1-27-101. Petition to be under oath; contents
(a) The petition for the writ of habeas corpus shall be sworn to and shall state:

(i) The person for whom the writ is sought is restrained of his liberty, by whom he is restrained and the place where he is restrained, stating the names of the parties if known and if unknown, describing them with as much particularity as practicable;

(ii) The cause or reason for the restraint according to the best information of the petitioner, and if it is by virtue of any legal process, a copy thereof must be annexed or a satisfactory reason presented for its absence;

(iii) The restraint is illegal;

(iv) The legality of the restraint has not been adjudged in a prior proceeding, of the same character, to the best knowledge and belief of the applicant, or if previously adjudged the facts of the prior proceeding with a copy of all the papers connected therewith or a satisfactory reason for the absence thereof; and

(v) Whether petition for the writ has been made to and refused by any court or judge, and if a petition has been made, a copy of the petition with the reason for the refusal appended or satisfactory reasons given for the failure to do so.

§1-27-102. Petition to be verified; presentation
The petition shall be sworn to by the person confined or by someone in his behalf, and presented to a court or officer authorized to allow the writ.

§1-27-103. Courts and judges allowing writ; services in any part of state
The writ of habeas corpus may be allowed by the supreme or district court or by any judge of those courts. It may be served in any part of the state.

§1-27-104. Petition to be made to nearest judge
Petition for a writ shall be made to the court or judge most convenient in point of distance to the applicant. A more remote court or judge may refuse the writ unless a sufficient reason is stated in the petition for not applying to the more convenient supreme or district court or judge.

§1-27-105. Writ to be allowed if grounds sufficient; contents of writ
(a) The writ shall be allowed if the petition shows a sufficient ground for relief and is in accordance with the foregoing requirements.

(b) The writ shall be directed to the person having custody of or who is alleged to be unlawfully restraining the petitioner, and shall command such person to produce the petitioner in person before the court or judge issuing the writ at the time and place specified in the writ. It shall further command such person to have with him the writ with his return thereon showing his doings in response thereto.

§1-27-106. Issuance of writ
When the writ is allowed by a court, it is to be issued by the clerk, but when allowed by a judge he must issue the writ himself, subscribing his name thereto without any seal.

§1-27-107. Reasons to be assigned for disallowance
If the writ is disallowed, the court or judge shall cause the reasons of the disallowance to be appended to the petition and returned to the person applying for the writ.

§1-27-108. Penalty for wrongful disallowance
Any judge, acting individually or as a member of a court, who wrongfully and willfully refuses the allowance of the writ when properly applied for, shall forfeit to the party aggrieved the sum of one thousand dollars ($1,000.00).

§1-27-109. Duty of court to issue writ without application in certain instances
Whenever any court or judge authorized to grant this writ has evidence from a judicial proceeding before it that any person within the jurisdiction of the court or judge is illegally imprisoned or restrained, the court or judge shall issue the writ or cause it to be issued though no application has been made.

§1-27-110. Service of writ
The writ may be served by the sheriff or by any other person appointed by the issuing court or judge for that purpose. If served by any person other than the sheriff, he possesses the same power and is liable to the same penalty for a nonperformance of his duty as though he were the sheriff.

§1-27-111. Manner of service
Service shall be made by leaving the original writ with the person to whom it is directed as defendant and preserving a copy on which to make the return of service. If the defendant cannot be found, or if he does not have the plaintiff in custody, service may be made upon any person having the plaintiff in his custody in the same manner and with the same effect as though he had been named defendant therein.

§1-27-112. Authorization to arrest defendant
If the defendant conceals himself or refuses admittance to the person attempting to serve the writ, or if he attempts wrongfully to carry the plaintiff out of the county or state after service of the writ, the person attempting to serve the writ may arrest the defendant and bring him and the plaintiff promptly before the judge or court before whom the writ is made returnable.

§1-27-113. Power of sheriff making arrest
In order to make the arrest, the sheriff or other person having the writ possesses the same power as a sheriff for the arrest of a person charged with a felony.

§1-27-114. Plaintiff may be taken in custody by officer; power of officer
If the plaintiff is found and no one appears to have charge or custody of him, the person having the writ may take him into custody and make return accordingly. To get possession of the plaintiff's person in such cases, he possesses the same power as given by W.S. 1-27-113 for the arrest of the defendant.

§1-27-115. Order for summary production of plaintiff
The court or judge to whom the petition for the writ is made may order the sheriff or any other person to bring the plaintiff promptly before the court or judge if convinced that the plaintiff will suffer irreparable injury before he can obtain relief by the proceedings authorized.

§1-27-116. Order for defendant's arrest for criminal offense
When the evidence is sufficient to justify the arrest of the defendant for a criminal offense committed in connection with the illegal restraint of the petitioner, the order shall also order the arrest of the defendant.

§1-27-117. Order for defendant's arrest for criminal offense; service of order of arrest
The officer or person to whom the order is directed must execute it by bringing the defendant, and the plaintiff if required, before the court or judge issuing it. The defendant shall make return to the writ of habeas corpus in the same manner as if the ordinary course had been pursued.

§1-27-118. Examination, commitment or discharge of defendant
The defendant may be examined, committed, bailed or discharged according to the nature of the case.

§1-27-119. Errors in writ to be disregarded
The writ of habeas corpus shall not be disobeyed for any defect or form or misdescription of the plaintiff or defendant if enough is stated to show the meaning and intent of the writ.

§1-27-120. Identity of defendant presumed
Any person served with the writ is presumed to be the person to whom it is directed, although it may be directed to him by a wrong name or description.

§1-27-121. Contents of defendant's answer
The defendant in his answer shall state simply and unequivocally whether he then has or at any time has had the plaintiff under his control and restraint, and if so, the reason therefor. If he has transferred him to another person, he shall state the fact, to whom and the time thereof, and the reason and authority therefor. If he holds him by virtue of a legal process or written authority, a copy thereof shall be annexed.

§1-27-122. Petitioner may reply to answer; trial by court
The petitioner may reply to the defendant's answer, and all issues joined thereon shall be tried by the judge or court.

§1-27-123. Evidence before magistrate may be reviewed
The reply may deny the sufficiency of the testimony to justify the action of the committing magistrate, on the trial of which issue all written testimony before the magistrate may be given in evidence before the court or judge in connection with any other testimony which may then be produced.

§1-27-124. Compelling attendance of witnesses; punishing for contempt
The judge issuing the writ of habeas corpus or the judge before whom it is tried has the same power as a court to compel the attendance of witnesses or to punish contempt of his authority.

§1-27-125. Certain proceedings not reviewable
Habeas corpus is not permissible to question the correctness of the action of a grand jury in finding a bill of indictment, or a petit jury in the trial of a cause nor of a court or judge when acting within their jurisdiction and in a lawful manner.

§1-27-126. When petitioner to be discharged
If no sufficient legal cause of detention is shown, the petitioner must be discharged.

§1-27-127. Errors in commitment to be disregarded

Although the commitment of the petitioner was irregular, if the court or judge is satisfied from the evidence that he ought to be held to bail or committed either for the offense charged or any other, an order may be made accordingly.

§1-27-128. Petitioner may be committed or admitted to bail

The petitioner may be committed, let to bail or his bail be mitigated or increased as justice requires.

§1-27-129. Custody of petitioner pendente lite

Until the sufficiency of the cause of restraint is determined, the defendant may retain the petitioner in his custody.

§1-27-130. Presence of petitioner at trial; waiver

The petitioner or his attorney may waive in writing his right to be present at the trial, in which case the proceedings may be had in his absence. The writ in such cases will be modified accordingly.

§1-27-131. Refusal of officer to deliver copy of process

Any officer refusing to deliver a copy of any legal process by which he detains the petitioner in custody to any person who demands a copy, shall forfeit five hundred dollars ($500.00) to the person detained.

§1-27-132. Transfer, removal or concealment of person with intent to avoid service

Whoever, having under his restraint any person for whose release a writ of habeas corpus has been issued or is being applied for, transfers that person to the custody or control of another or conceals the place of his confinement or restraint, or removes him from the jurisdiction of the court from which the writ is issued or sought, with the intent to avoid the service or effect of the writ, or whoever knowingly aids or abets in the commission of any such offense, shall be fined not more than one thousand dollars ($1,000.00) or imprisoned not more than ninety (90) days, or both.

§1-27-133. Papers to be filed; journal entry

When the proceedings are before a judge and the writ is allowed, all papers in the case shall be filed with the clerk of the district court of the county wherein the final proceedings are had, and the final order shall be entered by the clerk upon the journal as a vacation order.

§1-27-134. Fees and costs not to be advanced

No officer shall refuse to perform any of the duties required by law in habeas corpus proceedings because his fees are not paid in advance, but the judge or court to whom a petition is made may require the petitioner to give security for the payment of costs that may be taxed against him.

Current through the 2014 Budget Session

WISDOM IS THE KEY TO SUCCESS
Get Wise; Get a Smith's Guide™

Let Smith guide you step-by-step through the courts
and do it right the first time—every time.

All Smith's Guides are designed for the beginning pro se prisoner
and the practicing pro se litigator alike and are complete
with example pleadings from successful cases.

NEW! *SMITH'S GUIDE*™ *to State Habeas Corpus Relief for State Prisoners*

Provides detailed information and instructions for seeking relief via state habeas petition and for exhausting state-court remedies before proceeding to federal court to file a §2254 petition or an application to file a second or successive habeas petition. Includes state habeas rules and statutes for all 50 states. [578 pages]

SMITH'S GUIDE™ *to Habeas Corpus Relief for State Prisoners Under 28 U.S.C. §2254*

This book covers the entire process for filing the initial §2254 habeas petition to the final petition for a writ of certiorari in the U.S. Supreme Court. [380 pages]

NEW! *SMITH'S GUIDE*™ *to Second or Successive Federal Habeas Corpus Relief for State and Federal Prisoners*

For those seeking to file a second or successive habeas petition under §2244 or §2255, based on newly discovered evidence or retroactive effect of a U.S. Supreme Court case, this book provides detailed instructions for preparing the application. [352 pages]

SMITH'S GUIDE™ *to Executive Clemency for State and Federal Prisoners*

For those who have exhausted all legal remedies or have sentences that are too long to serve, this book lays out every aspect of the clemency process, self-development and personal transformation, communication skills, clemency campaign and promotional strategies, and much more. It is also applicable for parole hearings and could make the difference between freedom or additional incarceration. [288 pages]

SMITH'S GUIDE™ *to Chapter 7 Bankruptcy for Prisoners*

Get immediate freedom from liens against offender account (including from incarceration reimbursement judgment, halfway house costs, probation/parole intervention fees, and other debt) by filing chapter 7 bankruptcy. Includes blank bankruptcy forms and filing instructions. [256 pages]

All titles available online at Amazon.com

WISDOM IS THE KEY TO SUCCESS
Get Wise; Get a Smith's Guide™

Let Smith guide you step-by-step through the courts
and do it right the first time—every time.

All Smith's Guides are designed for the beginning pro se prisoner
and the practicing pro se litigator alike and are complete
with example pleadings from successful cases.

    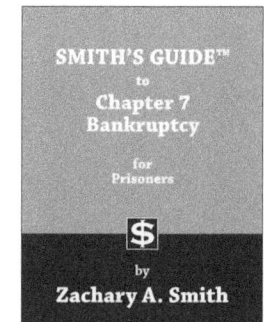

NEW! SMITH'S GUIDE™ to State Habeas Corpus Relief for State Prisoners

Provides detailed information and instructions for seeking relief via state habeas petition and for exhausting state-court remedies before proceeding to federal court to file a §2254 petition or an application to file a second or successive habeas petition. Includes state habeas rules and statutes for all 50 states. [578 pages]

SMITH'S GUIDE™ to Habeas Corpus Relief for State Prisoners Under 28 U.S.C. §2254

This book covers the entire process for filing the initial §2254 habeas petition to the final petition for a writ of certiorari in the U.S. Supreme Court. [380 pages]

NEW! SMITH'S GUIDE™ to Second or Successive Federal Habeas Corpus Relief for State and Federal Prisoners

For those seeking to file a second or successive habeas petition under §2244 or §2255, based on newly discovered evidence or retroactive effect of a U.S. Supreme Court case, this book provides detailed instructions for preparing the application. [352 pages]

SMITH'S GUIDE™ to Executive Clemency for State and Federal Prisoners

For those who have exhausted all legal remedies or have sentences that are too long to serve, this book lays out every aspect of the clemency process, self-development and personal transformation, communication skills, clemency campaign and promotional strategies, and much more. It is also applicable for parole hearings and could make the difference between freedom or additional incarceration. [288 pages]

SMITH'S GUIDE™ to Chapter 7 Bankruptcy for Prisoners

Get immediate freedom from liens against offender account (including from incarceration reimbursement judgment, halfway house costs, probation/parole intervention fees, and other debt) by filing chapter 7 bankruptcy. Includes blank bankruptcy forms and filing instructions. [256 pages]

All titles available online at Amazon.com

www.ingramcontent.com/pod-product-compliance
Lightning Source LLC
Chambersburg PA
CBHW080720230426
43665CB00020B/2564